THE
BLACK
STUDIES
READER

THE
BLACK
STUDIES
READER

Jacqueline Bobo
Cynthia Hudley
Claudine Michel

Editors

Routledge
New York & London

Published in 2004 by
Routledge
29 West 35th Street
New York, NY 10001
www.routledge-ny.com

Published in Great Britain by
Routledge
11 New Fetter Lane
London EC4P 4EE
www.routledge.co.uk

Routledge is an imprint of the Taylor & Francis Group.
Printed in the United States of America on acid free paper.

10 9 8 7 6 5 4 3 2 1

Library of Congress Cataloging-in-Publication Data

The Black studies reader / Jacqueline Bobo, Cynthia Hudley, Claudine Michel, editors.
    p. cm.
  ISBN 0-415-94553-4 (hardback) — ISBN 0-415-94554-2 (pbk.)
   1. African Americans—Study and teaching. 2. African Americans—History. 3. African Americans—Social conditions.   I. Bobo, Jacqueline. II. Hudley, Cynthia. III. Michel, Claudine.
E184.7.B56 2004
305.896'073—dc22

2003027162

CONTENTS

CREDITS

Bellegarde-Smith, Patrick, "Hormones and Melanin: The Dimensions of 'Race,' Sex and Gender in Africology; Reflexive Journeys." Copyright by the author

Bobo, Jacqueline, "*The Color Purple*: Black Women as Cultural Readers," in E. Deidre Pribram, ed., Female Spectators: Looking at Film and Television (London and New York: Verso, 1988), 90–109.

Brown, Elsa Barkley, "Womanist Consciousness: Maggie Lena Walker and the Indeoendent Order of Saint Luke," *Signs: Journal of Women in Culture and Society* 14:3 (spring 1989): 610–33.

Cannon, Katie Geneva, "Slave Ideology and Biblical Interpretation," *Semeia* 47 (1989): 9–22.

Cole, Johnnetta B., "Black Studies in Liberal Arts Education" in Johnnella E. Butler and John C. Walter, eds., *Transforming the Curriculum Ethnic Studies and Women's Studies* (Albany: State University of New York Press, 1991), 131–47.

Davis, Angela Y., "Black Women and the Academy: Defending Our Name 1894–1994," *Callaloo* 17:2 (summer 1994): 422–31.

duCille, Ann, "Dyes and Dolls: Multicultural Barbie and the Deep Play of Difference," *differences: A Journal of Feminist Cultural Studies* 6:1 (spring 1994): 48–68.

Grant, Jacquelyn, "Black Theology and the Black Woman," in Delores P. Aldridge and Carlene Young, eds., *Out of the Revolution: The Development of Africana Studies* (Lanham, Md.: Lexington Books, 2000), 427–43.

Hall, Stuart. "What Is This 'Black' in Black Popular Culture?" in Gina Dent, ed., *Black Popular Culture* (Seattle, Wash.: Bay Press, 1992), 21–33. (Now published by the New Press.)

Hammonds, Evelynn, "Black (W)holes and the Geometry of Black Female Sexuality"(More Gender Trouble: Feminism Meets Queer Theory), *differences: A Journal of Feminist Cultural Studies* 6:2–3 (summer–fall 1994): 126–46.

Harris, Robert L., Jr., "The Intellectual and Institutional Development of Africana Studies," in Robert L. Harris Jr., Darlene Clark Hine, and Nellie McKay, eds., *Three Essays: Black Studies in the United States* (New York: The Ford Foundation, 1990), 7–14.

Hudley, Cynthia, and Rhoda Barnes, "Home-School Partnership through the Eyes of Parents." Research paper supported by the Center for Black Studies at the University of California, Santa Barbara (1993).

Hull, Akasha Gloria, "DreadPath/LockSpirit," in Gloria Wade-Gayles, eds., *My Soul Is a Witness: African-American Women's Spirituality* (Boston: Beacon Press, 1995), 229–33.

Jennings, James, "Theorizing Black Studies: The Continuing Role of Community Service in the Study of Race and Class," in Manning Marable, ed., *Dispatches from the Ebony Tower* (New York: Columbia University Press, 2000), 177–85.

Johnson, Deborah J., "Racial Socialization Strategies of Parents in Three Black Private Schools," in Diana T. Slaughter and Deborah J. Johnson, eds., *Visible Now: Blacks in Private Schools* (New York: Greenwood Press, 1988), 251–67.

Kelley, Robin D. G., "How the West Was One: On the Uses and Limitations of Diaspora," *The Black Scholar* 30:3–4 (fall–winter 2000): 31–35.

Klotman, Phyllis R. "Military Rites and Wrongs: African Americans in the U.S. Armed Forces," in Phyllis R. Klotman and Janet K. Cutler, eds. *Struggles for Representation: African American Documentary Film and Video* (Bloomington: Indiana University Press, 1999), 34–70.

Knight, Frederick, "Justifiable Homicide, Police Brutality, or Governmental Repression? The 1962 Los Angeles Police Shooting of Seven Members of the Nation of Islam," *The Journal of Negro History* 79:2 (spring 1994): 182–94.

Lane, Alycee J., "Black Bodies/Gay Bodies: The Politics of Race in the Gay/Military Battle," *Callaloo* (1994): 1074–88.

McBride, Dwight A. "Can the Queen Speak? Racial Essentialism, Sexuality, and the Problem of Authority," in Devon W. Carbado, ed. *Black Men on Race, Gender and Sexuality: A Reader* (New York: New York University Press, 1999), 253–75.

Michel, Claudine, "Teaching Haitian Vodou," *Spring: A Journal of Archetype and Culture* 61 (1997): 83–99.

Miller, Randi L., "Desegregation Experiences of Minority Students: Adolescent Coping Strategies in Five Connecticut High Schools," *Journal of Adolescent Research.* 4:2 (Sage Publications, Inc., April 1989): 173–89.

Mueller, Carol, "Ella Baker and the Origins of 'Participtory Democracy,' " in Vicki L. Crawford, Jacqueline Anne Rouse, and Barbara Woods, eds., *Women in the Civil Rights Movement: Trailblazers and Torchbearers, 1941–1965* (Bloomington: Indiana University Press, 1993), 51–70. (Formerly published by Carlson Publishing, Inc., 1990, Brooklyn, N.Y.)

Mullen, Harryette, "African Signs and Spirit Writing," *Callaloo* 19:3 (1996): 670–89.

Robinson, Cedric J., "In the Year 1915: D. W. Griffith and the Whitening of America," *Social Identities* 3:2 (1997): 161–92. (Carfax Publishing Limited, P.O. Box 25, Abingdon, Oxfordshire OX14 3UE, United Kingdom.)

Ross, Marlon B., "Some Glances at the Black Fag: Race, Same-Sex Desire, and Cultural Belonging," *Canadian Review of Comparative Literature* 3 (1994): 191–219.

INTRODUCTION

Jacqueline Bobo, Cynthia Hudley, Claudine Michel

BLACK STUDIES, AS A SOCIALLY ENGAGED FIELD of scholarly inquiry, is the progeny of centuries of research that seeks to redress long-standing misconceptions of Black inferiority, African heritage, and cultural significance. As early as the nineteenth century, groundbreaking volumes containing radical reinterpretations of Black history were published. These studies included George Washington Williams's *History of the Negro Race* (1882), and *History of the Colored Race in America* (1887), by William T. Alexander. The esteemed historian, social critic, and political theorist W. E. B. Du Bois published *The Philadelphia Negro* (1899), and his highly influential *The Souls of Black Folk* first appeared in 1903. While director of the Atlanta University Conferences from 1897 to 1910, Du Bois produced more extensive analyses of Black culture. The early twentieth century witnessed the production of foundational scholarly studies: *The Negro in the History of the United States* (1905), by Harold M. Tarver; Benjamin Brawley's *A Short History of the American Negro* (1913); *The Negro from Africa to America* (1924), by Willis D. Weatherford; and other landmark works from Du Bois, including *Black Reconstruction in America* (1935) and *Black Folk, Then and Now* (1939).[1]

The noted Black scholar Carter G. Woodson left an indelible mark on Black history. He received his Ph.D. from Harvard in 1912 and founded the Association for the Study of Negro Life and History in Washington, D.C., in 1915. Woodson published the prestigious journals *Journal of Negro History* and *Negro History Bulletin* through this organization. Woodson also established Negro History Week, now celebrated annually throughout February as Black History Month. Woodson's publications include *The Education of the Negro prior to 1861* (1915); *A Century of Negro Migration* (1918); and the pioneering study *The Negro in Our History* (1922), which for many years was the standard text in Black history and is still considered one of the finest studies documenting Black people's culture and history.[2]

Historic social justice movements preceded the mid-twentieth-century grassroots activist endeavors that led to fundamental alterations in social and political organizations, including institutions of higher learning. The first contemporary initiatives toward the establishment of Black Studies programs on college campuses were ignited at Merritt Junior

College in Oakland, California, in 1963. Although the course entitled "Negro History" failed to meet the specifications of activists Huey Newton and Bobby Seale, their organizing efforts in response to the course led to the formation of Soul Students' Advisory Council, a precursor to latter-day Black student unions.[3]

At the instigation of the campus Black Student Union in 1967–1968, a Black Studies program started at San Francisco State College, the first such curriculum in the country. During the following year San Francisco State became the first institution of higher education in the nation to establish an autonomous Black Studies department.[4] Student actions at another California university led to the creation of an academic department and a research center shortly thereafter. On October 14, 1968, twenty members of the Black Student Union at the University of California, Santa Barbara, gained control of a campus building that housed the main computer center, potentially shutting down the entire university. The students' actions followed years of lobbying and negotiating with university administrators and faculty about the racist environment and practices rampant at the university. The students demanded the creation of a Black Studies department, a center for Black Studies, necessary financial support for library materials relating to Black Studies research, and sufficient educational resources and outreach efforts for prospective students of color. In fall 1969 the Department of Black Studies, along with the Center for Black Studies, became autonomous academic and research units at UCSB.

Between 1968 and 1975 over five hundred academic units (programs and departments) offering Black Studies courses were in place across the country.[5] Currently, there are approximately 400 Black Studies programs or departments with 140 offering undergraduate degrees, 24 with M.A. programs and 5 awarding Ph.D. degrees.[6] As Black students and other students of color, in unprecedented numbers, matriculated into predominately white colleges and universities, they challenged mainstream scholarly discourse. Specifically, the students confronted the false notions that scholarly investigations were objective and unbiased explorations of the range of human knowledge, history, creativity, artistry, and scientific discovery.

Battle lines were subsequently drawn against canonical texts perpetuating mainstream hegemonic perspectives conveyed by faculty who were, for the most part, white males educated at elite private institutions and determined to maintain an outmoded status quo. The student movements, following the pioneering leadership of the Student Nonviolent Coordinating Committee (SNCC) of the 1960s, were grounded in more fully articulated paradigms of scholarship closely connected to a range of human interests, rather than serving the vested concerns of a narrow stratum of wealth and power. That no segment of the population was protected from social and political imperatives became more pronounced in the late 1960s and early 1970s, when male students were placed in jeopardy through the military draft that would force them to fight in a war no one comprehended. Even still, communities and families of color were especially hard hit by the race and classed-biased policies of the military draft during the Vietnam War. Students in general protested university practices designed to serve war interests: required Reserve Officer Training Corps (ROTC) and academic research that fueled the military industrial machinery through corporations such as Dow Chemical (the manufacturer of the deadly chemical napalm).

In this charged atmosphere of dawning awareness of social inequities affecting people of color, women, the poor and disenfranchised, political activism of the time resonated with the questioning of traditional tenets by a range of students. Proponents of Black

Studies and Ethnic Studies, especially, pushed for scholarship that was accountable to various populations, that provided a critique of traditional politics, culture, and social affairs, that worked affirmatively for transformation of the existing social order.

The establishment of Black Studies, Chicana/o Studies, Asian American Studies, and Native American Studies as legitimate scholarly domains is the most enduring and valuable academic result of the 1960s political crusades. That these fields were born of social unrest in addition to academic initiatives sets them apart from other newly emergent scholarly areas of study. Traditionally, a new field takes off from the findings of scholars working in existing disciplines. Researchers working in complementary theoretical traditions, using differing methodologies and utilizing distinctly separate disciplinary approaches, will achieve conceptual and intellectual convergence that transcends existing disciplinary and departmental boundaries. Theories, methods, and findings—indeed all of the tools of scholarly inquiry that were once scattered across multiple literatures—can be more coherently linked in new conceptual paradigms.

Thus intellectual and scientific parameters are realigned (often painfully and contentiously), interdisciplinary programs conceived, corollary fields differentiated and reintegrated, and ultimately new academic disciplines and departments created. Recent examples range from the linkage of human prehistory and current social conditions by the study of evolutionary psychology to the uniting of the physical, biological, and medical sciences in biomedical engineering. Further innovations include the creation of new areas of research such as Diaspora Studies, Queer Studies and Environmental Racism, among other pressing subjects.

Markedly different origins can be delineated in the development of Black Studies. At the field's inception, scholars defined it as an intellectual necessity linked with political imperatives: student activism, collaboration among diverse Black communities, and scholarship in support of changes in the larger society. Progressively, Black Studies has evolved over the past thirty years as a unique and vital realm of research, training, and application, with documented intellectual integrity as autonomous academic departments and research centers granting undergraduate and advanced degrees.

PERSPECTIVES

Black Studies is fundamentally transdisciplinary. It is grounded in a range of traditional disciplines within the social sciences, humanities research, and natural and physical sciences. It exists not as a negotiation between or at the intersection of multiple coexisting disciplines, but as a separate yet integrated discipline concerned with questions that both encompass and transcend the individual fields, yielding areas of discoveries that offer unique research models, fresh syntheses, theoretical frameworks, methods, and insights applied to rigorous interrogation of all of human existence. It is an expansive, inclusive field of study.

Further, Black scholars have defined, articulated, and elaborated legitimate areas of scholarship, circumventing the restrictions of narrowly defined disciplines. The innovations of Black Studies research provide distinctive angles and critical perspectives from which facts and experiences are analyzed, presented, and written about. For example, research in American education has spawned an entire new discipline, the field of urban education that, at its inception, was simply a code phrase for the education of Black children.

In medical research, Black scientists have made significant inroads in controlling the devastating effects of sickle cell anemia. The ramifications for the study of other pernicious diseases are encouraging. In other areas, grassroots activism has spurred academic scrutiny. These include neighborhood resistance against the dumping of toxic waste materials in vulnerable communities.

The evidence is clear: core scholarship within the diverse areas of Black Studies expands, enhances, and enriches traditional disciplines in profound and significant ways. These complex tasks require both theoretical and methodological sophistication. Black Studies has met that challenge. The melding of cultures and research paradigms within Black Studies has demonstrated a commitment to issues of social, educational, and economic disparities, defining curricula vitally engaged with present-day societal issues. Interdisciplinary and multidivisional, these approaches create original and innovative bodies of knowledge, responding to the challenges of this country's increasingly divisive political, economic, and racialized climate that continues to exclude and marginalize those who are not considered part of mainstream America. Black Studies engages issues about historical and contemporary forms of resistance and resilience in response to local and global crises. Many lessons can be learned from cultural and literary expressions used by Black people to resist and exist in a society still ravaged by the ills of racism, sexism, homophobia, and classism.

The Black Studies Reader includes essays about the origins and institutionalization of the field, the history of Black people's military service, diverse religious and spiritual beliefs in Black life, cultural studies as an analytical paradigm, media and representation, communal values and responsibilities, educational reform, racial exclusion and inclusion, sexism, homophobia, and issues of social justice. The volume is divided into three parts: Theorizing Black Studies; Conceptualizing Culture and Ideology; and, Sexuality, Education, Religion. In the first part the sections are: "Evolution of Consciousness;" "Black Feminism: Acts of Resistance;" and, "Representing Black Men." The second part contains the following: "Text Creation and Representation" and "Interrogating Cultural Expressions." The final part includes: "Autonomy, Subjectivity and Sexuality;" "Education: Pedagogy and Practice;" and, "Religion in Black Life."

Part I: Theorizing Black Studies
The opening chapters present critical perspectives on the development and ongoing issues of Black Studies research. *Section A: Evolution of Consciousness* opens with a foundational essay by Robert L. Harris Jr., "The Intellectual and Institutional Development of Africana Studies." Written in 1990 as part of a Ford Foundation study of the contemporary state of Black Studies, Harris's article delineates four stages in the evolution of Black Studies as an area of scholarly inquiry: *(a)* the latter part of the nineteenth century up to the beginning of World War II; *(b)* the 1940s analyses by white scholars that were spurred by Gunnar Myrdal's two-volume study *An American Dilemma: The Negro Problem and Modern Democracy* (1944)—this second stage lasted through the early 1960s; *(c)* from the mid-1960s through the mid-1980s, during which Black Studies entered a period of legitimization and institutionalization; and *(d)* the contemporary period of theoretical refinement, analysis, and interpretation.

The next article sets forth the fundamental contributions of "Black Studies in Liberal Arts Education." Johnnetta B. Cole, former president of Spelman College, affirms the political nature of the field, asserting that Black people were enabled to look at themselves in new ways, to transmit Black values, and to pass on a dignified version of Black history. Cole maintains that Black Studies has served as a critique of educational institutions in American society, challenging what is taught in the liberal arts curricula of America's colleges and universities. "Black Studies in Liberal Arts Education" highlights the various ways in which Black Studies scholarship articulates proposals to help correct fundamental problems in American higher education and, consequently, in society.

Moving from an analysis of the innovative contributions of the field at its inception, James Jennings's "Theorizing Black Studies: The Continuing Role of Community Service in the Study of Race and Class" convincingly argues that programmatic links with neighborhood institutions and organizations are crucial to the purpose, theoretical grounding, and teaching of Black Studies. Attention to community service facilitates the growth and direction of intellectual inquiry, while furthering the impact on the analysis of political and economic issues facing Black communities and U.S. urban society. Jennings marshals the examples of the politically inspired work of the earlier preeminent Black scholars Charles V. Hamilton, Ida B. Wells-Barnett, Kenneth Clark, Harold Cruse, W. E. B. Du Bois, and others in a cogent assertion that Black Studies scholarship must be geared toward solving the social, economic, and political problems of Black communities.

The historian and cultural critic Robin D. G. Kelley probes the benefits and drawbacks of expansive analyses of Black people in "How the West Was One: On the Uses and Limitations of Diaspora." Kelley submits that Diaspora studies have existed since the mid-1950s and, with their current return to analytical prominence, invoke profound questions not only for a greater understanding of Black people worldwide, but for an altered perspective on the writing of histories of the modern West.

The specific nature of Black people's centuries-long struggles against oppression is examined in the articles in *Section B: Black Feminism: Acts of Resistance*. Mounting a challenge to white women's assessments of the role of Black women in feminist movements, the historian Elsa Barkley Brown presents the life story of an early Black feminist activist who combined sophisticated thinking about the advancement of Black people with practical, successful actions. Brown's article, "Womanist Consciousness: Maggie Lena Walker and the Independent Order of Saint Luke," details the collective activities of Black women in Richmond, Virginia, during the late nineteenth and early twentieth centuries toward economic, educational, social, and political freedom.

Yet another refutation of white feminists' claims of unity is expressed by Rosalyn Terborg-Penn in the article "Discontented Black Feminists: Prelude and Postscript to the Passage of the Nineteenth Amendment." The Fourteenth Amendment, passed in 1870, granted Black men the right to vote. Although white women were agitating for the right to vote, their concern was exclusively for white female enfranchisement, rather than for the rights of all women to vote. Terborg-Penn examines the concerted efforts of Black female suffragists to claim their full rights, including the right to vote contained through the passage of the Nineteenth Amendment in 1920, despite severe opposition from both white men and white women.

The leadership roles played by Black women in multiple arenas is examined fully by Carol Mueller in "Ella Baker and the Origins of 'Participatory Democracy.'" Ella Baker (1903–1986) was a guiding influence on several generations of civil rights workers. In the 1940s she was a field organizer for the NAACP in the South; during the 1950s she was the first organizer of the Southern Christian Leadership Conference; and in 1960 she was the founder of the Student Nonviolent Coordinating Committee. Baker was a proponent of the idea of "participatory democracy," a principle that involved people on the grassroots level in the decision-making process. For Baker, long-term political gains were possible when people were enabled to act on their own convictions and to develop their innate leadership capabilities.

Political activist and scholar Angela Y. Davis issues challenges to contemporary feminists of color in the article "Black Women and the Academy," derived from her closing address at the "Black Women in the Academy: Defending Our Name: 1894–1994" conference at the Massachusetts Institute of Technology. The occasion marked the 100th anniversary of the Black Women's Club Movement, initiated in 1894. Davis called on Black women in the academy to find ways to connect with and at the same time be critical of the work of their foremothers. The effort was needed to "affirm historical continuity and effect some conscious historical ruptures." Davis offers four challenging, affirming, and weighty truths that Black female scholars must address: the white establishment is no longer the single monolithic force that Black women have to position themselves against; Black women can no longer overlook the ways in which they reproduce the forms of domination which they attribute to others; Black women have to rid themselves of the habit of defining themselves with their status as victims; and the fervent defense of the name of Black women cannot be allowed to define Black women in opposition to Asian, Latina, Pacific Island, and Native American women.

Continuing challenges to families and communities, ever present throughout Black women's history in this country, are also manifest in the lives of Black men. The four articles in *Section C: Representing Black Men* offer an analysis of the various permutations of repression and resistance throughout history. That there were free Black people before the Civil War and scores of Black abolitionists in staunch opposition to slavery are little-known facts highlighted in Jacqueline Shearer's television documentary *The Massachusetts 54th Colored Infantry* (1991). The program presents the story of the first company of Black soldiers in the Union army, assembled because of agitation from the Black community in Boston in the nineteenth century. The documentary is as much the chronicle of the lives of free Black people in Boston as it is the story of the founding of the Massachusetts 54th. Shearer, writing from her long experience as a filmmaker, notes in her essay, "How Deep, How Wide?: Perspectives on the Making of *The Massachusetts 54th Colored Infantry*," that creating a film where men were the center of the story was a unique challenge for her. She observes that usually men *look* and women are *looked at*; in this case there was the opportunity to reverse the gaze. It was also a chance to portray a different aspect of the relationship between Black women and Black men: "something other than the posturing and sniping that too often wins the headlines."

The theme of Black people in military service is expanded upon in Phyllis R. Klotman's "Military Rites and Wrongs: African Americans in the U.S. Armed Forces." Klotman takes a closer look at Shearer's documentary of Black men fighting in the Civil War, then goes further in her exploration of how Black people have viewed their military service as inextricably connected to their ongoing struggles for freedom and equality. Klotman provides detailed evidence of her assertions through analyzing the films of William Miles who documented Black people's military service during World War I and World War II in the films *Men of Bronze* (1977), *The Different Drummer: Blacks in the Military* (1983), and *Liberators: Fighting on Two Fronts in World War II* (1992).

Frederick Knight, in "Justifiable Homicide, Police Brutality, or Governmental Repression? The 1962 Los Angeles Police Shooting of Seven Members of the Nation of Islam," draws attention to a watershed moment in the ideological development of Malcolm X and Los Angeles racial politics before the 1965 Watts rebellions. Knight argues that the Nation of Islam was targeted because the organization was a perceived threat to the racial order due to its growing national influence and its stands on police indifference to the violent repression of African-American human rights. Also, it was the only national grassroots organization not wholly opposed to the use of self-defense at the time and a force that could oppose police aggression. This particular shooting incident, Knight maintains, helped create a short-lived coalition among the various African-American groups across a wide political spectrum. However, the coalition was not able to sustain a prolonged, united struggle against police brutality and broader issues.

In a cogently argued essay, Marlon B. Ross looks at historical and cultural representations of Black lesbian and gay communities, with a specific concentration on representations of Black male sexuality. In his article, "Some Glances at the Black Fag: Race, Same-Sex Desire, and Cultural Belonging," Ross submits that "images of Black manhood that came to dominate . . . are always at the service of ideological purposes that can work for or against the advancement of African American communities."

Part II: Conceptualizing Culture and Ideology

The articles in Part II offer generative analyses relating to the effects of cultural representations during critical historical periods. *Section D: Text Creation and Representation* takes the role of cultural participants seriously. Rather than submitting to prevailing theories about the powerless objects of cultural imagery, these cultural scholars validate the ways social groups have strongly influenced the representations of their histories. In "*The Color Purple*: Black Women as Cultural Readers," Jacqueline Bobo explores how a specific audience can both recognize racist and stereotypical representations in mainstream Hollywood cultural productions, yet can also mentally reconstruct the work to resonate with critical areas of their own lives. She examines this phenomenon through contemporary cultural theories of audience analysis, specifically concepts about "cultural competencies" and "articulation" that provide an understanding of the means by which members of particular social groups, in their interactions with mainstream cultural forms, can subvert the oppressive ideologies embedded within the text. Alternatively, audience members, in this instance Black females, can form a collective alliance, through their affinities with a particular text, that allows the group to overcome repression in other aspects of their lives.

Analyzing the influences of a different cultural form, the media scholar Catherine Squires argues in "Black Talk Radio: Defining Community Needs and Identity" that within Chicago, WVON-AM radio is a vital and helpful institution for the Black public sphere. Her conclusions call into question the widely held pessimistic view of commercial media's role in the decline of the public sphere. Because the radio station is owned by Black people, it is able to draw and sustain a substantial and loyal audience. Not only does the station speak to Black issues, it speaks from a Black framework. Black ownership, Squires argues, breeds trust, and even more significantly, a sense of community ownership among its faithful listeners.

In "Chasing Fae: *The Watermelon Woman* and Black Lesbian Possibility," Laura L. Sullivan considers how this first feature film made by a Black lesbian filmmaker destabilizes viewers' preconceived notions of members of marginalized groups. Through its technical construction and subject matter, *The Watermelon Woman* (1996) engages viewers in a reconsideration of the unstable, complex, and contradictory nature of identity, specifically that of a figure that had been rendered invisible in dominant culture, that of the Black lesbian.

The esteemed Black feminist scholar Akasha Gloria Hull presents personal testimony of how Black people transcend exploitation to gain the strength to develop empowerment. Hull's groundbreaking essay, "DreadPath/LockSpirit," uncovers the relationship between dreads, spirituality, and states of consciousness. Recounting her experiences, she reveals how one may use dreads to release locked-in energy and make a fresh return to nature. This is a departure from a static state that is markedly different from the ever-changing dynamic that makes deadlocks so attractive in the first place. "Locking" is about new growth, new forms of being, positive flow of energy, and a renewed and transformed sense of self. It is also about faith, cleansing, healing, patience, discipline, about trusting a process and surrendering, all key elements to reaching spiritual consciousness. Hull submits that original responses and authenticity in general (dreading in this case) both require and lead to a degree of comfort with spiritual levels of existence.

Specific evidence of how cultural accretions have the potential for strategies of resistance are analyzed in the previous section and developed further in *Section E: Interrogating Cultural Representations*. The political scientist and cultural scholar Cedric J. Robinson provides substantial documentation of the ways a particularly pernicious film was able to naturalize a new American social order. The film director D. W. Griffith drew on a confluence of historical, social, and cultural circumstances to position his film *The Birth of a Nation* (1915) as the preeminent storehouse of false knowledge about Black people. Robinson details in "In the Year 1915: D. W. Griffith and the Whitening of America" how Griffith drew on the cooperation of President Woodrow Wilson and the novelist Thomas Dixon Jr. to present a "mythical national history" about white entitlement and privilege. This was to the long-term detriment of Black people and newly arrived immigrant populations because, according to Robinson, America, at the beginnings of the twentieth century, had emerged in the global economy as a major force. Race discourse functioned, in this new economic climate, to contain a vast and disparate labor force, through cultural discipline, social habituation, and political regulation.

In the latter part of the twentieth century, Cultural Studies, as a theoretical approach to understanding the position of specific social groups, became a predominant method of analysis. The British scholar Stuart Hall offers valuable insights about the politics of cultural representation and cultural criticism in "What Is This 'Black' in Black Popular Culture?" Hall's essay is derived from his presentation at the 1991 Black Popular Conference held at the Dia Center for the Arts and the Studio Museum in Harlem in New York City. At a historical moment when the United States is a world power and the center of global production and circulation, Hall reminds us that "popular culture has historically become the dominant form of global culture, so it is at the same time the scene, par excellence, of commodification, of the industries where culture enters directly into the circuits of a dominant technology—the circuits of power and capital." For Hall, the struggle is over cultural hegemony using cultural strategies that can make a difference, that can shift "the dispositions of power."

In "Dyes and Dolls: Multicultural Barbie and the Merchandising of Difference," the noted scholar Ann duCille recounts the history of the creation of the original Barbie doll, that of the first Black Barbies in the 1960s as well as the advent of the more "ethnically correct" Black Barbies of the 1990s. She ventures into an important historical phenomenon to offer an analysis of the commodity culture of which Barbie is both part and product. DuCille explains that there is always a subtext to these genderized, racialized, and sexualized dolls that has allowed them to acquire iconographical status. The very act of theorizing racial and gender differences, duCille declares, affirms the notion that there is a center—a mold for Barbie in this case—that raises questions about diversity and authenticity, about how Blackness is at once different and the same in dolls where plastic, dyes, and ethnic fabrics determine both the typical and stereotypical. For duCille, the demands of capitalism have, yet again, reduced mass-produced racially marked bodies to racialized-marketed bodies, the very signs of the difference it attempts to exploit.

The constellation of word choices and modes of expression are analyzed in the next article, "African Signs and Spirit Writing." The poet and critic Harryette Mullen argues that "any theory of African-American literature that privileges a speech-based poetics to the exclusion of more writerly texts will cost us impoverishment of the tradition." Mullen's assertions are a response to the widely known scholarship of literature scholar Henry Louis Gates (and others), positing that Black literary traditions privilege orality. While Mullen acknowledges the research from which Gates's claims emanate, she seeks to provide a fuller range of interpretations and an expansion of how knowledges circulated historically within Black life. Mullen feels it is necessary to reclaim the interlocking complexity of all African forms of cultural expression, without which traditions, values, and ethos would not be rendered to their greatest extent.

Part III: Sexuality, Education, Religion

Activists' endeavors toward self-determination for a diverse array of social groups are examined in Part III. The specific components of these efforts are presented in *Section F: Autonomy, Subjectivity, and Sexuality*. The first article shows how queer theory has allowed gay and lesbian people the means to interrogate different forms of sexualities. Traditionally, however, queer theory exhibits structured absences about people of color. In "Black (W)holes and the Geometry of Black Female Sexuality," Evelynn Hammonds critiques queer theory as presented by white theorists, then offers ways that queer theory can be opened up to explore Black lesbian sexuality, and, more broadly, Black female sexualities in general. Hammonds states that Black feminist theorists must develop a complex conception of racialized sexualities as a counter to the omissions within white queer theorizing and to reclaim that which was lost through the "production of silence," the historical legacy surrounding Black women's sexual past. The writings and theories presented by Black lesbians, with the focus on female desire and agency, are critical to any theories of Black female sexualities.

In "Black Bodies/Gay Bodies: The Politics of Race in the Gay/Military Battle," Alycee J. Lane cogently illuminates how many gay and lesbian advocates, during the battle to lift the ban on homosexuals in the military, conflated these struggles with the civil rights movement. Gay and lesbian activists' recourse to arguments used by African Americans in their fight for greater inclusion in American society, did not help to clarify the complexities with which the homophobic policy was constructed. Instead, by collapsing Black and gay and lesbian struggles and denying their fundamental differences, advocates decontextualized the specificity of both struggles. This helped to polarize those who supported civil rights and those who supported gay and lesbian rights, which in turn led to debates about the accuracy of conflating the two struggles. By redirecting focus away from the discriminatory practices of the military onto debates about the relationship between the gay and lesbian movement and civil rights struggles, the battle for eradicating the ban on gay and lesbian military service was weakened.

Traversing the continuum within which ideas about race, sex, and gender are considered, Patrick Bellegarde-Smith, in "Hormones and Melanin: The Dimensions of 'Race,' Sex, and Gender in Africology: Reflexive Journeys," argues against a biologistic viewpoint that, in the past, had colored ideologies prevalent in the West. African and African-derived cultures present essential differences in their civilizational processes as compared and contrasted with the Western world. This is particularly true as concerns sex, gender, and received notions regarding "race."

Dwight A. McBride, in "Can the Queen Speak? Racial Essentialism, Sexuality, and the Problem of Authority," argues against those Black intellectuals who presume to speak for "the race" and, in the process, exclude a full consideration of all aspects of Black communities, specifically, gay and lesbian populations. Additionally, McBride challenges the authority of those who have neglected a broad analysis of Black people. McBride examines the "political process that legitimates and qualifies certain racial subjects to speak for (represent) 'the race' and excludes others from that very possibility," and takes the field of Black Studies to task for the way in which it has "provided no serious and sustained discussion of the specificity of African American lesbian and gay folk."

The right of all students to quality education devoid of discriminatory practices is the focus of *Section G: Education: Pedagogy and Practice.* There is a consistent theme in education literature asserting that parents of poor and minority children are not involved in their children's schooling. However, most of those data represent the perspective of the school. The education scholars Cynthia Hudley and Rhoda Barnes surveyed parents of African-American children enrolled in grades K to 12 to understand parents' perspectives on their own participation. Their findings, reported in "Home-School Partnerships through the Eyes of Parents," reveal that parents were highly involved in their children's education, but these activities occurred at home rather than at the school site. As well, these parents felt that the schools should communicate more effectively with them and develop more culturally sensitive teaching practices at the school sites.

Studies of school desegregation all too often fail to consider the experiences of minority students and the extent to which these children are integrated into the larger social world of the school. Randi L. Miller explores the youth culture of Black adolescents attending desegregated high schools in "Desegregation Experiences of Minority Students: Adolescent Coping Strategies in Five Connecticut High Schools." This study describes four distinct strategies that African-American youth used in coping with the dominant youth culture in their predominantly white high schools. Results suggest that coping strategies varied systematically by school, and some schools were more successful that others in fostering positive interracial contact.

Black parents must not only develop strategies for coping with racism and discrimination, they must also successfully prepare their children to cope with issues of race while maintaining a positive sense of self. "Racial Socialization Strategies of Parents in Three Black Private Schools," by Deborah Johnson, examines how school environments either complement or obstruct parents' specific racial socialization practices. Findings indicate that parents socialize their children to use a broad range of racial coping strategies roughly categorized as reactive, proactive, or neutral. Further, when choosing a private school, parents deliberately choose schools that complement their preferred strategies.

The discussion of racial themes and injustice can lead to intense emotional responses from students in college classrooms. In "Talking about Race, Learning about Racism: The Application of Racial Identity Theory in the Classroom," Beverly Daniel Tatum discusses her experiences teaching a course to college students on the psychology of racism and racial identity development theory. She identifies three major belief systems that serve as sources of students' resistance to learning about race and racism: race as a taboo topic, America as an inherently fair society, and racism as unrelated to personal experience. Further, she discusses instructional strategies for overcoming resistance to the learning process.

Religion, in all its dimensions, has been an integral part of Black life. It has provided sustenance, hope, and community and is of vital importance to Black students. The articles in *Section H: Religion in Black Life* examine a diverse range of religious practices significant to Black people's history. The first article, written by a leading liberation ethicist, unmasks the rationales by which white antebellum Christians deluded themselves into protecting and sanctioning centuries of Black enslavement. Katie Cannon, in "Slave Ideology and Biblical Interpretation," validates that chattel slavery was a political and economic system that required the active support of white clergy, church governing boards, denominational missionary societies, and the rank and file of white church members. Cannon persuasively argues that despite white Christians' false religious legitimation, "Beneath their rhetoric and logic, the question of using the Bible to justify the subordination of Black people was fraught with their desire to maintain their dominance, to guarantee their continued social control. If the powerbrokers of the antebellum society were to continue benefitting from the privileges and opportunities the political economy provided, then the slaveholding aristocrats must, as a basic condition, maintain their domination over the ideological sectors of society: religion, culture, education, media."

Jacquelyn Grant, in "Black Theology and the Black Women," calls into question the prevailing actions of liberation theologians as well as Black theologians who profess to work in the name of the poor, the oppressed, and divine identification with those marginalized by the established social and political order, yet do not acknowledge the significance of Black women's historical oppression and value in Black churches. Grant contends that sexism is at the root of the sustained invisibility of Black females in Black churches and governing bodies and that the experiences of enslavement, oppression, and continual subjugation require theologians of all kinds to fully integrate Black women in the "theological enterprise." According to Grant, an authentic theology of divine liberation must, of necessity, ensure that Black women and men share jointly in the leadership in theology, in the churches, and in Black communities.

"Teaching Haitian Vodou" is a valuable recasting of the perceptions that this ancient religion is composed of superstitions, blood and sacrifice, sorcery and witchcraft. The Haitian scholar Claudine Michel provides a fuller understanding of Vodou in the lives and cultures of people of African descent throughout the disapora. Haitian Vodou is a religion of moral sustenance and coherence, of cosmological understandings, of humanism and communality. Haitian Vodou is a practical faith that is omnipresent and exists without the necessity of formal church and clergy, of written dogma and instructional material, and whose primary concerns are the well-being of the individual and the welfare of the group.

Richard Brent Turner, in "Islam in the African-American Experience," offers much needed information on a long-neglected scholarly investigation of Black people's religious experiences. Islam has existed in various forms in the life of Black people in this country and has had a profound impact on racial, ethical, and political relations. Turner examines pivotal figures and eras significant to Islam and Black people: (1) the African Muslims during enslavement who followed the religious and resistance practices of Bilali and Salih Bilali in the Georgia Sea Islands; (2) the twentieth-century urban-based Black Muslim activities; (3) the Ahmadiyya Movement in Islam, begun in the 1920s, the first multiracial American Islam alliance; and (4) the transmutation of the Nation of Islam through its origins in Detroit, through the leadership of Elijah Muhammad in Chicago, the widespread appeal of Malcolm X in the 1960s, and the contemporary activities of Louis Farrakan and Warith Dean Mohammed.

We thank those who embarked with us on this journey, principally the scholars whose articles are included in this volume. Appreciation also is due our editor, Karen Wolny, and assistants Sara Folks and Jaclyn Bergeron. Colleagues, family, and friends have been steadfast in their commitment to this project. Kudos to all.

NOTES

1. Manning Marable, *How Capitalism Underdeveloped Black America: Problems in Race, Political Economy and Society* (Boston: South End Press, 1983), 220.

2. Alvin White, "Godfather of Black History," *Sepia* (February 1976): 58–65.

3. Huey Newton and Bobby Seale would later start the Oakland-based organization The Black Panther Party for Self-Defense. Robert H. Brisbane, *Black Activism: Racial Revolution in the United States 1954–1970* (Valley Forge, Pa.: Judson Press, 1974), 195.

4. Robert H. Brisbane, *Black Activism*, 226.

5. Thomas J. La Belle and Christopher R. Ward, *Ethnic Studies and Multiculturalism* (Albany: State University of New York Press, 1996), 78.

6. Robert S. Boynton, "Out of Africa, and Back," *New York Times*, Section 4A, Education Life (April 14, 2002), 37.

PART I
THEORIZING BLACK STUDIES

1

THE INTELLECTUAL AND INSTITUTIONAL DEVELOPMENT OF AFRICANA STUDIES

Robert L. Harris Jr.

AFRICANA STUDIES IS THE MULTIDISCIPLINARY ANALYSIS of the lives and thought of people of African ancestry on the African continent and throughout the world. It embraces Africa, Afro-America, and the Caribbean, but does not confine itself to those three geographical areas. Africana studies examines people of African ancestry wherever they may be found—for example, in Central and South America, Asia, and the Pacific Islands. Its primary means of organization are racial and cultural. Many of the themes of Africana studies are derived from the historical position of African peoples in relation to Western societies and in the dynamics of slavery, oppression, colonization, imperialism, emancipation, self-determination, liberation, and socioeconomic and political development.

There have been four stages in the intellectual and institutional development of Africana studies as an area of scholarly inquiry. The first stage began in the 1890s and lasted until the Second World War. During this first stage, numerous organizations emerged to document, record, and analyze the history, culture, and status of African peoples. For example, the Bethel Literary and Historical Association of Washington, D.C., formed in 1881, sponsored lectures on numerous topics, such as the Egyptians, the Zulus, and various aspects of African culture, in addition to contemporary issues affecting African Americans. Other organizations functioned in a similar manner—for example, Philadelphia's American Negro Historical Society, established in 1897; Washington, D.C.'s American Negro Academy, also started in 1897; and New York's Negro Society for Historical Research, organized in 1911.

These early black literary and historical associations sought to preserve and to publicize the legacy of African peoples. They were superseded in 1915, when Carter G. Woodson formed the Association for the Study of Afro-American (formerly Negro) Life and History (ASALH), which still survives today. Woodson laid the groundwork for systematic study of African peoples through the association's annual meetings; the *Journal of Negro History*, launched in 1916; the national observance of Negro History Week (now Black History Month), started in 1926; publication of the *Negro History Bulletin*, begun in 1933; and the formation of Associated Publishers to print books on the Black experience in America and throughout the world. ASALH has been the premier organization in promoting historical consciousness and in generating greater understanding of African heritage in the United States.

In 1897 W. E. B. Du Bois initiated an ambitious program at Atlanta University to examine various categories of African-American life in ten-year cycles. He proposed that such studies be continued for at least one hundred years to provide knowledge and understanding of the Black family, church, social organizations, education, and economic development in the United States. From 1898 to 1914, the Atlanta University studies produced sixteen monographs, which consisted of more than 2,100 pages of research. Du Bois, Woodson, Lorenzo J. Greene, Charles H. Wesley, E. Franklin Frazier, Ralph J. Bunche, Charles S. Johnson, Abram Harris, Sterling Brown, and other pioneering Black scholars produced an impressive body of scholarship to correct the errors, omissions, and distortions of black life and history that prevailed among white academics and the American public.

The second stage for Africana studies began with the study of Black America by Gunnar Myrdal. This stage was in some respects a setback. Myrdal, who began his project for the Carnegie Corporation in 1939, confined his analysis to the American social, political, and economic order. There was growing concern about the role and place of the Black population during the Second World War, as a majority of African Americans became urban. Black migration northward, which had begun in large numbers during the 1890s, had accelerated during World War I, and had slowed during the Depression of the 1930s, mushroomed during World War II, making the Black presence in America more a national than a regional or primarily southern concern. Believing that Black people in the United States were fundamentally Americans who had no significant African cultural background or identity, Myrdal accepted the formulation of the University of Chicago School of Sociology that ethnic and racial contact led not only to conflict but also to inevitable assimilation and absorption into the dominant society. His two-volume study, *An American Dilemma: The Negro Problem and Modern Democracy*, published in 1944, had an important influence on scholarship, especially the work of white academics during this second stage.

White scholars, by and large, had ignored Black people. The Columbia University historian John W. Burgess had boldly stated: "[A] black skin means membership in a race of men which has never itself succeeded in subjecting passion to reason; has never, therefore, created any civilization of any kind." After World War II, as the Black population in the United States became predominantly urban and as scholarship in general shed notions of inherent racial inferiority and superiority with the Nazi debacle, white scholars devoted increasing attention to African Americans' status in the United States. They sought environmental rather than biogenetic explanations for African Americans' inferior status.

In *Mark of Oppression* (1951), Abram Kardiner and Lionel Ovesey hypothesized that African Americans emerged from slavery without a culture, with "no intra-psychic defenses—no pride, no group solidarity, no tradition." They argued: "The marks of his previous status were still upon him—socially, psychologically, and emotionally, and from these he has never since freed himself." Stanley Elkins in his book *Slavery* (1959) concluded that African Americans were not genetically inferior but were made inferior by the process of enslavement, which they internalized and passed on to succeeding generations. In *Beyond the Melting Pot: The Negroes, Puerto Ricans, Jews, Italians, and Irish of New York City* (1963),

Nathan Glazer and Daniel P. Moynihan attributed African-American status to the absence of middle-class values and norms among the Black population in general. Two years later, in *The Negro Family: The Case for National Action*, Moynihan wrote: "Three centuries of injustice have brought about deep-seated structural distortions in the life of the Negro American." He concluded that "the present tangle of pathology is capable of perpetuating itself without assistance from the white world."

Whereas Burgess had implied that Africans had never created anything of worth and therefore African Americans were descended from an inferior people, post–World War II white scholars, in the main, identified African-American status not with an inglorious African past but with deficiencies occasioned by slavery, segregation, and discrimination. It is important to note that these scholars believed that the end of racial oppression would not immediately produce racial equality, not because of lack of social opportunity but because of the accumulated pathological behavior of Black people. In other words, Black people were not divinely created inferior but were made inferior over time. The sum of racial oppression and its alleged internalization by Black people dramatically affected their lives across generations.

Another significant post–World War II development was the creation of African studies programs that had no real link to Black people in the New World. Although Melville Herskovits, a white anthropologist and proponent of African studies, tried to join the study of Africa with the lives of Black people in the New World, African studies became wedded to a modernization theory that measured African societies by Western standards. African history, culture, and politics were explored more within the context of the colonial powers than with any attention to African cultural continuities in the Western Hemisphere. This compartmentalization of knowledge regarding Black people departed significantly from the scholarship of individuals such as Du Bois and Woodson during the first stage in the development of Africana studies.

The civil rights revolution, the Black power drive, and the Black consciousness movement initiated a third stage of Africana studies. During this era, larger numbers of Black students entered predominantly white colleges and universities. Most of these students were the first generation of their families to attend college. They encountered faculties that were almost entirely white and a curriculum that was primarily Eurocentric in perspective. The "melting pot" thesis prevailed as the paradigm of American society in which all groups, regardless of background, assimilated to an ideal that was primarily white, Anglo-Saxon, and Protestant. Ironically, at a time when African nations were achieving independence from colonial rule, Africa seemed unrelated to Black people in the United States. If Africa was discussed in classes, it was generally as an adjunct to European imperialism. In large measure, Black people were seen as pawns rather than as actors, as victims more than as victors.

Together with many Black scholars from the first stage of Africana studies, Black college students challenged the prevailing orthodoxies on predominantly white campuses. They demanded the employment of Black professors and the establishment of Africana studies departments and programs. They pressed for the inclusion of African studies in the newly formed Africana studies programs. The inclusion of African studies was important for several reasons. First, African Americans have historically linked their destiny with the future of Africa. Second, the image of Africa has had significant consequences for the status of

African Americans. Third, African ancestry has informed the cultural heritage of African Americans as much as their presence in the United States. Fourth, the history, politics, and culture of Africa could stand as a counterweight to the dominance of Western culture in American education.

The Eurocentric focus of the college curriculum basically excluded people of African ancestry or studied them through a European filter. Eurocentrist scholars ignored the growth of civilization in Africa, especially in Egypt, or co-opted Egyptian civilization as part of a European rather than an African continuum. They also ignored the African heritage of African Americans, characterizing them as having begun their existence in North America as *tabulae rasae*—blank slates to be imprinted with Euro-American culture.

Although some colleges and universities were willing to establish Africana studies programs, they were less willing to organize Africana studies departments. Faculty within the traditional departments were reluctant to give up their prerogative of determining what constituted a course in history, literature, or government; who would take such courses; and how the professors teaching them would be evaluated for employment, promotion, and tenure. Advocates of Africana studies departments questioned how members of traditional departments that had not offered courses on the Black experience or hired Black faculty could sit in judgment on the nature and quality of work being done in this newly emerging field of study.

The third stage of Africana studies, from about the mid-1960s to the mid-1980s, was a period of legitimization and institutionalization. Few scholars were prepared to teach Africana studies courses. The shift in perspective from Eurocentrism to Afrocentrism required the recovery, organization, and accessibility of research materials that made Black people, their lives, and their thoughts the center of analysis and interpretation. Many white scholars in particular had assumed that there was not sufficient documentation on which to base sound judgments about the personal and collective experiences of Black people in the United States. However, with the new interest in black life and culture, federal, state, and local archivists combed their collections for materials on the African-American experience and published several useful guides. Major projects began assembling and publishing the papers of Black leaders, writers, and organizations. It is now clear that there are abundant materials (print, visual, and sound) to reconstruct and to interpret the African-American past.

The prodigious research of Black and white scholars has dramatically changed the manner in which we now view African Americans. Most scholars today acknowledge the persistence of African culture in the United States. They no longer accept the idea that African Americans passively acquiesced to oppression, recognizing that, on the contrary, they actively resisted oppression in a variety of ways. In large measure, scholars have come to accept the United States as a pluralistic society with multiple viable cultures, rather than as a "melting pot." We think more of acculturation, with give-and-take, than of assimilation—particularly in the form of total absorption into the dominant culture, which itself is now being redefined.

Africana studies has achieved legitimacy and has become institutionalized within higher education. It now has moved into a fourth stage of theoretical refinement and more sophisticated analysis and interpretation. The fundamental research tools have been developed, although there will certainly be a need to update and to supplement them as new materials become available. In general, the field is in fairly good condition, but there are some problems, or perhaps opportunities to improve it.

Because the formats for multidisciplinary programs vary from campus to campus, there will probably not be a single method of organization for Africana studies. The ideal format is the department structure, which allows for selection of faculty and development of curriculum. Programs with faculty in traditional departments can also be successful, provided that they have some control of faculty lines. The program, however, becomes a more complex arrangement, especially in decisions for hiring, promotion, and tenure. Joint appointments carry similar problems, especially for junior faculty. They are less burdensome for senior faculty, whose tenure has already been established. Cross-listing of courses is one means by which departments and programs can take greater advantage of faculty resources on their campuses. However, before such cross-listing can be effective, there must first be a strong core faculty within the department or program. Otherwise, the Africana studies curriculum becomes too dependent on the priorities of other departments.

One goal for the fourth stage of Africana studies should be to broaden and deepen the field of inquiry. This prospect becomes somewhat difficult for those departments and programs with limited numbers of faculty. Small faculties are stretched thin when they attempt to offer a major and to cover Africa, Afro-America, and the Caribbean. Offering a comprehensive program in Africana studies has meant that some departments and programs play primarily service roles in providing introductory courses that are used to fulfill one or more distribution requirements for graduation. These efforts have little opportunity to supply depth in the field of study. Faculty become very much occupied with servicing large introductory courses and have little time for research and writing in an area of specialization. There is a tendency for faculty to become generalists familiar with a broad range of knowledge rather than specialists who advance the frontiers of specific areas of knowledge.

As Africana studies moves into its fourth stage, as well as its third decade on predominantly white campuses, there is a need to reexamine the curriculum on many campuses. Some departments and programs offer a hodgepodge of courses that have evolved over time in response to student interest and faculty availability. Many departments and programs, particularly those with small faculties, need to determine what they can do best with their resources. Some have specific strengths upon which to build; others need to reconsider where they want to concentrate their resources. Unless they have the faculty and the administrative support, many departments and programs cannot offer successful comprehensive Africana studies courses. In a 1986 report on the "Status of Afro-American Studies in the State University of New York," Dr. Kenneth Hall showed that the preponderance of students are attracted by courses on Afro-American history, the civil rights movement, film, music, and contemporary Africa. Courses on history and culture (literature, music, film, drama, and dance) seem to appeal most to a cross section of students (Black and white), with politics close behind.

In many respects, Africana studies faculty need to return to the basic question: Africana studies for what? There was much discussion and debate on this question during the early days of organizing, when the focus was on the quest for legitimacy and institutionalization. On many campuses, Africana studies was to provide the Black presence, to supply role models for students, to have an active advising and counseling function, to organize film series, lectures, and symposia, and to influence traditional departments in the composition of their faculty and curriculum. This was a tall order that exhausted many Africana studies faculty. Having expended their energy on getting the new field off the ground, many faculty had not devoted sufficient time to research and publication and thus were caught short when evaluated for promotion and tenure.

Today, there is some debate about whether Africana studies faculty should play their former roles of counselors and mentors or give more time to research. Some of this tension would be eased if administrators supported campus-life specialists who would organize cultural activities for Black students in particular and for all students in general. Faculty development is an important element within the university, and it is especially important for Africana studies faculty, many of whom need to reorient themselves toward greater scholarship.

Public colleges that are clustered in metropolitan areas have a unique opportunity to foster scholarship in Africana studies by establishing master's degree programs and research institutes. Such projects might encourage Africana studies departments and programs to develop strengths in specific areas. These strengths could be drawn upon for graduate programs and research institutes to promote greater scholarship by identifying areas of investigation and by bringing together scholars with similar interests. Research institutes might also be a means to influence more students to pursue advanced degrees and expand the number of minority scholars.

Answers to the question of "Africana studies for what?" will have a significant effect on the shape and content of the curriculum. To address these issues, the National Council for Black Studies has already embarked on a program of summer institutes for college teachers. Such responses will also influence the role of Africana studies on different campuses. Africana studies will continue to vary from college to college. Ultimately, however, there is a need for greater clarification and understanding through more dialogue about its specific function on various campuses.

2

BLACK STUDIES IN LIBERAL ARTS EDUCATION

Johnnetta B. Cole

As an African American and as an educator, I turn with you to a critical assessment of Black Studies in liberal arts education.[1] I dare to do so not in conflict with but rather in concert with other scholars and activists in this process. The Curriculum Development Project of the Institute of the Black World; the Howard University Fifteen Year Assessment of Black Studies Conference; the symposium on Black Studies and Women's Studies entitled "An Overdue Partnership" organized by Smith College's Afro-American Studies Department and the University of Massachusetts' Women's Studies Program; and the ongoing work of the National Council of Black Studies are only a few of the many organized discussions of the state and potential of Black Studies. Thus my comments and analysis should be viewed as a part of this widespread and ongoing discussion.

This discussion of Black Studies is limited to liberal arts curricula in predominantly white institutions of higher education, but not because what takes place in Black colleges, elementary schools and high schools, and in community settings is unimportant. It is simply that clarity and conciseness require that we place some limitations on the boundaries of this discussion.

THE HISTORY OF BLACK STUDIES ONE MORE TIME

"Any attempt to discuss the question of what has come to be called Black Studies . . . outside of a political perspective is futile."[2] This is very obviously the case for the late 1960s surge for Black Studies. It is equally so when we review the prolonged history of what is the minimal call of Black Studies: "the inclusion of our point of view and our cultural heritage in educational curricula on a basis of equality . . ."[3] A political perspective is essential to an understanding of the most comprehensive meaning of Black Studies: the development of a fundamentally new way for Black people to look at themselves and be looked at by others; and a fundamentally new way for Black people to be actively involved in effecting positive changes in their condition, and thus in their society and in the world.

African-American concern about their formal education and their role in that process goes back at least to the creation of the Freedman Schools at the end of the Civil War. During the period of Reconstruction, when there was blatant white control of segregated Black educational institutions, Afro-Americans spoke out passionately for "a stronger, even a controlling voice in the process and institutions of education for our people."[4] Such was the view of C. E. Becker, expressed in a letter to Henry L. Morehouse, dated November 17, 1882:

> . . . we are willing to return thanks to the many friends who have assisted us in educating ourselves thus far, but we have now reached the point where we desire to endeavor to educate ourselves, to build school houses, churches, colleges, and universities, by our own efforts . . . ere we sacrifice our manhood.[5]

Today we would refer to our peoplehood, but the sentiment of this statement remains:

> . . . the desire to establish curricula to serve the needs of our people—to provide skills training, to transmit our values, to pass on a dignified version of our history and culture in a world in which our very persons were met (and are met) almost without exception with condescension, scorn, and hostility.[6]

When we turn to the most recent expression of the long-standing drive for Black Studies, that which began in the late sixties, the importance of placing the issue in a political context is extraordinarily clear. For as Julius Lester puts it:

> Black Studies carries the burden of its beginning. It was not invited into the curricula of colleges and universities because it was thought to have something new and vital to offer the humanistic body of knowledge. Indeed, it was not invited into curricula at all. It fought its way in through demonstrations in the sixties and seventies. Black studies was born because a man named King was assassinated.[7]

During the late sixties and early seventies, there was a substantial increase in the numbers of Black youths in American colleges and universities, two-thirds of whom were at white universities.[8] Their presence on college campuses was clearly related to the demands of the Civil Rights and Black Power movements of that period.

In ways unprecedented in our history, these young Afro-Americans forced us to confront the relationship between what was going on "in the streets" of America and what was going on, and in their view should go on, in the classrooms of U.S. educational institutions. These Black students recognized a relationship between their lives and the lives of the masses of Black people who were expressing their anger and frustration in the burnings and lootings of urban rebellions.

Black scholars, few in numbers on white campuses, joined with their students. In Vincent Harding's words: "When the students rose on the campuses and demanded our presence, or pressed for greater visibility and recognition for our work, we claimed, with them, indissoluble bonds to the heaving life of the Black masses."[9]

Black Studies must be understood as a part of that Black Student Movement—"the takeovers of computer centers, academic buildings and student unions; the creation of Black Student Unions and Black Cultural Centers; [and] the emergence of Black nationalist ideology within the potential Black petty bourgeois stratum."[10]

A full understanding of the rise of Black Studies also requires an appreciation of the influential interaction between the Black Student Movement and the general student movement of the sixties and seventies, and between the student movements and the resistance and revolt of the "anti-war movement."

THE FIVE CHALLENGES OF THE BLACK STUDIES CRITIQUE

The beginnings of Black Studies in liberal arts institutions are usually dated with the establishment of an Afro-American Studies Department at San Francisco State College in 1968. However, programs in Afro-American Studies existed at other white institutions before 1968; for example, Cornell University had a functioning program in 1967. Intimately tied to the Black Student Movement, and fueled by the Civil Rights and Black Liberation movements, Black Studies is fundamentally a critique of educational institutions in American society and a set of proposals for beginning the long and difficult process of change in those institutions.

The Black Studies critique explicitly addresses shortcomings, omissions, and distortions in liberal arts curricula and institutions as they affect Afro-Americans. It also charges that the liberal arts curricula falls far short of what is required to correctly educate white youth.

The Black Studies critique has taken the form of volumes of written and spoken words: explained before white faculties and administrators, written in the paragraphs of proposals for initiating programs and departments, analyzed in scholarly journals and popular articles, and debated in the string of conferences and symposia that took place all over the United States.

I suggest that the major points of the Black Studies critique can be summarized in terms of five challenges. Black Studies challenges *what* is taught in the liberal arts curricula of America's colleges and universities; *to whom* and *by whom* it is taught; *how* it is taught; and *why* it is taught. These challenges represent a sweeping critique, followed by plans, proposals, curricula, and projects designed to begin to correct certain fundamental problems in American higher education.

What Is Taught

Scholars and activists of Black Studies argue that a profound chasm separates the claim and the reality of what is taught in America's liberal arts institutions. The claim, simply put, is that liberal arts education is an objective, value-free exploration of the range of human history, activity, knowledge, and creativity. The reality is that this education is based on a Eurocentric perspective of the world, reflecting a racial, gender, and class bias that distorts African and African-American experiences.[11] "The history of America looks very different viewed from a cotton patch."[12]

There is no shortage of examples of these biases in mainstream scholarship. Among the examples frequently referred to are the notion in mainstream scholarship that Black culture is either nonexistent or merely a deviation from middle-class Euro-American culture; and the Moynihanian concept of the Black matriarchy. Another familiar example is the litanies of great classics that always refer to Mozart but never to Coltrane, to Conrad but not to Achebe, to Virginia Woolf but not to Margaret Walker, and to John Stuart Mill, but never to W. E. B. Du Bois.

The problem with the notions of "objectivity" and "value-free science" is that these sacred fetishes of Western scholarship are in reality, as Lewis King notes, ". . . a metaphor of the collective subjectivity of a particular group in history and the abstract representations of a singular race, sex and economic class".[13] Thus Black Studies argues for a corrective approach that would negate the myths and distortions inherent in traditional "White Studies" construction of Black people and indeed the world; explore all of history (and her-story as well); consistently address racism; and institutionalize a Black presence in American education.

Black Studies challenges what is traditionally taught and introduces a different curriculum.

> By its very nature Black Studies begins with the life and culture of Blacks, and in the American context that means a race of people brought into this country for one purpose and one only: to be slaves (I would not be in America if not for slavery, or if one of my ancestors had missed the boat). Thus the vantage point of Black Studies is qualitatively different from that of the traditional disciplines. Black Studies does not begin with the conquering of kingdoms, the decrees of monarchies, or the rhymed lines of a sonnet. It begins in a group experience of suffering and agony, of struggle and survival. When such is the crux of experience, definitions of life are vastly different.

> Black Studies is not only the study of the history, culture, and lives of Blacks. It is the point of view that comes from a reality so tenuous that one did not own even the very breath of his or her life. This reality is the heart of Black Studies. As W. E. B. Du Bois said almost 50 years ago: Instead of the university growing down and seeking to comprehend in its curriculum the life and experience, the thought and expression of the lower classes, it almost invariably tended to grow up and narrow itself to a sublimated elite of mankind.[14]

By Whom and To Whom

Black Studies during the 1960s and '70s took a critical look at the participants in American higher education. The ideal, often purported to be a reality, is that institutions of higher education choose professors because of their intellectual strengths and ability to contribute to the educational enterprise. Similarly, students are presumably selected because of their demonstrated abilities and intellectual potential. If this is indeed the case, Black Studies proponents ask, then why are almost all professors white male Ph.D.'s of a middle-class mind-set if not origin, who have been trained by scholars of a similar background? If intellectual potential really matters in the selection of students, and not simply demonstrated ability as indicated by culturally biased test scores and good grades in well-financed middle-class white schools, then why are there so few Black and other Third World students in America's colleges and universities? The truth, say the advocates of Black Studies, is that the overwhelming majority of the participants in liberal arts institutions reflect and reinforce the very streams of thought that dominate the curriculum: white, male, and middle class.

The reality of who teaches and who is taught in liberal arts institutions has led the proponents of Black Studies to make demands for a substantial increase in the number of Black faculty. They also ask that colleges and universities consider some individuals without academic degrees but with a wealth of practical and scholarly experience for faculty positions. Black Studies activists demand changes in admissions criteria, increases in financial aid, and expanded academic and other support services to give more Black students a fighting chance to go to college. Finally, advocates of Black Studies often fight for academic offerings for community residents to be held in community settings.

The call is very simply to bring about a Black presence in liberal arts institutions, such that Black students will have Black role models among their faculty and staff and all students will have the possibility to learn experientially about peoples, cultures, histories, and ideas that differed from their own.

How What Is Taught Is Taught

The Black Studies critique of liberal arts education also addresses questions of pedagogy. In short, not only is there a need to change what is taught, to whom and by whom, but also to qualitatively overhaul methods of teaching and learning. Thus Black Studies argues for a number of far-reaching reforms. There should be a greater emphasis on student participation in the teaching/learning process, rather than the banking process where the teacher deposits knowledge into students' heads and periodically (at exam time) makes withdrawals. There should be a closer relationship between the academy and "the outside world," in contrast to the traditional model of the academy as an isolated ivory tower. Thus students should be encouraged to engage in field projects and practicums that place them in dynamic interactions with communities. The competitive atmosphere that is so deeply embedded in the American educational process is also challenged. Black Studies proposes that students should be encouraged to engage in more cooperative learning experiences. Finally, the loyalty to disciplines over knowledge, the territoriality of departments, and the sanctity of specialized, indeed professional versus general education, are questioned. The call is for far greater dependence on an interdisciplinary approach. Julius Lester, a professor of Afro-American Studies, exemplifies this approach:

> . . . Black Studies cannot concern itself with the University as an apprenticeship system. This does not mean discouraging a student who wants to be a specialist in the field. However, it does not focus its energies on this student, [or] find its raison d'etre here. The mission of Black Studies is to invite and guide students into human experience as it has affected the lives of Blacks and to examine the variety of ways in which Blacks have responded.
>
> I am not interested, therefore, in creating intellectuals or for that matter in even teaching potential intellectuals. I am interested in that student who will leave the university and go into life, who will, in all likelihood, end up with a job rather than a career. Instead of demanding that this student write a critical analysis of *Native Son*, I ask something harder. I ask the student to learn what he or she feels freedom to be. What is instructive is how often the students have to be convinced that what they think matters.[15]

No discipline has a monopoly on understanding of what freedom is. The best theoretical formulation of freedom is sterile if it is not understood in practice. Finally, freedom, like effective education, is achieved most often when groups of human beings cooperate with each other, not when lone individuals compete against all others.

Why Teach What Is Taught

It is perhaps on this last point that the perspectives of Black Studies and the tradition of liberal arts education are at greatest odds. The issue is very simply that of purpose—the raison d'etre of education in our colleges and universities.

The dominant view is that the purpose of liberal arts education is to assist individuals, especially youth, to gain an understanding of the world in which they live. This is a process said to involve an understanding of how the world came to be as it is (history), its physical and natural elements (the sciences), the development and functioning of individuals and societies (the social sciences), and the creative expressions that are unique to the human species (the arts). As they engage in this process, to whom or to what are members of the academy accountable? The dominant view is that scholars are accountable to an abstract notion called "*TRUTH*," or more concretely, to an intellectual community. Professor Mike Thelwell further explores the issue:

> Scholarly objectivity is a delusion that liberals (of both races) may subscribe to. Black people and perceptive whites know better. The fact is that the intellectual establishment distinguishes itself by its slavish acceptance of the role assigned to it by the power brokers of the society. It has always been the willing servant of wealth and power, and the research done in the physical sciences, the humanities and social sciences has been, with very few honorable exceptions, in services to established power, which has, in this country, always been antithetical to the interests of Black people. The goals of the research undertaken, the questions asked, the controlling assumptions governing it, and consequently, the results obtained have always fitted comfortably into a social consensus which has been, by definition, racist.[16]

Black Studies, the intellectual arm of the Black Power Movement, articulates a very different perspective from that of the "intellectual establishment." Why study? Not simply to take a place in the world but to understand the world and to actively participate in helping to change it. To whom are scholars and students accountable? Black Studies advocates respond that Black teachers and students should be accountable to Black people as they struggle for a place of dignity, integrity, and equality in American society. By extension, they argue that all scholars and students must be accountable to the best interests of humankind.

A scholarship that is accountable to human interests is fraught with problems. Who defines these interests? How does one resolve conflicting notions of "best interest"? But on the question of racism, Black Studies advocates are absolutely positive that the perpetuation of this destructive system is not in the interest of any but a small elite.

Black Studies advocates argue, like C. Wright Mills, that we should strive to be objective, but we should not seek to be detached. Education, they argue, is one means by which Black youth could be prepared to play a significant role in the improvement of the conditions of Black communities. For these reasons, Black Studies proponents call for a strong activist component in the curriculum, and a close and dynamic relationship between the academy and African-American communities.

BLACK STUDIES IN LIBERAL ARTS EDUCATION: AN ASSESSMENT

Who has heard the critiques first voiced by the founders of Black Studies twenty years ago? Which Black Studies proposals have reached fruition? What is the best course of action for Black Studies advocates in the 1980s? How should we interpret the fact that the number of Black Studies programs and departments has declined over a twenty year period?

Our experiences over the past twenty years and the present realities in our country serve as a sobering context for an assessment of Black Studies. The times have changed. Since the inception of Black Studies programs and departments, governmental support of education and all other social services has markedly decreased. In a parallel and related development, North American society has become far less responsive even with token gestures to the needs of Black people. While the African Americans struggle has not ceased, the definitive turn to the right in American politics and the severity of economic conditions are among the factors that have made our struggle less public, and less national in scope than it was during the late 1960s.

Today, more than in the 1960s, there is a sense of the relationship between the struggle of African Americans in the United States and Third World peoples in other areas of the world. But there is also today the possibility of a shared doom among all peoples. Nuclear bombs are not designed to selectively destroy based on color, gender, or class coding. Clearly, our conditions today are not the same as those that reigned when Black Studies began.

We recall that Black Studies began during a period in which the Black Panther Party was organizing nationally and claiming to be a genuine challenge to the ruling power structure. It was a time of rapid increase in the number of Black students and faculty, largely due to Black students' pressures on administrators. It was also a time of rapid increase in the number of Black faces in industry, social service agencies, and government.

In the excitement of the late sixties and early seventies, many Black Studies participants acted as though these programs and departments would not only endure but also maintain access to resources, autonomy, and decision-making power within white liberal arts institutions. This stance was in some ways functional. By assuming the role of secure, confident administrators with power and financial commitments, many Black administrators and faculty were able to gain a degree of "legitimacy" for their programs. But such a stance clearly involved political myopia.

The euphoria of that period of rapid growth of Black Nationalism, the Black Student Movement, and Black Studies did not last. The systematic and violent repression of political groups such as the Black Panther Party and the assassination of national Black leaders tempered early optimism. Also contributing to the disillusionment were a decline in government programs for poor and minority people and the lessening of guilt-induced efforts by white institutions and individuals.

There has been a definitive decline in the number of Black Studies programs and departments. Today, according to the National Council for Black Studies, there are approximately 375 programs and departments of Black Studies, compared with about 800 in the early 1970s. Among Black Studies faculty, it is generally known that many of the programs and departments continue to exist under considerable strain. Budget cuts, denial of tenure and promotion, lack of academic support counselors, and, in some cases, active counseling against Black Studies all take their toll.

A new emphasis on vocationalism in American education has caused many Black as well as white students to question the "usefulness" of Black Studies, as compared to courses and majors in business, engineering, and computer science.

Twenty years after the first Black Studies department was founded, many academicians are still questioning the necessity and relevance of Black Studies. It is particularly interesting to note that similar doubts are not so frequently raised about area studies: American Studies, Middle Eastern Studies, East European Studies, African and Latin American Studies.

It is clear that Black Studies differs from area studies in several fundamental ways. In Black Studies, the scholars are, for the most part, of the same group as the people studied. They not only claim identity with the people being studied but, indeed, feel accountable to them. Such identity and accountability are less prevalent in area studies programs. Unlike Black Studies, area studies programs have access to sizeable research funds, faculty positions, and government contacts. In addition, the United States government frequently turns to area studies for information and advice.

Black Studies thus differs from area studies in certain fundamental ways, yet it is often judged by the same standards and expectations used to judge area studies programs. Obviously, Black Studies falls short.

In contrast to area studies, Women's Studies has fared more like Black Studies. Both Black Studies and Women's Studies were "granted" by university administrators in response to demands that were made during the sixties and seventies. Both had to overcome the traditionalists' self-fulfilling prophecy that since there were few readily available resources or qualified personnel, the focus on Black Studies and then on Women's Studies did not warrant expenditure of resources or the stamp of academic legitimacy. These issues, the traditionalist said, could be handled adequately within the regular liberal arts curricula and departments. Yet it was precisely because the traditional departments and curricula failed to deal adequately with issues of racism and sexism, and consistently demonstrated an unwillingness to hire Black or women staff, that a need for Black Studies and Women's Studies arose.

Thus the two programs exist on the fringe or periphery of the "regular" liberal arts curriculum. Many often perceive the departments as existing mainly to provide their clientele with psychic support, while relieving the pressure for more fundamental, university-wide curricula change.

The points made here concerning Black Studies and Women's Studies also hold for Comparative American Ethnic Studies programs and departments, such as Native American Studies, Chicano Studies, Puerto Rican Studies, and Asian American Studies.

Despite changes in American society and in liberal arts institutions that have not been conducive to the growth of viable Black Studies, many Black Studies programs and departments have survived. Survival is not necessarily a sign of the fittest. Nevertheless, there are concrete indices of healthy development in some Black Studies programs and departments. There are also important "by-products" of the ongoing Black Studies movement. Among the concrete accomplishments of Black Studies are a steady rise in the number of dissertations, books, and journal articles in Afro-American Studies and a growing number of scholarly journals and professional organizations in Black Studies.[17] Black Studies has also had some effect on the concepts, theories, and methodology of the traditional areas in the liberal arts curriculum.

The question of Black culture provides a specific example of the influence of Black Studies on social science. Charles Valentine, in a publication, *Black Studies and Anthropology: Political and Scholarly Interests*, defines the importance of Black Studies in correcting the position in anthropology (sociology and psychology, political science, history, and education as well) that Black folks have no culture. Prior to the publication of Melville J. Herskovits's *Myth of the Negro Past*, in 1941, the only position articulated within the ranks of established social science was the notion that Black folks were stripped of their culture before coming to the New World. According to this view, any remnants of African culture that reached these shores were wiped away by the brutality of the slavery experience.[18] Within mainstream scholarship this position was articulated in its modern version by scholars such as Gunnar Myrdal (*An American Dilemma*); E. Franklin Frazier (*The Negro Family in the United States, The Negro Church in America*, etc.); and Glazer and Moynihan (*Beyond the Melting Pot*). Glazer and Moynihan declare: "It is not possible for Negroes to view themselves as other ethnic groups viewed themselves because—and this is the key to much in the Negro world—the Negro is only an American and nothing else. He has no values and culture to guard and protect."[19] The contrary position to that articulated by Glazer and Moynihan was presented by Herskovits in his carefully documented *Myth of the Negro Past*. Despite detailed evidence of the retention of African cultural traits in the music, dance, folklore, religion, language, and social organization of New World Black folks, mainstream scholars insisted that Afro-Americans are simply imitators of white American ways.[20] Gunnar Myrdal put it bluntly in the summary statement to a series of chapters, "The Negro Community as a Pathological Form of an American Community." Myrdal said, "American Negro culture is not something independent of general American culture. It is a distorted development, or a pathological condition, of the general American culture."[21]

In the new version of Glazer and Moynihan's book, *Beyond the Melting Pot*, they explicitly state that Black Studies has been a source which corrected the theory of Black folks as "cultureless." And yet, the way they phrase their "change of heart" is an indication of the tenacity of their original view. Valentine, critically analyzing Glazer and Moynihan, writes:

> Students of the changing scholarly scene may be interested to find that in a second edition of their book, Glazer and Moynihan have edited the quoted statement to soften it somewhat without changing its basic message. Elsewhere in the new version of their book, these resourceful authors present a lengthy footnote on the same subject which is a small masterpiece of academic doubletalk. First they say they didn't really mean what they said in their original statement. Then they admit they made a mistake but blame it on "authoritative scholars, among them E. Franklin Frazier." Their mistake, as they see it, was to ignore "African survivals," and they give credit to "Afro-American and Black Studies" for challenging this, although they also condemn this field for "separatism." Eventually they conclude that "Out of American origins, one can create a distinctive subculture . . . This has certainly happened as a result of 300 years of Black American history, and could ["could," not "did"] serve as a sufficient basis for strong organization, regardless of the contribution of African origins. All this can surely be seen as a sign of the times, a tribute to effectiveness of the young field of Black Studies. Yet is is also a sharp reminder that the essential message of the traditional view remains intact and continues to be dominant outside Black Studies."[22]

There are other examples of the influence of Black Studies on mainstream attitudes, assumptions, and even theories. To note only a few, the pioneering work of Herbert Aptheker on slave revolts has received increased attention and has "become more possible as truth" as a result of widespread use of his material in Afro-American Studies and the dissemination of those ideas into communities outside the universities.

The Moynihan thesis on Black families has been severely challenged by Black Studies faculties and students; in fact there are few programs or departments that do not use the Moynihan theory as a teaching device for educating Black students about the convergence of "scholarly" and "ruling class political interests." The fact that Moynihan has become a known name in many Black communities is in some measure a result of the work of Black scholars associated with Black Studies.

Black Studies brought to the social sciences a different perspective, a perspective of the oppressed, the view of those without power, the view from the cotton patch.[23]

BLACK STUDIES AND LIBERAL ARTS EDUCATION: WHERE DO WE GO FROM HERE?

Many of the scholars and activists who helped found Black Studies programs and departments seriously critique what has transpired over the past twenty years. Joined by younger colleagues, students, and "drylongso" African Americans in communities throughout the United States, these scholars offer direction for the future of Black Studies.[24] These advocates of Black Studies openly criticize the continuing resistance to Black Studies by white administrators and faculty. They deplore the ways in which the financial hard times facing academic institutions and the conservative hostile environment in the United States adversely affect Black Studies. With no less honesty, these proponents of Black Studies turn inward and openly discuss those parts of the problem for which we ourselves may have the solutions.

Some of the points of discussion and debate are relatively new issues, others have been up for discussion since the very inception of Black Studies. For example, the issue of technology and African America is relatively new. How will various sectors of African-American communities be affected by this society's increasing dependence upon high technology and information as a product as well as a method of communicating? Given the potential for uneven access to high technology and for existing racial as well as gender and class inequalities, what should be the stance of Black Studies? Concretely, should Black Studies curricula take on instruction in computer and information science? Or should the Black Studies curricula continue to focus on the areas more traditionally covered in the liberal arts?

The question of race versus class as the focal point of Black Studies has been openly, indeed heatedly discussed and debated since the inception of Black Studies. What is new, and encouraging, is the growing rejection of the very formulation of a dichotomy such that it is either race *or* class that is *the* key concept for Black Studies: Black Nationalism *or* Marxism that is *the* correct perspective.[25]

To illustrate this dynamic of critical assessment within Black Studies, I choose an example that is particularly appropriate to this volume—the woman question within Black Studies.

THE WOMAN QUESTION WITHIN BLACK STUDIES

Black women as scholars and teachers, and Black women as an area of scholarship, appear to be caught between a rock and a hard place, that is, between the racial and ethnic bias of much of Women's Studies and the gender bias in much of Black Studies.

The situation in almost all of the Women's Studies programs and departments, where Black female professors are indeed rare, is summarized by Arlene Avakian in these terms:

> . . . most of the white women teaching and doing research in Women's Studies do not see Black and Third World women. Until very recently only the exceptional Women's Studies course included any women of color in its syllabus. Even rarer was any discussion at all of racism as a force in all of our lives. . . . Women of color are seldom included in our classes, journals or conferences, and when they are it is as if they are another species tacked on to the end of the course. It is rare to find women of color and their concerns fully integrated into a Women's Studies class or conference. And when Black and Third World women speak to this issue at conferences, the attitude of white women is generally one of annoyance, because their conference has been disrupted.[26]

The figures that confirm Avakian's point are found in the pages of *Who's Who and Where in Women's Studies.*

. . . between 1970 and 1973, courses which concerned minority women or which considered race and class in addition to gender comprised only 4 percent of women's studies courses. Three years later, within the 15 "mature" women's studies programs, only 11 percent of the courses were devoted to considerations of race and class, or to minority women's experiences. Within that number, there were some courses that specifically addressed the experiences of Black women; some of these were, in fact, jointly sponsored by Black studies and women's studies programs. Proportionately, however, they still "wouldn't fill a page."[27]

In 1978, not a single Black Studies program in a western land-grant college offered an independent course on Black women. Until 1982 and 1983, none of the few existing textbooks on Black Studies included specific discussions on Black women. The issues of Black women, when mentioned, are included under the topics of the Black family and traditional African societies. It is important to note that the most recent publication of *People's College* does include a fuller discussion of Black women's issues. This inclusion was clearly in response to criticisms raised by Black Studies scholars, especially women. Also, until recently, the course syllabi for Black Studies courses have drawn almost exclusively on male authors (Black and white) and the material of the syllabi rarely distinguishes Black women's experiences from those of Black men.

The paucity of scholarly attention to Black women within Black Studies is matched by the paucity of Black women as colleagues in these programs and departments. This is particularly important to note because within Black Studies, as in American society as a whole, there is a myth of Black female dominance. The reality is that there are very few Black women in leadership positions in Black Studies. The Black women who are involved in these programs and departments face very clear problems of gender inequality.

Professor Monica Gordon and I did a series of telephone interviews with Black women involved in Black Studies in the New England region. While we clearly did not conduct a rigorous study, nonetheless the women to whom we spoke articulated many of the same problems. The women interviewed believe that the inequities in promotion and salary experienced by Black women are a consequence of the myth that women are a "risk" because they will leave the workforce to have babies. The women deplored the insinuation that Black women who do hold positions in Black Studies gained them because they granted sexual favors (a variant on the myth that Black women have only advanced since slavery because they "give in" sexually to males). Some of the women we interviewed said that they are simply not taken seriously as scholars and as teachers. Finally, some of the women indicated that they are criticized within their Black Studies programs or departments and charged with divided loyalties because of their involvement in women's issues and Women's Studies. The reality is that most if not all Black women have differences with segments of the Women's Movement and with Women's Studies—both of which have been historically bound by middle-class white perspectives and values. But a rejection of those values does not eliminate the genuine concerns that Black women have *as women*.[28]

Until recently, Black Studies scholars and activists did not openly discuss these issues and concerns. In part, they did not raise these issues fearing that to do so would be divisive when cooperation between Black men and women is a prerequisite for the success of Black Studies. In addition, raising "the woman question," it was feared, would give the impression that there is only conflict or dissension between Black men and women in Black Studies when, in fact, there are many areas of cooperation. But ignoring or refusing to talk about problems rarely if ever makes them simply go away.

The issue of Black women in Black Studies has been brought out into the open. In Atlanta at the Institute of the Black World curriculum development conferences, and at the Howard University Fifteen Year Assessment of Black Studies Conference, the issues of Black women as colleagues and as subject matter in Black Studies were openly addressed. Similarly, at recent Women's Studies conferences these issues are receiving attention. The criticisms raised by Black women, and often by Black men as well as by white colleagues in Women's Studies, may well be heard and acted upon to the point that "more Black is put into Women's Studies, and more women are put into Black Studies."[29]

WITHOUT CONCLUSION

The "no conclusion" to this review of the beginnings, development, and current state of Black Studies in liberal arts institutions is that the Black Studies challenge remains, and the struggles it embodies continue. What can be said is captured in these words:

> Black studies offers a challenge to higher education far beyond the inclusion of black subject matter in the curriculum. Its challenge is how we view human existence itself. The question is, whose lives do we value? Black studies begins with the lives of black people and reaches out to all humanity. How many times I have had white students say to me at the end of a course. "I didn't know I would learn so much about myself by studying black literature."
>
> I knew, because within black literature, history and culture lie truths about America that can be found in no other place. I knew because universal truths lie within the black experience as certainly as these truths reside in the experiences of any people. Unfortunately, white academicians resist growing down into the black experience because to do so means an inevitable confrontation with the underside of America—racism. Yet, what more appropriate place for such a confrontation than the classrooms of universities and colleges.[30]

NOTES

1. A stipend from Oberlin College made it possible for Elizabeth H. Oakes to serve as my research assistant for this chapter.

2. Mike Thelwell, "Black Studies: A Political Perspective," *The Massachusetts Review*, (1969) Vol. 10(4): 703.

3. Eugene Terry, "Introduction," *Quadrennial Review of the Undergraduate Curriculum*, W. E. B. Du Bois Department of Afro-American Studies, University of Massachusetts at Amherst.

4. Ibid., 2.

5. Ibid.

6. Ibid.

7. Julius Lester, "Growing Down," *Change Magazine* (1979): 34.

8. In 1950, about 4.5 percent of the Black youth between the ages of eighteen and twenty-four attended U.S. colleges. By 1970, 15.5 percent of Black youth of this same age group were in colleges and universities. Only five years later, 20 percent of Black males and 21 percent of Black females between eighteen and twenty-four were in institutions of higher education. A decline began in 1976, reflecting the brutal attacks upon educational opportunities for African Americans. See Manning Marable, "Afro-American History: Post Reconstruction." Review Essay. Black Studies Curriculum Development Course Evaluations, Conference I: History and Political Economy, October 1–3, 1981, Institute of the Black World, Atlanta, Ga., 3.

9. Ibid., 4.

10. Ibid.

11. While the focus of this chapter is Black Studies and the African-American experience in higher education, the Eurocentic perspective similarly misrepresents the experience of other people of color and non-Western people.

12. Lester, "Growing Down," 37.

13. Lewis King, "The Future of Mental Health Research of the Black Population: Outline of an Alternative Deep Structure," *Research Bulletin*, Vol. 1(1).

14. Lester, "Growing Down," 35–36.

15. Ibid., 37.

16. Mike Thelwell, "Black Studies: A Political Perspective," 709.

17. Abdul Alkalimat, "Research and Evaluational Empirical Trends of Professional Development and Productivity in Black Studies" (delivered at "Symposium on Black Studies: A Fifteen Year Assessment," Howard University, Washington, D.C., December 1–2, 1982).

18. Although established social science argued the absence of Black culture, many Black scholars and writers have proclaimed a unique, and sometimes a superior, way of life. For a detailed discussion of this point see Herbert Aptheker's *Afro-American History: The Modern Era* (New York: The Citadel Press, 1971), 68–80.

19. Nathan Glazer and Daniel Patrick Moynihan, *Beyond the Melting Pot.* Cambridge, Mass.: MIT Press, 1970.

20. Frances S. Herskovits, ed., *The New World Negro* (Bloomington: Indiana University Press, 1966); Melville J. Herskovits, *The Myth of the Negro Past* (New York: Harper, 1941); J. C. Moore, "Religious Syncretism in Jamaica," *Practical Anthropology* 12 (1965): 63–70; Vera Rubin, ed., *Caribbean Studies: A Symposium* (Seattle: University of Washington Press, 1957); George E. Simpson, "The Belief System of Haitian Vodun," *American Anthropologist* 47 (1945): 35–59; Lorenzo D. Turner, *Africanisms in the Gullah Dialect* (Chicago: University of Chicago Press, 1949); Richard D. Waterman, "African Influence on the Music of the Americans," in *Acculturation in the Americas*, Sol Tax, ed. (Chicago: University of Chicago Press, 1952); Norman E. Whitten and John F. Szwed, *Afro-American Anthropology* (New York: The Free Press, 1964).

21. Gunnar Myrdal, *An American Dilemma* (London: Routledge & Kegan Paul, 1958).

22. Charles Valentine, *Black Studies and Anthropology: Scholarly and Political Interests in Afro-American Culture* (Reading, Mass.: Addison-Wesley).

23. Scholars of other Third World groups have made similar contributions. For example, the rise in Native American consciousness led to the work of Vine Deloria and others, in which the view of Native Americans presented is very different from that of the Bureau of Indian Affairs and many Euro-American anthropologists.

24. In his book *Drylongso: A Self Portrait of Black America* (New York: Random House, 1980), the anthropologist John L. Gwaltney uses the term to refer to the vast majority of Afro-Americans in the United States—regular, everyday people.

25. James B. Stewart, "Toward Operationalization of an 'Expansive' Model of Black Studies" (paper presented for the Black Studies Curriculum Development Project administered by the Institute of the Black World, Atlanta, 1982).

26. Arlene Voski Avakian, "Women's Studies and Racism," *New England Journal of Black Studies*, 1981: 33.

27. Charles P. Henry and Frances Smith Foster, "Black Women's Studies: Threat or Challenge," *The Western Journal of Black Studies*, 1982: 16.

28. "Rape cannot be a 'white' woman's issue when 60 percent of all women raped in the U.S. are Black. The issue of jobs and equal pay for equal work is not a white feminist issue, not when the median income of Black women is only 94 percent of that of white women, 73 percent of that of Black men, and 54 percent of that of white men" (Cole and Gordon, *New England Journal of Black Studies*, 1981: 7).

29. Johnnetta B. Cole, "Black Studies, Women's Studies: An Overdue Partnership" (luncheon address at the Conference on "Black Studies, Women's Studies: An Overdue Partnership." University of Massachusetts at Amherst, 1983).

30. Lester, "Growing Down," 37.

3

THEORIZING BLACK STUDIES

The Continuing Role of Community Service in the Study of Race and Class

James Jennings

THIS ESSAY PROPOSES THAT "COMMUNITY SERVICE" and related efforts to develop programmatic linkages with neighborhood institutions and organizations represent a key component in the theory and pedagogy of Black studies. Research paradigms that include community service and civic involvement reflect the description of Black studies as a discipline that is "descriptive, critical, and prescriptive," to use the words of Professor Manning Marable.[1] Attention to the pedagogy of community service on the part of scholars in Black studies is important for the growth of this field of intellectual inquiry as well as for its growing impact on the analysis of political and economic issues facing Black communities and U.S. urban society. Both theory and praxis are key to understanding how Black life experiences have molded, and are reflected, in United States society.

Theory refers to the building of predictive and projective knowledge about the experiences of Blacks in the African diaspora and how such experiences have influenced major national and global developments. The term *praxis* implies that theoretical understandings of Black life experiences in this society should be informed by the experiences of Blacks in ongoing political, economic, educational, and cultural struggles aimed at the expansion of racial and economic democracy. While this notion seems logical given the birth of Black studies in the post–World War II period, it is resisted at some levels in higher education. Within the field of Black studies, however, community service focuses on changing system-based and dominant/subordinate social and economic relations and improving living conditions for Blacks and, thereby, other communities. As a matter of fact, many Black studies programs in U.S. higher education were established during the 1960s and 1970s not only because of the need to examine race and political economy in urban settings but also to enhance the effectiveness of Black civic participation in the interests of social and racial justice. Indeed, this is still a distinguishing feature of many Black studies programs, although it is resisted somewhat, as suggested by Joy James in her article "The Future of Black Studies: Political Communities and the 'Talented Tenth'".[2]

Revisiting this traditional role of community service in the field of Black studies is a timely topic in that several doctoral programs offering courses of study in Black studies have been established recently. There are now doctoral programs in Black studies at Temple University, the Ohio State University, the University of Massachusetts, and the University of California at Berkeley. The call for the linkage of praxis with theory, and the pedagogy of community service, is an important component of these doctoral programs. The incorporation of community service within Black studies, furthermore, has been endorsed by many scholars presenting papers at recent professional and academic conferences focusing on Black studies.

The relationship between community involvement, or praxis, and the development of social and economic theory has been ignored or dismissed in other disciplines. But contrasted to this mainstream bias is the idea found in Black intellectual thought that scholarship must be in service to social democracy in civic life. Indeed, several Black studies departments and programs across the nation have designed curricula on the basis of building theory and knowledge linked to involvement with community-level experiences, preparing students to work in a variety of civic and professional settings. The recently established doctoral programs in this field suggest, through their faculty and curricula as well as their inaugural ceremonies, that scholarship about Black experiences in the United States should be pursued within a framework of theory, praxis, *and* community service.

Community service represents a significant component in the field of Black studies because it is actually an important research tool. Thus, the call for community service is viewed not solely as public service but as a key component for certain kinds of research. For instance, some focus on community service highlights the limitations in research concepts and paradigms utilized for the study of race and class within other disciplines such as political science, sociology, psychology, and economics. These limitations are associated, in part, with the separation of theory building from praxis and community service in the organization of these fields by traditional departments and universities. This is suggested in a publication by M. E. Hawkesworth, *Theoretical Issues in Public Policy Analysis*.[3] The author notes that the field of public policy can be described as in a state of intellectual crisis because its methodology and purpose have become obfuscated with a false scientism serving no useful social purpose in advancing democracy. Mainstream scholarship focusing on the economics of poverty or race relations in the United States has not been able to help develop public policy and civic participation that can allow the United States to overcome certain kinds of racial problems. At times scholarship reflects its own industry, separated from dialogue and activism aimed at advancing social democracy. Because community service within the field of Black studies is not disparaged or rejected as a component of research paradigms, it helps to inform and propel an intellectual understanding that may facilitate more effective civic responses to political and economic problems facing Black communities.

In the contemporary period there are several political conditions and issues that are of particular significance in determining the social and economic status of the U.S. urban Black community. The integration and utilization of community service in the field of Black studies contribute to a greater understanding of the nature of these conditions and how the civic sector can respond to these issues. These major political and economic issues facing Black communities include how its leadership should respond to national social policies—whether supported by Democrats or Republicans—that continue to weaken, institutionally and culturally, urban communities through the defunding of cities. Such policies include the adoption and implementation of laissez-faire or trickle-down approaches that usually focus on the development of downtown or benefits to corporate interests at the expense of neighborhoods.

Another challenge facing Blacks as a group is how the nation's intelligentsia, including media, educators, scholars, and cultural leaders, continue to approach Black urban communities as pathology, rather than recognize the significant cultural and intellectual contributions to U.S. society reflected in the nation's Black community. A relatively new political issue for the U.S. urban Black community is the status and future relations with other communities of color that are growing in number and potential social influence. Perhaps this particular issue can only be understood and responded to in the interest of advancing democracy within a context of praxis? Yet another challenge facing Black communities is how to respond to the renaissance of "color blindness" as a powerful and dominant ideology protecting the social and economic status quo. This ideology is becoming increasingly popular and influential in justifying a racial order born of segregation and slavery. And certainly the growing numbers and concentration of alienated youth without linkages to cultural or socially supportive institutions in their communities are another important challenge facing Black communities. While not an exhaustive listing, these are some of the basic social issues that community service pedagogy can target in the field of Black studies. I propose that community service, as an integral component of Black studies, is a fundamental tool for building effective theoretical frameworks and public policies.

BLACK STUDIES AND THE ROLE OF COMMUNITY SERVICE

The history of Black studies as a field illustrates that theory must be strongly linked to praxis, or community service. Planning and institutionalizing opportunities to pursue scholarship, praxis, and community service within an integrated framework was a major demand of students during the 1960s Black cultural renaissance and Black studies movement in U.S. higher education. In predominantly white universities the call for opportunities to pursue "community-based" research within programs of Afro-American studies can be summarized by the famous demands of Black students at San Francisco State University in 1968. These Black students, and other students as well, argued that the scholarship they were exposed to should be both informed by the everyday struggles of Black people for justice and economic survival and useful in preparing students to make contributions to society.

The suggestion that Black studies should reflect research concepts and paradigms based on community experiences is one of the strongest intellectual traditions within the Black struggle for educational equality and opportunity in the United States and abroad. This is the first theme explained by Charles V. Hamilton in his classic taxonomy of Black intellectual and philosophical traditions and values, *The Black Experience in American Politics*.[4] Historical and contemporary examples of how this theme is reflected in the work of a wide range of scholars can be found in William M. Banks's more recent book, *Black Intellectuals*.[5] In fact, the first editorial of the nation's first Black newspaper in 1827, *Freedom's Journal*, called for Black leaders to use education and scholarship as a civic and political resource aimed at the abolition of slavery and uplifting the Black masses. This was an important theme of Booker T. Washington's autobiography, *Up From Slavery*, published in 1895.[6] Washington explained that he decided to pursue education in order to return to his community with skills that would help uplift Blacks in the South. He argued further that this was a widely held belief in the Black community; that is, those Blacks fortunate enough to acquire an education were expected to return benefits to less fortunate Blacks by being involved with their community and receiving training that would advance this involvement.

This theme was reflected in the activism of the Black journalist and antilynching crusader Ida B. Wells-Barnett, who went much further than Booker T. Washington regarding the professional responsibility for community service on the part of the Black scholar and activist. While Washington generally felt that Black scholarship could be utilized to uplift the race, such uplifting could be carried out under the social and economic order of American society. Ida B. Wells-Barnett, however, believed that the *moral* responsibility of Black intellectuals meant not only trying, socially and economically, to uplift the community but also challenging a racist social order. According to Wells-Barnett, Black intellectuals even had moral license to consider those social situations that might require military action in order to redress wrongs committed against Blacks in America. Despite this important difference, however, in both instances scholarship and the pursuit thereof was tied to working with one's community.

The proposal that Black scholarship must be put at the service of solving the social, economic, and political problems of the community was certainly a strong theme in the life of W. E. B. Du Bois. His life reflects the belief that knowledge and intellect should be informed by praxis at the service of the Black community. Indeed, Du Bois's often misunderstood idea of the "talented tenth" was based on this very proposition. Du Bois certainly did not advocate that a Black elite be established as in a neocolonial bourgeoisie that would serve as a bridge or channel between powerful colonial powers and "the natives." He acknowledged that because of racism in American society it would be unlikely that the masses of Blacks would be educated and thereby equipped to challenge the racial, economic, and political order. What he proposed was that those few Blacks fortunate enough to break through the racial barriers of advanced education had a professional—and moral—obligation to help other Blacks break down the barriers of racial exclusion in ways that would change society for the better in terms of social and economic equality.

One of Du Bois's major intellectual works, and a critical study in defining the field of urban sociology today, is *The Philadelphia Negro*.[7] This work reflected a commitment to the pursuit of scholarship within a framework of praxis and community service. Decades later, Malcolm X argued eloquently that the purpose of education was to liberate the Black mind from mental slavery, but such education had to be grounded in the political and economic struggles to strengthen Black communities.

Between the turn of the twentieth century and the period of Malcolm X there were many educators, activists, and scholars who insisted that scholarship that would be useful to the advancement of Blacks in the United States must be grounded in praxis and community service. This is reflected in the works of St. Clair Drake and Horace Cayton, Oliver Cox, the late John Henrik Clarke, as well as the artistic contributions of individuals like Lorraine Hansberry and Paul Robeson.

There are numerous works on Black life in America in the 1960s that reflect the synthesis of scholarship, praxis, and community service. Although many examples could be cited, I have found two classics particularly useful for examining the role of community service within Black studies. One is Kenneth Clark's *Dark Ghetto*, published in 1965.[8] This important study, actually a sort of case study of a specific antipoverty program, HARYOU, laid the intellectual and conceptual foundation for numerous studies and books focusing on race relations and the nation's political economy today. The methodology used by Clark to produce *Dark Ghetto* reflects how community service can advance intellectual understandings of social and economic situations. Clearly, Professor Clark would not have been able to produce this insightful work about social and racial relations within and without a Black urban community without his community work and experiences in the HARYOU program.

Perhaps one of the most eloquent arguments for the pursuit of community-based research within Black studies is presented by Harold Cruse in his work *The Crisis of the Negro Intellectual*, also published in the midsixties.[9] Professor Cruse pointed to what Alexis de Tocqueville, David Truman, Robert Dahl, and many other white scholars had also concluded, namely, that the "group" is a fundamental social and cultural reality in American society. Cruse simply reminded Blacks that struggles for racial and economic justice should reflect this fundamental fact of U.S. society. Black intellectuals, or the professional sector, could only be effective in the long run if they were grounded in the theories and activism necessary to advance the group or the community. Blacks who were alienated, or disconnected, from their own community were, in fact, "ahistorical" beings. Individuals, as such, have very little opportunity to do anything that will move the community forward economically and politically. The Black community would not move forward, according to Professor Cruse, if they acted as a conglomeration of individuals rather than a cultural group, as have others who realized economic and political progress in the United States.

The importance of community service, and praxis, as a research tool within this field was echoed by Black studies professor Abdul Alkalimat in his introduction to *Paradigms in Black Studies: Intellectual History, Cultural Meaning and Political Ideology*: "There is one profound consistency in all fundamental modes of Black social thought: a focus on change. The key issue is changing the conditions that cause Black people's historical suffering."[10] This implies that individuals educated under the umbrella of Black studies must have opportunities to become involved in the challenges facing black communities, a key aspect of their education.

This fundamental role of Black studies, which involves training for civic action on the part of intellectuals and students, was also captured by another Black studies professor, Maulana Karenga, when he wrote in his classic work, *Introduction to Black Studies*,

> Black Studies advocates stressed the need for Black intellectuals who were conscious, capable and committed to Black liberation and a higher level of human life. They argued like Du Bois that the race would be elevated by its best minds, a "Talented Tenth" which did not sell itself for money and machines, but recognized and responded creatively to the fact of the indivisibility of Black freedom and their indispensable role in achieving it.[11]

Discussing the pedagogy of Black studies, Karenga explains that a major and "early objective" of the advocates of Black studies was "the cultivation, maintenance and continuous expansion of a mutually beneficial relationship between the campus and the community. . . . The intent here was to serve and elevate the life-conditions and the consciousness of the community and reinforce the student's relationship with the community through service and interaction."[12] Again, Alkalimat, in his previously cited work: "Afro-American Studies, as a field, is a partisan activity, an enterprise in which the objective is not merely to understand the world but also to help make it better."[13]

These statements are verified by many scholars examining the thoughts and writings of many Black intellectuals involved with advancing education. Historians Darlene Clark Hine, Wilma King, and Linda Reed substantively illustrate this point in their collection of case studies in the struggles of Black women, *We Specialize in the Wholly Impossible*.[14] This anthology shows that for many Black women educators the idea that scholarship should be, and is, strongly associated with activism is a dominant one. Other examples of Black women educators who based their intellectualism on community involvement are provided in the reference book by Gerda Lerner, *Black Women in White America: A Documentary History*.[15]

The importance of continuing to link Black studies and a community-based research agenda was reiterated at the 1990 Annual Meeting of the National Congress of Black Faculty. The keynote speaker for the annual meeting, the renowned sociologist James Blackwell, emphasized this theme in his discussion on the mentoring of Black students in higher education, arguing that students needed to be trained and educated for activism. According to the minutes and resolutions of the November 2, 1990, meeting of the Council of Community Relations, this topic is important for two reasons: (1) the presence of Black educators in American higher education is intricately and historically tied to Black community activism; and (2) the synthesis of the community's political, social, and educational agendas with the research agendas of Black scholars and teachers in academia can produce creative, significant, distinctive research projects beneficial to American society. This call does not mean that politics or political opinions take the place of scholarship. It simply means that theory is most effective, logical, and useful when it is informed by the real-life experiences of people. In fact, theory that is not informed by such experiences may not be useful in moving the Black community forward socially, economically, and culturally.

NOTES

1. Manning Marable, "Black Studies and the Black Intellectual Tradition," *Race and Reason*, vol. 4 (1997–1998): 3–4.

2. Joy James, "The Future of Black Studies: Political Communities and the 'Talented Tenth,' " *Race and Reason*, vol. 4 (1997–1998): 36–38.

3. M. E. Hawkesworth, *Theoretical Issues in Public Policy Analysis* (Albany: State University of New York Press, 1988).

4. Charles V. Hamilton, *The Black Experience in American Politics* (New York: Capricorn, 1973).

5. William M. Banks, *Black Intellectuals: Race and Responsibility in American Life* (New York: Norton, 1996).

6. Booker T. Washington, *Up From Slavery: An Autobiography* (New York: Doubleday, 1963).

7. W. E. B. Du Bois, *The Philadelphia Negro: A Social Study* (New York: Schocken, 1967 [1897]).

8. Kenneth Clark, *Dark Ghetto: Dilemmas of Social Power* (New York: Harper and Row, 1965).

9. Harold Cruse, *Crisis of the Negro Intellectual* (New York: William Morrow, 1967).

10. Abdul Alkalimat, *Paradigms in Black Studies: Intellectual History, Cultural Meaning, and Political Ideology* (Chicago: Twenty-first Century, 1990).

11. Maulana Karenga, *Introduction to Black Studies* (Los Angeles: Kawaida, 1982), 27.

12. Ibid.

13. Alkalimat, *Paradigms in Black Studies*.

14. Darlene Clark Hine, Wilma King, and Linda Reed, *We Specialize in the Wholly Impossible* (New York: Carlson, 1995).

15. Gerda Lerner, *Black Women in White America: A Documentary History* (New York: Pantheon, 1972).

4

HOW THE WEST WAS ONE

On the Uses and Limitations of Diaspora

Robin D. G. Kelley

MOST READERS of the *Black Scholar* know fully well that the concept of an African diaspora is hardly new. Even if we limit our discussion to scholarly investigations of the African diaspora, we will discover a rich discourse dating back at least to the 1950s and 1960s, if not before. It served as both a political term with which to emphasize unifying experiences of African peoples dispersed by the slave trade and an analytical term that enabled scholars to talk about Black communities across national boundaries. Much of this scholarship examined the dispersal of people of African descent, their role in the transformation and creation of new cultures, institutions, and ideas outside of Africa, and the problems of building Pan-African movements across the globe.[1]

Nevertheless, the diaspora has recently returned to analytical prominence in Black Studies, fueled in part by current debates about "globalization." Indeed, some of the latest efforts to develop a diaspora framework have profound implications not only for our understanding of the Black world but for the way we write the history of the modern West. The making of the African diaspora was as much the product of "the West" as it was of internal developments in Africa and the Americas. At the same time, racial capitalism, imperialism, and colonialism—the key forces responsible for creating the modern African diaspora—could not shape African culture(s) without altering Western culture.[2] The purpose of this very brief article is to map out points of convergence where the study of the African diaspora might illuminate aspects of the European–New World encounter. At the same time, I want to draw attention to the ways specific formulations of diaspora can also keep us from seeing the full range of Black transnational political, cultural, and intellectual links. I end with a few speculative remarks on how we might broaden our understanding of Black identities and political movements by exploring other streams of internationalism that are not limited to the black world.

One of the foundational questions central to African diaspora studies is to what degree are New World black people "African" and what does that mean? It is an old question posed as early as the publication of Sir Harry Johnston's amateur anthropological writings in his prodigious and enigmatic book, *The Negro in the New World* (1910).[3] Whether we employ

metaphors of survival, retention, exchange, transformation, acculturation, or conversation, the remaking of African New World cultures has enormous implications, not just for
the study of the African diaspora but for the Atlantic as a whole. We can ask similar questions and consider similar methodologies for studying the making of New World European and even Native American cultures, identities, and communities. The idea of a
"European" culture or even "English" culture is often taken for granted and hardly ever
problematized in the way that "African" is constantly understood as a social construction.
For example, we might follow Nahum Chandler's lead and think of early New World Euro-
Americans as possessing Du Bois's notion of "double-consciousness," say, English and
American, with whiteness as a means of negotiating this double-consciousness.[4] Or we
might consider the "New World" as a source of Pan-Europeanism in the way that it became
the source of Pan-Africanism—both fundamental for building modern racial identities
upon ethnic and national foundations.[5]

The question of New World cultural formation has also been critical for the study of
gender in New World African communities. For example, African historians have begun to
ask questions such as: How much of the idea of women as culture bearers embedded in
Western thought conflicts or resonates with ideas coming out of West and Central African
societies? In much of Africa spiritual access or power was not specifically gendered as male,
so women priests and diviners were fairly common. In the Caribbean one sees women
practitioners of vodun, myalism, and obeah; yet, in the institutional Black churches there
is a clear male-dominated gendered hierarchy. We might also consider the transfer of technology, especially in agriculture. In much of West and Central Africa women were cultiva-
tors; yet Europeans assumed that men were both responsible and knowledgeable about
cultivation—so how did Americans learn rice cultivation from Africans? Which Africans?
Did the passage of this knowledge to men change power relationships? And when we look
deeper at the gender division of labor under slavery, did women's participation in field
work, hauling, lifting, and the like free them of constraining notions of femininity, or was
it consistent with their gendered work and lives in Africa?[6]

On the other hand, the "Africanity" question has recently been met with caution, if not
outright hostility, by scholars concerned with essentialism and interested in locating hybridity and difference within Black cultures. This is understandable; thinking of cultural
change as a process of "destruction" or loss does more to obscure complexity than to illuminate the processes of cultural formation. Furthermore, emphasis on similarities and cultural continuities not only tends to elide differences in Black cultures (even within the same
region or nation-state), but also does not take into account the similar historical conditions
in which African people labored, created, and re-created culture. Forced labor, racial oppression, colonial conditions, and capitalist exploitation were global processes that incorporated Black people through empire building. They were never uniform or fixed, but did
create systems that were at times tightly coordinated across oceans and national boundaries.
This raises a number of questions. Were the so-called "cultural survivals" simply the most
effective cultural baggage Africans throughout the world used in their struggle to survive?
Or were they created by the very conditions under which they were forced to toil and reproduce? Are the anthropological studies from which many of these scholars draw their comparisons and parallels valid in view of the fact that they were made while Africa was under
colonial domination? Is Pan-Africanism simply the recognition that Black people share the

same timeless cultural values, as some nationalists would have us believe, or is it a manifestation of life under racism and imperialism?

Once we begin to talk about how diasporan identities are constituted, we are confronted with the limitations of "diaspora" as a way of comprehending the international contexts for "Black" identities and political movements. Too frequently we think of identities as cultural matters, when in fact some of the most dynamic (translational) identities are created in the realm of politics, in the way people of African descent sought alliances and political identifications across oceans and national boundaries. My point here is that neither Africa nor Pan-Africanism is necessarily the source of Black transnational political identities; sometimes they live through or are integrally tied to other kinds of international movements—Socialism, Communism, Feminism, Surrealism, religions such as Islam, and so on. Communist and Socialist movements, for example, have long been harbingers of Black internationalism that explicitly reaches out to all oppressed colonial subjects as well as to white workers. Although the relationships have not always been comfortable, the Communist movement enabled many different people to identify with other oppressed peoples and to reject patriotism and national identity. Black people across the globe could find each other, in some cases become African again, and they could also identify with the Spanish or Chinese or Cuban or even Russian Revolution.[7] Similarly, during the interwar period a group of Black intellectuals from the French-, Spanish-, and English-speaking world were drawn to Surrealism for its militant anticolonialism and fascination with the unconscious, the spirit, desire, and magic. Many figures, such as Aimé and Suzanne Césaire, the Afro-Chinese Cuban painter Wifredo Lam, René Menil, would go on to play a central role in the formation of *Négritude* or the promotion of African culture in the diaspora.[8]

Finally, let me close with some reflections on the usefulness of the African diaspora for constructing "global" narratives of the past. The concept of the African diaspora, for all of its limitations, is fundamental to the development of the "Atlantic" as a unit of analysis (which, we should recognize, is not new but a product of imperial history). Indeed, we might just as easily talk about a "Black Mediterranean" that is far more important in the Francophone and Italian worlds than in Britain.[9] Likewise, Edward Alpers and Joseph Harris have made significant contributions toward identifying, for want of a better term, a "Black Indian Ocean." Their work suggests, once again, that large bodies of water are not barriers but avenues for transnational, transoceanic trade, cultural exchange, and transformation. Indian Ocean crossings brought together many diverse peoples from East Africa, India, and the Arab world.[10]

We can see the promise of such a framework in studies by Peter Linebaugh and Marcus Rediker. In their forthcoming book, *The Many Headed Hydra: A History of the Atlantic Working Class*, they explore how merchant and industrial capital, with its attendant maritime revolution, and the rise of the transatlantic slave trade, created a brand new international working class of which Africans were a part, created misery and immiseration, and simultaneously gave birth to significant political movements such as republicanism, Pan-Africanism, and new, often suppressed, expressions of internationalism.[11] Likewise, Julius Scott's forthcoming book, *The Common Wind*, which examines New World Black people in the age of the Haitian Revolution, invokes the "sailing image" both literally and metaphorically to illustrate how networks of oral tranmission and shared memory were the crucial dimensions of Afro-diasporic politics and identity. The main characters in *The Common Wind* are Black republicans not long out of Africa, and they develop their own politically driven, relatively autonomous vision of an antislavery republicanism that is in many ways far more radical than anything being pursued in France or Philadelphia. Scott also demonstrates the level of ideological debate and international organization that existed among African Americans in the New World—a crucial element in the unfolding of the revolution. At the very least, Scott demonstrates how an Afro-diasporic approach can force us to rethink the creation of New World republicanism, systems of communication in the eighteenth and early nineteenth century, the political and cultural autonomy of African people in the West, and the crucial role that Black sailors played in the age of democratic revolutions.[12]

We need to move beyond unitary narratives of displacement, domination, and nation building that center on European expansion and the rise of "racial" capitalism. In some ways, destabilizing unitary narratives is what Paul Gilroy does in *The Black Atlantic* (1993) and what Cedric Robinson had already begun to do in his magnum opus, *Black Marxism: The Making of the Black Radical Tradition* (1983). Their work demonstrates not only how the rise of the transatlantic system helped forge the concept of Africa and create an "African" identity, but also that the same process was central to the formation of a European/"white" identity in the New World. These scholars and those who came before them see the fundamental importance of Black people to the making of the modern world: slave labor helped usher in the transition to capitalism; Black struggles for freedom indisputably shaped discourses on democracy and the rise of republicanism; and the cultures, ideas, epistemologies taken from Africa or created in the "New World" have deeply influenced, art, religion, politics, philosophy, and social relations in the West. Hence, just as Europe invented Africa and the New World, we cannot understand the invention of Europe and the New World without Africa and African people.

I am indebted to all who participated in "Transcending Traditions," especially its distinguished organizers, Tukufu Zuberi and Farah Jasmine Griffin. I owe my greatest debt to Tiffany Patterson; many of the ideas in this essay come out of my collaborations with Patterson, who coauthored a longer piece with me about the African diaspora, to appear in *The African Studies Review*.

NOTES

1. See George Shepperson, "African Diaspora: Concept and Context" and St. Clair Drake, "Diaspora Studies and Pan-Africanism," in Joseph E. Harris, ed., *Global Dimensions of the African Diaspora* (Washington, D.C.: Howard University Press, 1982); Jacob Drachler, *Black Homeland/Black Diaspora: Cross Currents of the African Relationship* (Port Washington, N.Y.: Kennikat Press, 1975); St. Clair Drake, *Black Folk Here and There: An Essay in History and Anthropology* (Los Angeles: Center for Afro American Studies, University of California, vol. I, 1987; vol. II, 1990); W. E. B. Du Bois, *The World and Africa: An Inquiry into the Part Which Africa Played in World History* (New York: Viking Press, 1947); John P. Henderson and Harry A. Reed, eds., *Studies in the African Diaspora: A Memorial to James R. Hooker (1929–1976)* (Dover, Mass.: Majority Press, 1989); Martin L. Kilson and Robert I. Rotberg, eds., *African Diaspora: Interpretive Essays* (Cambridge: Harvard University Press, 1976); Franklin Knight, *The African Dimension in Latin American Societies* (New York: Macmillan, 1974); Sidney J. Lemelle and Robin D. G. Kelley, eds., *Imagining Home: Class, Culture, and Nationalism in the African Diaspora* (London and New York: Verso Press, 1994); Vincent Thompson, *The Making of*

the African Diaspora in the Americas, 1441–1900 (1987); Robert Weisbord, *Ebony Kinship: Africa, Africans, and the Afro-American* (Westport, Conn.: Greenwood Press, 1973).

2. See Paul Gilroy, *The Black Atlantic: Modernity and Double Consciousness* (Cambridge: Harvard University Press, 1993); Peter Linebaugh, "All the Atlantic Mountains Shook," *Labour/Le Travailleur* 10 (autumn 1982): 87–121; Cedric Robinson, *Black Marxism: The Making of the Black Radical Tradition* (Chapel Hill: University of North Carolina Press, 1983); and an excellent essay by Kim D. Butler, "What Is African Diaspora Study?: An Epistemological Frontier," forthcoming in *Diaspora*.

3. Works that examine African survivals in the New World include: Melville J. Herskovits, *The Myth of the Negro Past* (Boston: Beacon Press, 1941); Sandra T. Barnes, ed., *Africa's Ogun: Old World and New* (Bloomington: Indiana University Press, 1989); Leonard Barrett, *Soul-Force: African Heritage in Afro-American Religion* (Garden City, N.Y.: Anchor Press, 1974); Roger Bastide, *African Civilisations in the New World* (London: C. Hurst, 1972); Roger Bastide, *The African Religions of Brazil: Toward a Sociology of the Interpretation of Civilisations* (Baltimore: Johns Hopkins University Press, 1978); George Brandon, *Santeria from Africa to the New World: The Dead Sell Memories* (Bloomington: Indiana University Press, 1993); Joseph Holloway and Winifred Vass. *The African Heritage of American English* (Bloomington: Indiana University Press, 1993); Joseph Murphy, *Santeria: African Spirits in America* (Boston: Beacon Press, 1988 and 1992); Joseph Murphy, *Working the Spirit: Ceremonies of the African Diaspora* (Boston: Beacon Press, 1994); Karen Fog Olwig, *Cultural Adaptation and Resistance on St. John: Three Centuries of Afro-Caribbean Life* (Gainesville: University of Florida, 1985); Sterling Stuckey, *Slave Culture: Nationalist Theory and the Foundations of Black America* (New York: Oxford University Press, 1987); Jim Wafer, *The Taste of Blood: Spirit Possession in Brazilian Candomblé* (Philadelphia: University of Pennsylvania Press, 1991); Sidney Mintz and Richard Price, *The Birth of African American Culture: An Anthropological Perspective* (Boston: Beacon Press, 1992); Gwendolyn Midlo Hall, *Africans in Colonial Louisiana: The Development of Afro-Creole Culture in the Eighteenth Century* (Baton Rouge: Louisiana State University Press, 1992); Carolyn Fick, *The Making of Haiti: The Saint-Domingue Revolution from Below* (Knoxville: University of Tennessee Press, 1990); Michael Mullin, *Africa in America: Slave Acculturation and Resistance in the American*

South and the British Caribbean, 1736–1831 (Urbana: University of Illinois Press, 1992); Joao José Reis, *Slave Rebellion in Brazil: The Muslim Uprising of 1835 in Bahia* (Baltimore: Johns Hopkins University Press, 1993); Monica Schuler, *Alas, Alas, Kongo: A Social History of Indentured African Immigration into Jamaica, 1841–1865* (Baltimore: Johns Hopkins University Press, 1980); Robert Farris Thompson, *Flash of the Spirit: African and Afro-American Art and Philosophy* (New York: Random House, 1983); Michael Gomez, *Exchanging Our Country Marks: The Transformation of African Identities in the Colonial and Antebellum South* (Chapel Hill: University of North Carolina Press, 1998).

4. Nahum Chandler, "Force of the Double: W. E. B. Du Bois and the Question of African American Subjection" (book manuscript, forthcoming).

5. There is a growing literature on whiteness and new ways of understanding Euro-American identities. Some of the best work includes Theodore W. Allen, *The Invention of the White Race; Volume One: Racist Oppression and Social Control* (New York and London: Verso, 1994); Alexander Saxton, *The Rise and Fall of the White Republic: Class Politics and Mass Culture in Nineteenth Century America* (London and New York: Verso, 1990); Noel Ignatiev, *How the Irish Became White* (New York and London: Routledge, 1995); Eric Lott, *Love and Theft: Blackface Minstrelsy and the American Working Class* (New York: Oxford University Press, 1993); Matthew Frye Jacobson, *Whiteness of a Different Color: European Immigrants and the Alchemy of Race* (Cambridge: Harvard University Press, 1998); George Lipsitz, *The Possessive Investment in Whiteness: How White People Profit from Identity Politics* (Philadelphia: Temple University Press, 1998).

6. See especially Claire Robertson, "Africa into the Americas?: Slavery and Women, the Family, and the Gender Division of Labor," in *More than Chattel: Black Women in Slavery in the Americas*, ed. Darlene Clark Hine and Barry Gaspar (Bloomington: Indiana University Press, 1996).

7. Lisa Brock, "Questioning the Diaspora: Hegemony, Black Intellectuals and Doing International History from Below," *ISSUE: A Journal of Opinion* (Vol. XXIV, No. 2, 1996): 10; Cedric Robinson, *Black Marxism: The Making of the Black Radical Tradition* (Chapel Hill: University of North Carolina Press, 2000 [orig. 1983]); Robin D. G. Kelley, "'This Ain't Ethiopia, but It'll Do': African Americans and the Spanish Civil War," in *Race Rebels: Culture Politics, and the Black Working Class* (New York: The Free Press, 1994); Robin D. G. Kelley,

Hammer and Hoe: Alabama Communists during the Great Depression (Chapel Hill: University of North Carolina Press, 1990).

8. Franklin Rosemont, ed., *André Breton: What Is Surrealism?: Selected Writings* (New York: Pathfinder, 1978), 37 passim.; "Murderous Humanitarianism," in *Negro: An Anthology*, ed. Nancy Cunard, (London: Wishart and Co., 1934); reprinted in *Race Traitor (Special Issue— Surrealism: Revolution against Whiteness)* 9 (summer 1998): 67–69; Max-Pol Fouchet, *Wifredo Lam* (Barcelona: Ediciones Polgrafa, S.A., 1989 [2nd ed.]); Robin D. G. Kelley, "Introduction: A Poetics of Anti-Colonialism" to *Discourse on Colonialism*, by Aimé Césaire, trans. Joan Pinkham (New York: Monthly Review Press, 2000); Tyler Stovall, *Paris Noir: African Americans in the City of Light* (Boston and New York: Houghton Mifflin, 1996); Brent Edwards, "Black Globality: The International Shape of Black Intellectual Culture" (Ph.D. dissertation, Columbia University, 1997); Michael Richardson, ed., *Refusal of the Shadow: Surrealism and the Caribbean*, trans. Michael Richardson and Krzysztof Fijalkowski (London: Verso, 1996); Cheikh Tidiane Sylla, "Surrealism and Black African Art," *Arsenal: Surrealist Subversion* 4 (Chicago: Black Swan Press, 1989), 128–29.

9. Cedric Robinson, *Black Marxism*; Brent Edwards, "Black Globality: The International Shape of Black Intellectual Culture" (Ph.D. dissertation, Columbia University, 1997).

10. Joseph Harris, *The African Presence in Asia: Consequences of the East African Slave Trade* (Evanston, Ill.: Northwestern University Press, 1971); Harris, "A Comparative Approach to the Study of the African Diaspora," in Joseph Harris, ed., *Global Dimensions of the African Diaspora* (Washington, D.C.: Howard University Press, 1982), 112–24; Edward Alpers, "The African Diaspora in the Northwestern Indian Ocean: Reconsideration of an Old Problem, New Directions for Research," *African Studies Review* (forthcoming 2000).

11. Peter Linebaugh and Marcus Rediker, *The Many-Headed Hydra: The Hidden History of the Revolutionary Atlantic* (Boston: Beacon Press, 2000); see also Peter Linebaugh, "All the Atlantic Mountains Shook," *Labour/Le Travailleur* 10 (autumn 1982), 87–121; Marcus Rediker, "*Between the Devil and the Deep Blue Sea": Merchant Seamen, Privates, and the Anglo-American Maritime World, 1700–1750* (Cambridge: Cambridge University Press, 1987).

12. Julius Scott, "The Common Wind: Currents of Afro-American Communications in the Era of the Haitian Revolution" (book manuscript, forthcoming).

5

WOMANIST CONSCIOUSNESS

Maggie Lena Walker and the Independent Order of Saint Luke

Elsa Barkley Brown

IN THE FIRST DECADES of the twentieth century Maggie Lena Walker repeatedly challenged her contemporaries to "make history as Negro women." Yet she and her colleagues in the Independent Order of Saint Luke, like most Black and other women of color, have been virtually invisible in women's history and women's studies. Although recent books and articles have begun to redress this,[1] the years of exclusion have had an impact more significant than just the invisibility of Black women, for the exclusion of Black women has meant that the concepts, perspectives, methods, and pedagogies of women's history and women's studies have been developed without consideration of the experiences of Black women. As a result many of the recent explorations in Black women's history have attempted to place Black women inside feminist perspectives, which, by design, have omitted their experiences. Nowhere is this exclusion more apparent than in the process of defining women's issues and women's struggle. Because they have been created outside the experiences of Black women, the definitions used in women's history and women's studies assume the separability of women's struggle and race struggle. Such arguments recognize the possibility that Black women may have both women's concerns and race concerns, but they insist upon delimiting each. They allow, belatedly, Black women to make history as women or as Negroes but not as "Negro women." What they fail to consider is that women's issues may be race issues, and race issues may be women's issues.[2]

Rosalyn Terborg-Penn, in "Discontented Black Feminists: Prelude and Postscript to the Passage of the Nineteenth Amendment," an essay on the 1920s Black women's movement of which Walker was a part, persuasively discusses the continuing discrimination in the U.S. women's movement and the focus of Black women on "uplifting the downtrodden of the race or . . . representing people of color throughout the world." Subsequently she argues for the "unique nature of feminism among Afro-American women." The editors of *Decades of Discontent: The Women's Movement, 1920–1940*, the 1983 collection on post–Nineteenth Amendment feminism, however, introduce Terborg-Penn's article by mistakenly concluding that these Black women, disillusioned and frustrated by racism in the women's movement, turned from women's issues to race issues. Using a framework that does not conceive of "racial uplift, fighting segregation and mob violence" and "contending with poverty" as women's issues, Lois Scharf and Joan Jensen succumb to the tendency to assume that Black women's lives can be neatly subdivided, that while we are both Black and female, we occupy those roles sequentially, as if one cannot have the two simultaneously in one's consciousness of being.[3] Such a framework assumes a fragmentation of Black women's existence that defies reality.

Scharf and Jensen's conclusion is certainly one that the white feminists of the 1920s and 1930s, who occupy most of the book, would have endorsed. When southern Black women, denied the right to register to vote, sought help from the National Woman's Party, these white feminists rejected their petitions, arguing that this was a race concern and not a women's concern. Were they not, after all, being denied the vote not because of their sex but because of their race?[4]

Black women like Walker who devoted their energies to securing universal suffrage, including that of Black men, are not widely recognized as female suffragists because they did not separate their struggle for the women's vote from their struggle for the Black vote. This tendency to establish false dichotomies, precluding the possibility that for many racism and sexism are experienced simultaneously, leads to discussions of liberation movements and women's movements as separate entities.

Quite clearly, what many women of color at the United Nations Decade for Women conference held in Nairobi, Kenya, in 1985, along with many other activists and scholars, have argued in recent years is the impossibility of separating the two and the necessity of understanding the convergence of women's issues, race/nationalist issues, and class issues in women's consciousnesses.[5] That understanding is in part hampered by the prevailing terminology: feminism places a priority on women; nationalism or race consciousness, a priority on race. It is the need to overcome the limitations of terminology that has led many Black women to adopt the term "womanist." Both Alice Walker and Chikwenye Okonjo Ogunyemi have defined womanism as a consciousness that incorporates racial, cultural, sexual, national, economic, and political considerations.[6] As Ogunyemi explains, "Black womanism is a philosophy" that concerns itself both with sexual equality in the Black community and "with the world power structure that subjugates" both Blacks and women. "Its ideal is for Black unity where every Black person has a modicum of power and so can be a 'brother' or a 'sister' or a 'father' or a 'mother' to the other. . . . [I]ts aim is the dynamism of wholeness and self-healing."[7]

Walker's and Ogunyemi's terminology may be new, but their ideas are not. In fact, many Black women at various points in history had a clear understanding that race issues and women's issues were inextricably linked, that one could not separate women's struggle from race struggle. It was because of this understanding that they refused to disconnect themselves from either movement. They instead insisted on inclusion in both movements in a manner that recognized the interconnection between race and sex, and they did so even if they had to battle their white sisters and their Black brothers to achieve it. Certainly the lives and work of women such as Anna Julia Cooper, Mary Church Terrell, and Fannie Barrier Williams inform us of this. Cooper, an early Africanamerican womanist, addressed the holistic nature of the struggle in her address to the World's Congress of Representative Women:

Let woman's claim be as broad in the concrete as in the abstract. *We take our stand on the solidarity of humanity, the oneness of life*, and the unnaturalness and injustice of all special favoritisms, whether of sex, race, country, or condition. If one link of the chain be broken, the chain is broken. . . . We want, then, as toilers for the universal triumph of justice and human rights, to go to our homes from this Congress, demanding an entrance not through a gateway for ourselves, our race, our sex, or our sect, but a grand highway for humanity. The colored woman feels that woman's cause is one and universal; and that not till . . . race, color, sex, and condition are seen as the accidents, and not the substance of life; . . . not till then is woman's lesson taught and woman's cause won—not the white woman's, nor the Black woman's, nor the red woman's, but the cause of every man and of every woman who has writhed silently under a mighty wrong. *Woman's wrongs are thus indissolubly linked with all undefended woe, and the acquirement of her "rights" will mean the final triumph of all right over might*, the supremacy of the moral forces of reason, and justice, and love in the government of the nations of earth.[8]

One of those who most clearly articulated womanist consciousness was Maggie Lena Walker. Walker (1867–1934) was born and educated in Richmond, Virginia, graduating from Colored Normal School in 1883. During her school years she assisted her widowed mother in her work as a washerwoman and cared for her younger brother. Following graduation she taught in the city's public schools and took courses in accounting and sales. Required to stop teaching when she married Armstead Walker, a contractor, she had been well prepared by her coursework to join several other Black women in founding an insurance company, the Woman's Union. Meanwhile, Walker, who had joined the Independent Order of Saint Luke at the age of fourteen, rose through the ranks to hold several important positions in the order and, in 1895, to organize the juvenile branch of the order. In addition to her Saint Luke activities, Walker was a founder or leading supporter of the Richmond Council of Colored Women, the Virginia State Federation of Colored Women, the National Association of Wage Earners, the International Council of Women of the Darker Races, the National Training School for Girls, and the Virginia Industrial School for Colored Girls. She also helped direct the National Association for the Advancement of Colored People, the Richmond Urban League, and the Negro Organization Society of Virginia.[9]

Walker is probably best known today as the first woman bank president in the United States. She founded the Saint Luke Penny Savings Bank in Richmond, Virginia, in 1903. Before her death in 1934 she oversaw the reorganization of this financial institution as the present-day Consolidated Bank and Trust Company, the oldest continuously existing Black-owned and Black-run bank in the country. The bank, like most of Walker's activities, was the outgrowth of the Independent Order of Saint Luke, which she served as Right Worthy Grand Secretary for thirty-five years.

The Independent Order of Saint Luke was one of the larger and more successful of the many thousands of mutual benefit societies that have developed throughout Africanamerican communities since the eighteenth century. These societies combined insurance functions with economic development and social and political activities. As such they were important loci of community self-help and racial solidarity. Unlike the Knights of Pythias and its female auxiliary, the Courts of Calanthe, societies like the Independent Order of Saint Luke had a nonexclusionary membership policy; any man, woman, or child could join. Thus men and women from all occupational segments, professional/managerial, entrepreneurial, and working-class, came together in the order. The Independent Order of Saint Luke was a mass-based organization that played a key role in the political, economic, and social development of its members and of the community as a whole.[10]

Founded in Maryland in 1867 by Mary Prout, the Independent Order of Saint Luke began as a women's sickness and death mutual benefit association. By the 1880s it had admitted men and had expanded to New York and Virginia. At the 1899 annual meeting William M. T. Forrester, who had served as Grand Secretary since 1869, refused to accept reappointment, stating that the order was in decline, having only 1,080 members in fifty-seven councils, $31.61 in the treasury, and $400.00 in outstanding debts. Maggie Lena Walker took over the duties of Grand Worthy Secretary at one-third of the position's previous salary.[11]

According to Walker, her "first work was to draw around me *women*."[12] In fact, after the executive board elections in 1901, six of the nine members were women: Walker, Patsie K. Anderson, Frances Cox, Abigail Dawley, Lillian H. Payne, and Ella O. Waller.[13] Under their leadership the order and its affiliates flourished. The order's ventures included a juvenile department, an educational loan fund for young people, a department store, and a weekly newspaper. Growing to include over 100,000 members in 2,010 councils and circles in twenty-eight states, the order demonstrated a special commitment to expanding the economic opportunities within the Black community, especially those for women.

It is important to take into account Walker's acknowledgment of her female colleagues. Most of what we know about the Order of Saint Luke highlights Walker because she was the leader and spokeswoman and therefore the most visible figure. She was able, however, to function in that role and to accomplish all that she did not merely because of her own strengths and skills, considerable though they were, but also because she operated from the strength of the Saint Luke collective as a whole and from the special strengths and talents of the inner core of the Saint Luke women in particular. Deborah Gray White, in her work on women during slavery, underscores the importance of Black women's networks in an earlier time period: "Strength had to be cultivated. It came no more naturally to them than to anyone. . . . If they seemed exceptionally strong it was partly because they often functioned in groups and derived strength from numbers. . . . [T]hey inevitably developed some appreciation of one another's skills and talents. This intimacy enabled them to establish the criteria with which to rank and order themselves." It was this same kind of sisterhood that was Walker's base, her support, her strength, and her source of wisdom and direction.[14]

The women of Saint Luke expanded the role of women in the community to the political sphere through their leadership in the 1904 streetcar boycott and through the *St. Luke Herald*'s pronouncements against segregation, lynching, and lack of equal educational opportunities for Black children. Walker spearheaded the local struggle for women's suffrage and the voter registration campaigns after the passage of the Nineteenth Amendment. In the 1920 elections in Richmond, fully 80 percent of the eligible Black voters were women. The increased Black political strength represented by the female voters gave incentive to the growing movement for independent Black political action and led to the formation of the Virginia Lily-Black Republican Party. Walker ran on this ticket for state superintendent of public instruction in 1921.[15] Thus Walker and many other of the Saint Luke women were role models for other Black women in their community activities as well as their occupations.

Undergirding all of their work was a belief in the possibilities inherent in the collective struggle of Black women in particular and of the Black community in general. Walker argued that the only way in which Black women would be able "to avoid the traps and snares of life" would be to "band themselves together, organize, . . . put their mites together, put their hands and their brains together and make work and business for themselves."[16]

The idea of collective economic development was not a new idea for these women, many of whom were instrumental in establishing the Woman's Union, a female insurance company founded in 1898. Its motto was "The Hand That Rocks the Cradle Rules the World."[17] But unlike nineteenth-century white women's rendering of that expression to signify the limitation of woman's influence to that which she had by virtue of rearing her sons, the idea as these women conceived it transcended the separation of private and public spheres and spoke to the idea that women, while not abandoning their roles as wives and mothers, could also move into economic and political activities in ways that would support rather than conflict with family and community. Women did not have to choose between the two spheres; in fact, they necessarily had to occupy both. Indeed, these women's use of this phrase speaks to their understanding of the totality of the task that lay ahead of them as Black women. It negates, for Black women at least, the public/private dichotomy.

Saint Luke women built on tradition. A well-organized set of institutions maintained community in Richmond: mutual benefit societies, interwoven with extended families and churches, built a network of supportive relations.[18] The families, churches, and societies were all based on similar ideas of collective consciousness and collective responsibility. Thus, they served to extend and reaffirm notions of family throughout the Black community. Not only in their houses but also in their meeting halls and places of worship, they were brothers and sisters caring for each other. The institutionalization of this notion of family cemented the community. Community/family members recognized that this had to be maintained from generation to generation; this was in part the function of the juvenile branches of the mutual benefit associations. The statement of purpose of the Children's Rosebud Fountains, Grand Fountain United Order of True Reformers, clearly articulated this:

> Teaching them . . . to assist each other in sickness, sorrow and afflictions and in the struggles of life; teaching them that one's happiness greatly depends upon the others. . . . Teach them to live united. . . . The children of different families will know how to . . . talk, plot and plan for one another's peace and happiness in the journey of life.
>
> Teach them to . . . bear each other's burdens . . . to so bind and tie their love and affections together that one's sorrow may be the other's sorrow, one's distress be the other's distress, one's penny the other's penny.[19]

Through the Penny Savings Bank the Saint Luke women were able to affirm and cement the existing mutual assistance network among Black women and within the Black community by providing an institutionalized structure for these activities. The bank recognized the meager resources of the Black community, particularly Black women. In fact, its establishment as a *penny* savings bank is an indication of that. Many of its earliest and strongest supporters were washerwomen, one of whom was Maggie Walker's mother. And the bank continued throughout Walker's leadership to exercise a special commitment to "the small depositor."[20]

In her efforts Walker, like the other Saint Luke women, was guided by a clearly understood and shared perspective concerning the relationship of Black women to Black men, to the Black community, and to the larger society. This was a perspective that acknowledged individual powerlessness in the face of racism and sexism and that argued that Black women, because of their condition and status, had a right—indeed, according to Walker, a special duty and incentive—to organize. She argued, "Who is so helpless as the Negro woman? Who is so circumscribed and hemmed in, in the race of life, in the struggle for bread, meat and clothing as the Negro woman?"[21]

In addition, her perspective contended that organizational activity and the resultant expanded opportunities for Black women were not detrimental to the home, the community, Black men, or the race. Furthermore, she insisted that organization and expansion of women's roles economically and politically were essential ingredients without which the community, the race, and even Black men could not achieve their full potential. The way in which Walker described Black women's relationship to society, combined with the collective activities in which she engaged, give us some insight into her understanding of the relationship between women's struggle and race struggle.

Walker was determined to expand opportunities for Black women. In fulfilling this aim she challenged not only the larger society's notions of the proper place of Blacks but also those in her community who held a limited notion of women's proper role. Particularly in light of the increasing necessity to defend the integrity and morality of the race, a "great number of men" and women in Virginia and elsewhere believed that women's clubs, movements "looking to the final exercise of suffrage by women," and organizations of Black professional and business women would lead to "the decadence of home life."[22] Women involved in these activities were often regarded as "pullbacks, rather than home builders."[23] Maggie Walker countered these arguments, stressing the need for women's organizations, saying, "Men should not be so pessimistic and down on women's clubs. They don't seek to destroy the home or disgrace the race."[24] In fact, the Richmond Council of Colored Women, of which she was founder and president, and many other women's organizations worked to elevate the entire Black community, and this, she believed, was the proper province of women.

In 1908 two Richmond men, Daniel Webster Davis and Giles Jackson, published *The Industrial History of the Negro Race of the United States*, which became a textbook for Black children throughout the state. The chapter on women acknowledged the economic and social achievements of Black women but concluded that "the Negro Race Needs Housekeepers . . . wives who stay at home, being supported by their husbands, and then they can spend time in the training of their children."[25] Maggie Walker responded practically to those who held such ideas: "The bold fact remains that there are more women in the world than men; . . . if each and every woman in the land was allotted a man to marry her, work for her, support her, and keep her at home, there would still be an army of women left uncared for, unprovided for, and who would be compelled to fight life's battles alone, and without the companionship of man."[26] Even regarding those women who did marry, she contended, "The old doctrine that a man marries a woman to support her is pretty nearly threadbare to-day." Only a few Black men were able to fully support their families on their earnings alone. Thus many married women worked, "not for name, not for glory and honor—but for bread, and for [their] babies."[27]

The reality was that Black women who did go to work outside the home found themselves in a helpless position. "How many occupations have Negro Women?" asked Walker. "Let us count them: Negro women are domestic menials, teachers and church builders." And even the first two of these, she feared, were in danger. As Walker perceived it, the expansion of opportunities for white women did not mean a corresponding expansion for Black women; instead, this trend might actually lead to an even greater limitation on the economic possibilities for Black women. She pointed to the fact that white women's entry into the tobacco factories of the city had "driven the Negro woman out," and she, like many of her sisters throughout the country, feared that a similar trend was beginning even in domestic work.[28]

In fact, these economic realities led members of the Order of Saint Luke to discuss the development of manufacturing operations as a means of giving employment and therefore "a chance in the race of life" to "the young Negro woman."[29] In 1902 Walker described herself as "consumed with the desire to hear the whistle on our factory and see our women by the hundreds coming to work."[30] It was this same concern for the economic status of Black women that led Walker and other Saint Luke women to affiliate with the National Association of Wage Earners (NAWE), a women's organization that sought to pool the energies and resources of housewives, professionals, and managerial, domestic, and industrial workers to protect and expand the economic position of Black women. The NAWE argued that it was vital that all Black women be able to support themselves.[31] Drawing on traditional stereotypes in the same breath with which she defied them, Walker contended that it was in the self-interest of Black men to unite themselves with these efforts to secure decent employment for Black women: "Every dollar a woman makes, some man gets the direct benefit of same. Every woman was by Divine Providence created for some man; not for some man to marry, take home and support, but for the purpose of using her powers, ability, health and strength, to forward the financial . . . success of the partnership into which she may go, if she will. . . . [W]hat stronger combination could ever God make—than the partnership of a business man and a business woman."[32]

By implication, whatever Black women as a whole were able to achieve would directly benefit Black men. In Walker's analysis family is a reciprocal metaphor for community: family is community and community is family. But this is more than rhetorical style. Her discussions of relationship networks suggest that the entire community was one's family. Thus Walker's references to husbands and wives reflected equally her understandings of male/female relationships in the community as a whole and of those relationships within the household. Just as all family members' resources were needed for the family to be well and strong, so they were needed for a healthy community/family.

In the process of developing means of expanding economic opportunities in the community, however, Walker and the Saint Luke women also confronted white Richmond's notions of the proper place of Blacks. While whites found a bank headed by a "Negress" an interesting curiosity,[33] they were less receptive to other business enterprises. In 1905 twenty-two Black women from the Independent Order of Saint Luke collectively formed a department store aimed at providing quality goods at more affordable prices than those available in stores outside the Black community, as well as a place where Black women could earn a living and get a business education. The Saint Luke Emporium employed fifteen women as salesclerks. While this may seem an insignificant number in comparison to the thousands of Black women working outside the home, in the context of the occupational structure of Richmond these women constituted a significant percentage of the white-collar and skilled working-class women in the community. In 1900 less than 1 percent of the employed Black women in the city were either clerical or skilled workers. That number had quadrupled by 1910, when 222 of the more than 13,000 employed Black women listed their occupations as typists, stenographers, bookkeepers, salesclerks, and the like. However, by 1930 there had been a reduction in the numbers of Black women employed in clerical and sales positions. This underscores the fact that Black secretaries and clerks were entirely dependent on the financial stability of Black businesses and in this re-gard the Independent Order of Saint Luke was especially important. With its fifty-five clerks in the home office, over one-third of the Black female clerical workers in Richmond in the 1920s worked for this order. The quality of the work experience was significantly better for these women as compared to those employed as laborers in the tobacco factories or as servants in private homes. They worked in healthier, less stressful environments and, being employed by Blacks, they also escaped the racism prevalent in most Black women's workplaces. Additionally, the salaries of these clerical workers were often better than those paid even to Black professional women, that is, teachers. While one teacher, Ethel Thomp-son Overby, was receiving eighteen dollars a month as a teacher and working her way up to the top of the scale at forty dollars, a number of Black women were finding good working conditions and a fifty-dollar-per-month paycheck as clerks in the office of the Indepen-dent Order of Saint Luke. Nevertheless, Black women in Richmond, as elsewhere, over-whelmingly remained employed in domestic service in the years 1890–1930.[34]

Located on East Broad Street, Richmond's main business thoroughfare, the Saint Luke Emporium met stiff opposition from white merchants. When the intention to establish the department store was first announced, attempts were made to buy the property at a price several thousand dollars higher than that which the Order of Saint Luke had originally paid. When that did not succeed, an offer of ten thousand dollars cash was made to the order if it would not start the emporium. Once it opened, efforts were made to hinder the store's operations. A white Retail Dealers' Association was formed for the purpose of crushing this business as well as other "Negro merchants who are objectionable . . . be-cause they compete with and get a few dollars which would otherwise go to the white mer-chant." Notices were sent to wholesale merchants in the city warning them not to sell to the emporium at the risk of losing all business from any of the white merchants. Letters were also sent to wholesale houses in New York City with the same warning. These letters charged that the emporium was underselling the white merchants of Richmond. Clearly, then, the white businessmen of Richmond found the emporium and these Black women a threat; if it was successful, the store could lead to a surge of Black merchants competing with white merchants and thus decrease the Black patronage at white stores. The white merchants' efforts were ultimately successful: the obstacles they put in the way of the em-porium, in addition to the lack of full support from the Black community itself, resulted in the department store's going out of business seven years after its founding.[35] Though its existence was short-lived and its demise mirrors many of the problems that Black busi-nesses faced from both within and without their community, the effort demonstrated the commitment of the Order of Saint Luke to provide needed services for the community and needed opportunities for Black women.

Maggie Walker's appeals for support of the emporium show quite clearly the way in which her notions of race, of womanhood, and of community fused. Approximately one year after the opening of the emporium, Walker called for a mass gathering of men in the community to talk, in part, about support for the business. Her speech, "Beniah's Valour; An Address for Men Only," opened with an assessment of white businessmen's and offi-cials' continuing oppression of the Black community. In her fine rhetorical style she queried her audience. "Hasn't it crept into your minds that we are being more and more oppressed each day that we live? Hasn't it yet come to you, that we are being oppressed by the passage of laws which not only have for their object the degradation of Negro man-hood and Negro womanhood, but also the destruction of all kinds of Negro enterprises?"

Then, drawing upon the biblical allegory of Beniah and the lion, she warned, "There is a lion terrorizing us, preying upon us, and upon every business effort which we put forth. The name of this insatiable lion is PREJUDICE. . . . The white press, the white pulpit, the white business associations, the legislature—all . . . the lion with whom we contend daily . . . in Broad Street, Main Street and in every business street of Richmond. Even now . . . that lion is seeking some new plan of attack."[36]

Thus, she contended, the vital question facing their community was how to kill the lion. And in her analysis, "the only way to kill the Lion is to stop feeding it." The irony was that the Black community drained itself of resources, money, influence, and patronage to feed its predator.[37] As she had many times previously, Walker questioned the fact that while the white community oppressed the Black, "the Negro . . . carries to their bank every dollar he can get his hands upon and then goes back the next day, borrows and then pays the white man to lend him his own money."[38] So, too, Black people patronized stores and other businesses in which white women were, in increasing numbers, being hired as salesclerks and secretaries while Black women were increasingly without employment and the Black community as a whole was losing resources, skills, and finances.[39] Walker considered such behavior racially destructive and believed it necessary to break those ties that kept "the Negro . . . so wedded to those who oppress him."[40] The drain on the resources of the Black community could be halted by a concentration on the development of a self-sufficient Black community. But to achieve this would require the talents of the entire community/family. It was therefore essential that Black women's work in the community be "something more tangible than elegant papers, beautifully framed resolutions and pretty speeches." Rather, "the exercising of every talent that God had given them" was required in the effort to "raise . . . the race to higher planes of living."[41]

The Saint Luke women were part of the Negro Independence Movement that captured a large segment of Richmond society at the turn of the century. Disillusioned by the increasing prejudice and discrimination in this period, which one historian has described as the nadir in U.S. race relations, Black residents of Richmond nevertheless held on to their belief in a community that they could collectively sustain.[42] As they witnessed a steady erosion of their civil and political rights, however, they were aware that there was much operating against them. In Richmond, as elsewhere, a system of race and class oppression including segregation, disfranchisement, relegation to the lowest rungs of the occupational strata, and enforcement of racial subordination through intimidation was fully in place by the early twentieth century. In Richmond between 1885 and 1915 all Blacks were removed from the city council; the only predominantly Black political district, Jackson Ward, was gerrymandered out of existence; the state constitutional convention disfranchised the majority of Black Virginians; first the railroads and streetcars and later the jails, juries, and neighborhoods were segregated; Black principals were removed from the public schools and the right of Blacks to teach was questioned; the state legislature decided to substitute white for Black control of Virginia Normal and College and to strike "and College" from both name and function; and numerous other restrictions were imposed. As the attorney J. Thomas Hewin noted, he and his fellow Black Richmonders occupied "a peculiar position in the body politics":

He [the Negro] is not wanted in politics, because his presence in official positions renders him obnoxious to his former masters and their descendants. He is not wanted in the industrial world as a trained handicraftsman, because he would be brought into competition with his white brother. He is not wanted in city positions, because positions of that kind are always saved for the wardheeling politicians. He is not wanted in State and Federal offices, because there is an unwritten law that a Negro shall not hold an office. He is not wanted on the Bench as a judge, because he would have to pass upon the white man's case also. Nor is he wanted on public conveyances, because here his presence is obnoxious to white people.[43]

Assessing the climate of the surrounding society in 1904, John Mitchell Jr., editor of the *Richmond Planet,* concluded, "This is the beginning of the age of conservatism."[44] The growing movement within the community for racial self-determination urged Blacks to depend upon themselves and their community rather than upon whites: to depend upon their own inner strengths, to build their own institutions, and thereby to mitigate the ways in which their lives were determined by the white forces arrayed against them. Race pride, self-help, racial cooperation, and economic development were central to their thinking about their community and to the ways in which they went about building their own internal support system in order to be better able to struggle within the majority system.

The Saint Luke women argued that the development of the community could not be achieved by men alone, or by men on behalf of women. Only a strong and unified community made up of both women and men could wield the power necessary to allow Black people to shape their own lives. Therefore, only when women were able to exercise their full strength would the community be at its full strength, they argued. Only when the community was at its full strength would they be able to create their own conditions, conditions that would allow men as well as women to move out of their structural isolation at the bottom of the labor market and to overcome their political impotence in the larger society. The Saint Luke women argued that it was therefore in the self-interest of Black men and of the community as a whole to support expanded opportunities for women.

Their arguments redefined not only the roles of women but also the roles and notions of manhood. A strong "race man" traditionally meant one who stood up fearlessly in defense of the race. In her "Address for Men" Walker argued that one could not defend the race unless one defended Black women. Appealing to Black men's notions of themselves as the protectors of Black womanhood, she asked on behalf of all her sisters for their "FRIENDSHIP, . . . LOVE, . . . SYMPATHY, . . . PROTECTION, and . . . ADVICE": "I am asking you, men of Richmond, . . . to record [yourselves] as . . . the strong race men of our city. . . . I am asking each man in this audience to go forth from this building, determined to do valiant deeds for the Negro Women of Richmond."[45] And how might they offer their friendship, love, and protection; how might they do valiant deeds for Negro womanhood? By supporting the efforts of Black women to exercise every talent;[46] by "let[ting] woman choose her own vocation, just as man does his";[47] by supporting the efforts then under way to provide increased opportunities—economic, political, and social—for Black women.[48] Once again she drew upon traditional notions of the relationship between men and women at the same time that she countered those very notions. Black men could play the role of protector and defender of womanhood by protecting and defending and aiding women's assault on the barriers generally imposed on women.[49] Only in this way could they really defend the race. Strong race consciousness and strong support of equality for Black women were inseparable. Maggie Walker and the other Saint Luke women therefore came to argue that an expanded role for Black women within the Black community itself was an essential step in the community's fight to overcome the limitations imposed upon the community by the larger society. Race men were therefore defined not just by their actions on behalf of Black rights but by their actions on behalf of women's rights. The two were inseparable.

This was a collective effort in which Walker believed Black men and Black women should be equally engaged. Therefore, even in creating a woman's organization, she and her Saint Luke associates found it essential to create space within the structure for men as well. Unlike many of the fraternal orders that were male or female only, the Order of Saint Luke welcomed both genders as members and as employees. Although the office force was all female, men were employed in the printing department, in field work, and in the bank. Principal offices within the order were open to men and women. Ten of the thirty directors of the emporium were male; eight of the nineteen trustees of the order were male. The Saint Luke women thus strove to create an equalitarian organization, with men neither dominant nor auxiliary. Their vision of the order was a reflection of their vision for their community. In the 1913 Saint Luke Thanksgiving Day celebration of the order, Maggie Walker "thank[ed] God that this is a *woman's* organization, broad enough, liberal enough, and unselfish enough to accord equal rights and equal opportunity to men."[50]

Only such a community could become self-sustaining, self-sufficient, and independent, could enable its members to live lives unhampered by the machinations of the larger society, and could raise children who could envision a different world in which to live and then could go about creating it. The women in the Order of Saint Luke sought to carve a sphere for themselves where they could practically apply their belief in their community and in the potential that Black men and women working together could achieve, and they sought to infuse that belief into all of Black Richmond and to transmit it to the next generation.

The Saint Luke women challenged notions in the Black community about the proper role of women; they challenged notions in the white community about the proper place of Blacks. They expanded their roles in ways that enabled them to maintain traditional values of family/community and at the same time move into new spheres and relationships with each other and with the men in their lives. To the larger white society they demonstrated what Black men and women in community could achieve. This testified to the idea that women's struggle and race struggle were not two separate phenomena but one indivisible whole. "First by practice and then by precept"[51] Maggie Lena Walker and the Saint Luke women demonstrated in their own day the power of Black women discovering their own strengths and sharing them with the whole community.[52] They provide for us today a model of womanist praxis.

Womanism challenges the distinction between theory and action. Too often we have assumed that theory is to be found only in carefully articulated position statements. Courses on feminist theory are woefully lacking on anything other than white, Western, middle-class perspectives; feminist scholars would argue that this is due to the difficulty in locating any but contemporary Black feminist thought. Though I have discussed Maggie Lena Walker's public statements, the clearest articulation of her theoretical perspective lies in the organization she helped to create and in her own activities. Her theory and her action are not distinct and separable parts of some whole; they are often synonymous, and it is only through her actions that we clearly hear her theory. The same is true for the lives of many other Black women who had limited time and resources and maintained a holistic view of life and struggle.

More important, Maggie Lena Walker's womanism challenges the dichotomous thinking that underlies much feminist theory and writing. Most feminist theory poses opposites in exclusionary and hostile ways: one is Black and female, and these are contradictory/

problematical statuses. This either/or approach classifies phenomena in such a way that "everything falls into one category or another, but cannot belong to more than one category at the same time."[53] It is precisely this kind of thinking that makes it difficult to see race, sex, and class as forming one consciousness and the resistance of race, sex, and class oppression as forming one struggle. Womanism flows from a both/and worldview, a consciousness that allows for the resolution of seeming contradictions "not through an either/or negation but through the interaction" and wholeness. Thus, while Black and female may, at one level, be radically different orientations, they are at the same time united, with each "confirming the existence of the other." Rather than standing as "contradictory opposites," they become "complementary, unsynthesized, unified wholes."[54] This is what Ogunyemi refers to as "the dynamism of wholeness." This holistic consciousness undergirds the thinking and action of Maggie Lena Walker and the other Saint Luke women. There are no necessary contradictions between the public and domestic spheres; the community and the family; male and female; race and sex struggle—there is intersection and interdependence.

Dichotomous thinking does not just inhibit our abilities to see the lives of Black women and other women of color in their wholeness, but, I would argue, it also limits our ability to see the wholeness of the lives and consciousnesses of even white middle-class women. The thinking and actions of white women, too, are shaped by their race and their class, and their consciousnesses are also formed by the totality of these factors. The failure, however, to explore the total consciousness of white women has made class, and especially race, nonexistent categories in much of white feminist theory. And this has allowed the development of frameworks which render Black women's lives invisible. Explorations into the consciousnesses of Black women and other women of color should, therefore, be a model for all women, including those who are not often confronted with the necessity of understanding themselves in these total terms. As we begin to confront the holistic nature of all women's lives, we will begin to create a truly womanist studies. In our efforts Maggie Lena Walker and Black women like her will be our guide.

My appreciation is expressed to Mary Kelley, Deborah K. King, Lillian Jones, and the participants in the Community and Social Movements research group of the 1986 Summer Research Institute on Race and Gender, Center for Research on Women, Memphis State University, for their comments on an earlier draft of this article.

NOTES

1. The recent proliferation of works in Black women's history and Black women's studies makes a complete bibliographical reference prohibitive. For a sample of some of the growing literature on Black women's consciousness, see Evelyn Brooks, "The Feminist Theology of the Black Baptist Church, 1880–1900," in *Class, Race, and Sex: The Dynamics of Control*, ed. Amy Swerdlow and Hanna Lessinger (Boston: G. K. Hall, 1983), 31–59; Hazel V. Carby, *Reconstructing Womanhood: The Emergence of the Afro-American Woman Novelist* (New York: Oxford University Press, 1987); Elizabeth Clark-Lewis, " 'This Work Had a' End': The Transition from Live-In to Day Work," Southern Women: The Intersection of Race, Class, and Gender Working Paper no. 2 (Memphis, Tenn.: Memphis State University, Center for Research on Women, 1985); Patricia Hill Collins, "The Social Construction of Black Feminist Thought," *Signs: Journal of Women in Culture and Society* 14, no. 4 (summer 1989), forthcoming; Cheryl Townsend Gilkes, " 'Together and in Harness': Women's Traditions in the Sanctified Church," *Signs* 10, no. 4 (summer 1985): 678–99; Deborah Gray White, *Ar'n't I a Woman? Female Slaves in the Plantation South* (New York: Norton, 1985). Also note: *Sage: A Scholarly Journal on Black*

Women, now in its fifth year, has published issues that focus on education, health, work, mother-daughter relationships, and creative artists.

2. On a contemporary political level, this disassociation of gender concerns from race concerns was dramatically expressed in the 1985 United Nations Decade for Women conference held in Nairobi, Kenya, where the official U.S. delegation, including representatives of major white women's organizations but not one representative of a Black women's organization, insisted upon not having the proceedings become bogged down with race and national issues such as apartheid so that it could concentrate on birth control and other "women's" issues. Delegates operating from such a perspective were unable to see African, Asian, and Latin American women who argued for discussion of national political issues as anything other than the tools of men, unfortunate victims unable to discern true women's and feminist struggles. For a discussion of the ways in which these issues were reflected in the Kenya conference, see Ros Young, "Report from Nairobi: The UN Decade for Women Forum," *Race and Class* 27, no. 2 (autumn 1985): 67–71; and the entire issue of *African Women Rising* 2, no. 1 (winter–spring 1986).

3. See Rosalyn Terborg-Penn, "Discontented Black Feminists: Prelude and Post-script to the Passage of the Nineteenth Amendment," 261–78; Lois Scharf and Joan M. Jensen, "Introduction," 9–10, both in *Decades of Discontent: The Women's Movement, 1920–1940*, ed. Lois Scharf and Joan M. Jensen (Westport, Conn.: Greenwood, 1983).

4. Terborg-Penn, 267. A contemporary example of this type of dichotomous analysis is seen in much of the discussion of the feminization of poverty. Drawing commonalities between the experiences of Black and white women, such discussions generally leave the impression that poverty was not a "feminine" problem before white women in increasing numbers were recognized as impoverished. Presumably, before that Black women's poverty was considered a result of race; now it is more often considered a result of gender. Linda Burnham has effectively addressed the incompleteness of such analyses, suggesting that they ignore "class, race, and sex as *simultaneously* operative social factors" in Black women's lives ("Has Poverty Been Feminized in Black America?" *Black Scholar* 16, no. 2 [March/April 1985]: 14–24 [emphasis mine]).

5. See, e.g., Parita Trivedi, "A Study of 'Sheroes,' " *Third World Book Review* 1, no. 2 (1984): 71–72; Angela Davis, *Women, Race, and Class* (New York: Random House, 1981); Nawal el Saadawi, *The Hidden Face of Eve: Women in the Arab World*, trans. Sherif Hetata (Boston: Beacon, 1982); Jenny Bourne, "Towards an Anti-Racist Feminism," *Race and Class* 25, no. 1 (summer 1983): 1–22; Bonnie Thornton Dill, "Race, Class, and Gender: Prospects for an All-Inclusive Sisterhood," *Feminist Studies* 9, no. 1 (spring 1983): 131–50; Evelyn Nakano Glenn, *Issei, Nisei, War Bride: Three Generations of Japanese American Women in Domestic Service* (Philadelphia: Temple University Press, 1986); Audre Lorde, *Sister/Outsider: Essays and Speeches* (Trumansburg, N.Y.: Crossing Press, 1984); Barbara Smith, "Some Home Truths on the Contemporary Black Feminist Movement," *Black Scholar* 16, no. 2 (March/April 1985): 4–13; Asoka Bandarage, *Toward International Feminism: The Dialectics of Sex, Race and Class* (London: Zed Press, forthcoming). For a typology of Black women's multiple consciousness, see Deborah K. King, "Race, Class, and Gender Salience in Black Women's Feminist Consciousness" (paper presented at American Sociological Association annual meeting, Section on Racial and Ethnic Minorities, New York, August 1986).

6. Alice Walker's oft-quoted definition is in *In Search of Our Mothers' Gardens: Womanist Prose* (New York: Harcourt Brace Jovanovich, 1983), xi–xii: "Womanist. 1. . . . Responsible. In Charge. *Serious*. 2. . . . Appreciates . . . women's strength. . . . Committed to survival and wholeness of entire people, male *and female*. Not a separatist, except periodically, for health. Traditionally universalist. . . . Traditionally capable. . . . 3. . . . Loves struggle. *Loves* the Folk. Loves herself. *Regardless*. 4. Womanist is to feminist as purple is to lavender." Cheryl Townsend Gilkes's annotation of Alice Walker's definition ("Women, Religion, and Tradition: A Womanist Perspective" [paper presented in workshop at Summer Research Institute on Race and Gender, Center for Research on Women, Memphis State University, June 1986]) has been particularly important to my understanding of this term.

7. Chikwenye Okonjo Ogunyemi, "Womanism: The Dynamics of the Contemporary Black Female Novel in English," *Signs* 11, no. 1 (autumn 1985): 63–80.

8. May Wright Sewall, ed., *World's Congress of Representative Women* (Chicago, 1893), 715, quoted in Bert James Loewenberg and Ruth Bogin, eds., *Black Women in Nineteenth-Century American Life: Their Words, Their Thoughts, Their Feelings* (University Park: Pennsylvania State University Press, 1976), 330–31 (emphasis mine). See also Anna Julia Cooper, *A Voice from the South: By a Black Woman of the South* (Xenia, Ohio: Aldine, 1892), esp. "Part First."

9. Although there exists no scholarly biography of Walker, information is available in several sources.

See Wendell P. Dabney, *Maggie L. Walker and The I.O. of Saint Luke: The Woman and Her Work* (Cincinnati: Dabney, 1927); Sadie Iola Daniel, *Women Builders* (Washington, D.C.: Associated Publishers, 1931), 28–52; Sadie Daniel St. Clair, "Maggie Lena Walker," in *Notable American Women, 1607–1960* (Cambridge: Harvard University Press, Belknap, 1971), 530–31; Elsa Barkley Brown, "Maggie Lena Walker and the Saint Luke Women" (paper presented at the Association for the Study of Afro-American Life and History 69th annual conference, Washington, D.C., October 1984), and " 'Not Alone to Build This Pile of Brick': The Role of Women in the Richmond, Virginia, Black Community, 1890–1930" (paper presented at the Midcontinental and North Central American Studies Association joint conference, University of Iowa, April 1983); Lily Hammond, *In the Vanguard of a Race* (New York: Council of Women for Home Missions and Missionary Education Movement of the United States and Canada, 1922), 108–18; A. B. Caldwell, ed., *Virginia Edition*, vol. 5 of *History of the American Negro* (Atlanta: A. B. Caldwell, 1921), 9–11; Rayford Logan, "Maggie Lena Walker," in *Dictionary of American Negro Biography*, ed. Rayford W. Logan and Michael R. Winston (New York: Norton, 1982), 626–27; Gertrude W. Marlowe, "Maggie Lena Walker: African-American Women, Business, and Community Development" (paper presented at Berkshire Conference on the History of Women, Wellesley, Mass., June 21, 1987); Kim Q. Boyd, " 'An Actress Born, a Diplomat Bred'; Maggie L. Walker, Race Woman" (M.A. thesis, Howard University, 1987); Sallie Chandler, "Maggie Lena Walker (1867–1934): An Abstract of Her Life and Activities," 1975 Oral History Files, Virginia Union University Library, Richmond, Va., 1975, Maggie Lena Walker Papers, Maggie L. Walker National Historic Site, Richmond, Va. (hereafter cited as MLW Papers). Fortunately, much of Walker's history will soon be available; the Maggie L. Walker Biography Project, funded by the National Park Service under the direction of Gertrude W. Marlowe, anthropology department, Howard University, is completing a full-scale biography of Walker.
10. Noting the mass base of mutual benefit societies such as the Independent Order of Saint Luke, August Meier has suggested that the activities of these organizations "reflect the thinking of the inarticulate majority better than any other organizations or the statement of editors and other publicists" (*Negro Thought in America, 1880–1915: Racial Ideologies in the Age of Booker T. Washington* [Ann Arbor: University of Michigan Press, 1963], 130).

11. *50th Anniversary—Golden Jubilee Historical Report of the R.W.G. Council I. O. St. Luke, 1867–1917* (Richmond, Va.: Everett Waddey, 1917), 5–6, 20 (hereafter cited as *50th Anniversary*).
12. Maggie L. Walker, "Diary," March 6, 1928, MLW Papers. My thanks to Sylvester Putman, superintendent, Richmond National Battlefield Park, and Celia Jackson Suggs, site historian, Maggie L. Walker National Historic Site, for facilitating my access to these unprocessed papers.
13. *50th Anniversary*, 26.
14. White (n. 1 above), 119–41. Although I use the term "sisterhood" here to refer to this female network, sisterhood for Black women, including M. L. Walker, meant (and means) not only this special bond among Black women but also the ties amongst all kin/community.
15. Of 260,000 Black Virginians over the age of twenty-one in 1920, less than 20,000 were eligible to vote in that year's elections. Poll taxes and literacy tests disfranchised many; white Democratic election officials turned many others away from the polls; still others had given up their efforts to vote, realizing that even if they successfully cast their ballots, they were playing in "a political game which they stood no chance of winning" (Andrew Buni, *The Negro in Virginia Politics, 1902–1965* [Charlottesville: University of Virginia Press, 1967], 77–88). The high proportion of female voters resulted from whites' successful efforts to disfranchise the majority of Black male voters, as well as the enthusiasm of women to exercise this new right; see, e.g., *Richmond News-Leader* (August–October 1920); *Richmond Times-Dispatch* (September–October 1920). Rosalyn Terborg-Penn (n. 3 above, 275) reports a similarly high percentage of Black female voters in 1920s Baltimore. In Richmond, however, Black women soon found themselves faced with the same obstacles to political rights as confronted Black men. Independent Black political parties developed in several southern states where the lily-white Republican faction had successfully purged Blacks from leadership positions in that party; see, e.g., George C. Wright, "Black Political Insurgency in Louisville, Kentucky: The Lincoln Independent Party of 1921," *Journal of Negro History* 68 (winter 1983): 8–23.
16. M. L. Walker, "Addresses," 1909, MLW Papers, cited in Celia Jackson Suggs, "Maggie Lena Walker," *TRUTH: Newsletter of the Association of Black Women Historians* 7 (fall 1985): 6.
17. Four of the women elected to the 1901 Saint Luke executive board were board members of the Woman's Union, which had offices in Saint Luke's

Hall; see advertisements in *Richmond Planet* (August 1898–January 3, 1903).

18. Some of the societies had only women members, including some that were exclusively for the mutual assistance of single mothers. For an excellent discussion of the ties among the societies, families, and churches in Richmond, see Peter J. Rachleff, *Black Labor in the South: Richmond, Virginia, 1865–1890* (Philadelphia: Temple University Press, 1984).

19. W. P. Burrell and D. E. Johnson Sr., *Twenty-Five Years History of the Grand Fountain of the United Order of True Reformers, 1881–1905* (Richmond, Va.: Grand Fountain, United Order of True Reformers, 1909), 76–77.

20. Saint Luke Penny Savings Bank records: Receipts and Disbursements, 1903–1909; Minutes, Executive Committee, 1913; Cashier's Correspondence Book, 1913; Minutes, Board of Trustees, 1913–1915, Consolidated Bank and Trust Company, Richmond, Va.; *Cleveland Plain Dealer* (June 28, 1914), in Peabody Clipping File, Collis P. Huntington Library, Hampton Institute, Hampton, Va. (hereafter cited as Peabody Clipping File), no. 88, vol. 1. See also Works Progress Administration, *The Negro in Virginia* (New York: Hastings House, 1940), 299.

21. This analysis owes much to Cheryl Townsend Gilkes's work on Black women, particularly her "Black Women's Work as Deviance: Social Sources of Racial Antagonism within Contemporary Feminism," working paper no. 66 (Wellesley, Mass.: Wellesley College Center for Research on Women, 1979), and " 'Holding Back the Ocean with a Broom': Black Women and Community Work," in *The Black Woman*, ed. LaFrances Rodgers-Rose (Beverly Hills, Calif.: Sage, 1980). Excerpt from speech given by M. L. Walker at 1901 annual Saint Luke convention, *50th Anniversary* (n. 11 above), 23.

22. The prevailing turn-of-the-century stereotype of Black women emphasized promiscuity and immorality; these ideas were given prominence in a number of publications, including newspapers, periodicals, philanthropic foundation reports, and popular literature. The attacks by various segments of the white community on the morality of Black women and the race at the turn of the century are discussed in Beverly Guy-Sheftall, " 'Daughters of Sorrow': Attitudes toward Black Women, 1880–1920" (Ph.D. diss., Emory University, 1984), 62–86; Darlene Clark Hine, "Lifting the Veil, Shattering the Silence: Black Women's History in Slavery and Freedom," in *The State of Afro-American History: Past, Present, and Future*, ed. Darlene Clark Hine

(Baton Rouge: Louisiana State University Press, 1986), 223–49, esp. 234–38; Willi Coleman, "Black Women and Segregated Public Transportation: Ninety Years of Resistance," *TRUTH: Newsletter of the Association of Black Women Historians* 8, no. 2 (1986): 3–10, esp. 7–8; and Paula Giddings, *When and Where I Enter: The Impact of Black Women on Race and Sex in America* (New York: William Morrow, 1984), 82–86. Maggie Walker called attention to these verbal attacks on Negro womanhood in her speech "Beniah's Valour: An Address for Men Only," Saint Luke Hall, March 1, 1906, MLW Papers (n. 9 above). It was in part the desire to defend Black women and uplift the race that initiated the formation of the National Federation of Black Women's Clubs.

23. Charles F. McLaurin, "State Federation of Colored Women" (n.p., November 10, 1908), Peabody Clipping File, no. 231, vol. 1.

24. Chandler (n. 9 above), 10–11.

25. Daniel Webster Davis and Giles Jackson, *The Industrial History of the Negro Race of the United States* (Richmond: Virginia Press, 1908), 133. Similar attitudes expressed in the *Virginia Baptist* in 1894 had aroused the ire of the leading figures in the national women's club movement. The *Baptist* had been particularly concerned that women, in exceeding their proper place in the church, were losing their "womanliness" and that "the exercise of the right of suffrage would be a deplorable climax to these transgressions"; see discussion of the *Baptist in Women's Era* 1, no. 6 (September 1894): 8.

26. M. L. Walker, "Speech to Federation of Colored Women's Clubs," Hampton, Va., July 14, 1912, MLW Papers (n. 9 above).

27. M. L. Walker, "Speech to the Negro Young People's Christian and Educational Congress," Convention Hall, Washington, D.C., August 5, 1906, MLW Papers.

28. Quotations are from M. L. Walker, "Speech to Federation of Colored Women's Clubs." These ideas, however, were a central theme in Walker's speeches and were repeated throughout the years. See, e.g., "Speech to the Negro Young People's Christian and Educational Congress" and "Beniah's Valour: An Address for Men Only" (n. 22 above). See also the *St. Luke Herald's* first editorial, "Our Mission" (March 29, 1902), reprinted in *50th Anniversary* (n. 11 above), 26.

29. Excerpt from speech given by M. L. Walker at 1901 annual Saint Luke convention, *50th Anniversary*, 23.

30. See "Our Mission" (n. 28 above).

31. The NAWE, having as its motto "Support Thyself—Work," aimed at making "the colored

woman a factor in the labor world." Much of its work was premised upon the belief that white women were developing an interest in domestic science and other "Negro occupations" to such an extent that the prospects for work for young Black women were becoming seriously endangered. They believed also that when white women entered the fields of housework, cooking, and the like, these jobs would be classified as professions. It therefore was necessary for Black women to become professionally trained in even domestic work in order to compete. Container 308, Nannie Helen Burroughs Papers, Manuscript Division, Library of Congress.

32. M. L. Walker, "Speech to Federation of Colored Women's Clubs" (n. 26 above).

33. See, e.g., "Negress Banker Says If Men Can, Women Can," *Columbus Journal* (September 16, 1909), Peabody Clipping File (n. 20 above), no. 231, vol. 7; see also Chandler (n. 9 above), 32.

34. In 1900, 83.8 percent of employed Black women worked in domestic and personal service; in 1930, 76.5 percent. U.S. Bureau of the Census, *Twelfth Census of the United States Taken in the Year 1900, Population Part 1* (Washington, D.C.: Census Office, 1901), *Thirteenth Census of the United States Taken in the Year 1910*, vol. 4: *Population 1910—Occupation Statistics* (Washington, D.C.: Government Printing Office, 1914), 595, and *Fifteenth Census of the United States: Population*, vol. 4: *Occupations, by States* (Washington, D.C.: Government Printing Office, 1933); Benjamin Brawley, *Negro Builders and Heroes* (Chapel Hill: University of North Carolina Press, 1937), 267–72; U.S. Bureau of the Census, *Fourteenth Census of the United States Taken in the Year 1920*, vol. 4: *Population 1920—Occupations* (Washington, D.C.: Government Printing Office, 1923); Ethel Thompson Overby, *"It's Better to Light a Candle than to Curse the Darkness": The Autobiographical Notes of Ethel Thompson Overby* (1975), copy in Virginia Historical Society, Richmond.

35. The business, which opened the Monday before Easter, 1905, officially closed in January 1912. Information on the emporium is found in *50th Anniversary* (n. 11 above), 55, 76–77; *New York Age*, March 16, 1905, Peabody Clipping File, no. 88, vol. 1, "Maggie Lena Walker Scrapbook," MLW Papers (n. 9 above); Daniels (n. 9 above), 41. The most detailed description of the opposition to the emporium is in M. L. Walker, "Beniah's Valour: An Address for Men Only" (n. 22 above), quote is from this speech.

36. M. L. Walker, "Beniah's Valour: An Address for Men Only."

37. Ibid.

38. Chandler (n. 9 above), 30.

39. M. L. Walker, "Beniah's Valour: An Address for Men Only."

40. Chandler, 30.

41. *New York Age* (June 22, 1909), Peabody Clipping File, no. 231, vol. 1.

42. Rayford W. Logan, *The Betrayal of the Negro from Rutherford B. Hayes to Woodrow Wilson* (New York: Collier, 1965; originally published in 1954 as *The Negro in American Life and Thought: The Nadir*).

43. J. Thomas Hewin, "Is the Criminal Negro Justly Dealt with in the Courts of the South?" in *Twentieth Century Negro Literature, or a Cyclopedia of Thought on the Vital Topics Relating to the American Negro*, ed. D. W. Culp (Toronto: J. L. Nichols, 1902), 110–11.

44. *Richmond Planet* (April 30, 1904).

45. M. L. Walker, "Beniah's Valour: An Address for Men Only" (n. 22 above).

46. *New York Age* (June 22, 1909), Peabody Clipping File, no. 231, vol. 1.

47. M. L. Walker, "Speech to the Federation of Colored Women's Clubs" (n. 26 above).

48. M. L. Walker, "Beniah's Valour: An Address for Men Only." This appeal for support of increased opportunities for Black women permeated all of Walker's speeches. In her last speeches in 1934 she continued her appeal for support of race enterprises (newspaper clipping [n.p., n.d.], "Maggie Laura Walker Scrapbook," MLW Papers [n. 9 above]). Maggie Laura Walker is Walker's granddaughter.

49. W. E. B. Du Bois, who explored extensively the connection between race struggle and women's struggle in "The Damnation of Women," also challenged men's traditional roles: "The present mincing horror of a free womanhood must pass if we are ever to be rid of the bestiality of a free manhood; *not by guarding the weak in weakness do we gain strength, but by making weakness free and strong*" (emphasis mine; *Darkwater, Voices from within the Veil* [New York: Harcourt, Brace, & Howe, 1920], 165).

50. M. L. Walker, "Saint Luke Thanksgiving Day Speech," City Auditorium, March 23, 1913, MLW Papers (n. 9 above).

51. M. L. Walker, "Address—Virginia Day Third Street Bethel AME Church," January 29, 1933, MLW Papers.

52. Ogunyemi (n. 7 above; 72–73) takes this idea from Stephen Henderson's analysis of the role of the blues and blues women in the Africanamerican community.

53. The essays in Vernon J. Dixon and Badi G. Foster, eds., *Beyond Black or White: An Alternate America* (Boston: Little, Brown, 1971) explore the either/or and the both/and worldview in relation to Africanamerican systems of analysis; the quote can be found in Dixon, "Two Approaches to Black-White Relations," 23–66, esp. 25–26.

54. Johnella E. Butler explores the theoretical, methodological, and pedagogical implications of these systems of analysis in *Black Studies: Pedagogy and Revolution: A Study of Afro-American Studies and the Liberal Arts Tradition through the Discipline of Afro-American Literature* (Washington, D.C.: University Press of America, 1981), esp. 96–102.

6

DISCONTENTED BLACK FEMINISTS
Prelude and Postscript to the Passage of the Nineteenth Amendment

Rosalyn Terborg-Penn

A SIGNIFICANT NUMBER of Black women and Black women's organizations not only supported woman suffrage on the eve of the passage of the Nineteenth Amendment but attempted to exercise their rights to vote immediately after the amendment's passage in 1920. Unfortunately for them, Black women confronted racial discrimination in their efforts to support the amendment and to win the vote. Consequently, discontented Black feminists anticipated the disillusionment that their white counterparts encountered after 1920. An examination of the problems Black women faced on the eve of the passage of the woman suffrage amendment and the hostility Black women voters endured after the amendment passed serves as a preview of their political status from 1920 to 1945.

The way in which Black women leaders dealt with these problems reveals the unique nature of feminism among Afro-American women. Black feminists could not overlook the reality of racism and class conflict as determining factors in the lives of women of their race. Hence, Black feminists of the post–World War I era exhibited characteristics similar to those of Black feminists of the woman suffrage era and of the late nineteenth-century Black women's club movement. During each era, these feminists could not afford to dismiss class or race in favor of sex as the major cause of oppression among Black women.

PRELUDE TO PASSAGE OF THE NINETEENTH AMENDMENT
On the eve of the passage of the Nineteenth Amendment, Black women leaders could be counted among other groups of women who had worked diligently for woman suffrage. At least ninety Black women leaders endorsed woman suffrage, with two-thirds of these women giving support during the decade immediately before passage of the amendment. Afro-American women organized suffrage clubs, participated in rallies and demonstrations, spoke on behalf of the amendment, and wrote essays in support of the cause. These things they had done since the inception of the nineteenth-century woman's rights movement. However, the largest woman suffrage effort among Black women's groups occurred during the second decade of the twentieth century. Organizations such as the National Federation of Afro-American Women, the National Association of Colored Women (NACW), the Northeastern Federation of Colored Women's Clubs, the Alpha Kappa Alpha Sorority,

and the Delta Sigma Theta Sorority actively supported woman suffrage. These organizations were national or regional in scope and represented thousands of Afro-American women. Some of the women were from the working class, but most of them were of middle-class status. Across the nation, at least twenty Black woman suffrage organizations or groups that strongly endorsed woman suffrage existed during the period.[1]

Three examples provide an indication of the diversity in types of woman suffrage activities among Black women's organizations. In 1915 the Poughkeepsie, New York, chapter of the Household of Ruth, a working-class, Black women's group, endorsed woman suffrage by sending a resolution to the New York branch of the National Woman's Party (NWP) in support of the pending state referendum on woman suffrage. With the need for an intelligent female electorate in mind, Black women of Texas organized voter leagues in 1917, the year Texas women won the right to vote. Among these was the Negro Women Voters' League of Galveston. Furthermore, in 1919, the Northeastern Federation of Colored Women's Clubs, representing thousands of women from Montreal to Baltimore, petitioned the National American Woman Suffrage Association (NAWSA) for membership.[2]

The enthusiastic responses of Black women to woman suffrage may seem astonishing when one realizes that woman suffrage was a predominately middle-class movement among native born white women and that the Black middle class was very small during the early twentieth century. Furthermore, the heyday of the woman suffrage movement embraced an era that historian Rayford Logan called "the nadir" in Afro-American history, characterized by racial segregation, defamation of the character of Black women, and lynching of black Americans, both men and women. It is a wonder that Afro-American women dared to dream a white man's dream—the right to enfranchisement—especially at a time when white women attempted to exclude them from that dream.[3]

The existence of a double standard for Black and white women among white woman suffragists was apparent to Black women on the eve of Nineteenth Amendment passage. Apprehensions from discontented Black leaders about the inclusion of Black women as voters, especially in the South, were evident throughout the second decade of the twentieth century. During the early years of the decade, Black suffragists such as Adella Hunt Logan, a club leader and suffragist from Tuskegee, Alabama; Mary B. Talbert, president of the National Association of Colored Women; and Josephine St. Pierre Ruffin, a suffragist since the 1880s from Boston and the editor of the *Woman's Era*, a Black women's newspaper, complained about the double standard in the woman suffrage movement and insisted that white suffragists set aside their prejudices to allow Black women, burdened by both sexism and racism, to gain political equality.[4]

Unfortunately, with little influence among white women, the Black suffragists were powerless and their words went unheeded. By 1916 Carrie Catt, president of the NAWSA, concluded that the South had to be conciliated if woman suffrage was to become a reality. Thus, in order to avoid antagonizing southern white women who resented participating in the association with Black women, she urged southern white delegates not to attend the NAWSA convention in Chicago that year because the Chicago delegation would be mostly Black.[5]

The trend to discriminate against Black women as voters continued, and in 1917 the *Crisis*, the official organ of the National Association for the Advancement of Colored People (NAACP), noted that Blacks feared white female voters because of their anti–Black woman suffrage and anti–Black male sentiments. Afro-American fears went beyond misgivings about white women. In 1918 the editors of the *Houston Observer* responded to Black disillusionment when they called upon the men and women of the race to register to vote in spite of the poll tax, which was designed especially to exclude Black voters.[6]

Skepticism about equality of woman suffrage among Blacks continued. Mrs. A. W. Blackwell, an African Methodist Episcopal church leader in Atlanta, estimated that about three million Black women were of voting age. She warned, however, that a "grandmother clause" would be introduced after passage of a suffrage amendment to prevent Black women, 90 percent of whom lived in the South, from voting.[7]

Disillusionment among Black suffragists became so apparent that several national suffrage leaders attempted to appease them with reassurances about their commitment to Black woman suffrage. In 1917 Carrie Catt and Anna Shaw wooed Black female support through the pages of the *Crisis*. In the District of Columbia, the same year, Congresswoman Jeannette Rankin of Montana addressed an enthusiastic group of Alpha Kappa Alpha Sorority women at Howard University. There she assured the group that she wanted all women to be given the ballot regardless of race.[8]

However, in 1917 while the New York state woman suffrage referendum was pending in the legislature, Black suffragists in the state complained of discrimination against their organizations by white suffragists during the statewide woman suffrage convention at Saratoga. White leaders assured Black women that they were welcomed by the movement. Although the majority of the Black delegates were conciliated, a vocal minority remained disillusioned.[9]

By 1919, the year before the Nineteenth Amendment was adopted by Congress, anti–Black woman suffrage sentiments continued to plague the movement. Shortly before the amendment was adopted, several incidents occurred to further disillusion Black feminists. Mary Church Terrell, a Washington, D.C., educator and national leader among Black club women, reported that white suffragists in Florida discriminated against Black women in their attempts to recruit support for the campaign. In addition, the NAACP, whose policy officially endorsed woman suffrage, clashed with Alice Paul, president of the NWP, because she allegedly said that "all this talk of Negro women voting in South Carolina was nonsense."[10] Later, Walter White, the NAACP's assistant to the executive secretary, complained to Mary Church Terrell about Alice Paul and agreed with Terrell that white suffrage leaders would be willing to accept the suffrage amendment even if it did not enfranchise Black women.[11]

Within a week after receiving Walter White's letter, Mary Church Terrell received a letter from Ida Husted Harper, a leader in the suffrage movement and the editor of the last two volumes of *The History of Woman Suffrage*, asking Terrell to use her influence to persuade the Northeastern Federation of Colored Women's Clubs to withdraw their application seeking cooperative membership in the NAWSA. Echoing sentiments expressed earlier by NAWSA president Carrie Catt, Harper explained that accepting the membership of a Black organization was inexpedient for NAWSA at a time when white suffragists sought the cooperation of white southern women. Harper noted that the major obstacle to the amendment in the South was fear among whites of the Black woman's vote. She therefore asked federation president Elizabeth Carter to resubmit the membership application after the passage of the Nineteenth Amendment.[12]

At its Jubilee Convention in St. Louis in March 1919, the NAWSA officially catered to the fears of their southern white members. In response to a proposal by the Kentucky suffragist Laura Clay that sections of the so-called Susan B. Anthony amendment that would permit the enfranchisement of Black women be changed, the convention delegates agreed that the amendment should be worded so as to allow the South to determine its own position on the Black female vote.[13]

During the last months before the passage of the Susan B. Anthony amendment, Black suffragists had been rebuffed by both the conservative wing of the suffrage movement, the NAWSA, and by the more radical wing, the NWP. Why then did Afro-American women continue to push for woman suffrage? Since the 1880s, most Black women who supported woman suffrage did so because they believed that political equality among the races would raise the status of Blacks, both male and female. Increasing the Black electorate, they felt, would not only uplift the women of the race but help the children and the men as well. The majority of the Black suffragists were not radical feminists. They were reformers, or what William H. Chafe calls social feminists, who believed that the system could be amended to work for them. Like their white counterparts, these Black suffragists assumed that the enfranchised held the key to ameliorating social ills. But unlike white social feminists, many Black suffragists called for social and political measures that were specifically tied to race issues. Among these issues were antimiscegenation legislation, Jim Crow legislation, and "lynch law." Prominent Black feminists combined the fight against sexism with the fight against racism by continuously calling the public's attention to these issues. Ida B. Wells-Barnett, Angelina Weld Grimké, and Mary Church Terrell spoke out against lynching. Josephine St. Pierre Ruffin and Lottie Wilson Jackson, as well as Terrell and Wells-Barnett, took steps to challenge jim crow facilities in public accommodations, and antimiscegenation legislation was impugned by Terrell, Grimké, and Wells-Barnett.[14]

Blacks understood the potential political influence, if not political power, that they could harness with woman suffrage, especially in the South. White supremacists realized it too. Although there were several reasons for southern opposition to the Nineteenth Amendment, the one common to all states was fear of Black female suffrage. This fear had been stimulated by the way in which Afro-American women responded to suffrage in states that had achieved woman suffrage before the passage of the federal amendment. In northern states with large Black populations, such as Illinois and New York, the Black female electorate was significant. Chicago elected its first Black alderman, Oscar De Priest, in 1915, the year after women won the right to vote. In 1917, the year the woman suffrage referendum passed the New York state legislature, New York City elected its first Black state assemblyperson, Edward A. Johnson. In both cities the Black female vote was decisive in the election. In the South, Texas Afro-American women mobilized in 1918 to effectively educate the women of their race in order to combat white opposition to their voting.[15]

By 1920 white southern apprehensions of a viable Black female electorate were not illusionary. "Colored women voter's leagues" were growing throughout the South, where the task of the leagues was to give Black women seeking to qualify to vote instructions for countering white opposition. Leagues could be found in Alabama, Georgia, Tennessee, and Texas. These groups were feared also by white supremacists because the women sought to qualify Black men as voters as well.[16]

Whites widely believed that Black women wanted the ballot more than white women in the South. Black women were expected to register and to vote in larger numbers than white women. If this happened, the ballot would soon be returned to Black men. Black suffrage, it was believed, would also result in the return of the two-party system in the South, because Blacks would consistently vote Republican. These apprehensions were realized in Florida after the passage of the Nineteenth Amendment. Black women in Jacksonville registered in greater numbers than white women. In reaction, the Woman Suffrage League of Jacksonville was reorganized into the Duval County League of Democratic Women Voters. The members were dedicated to maintain white supremacy and pledged to register white women voters.[17]

In Texas, where women could vote before the passage of the Nineteenth Amendment, Black women, nevertheless, were discriminated against. In 1918 six Black women had been refused the right to register at Forth Worth on the ground that the primaries were open to white Democrats only. Efforts to disfranchise Black women in Houston failed, however, when the women took legal action against the registrars who attempted to apply the Texas woman suffrage law to white women only. A similar attempt to disqualify Afro-American women in Waxahachie, Texas, failed also.[18]

Subterfuge and trickery such as the kind used in Texas were being used throughout the South by 1920. In North Carolina, the predictions of Mrs. A. W. Blackwell came true when the state legislature introduced a bill known as the "grandmother clause" for women voters. The bill attempted to protect illiterate white women from disfranchisement, but the legislators had not taken into account that "grandfather clauses" had been nullified by the Supreme Court. Nonetheless, Black leaders called to the women of the race to stand up and fight. This they did.[19]

In 1920 Black women registered in large numbers throughout the South, especially in Georgia and Louisiana, despite major obstacles placed against them by the white supremacists. In defense, Afro-American women often turned to the NAACP for assistance. Field Secretary William Pickens was sent to investigate the numerous charges and recorded several incidents which he either witnessed personally or about which he received reports. In Columbia, South Carolina, during the first day of registration Black women apparently took the registrars by surprise. No plan to disqualify them had been put into effect. Many Black women reported to the office and had to wait for hours while the white women were registered first. Some women waited up to twelve hours to register. The next day, a $300 tax requirement was made mandatory for Black women. If they passed that test, the women were required to read from and to interpret the state or the federal constitutions. No such tests were required of white women. In addition, white lawyers were on hand to quiz and harass Black women. Although the *Columbia State*, a local newspaper, reported disinterest in registering among Black women, Pickens testified to the contrary. By the end of the registration period, twenty Columbia Black women had signed an affidavit against the registrars who had disqualified them. In the surrounding Richland County, Afro-American women were disqualified when they attempted to register to vote. As a result, several of them made plans to appeal the ruling.[20]

Similar reports came from Richmond, Virginia, where registrars attempted to deny or successfully denied Black women the right to register. A Black woman of Newburn, North Carolina, signed an affidavit testifying to the difficulty she had in attempting to register. First she was asked to read and to write the entire state constitution. After successfully reading the document, she was informed that no matter what else she did, the registrar would disqualify her because she was Black. Many cases like this one were handled by the

NAACP, and after the registration periods ended in the South, its board of directors presented the evidence to Congress. NAACP officials and others testified at a congressional hearing in support of the proposed enactment of the Tinkham Bill to reduce representation in Congress from states where there was restriction of woman suffrage. White supremacy prevailed, however, as southern congressmen successfully claimed that Blacks were not disfranchised, just disinterested in voting. Hence, despite the massive evidence produced by the NAACP, the Tinkham Bill failed to pass.[21]

The inability of the NAACP to protect the rights of Black women voters led the women to seek help from national woman suffrage leaders. However, these attempts failed also. The NWP leadership felt that since Black women were discriminated against in the same ways as Black men, their problems were not woman's rights issues, but race issues. Therefore, the woman's party felt no obligation to defend the rights of Black women.[22]

That they would be abandoned by white female suffragists in 1920 came as no surprise to most Black women leaders. The preceding decade of woman suffrage politics had reminded them of the assertions of Black woman suffrage supporters of the past. Frederick Douglass declared in 1868 that Black women were victimized mainly because they were Blacks, not because they were women. Frances Ellen Watkins Harper answered in 1869 that for white women the priorities in the struggle for human rights were sex, not race. By 1920 the situation had changed very little, and many Black suffragists had been thoroughly disillusioned by the machinations of the white feminists they had encountered.[23]

POSTSCRIPT: BLACK FEMINISTS, 1920–1945

Afro-American Women continued to be involved in local and national politics during the post–World War I years. However, few organized feminist activities were apparent among the disillusioned Black feminists of the period. Afro-American women leaders and their organizations began to focus on issues that continued to plague both the men and the women of the race, rather than upon issues that concerned white feminists. The economic plight of Black women kept most of them in poverty and among the lowest of the working classes. Middle-class Black women were still relatively few in number. They were more concerned about uplifting the downtrodden of the race or in representing people of color throughout the world than in issues that were limited to middle-class feminists. Hence, during the 1920s there was little concern among Black women over the Equal Rights Amendment debate between the more conservative League of Women Voters (LWV) and the more radical NWP. Although the economic roles of many white American women were expanding, the status of Black women remained basically static between the wars. As a result, Black feminists identified more with the plight of Third World people who found themselves in similar oppressed situations. Former Black suffragists were more likely to participate in the Women's International League for Peace and Freedom (WILPF) or the International Council of Women of the Darker Races than in the LWV or the NWP.

In 1920 the Howard University professor Benjamin Brawley examined the economic status of Black women. He found that there were over one million Black females in the United States workforce in 1910. Fifty-two percent of them worked as farmers or farm laborers, and 28 percent worked as cooks or washerwomen. In essence, 80 percent of Black women workers were doing arduous, menial work. Brawley speculated that conditions had not changed much by 1920.[24] In 1922 the Black social worker Elizabeth Ross Haynes found that two million Black women in the nation worked in three types of occupations: domestic and personal service, agriculture, and manufacturing and mechanical industries. Of the two million, 50 percent were found in domestic service. Only 20,000 were found in semiskilled jobs in manufacturing and mechanical industries. Haynes's findings in 1922 were in keeping with Brawley's speculations.[25] Unfortunately, by 1945 the position of Black women in the workforce had not changed significantly. Black women ranked lowest on the economic scale among men and women, Black and white.

Geographically, during the period, the Black population was shifting from the rural South to the urban North and West. Nearly 90 percent of the adult Black female population lived in the South in 1920. By 1930 less than 80 percent of that population did. In 1940 the percentage had dropped to nearly 75 percent.[26] Even with this drop, however, three-fourths of the adult Black women of the nation remained in the South, where they were virtually disfranchised. The Black women who found their way north and west lacked the political influence necessary to change the status of Black women because of their economic powerlessness. What temporary gains Black women made in World War I industry quickly faded away during the postwar years.

In 1935 the average weekly wage for a Black domestic worker was three dollars and washerwomen received a mere seventy-five cents a week. Working conditions, as well as wages, were substandard, and Black women were exploited by white women as well as by white men. In observing the working conditions of New York City domestic workers, Louise Mitchell found that standards had not changed much by 1940. Some women worked for as little as two dollars a week and as long as eighty hours a week. Mitchell noted Women's Bureau findings that indicated that women took domestic work only as a last resort. She concluded that Black women were the most oppressed of the working classes.[27]

As the United States entered World War II, Black women found more opportunities in industry. However, jobs available to Black women were the ones for which white workers were not available. War industry jobs were often found in urban centers outside of the South. Consequently, the majority remained outside of the mainstream of feminist consciousness because feminist interests were not their interest, and those Black feminists of the woman suffrage era found little comfort from white feminists. Several of the Black feminists of the woman suffrage era remained in leadership positions during the 1920s and the 1930s, while others faded from the scene. In addition, new faces became associated with Black female leadership. Among these were Amy Jacques Garvey and Mary McLeod Bethune. Although all of these women either identified themselves or have been identified as feminists, their major concerns between the world wars were racial issues, with the status of Black women as a major priority.

A look at the 1920s reveals that most of the Black women's organizations that were prominent during the woman suffrage era remained so. Nonetheless, new groups were organized as well. Elizabeth Carter remained president of the Northeastern Federation of Colored Women's Clubs, which celebrated its twenty-fifth anniversary in 1921. The leadership of the NACW was in transition during the 1920s. Mary B. Talbert retired as president and was succeeded by a former suffragist, Hallie Q. Brown, in 1922. In the middle of the decade Mary McLeod Bethune assumed the presidency. In 1922 several NACW leaders organized the International Council of Women of the Darker Races. Margaret Murray Washington, the wife of the late Booker T. Washington and the first president of the National Federation of Afro-American Women, was elected president.[28]

In addition to these established Black women's organizations, there was the women's arm of Marcus Garvey's United Negro Improvement Association (UNIA). At its peak, in 1925, the UNIA had an estimated membership of two million and can be considered the first mass movement among working-class Black people in the nation. Amy Jacques Garvey, Marcus Garvey's wife, was the articulate leader of the women's division and the editor of the women's department of the UNIA official newspaper, *Negro World*. As a feminist in the international sense, Amy Jacques Garvey's feminist views embraced the class struggle as well as the problems of Third World women. A Black nationalist, Garvey encouraged women of color throughout the world to organize for the benefit of themselves as well as their own people. Although she gave credit to the old-line Black women's clubs, Garvey felt their approach to the problems of Third World women was limited. A Jamaican by birth, she called for revolutionary strategies that did not merely reflect the reform ideas of white middle-class women. Instead Garvey called upon the masses of Black women in the United States to acknowledge that they were the "burden bearers of their race" and to take the lead in fighting for Black independence from white oppression. Amy Jacques Garvey combined the UNIA belief in the power of the Black urban working class with the feminist belief that women could think and do for themselves. The revolutionary implications of her ideas are reflected in the theme of the women's pages of *Negro World*—"Our Women and What They Think." Garvey called for Black women's dedication to social justice and to national liberation, abroad as well as at home.[29]

Garvey was a radical who happened to be a feminist as well. Her views were ahead of her time; thus, she would have fit in well with the mid-twentieth-century radical feminists. However, the demise of the UNIA and the deportation of Marcus Garvey in 1927 shattered much of Amy Jacques Garvey's influence in the United States and she returned to Jamaica. In the meantime, the majority of Black feminists of the 1920s either joined the white social feminists, such as Jane Addams and the WILPF, or bypassed the feminists altogether to deal with race issues within Black organizations.

The leadership of the WILPF was old-line and can be characterized as former progressives, woman suffragists, and social feminists. Jane Addams presided over the organization before U.S. entry into World War I and brought black women such as Mary Church Terrell, Mary B. Talbert, Charlotte Atwood, Mary F. Waring, and Addie W. Hunton into the fold. Terrell had been a member of the executive committee since 1915. As a league representative, she was elected a delegate to the International Congress of Women held in Paris in 1919. Upon her arrival, Terrell was impressed with the conference delegates but noticed that there were none from non-Western countries and that she was the only delegate of color in the group. As a result, she felt obligated to represent the women of all the nonwhite countries in the world, and this she attempted to do. At the conference meeting in Zurich, Switzerland, Terrell agreed to represent the American delegation and did so by speaking in German before the largely German-speaking audience. In addition, she submitted her own personal resolution to the conference, despite attempts by American committee members to change her wording. "We believe no human being should be deprived of an education, prevented from earning a living, debarred from any legitimate pursuit in which he wishes to engage or be subjected to humiliations of various kinds on account of race, color or creed."[30] Terrell's position and thinking were in keeping with the growing awareness among black women leaders in the United States that Third World people needed to fight oppression together.

Although Mary Church Terrell remained an active social feminist, her public as well as private views reflected the disillusionment of Black feminists of the woman suffrage era. In 1921 she was asked by members of the WILPF executive committee to sign a petition requesting the removal of Black troops from occupied German territory, where they were alleged to be violating German women. Terrell refused to sign the petition because she felt the motives behind it were racist. In a long letter to Jane Addams, the executive committee chairman, Terrell explained why she would not sign the petition. She noted that Carrie Catt had investigated the charges against the Black troops and found them to be unfounded. The troops, from French colonies in Africa, were victims, Terrell contended, of American propaganda against Black people. Making a dramatic choice between the feminist organization position and her own loyalty to her race, Terrell offered to resign from the executive committee. Addams wrote her back, agreeing with Terrell's position and asking her not to resign.[31] In this case, when given the choice between the politics of feminism and the race pride, Terrell felt that her energies were needed to combat racism, and she chose to take a national position in the controversy.

Several other attempts were made at interracial cooperation among women's groups during the early 1920s, but most of these efforts were white-dominated and short-lived. An exception was the Cooperative Women's League of Baltimore, founded in 1913 by Sarah C. Fernandis. This group maintained relations with white women's civic leagues in connection with local health and sanitation, home economics, art, and education projects. In 1925 the league initiated its twelfth annual program.[32] This organization was quite conventional, a far cry from feminist—Black or white. However, the activities were, like most Black women's group activities of the times, geared to strengthen local Black communities.

Other Black-white cooperative ventures on a grander scale included the Commission on Inter-Racial Cooperation of the Women's Council of the Methodist Episcopal Church South. In October 1920 the commission held a conference on race relations. Only four Black women were invited and they were selected because of their husbands' prominence, rather than for their feminist views. The conference pledged a responsibility to uplift the status of Black women in the South, calling for a reform of the conditions under which Black domestics worked in white homes. The delegates passed resolutions supporting improved sanitation and housing for Blacks, fair treatment of Blacks in public accommodations, the prevention of lynching, and justice in the courts. Significantly, no mention of protecting Black women's suffrage was made. Several months later, the National Federation of Colored Women's Clubs met at Tuskegee, Alabama, and issued a statement that seemed to remind the Methodist Episcopal women of their pledge and called for increased cooperation and understanding from southern white women. Interestingly, the Black women included suffrage in their resolution.[33]

Nothing came of this attempt at interracial cooperation, for neither the social nor the economic status of Black women improved in the South during the 1920s. The trend toward interracial cooperation continued nevertheless, and in 1922 the YWCA appointed a joint committee of Black and white women to study race problems. Once, again, only four Black women were invited to participate. Principles were declared, but little came of the gathering.[34]

In the meantime, most Black women's organizations had turned from attempts to establish coalitions with white women's groups to concentrate upon pressing race problems. Lynching was one of the major American problems, and Black women organized to fight it. On the national front, Black women's groups used political strategies and concentrated their efforts toward passage of the Dyer Anti-Lynching Bill. In 1922 the Northeastern Federation of Colored Women's Clubs appointed a delegation to call on Senator Lodge of Massachusetts to urge passage of the Dyer bill. In addition, the Alpha Kappa Alpha Sorority held its national convention in Indianapolis and sent a telegram to President Warren Harding urging the support of his administration in the passage of the bill. Also that year, the NACW met in Richmond and appointed an antilynching delegation to make contact with key states needed for the passage of the Dyer bill in Congress. In addition, the delegation was authorized to meet with President Harding. Among the Black women in the delegation were the veteran antilynching crusader Ida B. Wells-Barnett, NACW president Hallie Q. Brown, and the Rhode Island suffragist Mary B. Jackson.[35]

Perhaps the most renowned antilynching crusader of the 1920s was the Spingarn Medal winner Mary B. Talbert. In 1922 she organized an executive committee of fifteen Black women, who supervised over seven hundred state workers across the nation in what Talbert called the Anti-Lynching Crusade. Her aim was to "unite a million women to stop lynching" by arousing the consciences of both Black and white women. One of Talbert's strategies was to provide statistics that showed that victims of lynching were not what propagandists called sex-hungry Black men who preyed upon innocent white women. The crusaders revealed that eighty-three women had been lynched in the United States since Ida B. Wells-Barnett had compiled the first comprehensive report in 1892. The Anti-Lynching Crusade was truly an example of woman power, for the crusaders believed that they could not wait for the men of America to stop the problem. It was perhaps the most influential link in the drive for interracial cooperation among women's groups. As a result of its efforts, the 1922 National Council of Women, representing thirteen million American women, resolved to "endorse the Anti-Lynching Crusade recently launched by colored women of this country."[36]

Although the Dyer bill was defeated, it was revised by the NAACP and introduced again in the House of Representatives by Congressman Leonidas C. Dyer of Missouri and in the Senate by William B. McKinley of Illinois in 1926. That year the bill failed again, as did similar bills in 1935, 1940, and 1942. However, it was the effort of Blacks and white women organized against lynching that pressed for legislation throughout the period. Without a doubt, it was the leadership of Black women, many of whom had been active in the late-nineteenth-century women's club movement and in the woman suffrage movement, who motivated white women in 1930 to organize the Association of Southern Women for the Prevention of Lynching. Although a federal antilynching bill never passed the Congress, by the end of the 1940s public opinion had been sufficiently convinced by the efforts of various women's groups that lynching was barbarous and criminal. Recorded incidents of lynching ceased by 1950.

Even though interracial cooperation in the antilynching campaign was a positive factor among Black and white women, discrimination against Black women by white women continued to plague feminists. In 1925, for example, the Quinquennial of the International Council of Women met at the Washington Auditorium in the District of Columbia. The council sought the cooperation of NACW president Mary McLeod Bethune and arrangements were made to have a mass choir of Black women perform. The night of the concert, Black guests were placed in a segregated section of the auditorium. Mary Church Terrell reported that when the singers learned of what was happening, they refused to perform. Foreign women delegates were in the audience, as well as white women from throughout the nation. Many of them were angry because the concert had to be cancelled. Terrell felt that this was one of the most unfortunate incidents of discrimination against Black women in the club movement. However, she agreed with the decision of her Black sisters not to sing.[37]

National recognition of Black women did not really come until 1936, when Mary McLeod Bethune was appointed director of the Division of Negro Affairs, National Youth Administration, under the Franklin D. Roosevelt administration. The founder of Bethune-Cookman Institute in Daytona, Florida, Bethune had been a leader in the Black women's club movement since the early 1920s. NACW president from 1924 to 1928, she founded the National Council of Negro Women (NCNW) in 1935. What feminist consciousness Bethune acquired was thrust upon her in the mid-1930s because for the first time, a Black woman had the ear of the president of the United States and the cooperation of the first lady, who was concerned not only about women's issues, but about Black issues. In 1936 Bethune took advantage of her new status and presented the concerns of the NCNW to Eleanor Roosevelt. As a result, sixty-five Black women leaders attended a meeting with Eleanor Roosevelt to argue the case for their greater representation and appointments to federal bureaus. They called for appointments of professional Black women to the Children's Bureau, the Women's Bureau, and each department of the Bureau of Education that dealt with the welfare of women and children. The NCNW also wanted the appointment of Black women to administrative positions in the Federal Housing Administration and Social Security Board. In addition, they called for enlarging the Black staff of the Bureau of Public Health and for President Roosevelt to suggest to the American Red Cross that it hire a Black administrator.[38]

The NCNW requests reflect two trends among middle-class women in the mid-1930s. First, they were calling for positions that Black women had never held, nor would achieve until a generation later; consequently, their ideas were revolutionary ones in terms of federal policies. Second, they were calling for policies to benefit not only their sex, but their race; hence, the NCNW reflected the position established by Black feminists a generation before.

Mary McLeod Bethune's leadership was acknowledged by Black women's groups throughout the nation, and she accepted the responsibility by referring to herself as the representative of "Negro womanhood." In 1937 she visited the Flanner House, a Black settlement house in Indianapolis whose Black woman superintendent, Clio Blackburn, said the institution's aim was to help Black people help themselves. If no other person represented this standard to Black women at this time, Mary McLeod Bethune did. The following year she met with the Alpha Kappa Alpha Sorority in Boston to assist them in a benefit for the Mississippi Health Project, a project to help Black people in that region which was sponsored by the national sorority.[39]

Middle-class Black women clearly reflected their dedication to uplifting the race at a time when most Afro-Americans were thwarted not only by race prejudice but also by economic depression. Although activities that involved race uplift were not feminist in orientation, many Black feminists took an active role in them. In an interview with Mary McLeod Bethune in 1939, Lillian B. Huff of the *New Jersey Herald News* asked her about the role of Black women leaders and how Bethune related to her leadership position. Bethune, who had come from humble origins, felt that Black women had room in their lives to be wives and mothers as well as to have careers. But most importantly, she thought, Black women should think of their duty to the race.[40]

Bethune's feelings were not unique to Black women, for most Black feminists and leaders had been wives and mothers who worked yet found time not only to struggle for the good of their sex, but for their race. Until the 1970s, however, this threefold commitment—to family and to career and to one or more social movements—was not common among white women. The key to the uniqueness among Black feminists of this period appears to be their link with the past. The generation of the woman suffrage era had learned from their late-nineteenth-century foremothers in the Black women's club movement, just as the generation of the post–World War I era had learned and accepted the experiences of the preceding generation. Theirs was a sense of continuity, a sense of group consciousness that transcended class. Racial uplift, fighting segregation and mob violence, contending with poverty, as well as demanding rights for Black women were long-standing issues of concern to Black feminists.

The meeting of the National Conference on Problems of the Negro and Youth at Washington, D.C., in 1939 was a good example of this phenomenon among Black women. Bethune called the meeting and invited a range of Black leaders from Mary Church Terrell and feminist Nannie Burroughs, who were both in their seventies, to Juanita Jackson Mitchell, the conference youth coordinator. The young Mitchell had been a leader among Black civil rights activists in the City-Wide Young People's Forum in Baltimore a few years before. Bethune noted the success of the meeting of young and old, all of whom had a common interest in civil rights for Afro-Americans.[41]

By 1940 Mary Church Terrell had written her autobiography. At the age of seventy-seven, she was one of the few living links with three generations of Black feminists. In her introduction, Terrell established her own interpretation of her life story, which in many ways reflected the lives of other Black feminists. "This is the story of a colored woman living in a white world. It cannot possibly be like a story written by a white woman. A white woman has only one handicap to overcome—that of sex. I have two—both sex and race. I belong to the only group in this country which has two such huge obstacles to surmount. Colored men have only one—that of race."[42]

Terrell's reference to her status as an Afro-American woman applied throughout United States history to most Black women, regardless of class. In view of this, it is not surprising that Black women struggled, often in vain, to keep the right to vote from 1920 to 1940. A brief reference to this struggle, a story in itself, reveals that they fought to keep the little influence they had although Black feminists anticipated that many of them would lose. Nonetheless, Black female enthusiasm was great immediately following the passage of the Nineteenth Amendment. In Baltimore alone, the Black electorate increased from 16,800 to over 37,400 in 1921, indicating that the number of Black women voters surpassed the number of Black men registered to vote. By 1922, however, attempts to thwart the influence of Black women voters were spreading across the South. As a result, the NACW recommended that all of its clubs lobby for the enforcement of the Nineteenth Amendment.[43]

By 1924 the feminist Nannie Burroughs had assessed the status of Black women of voting age and their relationship to white feminists. Burroughs noted that white women continued to overlook or to undervalue the worth of Black women as a political force in the nation. She warned white female politicians to tap the potential Black female electorate before white men exploited it.[44] With the exception of Ruth Hanna McCormick, who recruited Mary Church Terrell to head her 1929 Illinois campaign for the United States Senate, warnings such as Burroughs's did not seem to influence white female leaders. For example, disillusioned members of the Republican Colored Women State Committee of Wilmington, Delaware, protested unsuccessfully when they lost their representation on the state Republican committee. A merger of the Women's Advisory Committee, a white group, with the State Central Committee had caused the elimination of Black women representatives. The decline in Black women's participation in Republican Party politics was evident by 1928, when only 8 out of 104 black delegates to the Republican National Convention were women. The same year, the NACW program did not even bother to include suffrage among its priorities for women of the race.[45]

Although President Roosevelt made good his promise to Mary McLeod Bethune, so that by 1945 four Black women had received outstanding federal appointments, the political viability of Black women in the early 1940s was bleak. The list of Black elected officials from 1940 to 1946 included no women.[46] Agents of white supremacy continued to subvert what vestiges of political influence Blacks held. For example, in 1942 Congressman Martin Dies, chairman of the congressional committee investigating un-American activities, attempted to link several national Black leaders to the Communist Party. Among the group was Mary McLeod Bethune, who remained the only Black woman prominent in national politics.[47]

Hence, over twenty years after the passage of the Nineteenth Amendment racial discrimination festered in most areas of American life, even among feminists and women in political life. Prejudice did not distinguish between middle-class and working-class Black women, nor between feminists and nonfeminists who were Black. Although Black women continued to use what political rights they maintained, the small number of those politically viable made little impact upon public policies.

NOTES

1. See Rosalyn Terborg-Penn, "Nineteenth Century Black Women and Woman Suffrage," *Potomac Review* 7 (spring–summer 1977): 13–24; and Rosalyn M. Terborg-Penn, "Afro-Americans in the Struggle for Woman Suffrage" (Ph.D. dissertation, Howard University, 1977), 180–85.

2. *Indianapolis Freeman*, August 28, 1915; Monroe N. Work, ed., *The Negro Year Book, 1918–1919* (Tuskegee Institute, Ala.: The Negro Year Book Publishing Co., 1919), 57–59 (hereafter cited as *Negro Year Book*, by year); Rosalyn Terborg-Penn, "Discrimination against Afro-American Women in the Woman's Movement, 1830–1920," *The Afro-American Woman: Struggles and Images*, ed. Sharon Harley and Rosalyn Terborg-Penn (Port Washington, N.Y.: Kennikat Press, 1978), 26.

3. See Rayford W. Logan, *The Negro in the United States* (Princeton, N.J.: Van Nostrand, 1957); and Terborg-Penn, "Discrimination against Afro-American Women," 17–27.

4. Terborg-Penn, "Afro-Americans in the Struggle for Woman Suffrage," chap. 4.

5. David Morgan, *Suffragists and Democrats: The Politics of Woman Suffrage in America* (East Lansing, Mich.: Michigan State University Press, 1972), 106–7.

6. *Crisis* 15 (November 1917): 18; *Negro Year Book, 1918–1919*, 60.

7. Mrs. A. W. Blackwell, *The Responsibility and Opportunity of the Twentieth Century Woman* (n.p., n.d), 1–5. This pamphlet is housed in the Trevor Arnett Library, Atlanta University.

8. *Crisis* 15 (November 1917): 19–20; *New York Age*, May 10, 1917.

9. *New York Age*, September 20, 1917.

10. Walter White to Mary Church Terrell, March 14, 1919, Mary Church Terrell Papers, Box no. 3, Library of Congress, Washington D.C. (hereafter cited as MCT Papers); Charles Flint Kellogg, *NAACP: A History of the National Association for the Advancement of Colored People, 1909–1920* (Baltimore: Johns Hopkins Press, 1967), 208.

11. Walter White to Mary Church Terrell, March 14, 1919, MCT Papers, Box no. 3.

12. Ida Husted Harper to Mary Church Terrell, March 18, 1919, and Ida Harper to Elizabeth Carter, March 18, 1919, MCT Papers, Box no. 3.

13. Aileen Kraditor, *The Ideas of the Woman Suffrage Movement, 1890–1920* (Garden City, N.Y.: Anchor Books, Doubleday and Co., 1971), 168–69; *Crisis* 17 (June 1919): 103; Ida Husted Harper, ed.,

The History of Woman Suffrage, 1900–1920 (New York: J. J. Little and Ives Co., 1922), 580–81.

14. Terborg-Penn, "Afro-American in the Struggle for Woman Suffrage," chaps. 4 and 5.

15. Ibid., pp. 207, 217–18, 225.

16. *Crisis* 19 (November 1920): 23–25; *Negro Year Book, 1921*, 40.

17. Kenneth R. Johnson, "White Racial Attitudes as a Factor in the Arguments against the Nineteenth Amendment," *Phylon* 31 (spring 1970): 31–32, 35–37.

18. Terborg-Penn, "Afro-American in the Struggle for Woman Suffrage," 301–2.

19. Ibid., 303–04.

20. William Pickens, "The Woman Voter Hits the Color Line," *Nation* 3 (October 6, 1920): 372–73.

21. Ibid., 373; NAACP, *Eleventh Annual Report of the NAACP for the Year 1920* (New York: NAACP, 1921), 15, 25–30.

22. William L. O'Neill, *Everybody Was Brave* (Chicago: Quadrangle Press, 1969), 275.

23. Terborg-Penn, "Afro-Americans in the Struggle for Woman Suffrage," 311.

24. Benjamin Brawley, *Women of Achievement: Written for the Fireside Schools* (Nashville, Tenn.: Woman's American Baptist Home Mission Society, 1919), 14–17.

25. Elizabeth Ross Haynes, "Two Million Negro Women at Work," *Southern Workman* 15 (February 1922): 64–66.

26. United States Department of Commerce, Bureau of Census, *Population Trends in the United States, 1900–1960* (Washington, D.C.: U.S. Government Printing Office, 1964), 231, 234.

27. Gerda Lerner, ed., *Black Women in White America: A Documentary History* (New York: Random House, Pantheon Books, 1972), 226–27; Louise Mitchell, "Slave Markets Typify Exploitation of Domestics," *Daily Worker*, May 5, 1940.

28. *Negro Year Book, 1922–24*, 37.

29. *The Negro World*, October 24, 1925, March 5, 1927. See Mark D. Matthews, " 'Our Women and What They Think,' Amy Jacques Garvey and *The Negro World," Black Scholar* 10 (May–June 1979): 2–13.

30. Mary Church Terrell, *A Colored Woman in a White World* (Washington D.C.: Randsdell, Inc., 1940), 330–33.

31. Ibid., 360–64.

32. *Crisis* 30 (June 1925): 81.

33. *Negro Year Book, 1921–22*, 6–9.

34. *Negro Year Book, 1922–24*, 18–19.

35. Ibid., 37–38; *Crisis* 23 (March 1922): 218; *Crisis* 24 (October 1922): 260.

36. *Crisis* 24 (November 1922): 8.

37. Terrell, *A Colored Woman in a White World*, 370–71.

38. Mary McLeod Bethune, Vertical File, Howard University, Washington D.C., Clippings Folder, 1930, *Black Dispatch*, April 16, 1936 (hereafter cited as Bethune Vertical File and the source).

39. Bethune Vertical File, *Indianapolis Recorder*, December 14, 1937, *Boston Guardian*, October 18, 1938.

40. Bethune Vertical File, *New Jersey Herald News*, October 14, 1939.

41. Bethune Vertical File, *Black Dispatch*, January 28, 1939.

42. Terrell, *A Colored Woman in a White World*, first page of the introduction.

43. *Crisis* 23 (December 1921): 83; *Negro Year Book, 1922–24*, 37.

44. *Negro Year Book, 1922–24*, 70.

45. Terrell, *A Colored Woman in a White World*, 355–56; *Negro Year Book, 1922–24*, 70; *Negro Year Book, 1931–32*, 13, 92–93. Blacks did not vote the Democratic Party on a large scale until the second Franklin D. Roosevelt administration.

46. *Negro Year Book, 1947*, 286–87, 289–91.

47. Bethune Vertical File, *Black Dispatch*, October 10, 1942.

7

ELLA BAKER AND THE ORIGINS OF "PARTICIPATORY DEMOCRACY"

Carol Mueller

INTRODUCTION

The sources of ideas that guide the transformation and renewal of societies are often obscured by dramatic events and charismatic leaders that fit the media's emphasis on conflict and celebrity and the public's demand for mythic leaders and heroic sacrifice. Yet the beliefs that may ultimately inspire the mobilization of thousands (and millions) have often been tested and retested in obscure and out-of-the-way places by individuals who may never write manifestos, lead demonstrations, call press conferences, or stand before TV cameras. As Ella Baker said of herself, "you didn't see me on television, you didn't see news stories about me. The kind of role that I tried to play was to pick up pieces or put together pieces out of which I hoped organization might come. My theory is, strong people don't need strong leaders."[1]

In the 1960s, a complex of ideas coalesced under the label "participatory democracy," bringing together in a new formulation the traditional appeal of democracy with an innovative tie to broader participation. The emphasis on participation had many implications, but three have been primary: (1) an appeal for grassroots involvement of people throughout society in the decisions that control their lives; (2) the minimization of hierarchy and the associated emphasis on expertise and professionalism as a basis for leadership; and (3) a call for direct action as an answer to fear, alienation, and intellectual detachment. These ideas not only informed the student wing of the civil rights movement and the new left during the 1960s, but also the movements of the 1970s and 1980s that came to be called the "New Social Movements" in Western Europe and the United States.[2]

Participatory democracy legitimated an active public voice in a wide range of governmental decisions. Citizens now insisted on a voice in decisions regarding the composition of the Democratic Party—first in the challenge of the Mississippi Freedom Democratic Party in 1964 and later in the reforms of 1972; in the decisions of the government-sponsored Community Action Programs of the War on Poverty and the Model Cities Program; in the decision regarding foreign policy of the Vietnam War, the acquisition of new weapons systems such as the B-1 bomber and the MX missile as well as the later deployment of the Cruise and Pershing missile systems in Europe; and in the decisions regarding nuclear power and environmental pollution.

In addition, the ideas of participatory democracy encouraged a broader base for decision making within social movement organizations. Experimentation with direct democracy and consensus decision making ranged from the early voter registration projects of SNCC in Mississippi and Georgia,[3] to the ERAP projects of SDS in the slums of northern cities in the mid-1960s,[4] to the consciousness-raising groups of women's liberation in the late 1960s and early 1970s,[5] to the affinity groups associated with the antinuclear and peace movements of the late 1970s and early 1980s.[6] In many of these movements there has been a conscious effort to minimize hierarchy and professionalism.

Finally, this has been a period of unprecedented direct action.[7] Since the United States has had a long history of open resistance and rebellion (the slave revolts, the revolution against England, the Civil War, the labor movement, the Molly Maguires) and of civil disobedience (the women's suffrage movement of the World War I period, the nonviolent phase of the civil rights movement), it would be an obvious mistake to credit one particular formulation of ideas with legitimating direct intervention in the affairs of civil society or the state. Yet the ideas of participatory democracy frame the call to direct action—not as periodic response to crisis, but as part of a broader set of collective citizenship obligations.

These have been a powerful set of ideas, providing one of the major frameworks for legitimating, understanding, and stimulating the collective actions and protests of a period during which new resources combined with unprecedented political opportunity.[8] Despite the importance of these ideas, there is confusion and misunderstanding among historians regarding their origins. Particularly among some scholars studying the history of the Students for a Democratic Society (SDS), there is the assumption that participatory democracy originated with the intellectual core of students (Al Haber, Tom Hayden, Sharon Jeffrey, Bob Ross, Richard Flacks, and Steve Max) who participated most actively in drafting the Port Huron Statement of 1962.[9]

In contrast, I argue that the basic themes of participatory democracy were first articulated and given personal witness in the activism of Ella Baker. These ideas served as the basis for her decisive intervention in support of an independent student-led organization within the civil rights movement. The Student Nonviolent Coordinating Committee not only set much of the agenda for the civil rights movement during the next few years but also served as a model for later student-led political organizations such as SDS. During those years, SNCC also served as a laboratory field station directly testing the ideas of participatory democracy in daily practice. An appreciation of the role of Ella Baker in the creation of the participatory democracy frame is important for recognizing the source of transforming ideas in a context of ongoing struggle.

ELLA BAKER'S PARTICIPATORY DEMOCRACY

As was well known within the civil rights movement but not very far outside it, Ella Baker was one of its key leaders and the most important nonstudent involved in the phase of student activism that began with the formation of the Student Nonviolent Coordinating Committee following the dramatic sit-ins of the winter and spring of 1960. In dedicating his book *SNCC: The New Abolitionists* to Ella Baker, Howard Zinn (political scientist, then faculty member of Spelman College, and adviser to SNCC) wrote in his acknowledgments, "And finally, there is the lady to whom this book is dedicated, who is more responsible than any other single individual for the birth of the new abolitionists as an organized group, and who remains the most tireless, the most modest, and the wisest activist I know in the struggle for human rights today."[10] Writing his own history of SNCC at the close of the 1960s, James Forman, its executive director for most of that decade, begins "Book Two: A Bond of Sisters and Brothers, In a Circle of Trust" with a chapter on Ella Baker. It starts, "Ella Jo Baker, one of the key persons in the formation of SNCC, is one of those many strong Black women who have devoted their lives to the liberation of their people."[11]

When this strong, Black woman died in December 1986, after fifty years of political activism, a funeral service was held in Harlem where she had lived most of her adult life. The list of pallbearers gives eloquent testimony to her central role in SNCC and the high regard in which she was held by many of its leaders. They were (listed in alphabetical order as they were on the program for the service):

Jamil Abdullah Al-Amin—formerly H. Rap Brown, elected chair of SNCC in 1967 to
   succeed Stokley Carmichael.
Julian Bond—for five years communications director of SNCC in the Atlanta office and
   later state representative in the Georgia House of Representatives.
Vincent Harding—minister and close associate of Martin Luther King.
Doug Harris
Charles McDew—chair of SNCC from October 1960 until the election of John Lewis
   in 1963.
Reginald Robinson—one of the first SNCC members to begin voter registration work
   in McComb, Mississippi, in 1961; later worked with Ella Baker in mobilizing north-
   ern support for the challenge of the Mississippi Freedom Democratic Party.
Charles Sherrod—SNCC's first field secretary and leader of community work in south-
   east Georgia.
Kwame Toure—formerly Stokley Carmichael, elected chair of SNCC in 1966; gave voice
   to SNCC's emerging Black power orientation in the mid-1960s.
Robert Zellner—the first white field secretary hired by SNCC.

Honorary pallbearers included James Forman and Bayard Rustin, one of the key figures with Ella Baker in the organization of In Freedom, the northern support group for the Montgomery bus boycott who also worked with her in creating the Southern Christian Leadership Conference and one of her oldest political associates. The memorial service brought other civil rights leaders to pay their respects—Ralph Abernathy, cofounder of the SCLC and close associate of King; Wyatt T. Walker, who replaced Ella Baker as executive di-rector of the SCLC in 1960; and Bernice Johnson Reagon of the Albany Movement and the SNCC Freedom Singers. The service included special tributes from Percy Sutton; Jo Ann Grant, veteran SNCC worker and producer of *Fundi*, a documentary film of Miss Baker's life; Anne Braden, editor, with her husband, Carl, of the *Southern Patriot* newspaper pub-lished by the SCEF Education Fund, which Ella Baker served as a consultant; and Bob Moses, whose long years of organizing in the Mississippi project embodied, perhaps more than anyone else in SNCC, the philosophy of participatory democracy.

The words of Howard Zinn and James Farmer and the many who paid their respects at her funeral only begin to suggest the tributes to Miss Baker in the annals of the civil rights movement. Her lifetime of contributions to the goal of human freedom cannot be ade-quately chronicled here, but the major themes of her life are central to an understanding of the roots of participatory democracy as an outgrowth of active participation in the process of political struggle. The three themes of participatory democracy—grassroots involvement by people in the decisions that affect their lives; the minimization of hierarchy and professionalization in organizations working for social change; and direct action on the sources of injustice—grew out of more than twenty years of political experience that she brought to the fledgling student movement in the spring of 1960. The philosophy of social change that led her to insist on an independent student organization at the Raleigh Conference in April 1960 was the logical extension of these experiences combined with a southern upbringing based in a strong allegiance to family and community.

Her great sense of social responsibility was based in the traditions of the small North Carolina community where she moved in 1911 at the age of eight with her family.[12] The local church was presided over by her grandfather, a former slave, who had bought the land on which he once had served, vowing to provide amply for the needs of his family and neighbors. It was a commonplace for his household to take in the local sick and needy. Regardless of their social position, Miss Baker learned at an early age to be responsible for all of them.

Her sense of community and responsibility expanded after graduating from Shaw University in Raleigh, North Carolina, in 1927. Unable to afford graduate work in sociology at the University of Chicago, she moved to New York where she could rely for support on her network of kin. Refusing to follow the traditional woman's route of schoolteaching, she at first found it impossible to find a job doing anything other than waitressing or domestic service—despite her college degree. By 1929, the Depression had struck and the problems of the poor and needy multiplied around her.

EMPOWERMENT OF PEOPLE AT THE GRASS ROOTS

The type of solutions that Ella Baker sought in responding to the suffering of the Depression consistently reflected her belief that political action should empower people to solve their own problems. After several years of editorial work for the *American West Indian News* (1929–30) and the *Negro National News* (1932), she helped form the Young Negroes' Cooperative League, became its national director, and began organizing group buying through consumer cooperatives. Her experience as an organizer, speaker, and writer on consumer education led to her employment with the New Deal's Works Progress Administration (WPA). In the WPA, she continued to bring people together to augment their meager resources through collective buying.

Equally important, in the WPA, Ella Baker was exposed to the fermenting ideas on social change that were widely discussed in Harlem at this time. Miss Baker later said of those years, "New York was the hotbed of—let's call it radical thinking. You had every spectrum of radical thinking on the WPA. We had a lovely time! The ignorant ones, like me, we had lots of opportunity to hear and to evaluate whether or not this was the kind of thing you wanted to get into. Boy it was good, stimulating."[13]

The diversity of opinions that she characterized as "the nectar divine" apparently reinforced Ella Baker's commitment to social change through organizing people to act on their own behalf. In the late 1930s, as a young woman, she began working for the NAACP as a field organizer, traveling to cities, towns, and rural villages throughout the Deep South, speaking wherever she could find a group of people who were willing to listen.

In an interview with the historian Gerda Lerner, she described her work: "I used to leave New York about the 15th of February and travel through the South for four or five months.

I would go to, say, Birmingham, Alabama and help to organize membership campaigns . . . You would deal with whatever the local problem was, and on the basis of the needs of the people you would try to organize them in the NAACP."[14] In the early 1940s, she was made assistant field secretary for the NAACP and in 1943 she was named the association's national director of branches.

In her many years of travel for the NAACP trying to help people organize against the pervasive racial violence of the South, she was developing her own understanding of how people can collectively fight oppression. In the early 1970s, she described what she had learned from her many years as a field organizer:

> My basic sense of it has always been to get people to understand that in the long run they themselves are the only protection they have against violence or injustice. If they only had ten members in the NAACP at a given point, those ten members could be in touch with twenty-five members in the next little town, with fifty in the next and throughout the state as a result of the organization of state conferences, and they, of course, could be linked up with the national. People have to be made to understand that they cannot look for salvation anywhere but to themselves.[15]

Her belief in empowering people through their direct participation in social change assumed a new form when she took on the responsibility of raising her niece and gave up the annual six months of travel required of a field secretary. After several years of working in fund-raising for the National Urban League Service Fund, she was elected president of the New York branch of the NAACP. "We tried to bring the NAACP back, as I called it, to the people. We moved the branch out of an office building and located it where it would be more visible to the Harlem community. We started developing an active branch. It became one of the largest branches."[16]

When the Supreme Court's *Brown* decision came down in 1954, she was serving as chairman of the Education Committee of the New York branch of the NAACP. This committee began to fight segregation in the New York schools. Her view of what was successful about the work of this committee characteristically emphasized that "out of it came increased fervor on the part of the black communities to make some changes."[17]

She was critical of the national NAACP's failure to emphasize the development of self-sufficient local communities and, in 1944, initiated a series of regional leadership conferences, one attended by Rosa Parks of the Montgomery, Alabama, branch, to . . . "help local leaders develop their own leadership potential."[18]

She continued to emphasize meaningful participation and the development of the resources within individuals and institutions when she worked with the SCLC in the late 1950s. In its first project, the Crusade for Citizenship, a drive to register Black voters in the South, Miss Baker worked with its first executive director, Reverend John Tilley, in local communities to try to get churches to organize social action committees, set up voter clinics, and affiliate with the SCLC. She attempted to interest its ministerial leaders in citizenship classes to teach basic reading and writing skills so that Blacks could register to vote.[19] She argued that the classes could draw on the considerable resources that already existed at the local level in religious and educational groups of women. These as well as other suggestions to broaden the involvement of youth and women in SCLC fell on deaf ears and contributed to her dissatisfaction with its ministerial leadership.

The theme that later became a slogan, "Power to the People," served as Ella Baker's criterion for evaluating political work throughout her life. In the 1970s, when she was asked to comment on the movement for community control of schools, she saw it as part of a broad strategy:

> First, there is a prerequisite: the recognition on the part of the established powers that people have a right to participate in the decisions that affect their lives. And it doesn't matter whether those decisions have to do with schools or housing or some other aspect of their lives. There is a corollary to this prerequisite: the citizens themselves must be conscious of the fact that this is their right. Then comes the question, how do you reach people if they aren't already conscious of this right? And how do you break down resistance on the part of powers that be toward citizens becoming participants in decision making?
>
> I don't have any cut pattern, except that I believe that people, when informed about the things they are concerned with, will find a way to react. Now, whether their reactions are the most desirable at a given stage depends, to a large extent, upon whether the people who are in the controlling seat are open enough to permit people to react according to the way they see the situation. In organizing a community, you start with people where they are.[20]

GROUP-CENTERED LEADERSHIP
Ella Baker's impatience with the pretensions of hierarchy dated from her earliest childhood. Recalling her youth growing up in the South, she said:

> Where we lived *there was no sense of hierarchy*, in terms of those who have, having a right to look down upon, or to evaluate as a lesser breed, those who didn't have. Part of that could have resulted, I think, from two factors. One was the proximity of my maternal grandparents to slavery. They had known what it was to not have. Plus, my grandfather had gone into the Baptist ministry, and that was part of the quote, unquote, Christian concept of sharing with others. I went to a school that went in for Christian training. Then, there were people who "stood for something," as I call it. Your relationship to human beings was more important than your relationship to the amount of money that you made.[21]

This sense of equality contributed to her capacity to identify with people from all walks of life in her organizing work for the NAACP and later the SCLC and SNCC.

> On what basis do you seek to organize people? Do you start to try to organize them on the fact of what you think, or what they are first interested in? You start where the people are. Identification with people. There's always this problem in the minority group that's escalating up the ladder in this culture, I think. Those who have gotten some training and those who have gotten some material gains, it's always the problem of their not understanding the possibility of being divorced from those who are not in their social classification. Now, there were those who felt they had made it, would be embarrassed by the fact that some people would get drunk and get in jail, and so they wouldn't be concerned too much about whether they were brutalized in jail. 'Cause he was a *drunk*! He was a so-and-so. Or she was a streetwalker. We get caught in that bag. And so you have to help break that down without alienating them at the same time. The gal who has been able to buy her minks and whose husband is a professional,

they live well. You can't insult her, you never go and tell her she's a so-and-so for taking, for not identifying. You try to point out where her interest lies in identifying with that other one across the tracks who doesn't have minks.[22]

Miss Baker's antipathy to hierarchy combined with her commitment to grassroots organizing led to a particular concept of leadership that she called "group-centered leadership."[23] This pattern of leadership emphasized the role of the leader as a facilitator, as someone who brings out the potential in others, rather than a person who commands respect and a following as a result of charisma or status.

This view began in her organizing work in the South and continued as a source of tension in her many years with the NAACP. In commenting on the leadership of Walter White, she noted that, "Unfortunately, he also felt the need to impress government people. He had not learned, as many people still have not learned, that if you are involved with people and organizing them as a force, you didn't have to go and seek out the Establishment People. They would seek you out."[24]

She felt that some of this same attitude characterized the entire organization. In 1968, she told an interviewer:

> Basically, I think personally, I've always felt that the Association got itself hung-up in what I call its legal success. Having had so many outstanding legal successes, it definitely seemed to have oriented its thinking in the direction that the way to achieve was through the courts. It hasn't departed too far from that yet. So, I said to you that when I came out of the Depression, I came out of it with a different point of view as to what constituted success . . . I began to feel that my greatest sense of success would be to succeed in doing with people some of the things that I thought would raise the level of masses of people, rather than the individual being accepted by the Establishment.[25]

Miss Baker remained a tough critic of professionalized leadership throughout her association with the NAACP.[26] In particular, she criticized its emphasis on membership size without creating opportunities for members to be meaningfully involved in the program. At the time of her association in the early 1940s, much of the NAACP's membership of four hundred thousand primarily provided a financial base for its professional staff of lawyers and lobbyists. Payne's research into the reports of the association's field secretaries to the National Board has found a strong preoccupation with membership size rather than activities.[27] These tensions contributed to Ella Baker's resigning as its national director of branches in 1946 (as did accepting responsibility for raising her niece).

The same issues over organizational leadership led to her eventual departure from the SCLC in 1960. Having been instrumental in the founding of the SCLC in 1957, Miss Baker agreed to go to Atlanta to set up its first office. She originally served as its only staff member. Her first responsibility was to coordinate meetings throughout the South on Lincoln's Birthday 1958 to kick off the SCLC's first program, a Crusade for Citizenship, which would seek to double the number of Black voters in the South in one year.[28] With no resources and little support from the new ministerial associates of the SCLC, the fact that thirteen thousand people turned out in twenty-two cities "on the coldest night in 50 years" was miraculous.[29]

Ella Baker was the central figure in the SCLC Atlanta headquarters during the late 1950s.[30] She organized the office, carried on correspondence, and kept in touch with the local branches. With John Tilley, the executive director, she traveled throughout the South developing voter registration programs and SCLC affiliations that included a commitment to direct action.

It was not a compatible arrangement, however. Where Miss Baker had found earlier that professionalism and status concerns were an obstacle to group-centered leadership in the NAACP, she found in the SCLC that the emphasis on charismatic ministerial leadership was similarly at odds with her view of how organizations should be built to empower people to seek social change.

Despite considerably greater experience in working for social change than the ministers she worked for in the Atlanta office (she was fifty-four when she went to Atlanta), she was expected to handle administrative matters while her policy suggestions for greater emphasis on local organizing and the inclusion of women and youth were largely ignored.[31]

Although Tilley decided within a year to leave his post and return to his church in Baltimore, there was never any serious consideration of replacing him with Ella Baker. Instead, she was appointed acting director until an appropriate minister could be found. Reverend Wyatt Walker, who succeeded her, later told Morris, "When John Tilley left, it was within 90 days of his leaving or less [that] they knew they were going to hire me if they could get me, and Ella was just a holding action." Walker felt that Miss Baker could not fit into the preacher's organization: "It just went against the grain of the kind of person she is and was."[32]

The incompatibility between the SCLC and Ella Baker reflected their very different understandings of leadership and, thus, of programs. Miss Baker was very critical of placing great emphasis on a single leader, the organizing principle of the SCLC, focused as it was on the leadership of Martin Luther King Jr. Thus, Miss Baker opposed not only its organizational principle, but the specific leadership of King as well. Asked in the early 1970s why she had not had a more prominent position in the civil rights movement, she stated her general philosophy of leadership:

> In government service and political life I have always felt it was a handicap for oppressed peoples to depend so largely upon a leader, because unfortunately in our culture, the charismatic leader usually becomes a leader because he has found a spot in the public limelight. It usually means he has been touted through the public media, which means that the media made him, and the media may undo him. There is also the danger in our culture that, because a person is called upon to give public statements and is acclaimed by the establishment, such a person gets to the point of believing that he *is* the movement. Such people get so involved with playing the game of being important that they exhaust themselves and their time, and they don't do the work of actually organizing people.[33]

For Ella Baker, it was more important to serve "what was a potential for all of us," than to look after her own needs for status or position. She said, "I knew from the beginning that as a woman, an older woman, in a group of ministers who are accustomed to having women largely as supporters, there was no place for me to have come into a leadership role. The competition wasn't worth it."[34]

DIRECT ACTION

The third component of the participatory democracy framework was an emphasis on opposing violence and the intransigence of bureaucratic and legalistic obstacles by collective demonstrations of the "will of the people."[35] Designed to counter apathy, fear, and resignation through an assertion of independence, as well as to exercise influence on behalf of collective goals, for Ella Baker it was always a part of an overall strategy of empowering people, never an end in itself.

In the Deep South where she worked as an organizer for the NAACP, public affiliation with the organization in the 1940s and 1950s was itself an act of defiance that gave people a sense of strength through a collective effort. She said of those years:

> As assistant field secretary of the branches of the NAACP, much of my work was in the South. At that time, the NAACP was the leader on the cutting edge of social change. I remember when NAACP membership in the South was the basis for getting beaten up or even killed.
>
> You would go into areas where people were not yet organized in the NAACP and try to get them more involved. . . . Black people who were living in the South were constantly living with violence, part of the job was to help them to understand what that violence was and how they, in an organized fashion, could help to stem it.[36]

For years it was her job to convince people that they should take this risk.

Ella Baker saw direct action in the creation of an insurgent organization such as the southern NAACP in the 1940s. In 1955, however, mobilization of the Montgomery Improvement Association inspired her, Bayard Rustin, and Stanley Levison of the New York support group In Friendship to believe that a new stage of public mass action had arrived.[37] Following the integration of the Montgomery buses, Miss Baker worked with Rustin, Levison, and King on seven "working papers" that the New York group hoped would serve as the basis for discussion at the meeting of January 1957 that would lead to the formation of the SCLC. Although the meetings were officially entitled the "Southern Negro Leaders Conference on Transportation and Non-violence Interpretation," the working papers called for a broad strategy.

The strategy called for two principal tactics: voting power and mass direct action. Until more Blacks could vote, they argued, "we shall have to rely more and more on mass direct action as the one realistic political weapon."[38] Montgomery showed that the center of gravity had shifted from the courts to community action; the only question was what kind of mass action to use. The In Friendship group considered many of the tactics later developed by SNCC under Ella Baker's tutelage, particularly mass arrests and the creation of a "small disciplined group of non-violent shock troops to lead community mass actions."[39] These working papers failed to have a significant impact on the formation of the SCLC for a variety of situational reasons. Yet commenting later on those formative days of the SCLC, Miss Baker thought there were other reasons as well: "The other, I think, factor that has to be honestly said is that Martin was not yet ready for the kind of leadership that would inspire these men to really grapple with . . . ideological differences and patterns of organization."[40] Nevertheless, the working papers indicated the direction of the thinking among the more experienced organizers from New York. Particularly, they are important in showing the ideas that Ella Baker would shortly bring to SNCC.

During her tenure with the SCLC in the late 1950s, her own efforts were still directed toward direct action in the context of empowering local people. As associate director and later as acting executive director, she went to Shreveport, Louisiana, to help with voter registration drives. There she supported an all-day stand-in at Caddo Parrish, where a strong local movement sent 250 to register but only forty-six were interviewed and only fifteen were actually allowed to complete registration. She also worked with Dr. C. O. Simpkins, a local dentist, to prepare sixty-eight witnesses who gave testimonies at a Louisiana hearing.[41] Altogether, she spent five months in Shreveport working with local leaders to counter the countless reprisals against Blacks who tried to register.

Despite her efforts and those of many local leaders, Miss Baker felt that the SCLC at this time offered little support for a massive confrontation. Of her years with the SCLC's Crusade for Citizenship, she said, "It was very difficult to get it from being oriented in the direction of just big meetings; you know, having an annual conference, and a big meeting . . ."[42]

After Tilley left the position of executive director in April 1959, Ella Baker was named acting director. The following October, she wrote a memorandum expressing her frustration with the progress of the branches:

> The word Crusade connotes for me a vigorous movement, with high purpose and involving masses of people. In search for action that might help develop for SCLC more of the obvious characteristics of a crusade, a line of thinking was developed which I submit for your consideration. . . . To play a unique role in the South, SCLC must offer, basically, a different "brand of goods" that fills unmet needs of the people. At the same time, it must provide for a sense of achievement and recognition for many people, particularly local leadership.[43]

At this time Ella Baker already knew that the SCLC had not provided the leadership in direct mass action that she, Rustin, and Levison had hoped for. She also saw it as limited by a conception of leadership that inhibited mass participation and exalted the charismatic leader. She felt that both limitations failed to organize the people for self-sufficiency.

CONCLUSION

When the winter of 1960 brought a massive wave of sit-ins by Black college students throughout the South, it was Ella Baker who saw their potential more clearly than anyone else.[44] As conversations began within the civil rights organizations over how this new energy could be harnessed to fuel the lagging efforts of the movement, it was Ella Baker who called for an organizing conference of student sit-in leaders at her old alma mater, Shaw University. When the Raleigh meeting was held in April 1960, it was Ella Baker who insisted that the students who had created the sit-ins should decide their own future independently of the already established civil rights organizations.[45] When the Student Nonviolent Coordinating Committee was formed as a result of the Raleigh meeting, it was Ella Baker's unlabeled, but fully articulated, ideas on participatory democracy that were most compatible with the students' search for autonomous and active leadership roles in the civil rights movement.[46] As SNCC began to develop an office, a staff, and a program, it was Ella Baker who served as their chief adviser from 1960 through the challenge of the Mississippi Freedom Democratic Party in the summer of 1964. In the summer of 1960, she wrote of her hopes and dreams for the new student movements:

> By and large, this feeling that they have a destined date with freedom, was not limited to a drive for personal freedom, or even freedom for the Negro in the South. Repeatedly it was

emphasized that the movement was concerned with the moral implications of racial discrimination for the "whole world" and the "Human Race."

This universality of approach was linked with a perceptive recognition that "it is important to keep the movement democratic and to avoid struggles for personal leadership."

It was further evident that desire for supportive cooperation from adult leaders and the adult community was also tempered by apprehension that adults might try to "capture" the student movement. The students showed willingness to be met on the basis of equality, but were intolerant of anything that smacked of manipulation or domination.

This inclination toward group-centered leadership, rather than toward a leader centered group pattern of organization, was refreshing indeed to those of the older group who bear the scars of the battle, the frustrations and the disillusionment that come when the prophetic leader turns out to have heavy feet of clay.[47]

When hundreds and then thousands of northern white students supported the sit-ins or went south to view at first hand a student-led movement to end racial oppression, Ella Baker's ideas found another receptive audience and spread and spread and spread.

NOTES

1. Ellen Cantarow and Susan O'Mally, *Moving the Mountain: Women Working for Social Change* (New York: Feminist Press at the City University of New York: 1980), 55.

2. Claus Offe, "New Social Movements: Challenging the Boundaries of Institutional Politics," *Social Research* 52, 4 (winter 1975); Bert Klandermans and Sidney Tarrow, "Mobilization into Social Movements: Synthesizing European and American Approaches," in *From Structure to Action: Comparing Movement Participation Across Cultures* (Greenwich, Conn.: JAI Press, 1988).

3. James Forman, *The Making of Black Revolutionaries* (Washington, D.C.: Open Hand, 1985); Clayborne Carson, *In Struggle: SNCC and the Black Awakening of the 1960s* (Cambridge: Harvard University Press, 1981).

4. James Miller, *Democracy Is in the Streets* (New York: Simon and Schuster, 1987).

5. Joan Cassell, *A Group Called Women* (New York: David McKay, 1977); Jo Freeman, "The Tyranny of Structurelessness," in Jane S. Jaquette, ed., *Women in Politics* (New York: Wiley, 1974).

6. Steven E. Barkan, "Strategic, Tactical and Organizational Dilemmas of the Protest Movement Against Nuclear Power," *Social Problems* 27, 1 (October 1979).

7. See Craig Jenkins, "Interpreting the Stormy Sixties: Three Theories in Search of a Political Age," *Research in Political Sociology*, forthcoming, for a summary.

8. See John McCarthy and Mayer Zald, *The Trend of Social Movements in America: Professionalization and Resource Mobilization* (Morristown, N.J.: General Learning Press, 1973) on new resources; Craig Jenkins and Charles Perrow, "Insurgency of the Powerless," *American Sociological Review* 42 (April 1977); Doug McAdam, *Political Process and the Development of Black Insurgency* (Chicago: University of Chicago Press, 1982) on shifts in the political opportunity structure.

9. See especially James Miller, *Democracy Is in the Streets* (New York: Simon and Schuster, 1987).

10. Howard Zinn, *SNCC: The New Abolitionists* (Boston: Beacon Press, 1964), iii.

11. Forman, *Making of Black Revolutionaries*, 215.

12. Cantarow and O'Mally, *Moving the Mountain*.

13. Ibid., 64.

14. Gerda Lerner, "Developing Community Leadership," in *Black Women in White America* (New York: Pantheon, 1972), 347.

15. Ibid.

16. Ibid., 348.

17. Ibid., 349.

18. Charles Payne, " 'Strong People Don't Need Strong Leaders': Ella Baker and Models of Social Change" (unpublished paper, Northwestern University, Department of African American Studies, 1987).

19. Aldon Morris, *The Origins of the Civil Rights Movement* (New York: Free Press, 1984), 114.

20. Lerner, "Developing Community Leadership," 20.

21. Cantarow and O'Mally, *Moving the Mountain*, 60.

22. Ibid., 70.

23. See especially Payne, " 'Strong People Don't Need Strong Leaders.' "

24. Ella Baker, interview by John Britton, Civil Rights Documentation Project, Moorland-Spingam Research Center, Howard University, June 19, 1968, 6.

25. Ibid., 12.

26. Payne, " 'Strong People Don't Need Strong Leaders,' " 5.

27. Ibid., 36, n. 4.

28. David Garrow, *Bearing the Cross* (New York: William Morrow, 1986), 102–4.

29. Morris, *Origins of Civil Rights Movement*, 109.

30. Ibid., 102–8.

31. Ibid.

32. Ibid., 115.

33. Lerner, "Developing Community Leadership," 351.

34. Ibid.; also Britton, Interview with Ella Baker, 34.

35. Miller, *Democracy Is In the Streets*.

36. Lerner, "Developing Community Leadership," 346–47.

37. Garrow, *Bearing the Cross*, 85–87.

38. Ibid., 85–86.

39. Ibid., 86.

40. Ella Baker interview by Britton, 21.

41. Ibid., 25.

42. Ibid., 23.

43. Quoted in Morris, *Origins of Civil Rights Movement*, 112.

44. See Carson, *In Struggle*, 19–30; Morris, *Origins of Civil Rights Movement*, 195–223.

45. See especially Garrow, *Bearing the Cross*, 131–34.

46. See Carol Mueller, "From Equal Rights to Participatory Democracy: Frame Generation in a Cycle of Protest" (paper presented at American Sociological Association, August 1988).

47. Ella J. Baker, "Bigger than a Hamburger," *The Southern Patriot* (June 1960).

8

BLACK WOMEN AND THE ACADEMY[1]

Angela Y. Davis

I WANT TO THANK EVELYN HAMMONDS AND ROBIN KILSON for having devoted probably the last year of their lives to the organization of this absolutely magnificent gathering. This gathering has done so many things for all of us: we have been able to reconnect with friends and former colleagues and sister comrades and students, many of whom we might never have seen if not for Robin and Evelyn's determined organizing. And we have made new connections with new people, new ideas, new issues and new struggles. We have, at least for the last three days, constructed a powerful community of Black women and our sisters of color located within, around and against the academy. And we will go on record for having been here in all our wonderful, complicated and sometimes frustrating diversity. We have also agreed to let the Clinton administration know that we are indeed capable of formulating political demands. Whether we will follow up on them remains to be seen. But that is up to us.

It is an honor to have been invited to give a major address during this conference, especially since I speak from the same podium from which Johnetta Cole and Lani Guinier have offered us such inspiring and illuminating ideas. When I heard Lani Guinier tell her story about having been mistaken for Zoe Baird, I thought, well, at least the notion that "we all look alike" has become slightly more expansive than it used to be. Although I must admit that I continue to be astonished about the extent to which our community's knowledges are so thoroughly shaped by the visual media. Not very long ago a young Black woman clerk appeared quite excited that I was shopping at her store. "Aren't you the woman on 'A Different World'?" (Of course, there have been some white people who think I am Alice Walker or Whoopi Goldberg.) So, when I told the young woman my name, she said, "Oh, now I remember: the big afro!" I guess I am destined to go down in history as "The Big Afro"—although when I first started wearing it, the police often followed me because they thought I was Kathleen Cleaver (who, incidentally, has also been present at the conference this weekend).

We have gathered together these last few days in celebration of ourselves and in recognition of our foremothers who organized one hundred years ago around the motto "Defending Our Name." In the very recent period, we have been called upon to defend the names of many of our sisters in new and provocative ways.

We have defended the name of Anita Hill. And in this context, I would like to pay tribute to the women who gathered the names of scores of Black women for the *New York Times* ad, "Black Women in Defense of Ourselves."

We have had to defend the name of Lani Guinier—and, I think most of us will agree, we could have done a far better job of this defense than we did. As we could have done a better job of defending our sister Johnetta Cole, when she came under attack by the Right Wing.

We have had to defend the name of Joycelyn Elders. In this case, we might need to re-mind ourselves that, in light of the positions she recently has taken on drugs and the crim-inal justice system, we need to defend her today even more forcefully than when she faced the committee that considered her nomination to the post of U.S. Surgeon General.

Finally, I want to publicly thank my sister Toni Morrison. As our first Nobel Laureate and as Commander in the Arts and Letters Order in France, she has dramatically defended our name before the world.

These are very complicated times—in a sense the very fact that so many of us could come together as Black women academics—students, faculty, staff—is indicative of the vast strides that have occurred since 1862, when Mary Jane Patterson became the first African-American woman to be awarded a B.A. degree. After graduating from Oberlin College, she went on to teach at the Institute for Colored Youth in Philadelphia and later became principal of the Preparatory High School for Colored Youth in Washington, D.C. (which was the predecessor of Dunbar High School).[2] Thus, as so many Black women have done, she prepared younger generations for higher education. bell hooks, referring to Black women teachers in the South, wrote, "They were active participants in black community, shaping our futures, mapping our intellectual terrains, sharing revolutionary fervor and vision."[3]

But, while courageous people have organized and fought to make the walls of academia less impenetrable, these very victories have spawned new problems and foreshadowed new struggles. So today we are talking about defending our name within the system of higher education—as students, teachers, and workers.

Like Johnetta Cole did last night, I include workers—because it would be a mark of our having reproduced the very elitism which excluded and continues to exclude so many of us if we assumed that there is only one group of Black women whose names are worth de-fending in the academy. Why, in fact, is it considered more important to defend the name of the assistant professor who is refused tenure than the secretary who is kept in a dead-end job?—or the woman-of-color janitor who is not allowed to unionize?

Certainly the academy is an important site for political contestations of racism, sexism and homophobia. In relation to some issues we choose to address, the academy may be a strategic site, but it is not the *only* site, especially if we commit ourselves to defending the name of Black women.

Since we have all assembled this weekend around the motto "Defending Our Name," I suggest we look at the historical significance of the conference's organizing theme. As we know, this theme, which we associate with the turn-of-the-century Black women's club movement, was first formulated by Fannie Barrier Williams in an address she gave at a worldwide gathering of women during the 1893 Columbian World Exposition. That quote bears repeating now:

> I regret the necessity of speaking to the question of the moral progress of our women because the
> morality of our home life has been commented on so disparagingly and meanly that we are

placed in the unfortunate position of being defenders of our name . . . While I duly appreciate the offensiveness of all references to American slavery, it is unavoidable to charge to that system every moral imperfection that mars the character of the colored American. The whole life and power of slavery depended upon an enforced degradation of everything human in the slaves. The slave code recognized only animal distinctions between the sexes and ruthlessly ignored those ordinary separations of the sexes that belong to the social state. It is a great wonder that two centuries of such demoralization did not work a complete extinction of all the moral instincts.[4]

Williams continued to explain that Black southern women needed "protection": "I do not wish to disturb the serenity of this conference by suggesting why this protection is needed and the kind of men against whom it is needed."[5]

Williams' 1893 statement was admirable and courageous, but at the same time deeply influenced by the ideological climate of her time, which constructed womanhood—true womanhood—in explicitly middle class terms. Such constructions, as they were appropriated by African-American women, tended to conflate the much needed defense of Black women against white men's sexual abuse and working-class attitudes toward female sexuality.

When the National Association of Colored Women was founded in 1896, it chose for its motto "Lifting as We Climb." This motto called upon the most educated, the most moral and the most affluent African-American women to recognize the extent to which the dominant culture's racist perceptions linked them with the least educated, the "most immoral" and the most impoverished Black women. Mary Church Terrell described this cross-class relationship as a determination "to come into the closest possible touch with the masses of our women, through whom the womanhood of our people is always judged."[6] In other words, "[s]elf-preservation demands that [educated Black women] go among the lowly, illiterate and even the vicious, to whom they are bound by ties of race and sex . . . to reclaim them."[7] Such postures helped to produce a distinguished tradition of progressive activism among Black middle class women from the NACW to the National Council of Negro Women and similar organizations today, but what was and remains problematic is the premise that middle class women necessarily embody a standard their poorer sisters should be encouraged to emulate.

The Black women's club movement was especially concerned with "defending their name" against pervasive charges of immorality and sexual promiscuity. Given the extent to which representations of Black inferiority emanating from the dominant culture were bound up with notions of racial hypersexualization—the deployment of the myth of the Black rapist to justify lynching is the most obvious example—it is hard to imagine that women like Fannie Barrier Williams, Ida B. Wells and Mary Church Terrell could have been as effective as they were without defending the sexual purity of their sisters. Yet, in the process of defending Black women's moral integrity and sexual purity, sexual agency was almost entirely denied. We should remember that in the aftermath of slavery, sexuality was one of the very few realms in which masses of African-American women could exercise some kind of autonomy: they could, at least, choose their sexual partners—and thus they could distinguish their post-slavery status from their historical enslavement.

I want to suggest that this denial of sexual agency was in an important respect the denial of freedom for working class Black women. At the same time, I do not want to underestimate the historical importance of the campaigns organized by the Black women's club movement which attempted to affirm the morality of Black women and to defend Black women's names. Since the vast majority of Black women workers—from the end of slavery up to the late nineteen fifties—were domestic workers, sexual harassment and abuse were serious job hazards, particularly since white public opinion tended to shove the blame for any sexual activity between Black women and white men on the women rather than the men. But, in the process of conducting a much needed, righteous struggle against sexual abuse, focusing on the racist way in which Black women were depicted as inferior sexual animals, these ideological contestations tended to deny Black women's sexuality altogether.

I refer to this historical process for a reason, because I think similar problems emerge today. For example, most campaigns against teenage pregnancy fail to acknowledge the possibility and desirability of sexual autonomy in young Black women. In the most recent issue of *Jet Magazine* (January 10, 1994), there is an article announced on the cover as "Athletes for Abstinence Promotes 'Sexual Purity' for Teens Until Marriage." Consider also the program to distribute Norplant in the Baltimore school clinics. Female sexuality—young Black women's sexuality—is the hidden and unspoken factor in the debates around the distribution of Norplant in the public schools.

Last March, George Will wrote an article that appeared on the op/ed page of the *Washington Post* (March 18, 1993). Decrying sexual activity, he mobilizes statistics in an especially virulent and reifying way:

> This year 10 million teen-agers will engage in 126 million acts of sexual intercourse resulting in 1 million pregnancies, 406,000 abortions, 134,000 miscarriages and 490,000 births, about 64 percent (313,000 of them illegitimate). In 1988, 11,000 babies were born to females under 15. In 1990, 32 percent of ninth grade females (14 and 15) had sexual intercourse.[8]

He goes on to make racial distinctions, so as to support the extension of the Norplant program largely to young Black women:

> A white suburban teenager who becomes pregnant is apt to get an abortion and go on to college. A black inner-city teen-ager's pregnancy is not apt to disrupt similar expectations . . . Furthermore, the pregnant teenager is apt to have a supportive matriarchy to rely on if she decides to have the baby resulting from the unwanted pregnancy.
>
> But the prospects for such babies are at best problematic. Better the unwanted pregnancy had not occurred. And Norplant may be the most feasible preventative. . . .

In the debates against the distribution of Norplant in the schools, the specter of Black community genocide is often evoked by the opponents of this program. But what is omitted is a discussion of the young women themselves as subjects who might engage in sexual activity for a whole range of reasons. What is further omitted is a discussion of the need for education to assist the young women to protect themselves from HIV and AIDS as well as from other sexually transmitted diseases. Dr. Jocelyn Elders's promotion of the use of condoms is entirely ignored in these debates.

I want to return to the historical analysis I initially proposed. In "The Struggle of Negro Women for Sex and Race Emancipation," an article for a 1925 issue of *Survey Graphic*, Elsie Johnson McDougall wrote:

[The Negro woman's] emotional and sex life is a reflex of her economic station. The women of the working class will react, emotionally and sexually, similarly to the working-class women of other races. . . . Superficial critics who have had contact only with the lower grades of Negro women, claim that they are more immoral than other groups of women. This I deny. This is the sort of criticism which predicates of one race, to its detriment, that which is common to all races. Sex irregularities are not a matter of race, but of socio-economic conditions.[9]

Her attempt to shift the burden of sexuality—which, in its very acknowledgment, is equated with morality—from race to class ironically resonates with Will's argument and with contemporary patterns of racialization in which the role of race itself is denied.

As we approach the close of the only century that people of African descent have spent on this soil which has not seen slavery, we need to find ways to connect with and at the same time be critical of the work of our foremothers. There is no contradiction here. The most powerful way to acknowledge and carry on in a tradition that will move us forward is simultaneously to affirm historical continuity and effect some conscious historical ruptures. Therefore, I want to pose a question: What about the ideological tradition of "defending our name" do we wish to affirm and preserve? And what about it do we wish to break with? I only want to make a few points, and leave the rest to you.

Number 1. We can no longer assume that there is a single monolithic force against which we position ourselves in order to defend our name—i.e., the White Establishment. We have to defend our names in those places we consider home as well. Moreover, the corporate and political establishments are becoming increasingly integrated, while the structures of domination have become even more consolidated. They are even talking about Colin Powell as our—"our"?! whose?!—first serious presidential candidate. Because Black people were so instrumental in the election of Clinton, we often find it difficult to explore the extent to which the erasure of race by the new democrats mirrors previous arguments against affirmative action and the invocation of reverse discrimination by neoconservatives. In a sense, neo-liberalism and neo-conservatism are moving toward a dangerous embrace.

Number 2. We can no longer ignore the ways in which we sometimes end up reproducing the very forms of domination which we like to attribute to something or somebody else. "She ain't Black. She don't even look Black." Or else, "She's too Black. Listen to how she talks. She sounds more like a preacher than a scholar." Or, "Her work isn't really about Black women. She's only interested in lesbians." Or, more generally, "She's not a real scholar." It used to be that any work done by a Black person about Black issues was not acknowledged as "real scholarship." Consider how long it has taken us to compel the academy to recognize the work of W. E. B. Du Bois—or Zora Neale Hurston.

Number 3. We have to rid ourselves of the habit of assuming that the masses of Black women are to be defined in accordance with their status as victims. However, there are those of us who have made it into the academy—or into the corporate world or into the political establishment—who consider ourselves the examples, the exemplary Black women. "Don't judge us on the basis of what the Black woman drug addict does." Yet, when it is advantageous, we like to represent ourselves as victims, as when Clarence Thomas invoked the idea that he was the victim of a "hi-tech lynching."

Number 4. We cannot afford to commit ourselves so fervently to defending our names that we end up poising ourselves against our Asian, Latina, Pacific Island and Native American sisters. As Jackie Alexander put it, why do we not feel the need to develop a measure of fluency in the available literature by and about women of color other than ourselves. We are not the exemplary women of color. Ethnic solipsism is something we have always attributed to whiteness, Eurocentrism. Do we want simply to push aside one system of hierarchies in order to institute another? Do we want to accept the notion that discourses about race are essentially about Black/White relations? As if to suggest that if you are not either, then you are dispensable?

I could continue with this list—but I think you get the drift. The point is, let's try to take critical thinking seriously—not just narrowly in relation to scholarly projects, because a lot of us can be very critical when we are doing our research—but in relation to the ideologies that inform our ideas and our lives. And critical thinking, while revered in the academy, is not the academy's exclusive property. We thank Patricia Hill Collins for her brilliant work on the production of Black feminist knowledges in multiple cultural sites.

Having said all of this, I want to discuss a number of issues which have political implications for our research strategies and our organizing strategies.

The last point I made had to do with our positionalities as women of color. As not the only women of color, I should say. When we think of ourselves as women of color, that means we are compelled to think about a range of issue and contradictions and differences. Audre Lorde's work continues to challenge us to think about difference and contradiction not as moments to be avoided or escaped—not as moments we should fear—but rather as generative and creative.

In this context, I want to raise the issue of immigration before this conference. Immigrant women cross many borders—not only territorial ones. They cross racial and cultural borders as well. As Black women, how do we forge ties of political solidarity with Latina immigrant women, Asian immigrant women, Haitian immigrant women?

On the West Coast, we cannot claim, unfortunately, that African Americans have visibly and in significant numbers challenged support for the crackdown on undocumented immigrants from Mexico and Central America. Perhaps we need to remind our communities that the presently acceptable scapegoating of immigrants was preceded by overtly racist calls for increased vigilance of the California border by white supremacists like Tom Meztger. Perhaps we also need to remind our communities that Black migrants from the South were historically rejected in very much the same way as undocumented Latinos are rejected today. I want to argue that defense of immigrant rights is a Black women's issue. We need to speak out loudly against the anti-immigrant backlash. Joblessness in the Black community—and unemployment has reached crisis proportions—is not a result of immigrant workers taking Black jobs. As the L.A. Black community organizer Joe Williams III has pointed out:

> Like the Negro migrant, the Latino migrant today has become the scapegoat for a faltering capitalist economy. Perhaps it is not surprising that blacks, who find themselves at the bottom of the economic downturn, have all too readily bought the message. . . . But African Americans—both our leaders and our community—should condemn rather than support the anti-immigrant backlash. We should not allow politicians to reinvent the lie that was used against our own people 30 years ago.[10]

Many of you know that I try to be an unreconstructed activist, especially when it comes to capitalism. Just because socialist states have fallen—with the exception of Cuba—for reasons that had much more to do with the lack of democracy than with socialism itself, this does not mean that socialism is an obsolete political project. And it certainly does not mean that solidarity with working-class people is an obsolete political project.

In the workshop in which I presented, I distributed postcards and flyers about a boycott of the Jessica McClintock Corporation spearheaded by Chinese immigrant women in Oakland. The workers were not paid for the manufacture of McClintock garments after their immediate employer—a contractor with McClintock—folded his business. None of the garment corporations take responsibility for what happens to the workers who produce their profitable clothing. I suggest that we send a message of support to Asian Immigrant Women Advocates (AIWA) indicating that the 2,010 women—and men, thank you very much my brothers—who gathered here to discuss issues around Black women in the academy vow not to patronize Jessica McClintock until she changes her policies regarding workers' rights.

Another issue I want to raise here is the seductive representation of crime as the nation's single most important social problem. The contemporary law and order discourse is legitimized by democrats and liberals as well as republicans and conservatives. (It reminds me of the late 1960s and 1970s, of Richard Nixon and Ronald Reagan.) Communities of color are increasingly criminalized. In Latino communities, especially on the West Coast, the INS is a major disciplinary force along with the police and prison guards, who are the pivotal repressive agents for Black people. And, unfortunately, calls for more police and more prisons not only emanate from white circles. As a matter of fact, the first Black woman senator in U.S. history has sponsored a deleterious anti-crime bill. While it may be important to support her in various contexts, this does not mean we cannot challenge her. Write Carol Moseley Braun and strongly urge her to rethink this issue.

In a sense, Braun's support of the Senate Anti-Crime Bill response echoes contemporary ideological developments within Black communities. In a way that cuts across class, educational level, and party affiliation, African Americans are increasingly calling for more police and more prisons. At the same time, ever greater numbers of Black people are trapped within the criminal justice system. One million people are in jails and prisons and—as a further impetus for the participants in this conference to take up this issue—women constitute the fastest-growing sector of the imprisoned population.

Drugs play an important role in the ideological merging of racialization and criminalization. Black people, according to a study done by the National Institute on Drug Abuse, constitute about twelve percent of those who use drugs regularly, which exactly mirrors the Black proportion of this country's population. However, Black people represent more than 36 percent of those arrested for drug violations—and I am fairly sure that this is an underestimation. How, then, do national sentencing policies serve to racialize putative criminal groups? More than 90 percent of defendants in crack cases are Black, and Black people are about 25 percent of defendants in cases involving powdered cocaine. But the Omnibus Anti-Drug Abuse Act of 1986 requires five years in prison for possession of more than five grams of crack. In order to receive the same sentence on charges of possessing powdered cocaine, one must be caught with one hundred times as much. Drug policies criminalize in a process of concealed racialization.

On a related note, we need to think about the ideological representations of criminals that we all work with and to some degree perpetuate. When criminality is evoked, who are the people we imagine? Whom do we fear? Whom do we imagine as dangerous?

In the realm of material reality, prison construction is very big business. And we wonder why there is so little money for education, for scholarships, for research. In his State of the State Address, California Governor Pete Wilson devoted 20 out of 35–40 minutes to crime. He evoked the Polly Klaas case, positioning Richard Allen Davis, presently charged with the abduction and brutal murder of the little girl, Polly Klaas, as the quintessential criminal. Wilson used this case to call for a draconic crackdown on criminals. So, where do women—or, more specifically, Black women—fit into this scheme? Wilson argued that the best way to prevent crime was "a safe home with a nurturing two-parent family." So, in the final analysis, who is represented as responsible for crime?

Wilson went on to boast about having opened five new prisons during his tenure, and he asked for $2 billion more to open another six prisons. Prison construction is big, big business.

Where, again, do Black women figure in here? I want to refer once more to the project of defending the name of Surgeon General Joycelyn Elders. In the name of the war against drugs, we have witnessed an insane proliferation of jails and prisons, more police and military campaigns. And the only alternatives are those managed by the correctional system—whether state controlled or privatized. Dr. Elders has had the courage to place the issue of decriminalization of drugs on the political agenda. And because she has raised the only reasoned solution to the infinite proliferation of police and penal institutions—which do far more to reproduce crime than to deter it—she has been harshly rebuked by the White House. Clinton has employed the same "distancing" strategy in relation to Joycelyn Elders as in relation to Lani Guinier and Johnetta Cole.

Allow me a brief riff on Elders's decriminalization remarks, because I want to suggest something that I hope will be widely discussed here and placed on research and organizational agendas. What about the issue of abolishing jails and prisons for a substantial section of the criminalized population? We would begin with the incarcerated women's population and then move toward men's jails and prisons. The vast majority of women are in jails and prisons for non-violent crimes, drugs, prostitution, welfare fraud, etc. I am suggesting that we organize an abolitionist movement, and I use the term "abolitionist" because of its historical resonance with our struggles against slavery. Because, as a matter of fact, when slavery was abolished, it was abolished for all, except imprisoned individuals. In many ways, those structures of domination constructed during the era of slavery have survived, hidden away, behind the walls. The vast majority of states do not even allow inmates to vote. As a matter of fact, the state which is the site of this conference—Massachusetts—is one of the few that do allow inmates to vote: Maine, Massachusetts and Vermont. Considering present and ex-convicts, at least four million people in this country who do not have the right to vote, a disproportionate number of whom are Black and Latino. These are some of the issues we will be confronting both in our research and in our organizing.

Quite a few women in various disciplines are doing work on incarcerated women. But think about what it would mean not to accept the inevitability of prisons in our society—think about the kind of scholarly work that could be accomplished once we let go that notion that prisons are the only way we can deal with "criminals." The vast majority of people who are called criminals are there because of a criminalization process. There are many people we might justifiably call "criminals" who will never be immured in prisons because they are not subjected to—and in fact are immune to—this criminalization process.

I cannot close without invoking the international dimension of our work. I would like to reiterate the demand we plan to send to the White House for support of our sisters in

Haiti and of their struggle to guarantee the return of President Aristide. We are also calling for a new U.S.-Caribbean policy, which we especially need in relation to Cuba.

In conclusion, I want to ask a question: How will we remember this gathering? I know that I will go back to the sunny mountains of Santa Cruz, California, quite revitalized and renewed, and with a whole host of new questions on my mind, with a new sense of what it means to be associated with a powerful community of Black women. But I agree with Hortense Spillers, who urged us to tap the vast potential of this emerging community by doing follow-up organizing. The discussion about the specifics of this organizing will immediately follow my presentation.

I also want to suggest that as many of us as possible try to attend the 1995 Women's Conference in Beijing. If we were powerful, my sisters—and many of you who are here were in Nairobi in 1985—if we were powerful in 1985 in Nairobi, we can be devastating in 1995 in Beijing. Thank you.

NOTES

1. This essay was delivered as the Closing Address on January 15, 1994, at the "Black Women in the Academy: Defending Our Name: 1894–1994" Conference at the Massachusetts Institute of Technology, Cambridge, Mass.

2. Elizabeth L. Ihle, ed. *Black Women in Higher Education: An Anthology of Essays, Studies and Documents* (New York and London: Garland Publishing, Inc., 1992), x.

3. bell hooks, *Talking Back: Thinking Feminist, Thinking Black* (Boston: South End Press, 1989), 50.

4. *The Present Status and Intellectual Progress of Colored Women* (Chicago: Rand McNally, 1893); quoted in Eleanor Flexner, *Century of Struggle: The Woman's Rights Movement in the United States* (New York: Atheneum, 1974), 187–88.

5. Ibid., note 12, 358.

6. Mary Church Terrell, "What Role Is the Educated Negro Woman to Play in the Uplifting of Her Race?"; quoted in Paula Giddings, *When and Where I Enter: The Impact of Black Women on Race and Sex in America* (New York: William Morrow, 1984), 98.

7. Ibid.

8. Will cites the source of these statistics as Douglas Besharov and Karen Gardiner in *The American Enterprise Journal.*

9. *Survey Graphic*, 6.6 (March 1925): 691; quoted in Gerda Lerner, ed., *Black Women in White America* (New York: Vintage, 1970).

10. *Racefile*, 1.5 (November 1993).

9

HOW DEEP, HOW WIDE?

Perspectives on the Making of *The Massachusetts 54th Colored Infantry*

Jacqueline Shearer

EDITOR'S NOTE

In 1863 the first Black Union regiment was formed to fight in the Civil War. This was four years after John Brown, the abolitionist, led a raid on Harper's Ferry in Virginia, and two years after Confederate soldiers fired on a federal garrison in Charleston harbor, South Carolina, thus signaling the beginning of the Civil War.

The story of this first Black regiment, the Massachusetts 54th Colored Infantry, is given a fictionalized treatment in the film Glory (1989). The film starred Matthew Broderick as Robert Gould Shaw, the twenty-six-year-old commander of the regiment. Denzel Washington was featured as the character Trip, and Morgan Freeman played the part of a grave-digger who eventually becomes a Sergeant Major. Washington later won an Academy Award in the category of Best Supporting Actor for his role in the film.

The Massachusetts 54th Colored Infantry (1991) is a television documentary on the same subject. The program was a segment of the PBS series. The American Experience, *hosted by the historian David McCullough. The program was written, produced, and directed by Jacqueline Shearer, a Black woman who has been making films since the early 1970s. Her film. A Minor Alteration (1977) is considered a classic example of the work of Black women filmmakers.*

According to Joseph Glatthaar in The Journal of American History, The Massachusetts 54th *tells a more accurate story than did the film* Glory, *and contains fewer errors about the Civil War than did Ken Burns's documentary series on the war.[1] Glatthaar states: "Jacqueline Shearer and her team deserve kudos for their excellent research. The filmmakers scoured archives from Washington, D.C., to Massachusetts and located numerous fresh and exciting collections of letters from Black soldiers."[2]*

The documentary is structured using Morgan Freeman as the voice-over narrator who maintains the continuity of the story. On-camera interviewees are descendants of the Black men who fought in the Massachusetts 54th regiment. The Black historians Byron Rushing and Barbara Fields are also seen talking on camera. Fields was a historian used by Ken Burns for his series on the Civil War, and as Shearer relates in her article, Burns barely scratched the surface of Fields's extensive knowledge of the subject.

Rather than visual reenactments of the actual people, the documentary featured pho-
tographs of the soldiers and the abolitionists of that period that were discovered during the
research. Shearer also uses excerpts from their letters, diaries, and speeches. The excerpts are
read as voice-over dramatizations by Hollywood actors including Larry Fishburne, who played
the father in Boyz 'N the Hood *(1991); Carl Lumbly, one of the police officers on the television*
series Cagney and Lacey; *and Blair Underwood of the television series* L.A. Law.

The Black Union soldiers were denied positions as commissioned officers, even though they
were promised as much by the government. They were also paid a fraction of the amount paid
to the white soldiers. One of the misconceptions about the Massachusetts 54th that Shearer
corrects in the documentary concerns the length of time between the initial refusal of the Black
soldiers to accept a lower pay and their success in getting a fair wage. In the film Glory, *the sol-*
diers are portrayed protesting for a short period of time and their requests are granted. In actu-
ality, the Black soldiers fought for eighteen months before the government was pressured into
paying them the same amount given to white soldiers.

Shearer's documentary rectifies a second misconception that Glory *asserts. During the time*
of the Civil War, it was widely believed that the Black soldiers who fought with the Union
troops were attempting to prove their valor and demonstrate that Black people were worthy of
being freed. As Fields states in the documentary: "I don't think we have much reason to assume
that they were unaware that they were men. What they were aware of was that there were
some people who required extraordinary demonstrations of them in order to establish what,
for themselves, they considered to be self-evident."

The Massachusetts 54th Colored Infantry tells the story of the 178,975 Black men who
fought in the Civil War. It also tells the story of a very active Black abolitionist movement in
Boston during the nineteenth century.

DIGGING DITCHES

I have worked with a Black woman film editor who has a particular gift for metaphor.
Sometimes when the going gets tough in the editing room, Lillian[3] will deflate a metaphysi-
cal musing of mine with a question in response that puts things in their proper perspective.
Hunching her shoulders down to the task at hand, she'll ask me, "How deep, how wide?"

Filmmaking is a lot like digging ditches. It entails hard physical labor. Once you're past
the planning stage, progress happens on the real side. Either you have the piece of film you
need or you don't. Either you have the three extra seconds you need or you don't. Sometimes you hit a rock that breaks your shovel and you have to find another one. Everyone is
working against the pressures of budget and time and the more time you take, the greater
the strain on the budget. When you're done, the results are observable and measurable.

I feel caught up in the doing of filmmaking most of the time, so I appreciate the different
perspectives offered by critical discourse on the field. I value the insights that I might not otherwise have, or hear. It's always enlightening to hear from an audience, and often audiences in
the Academy will make connections and comparisons that are particularly illuminating and
useful. I also believe that that discourse is strengthened if it includes more thought and opinion from producers. It is in that spirit that I offer this report from the trenches.

INTRODUCTION

The Massachusetts 54th Colored Infantry is a one-hour documentary that I wrote and produced for the PBS television series *The American Experience*. It is the story of the first official

Union regiment of Black soldiers in the Civil War. I researched, wrote, directed, and produced the show from April 1990 to March 1991. We shot location photography and interviews in 16mm color negative, and the photographs and engravings in 35mm, edited in film, and transferred everything to videotape in the final stages of post-production. Professional actors performed all the voice-over recording, among them Morgan Freeman as the narrator; Larry Fishburne as the voice of the activist writer Martin Delany; Carl Lumbly as the abolitionist Frederick Douglass; and Blair Underwood as Douglass's son, Lewis.

The 54th was broadcast nationwide for the first time in October 1991 and is repeated at the will of local public television stations. It is also shown in high school and college classrooms and in various community-based settings. It takes its place in the body of African-American social history on film. Many of the documentaries produced each year cover some part of this ground. Every February, the airwaves are awash with this genre: biographies of race heroes, oral histories, portraits of cultural giants. These offer a scrapbook, sometimes piecemeal history of forgotten places and events.

Even though or maybe because the content of *The 54th* is not about women, I think that a look at its genesis and production yields some insight into the kind of work that many African-American women in the field do, and some of the power and decision-making dynamics that we face, both with the material and with all the people along the production chain that leads from conception to completion.

TRUE GLORY

One day I was interrupted by a phone call while at work on post-production for the second series of *Eyes on the Prize*.[4] The call was from Llew Smith, an African-American producer who had worked on the first series of *Eyes on the Prize* and was now story editor for *The American Experience*, a PBS television series on the country's history that is based at WGBH-TV in Boston. He asked if I had an hour that afternoon and I heard urgency in his voice. I like Llew, I could spare the time, so I went without asking any questions.

His boss, Judy Crichton, the Executive Producer of *The American Experience*, had a proposition for me. It was a few months after the successful release of *Glory* (1989), the Hollywood film with Matthew Broderick as Captain Robert Gould Shaw and Denzel Washington and Morgan Freeman as two of the soldiers in his regiment. Denzel Washington would win an Academy Award as Best Supporting Actor for his role in the film.

Judy wanted to do a "True Glory," a documentary about the men of the 54th infantry that would not take Hollywood's license with the facts. She also imagined that the piece would convey what the Black community of Boston in the mid-nineteenth century was like. I explained that my true passion in nineteenth-century African-American history lay in the Reconstruction period, not the Civil War. But Judy was clear about what she wanted. It would be the 54th or not.

This idea was a recent brainstorm of hers; the schedule would have to be tight if this show were to catch up with the others in the season, which had all had a head start. Judy said she would commit most of the $480,000 the show would take, and promised to support my fund-raising efforts for the rest. Not quite enough money, not quite enough time—but still a serious offer worth consideration. In a perverse kind of way, the fact that the schedule and budget were both short was a professional challenge to me: Would I be able to pull this off? More time and more money would have been better, but this way I wouldn't be able to linger too long, I would have to be crisp and decisive. I'd have to get in and get out. I was tired from the long haul of *Eyes on the Prize* and this meant that I wouldn't get the rest I badly needed. But I couldn't justify turning down an opportunity that other women of color, or even white men, would have died for.

Television documentary production is a world inhabited by many women, a disproportionately large number when compared to our scarcity in the field at large. Judy came from the old days at CBS, had worked with big shots, won many awards and now had her own highly respected and respectably funded series. Her second-in-command was also a woman. Many of the staff in *The American Experience* offices are women, as are many of the staff members at WGBH and other public television stations across the country.

I discovered right away that it was much more difficult for me to have an older woman boss because a "dutiful daughter" routine kicked in. Often, on a real unconscious, knee-jerk level, I cared more about pleasing Judy than was professionally appropriate. It was much more difficult for me to be assertive. I found myself susceptible to being intimidated by my own need to be polite. In light of these interpersonal dynamics, Judy had a subtle sway over me that a white man never would have. I hadn't had a female authoritarian over me since I'd left my mother's home. Surprisingly, none of this ultimately got in the way; it all functioned as neurotic grease to my wheels. It's a good thing Judy wasn't Black, otherwise I would have been in a world of trouble.

COLLECTIVE SHAME

I loved the "True Glory" concept of telling this story from an African-American perspective. Like many of us, I have no patience for the wrongheadedness that insists on relaying African American history through a white protagonist in order to sell it to a general (read white majority) audience. But while I basically agreed with the principle of the project, my initial reaction to the story itself was negative and not overly enthusiastic. A big yawn.

Why would I want to do a war story? I had always hated war movies, hated war stories, and had never been able to get beyond the basic absurdity of warfare. I could never get into the spirit of "Into the valley of death rode the six hundred . . ." And I hated the Civil War more than most other wars. I'd been an American history major at Brandeis and my aversion to this historic moment—a milestone for my country and my people—seemed personally neurotic at best, intellectually shortsighted, at worst. Why did I hate the Civil War?

I flashed back on my secondary education, my formal introduction to American history at an all-girls, mostly all-white high school. I remembered classmates stealing significant looks at me and the few other Black students when our American history course came to slavery and the Civil War. I knew the reason for the looks. The implication was clear. Black folks had brought a lot of grief and suffering to the nation with our need to be free. There's statue in Park Square in Boston of a tall, proud Abraham Lincoln bestowing freedom, or at least a congenial pat on the head, to two kneeling African figures. In the early hours of the morning, Black women would organize an informal street market in that park for day workers. In the late hours of the night, others gathered there looking for prostitution jobs. Boston was a hard place to nurture Black pride, and the image of those passive, helpless slaves as my forebears marked that square as especially infertile ground.

I once read an interview with the playwright August Wilson that gave me some much-needed insight into my visceral disdain for the Civil War. Apparently this contempt for the Civil War and its legacy of slavery surfaced in rehearsals for *Joe Turner's Come and Gone*:

Black folks have this thing about slavery. We don't want to hear that word. There's this shame. In "Joe Turner's Come and Gone," I had a line that says, "Ever since slavery got over with there ain't been nothing but foolish-acting niggers." And the actor refused to say it. He said "Ever since the Civil War got over with . . ." Night after night. So I asked the director what's going on? He said, "He don't want to say it." I talked to [the actor], and he said he'd try to say it. [That night] he said, "Ever since the Civil War got over with ain't been nothing but foolish acting niggers." He don't mind saying nigger. But the word slavery' he couldn't bring himself to voice it.[5]

Even before reading Wilson's insights, in thinking about *The American Experience* offer and my reactions to it, I had come to some kind of intuitive understanding that a big part of my resistance to the story was rooted in shame. Once I acknowledged that, I had no recourse but to confront it head-on.

ON THE RECORD
The other big part of my resistance had to do with my fear of becoming part of a deadly strain of hagiography in Black historical media making. I'm not comfortable with the ideological premise that anything Blacks have done is worth celebrating because Blacks did it. I spent a good part of my young adulthood protesting the war in Vietnam, spent a year in everyday terror that my brother would get killed over there, so why would I want to make a film that glorifies militarism and holds up for honor men ignorant enough to volunteer to fight for a country that enslaved them?

I knew that Blacks had always fought in every national war and had always acquitted themselves honorably, to borrow a phrase from the VFW. But was that something to be proud of? Would I be able to critique the role of the military in this society, or challenge the prevalence of warfare in this world? Would my politics have to experience a hiatus while I produced a puff piece on the honor of being cannon fodder?

I never silenced those lurid fantasies, but I was able to quell them by reassuring myself that no matter what I found out in the research, there would have to be a way to frame the truth so it would be respectful to the ghosts whose stories I was exhuming, and at the same time present the information as it would be useful and instructive to today's youth. Young people have always been my primary audience. I never really focused on the general programming for national television broadcast so much as on the years of Black History Month screenings at community groups, churches, secondary schools, colleges, and universities. Too often, young people are assaulted with a lot of mindless sentimentality parading as history. I knew from my experience with *Eyes on the Prize* that this piece would become part of the historical record.

A QUESTION OF STYLE
It's crucial to understand that a reflective look back over the production process misrepresents the true nature of things. Imagine a bumper-car ride at 90 mph at night with headlights that aren't always working or racing against a clock that vaporizes your prize money with every tick. Against such odds, aesthetics become a casualty of the war between what is desired and what is possible.

I'm always stumped when asked questions about an African-American cinematic style or an African-American women's cinematic style. I mainly think this is a question for the audience to answer, not me. I just dig the ditch, I don't know about its deeper dimensions. But lately, I've come to think of my work as quilt-making—a little bit of this and a little bit of that, eclecticism to the hilt. And like making quilts, the tone is not of high art, but folk art. This is art with a high use value, a way of using up all those pieces of cloth that might otherwise go to waste, to keep bodies warm that might otherwise be cold and provide something easy on the eye to contemplate at the same time. A quilt can be beautiful to look at, but I think the height of aesthetic appreciation of its beauty comes when you're wrapped up in it, warm and secure.

People now pay top dollar for these pieces of handiwork and museums treasure them as artifacts of folk life, but these are impositions on the quilts, not an inherent part of their design or intention. It's easy to demean this kind of work, and to romanticize it. But in any event it is always possible to judge them, the stitching, the colors and patterns of cloth used, the design holding everything together. Those women who made these quilts were putting themselves on the line with every stitch.

That's how I feel about my own work. As a child, I was groomed to be an intellectual and spent a lot of my youth in ardent philosophical debate. But the subjectivity of these pursuits was frustrating to me in their slipperiness. I welcomed the tangibility of filmmaking and today I use it to take stands, to say something definitive. I validate myself by producing a record of what I felt and thought about a subject at one time in history. If it were just an aperçu tossed out in conversation, I could always change it with my next breath. But a film is a developed line of thought and dramatic intention that has a life beyond me and my control. I appreciate its permanence and have always enjoyed being kept on my toes that way.

THE DOING OF IT

As an eldest daughter, I have no problem telling other people what to do. As a self-taught filmmaker, however, I keep myself open to suggestions and carefully gauge criticisms from others. This is how I've learned to develop my skills and my craft. Judy once paid my mother a compliment for having raised me with enough self-assurance to take criticism nondefensively. On some level, I tend to be confident that I'll be able to take what I need, toss out what I don't, and still maintain control of the film's overall direction.

I don't know if it's particularly gender-based, but it is a variation on the traditional macho to be able to absorb 360 degrees of opinion without entertaining any urge to lash out. My role as producer includes the task of absorbing everyone's problems and coming up with solutions. People look to me to create a work environment where they feel respected and are therefore able to give their best to the production. Like most other modern forms of production, I approach filmmaking as a twentieth-century art form where I set a vision on the creative assembly line and everyone along the way adds something. Sometimes, they strengthen the project with elements I would not have chosen or could not have foreseen, sometimes there are elements that I must discard. But always, the result winds up being much more than my original vision—a whole that is greater than the sum of its parts. This model of leadership is not about big displays of ego or rage, intimidation or manipulation. Sometimes I think it's a maternal tendency, that I worry too much about people who are supposed to be helping me. But if there has to be an imbalance, I prefer it on the side of the maternal rather than the tyrannical.

BEGINNING POINTS

Film, even documentary, works on an emotional level. It is a waste of the medium, therefore, not to consider the emotional subtext of a piece even while trying to figure out the practical details of plot and narrative flow. My own emotional subtext for *The 54th* began with the need to exorcise my own shame. My first intuitive groping toward a handle on this difficult emotion was to turn it on its head. This would not be a story about slavery, but a story about an irrepressible drive for freedom.

Once during the early planning stages for *The 54th*, I was having breakfast with one of the student interns who was working on *Eyes on the Prize*. He happened to have done some research on nineteenth-century Black history in Boston and I was picking his brain. I had asked him how he thought Black people in Boston before the Civil War felt about being Black in Boston. His one-word answer struck a chord in me: "vulnerable." Later, further research would confirm the veracity of this statement, but its emotional truth was powerfully clear on a totally intuitive level for me.

I am from Boston and although my roots there don't go back as far as the nineteenth century, even in the 1950s and 1960s Blacks were a small community with a proud but curiously timid voice. I remembered the terrible days of court-ordered school desegregation in the 1970s—the pervasive atmosphere of fear, the amazement in other parts of the country that liberal Boston was having these hateful problems.[6] I had just done a story on busing for *Eyes on the Prize II*[7] and found it curious to step back from this century to explore the similarities and differences in race relations in the nineteenth and twentieth centuries.

I could easily place myself in the setting of this story; I had walked the same streets, been in the same buildings that the mid-nineteenth-century African community in Boston had once inhabited. I believe that regions have certain tones, and I could understand the tone of the Boston Black community then—they were a small minority in a city that was at the same time more liberal in its racial attitudes and policies than many other places in the North. Nonetheless, this was still a place that could be dangerous for Blacks, a place where it was sometimes easier to make alliances with the Brahmins than with Irish immigrants. Ironically, I found some striking similarities between this Old World Boston and the city where I grew up.

A Black woman filmmaker who had worked on Ken Burns's series on the Civil War (which had not yet been broadcast) strongly recommended Barbara Fields as an historian. Burns had totally underused her in his series but her interviews were brilliant. As I was reading through some of Fields's work, the sentence "Freedom is more than the absence of slavery" jumped out and hit me in the head. I had a purely visceral reaction and knew that this statement marked the beginning of my journey.

Why would Blacks who enjoyed freedom in what was arguably the most liberal space in the free North risk life and limb to fight for the freedom of other Blacks? Of course many of them had formerly been slaves and quite likely still had family in slavery. But even those who had been born free understood that the freedom of Blacks in Boston wasn't the same as the freedom whites enjoyed. Particularly after passage of the Fugitive Slave Act,[8] all that separated free Blacks from slavery in Boston was the word of a slave-catcher. No, they weren't slaves, but they weren't truly free either.

I remembered James Baldwin's claim that as long as one Negro in this country was not free, then he was not free. Fields's statement, "Freedom is more than the absence of slavery," lies at the core of the African-American experience since our presence in this country. We have long understood our existence within a context of community and connection. Slavery, its individual and communal assault on African Americans, forged this bond between us all. We recognize it in one another and awkwardly avoid eye contact whenever we are forced to confront this legacy of shame. This shame cripples us and we find ourselves unable to say words like "slavery" or "nigger," we become restless and defensive in conversations about race and equality, or we develop curious contempt for particular wars and historic eras.

A MAN'S STORY

It wasn't until a few weeks into the project that it suddenly hit me that this was a story about men. I had been thinking about the big picture—freedom, slavery, abolitionism, retrenchment, Blacks in Boston—and it took some time to understand that the primary agents of this particular story were men. Their community esteemed women as vitally important (even then, Black families needed two incomes to make it), but it was the men who were at the center of the action. Now this was an important revelation for me. By this time, whenever I venture into a new project, my sensibilities kick into autopilot and foreground how this particular issue pertains to women, beginning, of course, with me. As had often been the case, my first insight with this topic emerged from my own insecurities about it. My inclination to underscore a woman's perspective in all aspects of history could serve me in this project as well but from a different angle. I recognized that having a strong position on the need for African-American women's empowerment does not automatically do away with the horror we all feel at the statistics of homicide, shorter life span, incarceration, and joblessness that outline the crisis of Black men in America.

I thought about the severity of their predicament—the endangered species of the African-American male. In my mind, those students who were my primary audience became young men. And what did I have to say to them? I could present Black men as credible heroes, not larger-than-life people, rich or famous or accommodating, but ordinary men who had hard lives but still put themselves on the line for the sake of principle and integrity—men whose heroism rested in their unrelenting resistance and militancy.

I felt honored that I had the resources to make a piece of media that in its own way would be designed to give Black men a mirror of their past selves—a reflection of their own potential from which they could draw pride and inspiration. I also seized this project as an opportunity to make a statement about the personal relationships between Black men and Black women as a counterpoint to the posturing and quibbling that too often wins the headlines. I looked forward to positioning warfare in relation to the home front—a look into the lives of Black soldiers and their importance to the women and children they'd left behind in the name of freedom.

Men are always making films about women, but women don't often have the opportunity to return the gaze. Women have a lot to say about men to men. Usually in the pieces I produce or direct, more of the perspective would be from women's viewpoints rather than from men's, but this would not be the case in *The 54th*. Fields is the only woman historian, and most of the descendants of Civil War veterans we interviewed are men, not women. Two women who are shown on camera, Ruth Jones and Helen Givens, make a strong impact and I have been told countless times how these older women have reminded viewers of their great-aunts and grandmothers. The abolitionist Charlotte Forten's is the only woman's voice we hear from the past. This imbalance of perspective is significantly different from my usual practice, but they were all conscious decisions. In various programs, male voices and perspectives dominate, usually because no one has made the effort to find female participants. But in this instance, the prevalence of the male voices in *The 54th* is a deliberate and affirmative statement.

CONSTRUCTION WORKERS

Who gets hired to do what is always an important political consideration in the construction of a film. Some argue that it is harder for a Black woman to get hired on a project headed by another Black woman. Also of concern to many is the gender distribution along the hierarchy of positions. I personally don't believe in hiring women exclusively, but I do pay attention to make sure that there's at least parity in leadership positions.

As part of my effort to seek out Black male perspectives, I created two in key positions; director of photography and cowriter.[9] Most of the scholars we consulted on the project were men, and I sought male opinions throughout the production.[10] But as is often the case, the new girls' grapevine was, as always, very helpful. It led me to Barbara Fields, who I might not have found on my own, and also put me in contact with the amazing array of actors who performed the voice-overs, including Morgan Freeman, Larry Fishburne, Blair Underwood, and Carl Lumbly.

STORYTELLING

I learned a lot about storytelling from my work on *Eyes on the Prize*. Henry Hampton, the executive producer, drummed it into our heads that what we were about was telling stories. If we could not pitch an idea to him in the story form—with a premise, a hook, characters, and dramatic rise and fall of action, in a pithy paragraph, then we didn't stand a chance of convincing him that it was something that belonged in the series. Hampton's rigor was good discipline. From my years of peer-review screening panels, I have come to understand that most documentaries produced in this country are mediocre because at the conceptual stage, right at the beginning of things, too many producers think that the issue is so compelling that it will tell itself. It never does.

This is the reason for the arduous work of ditch-digging, churning through mountains of material for the gold, searching for the clarity of the story. Where is the point of view located? Who are the protagonists? What is the conflict? What are the forces of good and evil? When I started shaping the story of *The 54th* from the research that had been culled, I found that I had much too much material. Unfortunately, all of it was good. The brunt of the story was the changing face of war. But the production subtext, as always, would be the tension between the ideal and the possible in terms of time and money. With me at the helm, I steadily floundered between wanting to put out all this great information I had discovered and knowing that I should emotionally distance myself to allow the story to breathe.

Apart from the various dimensions of history and production that the project entailed, the piece itself was about the evolution of the Civil War. But even more specifically, this was a battle waged by white men to preserve a slave-holding nation. Ironically, the slaves had to wage their own war to earn the right to fight. Once Blacks were allowed to enter the war, their fight no longer consisted only of Union and Confederate troops. Rather, they faced the formidable challenges of discrimination in their own ranks, most dramatically seen in the eighteen-month war the entire Black nation waged for pay equity between Black and white soldiers. This was one of the most flagrant inaccuracies in *Glory*, whereby the pay dispute for Black soldiers was seemingly resolved without incident. And finally, in the brutal reality of the battles themselves, these men, and the numerous communities they represented, risked everything to strike a blow for freedom.

Once the structure for the project was set, it was clear that this program would be narrated. I assumed the task of wordsmith and gradually pieced together the narrative strands of text. I have always felt deeply resolved that authorship is a profoundly feminist issue and having something to say can be empowering on numerous levels. But the power in writing comes not so much from style as from clarity, and I have always preferred a low-key, "nothing but the facts" tone, short on adjectives and superfluous emotion. When text is as concise and clear as it should be, each word matters very much.

There were a lot of words to manage in *The 54th*. I always feel a strong need to contextualize information, which ultimately causes a lot of narrative problems. The dramatic impulse is to cut to the chase, to start the story as much in the action as possible. This impulse clashes with the desire to set up the context of the narrative for some grounding and perspective. Somewhere amidst all the bits of history, personal details, and drama, I knew I also had to leave space for the emotional arias that Lillian, as an editor, builds so well. Through music and poignant images, Lillian could string together the myriad strands of information while also giving viewers time to settle comfortably into the developing story.

Writing to picture generates a particular kind of rhythm as you weave words in between images, music, and other sounds. Given the imperative to keep things moving, and my always didactic desire to say as much as I can, if not more, there is no time to make any point more than once. This is a different quality than writing for readers, where you can build and layer with much more substance. My working assumption when writing for programming is that I am raising questions and sowing seeds of interest that will give teachers material to work with and students an incentive to read more about the subject.

HISTORY: HAGIOGRAPHY OR REDEMPTION

For most filmmakers, the process of working on a project can be a spiritual journey of sorts. In my case, I never know where I'm going at the beginning or how I'm going to get there. I bob back and forth through waves of sheer terror and existentialist faith. I steady myself through pure faith—a persistent belief that I will be able to make it all work out if I keep a proper respect for the material and the process.

I guess it makes sense that the clarity I get from divining the story and then from executing its production is redemptive, as I feel lifted out of my ignorance and move away from the despair of not knowing. But this particular journey with *The 54th* came with two particular challenges in addition to the usual perils of the cinematic form. First, here were no visuals, an obstacle that only strengthened my resolve to picture it. Second, given the volatile nature of the subject under consideration. I lived daily with the fear that when all was said and done, I could end up creating something that turned out to be politically wrong.

We found the visuals. When we started gathering the photographs of the men of the 54th and other Union regiments, we were all amazed by how familiar these men seemed to us—so similar to men we knew and saw on the streets. It charged us all with a certain emotional urgency to tell the story: the characters became more real for us, people we could care about.

To complement these images, we found wonderful period music.[11] The music research that we did and the original recording of popular nineteenth-century African-American songs had proved to be a powerful tool in setting the tone for the piece. In preparing the soundtrack, we were all reminded of how critical music and song have been throughout the course of African-American history.

Much to my own relief, I found that there was nothing for me to be ashamed of in the story of Blacks and their participation in the Civil War. Black soldiers hadn't been the unwitting dupes I had once imagined them to be. It was these men who were the bedrock of abolitionism, not well-intentioned, benevolent whites as history has claimed. Blacks had pushed the issue of their freedom onto the national agenda and they were willing to fight for it no matter whose side they had to stand on. This substantial injection of Black soldiers helped Union troops win the war. Ultimately, through their courage and faith, we had won our own freedom.

NOTES

1. Joseph T. Glatthaar, "Movie Review: *The Massachusetts 54th Colored Infantry,*" *The Journal of American History* 78:3 (December 1991): 1167.

2. Ibid.

3. Lillian Benson, A.C.E., is the editor for *The 54th.* She is the first Black woman selected for membership in American Cinema Editors, the international organization of film editors. Lillian was also nominated for an Emmy award as the editor of "The Promised Land" segment of *Eyes on the Prize II.*

4. I was the producer/director for two segments of *Eyes on the Prize* II: "The Promised Land" and "The Keys to the Kingdom."

5. "Beating Our Heads against Concrete," *Newsday*, April 23, 1992, 109.

6. My film *A Minor Altercation* (1977) is a dramatization of the effects of busing on the families, Black and white, in Boston.

7. "The Keys to the Kingdom."

8. The Fugitive Slave Act became law in 1850. The act allowed slave-owners, or their agents, to capture and return runaway slaves, even if they had escaped to the North.

9. The director of photography is Arthur Jafa, who was also the director of cinematography for Julie Dash's *Daughters of the Dust* (1991). *Daughters of the Dust* was awarded the prize for Best Cinematography at the 1991 Sundance Film Festival. The cowriter of *The 54th* was Leslie Lee.

10. The academic advisors, in addition to Barbara Fields, included James Horton, George Levesque, and Leon Litwack.

11. The music for *The Massachusetts 54th* was actual music played and sung in the nineteenth century. Josephine Wright, from the College of Wooster, Ohio, served as musical consultant for the program. Also advising us was Horace Boyer, a musicologist at the University of Massachusetts, Amherst. We then re-created the music for an authentic sound. For the documentary, the music was performed by a conglomerate of accomplished musicians and performers including the Howard University Choir (directed by J. Weldon Norris), The Year of the Jubilee Choir (directed by Horace Boyer), the McIntesh County Shouters, and John Ross.

10

MILITARY RITES AND WRONGS
African Americans in the U.S. Armed Forces

Phyllis R. Klotman

Men of color to arms! Now or never.
Better to die free than to live slave.
                    –Frederick Douglass

They look like men . . . They look like men . . .
They look like men of war.
                    –"The Enlisted Soldiers"

African Americans have attempted in a number of ways to achieve the rights of full citizenship, including the right to bear arms in the service of their country. Nonetheless, what has been recognized as patriotic duty for white citizens has been looked upon with circumspection if not outright hostility when Black Americans have volunteered for military service that would place lethal weapons in their hands. "In the early history of New England, Blacks could not serve in the militias as combatants . . . the black military hero Peter Salem had to beg his master's permission to serve during the American Revolution."[1] In every subsequent conflict Blacks have demonstrated their patriotism by enlisting (or attempting to enlist) in every branch of the armed services, regardless of the military's official policy of segregation and the ubiquitous presence of discrimination. They have performed exemplary service, often without official acknowledgment of their presence or their contributions. Although disappointed again and again, African Americans have assumed that their service abroad would lead to freedom and equality at home. This chapter looks at the works of African-American documentarians who have chosen to contest the history that has made African Americans in arms invisible Americans by providing a powerful record of their achievements.

DO YOU KNOW IT? JACQUELINE SHEARER

Although Massachusetts was a hotbed of abolitionist activity before the Civil War, contradictions in that New England state abound: it was, in 1641, the first American colony to recognize the legality of slavery as an institution. And yet, it was in Boston that the first northern Black regiment was raised: the Massachusetts 54th Colored Infantry.[2] In 1991 Jacqueline Shearer brought her considerable talents to the production of a documentary on the Massachusetts 54th. Neither white nor male, Shearer may have seemed an unlikely filmmaker for this topic. Yet she grew up in Columbia Point, Dorchester, Massachusetts (she was bused to school in South Boston because there was no school in Columbia Point),[3] graduated with a degree in history from Brandeis University, and already had an impressive record at Blackside in Boston, coproducing two segments of *Eyes on the Prize II*, when she was approached by *American Experience*. In an interview in 1992, she was candid about her reaction to the idea: "I said I don't want to do that, but I'd love to do something on Reconstruction. Well, that didn't fit their menu for whatever reason, but it makes me want to go back and find the Reconstruction story that I want to tell. It's such an incredible period!"[4] *American Experience* wasn't wrong; she was the right person to make *The Massachusetts 54th Colored Infantry*. The tragedy is that her untimely death from cancer in 1993 meant that we would never see her vision of Reconstruction, that important post–Civil War period in American history.

In February of 1865, after the fall of Charleston, South Carolina (to which the Massachusetts 54th contributed), Martin Delaney, the first Black major commissioned in the United States Army, importuned the Port Royal ex-slaves in Charleston with these words: "Do you know that if it was not for the Black man this war never would have been brought to a close with success to the union and the liberty of your race if it had not been for the Negro. I want you to understand that. Do you know it? Do you know it? Do you know it?"[5] They are the words selected by Shearer (and spoken by Laurence Fishburne as Delaney) to underscore the political as well as military accomplishments of the men of the 54th. Delaney was not content to make it known that Black soldiers, including his son and the sons of Frederick Douglass, had fought valiantly in the service of the Union; he wanted acknowledgment that they had fought to put an end to slavery forever. He wanted not just those listeners but the world to know that Black men were the agents of their delivery; as the narrator (Morgan Freeman) says, they "had fought for the right to fight and they had won; they had fought for freedom and they had won."

What makes *The Massachusetts 54th* so effective is its clearly articulated political perspective: Shearer doesn't simply make this documentary a tribute to the gallant men of the regiment; she places their fight on the field and off in the context of the larger political battle to change the focus of the war from an economic and political struggle between white men of the North and white men of the South to a war against slavery. It is no accident that the first on-camera speaker who is *not* a descendant of one of the soldiers is Byron Rushing, an African-American Massachusetts legislator who says, "Before emancipation this was a war between groups of white people, white people in the North and white people in the South." Throughout the film the motives of the political establishment, with Lincoln as its chief spokesman, and those of the abolitionists, passionately articulated by Frederick Douglass (the voice of Carl Lumbly) are contrasted. Shearer works with parallel sequences, dramatizing arguments for and against emancipation by focusing on the photographic images of the "combatants" and building to the climatic moment when news of the Emancipation Proclamation is finally received in Boston on January 1, 1863.

Unlike the feature film *Glory* (1989) that preceded it, Shearer's documentary does not make the battle of Fort Wagner the centerpiece of the film.[6] She uses the traditional tools of the documentarian—archival footage, photographs, cartoons, quotations from historic texts, letters, and diaries (some of which she discovered herself), and interviews with experts as well as with descendants of the men of the 54th—to tell both the personal and the political story of the fight for freedom and dignity. In fact, the most compelling moments come from the off-the-field battles of the men and their families—the struggle for economic equity: When the men enlisted they were offered "equal pay and equal treatment in every respect save one: Blacks would not be commissioned as officers" (voice-over narrator). The pay was stipulated as $13, plus a $3.50 clothes allowance; however, on June 30, 1863, their first payday, the Black soldiers were offered $10 and at the same time were required to pay $3 for their clothes. They refused the offer: "Too many of our comrades' bones lie bleaching near the walls of Fort Wagner to subtract even one cent from our hard earned pay. As men who have fought to feed and clothe and keep warm, we must say that $10 by the greatest government in the world is an unjust distinction to men who have only a black skin to merit it."

Technically their act constituted mutiny, but even their white officer, Colonel Robert Gould Shaw, supported their action. They and their families suffered because of their principled stand. A descendant of Steven Swayle, one of the soldiers, describes on-camera the desperate straits of Swayle's wife and children, who were sent to the poorhouse because they received no money from him. It wasn't until August of 1864, months after their courageous but costly attack on Fort Wagner, that the men drew their first *equitable* pay; their protest had resulted in Congressional action. But it was too late for those who had died at Fort Wagner.

The men's refusal to accept secondary status with regard to their pay is dramatized in one scene in *Glory*, but the linear narrative drives toward the bloody charge on the barricades at Fort Wagner;[7] the focus is on the development of Shaw (Matthew Broderick) as an officer and leader of (Black) men and the voice-overs are mainly from his letters.[8] *Glory* perpetuates the misconception that the Black volunteers, with rare exceptions, were unable to read or write.[9] Yet we know early on in *The Massachusetts 54th* that Delaney's son, Douglass's sons Charles and Lewis Hayden, and Sojourner Truth's grandson James Caldwell—all of whom were literate—fought with the regiment; and that dockworkers,[10] farmers, sailors, carpenters, masons, house servants, *free* men with all different levels of education volunteered from the small free Black community in Boston. James Gooding, who had been a sailor, wrote poems; the letters he wrote as a member of the 54th were published in a column in his hometown newspaper. Thomas Ampey was killed in the assault on Fort Wagner, but his brother Isom wrote eloquent letters home to Indiana, the state from which they had been recruited. After that battle, Lewis Hayden Douglass (voice of Blair Underwood) wrote to his fiancée: "This regiment has established its reputation as a fighting regiment. Not a man flinched though it was a trying time. How I got out of that fight alive I cannot tell, but I am here. My dear girl, I hope again to see you. I must bid you farewell should I be killed. Remember, if I die, I die in a good cause. I wish we had 100,000 colored troops. We would put an end to this war."

Ultimately 178,975 African Americans served in the Grand Army of the Republic. The 54th's casualties were nearly 50 percent—yet no Black regiment was invited to participate when the victorious army passed in "grand review" in Washington, D.C., at the end of the war in spite of the fact that African Americans accounted for 10 percent of the men then under arms.

MUSIC AS METAPHOR

Hark! Listen to the trumpeters,
They call for volunteers;
On Zion's bright and flow'ry mount,
Behold the officers.
They look like men.
They look like men.
They look like men of war.
All arm'd and dress'd in uniform,
They look like men of war.

–"The Enlisted Soldiers"

Shearer's selection of music in the *Massachusetts 54th Colored Infantry* is as artful as it was in the segments of *Eyes on the Prize II*, which she coproduced.[11] "We did the music research and got the pieces and had a music consultant from Wooster, Ohio, a woman who knew a lot about 19th century Black music, make selections for us. And then we got two choirs, one from Howard University and one from U Mass, Amherst, both led by choir directors who knew a lot about 19th century Black musical styles, to perform the pieces." The hymn "The Enlisted Soldiers" frames the film. Performed by the Howard University Choir under the direction of J. Weldon Norris (who arranged it),[12] "The Enlisted Soldiers" sets the film's solemn yet magisterial tone, as well as the theme; it repeats as the credits roll. These men whose images the camera sets to music are *volunteers* in a war, not to preserve a Union that endorsed slavery, but to deal a death blow to slavery itself. The emphasis throughout the film is on their commitment to that cause despite the risks they faced and the conditions they endured. For example, if captured, they were tortured or put to death, never offered in prisoner exchange: "Any Negro taken in federal uniform will be summarily put to death," read a Confederate Congress proclamation.

When the choir later sings "We are coming, Father Abraham," the message is clear that Lincoln needs them to win the war. As Douglass admonished: "This is no time to fight with one hand when both are needed. This is no time to fight only with your white hand and allow your Black hand to remain tied." *The Massachusetts 54th* shows how Black men in the South, slave and free, also joined the struggle. Some, like Robert Smalls, were ingenious. A slave with navigating experience, he, with nine others, stole *The Planter*, a rebel gunboat, out of Charleston harbor and turned it over to the Union forces. "I thought *The Planter* might be of some use to Uncle Abe," he said.

WOMEN AND THE FAMILY

The Massachusetts 54th demonstrates the effect of the war on the families of the soldiers, the hardships suffered by wives and children, but it also considers how they coped. The historian James Horton discusses the women's ability to survive by working even longer hours than they usually did and coming together as a community to support each other. Unlike *Glory*, Shearer's film also makes clear that abolitionists were not all white and male. Charlotte Forten was among the New England teachers who went south to teach the Port Royal slaves in what was known as the "Port Royal Experiment" It was an experiment to prove that emancipation would work, that ex-slaves, such as those 10,000 abandoned by their masters, could learn to become self-sufficient. Forten was a staunch, assertive aboli-tionist who "craved anti-slavery food continually," and the story of her activism and her commitment to the cause is part of the seldom-told history of African-American women. Instead of the bloody and violent scenes of the Fort Wagner debacle that end *Glory, The Massachusetts 54th* continues with the story of the regiment that, in spite of tremendous losses, went on to engage in other battles, including the conflict at Olustee, Florida, and the siege of Charleston. The 54th was one of the first regiments to enter the city after the "Citadel of the South" finally fell. The documentary ends with an image of the family, fo-cusing in close-up on the photograph of a soldier reunited with his wife and children, ac-companied by "When Johnny Comes Marching Home."

Shearer's documentary was well received. Commenting in the *St. Louis Post-Dispatch* on the tenuous financial future of public television, Eric Mink included *The Massachusetts 54th Colored Infantry* in his list of *quality* public television films of 1991. In recommending the documentary, Zan Stewart of the *Los Angeles Times* pointed out that "the highly infor-mative, well-detailed program goes far beyond the specific unit, which assembled in Boston in 1863. . . . It also describes, with remarkably clear archival photographs, etchings from the period, interviews and narration by actor Morgan Freeman, the racial climate of the United States prior to, and after, the regiment's inception."[13]

Shearer came to film through the study of history and because of a strong political mo-tivation: "When I think of my own background in documentary—Boston Newsreel, part of a national new left organization, in the 1960s and 1970s—it has very much to do with film as a political tool and with my being politically motivated because I didn't learn film in school. I liked the notion of . . . learning it by doing it."[14] In all her work she brought the issues of race, gender, and class powerfully to the screen.

CHALLENGING THE RECORD: WILLIAM MILES

"I have always looked for situations where there is an imbalance, something important missing from the historical record."[15]

William Miles, who also learned by doing, is one of the filmmakers, along with Madeline Anderson and William Greaves, whom Jacqueline Shearer credited with having a profound impact on her. His *Men of Bronze* (1977) became a model for documentaries that put African Americans back into military history. His struggle to represent them on screen from *their* perspective began in the sixties.

Men of Bronze opens and closes with a parade—a highly successful structuring device. The marchers are proud African-American soldiers, "sons and grandsons of the old New York Infantry, the Harlem Hellfighters who became famous in France as the 369th, the old Rattlesnake Regiment." (Miles himself served in the 369th for twenty-one years, beginning in 1948.) Reaction shots of the crowd reveal the warm reception of the spectators with whom the film audience identifies. But there is much more to the "men of bronze" than a parade up Fifth Avenue. The camera cuts to the flag, an icon of both patriotic and ironic dimensions, focusing in close-up on a Black father and his young son. This is their day.

Eventually the camera comes to rest on the face of Melville T. Miller, a veteran of the 369th Infantry Regiment who enlisted to fight in World War I when he was just sixteen years old. It will be his story, that of Frederick Williams, another African-American veteran, and Hamilton Fish, a white captain who, like Robert Gould Shaw of Massachusetts, was assigned to a "colored" regiment. They will tell the story of the 369th, which began as the 15th New York National Guard, the first Black American combat troops to fight on French soil. Archival footage and photographs fill in the factual details, tracing the discrimination against African Americans in the military back to the Spanish-American War. State military law made no provisions for Black men, even veterans of that conflict, to join the New York National Guard. Legislation was passed in 1913 to amend the law, but it was not until June 1916 that the governor finally appointed William Hayward, a white colonel in the National Guard and public services commissioner of New York City, to recruit a "colored" regiment.

Over these historic images is the authoritative and resonant voice of Adolph Caesar, the film's narrator,[16] but Miles never lets the narration overshadow the recollections of the three men, Williams, Miller, and Fish. It is their oral narrative that makes the film memorable. The two enlisted men, Williams and Miller, are completely different in personality: Williams, who was wounded and unable to return with the other men to homecoming fanfare, grimly recalls the injuries of racism. At home the men had to train ignominiously with broomsticks—they weren't allowed guns; at home and abroad they were met with hostility from their own countrymen and were confined to the role of stevedores (labor troops) until they were finally assigned to the Fourth French Army.

At age ninety-three, Williams is extremely articulate. His story tells of a civilian life that embodies the experiences of thousands of African Americans who sought a better life in the North during the early part of the century—the period known as the Great Migration. Miller, at seventy-five, is the "baby": he tells with great glee how he was able to enlist at sixteen because the examining doctor falsified papers that "pushed up my age to nineteen and a half."[17] Former congressman Hamilton Fish is eighty-seven at the time of the filming. He recounts the threats against the men by an Alabama regiment with guns and ammunition ("We thought the war would start in America"), recalling matter-of-factly how the situation was defused when the Alabamans learned that the men of the 15th New York had munitions. Fish told his battalion: " 'If attacked fight back, if fired upon, fire back.' We were able to persuade the Alabama regiment it wouldn't be worthwhile to attack." Miles's respect for these men who volunteered in a war "to save the world for democracy" is apparent. They served in a racially segregated army which assumed that they were not real fighting men.

Thwarted as was the Massachusetts 54th, the 369th was finally offered the opportunity to fight with the French. Colonel Hayward had gone to Paris to advocate for his men, who had been trained to fight, not to stevedore. The War Department refused to mix white and Black troops, but the British and the French, who had been fighting since 1914, had lost thousands of men and needed replacements in the front lines. When Hayward returned he asked the men: "Do you want to be stevedores or do you want to fight?" Melville Miller says that the men answered with one voice. By the time they reached the Argonne Forest, three more Black regiments were fighting with the French; 3,925 were killed and wounded. Recalling how the 369th marched victoriously into Alsace-Lorraine, with famous musician James Reese Europe leading "the best band in the U.S. Army," Miller exults: "That day we were proud to be Americans, proud to be Black and proud to be in the New York Infantry." They had spent 191 days on the front line: "We had not lost a foot of ground or a prisoner. Every man in our outfit was given the Croix de Guerre by the French Government."

The soundtrack features the original music of the 369th band as the regiment, led by Lieutenant Europe, parades up Fifth Avenue on their return to New York, and it lends great power to the footage. Miller says: "That was one day there wasn't the slightest bit of prejudice in New York City." The camera supports that, freezing on the frame of a white soldier shaking the hand of Henry Johnson, one of the regiment's heroes. However, the reluctance of Congress to appropriate funds to build a monument to those left behind belies that rosy picture, for it took ten years before the monument was finally erected in France, in 1937. Even then it avoided specific recognition of African Americans with the generic inscription "To the men who died here." Albert Veyrenc, former French commander, conveys (through a translator) the sentiments of the French soldiers with whom the 369th fought: "We felt a great deal of respect for these men who had come 10,000 kilometers to save our country, but who also risked staying behind in the trenches where we lost so many soldiers, so many men. All my gratitude to our Black friends of 1918." Miles's respect for these veterans is reflected in the way he listens to their story, especially his willingness to allow time for silences between the words of Frederick Williams. Miles explained his strategy: "I always said to myself, no one can tell your story, so each individual that I have on camera, I figured, well, their experience is the thing that I want people to hear. It's not mine. So I stay out of their way. It seems as if when you hear it from the person that really lived that life, it has more meaning than if you come up with a script."[18]

Men of Bronze allows these courageous men the dignity they were so often denied even as they fought for "America, the Beautiful," sung soulfully as a finale by Ray Charles. It's voiced over the images of marching men and the flags of their regiment and their country.

Men of Bronze was first seen at the New York Film Festival in 1977 and aired on national public television later that year. Kudos came from fellow documentarian William Greaves in a review written by him and Dharathula H. Millender for *Film News:* "It has verve, it has élan, it has *music*"; in *Film Library Quarterly* Juanita R. Howard called attention to its "esthetic and technical symmetry"; and *Variety* praised it for its balance and objectivity: "In short, an excellent film."[19] In 1978 it was awarded an American Film Festival Red Ribbon, a CINE Golden Eagle, and an American Association of Local History Award of Merit.

Miles never intended to spend his filmmaking career documenting the contributions of African Americans to the military. After devoting twelve years to the making of *Men of Bronze*, he wanted to move on to other important aspects of Black history and achievement; however, he was importuned by a number of Black veterans: "I started getting these phone calls from guys in the Navy, the Marine Corps, Air Force guys, saying 'hey, man, how come you don't do our story?' "[20] Hence, *The Different Drummer: Blacks in the Military*, a three-part series for television which was completed in 1983, produced by Miles Educational Film Productions, Inc., for WNET/Channel 13.

The Different Drummer has all of the drawbacks as well as the virtues of historical surveys. Each segment opens with the same visuals, music and on-screen "prologue" showing how inclusive the series will be:

From Bunker Hill
To the Battle of New Orleans
At Shiloh and Antietam
From the Marne River
To the Rhine River

> To the Yalu in Korea
> Through all the offensives of Vietnam
> The Black American
> Has been a presence
> In all of America's Wars
> Sometimes as the Stranger
> The Outsider
> The Different Drummer

Instead of concentrating in depth on one branch of the service, or one period, *The Different Drummer* organizes a vast amount of material under the following topics: Part I. "The Unknown Soldier," Part II. "The Troops: Black American Troops in Modern Combat," and Part III. "From Gold Bars to Silver Stars." The first, which might well have been called "The Invisible Soldier," surveys African-American participation in all of the country's armed struggles from colonial times to the present—from Bunker Hill to Vietnam (the Gulf War had not yet been engaged). The second, the only one with a female narrator, looks at the various services African-American men *and women* have performed in those conflicts in the Army, Navy, Air Force, Marines, and Merchant Marines, from the most menial to the most combative and dangerous. The third introduces seventy-six high-ranking Black officers, and discusses the little-known facts of their existence. What unites the series is the nagging persistence of racism, the devaluation of African Americans in spite of their demonstrable ability and patriotism, the resistance to their participation in every period and every service unless the country was in peril. For his work on this series, Miles received the 1984 CEBA Award for Excellence and the D. Parke Gibson Award in Journalism.

LIBERATORS: RECONSTRUCTING HISTORY

It was in the process of making *The Different Drummer* that Miles first heard about the 761st Tank Battalion that fought in World War II. No film record had ever been made of their experiences or even of their existence. Miles shot some footage of the men of the 761st who wanted their story told, and documented their return to Europe for a reunion with some of the families they had met during the war, but he couldn't incorporate all of that into *Drummer*. It was footage he had never used. Then, in 1985 he happened on a letter to the editor in the *New York Times* by a man who "wanted to set the record straight." Benjamin Bender was a Holocaust survivor; he had been imprisoned in Buchenwald, one of the infamous death camps, and he was contesting a claim that several hundred inmates, "resistance fighters," had overwhelmed the guards forty hours before the American Third Army arrived:

> I was liberated at the Nazi concentration camp of Buchenwald on April 11, 1945. For me it was a glorious day, full of sunshine, an instant awakening of life after long darkness. The recollections are still vivid—Black soldiers of the Third Army, tall and strong, crying like babies, carrying the emaciated bodies of the liberated prisoners.
>
> The survivors of Buchenwald owe their lives to the American people and not to the "resistance fighters." The short resistance uprising took place hours before the Americans entered Buchenwald. The German SS guards, sensing the approaching defeat, escaped en masse on

bikes, on horses or just running. Credit for liberation belongs totally and unequivocally to the American people, and not to cheap propaganda trying to erase the shameful memories.[21]

Miles persuaded a reluctant Bender to tell his experiences on camera. It was Bender's description of his liberation that brought Miles to see a connection between the survivor's story and that of the African Americans who had fought so effectively with Patton's Third Army in the Battle of the Bulge—men of the 761st Tank Battalion and the 183rd Engineers. Had they been left out of the official record as liberators, as they were so often as soldiers? Miles remembered that someone from the 761st had said his tank went into a concentration camp.[22] It was this perceived connection that finally moved Miles to bring the story of African Americans as both skillful fighters and compassionate human beings to the screen. He invited Nina Rosenblum, another documentary filmmaker, to coproduce and the concept of *Liberators: Fighting on Two Fronts in World War II* (1992) began to take shape.

Liberators is a profoundly affecting film. Miles relied primarily on oral history, a strategy he had used successfully in a number of films, but most effectively in *Men of Bronze*. His experience gathering information about the heroism of the 369th Infantry Regiment in World War I had taught him to be wary of official records, which are often flawed or incomplete. *Liberators* tells two stories: one of Holocaust survival and the other of bravery under fire; of horror and humanitarianism; of genocide and racism. Told primarily from the point of view of survivors and some of the men who helped to liberate them, the film opens in the present at the site of one of Germany's most infamous concentration camps.

Benjamin Bender is an arresting presence: although his experience is individuated by his narrative, it also speaks to all survivors. When he takes two soldiers of the 761st, Leonard "Smitty" Smith and E. G. McConnell, through the "iron gate of Hell," Buchenwald becomes every concentration camp; we all descend into that inferno and do not emerge until the end of the film—a celebration of thanksgiving. But the men of the 761st and the 183rd have their own story to tell of patriotism and prejudice, of racism made in America but acted out on two fronts. The narrative alternates between these two stories of twentieth-century sin and redemption. Although the voice-over narration (by Denzel Washington and Louis Gossett Jr.) fills in the necessary historical background to the visuals, it is the presence of the witnesses to the drama that gives *Liberators* its power.

Using a garish Nazi poster of a caricatured Black saxophonist—"savage" face, huge earring, exaggerated lips—outlandishly dressed and wearing an oversized boutonniere with a Star of David superimposed on it (captioned *Entartete Musik: Degenerate Music*), *Liberators* effectively links Hitler's most despised. It was the Jews, Hitler claimed, who brought Negroes into the Rhineland for the purpose of bastardizing the white race. The poster is a startling visual representation of racism and anti-Semitism. Leon Bass links Blacks and Jews in a dramatic description of his experiences with American racism and Nazi barbarism. A retired high school principal and a member of the 183rd Combat Engineers, Bass is a major on-screen speaker. His address to an audience at Temple Israel in New Rochelle, New York, stands in counterpoint to the on-screen recollections of the tankers, mainly Smith and McConnell, William McBurney, Preston McNeil, Johnny Stevens. Most memorable are the scenes showing the return of a group of 761st veterans, with their wives, to a village near Liège for a reunion with the family who billeted the men during the war; and the reunion in New York forty-seven years after liberation of thirty survivors and forty African-American soldiers who helped to liberate them. When *Liberators* was shown on *The American Experience*, on November 11, 1992 (Veterans Day), it captured the imagination of audiences (3.7 million) and reviewers. John J. O'Connor in the *New York Times* called it "a remarkably illuminating documentary"; Tony Scott wrote in the cryptic prose of *Variety*: "*This is a fine docu*";[23] the International Documentary Association honored it for "outstanding documentary achievement"; it received an Oscar nomination; and Kareem Abdul-Jabbar with Laurel Entertainment optioned the book, written by Lou Potter with William Miles and Nina Rosenblum (which Jesse Jackson was to recommend be read by every child in the public schools), for a feature film.

CONTROVERSY: THE UNMAKING OF *LIBERATORS*

It is unlikely that Bill Miles and coproducer Nina Rosenblum set out to create a cause célèbre, but unlike Miles's other excursions into unofficial or unrecorded history, *Liberators* immediately struck a responsive chord. Not only was a new chapter in military history being written on the screen, but it seemed an occasion to repair strained relationships between Blacks and Jews and to reaffirm bonds established during the civil rights era. On December 17, a month after the film's initial airing, a special screening took place at the Apollo Theater in Harlem, arranged by Percy Sutton, Bill Lynch from then-mayor David Dinkins's office, and a representative of Time Warner. It was attended by 1,200 luminaries; Congressman Charles Rangel and Peggy Tishman, former president of the Jewish Community Relations Council, shared the podium. Speakers included, among others, Mayor Dinkins, District Attorney Robert Morgenthau of Manhattan, Jesse Jackson and Elie Wiesel (on video). Betty Shabazz, the widow of Malcolm X, was introduced from the audience. The presentations and screening were followed by a special *Neighbor-to-Neighbor* program, moderated by Charlie Rose, which was broadcast on cable. The underlying theme of the evening was "healing"—reconciliation between Blacks and Jews whose relationship had been at a particularly low ebb since the Crown Heights debacle.[24] Many saw it as a political maneuver to bolster Dinkins's ill-fated reelection bid. The particular political and racial situation in New York may well have played a role in intensifying the attack that was to come—a sometimes virulent assault on the film and its makers. According to writer Lou Potter, politics "took the controversy up to the next level."[25]

The controversy over the film took hold even before it was aired on national television. The film's detractors charged that it was historically inaccurate and misleading, and that African Americans had not liberated concentration camps. Charges and countercharges began to appear in the media—primarily in New York—from various sources. Veterans groups especially expressed concern about the dangers of misattribution and Holocaust revisionism. Members of the Sixth Armored Division, as well as other veterans, began a letter-writing campaign to public television stations around the country, as well as to WNET/13 and WGBH/Boston, after the film was broadcast. Many threatened to stop their contributions to public television if *Liberators* was not withdrawn. They contended that if the history of the liberation of the concentration camps is altered in any way—even to include additional information—it will fuel revisionism, and those who maintain that there was no Holocaust will be well served.

In letters to me, a veteran of the Sixth Armored Division stated unequivocally that the "U.S. Sixth Armored Div., 9th Armored Infantry Bn. were the first and *only* troops in Buchenwald on April 11, 1945 and part of the 12th"; another veteran insisted that the 42nd

Infantry Division and the 45th Infantry Division "are the Liberating Troops of Dachau, 29 April 1945." Yet, in a list of liberating units certified by the U.S. Army's Center of Military History in Washington, D.C., other troops also appear. For example, the 80th Infantry Division was also credited with being at Buchenwald on April 12, 1945; that unit had official documents to prove its presence within forty-eight hours of the first soldier's arrival, thereby meeting the criteria set by the center. In addition to the 42nd and the 45th Infantry Divisions, the 20th Armored was also present at Dachau on April 29, 1945, and is therefore certified as a liberating unit.[26]

Gail Frey Borden, author of the novel *Seven Six One* (1991), wrote a fifteen-page letter to journalists at four national publications, including the *Washington Post* and the *New York Times*, and to Herbert Mitgang of the Authors Guild, on January 24, 1993, detailing his research on the 761st. Borden expressed concern that the reputation of the battalion would be sullied: "I worry that the facts of the 761st's outstanding record . . . might be questioned if *Liberators*' central thesis is permitted to become accepted fact, and is then shown to be based upon what appears to be, at best, a foundation of questionable scholarship and shaky assertions."

Borden bases part of his argument on information from Jon Bridgman's *The End of the Holocaust: The Liberation of the Camps*, which names the units that liberated Buchenwald and Dachau: "elements of the 4th Armored Division first reached Buchenwald, and the 2nd Battalion of the 222nd Infantry Regiment first entered Dachau." However, he adds that Douglas Kelling, in *The Liberation of the Nazi Concentration Camps 1945, Eyewitness Accounts of the Liberators*, identifies the 45th and 42nd Infantry Divisions as the ones that liberated Dachau. These two statements are not consistent. Nor do they correlate with the list of divisions certified by the Center of Military History mentioned above, which credits the 4th Armored Division as the liberating unit of Ohrdruf, a Buchenwald *subcamp*, not Buchenwald itself;[27] and identifies the 6th Armored Division and the 80th Infantry Division as the liberating units of Buchenwald. To reiterate, the 42nd and the 45th Infantry Divisions are listed as liberating units of Dachau, but so also is the 20th Armored. It is not surprising that discrepancies with regard to the official historical record appear—that is one of the points made in *Liberators*.

It is not clear when the trouble began, nor exactly when E. G. McConnell decided to change his story about Buchenwald. Christopher Ruddy, a conservative journalist,[28] charged that the film was an "unholy hoax"; his article appeared in the *New York Guardian*, *Long Island Newsday*, the *New Republic* and the *Jewish Forward*. Researcher Asa Gordon lists a plethora of other attacks on the film by citing their hostile headlines: "The Liberators: Trendy Politics, Dubious History," *New York Post*, February 3, 1993; "The Exaggerators," the *New Republic*, February 8, 1993; "Concocting History," *New York Post*, February 6, 1993; "WWII Documentary on Black GIs Pulled," *Washington Post*, February 13, 1993; "Doubts Mar PBS Film of Black Army Unit," *New York Times*, March 1, 1993.

Kenneth Stern, program specialist on anti-Semitism and extremism of the American Jewish Committee, decided to investigate the charges himself. He issued "*Liberators*: A Background Report," February 10, 1993, that sought "to explore the historical accuracy of the film. It should also be understood that there is no claim here that either the survivors or the veterans of the 761st have lied about their recollections, nor that their recollections are unreliable . . . the problems are more complex." In regard to the 183rd he writes that "those who challenge whether the 183rd was a 'liberating' unit miss the point. The unit was there when it counted, in the first few days, helping helpless souls—true liberators in the second, less technical but equally humane meaning of the term."

Stern spoke with producers Miles and Rosenblum, some of the veterans and survivors, and with an archivist at the U.S. Holocaust Memorial Museum, Dr. Robert Kesting. Although his report addresses the difficulty of reconciling "inconsistent memories," Stern is insistent that "the film has serious factual flaws that go well beyond what can be written off as 'artistic license' " and that "the film and book make claims that are, at the most generous, negligently sloppy."

PBS issued a response to questions raised about the film, addressing particular charges and affirming Thirteen/WNET, WGBH and the *American Experience*'s "absolute confidence in the veracity of this outstanding film." Then, on February 11, 1993, they temporarily withdrew the film and in March an "Independent Review Team" was formed. It was headed by documentary filmmaker Morton Silverstein, assisted by Diane Wilson, a researcher and producer, and Nancy Ramsey, a freelance reporter and writer. Their thirteen-page report, "An Examination of *Liberators: Fighting on Two Fronts in World War II*,"[30] is dated August 19, 1993; Thirteen/WNET released a five-page statement regarding the committee's findings on September 7th. The press release included a statement of WNET's intention regarding *Liberators*: "Thirteen/WNET has advised the filmmakers of the review team's findings and of Thirteen/WNET's decision not to present the documentary again on public television until the errors in the film are rectified." Thirteen/WNET requested that it be removed from the film's production credits for nonbroadcast distribution "because the documentary does not meet Thirteen's standards of accuracy."

The review had concluded that the film's account of the liberation of Dachau and Buchenwald was seriously flawed. It "could not substantiate the presence of the 761st Tank Battalion at Buchenwald on its day of liberation, April 11, 1945, nor during the 48 hour period . . . criteria set forth by the U.S. Army Center of Military History." It also found a number of "less egregious" errors. For example, veteran Paul Parks's unit is identified as the 183rd Engineer Combat Battalion, while he was actually in the 365th; the narrator in the Bastogne sequence incorrectly identifies the Bastogne-Marche highway as the Brussels-Bastogne highway; the juxtaposition of some still photographs and narration misidentifies Dachau, Buchenwald, and Gardelegen, a lesser-known concentration camp.[31] The review did find evidence of the 761st at Gunskirchen Lager and of the 183rd at Dachau, although not within 48 hours of the first unit's entrance.

Members of the review team consulted with eight "archival sources" and spoke with veterans and survivors of the three camps mentioned in the film: Buchenwald, Dachau, and Gunskirchen Lager. Bender says that he spoke with Silverstein by telephone for nine hours, as well as with Ramsey. Yet he is mentioned in only two sentences in the report. On page 7: "Survivor Benjamin Bender recalls seeing Black soldiers at his liberation"; and on page 8: "It is possible, then, that Bender and other Buchenwald survivors who remember seeing Black soldiers on the first day of liberation do so because their day of liberation may have been after the 11th." Yet Bender is adamant that he was released from the hospital on April 11th after 11 A.M., and he saw Black soldiers enter the camp that afternoon. As additional proof he cites the photograph shot on April 11th by William Scott and recorded in Scott's diary that day.

A twenty-two-year-old African-American reconnaissance sergeant, photographer, and part-time historian in S-2 (intelligence), Scott was with the 183rd Combat Engineers. He is interviewed in *Liberators* and three of his photographs are used in the film. One is a hideous record of Nazi atrocities; it shows five Black soldiers, one of whom was Scott's friend Leon Bass, two white soldiers, and two inmates outside of an incinerator/crematorium building at Buchenwald. Bender explained: "When this picture was taken, I wasn't present, but on the day of the 12th in the morning, I was exploring the crematorium. Buchenwald was clean. So the Black forces couldn't have come on the 12th, 13th or 14th and taken the pictures. They were present on April 11, 1945."[32]

Scott, who died in March 1992, before *Liberators* was aired, had been speaking to student, synagogue, and church groups about his concentration camp experience long before he appeared in *Liberators*. In fact, he gathered together a number of the pictures he took at Buchenwald and published them in 1989 in a pamphlet entitled "World War II Veteran Remembers the Horror of the Holocaust." The cover has a telling sentence: "I remember the day—clear and sunny—riding in a convoy into Eisenach, Germany, *11 April 1945* [my emphasis], as World War II was ending; and, a Third Army courier delivering a message to us to continue on to a concentration camp (Buchenwald), 10 or more miles further east, near Weimar." In 1981 Scott and his friend Bass participated in a gathering of liberators and survivors at the State Department in Washington. In 1991, President George Bush appointed Scott to the United States Holocaust Memorial Council.[33]

Miles and Rosenblum responded on March 5, 1993, to Kenneth Stern's report and on September 7th to the Silverstein report and the findings of WNET:

> We do not feel that WNET has conducted an independent assessment of the program. We stand by the testimony of the liberators and survivors who have given substantive oral testimony. We support the report's conclusion that African-American soldiers played a critical role in the liberation. *Liberators: Fighting on Two Fronts in World War II* has been widely recognized nationally and internationally for its contribution to the subject and we continue to object to PBS censorship. We feel it is dangerous to limit historical inquiry, especially in light of recent revelations concerning the role of black troops in the military. A continuation of this dialogue is counter productive and only serves to denigrate the courageous concentration camp survivors and their heroic liberators.[34]

Writers on the *Liberators* project, Daniel Allentuck and Lou Potter, wrote letters defending the film, the witnesses, and the integrity of their work.[35]

THE 761ST TANK BATTALION

When I was a child in Alamo School in Galveston, Texas, Santa Anna was the villain and Sam Houston the hero. Texas was born in 1836 and "The Eyes of Texas" were always upon us. Wars and soldiers were a part of our study of history in our segregated junior and senior high schools. Heroes were white, and Black people were primarily contented slaves or invisible. Documentary films were not a part of school instruction, but *The March of Time*, along with radio, informed us that the country was preparing for war. Young men came to Texas from all over the country for basic training in segregated units. If Carlton Moss's *The Negro Soldier* (1944) was screened in Galveston, it would probably have been at one of the segregated theaters. As war entered our lives, we learned about great white military leaders: Eisenhower, Bradley, MacArthur, Patton. It is General Patton who, ironically, came to stand for the hopes and aspirations of those invisible soldiers whose stories never made it to the textbooks, the airwaves, or the screen. To fully understand how this segregated battalion, the first of its kind in the U.S. military, became the subject of a feature-length documentary, a bit of history is in order. We need to appreciate its relationship to the Army in general, and Patton in particular, and its depiction by witnesses to the liberation of the camps.

The first Black tank battalion in the United States Army was inaugurated in 1942. Its soldiers trained at Camp Claiborne in Louisiana and Camp Hood in Texas where they were treated to southern-style racism. The battalion was finally sent overseas in 1944 and was assigned to Patton's Third Army. Every account of their first encounter with the enemy in Morville-les-Vic, France, includes a speech by General Patton (November 2, 1944), who was in the habit of giving his men a pep talk before they went into battle. Trezzvant W. Anderson, African-American combat journalist,[36] recorded Patton's words to the 761st in his history of the battalion, which was published in Germany in 1945: "Men, you're the first Negro tankers to ever fight in the American Army. I would never have asked for you if you weren't good. I have nothing but the best in my Army. I don't care what color you are, as long as you go up there and kill those Kraut sonsabitches. Everyone has their eyes on you and is expecting great things from you. Most of all, your race is looking forward to you. Don't let them down, and, damn you, don't let me down!"[37] In his autobiography, *War As I Knew It*, Patton confirmed the talk (dating it October 31st), but gave no account of what he'd said. However, he did give his assessment of the men: "On the thirty-first, I inspected and made a talk to the 761st Tank Battalion. A good many of the lieutenants and some of the captains had been my sergeants in the 9th and 10th Cavalry. Individually they were good soldiers, but I expressed my belief at that time, and have never found the necessity of changing it, that a colored soldier cannot think fast enough to fight in armor."[38] It was not the only derogatory comment Patton made about Black troops, in spite of the fact that these men distinguished themselves, and the Armed Services, in the Third Army under his command.[39] Nevertheless, he remained an icon to the men of the 761st—the military man par excellence, "The Old Man" for whom they would risk their lives.

When Captain John Long,[40] commander, "B" Company of the 761st, was interviewed for the book *The Invisible Soldier: The Experience of the Black Soldier in World War II*, he reiterated the Patton speech but added two choice Patton sentences: "If you want me you can always find me in the lead tank. They say it's patriotic to die for your country, well let's see how many patriots we can make out of those German motherfuckers."[41] The men of the 761st did make a number of German "patriots," but were rarely given the recognition they had reason to expect for their efforts, perhaps because the 761st, as Long describes their function, "was a detached and self-sustained unit up for grabs by anyone who needed it in the 3rd Army." They spearheaded a number of Patton's advances into enemy territory. Long counters Ulysses Lee's version of the battle of Morville written for the government document *The Employment of Negro Troops*,[42] which credits a number of white officers with leading the battalion to victory:

> The victory of Morville-les-Vic belongs to the enlisted men and the junior officers of the 761st; they just happen to be Black. The two white senior officers of our unit [Lee] credits with Morville-les-Vic didn't have a goddamn thing to do with our victory. . . . Lieutenant Colonel Bates, our commanding officer, . . . was shot in the ass the night before and had to be evacuated. They never found out whether or not he was accidentally shot by an American soldier or hit by sniper fire. The next man in command, Major Wingo, the morning of the attack, turned

his tank around and went hell-bent in the opposite direction. He just plain chickened and that s.o.b. was evacuated for combat fatigue. Hell, we hadn't even been in battle yet.

WITNESSES[43]

As in many oral history reminiscences, the central moments of such experiences tend to be ineradicable memories, although details at the edges may grow fuzzy. this only emphasizes the importance of multiple witnesses.
                                            –Erik Barnouw[44]

Captain Long's attitude toward the Germans changed after he and his men *liberated* (his word) their first concentration camp:

Have you ever seen a stack of bones with the skin stretched over it? At the camp you could not tell the young from the old. When we busted the gate the inmates just staggered out with no purpose or direction until they saw a dead horse recently struck by a shell. . . . They tottered over to that dead carcass and threw themselves upon it, eating raw flesh. We cut ourselves back to one-third rations and left all of the food we could at the camp. There was just one thing wrong, we later learned our food killed many of them.

From this incident on Jerry was no longer an impersonal foe. The Germans were monsters! I have never found any way to find an excuse for them or any man who would do to people what I saw when we opened the gate to that camp and two others. We had just mopped them up before but we stomped the shit out of them after the camps.[45]

This interview, published in 1975, may be the first *written* record of the 761st as a liberating unit. Although Long does not say which camps he and his men liberated, he is clear about the experience. And yet there is apparently no validation in the morning reports (the "daily history" of a unit) or after-action reports to indicate that his unit took part in the liberation of Nazi victims.

Leonard "Smitty" Smith and E. G. McConnell, both of Company C, have as prominent a role in *Liberators* as Melville Miller and Frederick Williams have in *Men of Bronze*. Childhood friends who met again in the Army, they are witnesses in the film to Benjamin Bender's poignant recollections of Nazi brutality at Buchenwald, as well as to the exploits of the 761st, but they have become distinctly different witnesses in the controversy.

Smith has never wavered in his recollections of going into a concentration camp (the captain of the unit to which his tank was attached told the men it was Dachau). McConnell, on the other hand, said—after the film's release—that he was never at Buchenwald until he went with Miles and Rosenblum to shoot the film. However, McConnell met with survivors and other veterans in a reunion in midtown Manhattan in October 1991. George James reported in the *New York Times* a meeting with McConnell and Bender in that same month where the two men "remembered together": "E. G. McConnell, a soldier in the all-Black 761st Tank Battalion, found a sudden insight in the misery of Buchenwald. Like many of his Black colleagues, the young soldier from Jamaica, Queens, had gone into combat fired by the anger over racial indignities suffered in his own country and at the hands of his white comrades in arms. Looking at the end result of hatred, at its barely living survivors, he saw himself." McConnell was also quoted in the *Palm Beach Post*, February 18, 1992: " 'My country tis of thee, sweet land of bigotry' was the common feeling among

Black soldiers . . . [but] the soldiers knew they were a part of history when they marched into the concentration camps and broke into tears at the sight of emaciated prisoners." In addition, he made presentations at such places as the Jewish Museum, and was interviewed on a number of occasions. At a Holocaust memorial service at East Northport Jewish Center, he told the interviewer Don Crawford: "I was really astounded that a man could do this to another man. You couldn't tell the young from the old, the bodies lined up head to foot. . . . They were string beans, just wasted."[46]

McConnell attributes his belated repudiation of the film in part to the lack of supportive information in the morning and after-action reports, as do the organizations which petitioned successfully to have their divisions certified as liberating units.[47] Smith points to the fact that not everything went into those reports and gives the example of "rape call"—the ignominious order that allowed German women to pick from African-American troops but not from white troops, anyone they thought had violated them.

Corporal Horace Evans of "B" Company referred to a comparable experience: "I was called out of my tent at least a dozen times with other Black soldiers to stand in line to let some German girl look us over to see if we had raped her the previous night." Captain Gates, Black commander of "A" Company, was outraged that surveys were made in every area where there were Negro soldiers. When he was ordered to have his men stand in formation for rape call, he said, "I don't have my men fall out for anything like that."[48]

Trezzvant Anderson is clear on the issue of "complete and accurate reporting":

[The 761st Tank Battalion] received scant attention in histories of some of the infantry divisions with which it worked. . . . The 761st was mentioned *twice* by name, in the history of the 26th Division. And in the 103rd Division's "REPORT AFTER ACTION," published this year, our M-4 General Sherman tanks, were frequently pictured and referred to as "614th Tank Destroyers." This is the story of the 761st *Tank Battalion*, not a "towed" tank destroyer battalion, but a *Tank Battalion*, which fought and fought, and earned its place in the sun, by the sheer weight of its relentless drive, push and might, and by the sweat of the brows of dusky Negro soldiers, who . . . gave their blood and their lives on the field of battle, ASKING NOTHING, but HOPING that their sacrifices would not go unheeded and un-noticed, . . . and that their record would go down in history, as a contribution to the winning of World War II . . . .[49]

Benjamin Bender was the first survivor to point out, in the letter to the *New York Times* which first drew Miles's attention, that at least some of the claims of self-styled "liberators" were specious. He has never wavered from his original statements about seeing Black soldiers at Buchenwald on April 11, 1945. He painfully relived his concentration camp experience before the camera, returning to Germany in spite of misgivings, after being importuned by Miles and Rosenblum. After the attacks on *Liberators*, he wrote letters to the newspapers, to the War Department and to President Clinton, in addition to speaking for hours to the Thirteen/WNET review team.

Although the Buchenwald survivor Alex Gross did not have a prominent role in *Liberators*, he did appear in the reunion scene. He and William Scott had met in 1979 when they both responded to an invitation from Fred W. Crawford at Emory University. Crawford was attempting to locate veterans who had witnessed the Holocaust. In 1980 WAGA-TV taped and aired a session with Gross, Scott, and Crawford. Attacks on the credibility of the Holocaust prompted the Georgia Holocaust Commission to embark on an aggressive educational program in that state. Scott's pamphlet includes a picture of the two men (and the director of community relations, Atlanta Jewish Federation) at the 1981 Holocaust Memorial Services in Atlanta. Gross said that "he and one of his brothers were at Buchenwald when Scott's unit arrived and that he may be in the photo in this pamphlet of those leaving the camp." Their relationship existed long before *Liberators* and continued until Scott's death on March 7, 1992.[50] On April 11, 1995, Gross joined Leon Bass and Asa Gordon, William Scott's cousin, for a presentation at the United States Holocaust Memorial Museum in Washington, D.C.

In a report of his trip to Buchenwald in 1989, Henry Kamm wrote in the *New York Times* that East Germany made a national memorial of the camp, but the memorial doesn't "commemorate the victims for what they were, and it denies to the United States recognition for having liberated Buchenwald." In a legend created after the fact, he says, "Buchenwald was 'selbstbefreit' or 'self-liberated.' " In a telephone interview with Kamm, Elie Wiesel, the Nobel Prize–winning author, who was liberated at Buchenwald, gave a different account: "The most moving moment of my life was the day the Americans arrived, a few hours after the SS had fled, It was the morning of April 11. . . . I will always remember with love a big Black soldier. He was crying like a child—all the pain in the world and all the rage. Everyone who was there that day will forever feel a sentiment of gratitude to the American soldiers who liberated us."[51]

Gunther Jacobs, a survivor who spent three and a half years of his life in Buchenwald and other Nazi concentration camps, told Jeff Bradley, *Denver Post* critic-at-large: "The first Black people I ever saw in my life were the Black soldiers who liberated us on April 11, 1945." The article reports that Jacobs had never been able to speak about what happened at Buchenwald, but that he wanted to speak out now "on behalf of his Black liberators" whom he had never thanked. Jacobs, seventeen years old at the time, remembers the Black soldiers "coming to the camp with half-tracks and armored personnel carriers. About a half-dozen vehicles. These Black GIs came out and gazed at us—we were very malnourished and dehydrated and I was hardly able to walk."[52] It is not clear whether Jacobs was responding to the attacks on *Liberators*. In any case, there seems to be no reason why he would fabricate such a story; he had not appeared in the film and had no apparent reason to defend it.

An international lawyer and native of Bialystok, Poland, Samuel Pisar survived Nazi concentration camps for four years. In 1979, he published his memoirs, *Of Blood and Hope*, which begin with an encomium to Joe Louis: "We were ecstatic my classmates and I, when we heard in 1938 that the Black boxer Joe Louis had knocked out the Nazi Max Schmeling for the heavyweight championship of the world. So much for the 'Master Race.' " In the first three chapters he describes being thrown into the chaos and horror of the Nazi takeover of Bialystok, the murder of his father, mother and sister—the collapse of his world. Surviving for four horrific years (1941–1945) in labor and concentration camps in Poland and Germany, he was finally rescued in the vicinity of Dachau where the fleeing Germans had marched him and thousands of others to certain death. In the confusion of the German retreat before advancing Allied soldiers, Pisar and several of his friends escaped, but suddenly encountered a huge tank which they assumed to be German until Samuel realized that instead of a swastika the tank bore a five-pointed white star:

> With a wild roar . . . I leaped to the ground, and ran toward the tank. The German machine guns opened up again. The tank fired twice. Then all was quiet. I was still running. I was in

front of the tank, waving my arms. The hatch opened. A big Black man climbed out, swearing unintelligibly at me. Recalling the only English I knew, those words my mother had sighed while dreaming of our deliverance, I fell at the Black man's feet, threw my arms around his legs and yelled at the top of my lungs: 'God Bless America!' With an unmistakable gesture, the American motioned me to get up and lifted me in through the hatch. In a few minutes, all of us were free.[53]

Pisar appeared on the *Dick Cavett Show* shortly after the publication of his memoirs and touched the studio audience with his rendition of the story of his rescue by a "colored" American soldier who emerged from a tank that was still in the thick of battle *near Dachau.*

On May 7, 1995, Pisar briefly recounted the same story of his experiences in the death camps and his dramatic rescue by a Black American tanker in the *Washington Post,* "Escape from Dachau: My Own Private V-E Day." The article was taken from the keynote address he gave the next day at the U.S. Holocaust Memorial Museum in Washington.

More than a decade before the production of *Liberators,* as well as three and a half years after its release, Pisar described his liberation in the same way. Did he *invent* his story long before several 761st soldiers claimed that they were there? If it was not physically possible for 761st tanks to be deployed in the vicinity of Dachau, as several officers of the battalion have attested, who was that African-American tanker? Even though Pisar was young and had no personal contact with Americans, he knew who Joe Louis was and would hardly have made a mistake about race. What's more he claimed to have recognized the soldier, Bill Ellington, and personally thanked Ellington's widow at the Olympic Games in Atlanta. Yet his daughter, after attending a screening of *Liberators* at Harvard University, attacked the veracity of the film in the *Forward* (February 12, 1993), claiming that the effect was to give credibility to Holocaust revisionists: "The fear among many here is that inaccuracy, especially regarding a topic so sensitive as the Holocaust, might fuel revisionism and add support to those who claim the Holocaust never happened."

Holocaust deniers will feed on anything. But if the rules of recognition—only divisions can be designated as "liberating units"—prevail, then segregated battalions, regiments, companies, individuals are swallowed up and denied credit for one of the most humane acts performed by soldiers during World War II. Edward J. Drea's article, cited in note 28, includes an important point about smaller units: "Given the great number of U.S. Army units involved in the advance across Germany and the great number of camps, many were freed by small units subordinate to a division. . . . Thus an infantry regiment of division X might find itself *temporarily attached* [my emphasis] to an armored battalion of division Y as they pushed across the Third Reich." For that reason, they decided to credit only the "parent division."[54] Drea's statement about temporarily attached units reinforces the comments of a number of the men in both the 761st battalion and the 183rd regiment. Corporal Evans, "B" Company, 761st, was particularly bitter: "Overseas we were known as a bastard outfit. It meant we didn't belong to any group permanently; we fought with any outfit that needed us. . . . It was definitely a ploy to keep from committing us together as a battalion as much as possible; whole units get credit while a few isolated tanks, no matter whether they saved the day or not, are overlooked."[55]

The culture of segregation in the armed forces was responsible for the retention of long-held attitudes about the ability of African Americans to measure up to the challenges of war. If their often menial assignments were judged to be fit for second-class citizen/soldiers, why would their exemplary performance of those or much more meaningful tasks be worthy of recognition? Hollywood's *Patton* included one role for the fine African-American actor James Edwards—Patton's valet. It should be clear that the level of criticism and outrage occasioned by *Liberators* was due to complex historical and political factors—to attitudes and relationships—reaching far beyond the film itself. Regardless of its strengths and weaknesses *Liberators* provides a multiconscious view of World War II; it puts Black soldiers back into the field of battle and into the concentration camps that some of them helped to liberate.

Responding to *Liberators*, the film scholar/critic Annette Insdorf wrote in the *Washington Post*: "In 1993, we don't seem to be in danger of forgetting the Holocaust. But we are in danger of forgetting that all films—even documentaries—have a point of view, and that truth will always be partial." Insdorf added that *Liberators* is "certainly not the first—and probably won't be the last—Holocaust film to provoke heated discussion about the sanctity of the subject and the limitations not only of individual memory but of official records."[56]

If film theory offers useful insight into the way documentary presents a structured point of view, then critical race theory may provide a larger context for understanding the way that differing views of reality have contributed to the *Liberators* controversy. Critical race theory has emerged out of the desire of minority scholars in legal studies to construct an alternative way of explaining racial issues. In an attempt to attack racial subordination, some have developed a multiconsciousness analysis of phenomena that rejects efforts to harmonize diverse understandings. In fact, some scholars question whether objective reality matters when institutional structures, including the justice system, are designed to reflect the values of the dominant culture, ignoring or suppressing the perspectives of minorities.

Multiconsciousness analysis focuses on differences, not commonalities, in comprehending a given phenomenon. It posits competing versions of reality in part because our understanding of reality is based on different underlying assumptions and different belief systems.[57] Many critical race theorists "consider that a principal obstacle to racial reform is majoritarian mindset—the bundle of presuppositions, *received wisdoms*, and shared cultural understandings persons in the dominant group bring to discussions of race. To analyze and challenge these power-laden beliefs, some writers employ counterstories, parables, chronicles, and anecdotes aimed at revealing their contingency, cruelty, and self-serving nature."[58]

The controversy surrounding *Liberators* may invite analysis based on critical race theory that can help us understand the difficulties of reconciling such different views of reality. It is important to remember that, whatever its successes and failures, *Liberators* as a counterstory of World War II provides the privileged view of Black soldiers and Jewish survivors themselves—one that should not be disregarded. The intense debate over truth and factual accuracy may tell us a lot about institutional and alternative ways of constructing history, but should not overwhelm the legitimate values of the film.

LEGACY

A new generation of African-American documentary filmmakers may well inherit Miles's mantle. One candidate is Jerald Harkness who founded Visionary Productions in Indianapolis in June 1993. Following advice from his mentor Christopher Duffy, president and CEO of Wabash Valley Broadcasting, he embarked on a project to make a documentary on the first Black Marines—mentioned briefly in *The Different Drummer*—who trained in

North Carolina at Montford Point, a base built especially for the segregated training of "Negro" troops during World War II. When the Marines finally allowed Black volunteers to enlist, they set limits on how many could join and what jobs they could do. One thing was clear: No African American would be allowed to give orders to whites.

The Men of Montford Point: The First Black Marines[59] documents the story of the first African Americans to break the color barrier in the Marine Corps. A white marine who served during the Korean conflict, Duffy broached the idea to Harkness who researched it with Nora Hiatt, producer-writer on the project. They started working in April of 1996 and began production in June. Most of the interviews were shot in Kansas City at the Montford Point Annual Convention, the rest in October at Montford Point in Jacksonville, North Carolina. George Hobbs, a Black Marine with thirty years of service, acted as consultant. Harkness relies primarily on archival footage and on-screen interviews of the veterans of this token unit. Most speak candidly about why they left the Marines; the few who stayed tell why.

The themes that run through *The Men of Montford Point* echo those that emerged in all of the films discussed in this chapter: the struggle of African Americans to serve their country; the indignities suffered at the hands of civilians and military personnel alike; and the lack of recognition of their contributions.[60]

In *The Alchemy of Race and Rights* Patricia Williams articulates what so many African Americans in the U.S. Armed Forces painfully described for the documentarians who turned the cameras on their experience: "I wonder when I and the millions of other people of color who have done great and noble things or creative and scientific things—when our achievements will become generalizations about our race and seen as contributions to the larger culture, rather than exceptions to the rule."[61]

NOTES

1. Alton Hornsby Jr., *The Black Almanac* (Woodbury, N.Y.: Barron's Educational Series, 1972), xii.

2. Boston is also the site of the monument to Robert Gould Shaw and the 54th, erected in 1897. According to Christine Temin, the "initial design for the memorial was an equestrian statue of Shaw period—no Black soldiers. That was fine with [H. H.] Richardson [architect of Trinity Church and Boston's cultural czar] and [Augustus] Saint-Gaudens [the artist], but not with Shaw's family, who insisted that the men their son had commanded be included" ("Boston's Conscience Turns 100," *Boston Globe*, May 25, 1997, N1). Nonetheless, the statute is still known as the Robert Gould Shaw Memorial and the centennial celebration included a screening of *Glory*, not Shearer's documentary.

3. Taken from the tribute to Jackie Shearer published in Independent Television Service's *Buzzword* 2, no. 2 (winter 1994): 2.

4. Jacqueline Shearer interview conducted by Phyllis Klotman and Janet Cutler, June 29, 1992.

5. In the BBC docudrama *A Son of Africa: The Slave Narrative of Oloudah Equiano* (1995), Stuart Hall makes an important point about agency: "The historiography of the abolitionist movement itself has kind of written out the agency of Blacks themselves. It is as if abolition was really a gift by liberal and reforming whites to the enslaved peoples and not one in which slaves themselves played an active part." Shearer's film emphasizes the agency of slaves and former slaves in behalf of their own freedom, as does the narrator of William Miles's *The Different Drummer*, discussed later in this chapter, who says after numerous on-screen examples of their fight for freedom: "It is naive at best to even suggest that Abraham Lincoln, with a stroke of a pen, freed the slaves."

6. Jacqueline Shearer may not have intended to call into question the historical accuracy of the film *Glory*, produced by Freddie Fields; however, the fact that the feature film exists makes the comparison inevitable. Fields may have thought *Glory* needed a special marketing strategy to make a profit on his investment ("about $18,000,000," he responded to Dan Rather's question) since he agreed to have CBS's *48 Hours* crew at the Jekyll Island shoot. The

resultant "making of . . ." film is distributed by Carousel Film and Video as *48 Hours: Lights, Camera, War* (1989). The best thing about that film is its showcasing of Black stuntmen. Tri-Star Pictures, Inc. issued a *Glory* Collector's Edition in 1991: *Glory* plus *The True Story of Glory Continues*, "A Documentary of the 54th Regiment That Inspired the Oscar-Winning film *Glory*," narrated, like Shearer's film, by Morgan Freeman. The 54th turned out to be a real commodity.

7. Nothing in that staged battle is quite as horrific as Eli Biddle's description of his experience on the parapets. Pieces of burning flesh from the dying soldiers in front would fly onto the men behind them. When the men tried to pull it off, their flesh would come with it. Their sergeant instructed them: "Don't touch it—let it dry."

8. The film's major virtue is its cadre of fine African-American actors: Morgan Freeman as the natural leader of men, John "Pops" Rawlins; Denzel Washington in his Oscar-winning performance as "Trip," the one radical in the regiment; Andre Braugher as the only intellectual, Thomas Searles, who believed his status in Shaw's family (he and Robert were boyhood friends) would transcend the rigidity of Army and racial hierarchy.

9. The men in *Glory* appear to be much like those Colonel Thomas Higginson commanded and wrote about in his diary on December 11, 1862—the First South Carolina volunteers, the first slave regiment in the U.S. Army. Instead of a single educated soldier reading to the men, Higginson describes a camp laundress from a nearby plantation sitting in the firelight, in the center of a circle of men: "Sometimes the woman is reading slow monosyllables out of a primer, a feat which always commands all ears. Learning, to these men, is magic of the first magnitude, and the impressive syllables . . . command a respectful audience." *Army Life in a Black Regiment*, edited and abridged by Genevieve S. Gray (New York: Grosset and Dunlap, 1970), 19.

10. William Carney, a dockworker, was the first African American to win the Congressional Medal of Honor: "When Sgt. William Carney grabbed the regimental flags from the hands of the dying standard-bearer . . . he ran through a hail of fire." Wounded three times, Carney finally staggered into the field hospital, proud that the "dear old flag" had never touched the ground. Keith White, "*Glory* Short on Truth," Gannett News Service, January 19, 1990, Lexis-Nexis Universe.

11. In answer to a question about her film "signature," Shearer said: "I think music is my signature. I've . . . gotten a lot of favorable comments on the

soundtrack in *The Massachusetts 54th* for the *American Experience* series. The *American Experience* people were a little worried that I wasn't going to do a score, that I wanted to do the same thing I did with *Eyes* instead of doing wall-to-wall stuff. But I did do wall-to-wall stuff and the music was actually good. I mean, we liked it in the editing room; it wasn't just historically accurate, it was fun to play around with" (Shearer interview).

12. I am indebted to Professor Norris for furnishing me a copy of his arrangement of "The Enlisted Soldiers."

13. Eric Mink, "Public TV: Quality Now, Problems Later," September 22, 1991, 9G; Zan Stewart, " 'Colored Infantry' Views Race in 1860s," October 14, 1991, Calendar; Part F; 11.

14. Shearer interview.

15. Interview with Phyllis Klotman and Janet Cutler, 1992.

16. Coincidentally, Caesar would, in 1984, win an Oscar nomination for the best actor in a supporting role as Army noncommissioned officer Sgt. Waters in *A Soldier's Story*.

17. Miles confided that every time he would find one of the 369th veterans who served in World War I, he [Miles] "became a jinx," because by the time he got the money together to shoot the film, he would call up to confirm and be told, "he just passed." Interview with William Miles, conducted by Janet Cutler and Phyllis Klotman, New York City, June 30, 1992.

18. Ibid.

19. The *Film News* article appeared in the spring 1980 issue, 36; Howard's article is in the "Film Reviews" section of *Film Library Quarterly* 12, no. 4 (1979): 44–46; the *Variety* review by Land appeared in the September 28, 1977, issue, 22.

20. Miles interview.

21. Benjamin Bender's letter was published in the Late City Final Edition, Section A, page 18, column 4 of the *New York Times*, April 22, 1985.

22. Charles Baillou reported this comment in his article "PBS' documentary, 'Liberators,' portrays history of Blacks in WWII," *New York Amsterdam News*, November 14, 1992, 1.

23. "Review/Television: America's Black Army and a Dual War Front," *New York Times*, November 11, 1992, C24; *Variety* 349, no. 3 (November 9, 1992): 66(1).

24. Although New York had its own media feeding frenzy (Jesse Jackson's earlier remark characterizing the city as "Hymietown," for which he later apologized; Professor Jeffries's charges about Jews in the slave trade and the "Jewish Mafia" in Hollywood; and Jeffries's colleague Michael Levin at City

College espousing his theory of Black intellectual inferiority), the Crown Heights incident in Brooklyn was certainly in the national news. The violence in Crown Heights that exacerbated the tensions between Blacks and Jews occurred on August 19, 1991, a few months before the airing of *Liberators*: It was "triggered . . . when one of the cars in a three-car procession carrying the Lubavitcher Hasidic rebbe, the spiritual leader of the sect, ran a red light and swerved onto the sidewalk, striking and killing Gavin Cato, a 7-year-old Black boy from Guyana and injuring his sister" (*Plain Dealer*, October 26, 1995, 5E). Rumors that a Hasidic ambulance crew failed to help the children set off hours of rioting, and Yankel Rosenbaum, an Australian Hasidic scholar, was stabbed to death. The uncontrolled violence lasted for three days. The driver of the car was not indicted; Lemrick Nelson Jr., the young man who was arrested for the murder of Rosenbaum, was acquitted, but both Mayor Dinkins and Police Commissioner Lee P. Brown were strongly criticized by the Jewish community for their alleged mishandling of the crisis. They were also charged in a lawsuit by Orthodox Jewish groups with neglecting to protect them against attacks by Black demonstrators, but in 1997 a federal judge ruled that they could not be "personally liable for actions taken by the city during the 1991 racial unrest in the Crown Heights Section of Brooklyn" (*Houston Chronicle*, August 23, 1997, Section E, 25), much too late to help Dinkins's political career, but not too late for Lee Brown who was later successful in his bid for mayor of Houston.

25. Lou Potter interview conducted by Phyllis Klotman, July 18, 1997.

26. Col. James B. Moncrief Jr., USA-Retired, "PBS-Buchenwald Caper," *Super Sixer*, the Sixth Armored Division newsletter, undated (Moncrief also used the occasion to suggest that members advise their congressmen to reduce by 50 percent the funding for the Corporation for Public Broadcasting); Milton Harrison letter, August 21, 1997; Melvin Rappaport letter, July 12, 1997; the list, updated in January 1997, was sent to me on November 24, 1997, by Steven Luckert, curator of the Permanent Exhibition of the United States Holocaust Memorial Museum. Perhaps these veterans are unaware that the process of certification is, according to Luckert, an ongoing one. Edward J. Drea, chief of the Research and Analysis Division, U.S. Army Center of Military History, published an article explaining the rationale for recognition of divisions that liberated concentration camps: "to honor the officers and men of the liberating divisions and . . . to remember the victims of Nazi tyranny." Since the

U.S. Holocaust Memorial Museum would open in 1993, that was considered the appropriate time. Drea explained the process: petitioning by division associations or division veterans; verification of the data submitted by researching the division records held at the National Archives' Washington National Records Center (Suitland, Maryland); and reliance on *primary* sources. Neither oral history nor testimony would be sufficient, nor would secondary accounts or unit histories unless they could be verified by official records. And yet, for the sake of expediency—flags for the first ten divisions had to be ready in time for the April ceremony—"Center historians *had to rely* [my emphasis] on secondary sources to verify the unit list." The Center and the Council agreed at that time not to limit recognition to the first divisions to reach a camp, but to also include "follow-on" divisions that entered the same camp, or camp complex, within 48 hours of the initial division. "Recognizing the Liberators: U.S. Army Divisions Enter the Concentration Camps," *Army History: The Professional Bulletin of Army History*, PB–20–93–1, no. 24 (fall/winter 1992/1993): 1, 4–5.

27. According to Sgt. Edward Donald of "B" Company, the 761st had after three days of steady fighting "punched a hole through the Siegfried Line" so that the 4th Armored Division could push through to Germany. Patton then diverted the 761st north to stop the Germans in the Ardennes Forest. Cpl. Horace Evans, also of "B" Company, pointed out that "the 4th Armored received all the credit for the breakthrough on the Siegfried Line, and we did the work. The 761st did not even receive an honorable mention." Mary Penick Motley, ed., *The Invisible Soldier: The Experience of the Black Soldier, World War II* (Detroit: Wayne State University Press, 1975), 155–56.

28. According to Anthony Lewis in the *New York Times*, Ruddy is "one of the leading promoters of the notion that Mr. [Vincent] Foster was murdered" (December 29, 1997, A17).

29. "*Liberators* under Fire (A documentary wounded by friendly fire)," a 10-page paper, is available at http://members.aol.com/dignews/underfire.htm.

30. I am indebted to Colby Kelly of Thirteen/WNET for the final report prepared for Thirteen/WNET by Morton Silverstein. In her letter to me of September 8, 1997, Kelly referred to the "internal review of the *Liberators*"; the press release calls it an "internal review by an independent team." When I asked Silverstein to clarify that point, he referred me to the legal counsel at WNET (telephone conversation, December 30, 1997).

31. The historian Clement Alexander Price has written a critique of both *Liberators* and *Men of*

Bronze, faulting them for "factual errors" and, while acknowledging that "the world of traditional historiography has never been immune to using memory as the basis for fact," contending that the "world of historical movie documentation . . . is far more susceptible to error because it seeks not so much to render an accurate account of the past as to reintroduce us to feelings about the past"; ergo, "films like *Men of Bronze* and *Liberators* should especially serve a larger public need for scholarly objectivity to compete with historical passion." "Black Soldiers in Two World Wars: 'Men of Bronze' (1980) and 'Liberators' (1992)" was first published in *Historical Journal of Film, Radio and Television* 14, no. 4 (1994): 467–74. It was followed by "Clement Price, 'Liberators' and Truth in History: A Comment," by the historian Daniel J. Leab, which compliments Price's "reasoned and unemotional" argument and explores some of the same terrain as the Stern and Silverstein reports, although he was not given access to the latter. These two articles were published in essentially the same form, but with slightly changed titles, in *World War II: Film and History*, ed. John Whiteclay Chambers II and David Culbert (New York: Oxford University Press, 1996), although unless the reader checks the notes to the second article, it's not clear that they were published elsewhere. In both versions of Price's article *Men of Bronze* is incorrectly dated: 1980, instead of 1977. Leab's article refers to producer Nina "Rosenbaum" several times, but the producer's name is corrected in the version published by Oxford.

32. Benjamin Bender, Sara Bender, and Leonard "Smitty" Smith, interview conducted by Phyllis Klotman, June 1, 1997. I am indebted to the Benders and Leonard Smith for their willingness to share their personal collections and correspondence with me.

33. A copy of Scott's pamphlet, describing and picturing what he saw at Buchenwald, is in the Black Film Center/Archive and is available to researchers. Scott's first cousin, Asa Gordon, an aerospace engineer at the Goddard Space Flight Center, who founded the Douglass Institute of Government, an educational "think tank" in Washington, D.C., has set up an institute website, URL: http://members. aol.com/digasa/dig.htm. Articles on the *Liberators* controversy are available through a link to "*Liberators* under Fire—the Web Site/Research and Analysis" or directly at http://members.aol.com/dignews/ liberate.htm, including speeches Gordon has given on the subject. He has also put the entire Scott pamphlet ("World War II Veteran Remembers the Holocaust"), including pictures, on the Web. Gordon called my attention to an article in *USA Today*

in which the documentary filmmaker Ken Burns defended the accuracy of his *Baseball* series against charges by ESPN's Keith Olbermann that there were eighty-nine errors in the first five episodes. Burns said the same thing had been said about the *Civil War* series, comments he called "nitpicks" (September 26, 1994, 3D). However, as Gordon pointed out, those films were not taken off the air. He has continuously campaigned to have *Liberators* aired again nationally (telephone interview conducted by Phyllis Klotman, August 20, 1997).

34. Rosenblum continues to feel strongly that the attacks were racist and politically motivated— "New York politics really added fuel to it. . . . The controversy was different outside of New York"— and extended beyond *Liberators* to nationally supported funding agencies like the National Endowment for the Humanities and the Corporation for Public Broadcasting. She also pointed out that *Liberators* is still in distribution and still being shown; and that veterans and survivors, Smith and Bender, Bass and Robert Waisman (who identified Bass through the B'nai B'rith newsletter) continue to speak together about their experiences at various community functions. Nina Rosenblum interview conducted by Phyllis Klotman, March 27, 1997.

35. Allentuck and Potter, "To the Editor," *Newsday*, January 7, 1993; Allentuck, "Official WWII History Doesn't Tell All," February 9, 1993; Rosenblum and Miles, "The Filmmakers' Response to Kenneth Stern's report to the American Jewish Committee, March 5, 1993; Rosenblum and Miles, "To ID readers," *International Documentary*, March 1993, 11.

36. Trezzvant W. Anderson was with the 761st three times while they were in Europe: "being the last to visit them in November 1944, and the first to see them again in 1945, after six months of darkness had covered their whereabouts." Perhaps the fact that he didn't get back to the battalion until May explains why he didn't include in his book any of the concentration camp experiences that Captain Long later reported to Mary Penick Motley. In the conclusion he writes about the neglect of Black units: "Covered by a fog of obscurity, there were 32 different Negro COMBAT UNITS in service on the Western Front and in Italy. VERY FEW, VERY, VERY FEW of these were visited by Correspondents. One came for two days, the other for a day and a half. . . . No glamorous accounts of their stirring deeds emblazoned the front pages of the newspapers" even though the 761st was on the front lines for 183 days. *Come Out Fighting: The Epic Tale of the 761st Tank Battalion, 1942–1945* (Tiesendorf, Germany: Salzburger Druckerei und Verlag, 1945), 125.

37. Anderson, 21.

38. George S. Patton Jr., *War As I Knew It* (Boston: Houghton Mifflin, 1947), 159–60.

39. Patton was even more negative in his assessment of Jews. In his biography of the general, *Patton: A Study in Command* (New York: Charles Scribner, 1974), 237, H. Essame quotes this section from Patton's diary: "Everyone believes that the displaced person is a human being, which he is not, and this applies particularly to the Jews who are lower than animals. Either the displaced persons never had a sense of decency or else they lost it during their period of internment by the Germans. My personal opinion is that no people could have sunk to the level of degradation these have reached in the short space of four years." Lou Potter also quotes Patton's words in the book *Liberators: Fighting on Two Fronts in World War II* (New York: Harcourt Brace Jovanovich, 1992), 221.

40. John Long and Ivan Harrison were the first two Black lieutenants in the United States Tank Corps. A soldier who rose from the ranks, Long was a cook at Fort Knox, Kentucky, when he was accepted for Officer Candidate School (OCS). Motley, 151.

41. Ibid., 152.

42. Lee, *United States Army in World War II, Special Studies: The Employment of Negro Troops* (Washington, D.C.: Office of the Chief of Military History, United States Army, 1966), 662–66. Lee does however confirm that Lt. Colonel Bates was wounded and evacuated from the field the first day of the attack, November 7, 1944; he was hospitalized until mid-February 1945. Lee, 663.

43. This section is a random sampling of witnesses, both veterans and survivors; not all of whom appeared in *Liberators*. Some responded to the reunion invitation extended by the filmmakers and Thirteen/WNET, where most of the interviews were shot.

44. Barnouw, "In Defense of *Liberators*," Letter to *International Documentary*, April 1993, 5.

45. Motley, 155.

46. "Nazi Survivors Reunite with Black Liberators," October 7, 1991, B1; News 12, Long Island, N.Y. (Videotapes of live interviews with veterans and survivors; reunions, celebrations, presentations, meetings connected with the development of *Liberators* and the subsequent controversy; as well as outtakes, were made available by Rosenblum and Miles through Miles Educational Film Productions, Inc. They are accessible for research and study at the Black Film Center/Archive, Afro-American Studies Department, Indiana University.) In answer to my question "Did you say you had gone to some of the camps?" E. G. McConnell responded, "I didn't say Dachau or Buchenwald.

Only once, I did mistakenly, I stated that, before I found out positively" (telephone interview, August 14, 1997).

47. In March 1993, McConnell told Stephen J. Dubner that he had phoned the mayor's office before the Apollo event, because he thought as a "Black man [it was his] duty to warn Mayor Dinkins and Jesse Jackson about this thing," but they "treated him like [he] was some kind of a kook" (*New York*, March 8, 1993, 51). Several officers of the 761st, Lt. Colonel Bates and Captains Charles Gates and David Williams (author of a novel about the 761st, *Eleanor Roosevelt's Niggers*) have also denied that any of the men of the 761st were involved in the liberation of Buchenwald or Dachau. They did not mention Gunskirchen Lager.

48. Smith interview; Motley, 160; Studs Terkel, *The Good War: An Oral History of World War Two* (New York: Pantheon Books, 1984), 268.

49. Anderson, 127. He also lists the number of awards the men received (eleven Silver Star medals, sixty-nine Bronze Star medals, with four clusters; three Certificates of Merit; 296 Purple Hearts, with eight Clusters—a total of 391 battle awards), but he couldn't have known that it would take thirty-three years for the 761st to receive the Presidential Unit Citation (January 24, 1978, signed by President Jimmy Carter). Gates told Terkel: "We had discovered that at least twelve other units to which we had been attached had received Presidential Unit Citations. About eighteen had received the French Croix de Guerre. How easy it has been all through the years to conceal the history of the Negro Soldier." Terkel, 268. Borden questions why the 761st didn't include anything about liberating camps in their record when they petitioned for the Presidential Unit Citation (Borden letter). More appropriate questions would be: Were unit citations given for anything other than battle records? How many other units had to wait thirty-three years to be recognized?

50. Gross gave one of the eulogies at Scott's funeral, and Scott's widow told me that he often called her husband "his angel" (telephone interview, December 30, 1997). In "The Filmmakers' Response to Kenneth Stern's Report to the American Jewish Committee" March 5, 1993, Miles and Rosenblum included a reference to Gross: "To this day, Alex Gross adheres to his recollection that he saw a Black soldier emerge from 'the first American tank that approached my part of the camp.' (See the attached letter of Alex Gross to *The New Republic*, to date unpublished.)" Sylvia Wygoda of the Georgia Holocaust Commission has prepared a traveling exhibit entitled "William A. Scott III: Witness to the Holocaust—World War II" as a part of the

commission's ongoing education program. They continue to show *Liberators* on their programs (telephone interview, January 9, 1997).

51. Kamm, "No Mention of Jews at Buchenwald," *New York Times*, March 25, 1989, Section 1, 8:1.

52. Bradley, "Black Troops First to Reach Death Camp," *Denver Post*, March 7, 1993.

53. Samuel Pisar, *Of Blood and Hope* (Boston: Little, Brown and Company, 1979), 27, 91.

54. Drea, 2–3.

55. Motley, 163.

56. Annette Insdorf, "Truths Lost in the Night and Fog," *Washington Post*, September 26, 1993, G4.

57. Patricia J. Williams's *The Alchemy of Race and Rights* (Cambridge: Harvard University Press, 1991) is especially useful to an understanding of critical race theory.

58. Richard Delgado and Jean Stefancic, "#461 Critical Race Theory: An Annotated Bibliography," *Virginia Law Review*, March 1995: 1. The bibliography is an impressive list of work on critical race theory by the legal scholars Derrick Bell, Kevin Brown, Kimberle Crenshaw, Lani Guinier, and others.

59. Aired once on WNDY-TV, Indianapolis, *The Men of Montford Point* (in its 90-minute format) was favorably reviewed by Steve Hall in the *Indianapolis Star*, February 18, 1997. Harkness considers it a work in progress and would like to cut the film to one hour (Jerald Harkness telephone interviews, conducted by Phyllis Klotman, November 20 and 27, 1997). Steve Crump of Charlotte, North Carolina, has also taken up the cause of African Americans in the military. *Airmen and Adversity* (1998), a documentary which he produced, directed, and narrated for WTVI, Charlotte public television, is the story of the "Tuskegee Airmen," African Americans who enlisted in the Air Force during World War II. Veterans on camera relate their struggle to become an integral part of the Air Force. A segregated unit, they were assigned to escort bombers piloted by whites; in two hundred missions they never lost a bomber. Like the men of the 761st, they had to endure discrimination—the daily insults of segregation, not the least of which was seeing Nazi POWs being allowed access to all of the camp facilities which they were denied.

60. Black troops during World War II were especially offended by the differential treatment they and prisoners of war were given: German and Italian prisoners were allowed to use facilities, like the PX, to "fraternize" with white women (in North Carolina and in England). African Americans, whether Marines, tankers, or infantrymen, were not. They were especially outraged when a German officer was given a full military funeral.

61. Williams, 113.

11

JUSTIFIABLE HOMICIDE, POLICE BRUTALITY, OR GOVERNMENTAL REPRESSION?

The 1962 Los Angeles Police Shooting of Seven Members of the Nation of Islam

Frederick Knight

ON THE NIGHT OF APRIL 27, 1962, scores of policeman ransacked the Nation of Islam Mosque in Los Angeles and wounded seven unarmed Muslims, leaving William Rogers paralyzed and Ronald Stokes dead. Newspapers from New York to Los Angeles printed the story in their headlines, presenting the gruesome image of the slain Muslim, suited, face-down, handcuffed, swimming in a pool of his own blood. The political struggles which erupted after the shooting soon overshadowed this story of human pain and suffering. And the headlines of local and national newspapers quickly recognized that the siege was certainly not the normal police brutality case.

To many white political leaders, the conflict substantiated their worst fears about the violent nature of the Nation of Islam. On the other hand, many Black leaders condemned the police for what they considered to be a racially motivated assault. Though contemporaries viewed the shooting from different perspectives, they agreed on the importance of the attack and its aftermath. Several recent scholars have marked the event as a watershed event in the ideological development of Malcolm X and in Los Angeles racial politics preceding the Watts Rebellion of August 1965. This study synthesizes the current scholarship and taps new sources to show that the fatal shooting of Ronald Stokes has even deeper roots and wider implications than any single scholar has suggested.

Biographers have shown that the shooting catalyzed Malcolm's growing disenchantment with the eventual break from the Nation of Islam. George Breitman, editor of Pathfinder Press, reveals that the shooting may have created the tension that caused the split between Elijah Muhammad and Malcolm X.[1] Peter Goldman and Benjamin Karim describe the inner struggle that Malcolm felt because of the Nation of Islam's "inaction" after the shooting.[2] Eugene Wolfenstein provides an unmistakably Marxist analysis in interpreting Malcolm X's response to the failure of the Nation of Islam to retaliate against the police.[3] And in what he proclaims as "the first complete biography" of the slain leader, Bruce Perry gives an account of the shooting and Malcolm's surface response, but he does not provide any substantial analysis.[4]

Several other authorities provide deeper analyses of the shooting of Ronald Stokes and its aftermath. Bruce Tyler places the conflict within the wider context of the volatile Los Angeles racial politics which erupted into the Watts uprising of 1965.[5] In his study of the governmental plot to assassinate Malcolm X, Karl Evanzz provides the most thorough analysis to date.[6] Relying most heavily upon FBI records, Evanzz brilliantly captures the national and international response, yet he fails to explore the origins of or local protest to the attack. This study taps new sources to show that the assault on the Los Angeles Muslims had even deeper roots and wider implications than any single scholar has suggested.

In providing their accounts of the shooting, the previously mentioned authorities share a variety of primary sources. Of course they reference the *Autobiography of Malcolm X*. Most of them cite Hakim Jamal's *From the Dead Level*, which is a moving autobiography of a Muslim who left the Los Angeles Mosque because of his disappointment over the Nation of Islam's "inaction" after the shooting. Evanzz, Goldman, and Wolfenstein utilize Louis Lomax's *To Kill a Black Man: The Shocking Parallel in the Lives of Malcolm X and Martin Luther King, Jr.* Overall, Perry, Wolfenstein, Evanzz, and Breitman use a carefully selected combination of biographies, government documents, interviews, newspapers, and audio tapes.

Several of these sources proved to be useful, especially the *Autobiography of Malcolm X*, Lomax's work, and Jamal's biography. But for the purposes of this study, other sources needed to be tapped. The official organ of the Nation of Islam, *Muhammad Speaks*, and the *Los Angeles Times* were indispensable in providing chronology, detail, and a wide assortment of perspectives. Most importantly, the traditional Black press, including the *Pittsburgh Courier, New York Amsterdam News, Los Angeles Sentinel*, and *California Eagle*, provides invaluable information on the local and national protest to the shooting. A variety of other sources, including the papers of the Student Non-Violent Coordinating Committee, government reports, secondary sources, and general dialogue with fellow students and mentors revealed important insights. Unfortunately, the Muslims who were at the scene of the shooting were not available for interviews. Despite the absence of their testimony, this study still provides greater scope than previous works.

The shooting of Ronald Stokes in April 1962 can perhaps be best understood as part of a larger historical tradition of American violence against Blacks. From the torturous slave trade to the lash of the slaveholder to the noose of the Ku Klux Klan, Blacks, irrespective of gender or class, have withstood seemingly constant violence from the hands of white America. Racist violence followed Blacks as they made the Great Migration from the South to the North. By the mid-twentieth century, Black ghettoes were being described by some as internal American colonies. In this context, the police department served not as protector of the peace but as an occupying army which could reign terror without fear of reprimand.[7] And Blacks were expected to remain passive and stand defenseless in the face of such racist assault.

As an essentially northern grassroots movement, the Nation of Islam was certainly no stranger to police brutality. The brutal murder of Ronald Stokes was to become the most vivid example, but the antagonism between the Nation of Islam and the police predates the Los Angeles shooting. For example, because many of the members of the Nation of Islam were ex-convicts, surely some of them had been victims of the capricious acts of the police or prison guards. In addition, the movement was embroiled in a 1957 brutality case in New York City. Hinton Johnson, a member of the Nation of Islam, was beaten and then arrested by a police officer. Malcolm X, then the local New York minister, led dozens of members of

Muhammad's Mosque No. 7 and many curious bystanders on a march on the Harlem police precinct, where they demanded proper medical attention for their fallen brother, who was mauled so severely that surgeons were required to use a steel plate to repair his cracked skull. The message quickly spread among Black New Yorkers that the Nation of Islam was nothing to play with; and police departments and federal investigators became increasingly concerned that the "Black Muslim Movement" was a subversive organization.[8]

It did not take long for members of the Nation of Islam Mosque No. 27, established in 1957, in Los Angeles, to experience their first confrontation with law enforcement. On September 2, 1961, several Muslims were selling their national newspaper, *Muhammad Speaks*, in South Central Los Angeles at Venice Plaza in the parking lot of a Safeway grocery store when they were accosted by two white store detectives. The *Los Angeles Times* reported that detectives were stomped and beaten after they tried to stop the Muslims' solicitations. "We've been having trouble for 10 months. . . . Groups of Muslims block the market doorways and try to sell their newspaper," said one detective. Reporting the story, the *Los Angeles Times* printed on the cover of its September 3 Metropolitan section a picture of a Los Angeles policeman reading a copy of one of the confiscated newspapers. Ironically (or perhaps fittingly), on the cover of that month's *Muhammad Speaks* appeared the headline: "MUSLIMS SET FOR CHRISTIAN ATTACK".[9]

An article in the May 1962 issue of *Muhammad Speaks* describes the incident quite differently:

> According to witnesses, two white "store detectives" employed by the Safeway store came onto [sic] the lot and tried to chase the Muslims away. When they refused, saying they had permission from the owner to sell the paper there, the two "detectives" produced guns and attempted to make a "citizen's arrest." Grocery packers rushed out to help the detectives, who were identified as Fred Pendergast and King Marsh, and Black residents of the area who had gathered also became involved. For 45 minutes bedlam reigned.

It took forty policemen to disperse the crowd of bystanders before arresting five Fruit of Islam, Louis (5X) Faison, twenty-four; William (X) Orr, nineteen; Raymond (6X) Phillips, twenty-two; Donald (6X) Caffey, twenty-two; and Wade (X) Morris, twenty-five; and one onlooker, Fred Perkins, forty-seven. Further research will determine who threw the first blow. But it is important to note that when the case went to trial the store's owner and manager submitted an affidavit that stated they had permitted paper sales, thus exonerating the Muslim defendants. After less than two hours of deliberation, an all-white jury acquitted the Fruit of Islam of assault and battery charges; the Muslims subsequently filed a lawsuit against Safeway in excess of one million dollars.[10]

The May 1962 issue of *Muhammad Speaks* not only reported the 1961 Los Angeles conflict but also cited a recent report by the United States Commission on Civil Rights that concluded that "Negroes are the victims of (police) brutality far more, proportionately, than any other group in American society." It is rather ironic that these two articles were published in May 1962, only four days after the fatal shooting of Ronald Stokes and the wounding of six other Muslims. Obviously, the paper had gone to press before the April 27, 1962, shooting. But importantly, that issue shows the consciousness of the paper's editor (if not the entire organization) of the friction between law enforcement and the Muslims, and, more generally, the volatile relationship between the police and the Black community.

Such tension was felt in the North and the South, in the East and the West. In 1961, in Los Angeles, the tension erupted when on May 31, a gathering of nearly two hundred Blacks who were enjoying a Memorial Day barbecue at Griffith Park was confronted by seventy-five policemen. Most accounts reveal that the "miniriot" that ensued was the fault of police overreaction. The unrest occurred just a few days before the city's mayoral Democratic primary election between Samuel Yorty and the incumbent Norris Poulson. Yorty's criticism of the current administration's record in law enforcement helped him gain some of the undecided vote, solidify the Black vote, and carry the primary.[11] After the election, answering a question about police chief William H. Parker, Yorty remarked:

> I stand all right with Chief Parker. I got him a double (pay) raise that he wouldn't have gotten otherwise. I'm planning on keeping him, but I want [him] to enforce the law and stop making remarks about the minority groups in this community, because the police have had very poor public relations with the minority groups.
>
> This is not good for this community. We're not living in the South and I expect everybody to be treated equally and fairly and I expect police to enforce the law and I will expect they will do so.
>
> I know the minority groups have confidence in me and I have confidence in them, and we are going to have good public relations with all the groups in this community and act like a grownup [sic] city.[12]

The exigencies of office would make Mayor Yorty eat his words.

Yorty entered a government that seemed to have no conscience—certainly it would not be disturbed by the murder of a member of the Nation of Islam at the hands of the police. For by the 1960s, the government, on the federal, state, and local levels, had developed an expertise in conducting surveillance, destroying the lives of "subversives," and dismantling organizations, all under the guise of "nabbing communists." The Nation of Islam, though not considered a communist organization, was put on the government's list of dangerous organizations. In fact, during the 1940s, Yorty chaired the California Committee on Un-American Activities, which by the early 1960s targeted the Muslims.[13]

Two documents are indicative of the federal government's viewpoints on the "Black Muslims." In a seventy-three-page report, Black FBI agent J. P. Mathews describes the ambivalent feelings the Nation of Islam had toward violence. Mathews observed that while leaders preached nonviolence publicly and often admonished their followers to obey the white man's law, local ministers would tell their followers, "Blood must be shed to get our rights. We mean business."[14] Such statements confounded the FBI.

Concern about the Nation of Islam reached the top of the FBI. In his September 18, 1968, statement to the National Commission on the Causes and Prevention of Violence, FBI director J. Edgar Hoover argued that the Nation of Islam's "meetings are replete with condemnations of the white race and vague references to the physical retribution that will be meted out to oppressors."[15] Some in the bureau saw the Nation of Islam as a threat, but several factors spared it from more intense scrutiny: the organization had religious grounding, it publicly denounced or equivocated on the question of violence, and the bureau was primarily concerned with the Communist Party and the civil rights movement.

On the state level, the Nation of Islam was among the organizations included in the eleventh report of the California Senate Factfinding Committee on Un-American Activities. Essentially, the committee asked whether the Nation of Islam had communist affilia-tions. Though this fear was allayed, they still concluded that there was an "interesting par-allel between the Negro Muslim movement and the Communist Party, and that is the advocacy of the overthrow of a hated regime by force, violence or any other means. . . ."[16] The state committee, once chaired by Mayor Yorty, evoked fear of the Nation of Islam that may have trickled down to the local level.

As a neighbor of Los Angeles, the San Diego Police Department established a method of identifying and confronting members of the Nation of Islam and forewarned its officers about possible confrontations. According to their officer training manual:

> The nucleus of the Nation of Islam is comprised of 20 to 30 year old men called, "the Fruit of Islam." These men are selected for their physical prowess and are adept for their aggressive tac-tics and judo. They are psychotic in their dedication and hatred of Caucasians and are compa-rable to the Mau Mau or Kamikaze in their dedication and fanaticism. It has been reported that many temples have gun clubs in which this militant group is trained in weapons.
>
> The Muslims in the Los Angeles area, like their cult elsewhere, are highly disciplined. *The "clean cut" Negro, well dressed and groomed, is the most likely member of the organization*; male members of the inner circle wear dark suits, white shirts and maroon ties. Many are well-edu-cated, all are well trained. . . .
>
> Officers should, however, be apprehensive and alert to any eminent threat to these fanatics. Patrol Officers should request "back-up" on any investigation or police incident involving a possible MUSLIM, *regardless of how trivial the incident. . . .*[17]

Their method of identification and analysis was dangerously vague. First, their assertion that mosques had "gun clubs" implied that Muslims were armed and therefore a threat to patrolmen. Second, their use of terms such as "fanatic," "aggressive," and "psychotic" painted the picture to trainees that the Fruit of Islam would not fear using their alleged weapons and made the Muslims justifiable targets for police attack. Third, their statement that " 'the clean cut' Negro, well dressed and groomed, is the most likely member of the organization" is sufficiently nebulous that almost any Black man dressed in a dark suit could be targeted, whether a Fruit of Islam, a lawyer, or a Baptist preacher. The national and state paranoia may have aroused the San Diego Police Department's anxiety. But since San Diego did not have a substantial Muslim population, why did they express such concern?

The Los Angeles Police Department may have cautioned the San Diego Police Depart-ment. In an April 1962 interview by Donald McDonald of the Center for the Study of Democratic Institutions, Los Angeles police department chief William H. Parker admitted his concern over racial tensions in Los Angeles. A published interview reads:

> **Parker:** You can't ignore these problems [racial tensions]. I am reading a book now dealing with an organization which is totally anti-Caucasian. We have been watching it with concern for a long time.
> **Q:** Do you Mean the Muslims?
> **Parker:** Yes, the Black Muslims of America [sic]. The Negro author of this book [C. Eric Lincoln] does an apparently objective analysis of this problem. Of course, our primary job is to enforce the law. . . . But we ought to also be interested enough in our work to look into some of the causes of these problems.[18]

Less than one year after police were called in to repress the struggle between Muslims and Safeway detectives and during the very month of the shooting, the chief of police admitted that he was conducting surveillance of the Nation of Islam.

The tension between the Los Angeles Police Department and the Nation of Islam eventually exploded on April 27, 1962, with the shooting of Ronald Stokes and six other Muslims. The *Los Angeles Times* initially reported the story as a "blazing gunfight" though the Muslims were unarmed.[19] Such headlines proved to be emblematic of their coverage. As it reported the trial of the fourteen Muslims charged in the melee (Robert L. Buice, Arthur Coleman, John Shabazz, Raymond Wiley, Elmer Craft, Fred Jingles Jr., Nathaniel Rivers, William Rogers, Randolph Sidle, Charles H. Zeno, Roosevelt Walker, Robert Rogers, Troy Augustine, and Monroe Jones), it privileged the testimony of the police under the district attorney's questioning and, when it included the cross-examination, relegated to the end of its articles any contradictions that may have arisen under the defense attorney's questioning. Before, during, and after the trial, the major Los Angeles electronic and print media, and institutions which wielded the most power and held the greatest claim to "objectivity," came down decidedly on the side of the police.[20] The coverage was so one-sided that John Shabazz, minister of Muhammad's Mosque No. 27 and one of the defendants, declared that the Muslims were "not only PERSECUTED, and PROSECUTED, but worst of all we were PRESSECUTED."[21]

Bruce Perry in his biography of Malcolm X provides an account of the shooting. He contends that at around midnight on April 27, 1962, two Los Angeles patrolmen, Stanley Kensic and Frank Tomlinson, confronted two Black men whom they deemed suspicious. Perry asserts that the policemen stopped to interrogate the men because there was a rash of clothing store burglaries in the area. The two Black men whom they saw take some clothing from a parked car thus became immediate suspects. "What happened next has been disputed," says Perry. But he then provides a lengthy account of what he thinks happened. Because he does not provide a historical backdrop behind the shooting and because his narrative flows largely from the perspective of the police officers, Perry, whether he knows it or not, presents the police as victims.[22]

The murder of Ronald Stokes and the shooting of six other Muslims at the hands of the Los Angeles police department can not be understood outside of a historical context. First, the Nation of Islam was a targeted organization. The increased national exposure and the previous clashes between the Nation of Islam and law enforcement had drawn the attention of Los Angeles police chief Parker. Second, the police felt a general disregard for the human rights of Blacks to live free from violent repression: in fact, by the mid-twentieth century, many perceived the police as the new bearers of the "American tradition" of violence. Third, as a grassroots organization in the urban "colony" and the only national Black organization that broached the subject of self-defense, the Nation of Islam served as an antithesis to the police. This combination of ingredients exploded.

Certainly it is a difficult task to re-create what happened at approximately midnight on April 27, 1962, just one block from the Nation of Islam Mosque. Emotions were flaring and subsiding, things occurred simultaneously, and those on the inside were not aware of everything that surrounded them. Sources correspond on several facts and are in conflict on others; what no one disputes is that after the two officers confronted two Muslims, one being Monroe Jones, a struggle ensured. A bullet from the arresting officer Stanley Kensic's revolver struck his partner Officer Frank Tomlinson in the elbow. Later in the conflict, from approximately six feet away, Officer Donald Weese fatally shot the unarmed Ronald Stokes through the heart as he walked toward the officer with his hands raised in the air. William Rogers was shot in the back and paralyzed. And five other Muslims, Robert Rogers, Arthur Coleman, Roosevelt Walker, Fred Jingles Jr. and Monroe Jones, were shot. Who provoked the conflict? Who shot Officer Tomlinson? These questions will be left for further research. But the evidence suggests that perhaps the most important question can be answered: Was the shooting of the seven Muslims justifiable homicide (as the white media, Bruce Perry, and the Los Angeles grand jury contend), a case of police brutality (as most Blacks concluded), or an instance of racist governmental repression against the Black struggle for freedom?

Reports from *Muhammad Speaks*, several other Black newspapers, and other primary sources present damaging evidence against the police department. Testimony from the trial of the Muslims suggests that a Black off-duty security guard, noticing the conflict, fired the bullet which struck officer Tomlinson. In a speech delivered to a mass meeting, Malcolm X asserted that after the original struggle between the police and the Muslims outside of the mosque, a call went out to the police department. However, they did not report to the original scene of the conflict. Rather, they stopped a block away at the Muslim mosque, where Muslims began to filter out of the Mosque.[23]

Policemen shot their way into the mosque, wounding Robert Rogers, Roosevelt Walker, Arthur Coleman, Clarence Jingles, and Monroe Jones and paralyzing William Rogers. Officer Donald Weese shot to silence the Muslims as they declared in Arabic, "Allah O Akbar," which simply means "God is Great." Inside the mosque, Minister John (Morris) Shabazz called for medical attention and handed the phone to Stokes and then rushed outside to tend to the fallen brothers. When he found that the wounded Clarence Jingles was already rushed off to the hospital, Minister Shabazz reentered the mosque to ensure the safety of the Muslim women.[24]

In the meantime, Stokes went outside to make sure that his wife was safe and to carry the downed Roosevelt Walker from the scene. The police immediately demanded Stokes to stop. Stokes, secretary of Mosque No. 27, then dropped Walker's feet and walked forward with his hands raised to plead with the police to stop shooting. Officer Donald Weese, ignoring Stokes's pleas, shot him through the heart. "I shot to kill," Weese testified in the grand jury hearings held against the police. Later, a Muslim inside the mosque overheard a policeman brag, "We got one of their top officials."[25]

Inside the mosque, a policeman poked a gun to Minister Morris's back. He overheard Officer Reynolds say, "*We ought to burn this place down. They're going to declare it subversive in the next few days anyway*" [italics mine]. He then exhorted, "Let's tear those pretty suits off those niggers." They then ripped the Muslims' clothes off in an alleged search for weapons. Not one weapon was found.[26]

The police proceeded to kick, slap, hit with their night sticks, and handcuff the wounded Muslims who were left to lay in their own blood, scattered along the sidewalk outside the mosque. Approximately one hour expired before ambulances arrived at the scene, and then whites were treated first. As one of the Muslims was being carried off the scene, one of the attendants remarked to a policeman: "Why don't you kill the nigger. I'll say that he tried to grab your gun." The officer then said, "Take the long way to the hospital and drive real slow and this nigger will be dead by the time we get there [the hospital]."[27]

When in custody at the police headquarters, a Muslim overheard officers boasting about how they shot up the mosque. One allegedly said: "We should have gotten more of those nigger M[other] F[ucker]'s." Reminiscent of the scene in New York with Hinton Johnson, three Muslims who suffered gunshot wounds were held in jail for two days and denied sufficient medical treatment until their $10,000 bond was posted.[28] Was the shooting "justifiable homicide"? If one believes the reports in the *Los Angeles Times*, one might respond, "Yes, the police were justified." But if the information in *Muhammad Speaks* and *California Eagle* is correct, the only rational conclusion that can be drawn is that the shooting was a case of police brutality and a religious, political, and racial attack.

The crisis that followed the shooting can be best described within the context of the tensions between the Black masses and various forms of "leadership" on the question of self-defense and self-determination during the civil rights era. The white power structure, including the press, the mayor, and the police chief, attempted to direct the energy of the masses and prevent a riot. Members of the local Black leadership distanced themselves from the violent image of the Muslims but capitalized on the headlines the shooting drew to deal with the issue of police brutality. And some followed more closely the philosophy of the militant civil rights activist Robert Williams, who provided the keen insight that self-defense is an "American tradition."[29]

The written word is not sufficient to express the rage Malcolm X vented in responding to the shooting of Ronald Stokes. In a Harlem "Unity Rally," Malcolm exhorted: "This is a Black man [Ronald Stokes], a Korean vet; went to war in Korea fightin' for America . . . and came back to this country and was shot down by the white man like a dog. Not from Ku Klux Klansmen, down in Mississippi! This Black man was shot through the heart by policemen in Los Angeles, California. And they are dumb enough to think we have forgotten it. . . . We'll never forget!!!" Throughout the speech, he roused his audience's emotions, declaring at one moment that God will bring retribution but in the next proclaiming the right for personal self-defense.[30]

Malcolm felt a personal loss in the slaughter at the mosque that he helped to establish five years earlier. For Ronald Stokes was innocent: a college man, a Korean veteran, a husband, and a father of a three-month-old girl, Saudia. Malcolm described Stokes as "one of the most religious persons who displayed the highest form of morals of any black person anywhere on this earth." To Malcolm, the assault on the Muslims deserved a call to action.[31]

Some Muslims saw the cold-blooded shooting of Ronald Stokes as their call to start the battle of Armageddon. In *To Kill a Black Man*, Louis Lomax reports that Malcolm X left New York the day after the shooting with the intention of directing the attack. However, Elijah Muhammad stayed his hand.[32] Hakim Jamal, a member of Mosque No. 27, described the scene that Malcolm met in Los Angeles two days after the shooting by stating plainly:

> I never knew there were that many Muslims in America, never mind Los Angeles—we were everywhere. Many brothers had guns in their pockets, others were sharpening knives. Still others were in corners of the mosque limbering up and practicing judo and karate chops on imaginary devils' necks.
>
> We were all ready to kill.
>
> Very few talked of dying. Everyone smiled at each other in a strange way. Most of us knew we would probably get killed, but we knew that we were at war with the devil. The time had arrived to kill.[33]

As the crowd grew restless, Malcolm mounted the podium to give the word. With the message from Elijah Muhammad, he exclaimed: "We are going into the streets now to begin war with the devil. Not the kind of war he expects . . . no, we are going to let the world know he is a devil: we are going to sell newspapers."[34] They went out and sold the newspaper; but the picture of Ronald Stokes lying in his own blood became a moral symbol and a painful reminder to the Nation of Islam.

Some of the Muslims were not satisfied. A number of them formed a "band of angels" to beat up white drunkards on the Fifth Street skid row. "Ten brothers would get together, drive down there and watch until a devil came out of a barroom; karate chops would land on white necks; a devil would die or damn near die." When Malcolm found out about Fifth Street, he chastised the "band of angels" for being cowardly.[35] Unable to retaliate, Malcolm embarked on a personal campaign to unify Black leaders and the urban masses, inviting the leaders of the Congress of Racial Equality (CORE), the NAACP, SCLC, Urban League, and other leaders to mass rallies in Los Angeles and eastern cities. In a letter to James Farmer, National Director of CORE, Malcolm wrote, "It is a disgrace for Negro leaders not to be able to submerge out 'minor' differences in order to seek a common solution to a common problem posed by a *Common Enemy.*"[36]

Biographers have acknowledged that the shooting deeply affected Malcolm, but they do not always recognize that the inner struggle reached throughout the ranks of the Nation of Islam. The "band of angels" were carrying out their "little deaths" against the white man. Hakim Jamal, who reported this scene, and other Muslims soon defected from the mosque. Muslims who witnessed the massacre had its image forever etched into their minds and hearts. And an angry member chastised the *Amsterdam News*: "Your failure to make any comment in your paper on the brutal wanton murder of our beloved Muslim brother is indicative of your callous indifference to the militant, determined stand of courageous Black men for freedom, justice, and equality, regardless of cost."[37]

Elijah Muhammad has been roundly criticized for his inaction. Malcolm and many in the rank and file were dissatisfied with Elijah's statement on self defense:

In the case of the so-called American Negro, we have nothing to fight back with. If you come to the door shooting, we have no guns here to shoot back, so, therefore, the right is with God, as it is written in the Book.

He will defend us if we believe in Him and trust in Him, and we're not going to start fighting with any one to have Him to defend us. *But if we are attacked, we depend on Him to defend us . . .*" [italics mine].

However, an earlier statement reveals a quite different sentiment: "There is no justice in the sweet bye and bye. Immortality is NOW, HERE. We are the blessed of God and we must exert every means to protect ourselves. . . ." Ultimately, Muhammad used the shooting as further evidence against "the white man" and to push his program.[38] To Elijah Muhammad, retaliation was out of the question.

Under pressure from Mayor Yorty, Elijah Muhammad admonished Malcolm to tone down his rhetoric. Indeed, the same Mayor Samuel Yorty who courted the Black vote for his 1961 election tried to silence major Black voices. For example, he realized the power of the printed word. Formerly a critic of the tactics of the police force and an advocate of improved race relations in Los Angeles, Yorty was to become an outspoken defender of the police department and a staunch critic of the Black press. In response to requests by Black civic leaders to fire Chief Parker, he remarked, "I don't want the Negro community to appear as if it's [sic] only objective is the firing of Chief Parker because Parker is highly respected by the white community." Also, in response to a question calmly posed by Malcolm X at a symposium in New York, Yorty pronounced, "I'm having the police investigate the Negro Press in Los Angeles because of articles they feed the Negro community. . . . The Negro press inflames the community against the police by printing lies about the police."[39]

Yorty's response was indicative of the general paranoia which reigned in the aftermath of the shooting. On May 1, the San Diego Police Department reported that it sighted 180 members of the Nation of Islam cross the border into Mexico. The following day, it sighted fifteen to twenty Muslims return. But on May 3, to its own embarrassment, it admitted that its "suspects" may have been just a group of Blacks who were there for a funeral.[40] Less than two weeks after the shooting, Los Angeles district attorney William B. McKesson joined the mayor in his request for an investigation. He called upon the California state attorney general Stanley Mosk to probe the "Muslim Conspiracy in California."[41] This defender of "innocent before proven guilty" seemed to have concluded that the Nation of Islam was a "conspiracy" even before an investigation was made. Such was the paranoia and defensiveness of the white Los Angeles power structure (including the police chief, the mayor's office, the attorney general, and the press) immediately after the shooting.[42]

Not all whites aligned themselves against the Black community. In a letter dated July 6, 1962, twenty middle-class whites addressed a letter to the editor of the *New York Times* arguing that "we who are not Negroes believe that we cannot stand aside and allow the protest against these brutal acts to remain the responsibility of the Negro community alone." Two of the cosigners, Drs. Kathleen and David Aberle, resigned from their positions at Brandeis University because the school's president censored Dr. Kathleen Aberle for remarks she made criticizing police brutality.[43]

With but minor dissent from white circles, the Los Angeles power structure tried to silence the Black community. During the 1950s, this tactic may have worked. In *Here I Stand*, Paul Robeson wrote that when whites mounted racist attacks, the Black community often did not respond. "*Where are the other Negroes?*" he implored.[44] However, the civil rights movement emboldened many within Black communities. Thus, national civil rights leaders spoke out against the shooting, and local Black leaders refused to be silenced.

At least two of the mainstream civil rights organizations expressed their concern; however, they did so with qualification. James Farmer, chairman of the Congress of Racial Equality (CORE), "stated that CORE stood shoulder-to-shoulder with the NAACP and other human rights organizations 'in condemnation of such police brutality.' " On the local level, national vice chairman Earl Walter of Los Angeles observed that CORE could learn from the Nation of Islam; he proposed that the issue of police brutality be used to rally the Black community behind CORE's agenda.[45] So when Los Angeles CORE, which at the time was three-fourths white, protested police brutality by picketing outside the trial of the fourteen Muslims, it may have come as much from self-interest as from altruism.

Roy Wilkins, executive director of the National Association for the Advancement of Colored People (NAACP), wrote an open letter condemning the shooting. However, a statement released to the press underscores his still conservative nature. "Why did they [the police] have to use their guns?" he asked. "Didn't they have billy clubs?" He received the support of the national body. Meeting in Atlanta, Georgia, the national convention of the NAACP approved a resolution which stated, "This convention approves the vigorous protest entered by the Los Angeles Branch of the Association and Executive Director Roy Wilkins in this instance against the use of obsessive [sic] force by police officers. . . ."[46]

The Nation of Islam hoped to take the issue onto the international stage. A Korean newspaper circulated petitions which read:

> All freedom loving people of all races and nationalities who believe in equality must demand justice for the Muslims. . . .
>
> The undersigned respectfully request that this great injustice be presented to the public opinion of the world. . . .
>
> We further request that the Commission on Human Rights investigate the police brutality charges. These charges are being heard in an atmosphere of hate and prejudice by the racist press, radio and television of the area. . . ."[47]

According to Evanzz, leaders from the newly independent African nations, with whom Malcolm was beginning to establish connections, publicly condemned the shooting. *Muhammad Speaks* made a strong case that the shooting of Ronald Stokes and six others could be classified as an act of genocide as defined by Articles II and III of the United Nations Convention of the Prevention and Punishment of the Crime of Genocide. And the noted civil rights lawyer Paul Zuber suggested that he would press the United Nations to investigate the death of Ronald Stokes and the shooting of six others. He "stated that he would personally take the case before the Afro-Asian bloc if no action were forthcoming" from the UN Secretary General, U Thant.[48]

Though it reached national and international quarters, the reaction to the shooting was the most dynamic on the local level. The local power structure continued to antagonize the Black community and, more specifically, members of the Nation of Islam. In the aftermath of the shooting, Police Chief William Parker called for two-man patrols in "sensitive areas until such a time as the potentially dangerous emotional reactions abate."[49] In May 1963, as the trial proceeded, Malcolm X and another Muslim were followed from the airport by Los Angeles police officers. They forced Malcolm and the driver off the road at gunpoint and searched their car for weapons.[50] Despite such efforts, the Los Angeles power structure could not silence the Black leadership.

For a brief moment, the Black community answered calls for unity as they mobilized around the issue of police brutality. Middle-class Blacks, including the political candidates Mervyn Dymally and Augustus Hawkins, Broadway Federal Savings and Loan president Dr. Claude Hudson, and the Black legal association, the Langston Law Club, condemned the injustice.[51] However, the unity began to splinter when a group of Black clergy distanced themselves from the Nation of Islam and sought to negotiate with Yorty and Parker on the issues facing the Black community. On May 25, from a manifesto representing more than five hundred Black churches and ninety Los Angeles preachers, a leading A.M.E. minister, Hartford Brookins, read the following:

> We want it clearly understood that we are in no way related to the Muslim movement. We repudiate its total doctrine of Black supremacy and the attempt to place one American against

another. We suspect that the Muslim movement wears the garb of religion but in reality is just another nationalistic movement.[52]

The statement soon drew the praise of Mayor Yorty and the editor of the *Los Angeles Times*. However, the Muslims and many among the masses saw the manifesto as a sellout. At a meeting at the Garden of Prayer Baptist Church, nearly seven hundred people protested against the position taken by the preachers. One woman cried aloud that the ministers were "handkerchief heads." As the unity of Blacks crumbled, Earl Warren, president of the local chapter of the NAACP, and Earl Walter, leader of the local CORE chapter, tried unsuccessfully to keep the factions together.[53] Ideological differences shattered the tenuous unity as several Black leaders were co-opted by the power structure. Blacks lost a chance for a consolidated struggle against police brutality and perhaps against broader issues. Individuals made various attempts, through commissions and official meetings, to get redress. However, as unity broke down, so did momentum.

When Watts erupted into rebellion in the long, hot summer of 1965, the police made another repressive attack on the Nation of Islam Mosque, firing one hundred rounds blindly into the place of worship. And authorities have cited the recurrence of police brutality, as an underlying cause of the Watts Rebellion. The two issues which racked the city in 1962 were still alive in 1965. Blacks failed to resist the power structure, capitalize on the crucial issue of police brutality, and build an enduring unity. Tragically, the Los Angeles Police Department was able to continue its assault on Blacks, most viciously against the Black Panther Party. Thus Ronald Stokes appears to have died in vain.

NOTES

1. George Breitman, *The Last Year of Malcolm X: The Evolution of a Revolutionary* (New York: Pathfinder Press, 1967), 17. Breitman refers to a statement made by Malcolm X during the question-and-answer period after a talk with a group of young people from McComb, Mississippi. Malcolm X asserted: "That's what caused the Black Muslim movement to be split. Some of our brothers got hurt, and nothing was done about it, and those of us who wanted to do something about it were kept from doing something about it. So we split."

2. Peter Goldman, *The Death and Life of Malcolm X*, 2nd ed. (Urbana: The University of Illinois Press, 1979; reprint, 1973), 92–101; Benjamin Karim, *Remembering Malcolm: The Story of Malcolm X from Inside the Muslim Mosque*, with Peter Skutches and David Gallen (New York: Carroll and Graf Publishers, Inc., 1992), 133–42.

3. Eugene Victor Wolfenstein, *The Victims of Democracy* (Los Angeles: The University of California Press, 1981), 273–81.

4. Bruce Perry, *Malcolm: The Life of a Man Who Changed America* (New York: Station Hill, 1991), 191–94.

5. Bruce Tyler, *Black Radicalism in Southern California, 1950–1982*, (Ph.D. thesis, University of California, Los Angeles, 1983), 14, 312.

6. Karl Evanzz, *The Judas Factor: The Plot to Kill Malcolm X* (New York: Thunder's Mouth Press, 1992), 117–24.

7. For lengthy authoritative descriptions of the Nation of Islam movement, consult C. Eric Lincoln, *The Black Muslims in America*, rev. ed. (New York: Kayode Publications, Ltd., 1991; reprint, 1973); and E. U. Essien-Udom, *Black Nationalism: A Search for Identity in America* (Chicago: The University of Chicago Press, 1962); for a discussion of the perception of the police as a colonizing army, refer to George Jackson, *Blood in My Eye* (Baltimore: Black Classic Press, 1981; reprint, 1972), and Louis E. Tackwood and the Citizens Research and Investigation Committee, *Center for the Analysis of Law Enforcement Practices: The Glass House Tapes* (New York: Avon Press, 1973); Robert M. Fogelson disputes the claim that the urban ghetto was a colony in his article "Violence as Protest," *The Underside of American History, Volume II: Since 1865*, 229–53, Thomas Frazer, ed.

(New York: Harcourt Brace Jovanovich, Inc., 1974), 237–38.

8. Malcolm X, *The Autobiography of Malcolm X* (New York: Ballantine Books, 1992, reprint, 1965), 233–35; Goldman, 55–60.

9. *Los Angeles Times*, September 3, 1961, sec. C, 1 and 3; *Muhammad Speaks*, May 1962, 5 and 6.

10. Ibid.

11. John C. Bollens and Grant B. Geyer, *Yorty: Politics of a Constant Candidate* (Pacific Palisades, Calif.: Palisades Publishers, 1973), 132.

12. *Los Angeles Times*, June 2, 1961, sec. 1, 1 and 8.

13. Clayborne Carson, *Malcolm X: The FBI File* (New York: Carroll and Graf Publishers Inc., 1991), 25–30; see Tyler, *Black Radicalism*, chap. 3, for a thorough analysis of Yorty's repressive Cold War activities.

14. J. P. Mathews, "Nation of Islam," 1965, J. P. Mathews Papers, Special Collections, William R. Perkins Library, Duke University, Durham, N.C.

15. Statement of J. Edgar Hoover, director, Federal Bureau of Investigation, before National Commission on the Causes and Prevention of Violence," September 18, 1968, J. P. Mathews Papers.

16. California Legislature. Joint Factfinding Sub-Committee on Un-American Activities, *Un-American Activities in California*, Eleventh Report, 1963, 131–38.

17. *Muhammad Speaks*, June 1962, 11.

18. William Parker, "The Police," interview by Donald McDonald (Center for the Study of Democratic Institutions, April 1962), One of a series of interviews on the American Character, 18.

19. Karim, *Remembering Malcolm*, 133.

20. *Los Angeles Times*, April, May, June, and July 1962 and April, May, and June 1963.

21. *Muhammad Speaks*, July 5, 1963, 3 and 4. A review of articles from the *Los Angeles Times* reveals the accuracy of the following statement by John Shabazz, one of the defendants and minister of Muhammad's Mosque No. 27: "THE ANTI-BLACK white press not only tried the case and found all guilty before a trial date was set, but covered the trial by giving complete credence to the prosecution's side of the case and playing down the side of the defense."

22. Perry, *Malcolm*, 191–92.

23. Malcolm X, "Los Angeles Press Conference," audio tape, May(?) 1962; *Muhammad Speaks*, July 1962, 2; *California Eagle*, May 30, 1963, 1, 4.

24. *California Eagle*, May 23, 1963, 1, 4.

25. *California Eagle*, May 16, 1963, 1–4; *Muhammad Speaks*, July 1962, 2.

26. *California Eagle*, May 23, 1963, 1, 4.

27. Ibid.; *Muhammad Speaks*, July 1962, 5 and 6.

28. Ibid.; *Muhammad Speaks*, July 5, 1963, 2.

29. Robert F. Williams, *Negroes with Guns* (New York: Marzani and Munsell, Inc., 1962), 110.

30. Malcolm X, audio tape, "Unity Rally," Harlem, New York, 1963(?).

31. *Muhammad Speaks*, June 1962, 2; Malcolm X, "Los Angeles Press Conference"; Karim, *Remembering Malcolm*, 134.

32. Louis Lomax, *To Kill a Black Man: The Shocking Parallel in the Lives of Malcolm X and Martin Luther King, Jr.* (Los Angeles: Holloway Publishing Co., 1987; reprint, 1968), 97.

33. Hakim Jamal, *From the Dead Level* (New York: Random House, 1972), 219.

34. Ibid., 221.

35. Ibid., 222–23.

36. Malcolm X to James Farmer, July 29, 1963, Congress of Racial Equality Papers (Microfilming Corporation of America), Series 1, Reel 3:34, Frame 424.

37. *Amsterdam News*, May 26, 1962, 10.

38. *Muhammad Speaks*, July 1962, 7, and May 24, 1963; Elijah Muhammad also refers to the shooting in *Message to the Blackman in America* (Chicago: Muhammad's Mosque No. 2), 211–15. Refer to the 1962 and 1963 issues of *Muhammad Speaks* to see how Muhammad used the shooting to push his program.

39. *Muhammad Speaks*, August 15, 1962, 3; *Los Angeles Times*, May 9, 1962, sec. II, 1; Evanzz, *The Judas Factor*, 121; Ed Ainsworth, *Maverick Mayor: A Biography of Sam Yorty of Los Angeles* (Garden City, New York: Doubleday & Company, Inc., 1966), 199–200. It is no coincidence that on October 12, Mayor Yorty and Chief Parker placed a request to the city council for three thousand riot helmets. A passage in Ainsworth's work reads: "In the budget for 1963–64 an item of $50,930 was included and approved for the purchase. These helmets were kept in readiness in the event of necessity." The "necessity" arose three years later with the eruption of the Watts rebellion of 1965.

40. *Los Angeles Times*, May 2, 3, and 4, 1962, sec. I, 1.

41. *Los Angeles Times*, May 10, 1962, sec. II, 1.

42. One white woman, Helen Herbert, became so distressed about the possibility of a Muslim attack that on July 5 she offered $11,427 to join the Nation of Islam for personal protection. Of course her offer was rejected. *Amsterdam News*, July 14, 1962, 9.

43. SNCC Papers, Box 11, File 8, Martin Luther King, Jr. Center for Nonviolent Social Change, Atlanta, Georgia, *Muhammad Speaks*, April 29, 1963.

44. Paul Robeson, *Here I Stand* (Boston: Beacon Press, 1971; reprint 1958), 93.

45. August Meier and Elliot Rudwick, *CORE: A Study in the Civil Rights Movement, 1942–1968* (New York: Oxford University Press, 1973), 194 and 198; *Muhammad Speaks*, June 7, 1963, 3.

46. *Muhammad Speaks*, June 1962, 5; August 31, 1962, 3; see Evanzz, *The Judas Factor* for further discussion of the responses of national civil rights leaders.

47. *Muhammad Speaks*, May 13, 1963, 1 and 2.

48. Evanzz, *The Judas Factor; Muhammad Speaks*, June 1962, 10; July 1962, 5. A section of the resolution follows:

> **ARTICLE II**
>
> In the present Convention, genocide means any of the following acts committed with intent to destroy, in whole or in part, a national, ethnic, racial or religious group as such:
>
> a. Killing members of the group;
> b. Causing serious bodily or mental harm to members of the group;
> c. Deliberately inflicting on the group conditions calculated to bring about its physical destruction in whole or in part;
> d. Imposing measures intended to prevent births with the group;
> e. Forcibly transferring children of the group to another group.
>
> **ARTICLE III**
>
> The following acts shall be punishable:
>
> a. Genocide;
> b. Conspiracy to commit genocide;
> c. Direct and public incitement to commit genocide;
> d. Attempt to commit genocide;
> e. Complicity in genocide.

49. *Los Angeles Times*, May 11, 1962, part II, 1.

50. *Muhammad Speaks*, June 7, 1963, 3.

51. *Los Angeles Sentinel*, May 10, 1962, A4; May 17, 1962, A3, 5; *California Eagle*, May 24, 1962, 4.

52. *Pittsburgh Courier*, June 2, 1962, 4.

53. *California Eagle*, May 31, 1962, 1 and 4.

12

SOME GLANCES AT THE BLACK FAG
Race, Same-Sex Desire, and Cultural Belonging

Marlon B. Ross

This was how the people accepted it in the community. Nobody could be shocked at people being faggots. Nobody thought there was anything so crazy about it.
—Claude Brown

Mass media images of contemporary Harlem reveal only a part of the actual texture of the lives of the people who inhabit that vast, richly varied, infinitely complex, and endlessly fascinating area up-town Manhattan. Those who create such images almost always restrict themselves to documenting the pathological.
—Albert Murray

When an open and autonomous culture of gays and lesbians began to form in America's urban centers during the late 1960s, there already existed largely integrated within the African-American community an established and visible tradition of homosexuality. The consolidation of an openly gay culture had a direct impact on the ways in which Black gays and lesbians could position themselves within the African-American community, in relation to the emergent gay community, and in relation to American society at large. Given the ways in which European-American society has projected its own anxieties about sexual pathology and conformity onto African-American culture, it is not surprising that issues of sexual diversity would be intimately tied to matters of racial community within the United States. The legitimate theoretical link between racial liberation and sexual liberation immediately became confused by the American tendency to associate sexual license with African-American culture. If racial integration was projected as a threat to social order based on the myth of the African American as a promiscuous, pathological other, then it was a short step to conflating the social transgressions of homosexuality with deep-seated anxieties surrounding Black sexuality. As the fear of cross-racial sexuality was intensified by the integration-oriented civil rights movement during the 1950s and 1960s, the fight for racial integration set the stage for viewing gay liberation in a similar light: as a crossover phenomenon that operated by disrupting a social order based on maintaining the nuclear family, proper gender roles, and solid racial boundaries. The open display of homosexuality in the cities seemed to be but another symptom (and proof) of the break-down of social order brought on by white America's impending loss of cultural control over black America.

Furthermore, by the 1960s a strong link had been established between African-American culture and greater tolerance of homosexuality due to a long historical relation between more open urban homosexuals and African-American urban communities. In the 1960s homosexuality was still largely an unspoken phenomenon in American society, even though its visibility had increased in larger cities since World War II. For some of the same reasons that African Americans had migrated from the rural South to northern urban cen-ters, gay men and lesbians had begun a pattern of migration from rural areas to major urban centers.[1] Homosexual activity was less hidden to African-American eyes because those gays who were more open about their sexuality were beginning to share the same geo-graphic terrain with blacks in northern urban centers. The relation between white homo-sexuals and the African-American community is a complicated, vexed history that can be traced at least as far back as the 1920s, but the African-American community's reluctance to ostracize black homosexuals in the puritan European-American mode may go back much further.[2] On the one hand, white homosexuals, like bohemians and hipsters, saw African-American communities as hip places to test their avant-garde status. Whites invaded Black urban communities to make themselves feel more cosmopolitan, to give themselves license to feel unencumbered by the puritanism and commercialism of middle-class white society. A significant aspect of this cosmopolitan ambiance was projected as sexual license—merely extenuating into vicarious pleasure the fearful tendency of white Americans to fantasize Africans as possessing a more deviant, and thus freer and richer, sexual life. Given the racial conditions, it is not surprising that white exploitation characterized one aspect of the rela-tion between white homosexuals and the Black community—a fact that has made any coali-tion between the two communities much more problematic.[3] On the other hand, the African-American community was also seen as a genuinely safer place to experience homo-sexual relations without the stigma and judgment of middle-class white society. It provided a model of tolerance not available elsewhere in American society.

In "A Spectacle in Color: The Lesbian and Gay Subculture of Jazz Age Harlem," Eric Garber summarizes the attitude of white lesbians and gays who trekked up to Harlem to enjoy the liberties it afforded:

> With its sexually tolerant population and its quasi-legal nightlife, Harlem offered an oasis to white homosexuals. For some, a trip to Harlem was part of a larger rebellion against the Pro-hibition Era's conservative moral and political climate. For Van Vechten, and for many other white lesbians and gay men, Harlem offered even deeper rewards. Blair Niles based her [novel] *Strange Brother* on her friend and confidant Leland Pettit, a young, white, gay man from Mil-waukee and the organist at Grace Church. According to *Strange Brother*, Pettit frequented the homosexual underworld in Harlem because he found social acceptance, and because he iden-tified with others who were also outcasts from [white] American life. This identification and feeling of kinship, undoubtedly shared by other white lesbians and gay men, may have been the beginnings of homosexual "minority consciousness." (329)[4]

Garber's insight that gay "minority consciousness" may have formed in the Black commu-nity's homosexual networks has much to recommend it—though we might question the way in which Garber segregates Black same-sex activity to an "under-world."[5] The whole of pre–civil rights Black life, from a white perspective, could be, and frequently has been, viewed as an "underworld." This relation between Black neighborhoods and white homosexuals was by no means limited to Harlem, but was common in many urban centers. As a result, when gay men began to consolidate their own open communities in the 1960s, these communities often bordered the neighborhoods of Blacks (and other people of color), and in most cases were developed not coincidentally in the midst of areas undergoing urban "blight." (In addition to New York City, this was the case in San Francisco, Chicago, Los Angeles, Detroit, Cleveland, Philadelphia, Washington, D.C., Boston, St. Louis, Milwaukee, New Orleans, Miami, Atlanta, Seattle, and Houston, as well as many smaller cities.) This "border" relationship helped to establish a further dialogue between white homosexuals and the Black community, a complicated dialogue that academe and the media have not noticed until recently, and now tend to notice only in the most superficial, sensationalistic ways. This dialogue is most frequently characterized as contentious, pitting each side against the other by the press in such a way that both sides are wrong and neither side can win. The media tend to characterize Blacks as being more homophobic than nonBlacks— an astonishing conclusion, considering the history of relatively greater tolerance within the African-American community. Gay men are characterized by the media as preying on the Black community—taking attention away from the racial struggle and exploiting the successes of Black civil rights in an attempt to parlay similar successes for themselves. Gay people are always portrayed in this context as all white and as male; the only Blacks the media tend to interview are more socially conservative (male) ministers. As a result, the argument looks as though it is between the two figures that the media have portrayed as most frightening to mainstream America: the strong Black (straight) male and the militant (white) gay male. The argument gets framed in such a way that the dominant stereotype of each figure is reinforced. The Black (straight) male cannot protect his turf (the city) even against a faggot. The (white) homosexual is framed as an exploitative, narcissistic interloper, one who is more concerned about getting his sexual preference, that is, his sexual license, validated than about the more serious problems of crime, unemployment, impoverishment, and genocide in the inner city. The media react as though the dialogue concerning the relation between homosexuality and race is a new phenomenon, one that came into existence only after mainstream white society was forced to begin to deal with questions of gay rights.

We should not be surprised by the media's distorted treatment of the relationship between white gays and the African American community. The media are simply doing what they always do well, picking up on a strain between two oppressed groups, and exploiting that strain to the disadvantage of each group and to the advantage of the status quo. In fact, there is a long, complicated history at stake, a history that tells us as much about the representation of Black male sexuality as it does about the interplay of sex and race in American politics. The strain between white gays and the Black community grows out of this history. When white gay men migrated to the cities, they came at an opportune moment. By concentrating their numbers in the cities, they were able to become an influential political block, both economically and at the ballot box, due to their relative affluence and to their growing visibility and political organization. In a sense, they began to replace the white "ethnics," who had begun to leave the urban centers for the suburbs, in competition with racial minorities for political control and influence in the cities. This political rivalry could only be intensified by the fact that gays have relied heavily on strategies, laws, and rhetoric originally fostered by Black Americans in their fight for civil rights and group empowerment. The media's sensationalist and noisy attention to this rivalry, however, has silenced other aspects of this relationship, and has helped to suppress the rich, entangled history tying homosexual consciousness to the African-American struggle for unity and empowerment. The broader and deeper nature of this relationship can be understood only through a double focus. First, we must clarify what the white homosexual, as a cultural concept and as a political entity, gains from a literal and figurative "border" relation to African-American culture. Second, we must bring into view the cultural role of the Black faggot, the male figure who is most frequently suppressed in the media's staging of an argument. The Black homosexual does not obliterate the easy opposition between Black and white, straight and gay, which fuels the American imagination and greases the oppressive engine of American politics, but this figure complicates those oppositions and helps us to flesh out a history in which homosexuality and race are not natural enemies.

Obviously, gays and lesbians looked to the civil rights movement as a model for their own awakening into social and political consciousness. More subtly, however, the more significant influence may have been the actual experience of how an outcast status could enable greater group solidarity and greater freedom within the group, a phenomenon that white gays experienced secondhand when visiting the homosexual networks of the Black community. In homosexuals' attempt to establish a permanent, viable, open culture virtually from scratch against the grain of oppression and obscurity, the long history of African American culture had to prove a valuable resource for a homosexual consciousness in search of ways to consolidate and mobilize a fragmented, distorted, hidden protoculture in which individuals necessarily start out as lonely queers bereft of a sympathetic community.

What did white homosexuals gain during the 1940s and 1950s by staying in and flocking to the urban centers at a point when these centers were being vacated by whites and were becoming unrespectable places to live from the viewpoint of an oppressing dominant culture?[6] Beyond the advantage of being left alone, white homosexuals gained, in effect, a nascent new identity as an oppressed group willing to acknowledge and work against its own oppression. Sharing the stigma of an inferior status with their neighbors of color, white homosexuals could attain the value of that stigma validated through their association with groups whose strength in adversity had been long proven, turning that stigma into a badge of cultural belonging. In his groundbreaking study *The Homosexual in America* (1951), Donald Webster Cory was the first to put forward a fully worked out theory of gay "subculture" based solely on the idea that gays and lesbians constitute an "unrecognized minority." Cory demonstrates how homosexuals already constituted a "minority" group, though not yet recognized as such, and, more fundamentally, a cultural group, though one whose culture was "submerged" or malformed due to the peculiar pressures of sexual oppression. At every turn of his elaborate and forceful argument, Cory relies on the comparison to African-American "minority" culture to establish the legitimacy of a homosexual culture—the dominant strategy still relied on today by gay and lesbian activists of all political stripes.

Also at the heart of Cory's argument, however, is the idea that gays and lesbians constitute a fluid minority, whose particular virtue grows out of the fact that they exist inside of every other cultural group.

The homosexual, cutting across all racial, religious, national, and caste lines, frequently reacts to rejection by a deep understanding of all others who have likewise been scorned because of belonging to an outcast group. "There, but for the grace of God . . ." it is said, and the homosexual, like those who are part of other dominated minorities, can "feel" as well as understand the meaning of that phrase. The person who has felt the sting of repudiation by the dominant culture can reflect that, after all, he might have been another religion or race or color, an untouchable in India, one of the mentally or physically handicapped. It is not for him to join with those who reject millions of their fellowmen of all types and groups, but to accept all men, an attitude forced upon him happily by the stigma of being cast out of the fold of society.

It is no wonder, then, that a true and genuine democracy so frequently pervades the activities of the homosexual group . . . And today, the deeprooted prejudices that restrict marriages and friendships according to social strata—family, wealth, religion, color, and a myriad of other artifices—are conspicuously absent among the submerged groups that make up the homosexual society. (151–52)

Multiculturalism is conceptualized here as an intrinsic and definitive determinant of gay culture, thus making the crossover dynamic a founding principle of homosexuality. A culture that is ironically defined by its lack of cultural boundaries, rather than by its cultural singularity, becomes a guiding ideal within the gay and lesbian community. Cosmopolitanism defines this concept of open gay culture for whites in four interrelated ways.

First, as Cory points out, gays and lesbians represent every imaginable cultural group, and they bring this traditional cultural orientation with them when they enter into gay/lesbian culture. Second, their gay cultural affiliation is both secondary (always succeeding acculturation in some other racial, ethnic, religious group) and also invisible. Not only do nongays tend to project heterosexuality onto others; they also tend to defend against the invisible nature of the homosexual disposition by concocting elaborate myths about how homosexuals can be easily spotted. This means that a gay person can experience the stigma of oppression while appearing to be part of the dominant culture that oppresses. Whereas this experience of "passing" is also an option within other groups, it is an exception that requires the individual to abandon the formative culture. For the gay person, passing is the rule, not the exception, and the process and effect are just the opposite. Rather than abandoning the original cultural group in order to pass, the gay person passes by remaining totally assimilated by the original group. The gay person ceases to pass in a process of abandoning the original cultural group or in challenging its cultural priority and totality by coming out and identifying openly with gay/lesbian culture. For Cory this chameleon capacity forces the homosexual to cross boundaries and empathize with others in the most downcast groups ("an untouchable in India") without necessarily having to experience the external markers of that oppression. Whereas homosexuals from racially oppressed groups are used to the experience of being outcast from dominant society while being empowered within their own culture, for white homosexuals (especially men), this is a new experience.

Third, once homosexuals accept their variance (perceived as "deviance" in the 1950s and 1960s, as "difference" in the 1980s and 1990s), they not only are compelled to identify with downcast groups, but also are drawn into connections with individuals from these groups who also happen to be gay. The more openly gay the individual, the more she or he is pressed into relations with others who are also escaping the straightjacket of their original groups.

Finally, the more openly gay the individual, the more she or he will become geographically marginalized in relation to the dominant culture, pressed into contact with those at the bottom of the American social scale in the urban centers. At each step and at every level in the gay person's developing awareness, the cosmopolitan impulse supposedly intensifies.[7]

Although we should not underestimate this utopian aspect of gay and lesbian settlement in the inner city, we should also remember that, as the most despised group in society, they had no choice but to settle among racial groups already outcast based on class and color. The diversity of homosexuality that gays and lesbians the most easily assimilable group also suggests an ideal—nowhere approached in practice—of "true and genuine democracy," once they begin to establish open geographic communities. Hoping that homosexuals will be able to stake a claim to a special contribution in the larger culture of America, Cory focuses on this innate cosmopolitan diversity and its attendant "democratic spirit" as axiomatic. "It is in this . . . that we find a reaction to being gay that is strength born of handicap. The sympathy for all mankind—including groups similarly despised in their own right—that is exhibited by so many homosexuals, can be a most rewarding factor, not only for the individual, but for society" (152).

This hope that gay culture will be instrumental in spreading cosmopolitan democracy is not as original as it first appears. For even in this cultural characteristic, gay/lesbian communities have been deeply influenced by the role of African-American culture (as well as Jewish culture), especially since the 1920s, in creating the vanguard of modern cultural expression admired and imitated throughout the entire world.[8] By associating with African Americans from the 1920s to the 1940s and by actually settling open communities next to them in the 1950s and 1960s, homosexuals embarked on making visible the otherwise concealed mark of sexual deviation, and thus making valid, in the minds of white homosexuals, the *group* "identity" of homosexuality, which was normally considered a solitary, individual affliction. A white person venturing into a Black neighborhood is already conspicuous, and any stigma and judgment brought down on him by African Americans would necessarily be different in effect, if not in kind. For a white person to be judged by Blacks could not have the same ostracizing effect as being condemned by dominant white society. What white homosexuals gained from these largely economically impoverished African-American neighborhoods was a cultural model for social tolerance, solidarity despite variance within the group, dignity in the face of oppression, and a drive for cultural expression that could determine the standard for cosmopolitanism.

The myth of greater sexual license within African-American culture was easily confused with the reality of African-American culture's great tolerance of Black homosexuals. How could white homosexuals not observe with some envy the ways in which African-American communities refused to ostracize even those native sons who were most "flamboyantly" homosexual? They could never have such freedom in their own mainstream white communities. How could the white homosexual understand that Black society's embracing of their homosexual sons was not the same as Black society's embracing of homosexuality itself?[9] What white homosexuals would have difficulty seeing is that the greater acceptance within the Black community was not a result of greater sexual license per se, but instead was a result of a cultural value long held among African Americans that racial freedom could be gained only through racial solidarity, an understanding that the need for racial solidarity was much more important than the impulse to ostracize individuals whose sexuality seemed to vary from the norm. In effect, that "norm," like the rule of law itself, has been much more contested within African-American culture, exactly because Blacks have had to be wary of the endless attempts of mainstream society to whitewash Black culture by imposing a standard of normalcy that is really just an excuse for oppressive behavior.

Unlike white homosexuals, who had the comparative luxury of being able to escape to urban centers and occasionally to go "slumming" in Black neighborhoods within the city, Black homosexuals had no such option before the 1960s, unless, as we shall see, they consented to becoming dependent, kept lovers of white gay men. If a Black homosexual were to be ostracized from his community, where on earth could he go? This dramatic difference in social, economic, and historical conditions between the Black and white homosexual necessarily has led to a different conception of sexual orientation and coming out. For the white homosexual, integrating same-sex desire into one's sense of self meant necessarily leaving one's community behind for a new community in a mixed urban environment. For the Black homosexual, nothing could be further from the case. Integrating same-sex desire within the self meant finding a way to remain integrated within the home community while remaining true to one's desire. Even the Black homosexual who might leave the rural South in search of homosexual community would possess a continuity not imaginable for the white homosexual. For even as Black homosexuals might leave home behind, they would find it waiting for them in the Black communities of the urban North. For the Black homosexual, same-sex desire was a matter of finding a way to reaffirm continuity, rather than a matter of breaking with a dominant culture in order to gain a new identity through an awakened consciousness shared with others of a similarly oppressed status. After all, how could Black gays break with dominant culture, since they had never been part of it?

This is why James Baldwin's refusal to identify as a homosexual is not necessarily the contradiction it is often seen as being. Though Baldwin felt compelled to expose the scandal of normalcy by bringing the reality of desire to the surface, he did not consider himself a homosexual. "Homosexual," he reminded us, is properly an adjective, not a noun. What Baldwin meant by this is that he viewed homosexuality as a practice or disposition of desire, not as an identity defining the existence of an individual's cultural belonging.

> A Black gay person who is a sexual conundrum to society is already, long before the question of sexuality comes into it, menaced and marked because he's Black or she's Black. The sexual question comes after the question of color; it's simply one more aspect of the danger in which all Black people live. I think white gay people feel cheated because they were supposed to be safe. The anomaly of their sexuality puts them in danger, unexpectedly. Their reaction seems to me in direct proportion to the sense of feeling cheated of the advantages which accrue to white people in a white society. There's an element, it has always seemed to me, of bewilderment and complaint. (In Goldstein 180)

Ironically, Baldwin's view of homosexuality is, in some ways, more similar to that of the Black nationalists who blasted him than the white gay community, which has fully embraced the "gay" aspects of his work. Baldwin sees African-American identity as both prior and more grounding. The same-sex disposition is, for him, not so much an identity as it is a variation within and among the bedrock of racial identity. Like Cory, he conceptualizes homosexuality as a fluid characteristic that traverses other identities that are assumed to be more stable, solid, and total. This idea that race is a more stable block of identity and that homosexuality is a more fluid, historically varied form of identity lives on in the 1990s and undergirds much of the academic and popular discourse on race and sexuality.[10] Often, this means that sexuality becomes a matter of "lifestyle," unfixable postmodern identification, and traveling alliances, whereas race becomes a matter of cultural tradition, fixed historical identification, and originary ties to specific geographical spheres (whiteness in Europe, Blackness in Africa, etc.). Depending on the context, sexuality's unfixable nature is seen either as an advantage, especially when it is used as the exemplary characteristic that proves the cultural construction of identity, or as a disadvantage, especially when it is reduced to a mere lifestyle choice in practical debates over civil rights legislation. For Black homosexuals before the 1970s, to break with their racial culture as a way of embracing their variant desire made no sense. However, after the more militant movements of both Black nationalism (which tended to scapegoat homosexuality) and gay liberation (which offered a rhetoric of racial inclusion) in the late 1960s and early 1970s, embracing European-American style autonomous gay identity began to make some sense for some Black homosexuals. At first glance, it might appear to be the ultimate irony that Baldwin, the most famous openly gay Black man and the one most responsible for initiating a popular discussion of homosexuality, did not believe in the existence of gay culture. But this irony is swept away once we remind ourselves of Baldwin's historical situation. However much homosexuality was damned to the inner "extremities" (the urban centers) of mainstream culture, the Black who happened to be homosexual was already at home within those inner "extremities." As long as he remembered where he came from as a Black man, homosexuality would normally not become a reason for his being banished from his own culture.

Within American society, there was every reason for a gay culture (or subculture) not to exist. Gays and lesbians did certainly have traditions, ways of thinking, even institutions (such as bars) before the 1960s (and perhaps even as early as the seventeenth century in Europe), but the important point is that these conditions existed in a strange limbo, a culture not yet born and yet always potentially operative.[11] This limbo was a comparatively safe place for them to visit temporarily in an escape from the hostilities of "real" culture, not a place to live, grow, work, prosper, and educate the next generation. Because gays and lesbians were thought to have no vital relation to procreation, they could have only a tangential relation to what was seen as legitimate culture, and, in the context of their own group, they were seen as isolated, lonely, misplaced individuals wrongly or rightly outcast from the permanence of real culture. At best, their social relations to each other could only diminish temporarily their loneliness by stressing the deeper reality of their essentially permanent isolation from culture. This mainstream American attitude toward the homosexual dominated through the 1960s. It is apparent in sociological and psychoanalytic studies on homosexuality, as well as in literary representations of homosexuality in novels like Gore Vidal's *City and the Pillar*, Chester Himes's *Cast the First Stone*, Baldwin's *Giovanni's Room*, James Barr's *Quatrefoil*, Fritz Peters' *Finistère*, Charles Wright's *The Messenger*, or the writings of Tennessee Williams, Truman Capote, and James Purdy. Even though all of these writers are sympathetic, they tend to disparage the social network available to homosexuals as a culture manqué, rather than a culture outright.

The best articulation of this dominant attitude comes not surprisingly from the most influential theoretical anthropologist of the '50s and '60s, Claude Lévi-Strauss. In his most popular book, *Tristes Tropiques* (1955), Lévi-Strauss searches for a way to describe the "weirdest" site of his travels into "primitive" South America, and he finds an appropriate geographic-anthropological analogy in Fire Island:

Both express the same kind of geographical and human absurdity, comic in the one instance and sinister in the other. Fire Island might have been invented by Swift. . . . The dunes on Fire Island are so shifting, and their hold on the sea so precarious, that further notices warn the public to keep off in case they should collapse into the water below. The place is like an inverted Venice, since it is the land which is fluid and the canals solid.

The "aquatic desert" of Porto Esperança is, like Fire Island's inverted relation between water and land, a freak of nature, a structure with "no reason for its existence" (169). The human factor in this absurd site is, of course, the homosexual population of Fire Island's major village, Cherry Grove, one of the earliest white American openly gay communities.

To complete the picture, I must add that Cherry Grove is chiefly inhabited by male couples, attracted no doubt by the general pattern of inversion. Since nothing grows in the sand, apart from broad patches of poisonous ivy, provisions are collected once a day from the one and only shop, at the end of the landing-stage. In the tiny streets, on higher ground more stable than the dunes, the sterile couples can be seen returning to their chalets pushing prams (the only vehicles suitable for the narrow paths) containing little but the weekend bottles of milk that no baby will consume. (168–69)

Characterized by "farcical gaiety," Cherry Grove society is a parody of real culture solely because male couples cannot procreate. Lévi-Strauss's clever portrait of male couples pushing baby carriages laden with bottles of milk, instead of babies, assumes that any cultural group brought together without a procreative base will be sterile, both symbolically and literally. These fake couples are "attracted no doubt to the general pattern of inversion" on Fire Island. Underlying the farcical effect of this "sterile" community is a more sinister poisonousness. Just as the sterile couples must import their food because nothing but poison ivy grows on the island, so they must import their social relations from mainstream culture as they absurdly mock the heterosexual couple. For Lévi-Strauss this is all laughable only because it is so contained, so sterile, so unnatural, offering no real threat to real culture.

Lévi-Strauss's portrait of gay Fire Island relies on a confusion between the literal and the symbolic, a grounding fallacy in Western anthropological thinking.[12] Gay males are not literally sterile, and to call their relationships sterile can only make sense if the sole purpose for bonding is procreation, symbolic or literal. According to his logic, gay men must be literally attracted to literally sterile habitats, because homosexuals symbolize the inversion of culture's total purpose, the procreative drive. The symbolic correlation between social structure and geographic structure reveals, for the anthropologist, the literal relation between procreation and the reproduction of genuine cultural knowledge.

The Lévi-Strauss school of structural anthropology has been criticized for basing the reproduction of culture on abstract concepts and patterns that seem to diminish the role of instinct, practical physical needs, and the tactical give-and-take struggle that exists within any culture.[13] Actually, however, Lévi-Strauss's concept of culture places physical procreation as the cornerstone of legitimate culture in no less a way than his predecessors. His Cherry Grove example is not a whimsical aside, but a telling analogy. In his need to explain (and thus explain away) the existence of homosexuality among the Nambikwara, a native tribe of central Brazil, Lévi-Strauss again reveals the procreative logic at the heart of his anthropological system. Of course, this reveals nothing about the Nambikwara and everything about the peculiarly Western assumptions undergirding Lévi-Strauss's "science." According to Lévi-Strauss, the Nambikwara resort to homosexuality only as a clever way of solving the problem of a scarcity of female partners for young men, as a result of the practice which grants to the chief the privilege of polygamy:

> Such relationships are frequent between young men and take place far more publicly than *normal* relationships. The two partners do not withdraw into the bush like adults of opposite sexes. They settle down near the camp fire, while their neighbours look on with amusement. Such incidents are a source of jokes, which generally remain discreet; homosexual relationships are considered to be childish pastimes and little attention is paid to them. (354, italics added)

The anthropological question here *should be* what constitutes "normal relationships" for this tribal group; instead, it becomes a priori a matter of figuring out how behavior (male-male sexual relations) already defined by the anthropologist as abnormal can happen among such innocent primitives. If such relations are routine within Nambikwara society, then why is not such routineness itself a clue for the "normalcy" of such behavior? Among the Nambikwara, homosexuality is integrated within the culture in such a way that it is strange and threatening to Lévi-Strauss's observant Western eyes, but not so threatening as to alter his understanding of same-sex desire. In effect, he responds the same way to both the culturally integrated same-sex desire of the Nambikwara and the culturally segregated homosexuality of Cherry Grove. Given his assumptions, neither can be seen as deep structures within the cultural system; both are merely improvised rationales that, despite their instrinsic absurdity, give credence to the deepest structure of male-female bonding and procreation.

Lévi-Strauss's attitude was shared uniformly among social scientists throughout the 1950s and 1960s. As long as same-sex desire was seen as a form of inverted individual behavior dependent upon normal culture for its rationale, it could not be seen as a form of group behavior. In Western thinking, same-sex desire comes to make sense in itself only once it has been raised to the level of a cultural phenomenon, only once it is studied as a culture unto itself. Since Cory's study, white American gays and lesbians have understood that the only way to legitimate homosexual desire was first to segregate it culturally and demonstrate not only its "minority" status but also its cultural value to the larger American society. This is difficult, if not impossible, to do by conceiving of homosexuality on an individual basis, for as individuals, gays and lesbians, according to the procreative logic of dominant society, will always be extraneous and detached loners. In the introduction to *Gay Culture in America*, Gilbert Herdt writes:

> It seems ideologically significant that a hundred years of research on homosexuality, marking its beginnings with Karl Ulrichs's twelve-volume study in the nineteenth century, have so very often been concerned with the causes rather than the outcomes of "homosexuality." To ask, for instance, why people desire the same sex is very different from asking whether they are happy, or successful, or competent. Particularly in medical research and disease discourse, the issue has been fixated on individual development more than on the formation of a gay cultural community. Gradually, however, the focus of such studies—and the source of these studies as well—has shifted. Scholars of "homosexuality" are more and more gays or lesbians themselves, and they are concerned, not with the etiology of a "disease," but with the cultural history of lesbians and gays. (4–5)

The anthropological field essays in *Gay Culture in America* are themselves excellent examples of the shift Herdt refers to. It is not until after the actual formation of an open gay culture that this shift in scholarly procedure could take place, however.

While the focus on autonomous gay/lesbian culture works well for a post-Stonewall view of white homosexuality, it necessarily fails to account for the more integrated experience of same-sex desire within traditional African-American culture, especially before the 1960s. The problem is that, once autonomous white gay and lesbian culture became the norm, as the object and subject of study, for understanding homosexuality, the same autonomous-culture approach was automatically applied to same-sex desire within African-American communities. Attempts to apply the same autonomous-culture approach to Black homosexuality, however, necessarily misrepresent the conditions of same-sex desire within the African-American community. Predictably, the one essay on Black gay men in *Gay Culture in America* returns to an individualist, causative approach, citing woefully inadequate statistics to try to understand why Black gay men supposedly are less prone to come out, form relationships, and participate in the (white) lesbian/gay community. White homosexual culture becomes an unspoken norm which allows the anthropologist to understand (or misunderstand) same-gender relationships among African Americans. "Virtually all the data on sexual behavior of Black men in the United States are confined to studies on their sexual behavior with females," John L. Peterson writes. "Similar studies of the same-sex behavior of Black males have been largely neglected. This neglect results in insufficient knowledge of the social and psychological factors that influence same-sex behavior among Black males" (147). These first sentences of the essay admit that there is not much statistical evidence about Black gay men, so how can the statistical approach, used in Peterson's essay, provide anything more than speculative stereotypes, based on a flawed logic of etiology? If comparisons are to be made, it would be more appropriate to consider Black homosexuality as a phenomenon more integrated into Black life similar to the traditional culture of the Nambikwara, but in doing so, we must also steer clear of the kind of absurd Western assumptions besetting the observations of Lévi-Strauss.

Claude Brown's controversial 1965 documentary autobiography *Manchild in the Promised Land* is a much more compelling and helpful guide to understanding the relation between same-sex desire, Black community, and masculinity. I am not suggesting that Brown, or any individual, can give us the key to knowing the "real" Black fag. Cultural knowledge, as I have suggested in the Introduction, is always hedged in by the cognitive processes of synecdoche, metonymy, and projection.[14] Furthermore, my larger point has been and is that images of Black manhood which come to dominate, though they may be based in reality, are always at the service of ideological purposes that can work both for and against the advancement of African-American communities. I would not, however, go as far as Albert Murray, who argues that books like Claude Brown's and James Baldwin's merely repeat the pathology-oriented case studies favored by the social science "ghettologists." According to Murray, such authors are obsessed with proving that African-American culture is sick in order to gain sympathy and money for fixing it (see 98–99). The ideological purpose of Murray's book is to suggest that Blacks are American first, African second, like any other ethnic group, and that the real solution to economic and social problems within African-American communities is to encourage advancement into the wrongly maligned Black middle-class.[15] Murray wants to normalize the race by representing it as not really a race at all, but as a group of "omni-Americans" who contain within themselves everything that is in America, and whereby nothing that is in them is not also in all other Americans. In effect, this becomes another way of representing respectability. Traditionally, the Black middle class has tried to hide or downplay those aspects of African-American culture that might be seen as questionable to mainstream society. Ironically, during the civil rights era, these same cultural variations became exhibit A; they were now put forward by the Black middle class as prime examples of why social reforms, like integration, needed broad political support. Whereas Murray sees through the flawed logic of exhibiting pathology as a basis for social change, Murray's shift to a focus on the continuity (good and bad aspects) between African-American culture and mainstream American culture—assuring that the American norm is the African-American norm—has its own liabilities, most notably a failure to question the legitimacy of norm-focused politics in any movement for social justice and self-empowerment.

Murray's criticism is instructive, however, in that it helps us to keep in mind that tendency in the social sciences, already pointed out in Lévi-Strauss, to pathologize every aspect of communities that are seen as deviating from mainstream European-American cultural practices. It is also true that at the height of the integrationist civil rights movement (mid-1950s to mid-1960s), African-American authors developed a trend of exhibitionist writing. Geared toward making whites understand the predicament of Black America, this trend encourages writers to exhibit in rich detail the social and sexual habits of life "on the street," in the "ghetto," or in the prison.[16] These ghettoized sites appeal to puritan-prurient white tastes exactly because they display Black life as largely cut off from orderly mainstream America while also allowing white readers to experience vicariously what it might be like to lead a life that breaks the rules of an oppressive, hum-drum, work-driven, procreative social order. As Murray points out, Brown's book can be read within this trend, as can other such books that were popular during the time, including *Native Son* (perhaps the progenitor), Chester Himes, Ann Petry, Charles Wright, and, of course, James Baldwin.[17] But the more militant writers of the mid-1960s to early 1970s can also be read in this light, including Eldridge Cleaver, George Jackson, Malcolm X, and the early work of Imiri Baraka. Where Murray goes wrong is to discount totally the material discussed in these books due to the problematic nature of the trend in which they partake. Rather than suggesting that such books "distort" African-American experience by stressing only the underside of it (as Murray contends), we would do better to consider how books like Brown's, even as they strive toward a necessarily flawed rhetorical strategy of nonjudgmental reportage, fall prey to the limitations inherent in the politics of cultural representativeness. The problem is that even though reportage might enable the writer to represent a slice of life as indexing a community spirit, such reportage gets transformed into an act of revelation. An African American, who necessarily lives his version of that experience, does not need it revealed as an experience. He does need, however, journalistic and artistic representations of that experience which can reveal its value and its shortcomings as a common, representable experience. Dependent largely upon a white media, a white publishing establishment, and a white critical response, the record of one man's experience of racial community inevitably gets contextualized as the Black writer's astonishing revelation of salacious racial characteristics. Furthermore, it is difficult to disentangle the rhetorical strategy of reportage from the mainstream cultural value of scientific objectivity. It becomes easy for even African Americans to forget that what the writer reports is not some objectively validated, statistically justifiable social science reality, or that such a thing can even exist, but instead what he reports is his own subjective experience of an objectifiable reality, one which can be reported on at all only when it is, in some sense, objectified. Brown's book especially seeks not only to explore what it is like on the street, but also what it means to view oneself on the street and what it means to represent the street as a sign of racial community.[18] Brown is clearly concerned with recording the conditions which enable a sense of community even under the most degrading and threatening circumstances, and thus with indexing a common experience of a people whose lives have been increasingly represented reductively by the media in terms of violence, despair, and moral rootlessness. The cultural index offers a slice of experience as a way of pointing toward and pointing out what the community at large may need to address as crucial; unfortunately, readers will tend to take this index as a wholistic representation of the race and will project the pressures bearing on the community at large as racial characteristics inhering in a racial whole. In effect, *Manchild* must be viewed in this context of the burden of cultural representation, as well as taken as an index that seeks to (re)present a frameable portrait, a readable account, of one aspect of African-American experience.

Reflecting on his youth in Harlem during the 1940s and 1950s, Brown gives us a personal view from the inside of grassroots African-American culture. His comments reflect, contrary to Murray's critique, no passing interest either in pathologizing or normalizing what he sees. His depiction helps us to see to what extent homosexuality has been a recognized, ordinary aspect of life within the African-American community. This recognition of same-sex desire and sexual variance more generally hinges on a principled refusal to make sexual identity an overriding concern in an individual's makeup. Black cultural survival has depended much more on keeping "family" intact than on enforcing sexual norms that emphasize procreation within (white-identified) nuclear families. Rejecting or purging individuals who evidenced interest in same-sex desire would have also meant rejecting the talents and special gifts which such individuals might offer to the community at large. Even today, in a climate of sometimes heightened intolerance, homosexual individuals often take the role of providers for the young or as caretakers for the elderly in situations where parents or other adults cannot afford (in terms of time, money, and energy) to do so. In such situations, the attitude in the community tends to be to overlook the person's sexual disposition as irrelevant. Just as the individual's talents are seen as coming specially from God, so is the sexual disposition ("that God's doing"), which enables him to contribute in this special way. The community tendency to overlook homosexuality manifests itself in acknowledging the reality of the homosexual's existence but looking away, discounting its potential negative meaning in terms of religious and mainstream dogma, while valuing its positive significance in helping to fulfill needs in the community that might otherwise go unmet. This gesture of overlooking is virtually the opposite of the conventional European-American response in the decades before the 1970s. The convention there was to overlook as an act of totalized surveillance, whereby legally, politically, and socially the aim was to detect, ostracize, silence, and purge any sign of same-sex desire. In effect, African-American culture has generally refused to treat homosexual individuals as an abstract phenomenon that threatens community survival and welfare, fully aware that the real threat to survival and welfare comes from economic deprivation, racist policies, and myriad other causes. Notably, recent attacks on homosexual individuals have come largely from an ideological camp, the Afrocentrists, who argue that homosexuality should be viewed as an abstract, segregatable phenomenon spawned and spread by a conspiracy of European-American origins. The most cogent, if not persuasive, statement of this case has been made by Nathan and Julia Hare in *The Endangered Black Family* (63–68). Significantly, the Hares advocate reattaching the value of sexuality to procreation (125–36), as well as a return to strict gender-coded roles in terms of courtship, family, non-occupation-related activities (137–50). However, even the Hares, illogically against the grain of their argument, reject the idea of ostracizing or purging homosexual individuals—recognizing, as they must, that this would go counter to what is best in African-American history and counter to the objective of survival and unity (65).[19]

While Brown's refusal to exclude homosexuality from his documentary reflects a prag-matist and survivalist cultural attitude in which priorities are based on countering real threats and fulfilling basic needs, the contradictions in Brown's representation of Black faggotry help us to see how the categories of sissy and swish and the tensions surrounding sexual respectability play themselves out, how such categories are constantly mediated by the common and varied experiences of African-American people in everyday life.[20] The autobiography begins grippingly with Sonny, the author-observer-hero, being shot and then being awakened in the hospital:

> On my fourth day in the hospital, I was awakened by a male nurse at about 3 A.M. When he said hello in a very ladyish voice, I thought that he had come to the wrong bed by mistake. After identifying himself, he told me that he had helped Dr. Freeman save my life. The next thing he said, which I didn't understand, had something to do with the hours he had put in working that day. He went on mumbling something about how tired he was and ended up asking me to rub his back. I had already told him that I was grateful to him for helping the doctor save my life. While I rubbed his back above the beltline, he kept pushing my hand down and saying, "Lower, like you are really grateful to me." I told him that I was sleepy from the needle a nurse had given me. He asked me to pat his behind. After I had done this, he left. (10–11)

As the narration moves through this episode, it does not skip a beat, but remains in the same routine, fast-paced, matter-of-fact reportage. The casual attitude toward such an encounter is unusual in the dominant culture, to say the least, and is rarely found even within white dominant culture today. Straight white men are expected to protest, to overprotest, any prox-imity to homosexuality, especially in a situation where the gay man has an advantage over the straight one, or is beholden to him. The treatment of the episode suggests, without having to say it, that this male nurse swish is part of the common fabric of African-American life.

More importantly, it suggests that various forms of hyperaversion, the response ex-pected within mainstream culture even today, would have been rude in the context nar-rated here. The nurse asks Sonny to pat his behind; Sonny obliges. Sonny loses nothing in obliging, despite the fact that he has nothing to gain in obliging. The gesture of embracing the nurse's need to be touched is made significantly without protest, either by attempting, or overattempting, to segregate the nurse either as an object of suspicion, scorn, or de-viancy within the narrative sequence or as a discursive subject for focused attention out-side of the narrative sequence. Brown does not use the introduction of this character as an opportunity to step outside of the narrative to discuss homosexuality, positively or nega-tively, as would be expected. In fact, the nurse is more a "character" in the sense of being a mildly amusing eccentric, whose impact is real but nonthreatening, than in the sense of a fictional construct placed within the narrative for the purposes of exploring the whys and hows of what makes such a "type" tick. The etiology of homosexuality is not an issue here. The episode is communicated literally as a real-life encounter, an impressionable one well remembered and casually retold.

On the one hand, the episode is matter-of-fact and inclusive—making the nurse as legitimate a part of Harlem life as any other person we encounter. On the other hand, we understand that the nurse is a swish, and our understanding is based on the stereotypical portrayal (the "ladyish" voice, the flaunting behavior, the self-parody). Furthermore, we understand that Sonny has no sexual interest in the nurse. This understanding is communicated playfully, not at the expense of the homosexual, who, after all, is the one who is playing around with Sonny's sexuality. As author, Brown only needs the slightest cue to indicate his sexual noninterest: "I rubbed his back above the beltline." As a character in the story, his noninterest is expressed in the same mild terms. In mainstream culture, a straight man's noninterest in homosexual desire is normally overemphasized by turning the homosexual into an object of verbal and/or physical violence. Moreover, this kind of violence is often acted out against men merely perceived to be gay, men who are not flaunting, who are not propositioning the straight, or showing any interest in the straight. Contrary to this mainstream attitude, Sonny communicates his noninterest in exactly the opposite way, through gentle touching, through verbally acknowledging the legitimacy of the swish's desire, and through playful setting of limits. The rejection of the swish's advances is carried out literally through inclusive verbal and physical gestures.

One of the stereotypes of the swish in African-American folk culture is that he is always testing the boundaries and limits—not just sexually, but in all kinds of outrageous ways. He is always searching for sexual outlets without regard to rigid categories of sexual orientation. This is because he never knows when he might strike gold. Because homosexuality has tended to be more integrated into African-American communities, there is naturally more interplay between "straight" men and gays, sexually and nonsexually.[21] Straight men can have sex with gay men and remain straight. Especially before the 1960s, there would be less psychological compulsion and less social pressure for the straight man to define his cultural orientation against homosexuality as an abstract unknown, since homosexual individuals were obviously integral contributors to the culture at large. Arbitrary violence against gay individuals was normally out of the question—unfortunately no longer the case in the volatilely mixed urban areas during the 1980s and 1990s. A swish could afford to be more casual and playful about what he desired from the object of his attention, who may be gay and interested, gay and not interested, straight and interested, straight and not interested, a circumspect sissy and interested, a circumspect sissy and not interested. Knowing that the swish's playful testing of limits is no reflection on the sexuality of the "straight" object of attention (which would be the normal presumption in white American culture), Sonny can reply just as playfully—without any hint of aversion or violence. The straight man can be just as playful about what he does not want as the swish can be about what he does.

Even more instructive than the episode itself is the response to it by Sonny's macho friends. Not only does Sonny casually tell us, his readers, about the swish; he just as casually tells his running buddies about the encounter in exactly the same tone:

> The next day when the fellows came to visit me, I told them about my early-morning visitor. Dunny said he would like to meet him. Tito joked about being able to get a dose of clap in the hospital. The guy with the tired back never showed up again, so the fellows never got a chance to meet him. Some of them were disappointed. (11)

Sonny's best pals, all of whom are straight, have their interest left tantalizingly piqued. Dunny's interest could be mere curiosity, or it could be more an interest in harmless sexual teasing to match the swish's own camp playfulness, or it could be genuine sexual interest. We have no way of knowing, just as the swish has no way of knowing without testing the waters and wading in to find what the actual circumstance brings up.

Tito's joke also indicates the flexibility of sexual encounters between swishes and straights in the Black community. In the 1940s and 1950s, the folk wisdom was to be careful about going with gay men because many were supposedly infected with gonorrhea. (An obvious analogy could be made to AIDS in the 1980s, though there are significant differences due to both the deadly nature of the disease and the changed discourse on homosexuality in the Black community by the 1980s.) This is a matter of the word on the street—from guys who know because they have been there. Tito's joke, however, suggests not only a caution to the wise, but also a humorous taunt that embraces, more than ridicules, the nurse. At the heart of the joke is the imaginable probability of sexual intercourse with the nurse: Is it not funny that you could go with this guy and get the clap right here in the hospital from the punk nurse who is supposed to be healing you? Despite their looking down on the swish as a kind of outrageous "character," Sonny and his friends clearly admire his boldness, and want to be entertained by the swish, who himself is entertained by entertaining them. This episode, and the ones that follow in the autobiography, contradict the common idea, expressed by Peterson, that the more flexible interplay between gay Black men and straight Black men is merely a matter of deprivation on the part of the straights. There is a much more fundamental cultural variation at stake here, one not easily explained away by applying European-American models of strict sexual labeling and white attitudes based on concepts of autonomous gay culture and segregated homosexual desire.

It is in juvenile prison that Sonny learns in depth about things he had taken for granted on the streets. "You learned something new from everybody you met" (144). Once again, homosexuality is just another case. Sonny comes to appreciate and understand something that he had taken for granted on the streets. It is with this coming into deeper awareness that we can begin to understand some of the African-American cultural tensions that arise from overlaying the image of homosexuality over the actual experience of the Black faggot.

> One of the most interesting things I learned was about faggots. Before I went to Warwick, I used to look down on faggots like they were something dirty. But while I was up there, I met some faggots who were pretty nice guys. We didn't play around or anything like that, but I didn't look down on them any more.
>
> These guys were young cats my age. It was the first time I'd been around guys who weren't afraid of being faggots. They were faggots because they wanted to be. Some cats were rape artists because they wanted to be, some cats were flunkies, some cats were thieves, and some cats were junkies. These guys were faggots because they wanted to be. And some of the faggots up there were pretty good with their hands. As a matter of fact, some of them were so good with their hands, they had the man they wanted just because he couldn't beat them.
>
> At Warwick, there was even a cottage just for faggots. If a cat came up there acting girlish, they'd put him right in there. They had a lot of guys in there—Puerto Ricans, white, colored, everything—young cats, sixteen and under, who had made up their minds that they liked guys, and that's all there was to it. (146–47)

There are obvious tensions between how Sonny has rather nonjudgmentally represented faggots before the prison meditations and the way he feels he has unfairly misjudged them in his own previous thinking. His behavior has been much less harsh toward gay men than his judgment is toward himself for merely thinking, not expressing, harsh things about them. In his mind, he thought dirty things about them, but in his behavior he has been more than tolerant. Once again, we have to remember that Sonny's behavior has been tolerant because he knows that homosexuals are not a real threat. Nonetheless, in his unexpressed, unformulated thinking about them, he thoughtlessly has imbibed the dominant image and prejudice espoused by some of the most "respectable" people in the community, inculcated by dominant culture, and enforced by the white legal establishment. To some extent, this is an expected tension between cultural doctrine (what respectable people think they ought to believe) and cultural practice (how respectful people negotiate firm beliefs into reasonable behavior). But at stake here is a much finer distinction between homosexual individuals who are an integral part of the community and the abstract concept of homosexuality as a segregated cultural identity, as a way of life significantly different from others' lives in the community.

There is tension between his portrayal of the gay nurse and his statement that "[i]t was the first time that I'd been around guys who were not afraid of being faggots." The nurse does not seem afraid; in fact, he seems outright self-confident. I would suggest that this is a tension between the African-American projection of the swish's image and the actual, ordinary experience on the street. The projection is that the swish expects to be looked down on and is looked down on. The reality, not so much contradicting as overriding this image, is that the swish is admired for his daring testing of the waters, and that he knows how to play on that admiration. There is also a tension between the persistent viewing of the faggot as girlish and the awareness that some gay men can do macho things better than straight men. The prison officials immediately segregate the guys who act "girlish" in the "cottage just for faggots," despite the fact that you cannot tell the faggots from the straight men based on who is better at manly sports like boxing: "[S]ome of them were so good with their hands, they had the man they wanted just because he couldn't beat them" (147). Sexual variance was not a reason for segregating individuals in the Black community. White society, on the other hand, has enforced its abstract concept of homosexuality as difference and deviation by enacting the same kind of policy against queer inmates that the American system enacted against African Americans in larger society. Segregation is the most efficient way to enforce categorical differences that otherwise might become insignificant as merely variable characteristics of a population. How ironic that the segregation of gay culture as an autonomous identity that occurred with the emergence of the gay rights movements should lead both to greater freedom and tolerance for homosexual expression in the larger society and to greater segregation and intolerance within the African-American community.

NOTES

This essay is excerpted from my study entitled *The Color of Manhood: Representations of Black Men in the Civil Rights Era*, which examines a complex of dialectically paired images of Black masculinity—addict and entrepreneur, sissy and swish, agitator and athlete, integrationist and militant, prisoner and cop—and how they shape and are shaped by the racial and sexual politics of the civil rights era.

1. The cultural origins of the modern gay/lesbian community have been traced by a variety of scholars. See, for instance, John D'Emilio's *Sexual Politics, Sexual Communities*; Barry Adam's *The Rise of* a Gay and Lesbian Movement; Dennis Altman's *The Homosexualization of America, the Americanization of the Homosexual*; and Toby Marotta's *The Politics of Homosexuality*.

2. For a discussion of homosexuality in early African-American culture, see Nero 233–35. Not surprisingly, reliable evidence concerning Black male sexuality in early America is scant, but what evidence does exist makes absurd any presumption that there was no same-sex expression of desire.

3. For a concise, but incisive summary of the divisions between some leading African Americans and

the gay/lesbian movement, see Henry Louis Gates Jr.'s *New Yorker* essay "Blacklash." This observation is especially helpful: "Much of the ongoing debate over gay rights has fixated, and foundered, on the vexed distinction between 'status' and 'behavior.' The paradox here can be formulated as follows: Most people think of racial identity as a matter of (racial) status, but they respond to it as behavior. Most people think of sexual identity as a matter of (sexual) behavior, but they respond to it as status." (43)

The answer is not only to decode the false status-behavior dichotomy, but also, and more fundamentally, to demonstrate how "identity" historically comes to pit varying characteristics of and within cultural groups, of and within individuals, against one another.

4. Michael Bronski makes a similar point in *Culture Clash: The Making of Gay Sensibility* (72–76). Bronski points out also an important class difference within the Black community: "Middle class Blacks did not approve of the social or entertainment aspects of Black culture that white cultural radicals were so enamoured of. This distaste continued through the 60s, when Black nationalists demanded that Harlem's Apollo Theater cease its presentation of drag shows because 'it glorified the homosexual . . . and was a threat to Black life and the Black family' " (75–76). Bronski is right that the objection to overt homosexuality in the Black community has a class basis, but the objection coming from Black nationalists is more complicated. Black nationalism traditionally has sprung primarily from the grass roots, not from the more integration-oriented middle class, but, as we'll see in the next chapter, it does borrow its homophobia from middle-class concepts of family. For another account of a white gay trying to find community by turning to Blacks, see Seymour Kleinberg's fascinating analysis of gay subcultures in Detroit and New York during the '60s and '70s in *Alienated Affections* (especially chapters 1 and 2).

5. I use the term "network" rather than "enclave" or "subculture" because network indicates both an active assembly constantly in motion and a group not segregated from the larger community but intimately tied to it while sustaining ties among themselves.

6. Another aspect of this question is dealt with later in the chapter in a section not included here. I argue that the white gay man turned the inner city into a "frontier" to be conquered with all of the connotations that accompany that concept in American culture and politics. By moving into the wilderness of the inner city, the white gay man proved his manhood to mainstream America, proved that he could survive the "extreme" conditions and make profitable and civilized settlements in a territory scarred by crime, violence, and declining profits. The reward for this frontiersmanship was increasing political clout. Once the (white) gay man had conquered the inner city, he too could begin to move back into mainstream culture (into the suburbs), where his money and talents would be increasingly more accepted.

7. Much has been written on this utopian impulse in the early gay liberation movement, an impulse defined among white gay men as romantic and sexual license, the ability to bond with a variety of men from every racial, ethnic, and class background in an egalitarian setting. This cosmopolitan ideal was often seen as embodied in the gay bathhouse, a site where all men were equally welcome and where all were equally desirable, desiring, and desired. Dennis Altman's *The Homosexualization of America* traces the history of, and offers an excellent critique of, this concept as it gets elided with the exploitative logic of consumer capitalism.

8. I do not mean to suggest here that African cultural expression was not influential before the 1920s; only that it was in this period that people of African descent became more self-aware of their central role in world culture throughout history, thus forcing some whites (the bohemians and later the hipsters, beatniks, and hippies) to begin to recognize their own reliance on African forms of expression.

9. For instance, although Garber is careful to sketch the risks of being Black and gay in Harlem during the 1920s, he still tends to conflate the Black community's greater acceptance of Black homosexuals with greater acceptance of homosexuality in general.

10. Biddy Martin has argued that much recent "queer theory" tends to rely on this dichotomy between race and sexuality, whereby race becomes the more totalized, determined experience of identity over against a playful, sophisticated, postmodern sexuality that is self-conscious of its own cultural construction.

11. Alan Bray has documented the presence of an urban homosexual subculture in England during the seventeenth century, as well as attempts made by governmental agencies to control and purge this subculture in his study *Homosexuality in Renaissance England*. See also Norton; and Trumbach. In many traditional African and Native American cultures, homosexuality was integrated into the "mainstream" of the cultures in various customs. Perhaps the most famous of these same-sex customs is the *berdache*, cross-dressing individuals who held an honorable status and were often taken as spouses by same-sex partners within many Native tribes. On the *berdache* tradition, see Williams;

and Allen. A good compendium bringing together the extensive research on the variety of same-sex practices and homosexual expression in traditional cultures can be found in Greenberg 25–88.

12. By this I mean that anthropologists are necessarily very selective when it comes to explaining why a culture engages in its behaviors. What determines which behaviors need explanation and which behaviors are self-explanatory? The norm or standard of behavior already established in the anthropologist's own culture becomes the basis for selection and explanation.

13. See, for instance, Clifford Geertz's famous critique of Lévi-Strauss in The *Interpretation of Cultures* (345–59). Geertz writes: "For what Lévi-Strauss has made for himself is an infernal culture machine. It annuls history, reduces sentiment to a shadow of the intellect, and replaces the particular minds of particular savages in particular jungles with the Savage Mind immanent in us all. It has made it possible for him to circumvent the impasse to which his Brazilian expedition led—physical closeness and intellectual distance—by what perhaps he always really wanted—intellectual closeness and physical distance." (355–56)

14. In the introduction to my work in progress, *Color of Manhood*, I offer a concept of cultural knowledge based on the interdependent cognitive processes of synecdoche, metonymy, and projection. I define synecdoche as the tendency to view specific characteristics perceived as common among a particular group as constituting a whole that can then be extrapolated back to every individual associated with the group. Cognitive metonymy is the tendency to exchange partial knowledge and ignorance about individuals perceived as belonging to a group for full knowledge about those individuals. Projection is the tendency to throw onto oppressed groups that which is most feared within an oppressing group as a form of scapegoating.

15. Murray is so uneasy with class analysis that he goes so far as to suggest that it is impossible to identify a Black middle class, and yet his argument seems to rely on the need for a middle class (see his section the "Illusive Black Middle Class" in The *Omni-Americans* 86–96). For an analysis of the Black middle class at the opposite end of the pole, see Cruse (especially 267–336); and Frazier. It is also ironic that Murray criticizes writers like Brown, Baldwin, and Cleaver for writing for white people when his own book is clearly written for white people in order to remold the image of African-American culture into one of ethnic respectability.

16. Exhibitionist writing is closely related to the protest tradition in African-American literature, a tradition which tends to represent the author as a spokesman for the race addressing a predominantly white audience. In *The Way of the New World*, Addison Gayle Jr. develops a sophisticated cultural history of the African-American novel based on the progression from protest to rebellion to revolution, as a progression from the desire for assimilation and American liberty to the reclamation of cultural identity and self-directed social revolution. From this perspective, exhibitionist writing like Baldwin's and Brown's becomes atavistic, going against the grain of African-American literary history.

17. White interlopers in the Black community also wrote books on the urban ghetto contributing to this trend. Murray uses Warren Miller's *The Cool World* (1959) as the prime example (see Albert Murray 127–83). Miller's portrayal of Black men's sexual license, analyzed later in the chapter, participates in a tradition that goes at least as far back as Carl Van Vechten's 1926 novel about Harlem, *Nigger Heaven*.

18. Brown's 1973 book, *The Children of Ham*, is comprised of a series of interviews with young gang members, who talk about their lives on the street. As with *Manchild*, Brown aspires toward a documentary form, dissuading a judgmental response and encouraging vicarious sympathy, as a way of understanding the broader pressures bearing on the community at large. Mumps's description of prison homosexuality is noticeably different from the description given by Sonny, as Mumps relies much more on mainstream conventions of homophobia, rather than on attitudes toward sexual diversity indigenous to African-American culture before the 1960s. This brief discussion of homosexuality in *Children of Ham* may index the attitudinal shift toward sexual variance resulting from a variety of changes within the African-American community and within mainstream society concerning the status of gay men and lesbians (see 98–100)

19. In stressing the procreative value, and thus the father's place as inseminator or provider, Afrocentrists like the Hares are going against a long-honored, indigenous tradition within African-American culture of stressing individual talent as contribution to community rather than strictly coded roles as the source of community stability. Traditionally, an individual gives according to the gifts and special talents given to him or her by God, not according to a social role predetermined by gender or sexuality and coded strictly according to one's place in a nuclear family. In this tradition, a homosexual or female provider is not a threat, but a necessity for mutual survival. According to the logic of some Afrocentrists, as in mainstream white culture, the individual who provides

outside of the prescribed gender role becomes a threat to patriarchal fathering and procreation.

20. In chapter 2 of the *Color of Manhood*, I discuss in some detail the dialectically opposed images of the sissy and the swish, the two dominant representations of male homosexuality within African-American culture. The sissy is an aspiring middle-class man who is very discreet about his same-sex desire. He courts and achieves respectability within the African-American community, especially through the influential religious, educational, and social service institutions, either limiting or sacrificing his sexual expression for the sake of advancing the race. As a pillar of the community, he becomes a role model presentable to white America. The swisher, or swish, is as flamboyant and defiant as the sissy is circumspect and subservient. He is associated usually with life on the streets, and cultivates a crossover dynamic with white homosexuals parallel to the sissy's crossover influence as a representative spokesman for the race.

21. According to Peterson, "Black males have extensive homosexual experience, but it may not affect their homosexual identity" (149). This is one statistical notion that seems easily borne out in terms of the qualitative and representational literature on male homosexuality in the African-American community. Nevertheless, Peterson goes on to apply inappropriate autonomous-culture models to this behavior, assuming—in a similar way that Lévi-Strauss does

about the Nambikwara—that same-sex bonding behavior among men not self-identified as gay has to be explained away as acts of deprivation. "These heterosexual men may not label themselves homosexual because of the reasons they engage in homosexual behavior" (149). Peterson goes on to list economic motivations, high unemployment, and lack of access to female partners as the reasons for sex between self-identified gay Black men and "heterosexual" Black men. Peterson fails to see that the whole issue of labeling sexuality is different and plays a radically different role in African-American culture from that in the dominant white culture. A similar pattern of behavior has been noted among Latino men. For a discussion of this issue in Chicano culture, see Almáquer; and Carrier. Carrier writes, "One effect of homosexual role playing in Mexican society is that only the feminine male is labeled a 'homosexual.' By societal standards, the masculine self-image of Mexican males is not threatened by their homosexual behavior as long as they play the anal insertive role and also have a reputation for having sexual relations with women" (206). Carrier also points out that "[t]he major effect of this is that 'straight' Anglo males in general appear to be far more concerned about being approached by homosexual males than do 'straight' Mexican males. 'Queer bashing,' for example, is an Anglo phenomenon that occurs only rarely in Mexico" (207).

WORKS CITED

Adam, Barry D. *The Rise of a Gay and Lesbian Movement.* Boston: Twayne, 1987.

Allen, Paula Gunn. *The Sacred Hoop: Recovering the Feminine in Native American Traditions.* Boston: Beacon Press, 1986.

Almáquer, Tomás, "Chicano Men: A Cartography of Homosexual Identity and Behavior." *differences* 3.2 (1991): 75–100.

Altman, Dennis. *The Homosexualization of America, the Americanization of the Homosexual.* New York: St. Martin's Press, 1982.

Bray, Alan. *Homosexuality in Renaissance England.* London: Gay Men's Press, 1982.

Bronski, Michael. *Culture Clash: The Making of Gay Sensibility.* Boston: South End Press, 1984.

Brown, Claude. *Manchild in the Promised Land.* New York: Signet, 1965.

———. *The Children of Ham.* New York: Stein and Day, 1973.

Carrier, Joseph. "Miguel: Sexual Life History of a Gay Mexican American." In *Gay Culture in America*, Ed. Gilbert Herdt. Boston: Beacon Press, 1992, 202–24.

Cory, Donald Webster. *The Homosexual in America: A Subjective Approach.* New York: Greenberg, 1951.

Cruse, Harold. *The Crisis of the Negro Intellectual.* New York: Quill, 1984.

D'Emilio, John. *Sexual Politics, Sexual Communities: The Making of a Homosexual Minority in the United States, 1940–1970.* Chicago: University of Chicago Press, 1983.

Frazier, E. Franklin. *Black Bourgeoisie: The Rise of a New Middle Class in the United States.* New York: Macmillan, 1957.

Garber, Eric. "A Spectacle in Color: The Lesbian and Gay Subculture of Jazz Age Harlem." In *Hidden from History: Reclaiming the Gay and*

Lesbian Past. Ed. Martin Bauml Duberman, Martha Vicinus, and George Chauncey Jr. New York: New American Library, 1989, 318–31.

Gates, Henry Louis Jr. "Blacklash?" *The New Yorker*, May 17, 1993, 42–44.

Gayle, Addison Jr. *The Way of the New World: The Black Novel in America*. Garden City, N.Y.: Anchor/Doubleday, 1975.

Geertz, Clifford. *The Interpretation of Cultures*. New York: Basic Books, 1973.

Goldstein, Richard. "Go the Way Your Blood Beats: An Interview with James Baldwin." In *James Baldwin: The Legacy*. Ed. Quincy Troupe. New York: Simon and Schuster, 1989, 173–85.

Greenberg, David F. *The Construction of Homosexuality*. Chicago: University of Chicago Press, 1988.

Hare, Nathan, and Julia Hare. *The Endangered Black Family: Coping with the Unisexualization and Coming Extinction of the Black Race*. San Francisco: Black Think Tank, 1984.

Herdt, Gilbert, ed. *Gay Culture in America: Essays from the Field*. Boston: Beacon Press, 1992.

Kleinberg, Seymour. *Alienated Affections: Being Gay in America*. New York: St. Martin's Press, 1977.

Lévi-Strauss, Claude. *Tristes Tropiques*. New York: Washington Square Press, 1955.

Marotta, Toby. *The Politics of Homosexuality*. Boston: Houghton Mifflin, 1981.

Martin, Biddy. "Sexualities without Genders and Other Queer Utopias." University of Michigan. April 1, 1993.

Murray, Albert. *The Omni-Americans: Black Experience and American Culture*. New York: Vintage, 1970.

Murray, Stephen O. "Components of Gay Community in San Francisco." In *Gay Culture in America*. Ed. Gilbert Herdt. Boston: Beacon Press, 1992, 107–46.

Nero, Charles I. "Toward a Black Gay Aesthetic: Signifying in Contemporary Black Gay Literature." In *Brother to Brother: New Writings by Black Gay Men*. Ed. Essex Hemphill. Conceived by Joseph Bean. Boston: Alyson, 1991, 229–52.

Norton, Rictor. *Mother Clap's Molly House: The Gay Subculture in England 1700–1830*. London: GMP, 1992.

Peterson, John L. "Black Men and Their Same-Sex Desires and Behaviors." In *Gay Culture in America*. Ed. Gilbert Herdt. Boston: Beacon Press, 1992, 147–64.

Ross, Marlon B. *The Color of Manhood*. In progress.

Trumbach, Randolph. "The Birth of the Queen: Sodomy and the Emergence of Gender Equality in Modern Culture, 1660–1750." In *Hidden from History: Reclaiming the Gay and Lesbian Past*. Ed. Martin Bauml Duberman, Martha Vicinus, and George Chauncey Jr. New York: New American Library, 1989, 129–40.

Williams, Walter L. *The Spirit and the Flesh: Sexual Diversity in American Indian Culture* Boston: Beacon Press, 1986.

PART II
CONCEPTUALIZING CULTURE AND IDEOLOGY

13

THE COLOR PURPLE

Black Women as Cultural Readers

Jacqueline Bobo

TONY BROWN, a syndicated columnist and the host of the television program *Tony Brown's Journal* has called the film *The Color Purple* "the most racist depiction of Black men since *The Birth of a Nation* and the most anti-Black family film of the modern film era." Ishmael Reed, a Black novelist, has labelled the film and the book "a Nazi conspiracy."[1] Since its première in December 1985, *The Color Purple* has provoked constant controversy, debate and appraisals of its effects on the image of Black people in the United States.

The film also has incited a face-off between Black feminist critics and Black male reviewers. The women defend the work or, more precisely, defend Alice Walker's book and the right of the film to exist. Black males vehemently denounce both works and cite the film's stereotypical representations. In the main, adverse criticisms have revolved around three issues: *(a)* that the film does not examine class; *(b)* that Black men are portrayed unnecessarily as harsh and brutal, the consequence of which is to further the split between the Black female and the Black male; and *(c)* that Black people as a whole are depicted as perverse, sexually wanton, and irresponsible. In these days of massive cutbacks in federal support to social agencies, according to some rebukes, the film's representation of the Black family was especially harmful.

Most left-wing publications in the United States, the *Guardian, Frontline*, and *In These Times*, denounced the film, but mildly. *The Nation*, in fact, commended the film and its director for fitting the work's threatening content into a safe and familiar form.[2] Articles in the other publications praised particular scenes but on the whole disparaged the film for its lack of class authenticity. Black people of that era were poor, the left-wing critics stated, and Steven Spielberg failed to portray that fact. (Uh-uh, says Walker. She said she wrote here about people who owned land, property, and dealt in commerce.)

Jill Nelson, a Black journalist who reviewed the film for the *Guardian*, felt that the film's Black protestors were naïve to think that "at this late date in our history . . . Hollywood would ever consciously offer Black Americans literal tools for our emancipation."[3] Furthermore, Nelson refuted the charge that the film would forever set the race back in white viewers' minds by observing that most viewers would only leave the theatre commenting on whether or not they liked the film. Articles counter to Nelson's were published in a following issue of the *Guardian* and they emphasized the film's distorted perspective on class and the ideological use to which the film would be put to show the Black family's instability.

The December première of *The Color Purple* was picketed in Los Angeles by an activist group named the Coalition Against Black Exploitation. The group protested against the savage and brutal depiction of Black men in the film.[4] That complaint was carried further by a Black columnist in the *Washington Post*, Courtland Milloy, who wrote that some Black women would enjoy seeing Black men shown as "brutal bastards," and that furthermore, the book was demeaning. Milloy stated: "I got tired, a long time ago, of white men publishing books by Black women about how screwed up Black men are."[5] Other hostile views about the film were expressed by representatives of the NAACP, Black male columnists, and a law professor, Leroy Clark of Catholic University, who called it dangerous. (When Ntozake Shange's choreopoem *For Colored Girls Who Have Considered Suicide/When the Rainbow Is Enuf* opened on Broadway in autumn 1976, the response from Black male critics was similar.)

Black female reviewers were not as critical of the film in its treatment of gender issues. Although Barbara Smith attacked the film for its class distortions, she felt that "sexual politics and sexual violence" in the Black community were matters that needed to be confronted and changed.[6] Jill Nelson, emphasizing that those who did not like what the messenger (the film) said about Black men should look at the facts, provided statistics on female-headed Black households, lack of child support, and so on.[7]

Michele Wallace, a professor of Afro-American literature and creative writing at the University of Oklahoma and author of *Black Macho: The Myth of the Superwoman*, stated that the film had some "positive feminist influences and some positive import for Black audiences in this country."[8]

However, in an earlier article in the *Village Voice*, March 18, 1986, Michele Wallace was less charitable to the film. Although she gives a very lucid explication of Walker's novel, citing its attempt to "reconstruct Black female experience as positive ground," Wallace wrote of the film, "Spielberg juggles film clichés and racial stereotypes fast and loose, until all signs of a Black feminist agenda are banished, or ridiculed beyond repair." Wallace also noted that the film used mostly cinematic types reminiscent of earlier films. She writes: "Instead of serious men and women encountering consequential dilemmas, we're almost always minstrels, more than a little ridiculous; we dance and sing without continuity, as if on the end of a string. It seems white people are never going to forget Stepin Fetchit, no matter how many times he dies."[9]

Wallace both sees something positive in the film and points to its flaws. I agree with her in both instances, especially in her analysis of how it is predictable that the film "has given rise to controversy and debate within the Black community, ostensibly focused on the eminently printable issue of the film's image of Black men."

In an attempt to explain why people liked *The Color Purple* in spite of its sometimes clichéd characters, Donald Bogle, on the Phil Donahue show, put it down to the novelty of seeing Black actors in roles not previously available to them:

> for Black viewers there is a schizophrenic reaction. You're torn in two. On the one hand you
> see the character of Mister and you're disturbed by the stereotype. Yet, on the other hand, and
> this is the basis of the appeal of that film for so many people, is that the women you see in the
> movie, you have never seen Black women like this put on the screen before. I'm not talking

about what happens to them in the film, I'm talking about the visual statement itself. When you see Whoopi Goldberg in close-up, a loving close-up, you look at this woman, you know that in American films in the past, in the 1930s, 1940s, she would have played a maid. She would have been a comic maid. Suddenly, the camera is focusing on her and we say, "I've seen this woman some place, I know her."[10]

It appears to me that one of the problems most of the film's reviewers have in trying to analyze the film, with all of its faults, is to make sense of the overwhelming positive response from Black female viewers.

The Color Purple was a small quiet book when it emerged on the literary scene in 1982. The subject of the book is a young, abused, uneducated Black girl who evolves into womanhood and a sense of her own worth gained by bonding with the women around her. When Alice Walker won the American Book Award and the Pulitzer Prize for Fiction in 1983, the sales of the novel increased to over two million copies, placing the book on the *New York Times* best-seller lists for a number of weeks.[11] Still the book did not have as wide an audience or the impact the film would have. In December 1985 Steven Spielberg's *The Color Purple* exploded with the force of a land mine on the landscape of cultural production. Many commentators on the film have pointed out that the film created discussion and controversy about the image of Black people in media the likes of which had not been seen since the films *The Birth of a Nation* (1915) and *Gone with the Wind* (1939).

One of the reasons Alice Walker sold the screen rights was that she understood that people who would not read the book would go to see the film. Walker and her advisers thought that the book's critical message needed to be exposed to a wider audience. The readership for the novel was a very specific one and drastically different from the mass audience toward which the film is directed. However, the film is a commercial venture produced in Hollywood by a white male according to all of the tenets and conventions of commercial cultural production in the United States. The manner in which an audience responds to such a film is varied, diverse, and complex. I am especially concerned with analyzing how Black women have responded.

My aim is to examine the way in which a specific audience creates meaning from a mainstream text and uses the reconstructed meaning to empower themselves and their social group. This analysis will show how Black women as audience members and cultural consumers have connected up with what has been characterized as the "renaissance of Black women writers."[12] The predominant element of this movement is the creation and maintenance of images of Black women that are based upon Black women's constructions, history, and real-life experiences.

As part of a larger study I am doing on *The Color Purple* I conducted a group interview with selected Black women viewers of the film.[13] Statements from members of the group focused on how moved they were by the fact that Celie eventually triumphs in the film. One woman talked about the variety of emotions she experienced: "I had different feelings all the way through the film, because first I was very angry, and then I started to feel so sad I wanted to cry because of the way Celie was being treated. It just upset me the way she was being treated and the way she was so totally dominated. But gradually, as time went on, she began to realize that she could do something for herself, that she could start moving and progressing, that she could start reasoning and thinking things out for herself." Another woman stated that she was proud of Celie for her growth: "The lady was a strong lady, like I am. And she hung in there and she overcame."

One of the women in the group talked about the scene where Shug tells Celie that she has a beautiful smile and that she should stop covering up her face. This woman said that she could relate to that part because it made Celie's transformation in the film so much more powerful. At first, she said, everybody who loved Celie [Shug and Nettie], and everyone that Celie loved, kept telling her to put her hand down. The woman then pointed out "that last time that Celie put her hand down nobody told her to put her hand down. She had started coming into her own. So when she grabbed that knife she was ready to use it." This comment refers to the scene in the film at the dinner table, when Celie and Shug are about to leave for Memphis. Mister begins to chastise Celie telling her that she will be back. He says, "You ugly, you skinny, you shaped funny and you scared to open your mouth to people." Celie sits there quietly and takes Mister's verbal abuse. Then she asks him, "Any more letters come?" She is talking about Nettie's letters from Africa that Mister has been hiding from Celie and that Celie and Shug had recently found. Mister replies, "Could be, could be not." Celie jumps up at that point, grabs the knife, and sticks it to Mister's throat.

The woman who found this scene significant continued: "But had she not got to that point, built up to that point [of feeling herself worthwhile], she could have grabbed the knife and turned it the other way for all that it mattered to her. She wouldn't have been any worse off. But she saw herself getting better. So when she grabbed that knife she was getting ready to use it and it wasn't on herself."

Other comments from the women were expressions of outrage at criticisms made against the film. The women were especially disturbed by vicious attacks against Alice Walker and against Black women critics and scholars who were publicly defending the film. One of the women in the interview session commented that she was surprised that there was such controversy over the film: "I had such a positive feeling about it, I couldn't imagine someone saying that they didn't like it." Another said that she was shocked at the outcry from some Black men: "I didn't look at it as being stereotypically Black or all Black men are this way" (referring to the portrayal of the character Mister).

Another related a story that shows how two people can watch the same film and have opposite reactions: "I was thinking about how men felt about it [The Color Purple] and I was surprised. But I related it to something that happened to me sometime ago when I was married. I went to see a movie called Three in the Attic. I don't know if any of you ever saw it. But I remember that on the way home—I thought it was funny—but my husband was so angry he wouldn't even talk to me on the way home. He said, "You thought that was funny." I said that I sure did. He felt it was really hostile because these ladies had taken this man up in the attic and made him go to bed with all of them until he was . . . blue. Because he had been running around with all of these ladies. But he [her husband] was livid because I thought it was funny. And I think now, some men I talked to had a similar reaction to The Color Purple. That it was . . . all the men in there were dummies or horrible. And none of the men, they felt, were portrayed in a positive light. And then I started thinking about it and I said, 'well . . . I felt that somebody had to be the hero or the heroine, and in this case it just happened to be the woman.' "

I have found that on the whole Black women have discovered something progressive and useful in the film. It is crucial to understand how this is possible when viewing a work made according to the encoding of dominant ideology. Black women's responses to The

Color Purple loom as an extreme contrast to those of many other viewers. Not only is the difference in reception noteworthy but Black women's responses confront and challenge a prevalent method of media audience analysis that insists that viewers of mainstream works have no control or influence over a cultural product. Recent developments in media audience analysis demonstrate that there is a complex process of negotiation whereby specific members of a culture construct meaning from a mainstream text that is different from the meanings others would produce. These different readings are based, in part, on viewers' various histories and experiences.

OPPOSITIONAL READINGS

The encoding/decoding model is useful for understanding how a cultural product can evoke such different viewer reactions. The model was developed by the University of Birmingham Centre for Contemporary Cultural Studies, under the direction of Stuart Hall, in an attempt to synthesize various perspectives on media audience analysis and to incorporate theory from sociology and cultural studies. This model is concerned with an understanding of the communication process as it operates in a specific cultural context. It analyzes ideological and cultural power and the way in which meaning is produced in that context. The researchers at the Centre felt that media analysts should not look simply at the meaning of a text but should also investigate the social and cultural framework in which communication takes place.[14]

From political sociology, the encoding/decoding model was drawn from the work of Frank Parkin, who developed a theory of meaning systems.[15] This theory delineates three potential responses to a media message: dominant, negotiated, or oppositional. A dominant (or preferred) reading of a text accepts the content of the cultural product without question. A negotiated reading questions parts of the content of the text but does not question the dominant ideology which underlies the production of the text. An oppositional response to a cultural product is one in which the recipient of the text understands that the system that produced the text is one with which she/he is fundamentally at odds.[16]

A viewer of a film (reader of a text) comes to the moment of engagement with the work with a knowledge of the world and a knowledge of other texts, or media products. What this means is that when a person comes to view a film, she/he does not leave her/his histories, whether social, cultural, economic, racial, or sexual at the door. An audience member from a marginalized group (people of color, women, the poor, and so on) has an oppositional stance as they participate in mainstream media. The motivation for this counter-reception is that we understand that mainstream media have never rendered our segment of the population faithfully. We have as evidence our years of watching films and television programs and reading plays and books. Out of habit, as readers of mainstream texts, we have learned to ferret out the beneficial and put up blinders against the rest.

From this wary viewing standpoint, a subversive reading of a text can occur. This alternative reading comes from something in the work that strikes the viewer as amiss, that appears "strange." Behind the idea of subversion lies a reader-oriented notion of "making strange."[17] When things appear strange to the viewer, she/he may then bring other viewpoints to bear on the watching of the film and may see things other than what the filmmakers intended. The viewer, that is, will read "against the grain" of the film.

Producers of mainstream media products are not aligned in a conspiracy against an audience. When they construct a work they draw on their own background, experience, and social and cultural milieu. They are therefore under "ideological pressure" to reproduce the familiar.[18] When Steven Spielberg made *The Color Purple* he did not intend to make a film that would be in the mould of previous films that were directed by a successful white director and had an all-Black or mostly Black cast.

Spielberg states that he deliberately cast the characters in *The Color Purple* in a way that they would not carry the taint of negative stereotypes:

> I didn't want to cast traditional Black movie stars, which I thought would create their own stereotypes. I won't mention any names because it wouldn't be kind, but there were people who wanted to play these parts very much. It would have made it seem as if these were the only Black people accepted in white world's mainstream. I didn't want to do that. That's why I cast so many unknowns like Whoopi Goldberg, Oprah Winfrey, Margaret Avery.[19]

But it is interesting that while the director of the film made a conscious decision to cast against type, he could not break away from his culturally acquired conceptions of how Black people are and how they should act. Barbara Christian, professor of Afro-American Studies at the University of California, Berkeley, contends that the most maligned figure in the film is the character Harpo. She points out that in the book he cannot become the patriarch that society demands he be.[20] Apparently Spielberg could not conceive of a man uncomfortable with the requirements of patriarchy, and consequently depicts Harpo as a buffoon. Christian comments that "the movie makes a negative statement about men who show some measure of sensitivity to women." The film uses the husband and wife characters, Harpo and Sofia, as comic relief. Some of the criticisms against the film from Black viewers concerned Harpo's ineptness in repairing a roof. If the filmmakers have Harpo fall once, it seems they decided that it was even funnier if he fell three times.

In her *Village Voice* review, Michele Wallace attributed motives other than comic relief to the film's representations of the couple. Wallace considered their appearances to be the result of "white patriarchal interventions." She wrote:

> In the book Sofia is the epitome of a woman with masculine powers, the martyr to sexual injustice who eventually triumphs through the realignment of the community. In the movie she is an occasion for humor. She and Harpo are the reincarnations of Amos and Sapphire; they alternately fight and fuck their way to a house full of pickaninnies. Harpo is always falling through a roof he's chronically unable to repair. Sofia is always shoving a baby into his arms, swinging her large hips, and talking a mile a minute. Harpo, who is dying to marry Sofia in the book, seems bamboozled into marriage in the film. Sofia's only masculine power is her contentiousness. Encircled by the mayor, his wife and an angry mob, she is knocked down and her dress flies up providing us with a timely reminder that she is just a woman.[21]

The depiction of Sofia lying in the street with her dress up is almost an exact replica of a picture published in a national mass-circulation magazine of a large Black woman lying dead in her home after she had been killed by her husband in a domestic argument. Coincidence or not, this image among others in the film makes one wonder about Spielberg's unconscious store of associations.

BLACK PEOPLE'S REPRESENTATION IN FILM

While a filmmaker draws on her/his background and experience, she/he also draws on a history of other films. *The Color Purple* follows in the footsteps of earlier films with a Black storyline and/or an all-Black cast that were directed by a white male for mass consumption by a white American audience. The criticisms against the film repeatedly invoked the names of such racist films as *The Birth of a Nation* (1915), *Hallelujah* (1929), and *Cabin in the Sky* (1943). One reviewer in the *Village Voice* wrote that *The Color Purple* was "a revisionist *Cabin in the Sky*, with the God-fearing, long-suffering Ethel Waters (read Celie) and the delectable temptress Lena Horne (known as Shug Avery) falling for each other rather than wrestling over the soul of feckless (here sadistic) Eddie Anderson."[22]

According to Donald Bogle in *Toms, Coons, Mulattoes, Mammies and Bucks*, Nina Mae McKinney's character in *Hallelujah* executing "gyrations and groans" and sensuous "bumps and grinds" became a standard for almost every Black "leading lady" in motion pictures, from Lena Horne in *Cabin in the Sky* to Lola Falana in *The Liberation of L.B. Jones*.[23] The corollary of this stereotype can be seen acted out by Margaret Avery as Shug in the juke joint scenes in *The Color Purple*. Here we see Shug singing in the juke joint and later leading the "jointers" singing and prancing down the road to her father's church. One viewer of The Color Purple wondered, in reference to this scene, if it were obligatory in every film that contained Black actors and actresses that they sing and dance.[24]

As Spielberg called on his store of media memories in making *The Color Purple*, he used a cinematic technique that made D. W. Griffith famous, cross-cutting, toward the same end as Griffith—that of portraying the "savage" nature of Black people. At the beginning of *The Color Purple* the young Celie gives birth to a child fathered by the man she thinks is her father. The viewer can recall the beads of sweat on Celie's face and the blood in the pan of water as Nettie wrings out the cloth she is using to wash Celie. The next shot of blood is on the rock that one of Mister's bad kids throws and hits the young Celie with. We look at Celie and then there is a close-up of the blood on the rock. Later in the film, there is a scene of the grown Celie taking up a knife that she will use to shave Mister. It should be noted that this scene was not in the book and was entirely the film's invention. As Celie brings the knife closer to Mister's neck there is continual cross-cutting with scenes of the initiation rites of Adam (Celie's son) and Pasha in Africa. This cross-cutting is interspersed with shots of Shug dressed in a red dress running across a field to stop Celie from cutting Mister's throat. As the back-and-forth action of the three scenes progresses, the kids' cheeks are cut and we see a trickle of blood running down one of their faces.

In fictional filmmaking, scripts utilize what is known as the rule of threes: first there is the introduction to a concept that is significant, then the setup, then the payoff. Without reaching too hard for significance, we can see in the meaning of the shots of blood with the blood-red of Shug's dress as she runs to rescue Celie, and then the bloodletting of the African initiation rite, that these shots and their use of red culminate in the payoff: these are "savage" people. This connects up later in the film with the overall red tone to the juke joint sequences and the red dress that Shug wears while she is performing there. As Barbara Christian put it, the gross inaccuracy of the African initiation ceremony coupled with the shots of Celie going after Mister with the sharpened knife seemed intended to depict a "primordial blood urge shared by dark peoples in Africa and Afro-Americans."

Other films that have formed the foundation of Black people's demeaning cinematic heritage are *Hearts of Dixie* (1929), *The Green Pastures* (1936), *Carmen Jones* (1954) and

Porgy and Bess (1959). *Porgy and Bess* is especially interesting because of the similarity of its reception to that of *The Color Purple*. The playwright Lorraine Hansberry figures prominently in Black people's negative reaction to *Porgy and Bess*. Hansberry was the only Black person who confronted the director, Otto Preminger, in a public debate about the film. At the time of the debate, Hansberry was well known because of the success of her play *A Raisin in the Sun* (1959). Hansberry's condemnation of the film and its director was the catalyst for a scathing article in *Ebony* magazine, criticizing not only the makers of the film but also the Black stars who had defended the film as a commendable work of art.[25]

There is a sense of déjà vu in considering the success of Lorraine Hansberry, her view of Black people's representation in commercial films, and her deliberations about having her work turned into a Hollywood property. Hansberry's concern almost twenty-five years before the release of *The Color Purple* reads as if it could have been written about the contemporary film. Both Hansberry and Alice Walker were hesitant about turning their works, which were successful in another medium, over to a white director in Hollywood. Hansberry wrote about this in 1961:

> My twenty years of memory of Hollywood treatment of "Negro material" plus the more commonly decried aspects of Hollywood tradition, led me to visualize slit skirts and rolling eyeballs, with the latest night club singer playing the family's college daughter. I did not feel it was my right or duty to help present the American public with yet another latter-day minstrel show.[26]

The negative assumptions that Hansberry was confronting and that she countered in her works are the myth of the exotic primitive.[27] I label it a myth not because of the concept's falseness but because of its wide acceptance, and because of the manner in which it functions as a cultural belief system.

In contemporary terms, a myth is a narrative that accompanies a historical sequence of events or actions. A body of political writings and literature develops around this narrative. This becomes the formulated myth. The myth is constructed of images and symbols which have the force to activate a cultural belief system. This means that if a culture believes a myth to be true or operable in their society, a body of tradition, folklore, laws, and social rules is developed around this mythology. In this way myths serve to organize, unify, and clarify a culture's history in a manner that is satisfactory to a culture.

Mark Schorer, in *Myth and Mythmaking*, states that all convictions (belief systems), whether personal or societal, involve mythology. The mythology, although historically grounded, does not have to be historically accurate. The truth or falsity of the myth is not important when considering the function of the myth (that of validating history), as the cultural system of beliefs is not rational but based on the assumptions in the myth-making process. As Schorer indicates: "Belief organizes experience not because it is rational but because all belief depends on a controlling imagery and rational belief is the intellectual formalization of that imagery."[28] In other words, we believe first, and then we create a rationale for our beliefs and subsequent actions. The formal expression of our beliefs can be seen in the imagery used by a culture.

The characteristics of the myth of the exotic primitive are these: *(a)* Black people are naturally childlike. Thus they adjust easily to the most unsatisfactory social conditions, which they accept readily and even happily. *(b)* Black people are oversexed, carnal sensualists dominated by violent passions. *(c)* Black people are savages taken from a culture relatively low on the scale of human civilization.[29]

As a panelist on *The Negro in American Culture*, a radio program aired on WABI-FM, in New York in January 1961, Lorraine Hansberry spoke eloquently about mainstream artists' need to portray Black people in a negative light:

> And it seems to me that one of the things that has been done in the American mentality is to create this escape valve of the exotic Negro, wherein it is possible to exalt abandon on all levels, and to imagine that while I am dealing with the perplexities of the universe, look over there, coming down from the trees is a Negro who knows none of this, and wouldn't it be marvelous if I could be my naked, brutal, savage self again?[30]

Knowing that this concept of exoticism underlies the products of mainstream cultural production, I think this is one of the reasons that many viewers of a film such as *The Color Purple* have what Bogle described earlier as a schizophrenic reaction. The film did have something progressive and useful for a Black audience but at the same time some of the caricatures and representations cause the viewer to wince. It is my contention that a Black audience through a history of theatregoing and film watching knows that at some point an expression of the exotic primitive is going to be presented to us. Since this is the case, we have one of two options available to us. One is to never indulge in media products, an impossibility in an age of media blitz. Another option, and I think this is more an unconscious reaction to and defense against racist depictions of Black people, is to filter out that which is negative and select from the work elements we can relate to.

BLACK WOMEN'S RESPONSE

Given the similarities of *The Color Purple* to past films that have portrayed Black people negatively, Black women's positive reaction to the film seems inconceivable. However, their stated comments and published reports prove that Black women not only like the film but have formed a strong attachment to it. The film is significant in their lives.

John Fiske provides a useful explanation of what is meant by the term "the subject" in cultural analysis. "The subject" is different from the individual. The individual is the biological being produced by nature; the "subject" is a social and theoretical construction that is used to designate individuals as they become significant in a political or theoretical sense. When a text—a cultural product—is being considered, the subject is defined as the political being who is affected by the ideological construction of the text.[31]

Black women, as subjects for the text *The Color Purple*, have a different history and consequently a different perspective from other viewers of the film. This became evident in the controversy surrounding the film, and in the critical comments from some Black males about what they perceived as the detrimental depiction of Black men. In contrast to this view, Black women have demonstrated that they found something useful and positive in the film. Barbara Christian relates that the most frequent statement from Black women has been: "Finally, somebody says something about us."[32] This sense of identification with what was in the film would provide an impetus for Black women to form an engagement with the film. This engagement could have been either positive or negative. That it was favorable indicates something about the way in which Black women have constructed meaning from this text.

It would be too easy, I think, to categorize Black women's reaction to the film as an example of "false consciousness"; to consider Black women as cultural dupes in the path of a media barrage who cannot figure out when a media product portrays them and their race in a negative manner. Black women are aware, along with others, of the oppression and harm that comes from a negative media history. But Black women are also aware that their specific experience, as Black people, as women, in a rigid class/caste state, has never been adequately dealt with in mainstream media.

One of the Black women that I interviewed talked about this cultural past and how it affected her reaction to the *The Color Purple*: "When I went to the movie, I thought, here I am. I grew up looking at Elvis Presley kissing on all these white girls. I grew up listening to 'Tammy, Tammy, Tammy.' [She sings the song that Debbie Reynolds sang in the movie of the same name.] And it wasn't that I had anything projected before me on the screen to really give me something that I could grow up to be like. Or even wanted to be. Because I knew I wasn't Goldilocks, you know, and I had heard those stories all my life. So when I got to the movie, the first thing I said was 'God, this is good acting.' And I liked that. I felt a lot of pride in my Black brothers and sisters. . . . By the end of the movie I was totally emotionally drained. . . . The emotional things were all in the book, but the movie just took every one of my emotions. . . . Towards the end, when she looks up and sees her sister Nettie . . . I had gotten so emotionally high at that point . . . when she saw her sister, when she started to call her name and to recognize who she was, the hairs on my neck started to stick up. I had never had a movie do that to me before."

The concept "interpellation" sheds light on the process by which Black women were able to form a positive engagement with *The Color Purple*. Interpellation is the way in which the subject is hailed by the text; it is the method by which ideological discourses constitute subjects and draw them into the text/subject relationship. John Fiske describes "hailing" as similar to hailing a cab. The viewer is hailed by a particular work; if she/he gives a cooperative response to the beckoning, then not only are they constructed as a subject, but the text then becomes a text, in the sense that the subject begins to construct meaning from the work and is constructed by the work.[33]

The moment of the encounter of the text and the subject is known as the "interdiscourse." David Morley explains this concept, developed by Michel Pêcheux, as the space, the specific moment when subjects bring their histories to bear on meaning production in a text.[34] Within this interdiscursive space, cultural competencies come into play. A cultural competency is the repertoire of discursive strategies, the range of knowledge, that a viewer brings to the act of watching a film and creating meaning from a work. As has been stated before, the meanings of a text will be constructed differently depending on the various backgrounds of the viewers. The viewers' position in the social structure determines, in part, what sets of discourses or interpretive strategies they will bring to their encounter with the text. A specific cultural competency will set some of the boundaries to meaning construction.

The cultural competency perspective has allowed media researchers to understand how elements in a viewer's background play a determining role in the way in which she/he interprets a text. Stuart Hall, David Morley, and others utilize the theories of Dell Hymes, Basil Bernstein, and Pierre Bourdieu for an understanding of the ways in which a social structure distributes different forms of cultural decoding strategies throughout the different sections of the media audience. These understandings are not the same for everyone in the audience because they are shaped by the individual's history, both media and cultural, and by the individual's social affiliations such as race, class, gender, and so on.[35]

As I see it, there can be two aspects to a cultural competency, or the store of understandings that a marginalized viewer brings to interpreting a cultural product. One is a positive response where the viewer constructs something useful from the work by negotiating her/his response, and/or gives a subversive reading to the work. The other is a negative response in which the viewer rejects the work. Both types of oppositional readings are prompted by the store of negative images that have come from prior mainstream media experience; in the case of *The Color Purple*, from Black people's negative history in Hollywood films.

A positive engagement with a work could come from an intertextual cultural experience. This is true, I think, with the way in which Black women constructed meaning from *The Color Purple*. Creative works by Black women are proliferating now. This intense level of productivity is not accidental nor coincidental. It stems from a desire on the part of Black women to construct works more in keeping with their experiences, their history, and with the daily lives of other Black women. And Black women, as cultural consumers, are receptive to these works. This intertextual cultural knowledge is forming Black women's store of decoding strategies for films that are about them. This is the cultural competency that Black women brought to their favorable readings of *The Color Purple*.

BLACK WOMEN'S WRITING TRADITION: COMMUNITY AND ARTICULATION

The historical moment in which the film *The Color Purple* was produced and received is what one Black feminist scholar has categorized the "renaissance of Black women writers" of the 1970s and 1980s. Within this renaissance the central concern of the writers has been the personal lives and collective histories of Black women. The writers are reconstructing a heritage that has either been distorted or ignored. In this reconstruction, Black women are both audience and subject.[36]

A major difference in the current period of writing from that of the well-known Harlem Renaissance of the 1920s, the protest literature of the 1940s and the Black activist literature of the 1960s, is that Black women writers are getting more exposure and recognition today, and the target of their works is different. In the earlier periods of Black writing, male writers were given dominant exposure and the audience to whom they addressed their works was white. The writers believed that because Black people's oppression was the direct result of white racism, exposing this fact to white people would result in change. By contrast, for Black women writers within the last forty years, the Black community has been the major focus of their work.

Hortense J. Spillers writes that the community of Black women writing is a vivid new fact of national life. Spillers includes in this community not only the writers but Black women critics, scholars, and audience members. This community, which Spillers labels a community of "cultural workers" is fashioning its own tradition. Its writers and its readers are, she writes, creating their works against the established canons and are excavating a legacy that is more appropriate to their lives. Spillers argues compellingly that traditions are made, not born. Traditions do not arise spontaneously out of nature, but are created social events. She insists that traditions exist not only because there are writers there to make them, but also because there is a "strategic audience of heightened consciousness prepared to read and interpret the works as such."[37]

Spillers adds that traditions need to be maintained by an audience if they are to survive, and she argues that this is currently happening. She writes that "we are called upon to witness" the formation of a new social order of Black women as a community conscious of itself. This is not a random association of writers creating in isolation or readers consuming the works in a vacuum. According to Spillers, the group views itself as a community and is aware that it is creating new symbolic values and a new sense of empowerment for itself and the members of the group.

Stuart Hall has defined the principle of "articulation," developed by Ernesto Laclau, to explain how individuals within a particular society at a specific historical moment wrest control away from the dominant forces in a culture and attain authority over their lives for themselves and for others within their social group. The way in which an articulation is accomplished, and its significance, has bearing on this examination of the film *The Color Purple*. An articulation is defined as the form of a connection, a linkage, that can establish a unity among different elements within a culture, under certain conditions.[38] In the case of a cultural product such as the film *The Color Purple*, the unity that is formed links a discourse (the film) and a specific social group (Black women or, more precisely, what Spillers has defined as the Black women's writing community). Such unity is flexible, but not for all time. It must constantly be strengthened. The strength of the unity formed between a discourse and a social alliance comes from the use to which the group puts the discourse, or the cultural product. In the case of *The Color Purple*, the film has been used to give new meaning to the lives of Black women.

Articulation, as it is normally defined, can have two meanings: "joining up" in the sense of the limbs of a body or an anatomical structure, or "giving expression to."[39] Hall disagrees with the use of articulation to mean "giving expression to" because it implies that a social group shares an expressive unity which Hall believes it does not. An articulation results from a coming together of separate discourses under certain specific conditions and at specific times. The use of articulation to mean "giving expression to" implies that the two elements that are linked are the same, but for Hall they are not. The unity formed "is not that of an identity where one structure perfectly reproduces or recapitulates" the other. The social group and the signifying text are not the same. An articulation occurs because a social alliance forms it, in a political act which makes the group a cohesive one for a time, as long as it goes on acting for a political purpose.

When an articulation arises, old ideologies are disrupted and a cultural transformation is accomplished. The cultural transformation is not something totally new, nor does it have an unbroken line of continuity with the past. It is always in a process of becoming. But at a particular moment the reality of the cultural transformation becomes apparent. The group that is the catalyst for it recognizes that a change is occurring and that they are in the midst of a cultural transition. The formal elements of the transformation are then recognized and consolidated.

The Black women's writing tradition laid a foundation for the way in which Black women formed an articulation through which they interpreted the film *The Color Purple*. The boundaries of the tradition are set from 1850 onward. Although Black women were socially and politically active from the beginning of their enforced presence in the "new world," their writings, speeches, and lectures, their "public voice," as Hazel Carby describes it, was not being recorded and preserved. Carby makes the critical point, however, that Black women's voices were being heard.[40] The public voice of nineteenth-century Black women activists resounds now in the creative works of Black women in the 1970s and the 1980s, thus giving contemporary texts all the elements of a tradition.

Barbara Christian's *Black Women Novelists* (1980) was instrumental in identifying the presence of the tradition. In her book Christian not only demonstrated that there was indeed a Black women's writing tradition, but she also proved convincingly, I think, that the reasons that these Black women were little known was that the two established critical institutions, African-American literature and mainstream white literature, had placed Black women in the shadows of literary scholarship. She proved, as Spillers indicated, that tradition is a man-made product and that Black women had been left out.

Christian also looks at the elements of Black women's writing that foreshadowed and formed a foundation for the contemporary writers that she finds most influential: Paule Marshall, Toni Morrison, and Alice Walker. The elements of Black life that they portray seem to strike a resonance in the audience for whom the works are written, Black women. Christian argues that Black women's literature is not just a matter of discourse, but is a way of acknowledging one's existence: "it has to do with giving consolation to oneself that one does exist. It is an attempt to make meaning out of that existence." And further, "The way in which I have often described this for myself, as a Black woman, is that this literature helps me to know that I am not hallucinating. Because much of one's life from the point of view of a Black woman could be seen as an hallucination from what society tells you." She said the way in which the literature connects up with the experiences of other Black women is that, in giving Black women a place as subject, it "therefore gives them a sense that their lives are in fact *real.*"[41]

Toni Morrison writes of one of her characters: "She had nothing to fall back on; not maleness, not whiteness, not ladyhood, not anything. And out of the profound desolation of her reality she may well have invented herself."[42] Out of the profound desolation of Black women's reality, to paraphrase Toni Morrison, Black women cultural producers are beginning to create works more appropriate to their lives and to the daily reality of other Black women. In Ntozake Shange's choreopoem *For Colored Girls Who Have Considered Suicide/When the Rainbow Is Enuf* (1976), one of the characters, the lady in orange, tells her former boyfriend:

> ever since i realized there waz someone callt
> a colored girl an evil woman a bitch or a nag
> i been trying not to be that & leave bitterness
> in somebody else's cup/come to somebody to love me
> without deep & nasty smellin scald from lye or bein
> left screamin in a street fulla lunatics/whisperin slut bitch bitch niggah/ get outta
> here wit alla
> that/ . . .

Later in the passage the lady in orange delivers what I think is a sign for Black women that the status quo is not for them and that something different is required:

. . . /but a real dead

lovin is here for you now/cuz i don't know anymore/how to avoid my own face wet wit my tears/
   cuz i had convinced

myself colored girls had no right to sorrow/ & i lived

& loved that way & kept sorrow on the curb/ allegedly

for you/ but i know i did it for myself/

i cdnt stand it

i cdnt stand bein sorry & colored at the same time it's so redundant in the modern world.[43]

"I couldn't stand it," the lady in orange says, and she issues an ultimatum that the Black woman was evolving from one place in society's conception of her to another of her own choosing. The Black woman was changing from victim to victor, was placing herself outside of the cocoon for others' constructions of her and, as Alice Walker's character Celie says in *The Color Purple*, entering into "the Creation."

Celie's declaration contains the essence of Black women's response to the film *The Color Purple*. There has been a long march from early images of the Black woman in creative works to the reconstruction of the character Celie in Alice Walker's novel. Celie tells Mister, at a turning point in the novel, that she is leaving the prison that he has created for her and entering into a freer place where she has more control over her own destiny. Black women responded to Celie's statement in their overwhelming positive reaction to both the novel and the film.

Black women's positive response to the film *The Color Purple* is not coincidental, nor is it insignificant. It is in keeping with the recent emergence of a body of critical works about the heritage of Black women writers, the recent appearance of other novels by Black women written in the same vein as *The Color Purple* and, very importantly, the fact that there is a knowledgeable core of Black women readers of both literary and filmic texts. This community of heightened consciousness is in the process of creating new self-images and forming a force for change.

NOTES

1. Phil Donahue read a quote by Tony Brown with this statement on his show, *The Phil Donahue Show*, April 25, 1986. Brown was part of a panel along with Donald Bogle, Michele Wallace, and Willis Edwards, debating the film. Ishmael Reed's statement was quoted by Tony Brown on his show *Tony Brown's Journal*, when Reed was a guest there. Reed was debating Barbara Smith on the topic of the show: "Do Black Feminist Writers Victimize Black Men?' (repeat program), November 2, 1986.

2. Andrew Kopkind, "The Color Purple," *The Nation*, February 1, 1986, 124. The *Guardian* is a radical journal in the United States.

3. Jill Nelson, "Spielberg's 'Purple' Is Still Black," *Guardian*, January 29, 1986, 1.

4. E.R. Shipp, "Blacks in Heated Debate over *The Color Purple*," *New York Times*, January 27, 1986, A13.

5. Courtland Milloy, "A 'Purple' Rage Over a Rip-Off," *Washington Post*, December 24, 1985, B3.

6. Barbara Smith, "*Color Purple* Distorts Class, Lesbian Issues," *Guardian*, February 19, 1986, 19.

7. Jill Nelson, *Guardian*, 17.

8. Michele Wallace, *The Phil Donahue Show*, April 25, 1986.

9. Michele Wallace, "Blues for Mr Spielberg," *Village Voice*, March 18, 1986, 27.

10. Donald Bogle, *The Phil Donahue Show*, April 25, 1986.

11. William Goldstein, "Alice Walker on the Set of *The Color Purple*," *Publishers Weekly*, September 6, 1985, 48.

12. Mary Helen Washington, "Book Review of Barbara Christian's *Black Women Novelists*," *Signs: Journal of Women in Culture and Society*, vol. 8, no. 1 (August 1982): 182.

13. I am at present writing a dissertation on Black women's response to the film *The Color Purple*. As part of the study I conducted what will be an

ethnography of reading with selected Black women viewers of the film in December 1987 in California. All references to women interviewed come from this study. For a discussion of the issues of readers' response to texts in media audience analysis see Ellen Seiter et al. "Don't Treat Us Like We're So Stupid and Naive: Towards an Ethnography of Soap Opera Viewers," in *Rethinking Television Audiences*, Ellen Seiter, ed. (Chapel Hill: University of North Carolina Press, forthcoming). See also Seiter's use of Umberto Eco's open/closed text distinction to examine the role of the woman reader. Seiter uses Eco's narrative theory to argue for the possibility of "alternative" readings unintended by their producers in "Eco's TV Guide: The Soaps," *Tabloid*, no. 6 (1981): 36–43.

14. David Morley, "Changing Paradigms in Audience Studies," in *Rethinking Television Audiences*, Ellen Seiter, ed. (Chapel Hill: University of North Carolina Press, forthcoming).

15. David Morley, "Changing Paradigms," 4.

16. Lawrence Grossberg, "Strategies of Marxist Cultural Interpretation," *Critical Studies in Mass Communication*, no. 1 (1984): 403.

17. Christine Gledhill explains the idea of "making strange" in two articles: "Developments in Feminist Film Criticism," *Re-Vision: Essays in Feminist Film Criticism*, Mary Ann Doane, Patricia Mellencamp, and Linda Williams, eds., (Frederick, Md.: University Publications of America, in association with the American Film Institute, 1984); and "Klute 1: A Contemporary Film Noir and Feminist Criticism," in *Women in Film Noir*, E. Ann Kaplan, ed., (London: British Film Institute, 1984).

18. Lawrence Grossberg, 403.

19. Steven Spielberg, BBC documentary, *Alice Walker and The Color Purple*, 1986.

20. Barbara Christian, "De-Visioning Spielberg and Walker: *The Color Purple*—The Novel and the Film," Center for the Study of Women in Society, University of Oregon, May 20, 1986.

21. Michele Wallace, "Blues for Mr Spielberg," 25.

22. J. Hoberman, "Color Me Purple," *Village Voice*, December 24, 1985, 76.

23. Donald Bogle, *Toms, Coons, Mulattoes, Mammies and Bucks: An Interpretive History of Blacks in American Films* (New York: Viking Press, 1973), 31.

24. Julie Salamon, ". . . As Spielberg's Film Version Is Released," *Wall Street Journal*, December 19, 1985, 20.

25. Era Bell Thompson, "Why Negroes Don't Like 'Porgy and Bess,' " *Ebony*, October 1959, 51. A run-down of Lorraine Hansberry's debate with Otto Preminger is also given by Jack Pitman, "Lorraine Hansberry Deplores 'Porgy,' " *Variety*, May 27, 1959.

26. Lorraine Hansberry, "What Could Happen Didn't," *New York Herald Tribune*, March 26, 1961, 8. In this article Lorraine Hansberry writes about the experience of turning her play *A Raisin in the Sun* into a Hollywood movie. Hansberry wrote the screenplay herself and, as far as I know, was the first Black woman to have a Hollywood film based on her work. For a further examination of the political and historical significance of Hansberry, see Jacqueline Bobo, "Debunking the Myth of the Exotic Primitive: Three Plays by Lorraine Hansberry," (unpublished M.A. thesis, San Francisco State University, 1980).

27. The anthropologist Melville Herskovits gives broader scope to the myth, designating it as the myth of the Negro past. The trait of exotic primitivism can be extrapolated from Herskovits's definition and considered a myth itself in that both concepts are of sufficient potency that the effect in a culture is the same: validating the social processes whereby Black people are considered inferior. Melville Herskovits, *The Myth of the Negro Past* (Boston: Beacon Press, 1958), 1.

28. Mark Schorer, "The Necessity of Myth," in *Myth and Mythmaking*, Henry A. Murray, ed., (New York: George Braziller, 1960), 356.

29. Herskovits, 1.

30. Lorraine Hansberry, "The Negro in American Culture," reprinted in *The Black American Writer*, C. W. E. Bigsby, ed., (Deland, Florida: Everett/Edward, 1969), 93.

31. John Fiske, "British Cultural Studies and Television," in *Channels of Discourse: Television and Contemporary Criticism*, Robert C. Allen, ed., (Chapel Hill: University of North Carolina Press, 1987), 258.

32. Barbara Christian, University of Oregon, May 20, 1986.

33. John Fiske, "British Cultural Studies and Television," 258.

34. David Morley, "Texts, Readers, Subjects," in *Culture, Media, Language*, Stuart Hall, Dorothy Hobson, Andrew Lowe, and Paul Willis, eds., (London: Hutchinson, 1980), 164.

35. David Morley, "Changing Paradigms in Audience Studies," 4.

36. Barbara Christian, Seminar: "Black Women's Literature and the Canon," University of Oregon, December 7, 1987.

37. Hortense J. Spillers, "Cross-Currents, Discontinuities: Black Women's Fiction," in *Conjuring: Black Women, Fiction, and Literary Tradition*, Marjorie Pryse and Hortense J. Spillers, eds. (Bloomington: Indiana University Press), 1985, 250.

38. Stuart Hall discusses the principle of "articulation" in two articles: "Race, Articulation and

Societies Structured in Dominance," in *Sociological Theories: Race and Colonialism*, (Paris: UNESCO, 1980), 305–45. Also, Lawrence Grossberg, ed., "On Postmodernism and Articulation: An Interview with Stuart Hall," *Journal of Communication Inquiry*, vol. 10, no. 2 (summer 1986): 45–60.

I explore the principle of "articulation" further in the larger study that I am doing on Black women's response to *The Color Purple*. I see the articulation between Black women as audience, the Black women's writing community and Black women's collective response to the film as constituting a social force that will affect other areas in Black people's lives: politically, economically, and socially.

39. Hall, "Race, Articulation and Societies Structured in Dominance," 328.

40. Hazel V. Carby, *Reconstructing Womanhood: The Emergence of the Afro-American Woman Novelist* (New York: Oxford University Press), 1987. Other critical works that examine the Black women's writing tradition are: *The Black Woman* (1970), by Toni Cade; *Black-Eyed Susans* (1975) and *Midnight Birds* (1980), by Mary Helen Washington; *Black Women Writers at Work* (1983), Claudia Tate, ed.; *Black Women Writers* (1984), by Mari Evans; *Invented Lives* (1987), by Mary Helen Washington; and *Specifying* (1987), by Susan Willis.

41. Barbara Christian, seminar, University of Oregon, December 7, 1987.

42. Toni Morrison, cited in Mary Helen Washington, *Black-Eyed Susans: Classic Stories by and about Black Women* (New York: Anchor Press/Doubleday, 1975), vii.

43. Ntozake Shange, *For Colored Girls Who Have Considered Suicide/When the Rainbow Is Enuf* (New York: Macmillan, 1976), 43.

14

BLACK TALK RADIO
Defining Community Needs and Identity

Catherine R. Squires

This article presents research concerning the relationship between media and public spheres through an investigation of an African-American-owned and -operated talk-radio station in Chicago. The article concludes that contrary to some scholars' pessimistic view of commercial media's role in the decline of the public sphere, the radio station portrayed here is an integral and useful institution for the Black public sphere in Chicago. The study reveals how African-American community members and listeners use the station as a public forum wherein traditional political concerns, as well as identity politics, are aired and discussed. Furthermore, the article argues that it is precisely because the station is owned and operated by Blacks that it is able to draw and sustain a substantial and loyal audience. Because they trust the station to "talk their talk," community members are enthusiastic about participating in the station's conversational activities and are even willing to make personal financial contributions when advertising revenue is low.

Although many researchers have investigated the negative impact of traditionally white-controlled mass media on white attitudes toward Blacks* (see Entman 1992; Peffley et al. 1996), the question of how Black-controlled mass media shape Black public life has not been as rigorously investigated. As Michael Dawson notes, "How and to what extent the circulation of and participation in debates within social movements, indigenous organizations, *and Black media* and artistic outlets influence political attitudes of individuals is an empirical question" that has yet to be answered (Dawson 1994:217, emphasis added). Building on Dawson's suggestion, I explore the relationship between Black mass media and Black publics through a study of WVON-AM radio, the only Black-owned talk-radio station in Chicago. Results of a survey and an ethnographic research study suggest that WVON and its listeners create alternative conversational and physical public spheres in

---

*In this article, I use "Black," "African-American," and "black" interchangeably to reflect the use of all three of these terms by different peoples in Black communities.

which members of the audience (also known as "the WVON family") circulate informa-tion and provide opportunities for community interaction and political involvement.

TALK RADIO

Most studies of talk radio either focus on nationally broadcast, celebrity hosts, such as Rush Limbaugh, or use large, random national samples to extract information about the talk-show audience and talk-show texts (Davis 1997; Hofstetter and Gianos 1997; Hollander 1997; Owen 1997). These approaches have resulted in a lopsided picture of the talk-show phenom-enon: that is, that the shows are overwhelmingly enjoyed by white conservative males (often associated with the Gingrich "revolution") and that the content is also mainly conservative. Not surprisingly, this picture resonates with liberal politicians' and commentators' com-plaints about the "new" influence talk shows have on voters and the irresponsibility of politi-cal journalists. These studies do not fully explain the reemergence of talk-show popularity, nor do they encompass the wide range of hosts, formats, and audiences involved in this phe-nomenon. Their focus on and concern with the behavior of white conservative listeners has fueled the fire over "hate radio" without revealing the differences that exist across stations and audiences. By exploring local radio stations in addition to the national broadcasters, we will gain a more nuanced understanding of talk radio's function in both the lives of its audi-ences and its effects on political processes.

Black talk radio, largely ignored by media scholars, has been growing steadily around the country. In addition to the popularity of the nationally syndicated host Tom Joyner, many local Black-owned stations have included talk programming for years. Earlier in the century, Blacks who were able to buy airtime in large cities, like Jack Cooper's pioneering efforts in Chicago, or who were hired at stations that played Black music created talk shows for their Black listeners (Cantor 1992; Newman 1988). However, these traditions in pro-gramming and African-American audience have been overlooked and underrepresented in national sample surveys and are rarely mentioned in editorial discussions concerning talk radio.

Below, I present some of the results of a long-term study of WVON-AM in Chicago, combining ethnographic and survey research methods to begin constructing a more di-verse picture of the talk-radio phenomenon. Furthermore, I intend for my description of this particular audience to advance Susan Herbst's contention that studies of talk radio should attempt to discern why they are an attractive means of "discursive political partici-pation" and how the talk show "illuminates debates about the nature of the public sphere" (Herbst 1995:264). At the end of her article, Herbst suggests that part of the attraction for the conservative white listeners is their distrust of mainstream media, creating the desire for an alternative forum. I find that Black listeners at WVON also distrust mainstream white media, but their attraction to an alternative sphere of discourse has other roots as well—roots that reach back to the birth of a separate (yet overlapping and interactive) Black public sphere.

THE PUBLIC SPHERE(S)

The translation of Jurgen Habermas's *The Structural Transformation of the Public Sphere* (1989) has inspired many scholars to rethink the idea of the public forum, the importance of public discourse, the nature of public opinion, and the role of the mass media in the production of all three. Habermas proposes the existence of a single public sphere where participants leave behind status markers in order to engage in rational critical discourse. His idealized conception, based in eighteenth-century Europe, does not echo Black experiences with public spaces or the media. African Americans have had neither the luxury of leaving the status marker of race behind (unless they could "pass" for white), nor have they had access or been welcome to speak and participate in the dominant public sphere until very recently in American history. Hence, Blacks have created alternate forms of publicity in the face of a hostile and often threatening white public. Blacks made their own sequestered and semisequestered spaces for deliberation, resistance, and sustenance to survive in America. This history of African Americans and the public sphere demands a more complex vision of public spaces and deliberation than Habermas's ideal type provides.

Like Dawson, I consider the Black public sphere to be closer to Nancy Fraser's vision of a subaltern counterpublic (1992). In her critique of Habermas, Fraser demonstrates that rather than insisting upon the existence of a single public sphere, it is more useful to envision multiple public spheres coexisting, overlapping, and competing in stratified societies like the United States. There is a dominant public sphere that "will tend to operate to the advantage of dominant groups and the disadvantage of subordinates" (Fraser 1992:122). However, subordinates are not rendered completely silent. Rather, they create their own discursive arenas, which Fraser calls "subaltern counterpublics." Dawson uses Fraser's general depiction of a subaltern counterpublic to create a specific operationalization of the Black counterpublic and its goals:

> The Black public sphere [is] . . . a set of institutions, communication networks and practices which facilitate debate of causes and remedies to the current combination of political setbacks and economic devastation facing major segments of the Black community, and which facilitate the creation of oppositional formations and sites. (Dawson 1994:197)

Dawson, like other Black political and cultural theorists, believes that the current state of the majority of Blacks in the United States necessitates an oppositional sphere. Counterpublics give oppressed and/or marginalized groups arenas for deliberation outside the surveillance of the dominant group. Here, they can

> invent and articulate counterdiscourses to formulate oppositional interpretations of their identities, interests and needs. . . . On the one hand, [subaltern counterpublics] function as spaces of withdrawal and regroupment; on the other, they function as bases and training grounds for agitational activities directed toward wider publics. (Fraser 1992:123–24)

Daniel Brouwer provides three additional reasons for the existence and importance of subaltern publics: (1) when the standards for participation are perceived by marginal cultures to be restrictive or unfairly applied; (2) when official public forums are perceived "not to be adequate sites for the redress of sociopolitical or cultural grievances"; and (3) when the representations of subaltern publics produced by mainstream sources are "inaccurate, offensive, limiting, or dangerous" (Brouwer 1995). So, while African Americans have made great legal gains in this society, there are still structural and cultural barriers to full equality (see Marable 1991; Omi and Winant 1994; West 1993). In addition, harmful narratives and images concerning blacks are still circulated in mainstream and other media (Dates and Barlow 1990; Entman 1992; Gilens 1996; Morrison 1992). Therefore, there is still a need for an alternate sphere (or spheres) for Blacks in the United States, as well as alternative black media.

However, Dawson concludes in his overview of the state of the Black community that such a sphere has not existed since the early 1970s. Furthermore, he questions whether there can be a single Black public sphere any longer, given division along class and gender lines. Hence his call for a new program of research into the institutions that undergird a counterpublic and investigations of Black public opinion to spur on the revitalization of such a public (or publics). In this article, I present evidence that the activities at a particular talk-radio station are providing sites for the creation of communication networks and oppositional sites for political organization. WVON radio is an institution that serves a Black public sphere occupying a particular niche in the Chicago radio market at the frequency 1450 AM.

AUDIENCE AS (SUBALTERN) PUBLIC; AUDIENCE AS A NICHE MARKET

James Webster and Patricia Phalen note that in American media policy debates, the public is conceived as a large collection of citizens, unknown to each other and unseen by the government—except, perhaps, as poll data. This concept of the public bears obvious similarities to the mass audience (Webster and Phalen 1994:21). Their observation is built on Susan Herbst and James R. Beniger's observation that as politicians in the twentieth century increased their use of media to reach the public, the media audience became analogous for the publics they were trying to persuade. Because "mass media now transmit much of the information needed to formulate opinions . . . , publics might be viewed as bodies formed through communication" (Herbst and Beniger 1994:109, 97). In the age of mass media, the terms *audience* and *public* have become interchangeable.

Habermas, however, depicts modern mass media as distraction from rather than preparation for rational critical debate. This critique is based on the assumption that media are no longer produced by the public itself and are entangled in commercial interests that run counter to the ideals of public education and debate (Habermas 1989:188). Many scholars of media and democracy would agree with Habermas's critique that today's news media are debilitating rather than energizing the public sphere. Robert Entman, for instance, describes the media as heavily dependent on elites and politicians for information and focused on profit maximization rather than public service (1989). Others' accounts, whether they tend toward conspiracy (Chomsky 1992; Parenti 1993) or pragmatism (Bennett and Paletz 1994; Page 1996), also focus on the problematic relationships between political elites, news producers, and commercialism. However useful these analyses of mainstream media are, though, they operate within a singular public sphere model. To get a more complete look at how different sectors of the populace use media and discuss public issues, we use a model of multiple public spheres. One must then investigate each particular sphere's production and consumption of media (in addition to its relationship to the media of the dominant sphere) to ascertain the utility of the media to that particular public.

William Gamson states that "because media discourse is so central in framing issues for the attentive public, it becomes . . . 'a site on which various social groups, institutions, and ideologies struggle over the definition and construction of social reality.' " However, acknowledging this function of the media "doesn't tell us how and in what ways it operates on different parts of the audience. . . . Media practices both help and hurt social movement efforts in complex ways that differ from issue to issue" (Gamson 1992:71). I would amend

Gamson's statement to add that media practices help and hurt social movement efforts in ways that differ from medium to medium, from public to public. In other words, one might hypothesize that media created by and for subaltern publics will operate differently than media created by and for dominant publics. The talk-show format, which allows the audience to participate in constructing social texts and assigning meanings, may assist the social and political goals of different publics in different ways. The management and production teams of WVON believe that the talk-show format is a catalyst for, not a hindrance to, its audience's political and social goals.

In the case of WVON, the distinctions between producer and audience are not as stark as with the mainstream commercial media firms critiqued by the authors mentioned above. First, WVON grounds itself in a community ethic and a commitment to disseminating information shared by its listeners. Second, the talk-show format itself is an opportunity for a dynamic process of joint creation of texts and reciprocal information sharing between audience, guests, and station staff. Through this particular media environment, the audience participates in a Black public sphere created in multiple ways: through the discursive space of the talk show, the physical spaces of community forums sponsored by or announced by WVON, and membership in the WVON family, a subset of a larger Black collective.

From the publication of *Freedom's Journal* in 1827 to the ascendancy of the *Chicago Defender* in the 1920s, the role of the black media has been to "serve, speak, and fight for the Black community" (Wolseley 1971:3). Not only has the Black media spoken to and for Black publics, presenting an alternate portrayal of black life, but it has also provided an alternative, autonomous discursive public sphere for Blacks from Chicago to the Deep South (Suggs 1996; Washburn 1986).[1] Dawson calls for researchers to focus their attention on the importance of such institutions to a Black public sphere, noting that

> a multiplicity of Black institutions have formed the material base for a subaltern counterpublic. *An independent Black press*, the production and circulation of socially and politically sharp Black music and the Black church have provided institutional bases for the Black counterpublic since the Civil War. (Dawson 1994:210, emphasis added)

In the past, the Black press and other media have enriched the Black public sphere, even though they targeted a wide swath of the Black public and depended on subscriptions and advertisements for revenue (Squires 1999). Creating oppositional frameworks for African Americans and rearticulating Black identity, the Black press served as a site for grievances to be aired when even letters to the editor were segregated, spread the word for activists and scholars, and allowed blacks to use their expertise and modes of expression without as much censure from the dominant public.[2] Despite this historical legacy, little work has been done on the role of contemporary Black talk radio in Black political discourse. Two studies of Black radio's educational impact on Black communities currently available (Johnson 1992; Johnson and Birk 1993) find that Black radio managers report a high level of community involvement. In particular, these studies by Phylis Johnson and her colleagues find that concern for the health and welfare of Black communities guides many decisions about promotions and special events put on by Black-owned stations.[3] In light of the history of Black-owned media and current activities in radio, it is not surprising to find

WVON catering talk shows to a niche of the Black community in Chicago. This study suggests that WVON is continuing the legacy of the Black press via radio, creating an institution with the potential to meet Dawson's criteria for a revitalization of the Black counterpublic. This article centers on the following issues and questions:

1. Does the programming on WVON provide useful information to listeners and staff in terms of critical debate and public action?
2. What relationships to the Black community/public do listeners and station staff expect from Black media?
3. How does the station imagine the Black public it serves, and how do audience members imagine that public?

METHODS

This article began with fieldwork at WVON in the summer of 1995. Through participant observation, interviews with staff and listeners, and analysis of broadcasts, I was immersed in its motives and history.[4] In this article, I share both the results of this ethnographic research and a 1996 survey that focused on audience members who reside in Chicago. The list of audience members was generated through WVON's first subscription drive of late 1995. From this database (WVON's only official listing of any of its listeners), I randomly selected 515 names. Fifteen were used to pretest the questionnaire,[5] and the remaining five hundred were sent surveys with return postage and mailing included. The response rate was 46 percent ($N = 232$), a rather high rate for a mail survey of this type. The questionnaire contained open-ended items, dichotomous choice questions, and Likert scale–styled questions that required respondents to answer whether they strongly agreed or disagreed with statements about WVON and other media.

I also analyzed the conversations between hosts, listeners, and guests on the station. The excerpts related here come from a collection of tapes I recorded while I was a volunteer production assistant at the station. I worked two days a week at the station and recorded Cliff Kelley's drive-time show, *World Objectives*, each of those days (6 A.M. to 10 A.M.). In addition to those tapes, I also recorded shows that concerned historically important events (e.g., the O.J. Simpson verdict, the Million Man March) and interviews with important national figures (e.g., Jesse Jackson, Dick Gregory, former senator Carol Moseley-Braun). I then transcribed the tapes and read them closely for recurrent themes and controversies. I also listened to the tapes repeatedly to recall the tones of the conversations, vocal emphases, and the like to create better descriptions of the conversations I was transcribing. Through this close listening and reading, I was able to discern recurrent themes, concerns, and controversies that illuminated the station's role in its audience members' lives.

WVON AS A SITE FOR DISCOURSE AND FOR ORGANIZATION

WVON seems to have a high degree of utility for respondents. It seems to be living up to one of its slogans: "Bringing the Community Together."

A large majority of respondents have become involved with community events and organizations after listening to or participating in WVON's discussions. Beyond being a site for "just talk" on the airwaves, WVON provides links to other physical and discursive public forums. In addition to informing listeners about community happenings and organizations, WVON regularly sponsors its own community events: breakfasts with speakers, aldermanic debates, and panel discussions about issues ranging from economic renewal to affirmative action to male-female relationships. In addition, WVON's hosts and callers provide information about rallies, protests, seminars, and entertainment events in the Black community and in Chicago at large. Here, for example, are excerpts from the drive-time show on October 5, 1995, where a caller thanks Cliff for discussing the murder of a Black homeless man by a white Chicago policeman instead of concentrating on the O.J. Simpson trial.

> **Cliff:** Getting to other racial bombs . . . Becker, the off-duty pig—I mean, cop—who shot the homeless gentleman [Joseph Gould]. Judge John Brady yesterday refused to raise Becker's bond. . . . Now you know exact—this is why people don't have any faith in the system. Black people, that is. Because you know what would happen if Gould had shot Becker: There wouldn't be any bond. He'd be in jail—if he ever even got to jail. . . . That judge is a threat to justice. That's why we have to remember these names, folks. . . .
>
> 591–5990 is the number. We've got [Caller 1] with us now. How are you today?
>
> **Caller 1:** I'm super, and that's because you addressed the Becker issue this morning and I was afraid people were getting away from it. We still need to keep the pressure on here because even if the trial comes up, this man can only be convicted of manslaughter. And that is not equal to the crime. . . .
>
> Have you heard about the [push] to increase the charges to murder? Because justice will not be served unless we Black people jump on that band-wagon. . . .
>
> **Cliff:** That [process of increasing the charges] is the sole responsibility of the county prosecutor, who you know is Mr. O'Malley, who many of you think—the only reason we have anything [a manslaughter charge] is because of outside agitation. He claims, of course, that's not the case, but outside agitation needs to continue to achieve the goal you are speaking of. Otherwise it's not gonna happen.
>
> **Caller 1:** I just got a letter from Telli Imani's organization, and I was very disappointed because it had a lot of [additional] riders on it. And I thought that, if we were gonna be effective, we need to be focused on increasing the charges and dealing with these judges, because . . . the only way you can remove them is during election time. . . . .
>
> **Cliff:** You're right. The only way to do it is during retention, which is—that's why I'm saying . . . what we will have to do is keep these names out front so people can remember. And I promise I will certainly be doing that when the election comes up.[6]

As this exchange shows, not only is the caller interested in learning new information about the Gould murder, but both he and Kelley are invested in continuing the community protests and increasing pressure on the Cook County state's attorney. And not only is protest deemed necessary, but Black involvement specifically. Finally, the caller mentions his contact with a particular organization headed by Telli Imani, which is organizing around the issue, and he gives his critique of their tactics.

On another show, listeners and politicians called in to respond to what they felt was a questionable endorsement of Dick Devine, a white candidate for state's attorney, over a Black candidate, Judge Eugene Pincham. The guest, Artensa Randolph, is the president of a Chicago Housing Authority (CHA) community group that registers voters and makes endorsements for Chicago elections.

Cliff: How are you, sir?

Caller: Fine, thank you. Good morning Miss Randolph!

Artensa: Good morning!

Caller: Listen! When I heard you say that you were supporting Devine, you scared the life out of me! I grabbed this phone quick! Listen! I can't think of anything worse than folks in the projects and CHA citizens voting for Devine. I can't. And I would hope that somebody from Judge Pincham's campaign would get in touch with you right away. . . .

Cliff: Well, let me say this, Reggie. Not only do I agree with you, and that's why I told Miss Randolph when she said nothing's in stone, and she said "at this point," Judge Pincham called in while we were off the air and said that he certainly wanted to meet with you. . . .

Another caller, Ann, calls in to voice her disapproval of the endorsement.

Ann: I hope that you turn your endorsement around because so many people look to you for leadership and guidance. . . .

Later in the show, Alderman Anna Langford calls in to remember when she and other activists went door-to-door to get voters out at the CHA buildings represented by Randolph's organization:

Anna: We went to five of the buildings in Robert Taylor. We covered every floor and every door, until eleven o'clock that night. Ralph Metcalf won by about nineteen votes or something like that. We got those buildings out of it, so there's voting strength in those buildings; it's very significant.

Artensa: Sure is!

Anna: However, and I'm glad that you got those five thousand people, but I would hate to think that those five thousand people are going to vote for the opposition and the enemy. Divine . . . has done a terrible disservice by having his law firm vote against remap. And we can't have that. And Judge Pincham I've known ever since he was practicing law.[7]

These sorts of exchanges happen daily on WVON as topics of the day and are brought up by host, guest, and caller alike. Thus it seems that the audience, as evidenced by the survey results and the exchanges above, are attending events, meeting people, circulating in the other public spaces WVON clues them in on. This social circulation is key to a healthy public sphere. The statistics on WVON audience involvement support the notion that "audience discussion programs . . . may offer a constructive experience which demands analysis rather than dismissal . . . [because] the programs have many unintended consequences which only audience research can discover" (Livingstone and Lunt 1994:2). On the talk show, listener involvement and feedback is immediate and required for the success of the show. Even those who do not personally call in may have their concerns aired by their peers in the audience who do choose direct participation. The studio audience; Livingstone says, in effect "becomes a joint author . . . to debate social, moral, and political topics" (Livingstone and Lunt 1994:4). Furthermore, as illustrated by the preceding conversation and survey responses, the callers and listeners do not stop at participation in political talk; they take the next step to connect themselves to opportunities for public action.

IMAGINING AND ADDRESSING A BLACK AUDIENCE

WVON serves as a locus both for information crucial to community activities and political education and for the formation and sustenance of a Black identity. Not only does WVON speak to "Black issues," it also seeks to address all issues with a Black framework. There are many reasons for this. There is a great distrust of mainstream/white media, both among listeners and staff. Looking to audience responses in the questionnaires, WVON listeners discern a need for Black media in their lives and in the life of the larger Black collective. More evidence of this desire for an independent Black media comes in the form of financial contributions during the station's yearly subscription drives. Begun in 1995, subscription drives at WVON have brought in more than $180,000 over the last three years. As the following quotes from the survey reveal, most listeners who answered the open-ended questions felt that white-owned and mainstream media sources continue to misconstrue the Black community, whether through ignorance, malice, or neglect, while WVON gives a fairer view of their communities.

> Unlike white-owned media, you can count on WVON to inform and inspire its audience with truth on all issues discussed, especially those issues Afro-Americans need to hear (e.g., improve their economic standing, their educational pursuits, etc.).
>
> The white-owned media is not at all objective in its assessment of what is news in the Black community. It appears they almost always focus on the negative, or that which demeans us. . . . WVON fights back!
>
> Community issues are discussed in depth. WVON serves as a forum for the Black perspective [which is] rarely understood by whites.
>
> WVON is more relevant [to Blacks].

As this testimony illustrates, the white-owned media fall short of these listeners' expectations. In addition to the free responses, Table 2 illustrates that respondents also overwhelmingly agreed that the station did a better job than mainstream media in reflecting their concerns and giving a broader view of Black opinions and life.

WVON provides a wide range of topics and guests to its listeners, week in and week out. Local and national Black elected officials, leaders, artists, authors, scholars, and activists are interviewed and talk with listeners on a regular basis. But more important, these participants come from varied ideological backgrounds and support bases. For instance, representatives from the Nation of Islam, the Rainbow Coalition, the Urban League, the National Black Gay and Lesbian Leadership, and the NAACP have all been guests. Local grassroots activists like Conrad Worrill, as well as national figures like Reverend Jesse Jackson, have been interviewed and have called in to participate in discussions or to spread the word about events or important issues. Elected and appointed officials also populate the WVON landscape. Here is a sampling from the September 1997 schedule:

Katy Meaker Menges, National Center for Policy Analysis
Hedy Ratner, Women's Business Symposium
Roland Burris, gubernatorial candidate
Dr. Earl Ofari Hutchinson
Eleanor Chapman, Africa Travel Advisors
Alderman Robert Shaw, Chicago City Council Black Caucus

Asia Coney, Million Woman March co-organizer

Prime Minister Hage Geingob, Republic of Namibia

Haki Madhabuti, founder of Third World Press

Erayne Gee, NAACP student organizer, University of Texas at Austin

Philip Jackson, chief of staff, Chicago Public Schools

Theresa Welch, housing organizer, South Austin Coalition

The Christian Explainers, a South African Choir

Renae Ogletree, People of Color Coalition

Through its talk programs, WVON airs views from the mainstream to the underground. Callers, hosts, and guests together create a spectrum of opinions and ideas that run the gamut from socialism to nationalism to neoconservatism. Talk is not restricted to traditionally defined politics, such as elections. WVON addresses social trends, economics, health issues, scholarly and popular literature, and entertainment in its discussions, and the political implications of issues related to these are often revealed in the discussions that occur.

For the guests listed above, topics included local electoral politics; COINTELPRO; travel in Africa; public school policies; fair housing laws; AIDS and health care; supporting Black businesses; and current political and economic trends in African nations. Many of the topics aren't just "Black" topics, as defined by the mainstream media, or complaints about white oppression. Producer Keisha Chavers explains:

> I guess one thing that the [greater Chicago] community needs to know about us is that we don't spend our time dealing with white—you know, dogging white people. We try to get, we try to become issue oriented. . . .
>
> They'll poll us if it's a racial or if it's a, you know, criminal issue, something of that matter. But they won't come and poll us when it's regarding health care or when it's regarding some of the other items that, you know, that the mainstream community is talking about. They won't come and poll us.
>
> So I think that we are able—I mean in my capacity as a producer at WVON—I'm able to offer the programming you know, for members of our community just to call in and discuss as they would at WLS. Medicare, education, politics, today we did the piece on the environment. You know what I'm saying? And those are the types of things that the mainstream [media] don't come, they don't come to our community just to discuss it with us until it becomes a racial issue.[8]

In the mainstream public sphere, Blacks, like other nonwhite groups, are considered "special interest," not included in the category of everyday citizens. Hence, conversations concerning issues that are pertinent to the entire body politic are often considered relevant only to members of the class considered "typical" citizens: whites.[9] In addition, the pool of experts consulted regularly by mainstream media outlets is predominantly white. Getting a Black expert on economics on CNN is largely unheard of, unless the topic is somehow coded "Black." WVON allows the community to hear a larger range of Black expertise on civic topics than mainstream information sources. Furthermore, WVON gives listeners an opportunity to speak with these people—most of whom are rarely interviewed in mainstream venues—and they hear them talking one-on-one with Black people. This makes a huge difference to the audience and to the staff. As producer Keisha Chavers told me when I asked her why she tries to book Black experts,

> Outside the obvious that we're a Black radio station, the other thing is that, in the mainstream, what do you see? You know, nothing but white experts, unless it's a racial issue or even a criminal issue. . . . The criteria I've set is to get the Black expert first, the one who could talk about it as well as a white expert, who could relate it to our community. . . .

Hosts Cliff Kelley and Lu Palmer reiterate the need for Blacks to provide information for Blacks to compensate for the omissions and misrepresentations in mainstream media.

> It is the only Black talk radio in the city. We give Black people a method of communication we wouldn't have otherwise, because many stations would not even have the people that we have on. They wouldn't recognize them as important.[10]

> You have to understand also that I've always been what's called an advocacy journalist. See, you're taught in school that you are supposed to be objective and never advocate any cause. . . . All crap. And that's all that is, crap, because it's impossible to be objective.[11]

According to these responses, WVON is fulfilling the task of the traditional oppositional Black press, presenting Blacks in a different light than the mainstream media, as well as compensating for the omissions in the dominant press. Given the history of representation of African Americans in the American mainstream media, this is no surprise. But the impetus to provide "in-house" information has other motives as well. Listeners and staff feel that information regarding specific Black events and concerns is rarely given airtime or column space in the mainstream media. Hence, WVON provides them with information and encouragement they cannot rely on or trust the white press to present.

Listeners and staff expect Black media to perform many tasks. First, they expect Black journalists to undo the damage done by their white counterparts. Second, they demand coverage of Black issues and Black accomplishments. Third, they expect the Black press to advocate Black progress. It is this last aspect where important differences within the Black public arise. What the next or best strategy is for the Black public is a matter of debate based on one's vision of Black identity and political ideology. Listeners and staff have strong views about Black loyalty that echo Dawson's depiction of one problematic aspect of the Black public sphere: an insistence on race loyalty that can serve to suppress oppositional or diverse viewpoints and squelch certain attempts to build bridges outside of the Black sphere (Dawson 1994:215; West 1993). President and general manager Melody Spann sums it up concisely here:

> Some [Black journalists] are just plain lazy. They're not gonna go beyond the call of duty to help you . . . But I think they need to have a commitment to enhance anything that is owned by anybody who looks like them.
>
>   And when they lose sight of that commitment, they might as well not be Black and working in the industry.[12]

The accusation of effectively losing one's Blackness if one is not committed to a partic-ular vision of Black advancement is extended to Blacks who disagree with certain views and policy preferences. Although this is not a constant feature of WVON's programs, it ex-ists in proportion to the larger Black collective's debates over identity and politics. Al-though WVON's management and hosts follow the ideal of "agree to disagree" when addressing listeners and guests who are ideologically dissimilar, this credo becomes more or less strained, depending on the issue at hand. For example, affirmative action is a volatile issue at WVON, as it is across the nation. During the show on February 9, 1996, a white author of a book opposing affirmative action was taking calls with Cliff Kelley. When this caller chimed in, one could hear some animosity between host and caller as they try to engage in egalitarian debate.

> **Caller 1:** What this gentleman [the guest] is saying is, to make things equal, everybody has to be playing by the same rules. And it is time for us as Black Americans to start playing by the same rules as everybody else. And affirmative action ain't doing us any favors. And I'd like to point out that when the gentleman is trying to make a point, Cliff, that you should let him fin-ish his sentence, and don't interrupt him. It would be easier for all of us to understand what he's saying.
>
> **Cliff:** Well it would be nice if we both did that, but you're right. . . . I think I do a good job at that [Caller 1] . . .
>
> **Caller 1:** I think there's more truth in what he's saying than we as Black people are willing to admit.
>
> **Cliff:** Thanks for your call. I disagree with you, but I appreciate your call. [Hangs up on Caller 1.] [Caller 2], you're on with Attorney Stratton.
>
> **Caller 2:** Good morning, Mr. Kelley. . . . He [the first caller] is in the minority. As for the gentle-man who just called, when he is swiped from the shelf, then people will have a different attitude.
>
> **Cliff:** Well, you know, there are some people, when the master dies, they go out and the first thought is, "Where's the next master?" . . . There are people who are psychologically crippled who believe anything someone says as long as they are of a lighter hue.
>
> **Caller 2:** Right, right. . . . And that's the most dangerous weapon they [white people] have is the pen and paper, the twisting and turning of language and phrases. See, they can take some-thing and turn it right around and make it something other than what it actually meant.

While Kelley certainly tries to remain civil to the first caller, he is very obvious in his agreement with and approval of the second caller's views. They assert a view of what Black concerns should be, which clashes with the first caller's, questioning his race loyalty and fitness in the process. Kelley and the second caller use a metaphor of slavery's varied effects on the psyche of Blacks and find some to be brainwashed and subservient (the first caller) and others (themselves) resistant to white trickery. Callers and hosts feel free to label other listeners, political figures, and others along these lines. For example, Senator Carol Mose-ley-Braun and Clarence Thomas have been labeled race traitors or too close to whites on air by staff and listeners. Vernon Jordan was subject to the same judgment during an inter-view with June Cross, a Black television producer.

> **Cliff:** I think he was talking to some people I know [laughter].
>
> **June:** Yeah, we all know those people.

Cliff: When you talk about him going out and trying to mentor some young Black children in the inner city, or going out to help somebody get elected, they look at you like you're nuts. . . .
June: Oh, God. I heard a great quote last night, if I would remember what it is. Everything in this country comes down to race, even things that don't appear to be of that race; and when we start to talk about race, we talk about everything except race!
Cliff: You know, that's very true.
June: And I think it does kind of come down to that. Um, it is an American problem. It's always been an American problem, and I think a part of what we're seeing is that there's a certain group of Black Americans who've been admitted to the club of Americans, you know? Like Brother [Vernon] Jordan is an American now, he's not a Black American anymore [both laugh at this], at least he was until he got caught up with Bill in this thing. So now they're going to separate him out again, because he got caught with Bill covering up this thing. . . .

And, you know, there is a question that we hope the documentary raises and starts people thinking about, is, do we want to become Americans if the cost of becoming an American is that we become self-centered people who don't care about anybody else.
Cliff: Yeah, particularly our own.[13]

The station's staff believes (with much evidence, I think) that its audience is not only intelligent but politically aware and committed to Black advancement. Survey results, interviews, as well as caller exchanges on the air support their vision of the listening public. In addition to assuming a level of commitment to Black struggles, listeners and staff assume a common memory among the WVON family. Listening to any broadcast takes not only basic knowledge of current events, but familiarity with Black history and Black cultural forms. If you aren't in the know, many exchanges on the air, as well as the texts of some station identifications and advertisements, will be opaque. References to slavery, use of Black vernacular, and excerpts from famous jazz, blues, and funk songs are constantly woven through broadcasts, flavoring the discourse for the insider. During the Million Man March broadcast, for example, we played key James Brown and Aretha Franklin tunes to fade in and out from commercials.[14] In addition, many callers linked the march to important events and figures in Black history as they celebrated or critiqued the march. One caller used prophetic language, comparing the march to the return of Nat Turner. Others invoked the legacy of Rosa Parks, Ida B. Wells, and other strong Black women to counteract the assumptions that Black women were acquiescing to the desires of Black men.[15] Other callers and guests just took some time out to reminisce, "drop some science," or remark on the music played for intros, as this caller did: (Voices are talking together at times, overlapping.)

Caller: Hi Cliff!
Cliff: Hi, how are you?
Caller: . . . and Ahmad Jamal?
Cliff: Hey hey! You've got it!
Caller: [Jamal is] the greatest. You're dating yourself—
Cliff: I love it! I love it, too.
Caller: Israel Crosby, you remember him?
Cliff: Yes!
Caller: Yeah . . .
Cliff: Absolutely!
Caller: I learned a lot from him. . . .[16]

This guest included a little Black history lesson in his commentary:

Caller: So [the term] *African-American* is not new. Actually, you can go back to T. Thomas Fortune, who was a famous Black journalist in the 1890s, with the Afro-American, and the National Afro-American Council, which had in its very name the term *Afro-American*. So, a lot of these terms come out of our struggle and our attempt to define ourselves. . . .[17]

These exchanges reveal the assumption of a shared cultural background or the shared cultural interests of Black folks. These bits of talk and information that underscore a shared Black heritage allow Black listeners to feel secure that the station and the community of listeners "talk their talk."

CONCLUSIONS

This study suggests that (1) the audience and WVON have constructed a community of listeners within the public spheres produced by the station and members of the audience; (2) the community of listeners and the staff view WVON as an important source of information and perspectives relevant to Black public life; and (3) WVON provides an institutional basis for Black discourse and links to certain forms of political action and organization. From this study of a specialized audience, I argue that commercial media can play a positive role in forming and sustaining serious discourse within a subaltern public sphere, especially through a small-market or niche format like WVON's. By constructing and attracting a dedicated "family" of media consumers, WVON and its listeners have created a media environment whose commercial and community goals overlap. Cultivating such an environment, WVON has produced a community/commodity to show advertisers. At the same time, listeners, activists, and community leaders can use the interactive discursive space provided by the station to effectively distribute information and ideas to other active members of the community.

However, my analysis thus far has not sufficiently addressed a key question posed both by Dawson and by other scholars: How can a single counterpublic serve all of its constituents when within itself exist its own cleavages along class, gender, and generation lines? Even if WVON provides institutional support and discursive opportunities, how can it address this issue of dealing with disagreements within, let alone relations to non-Black publics? As for the first concern, the affirmative action debate excerpted above raises a key issue: How can a Black political discourse (or any minority discourse) be constructed without stifling differences under oppressive, convenient essentialisms and "race traitor" accusations? The discourses surrounding Anita Hill and Clarence Thomas, Mike Tyson, and Marion Berry all serve as examples of the dangers of what Cornel West terms "racial reasoning," but can we really expect to find a racial politics devoid of a sense of some shared identity?[18] The second concern is linked to the first: How can coalition politics be fostered more successfully? After a century of ebbing and flowing cross-racial partnerships, how can we construct new ways of approaching the discourse within and across public spheres to facilitate more cross-cultural understanding and political organization? As Melody Spann said in a conversation concerning the white financial investment in Spike Lee's film *Get On the Bus*, "You can't do anything in this society without dealing with white people!" While this blanket statement may certainly be disproved in various contexts, the message is clear: in a pluralist society, one will eventually have to deal with one's adversaries, as well as one's allies, who have healthy disagreements with one's position.

Again we return to the question, How can one support the notion of ethnic or racial solidarity without subsuming the identities of individuals and particular subgroups under an
oppressive form of essentialism?[19] In addition to concerns about the implications of inter-
and intragroup politics for public spheres, this project leads me to further question the
definition of the audience. What are the main distinctions between audiences and publics
in modern mass-mediated society? Although I agree with Herbst and Beniger's statement
that publics today are more likely to be composed of audiences, are the two truly synonymous
in all cases? And if they are interchangeable, how durable is this audience/public? When are
they merely "imagined communities," as described by Benedict Anderson (1991), and when
are they truly organized and interactive toward political ends?

Rather than add to the debate over whether talk is truly political action, I propose we
speak of multiple publics that take on different modes of discursive and political actions,
depending on social and political conditions. So we can speak of a public *enclaving* itself,
hiding its antiestablishment ideas and strategies to avoid sanctions, but internally producing lively debate and planning; we can also imagine a public *oscillating* to engage in debate
with outsiders, to test ideas. A public that engages in mass actions to assert its needs would
be a *counterpublic*, using traditional social movement tactics (boycotts, civil disobedience)
to make demands on the state. Finally, we can envision a public working in conjunction
with other publics on equal footing enjoying a *parallel* status. With these four labels, I hope
to offer scholars a more flexible and descriptive vocabulary to employ when analyzing the
various actions of a particular public or group of publics.[20]

As regards WVON, we can see how this talk-radio station could be—and is—useful to
the Black public sphere in all of these modes. Although the station is broadcast and can be
heard by anyone, its African-American staff and majority Black listenership make callers
feel comfortable that they are safer from sanction than in other forums (enclave). Through
interviews with non-Black guests, ideas can be exchanged and concerns can be aired to
those in power outside the Black public sphere (oscillating). WVON also serves as a mobilizing tool, announcing and facilitating community meetings that may result in social
movement–type actions, such as the protests in response to the Joseph Gould murder
(counterpublic). As for parallel activities, the station could facilitate similar meetings with
members of other publics if the opportunity arose. In these examples and in this study, we
see how WVON's audience can be transformed into an active public in the traditional
sense as well as being a talking public and an imagined public. Membership in "the WVON
family"—both of fellow listeners and the larger imagined Black community—serves as a
strong bond for listeners. This bond compels them to participate in the talk and activities
made available through WVON, as well as linking them to other community sites, cultural
events, and political activities. Notions of shared Black culture and identity and political
interests serve as bonds beyond media exposure. Hence, even after one's exposure to the
station ends, one still feels like a part of a larger Black collective with more complex cultural ties than the traditional notion of audiences connected only through common media
exposure.

To get a more nuanced picture of how the media influence public spheres, we should
use a model of coexisting, multiple spheres, which can describe various activities and roles
in their interactions with the state and other publics. We must also examine how different
publics create, consume, and use particular media products. As the WVON case demonstrates, a commercial media enterprise does not necessarily create the contradictions between public goods and private gain that Habermas and Entman lament. Rather, WVON

exists in response to the poor public service Blacks feel they receive from mainstream media providers. Its commercial success rests on listener loyalty, which can only be had through public-minded programming, awareness, and celebration of Black culture and through a commitment to community service.

ACKNOWLEDGMENTS

Earlier versions of this paper were presented at the 1996 meeting of the Midwest Political Science Association in Chicago and the 1997 meeting of the International Communication Association in Montreal. This research was supported by awards from the Joan Shorenstein Center and Northwestern University. I thank David Brouwer, Susan Herbst, and Jacqueline Bobo for their insightful comments on earlier versions of the paper.

NOTES

1. The *Defender* was one of many Black northern newspapers that were circulated widely between urban and rural Black publics both by subscription and by other means. In the days of Jim Crow, many copies of the *Defender* made their way south via Pullman porters who smuggled them to relatives who feared white repression if a *Defender* subscription was discovered (Senna 1993; Walker 1996).

2. Of course, in certain cases even the segregated newspapers did not provide safe haven. Ida B. Wells's offices were destroyed by a white mob; subscription agents for the *Defender* were beaten and threatened in the South; and Black publications were threatened with sedition charges for printing editorials about racism in the armed forces during World War II (Washburn 1986; Wolseley 1971).

3. Trade publications have also commented on the Black and "urban format" stations' community focus. See Walt Love, "WDAS Brings Philly Together: Twelfth Annual Unity Day Focuses on Community, Youth, and Family Fun," *Radio and Records*, September 27, 1991, 50; Walt Love, "WVEE Wages War against Violence," *Radio and Records*, December 6, 1991, 36; and Brown 1990.

4. At the time of my research, WVON was a 1,000-watt station. WVON shared its frequency with WCEV ("Chicago's ethnic voice"), switching to WCEV from 1 P.M. to 10 P.M. Thus, WVON had the morning drive-time hours, a lucrative position in the Chicago market. The signal reached the south and west sides of the city and the southwest suburbs easily, thus covering most of the Black neighborhoods in the area. Reception was not as good on the north side of the city at that time, but a new transmitter installed in late 1998 cleared up that problem.

5. The pretest revealed that two ranking questions concerning the O.J. Simpson trial and the Million Man March were too confusing for respondents, so these were eliminated.

6. *World Objectives.* Broadcast aired October 5, 1995.

7. *World Objectives.* Broadcast aired October 4, 1996.

8. Keisha Chavers, executive producer, WVON-AM, interview, October 20, 1995, WVON studios, Chicago, Illinois. Tape recording.

9. See Michael Warner's discussion of the citizen body and the public sphere (1992). Warner contends that the historical position and privilege of white propertied males created a public sphere in which only some (white males) are allowed to take on the role of "citizen," and nonwhite males are marked noncitizen and biased by their particular racial, ethnic, or gender differences. Hence, nonwhites have the burden of being seen as pursuing "special interests" rather than the public good.

10. Cliff Kelley, talk-show host, WVON-AM, interview, March 5, 1995, Nick's Restaurant, Chicago, Illinois. Tape recording.

11. Lu Palmer, talk-show host, WVON-AM, telephone interview, March 8, 1995. Tape recording.

12. Melody Spann, president and general manager, WVON-AM, interview, October 18, 1996, WVON Studios, Chicago, Illinois. Tape recording.

13. *World Objectives.* Broadcast aired February 9, 1998.

14. I use the pronoun *we* here because I was assistant producer on the *Sisters at Sunrise* broadcast and was active in the choice of music that day. However, this sort of musical call and response with show subjects is a regular attribute of the shows. Cliff Kelley's show, for example, is always introduced by jazz music, often the music of Gene "Jug" Ammons, which listeners name and comment on before making comments on the topic at

hand. Also, in program identification spots, Cliff is often referred to as "Jug." A non-Black friend of mine who listened to the broadcast with me one morning asked me why Cliff would want to be referred to as a jug. For him, *jug* denoted "Jughead" from the Archie comic strip, not jazz music, saxophone players, and the like.

15. *Sisters at Sunrise.* Broadcast aired October 16, 1996.

16. *World Objectives.* Broadcast aired October 6, 1995.

17. *World Objectives.* Broadcast aired January 5, 1998.

18. Cornel West describes the skewed results of racial reasoning as decisions that subordinate common sense and compassion to the idea that all Black

"leaders" (especially Black males) should be defended despite the potentially disastrous ramifications (1993). The classic example is the defense of Clarence Thomas in the face of his conservative stance on most civil rights issues.

19. Following the argument of Craig Calhoun, Gayatri Spivak, and others that there are many essentialisms that can be deployed strategically, I believe that essentialism in the service of solidarity can be useful in particular situations, just as it can stifle dissent in others (Calhoun 1994).

20. These labels are taken from my dissertation on the Black public sphere and will be more fully explicated in a future paper excerpted from the dissertation.

REFERENCES

Anderson, Benedict. 1991. *Imagined Communities.* London: Verso.

Bennett, W. Lance, and David L. Paletz, eds. 1994. *Taken by Storm: The Media, Public Opinion, and U.S. Foreign Policy in the Gulf War.* Chicago: University of Chicago Press.

Brouwer, Daniel C. 1995. "The Charisma of 'Responsibility': A Comparison of U.S. Mainstream Representations of Gay Men with AIDS in U.S. AIDS 'Zines." Master's thesis, Northwestern University.

Brown, Fred, Jr. 1990. "African American Broadcasters: The Link to Their Communities." *Pulse of Radio: Radio's Management Weekly* 5(46): 22–24.

Calhoun, Craig, ed. 1994. *Introduction to Social Theory and the Politics of Identity.* Oxford: Blackwell.

Cantor, Louis. 1992. *Wheelin' on Beale: How WDIA Memphis Became the Nation's First All-Black Radio Station and Created the Sound That Changed America.* New York: Pharos.

Chomsky, Noam. 1992. *Deterring Democracy.* New York: Farrar, Straus and Giroux.

Dates, Jannette L., and William Barlow, eds. 1990. *Split Image: African Americans in Mass Media.* Washington, D.C.: Howard University Press.

Davis, Robert. 1997. Introduction to the symposium "Understanding Broadcast Political Talk." *Political Communication* 14(3): 323–32.

Dawson, Michael. 1994. "A Black Counterpublic? Economic Earthquakes, Racial Agenda(s), and Black Politics." *Public Culture* 7(1): 195–224.

Entman, Robert. 1989. *Democracy without Citizens: Media and the Decay of American Politics.* New York: Oxford University.

———. 1992. "Blacks in the News: Television, Modern Racism, and Cultural Change." *Journalism Quarterly* 69(2): 341–61.

Fraser, Nancy. 1992. "Rethinking the Public Sphere: A Contribution to the Critique of Actually Existing Democracy." In *Habermas and the Public Sphere,* ed. Craig Calhoun. Cambridge: MIT Press.

Gamson, William. 1992. "The Social Psychology of Collective Action." In *Frontiers in Social Movement Theory,* ed. Aldon D. Morris and Carol McClurg Mueller. New Haven, Conn.: Yale University.

Gilens, Martin. 1996. "Race and Poverty in America." *Public Opinion Quarterly* 60: 515–41.

Habermas, Jurgen. 1989. *The Structural Transformation of the Public Sphere: An Inquiry into a Category of Bourgeois Society.* Trans. Thomas Burger. Cambridge: MIT Press.

Herbst, Susan, 1995. "On Electronic Public Space: Talk Shows in Theoretical Perspective." *Political Communication* 12: 263–74.

Herbst, Susan, and James R. Beniger. 1994. "The Changing Infrastructure of Public Opinion." In *Audiencemaking: How the Media Create the Audience,* ed. James Ettema and D. Charles Whitney. London: Sage.

Hofstetter, C. R., and Christopher L. Gianos. 1997. "Political Talk Radio: Actions Speak Louder than Words." *Journal of Broadcasting and Electronic Media* 41(4): 501–15.

Hollander, Barry A. 1997. "Fuel to the Fire: Talk Radio and the Gamson Hypothesis." *Political Communication* 14(3): 355–70.

Johnson, Phylis. 1992. "Black/Urban Radio Is in Touch with the Inner City: What Can Educators Learn from This Popular Medium?" *Education and Urban Society* 24(4): 508–18.

Johnson, Phylis, and Thomas A. Birk. 1993. "The Role of African American–Owned Radio in Health Promotion: Community Service Projects

Targeting Young African Males." *Urban League Review* 16(2): 85–94.

Livingstone, Sonia, and Peter Lunt. 1994. *Talk on Television: Audience Participation and Public Debate.* London: Routledge.

Marable, Manning, 1991. *Race, Reform, and Rebellion: The Second Reconstruction in Black America, 1945–1990.* 2nd ed. London: University Press of Mississippi.

Morrison, Toni, ed. 1992. *Race-ing Justice, En-gendering Power: Essays on Anita Hill, Clarence Thomas, and the Construction of Social Reality.* New York: Pantheon.

Newman, Mark. 1988. *Entrepreneurs of Profit and Pride: From Black-Appeal to Radio Soul.* New York: Praeger.

Omi, Michael, and Howard Winant. 1994. *Racial Formation in the United States.* 2nd ed. New York: Routledge.

Owen, Diana, 1997. "Talk Radio and Evaluations of President Clinton." *Political Communication* 14 (3): 333–54.

Page, Benjamin I. 1996. *Who Deliberates? Mass Media in Modern Democracy.* Chicago: University of Chicago Press.

Parenti, Michael. 1993. *Inventing Reality: The Politics of News Media.* 2nd ed. New York: St. Martin's Press.

Peffley, Mark, Todd Shields, and Bruce Williams. 1996. "The Intersection of Race and Crime in Television News Stories: An Experimental Study." *Political Communication* 13(3): 309–27.

Senna, Carl. 1993. *The Black Press and the Struggle for Civil Rights.* New York: Franklin Watts.

Squires, Catherine. 1999. "Searching Black Voices in the Black Public Sphere: An Alternative Approach to the Analysis of Public Spheres." Ph.D. diss., Northwestern University.

Suggs, Henry L., ed. 1996. *The Black Press in the MiddleWest, 1865–1985.* Westport, Conn.: Greenwood Press.

Walker, Juliet E. 1996. "The Promised Land: The Chicago Defender and the Black Press in Illinois, 1862–1970." In *The Black Press in the Middle West, 1865–1985*, ed. Henry L. Suggs. Westport, Conn.: Greenwood Press.

Warner, Michael. 1992. "The Mass Public and the Mass Subject." In *Habermas and the Public Sphere*, ed. Craig Calhoun. Cambridge: MIT Press.

Washburn, Patrick S. 1986. *A Question of Sedition: The Federal Government's Investigation of the Black Press during World War II.* New York: Oxford University Press.

Webster, James, and Pat Phalen. 1994. "The Mass Audience: Rediscovering the Dominant Model." Unpublished manuscript.

West, Cornel. 1993. *Race Matters.* New York: Vintage.

Wolseley, Robert E. 1971. *The Black Press, U.S.A.* Ames: Iowa State University.

15

CHASING FAE

The Watermelon Woman and Black Lesbian Possibility

Laura L. Sullivan

CHERYL DUNYE'S 1996 FILM, *The Watermelon Woman*, is a groundbreaking, and rule-breaking, film. The first feature film made by a Black lesbian filmmaker (McAlister), the film employs both deconstructive and realist techniques to examine the way that identity in contemporary U.S. culture is shaped by multiple forces, primarily race, gender, and sexual orientation. Encouraging viewers to consider the unstable, complex, and often contradictory nature of identity, the film is humorous yet politically engaging. In this paper, I consider the ways that the film works simultaneously to represent and to decenter the identity and history of a figure most invisible in the textual production of the dominant culture–the Black lesbian.

The Watermelon Woman, an independent film made on a shoestring budget, experimentally combines narrative and documentary forms. The film's storyline centers on the life and work of Cheryl, a Black lesbian woman filmmaker living in Philadelphia. Cheryl works in a video store and in an independent video business with her acerbic friend Tamara, also Black and lesbian. Cheryl is making a film about an African-American actress named Fae "The Watermelon Woman" Richards, who appeared in Hollywood films in the 1930s and 1940s. The central narrative's plot concerns Cheryl's relationship with a white woman, Diana, and the parallels between Cheryl's experiences and the subject matter of her research: the life and work of Fae Richards, who was not only a Black woman involved in film, but a lesbian who once had an affair with one of her white directors, a woman named Martha Page. Metafictionally, Cheryl often directly addresses the camera as she describes her progress in making the film within the film, and the film presents us with scenes of Cheryl creating her film, performing interviews, and undertaking archival research. The primary tension in the film occurs at the intersection of race and sexual orientation and addresses the feasibility—and politics—of Black-white lesbian relationships.

The film also reworks filmic conventions, both traditional and postmodern, as it provokes the viewer's curiosity about this unknown "watermelon woman" actress. Many viewers find it "simply fascinating to follow along with Cheryl's detective work" as she searches for clues about this unknown Black actress (McAlister). We participate in Cheryl's process of discovery as she learns about this historical figure with whom she increasingly identifies. The viewer does not discover until the film's end that the actress Fae "The Watermelon

Woman" Richards never existed, and is, in fact, the creation of the film's writer and director, Dunye. I explore the implications of the way that the film draws upon and questions both fictional and documentary forms in more detail below. First, a consideration of how this film addresses the representation of members of marginalized groups.

DE/RECONSTRUCTING IMAGES OF BLACK WOMEN

In *Black Women as Cultural Readers*, Jacqueline Bobo asserts that "Black women are . . . knowledgeable recorders of their history and experiences and have a stake in faithfully telling their own stories" (36). In her first direct address of the viewer, Cheryl speaks to this imperative as she muses about what subject to use as the focus of her film: "I know it has to be about Black women, because our stories have never been told." As this remark indicates, Cheryl Dunye recognizes that the voices of Black women have been absent from the dominant cultural production of texts in this century; her film seeks to address this elision.

Recent cultural critics point out that the primary images of Black women in film have been largely harmful and inaccurate stereotypes. Bobo explains that throughout the history of Hollywood cinema, we find "a venerable tradition of distorted and limited imagery" of representations of Black women, who have been limitedly characterized "as sexually deviant, as the dominating matriarchal figure, as strident, eternally ill-tempered wenches, and as wretched victims" (33). Bobo specifies that within this last category, classical Hollywood portrayed Black women as domestic servants, while more recent texts focus on Black women as " 'welfare' mothers" (33). In *The Watermelon Woman*, viewers are exposed to this history while they are also asked to critique it.

The film's central character, Cheryl, is fascinated by the unknown Black actresses of early Hollywood cinema, while her friend Tamara chastises her for her interest in "all that nigga-mammy shit from the '30s." In her first monologue about her documentary, Cheryl tells viewers that she has been viewing tapes of 1930s and 1940s movies that have Black actresses in them, exclaiming that she is "totally shocked" to discover that "in some of these films, the Black actresses aren't even listed in the credits." In this way, Dunye the filmmaker comments on a real phenomenon, the historical invisibility of Black women in film as well as the devaluation of their labor and identities, before she introduces us to the (fictitious) film that currently has her character Cheryl's attention. Cheryl relates that when she first watched this film, she "saw the most beautiful Black mammy, named Elsie." Clearly intrigued by this actress, Cheryl insists that she show us a clip. Yet the "clip" from the video is typically racist and demeaning, containing a Civil War scene in which the mammy comforts a white woman, "Don't cry Missy, Massa Charles is coming back—I know he is!" This constructed excerpt is familiar to us, as heirs to a media culture that routinely assigned Black actresses to such roles, not that many decades ago, as emblematized by Hattie McDaniel in *Gone with the Wind* (1939). While Cheryl is aware of the exploitation of Black women in cinema, she is still seduced by these images. As she explains to the viewer, she is going to make a film about this actress, known as "the watermelon woman" because "something in her face, something in the way she looks and moves, is serious, is interesting."

Bobo notes that "Black female creative artists bring a different understanding of Black women's lives and culture, seeking to eradicate the harmful and pervasive images haunting their history" (5). Dunye's film directly acknowledges the negative effects of the oppressive stereotypes with which Black women have been imaged in the history of film. The title of the Fae Richards film with which Cheryl is most fascinated is telling in this regard, *Planta-*

tion Memories. Through mechanisms such as the naming of this (fictional) film, Dunye comments on the historical continuity of the oppression of Black women. She reflects how the legacy of slavery affects the lives of Black women in the twentieth century (and how this legacy also shapes the representations of such lives). She also reminds us that early stereotypical depictions of Black women continue to impinge on the lived experiences of Black women today and continue to delimit the options available for Black women producers of contemporary cultural texts.

In the case of Black lesbian women, however, what is "haunting their history," to use Bobo's phrase, is not so much a history of damaging and false images, but, is, instead, a certain absence of participation in the representations of the mainstream media. Jewelle Gomez comments on the Black lesbian's "invisibility in American society" and explains that Black lesbians "are the least visible group not only in the fine arts, but also in the popular media, where the message conveyed about the Lesbian of color is that she does not even *exist*, let alone use soap, drive cars, drink Coke, go on vacations, or do much of anything else" (110). Thus, Dunye's film serves first to document the existence of Black lesbians, in much the same way as Julie Dash's film *Daughters of the Dust* (1992) was unique in featuring a group that is not typically the visual or diegetic focus of most films—Black women. As bell hooks comments in a dialogue with Julie Dash, "To de-center the white patriarchal gaze, we indeed have to focus on someone else for a change. And . . . the film takes up that group that is truly on the bottom of this society's race-sex hierarchy. Black women tend not to be seen, or to be seen solely as stereotype" (40). Dash and hooks discuss the discomfort of some viewers of *Daughters* . . . in having to "spend . . . two hours as a Black person, as a Black woman" (40). While Black women flocked to the film in droves (Bobo 9), Black men and nonBlack viewers needed to connect with the film through mechanisms other than direct identification (Dash and hooks 40). Viewers from these subject positions were thus called upon to be more actively involved in the process of textual reception.

Dunye's film likewise calls upon an active viewer, but with the added dimension of sexual orientation. For if the Black woman has been invisible or stereotyped in popular culture, the Black lesbian woman has been even more invisible, and, when present, this figure has caused even Black women discomfort. (For example, Dash reports that the actress who played one of the Black lesbian lovers in her film, Yellow Mary, later denied that her character was gay (Dash and hooks 66).) *The Watermelon Woman* foregrounds Black lesbian identity throughout, but it does so in a way that invites the reader to connect the history of the Black lesbian actress who rose to fame through a series of denigrating roles as servant and slave, with the present Black lesbian filmmaker before us, Cheryl Dunye, who is playing a version of herself.

For example, in scenes filmed in Cheryl's home, the tape of *Plantation Memories* plays on the television, while Cheryl, a bandana tied around her head, lip-syncs the mammy's part in the film's scene, exaggeratedly mimicking the fawning pretense of the Black servant played by Fae Richards. Likewise, in another series of scenes in the film, Cheryl sits in front of her video camera, holding several postcards and pictures of the Watermelon Woman in her hands, hiding her face. The camera is tightly focused on the images of the Watermelon Woman that Cheryl leafs through, showing these pictures to the viewer, but Cheryl is visible in the background, an eye peering around these representations of the actress, a gesture of connection. Yet in the end what we have is a constructed history connected to a constructed but "real" figure, Cheryl the character standing in for Cheryl Dunye the filmmaker.

Commenting on the uniqueness of *Daughters of the Dust*, hooks notes that there are "very few other films where the camera really zooms in on Black women's faces" (52). Dunye also employs this technique, and there are many scenes in which the faces and bodies of Black women, in this case Black lesbians, are prominent. These typically invisible bodies are rendered visible in a number of ways. First, there are many close-ups of Cheryl in the segments where she directly addresses her video camera. Second, there are explicit love scenes that break new ground. For while viewers of alternative cinema have previously seen the naked bodies of white lesbians, such as Patricia Charbonneau and Helen Shaver in Donna Deitch's *Desert Hearts* (1985), and even including *The Watermelon Woman*'s Guin Turner who starred in the white lesbian film *Go Fish* (1994), love scenes that feature Black lesbian women are rare. Patricia Rozema's *When Night Is Falling* (1995) is a notable exception in this regard, as it depicts a romance between a Black lesbian woman and a previously straight white French woman. However, while that film's focus is on the white woman's "conversion" to lesbianism, *The Watermelon Woman* centrally engages the interracial dimension of its lesbian romances. The subjects of Cheryl's interviews about Fae Richards debate the nature of her relationship with Martha Page, and Fae's last lover, June Walker, refers to Page as "that white woman." More relevant to this discussion is the way that Dunye's film visually highlights the racial aspect of the lesbian relationship between Cheryl and Diana, in scenes technically reminiscent of Spike Lee's *Jungle Fever* (1991). Viewers are treated to tight close-ups of Cheryl and Diana's Black and white bodies pressed together in explicit sex scenes. Their hands roam across each other's naked bodies as the women kiss. At one point, the camera zooms in on the interlocked Black and white hands of the two characters in bed. In this way, the film not only requires that Black lesbians be acknowledged; it also documents the existence of interracial lesbian romances.[1]

AVOIDING ESSENTIALISM

Queer female producers of cultural texts must wrestle with the nature of lesbian subjectivity. In the wake of the complete destabilizing of subject formation that has resulted from the theoretical insights provided by a postmodern perspective, such artists face the challenge of "reconstruct[ing] lesbian subject positions without reinstating essentialisms" (Dolan 42). Dunye has risen to this challenge, as the characters in *The Watermelon Woman* do not present a monolithic view of any featured group. As Dolan argues, "Lesbians disappear under the liberal humanist insistence that they are just like everyone else. Difference is effectively elided by readability" (44). In this film, there is no unified lesbian subject position, either Black or white. Cheryl, Tamara, their white video store coworker Annie. Tamara's Black girlfriend Stacy, and Diana are all very different types of lesbians. They have different styles of fashion, different race and gender politics, and distinctive personalities. For example, Cheryl and Tamara have short, close-shaven haircuts, while Diana has long hair and wears lipstick. Stacy is a student finishing her M.B.A. degree at Wharton; Tamara is obsessed with sex; Cheryl is passionate about filmmaking; and Diana wants to "figure out her life."

However, the film moves beyond merely presenting the wide variety of lesbian subject positions. The film addresses what is required "to reconstruct a tenable lesbian subject position . . . somewhere between deconstruction and essentialism" (Dolan 53). Dolan specifies what this new representation of lesbian subjectivity will entail:

Reconstructing a variable lesbian subject position that will not rise like a phoenix in a blaze of essentialism from the ashes of deconstruction requires emptying lesbian references of imposed truths, whether those of the dominant culture or those of lesbian radical feminist communities which hold their own versions of truth. The remaining, complex, different referent, without truth, remains dependent on the materiality of actual lesbians who move in and out of dominant discourse in very different ways because of their positions within race, class, and variant expressions of their sexuality—dragging at the margins of structure and ideology. (53)

The Watermelon Woman answers Dolan's call, by refusing to accept the heritage of racist and heterosexist Hollywood cinema, by interweaving questions of sexuality and race, and by presenting lesbians who have conflicted relationships to dominant ideology. Additionally, the binary oppositions of "good" and "bad" identities are similarly deconstructed, as the film avoids simply reversing the dominant characterizations that attribute positive connotations to straight and/or white people and negative ones to gay and/or Black people.

Although Black lesbians, real and imagined, present and historical, are the focus in this text, the film presents a more complex view of lesbian subjectivity. The contrast between Cheryl and Tamara, for example, not only reflects the variety of subject positions of Black lesbians; it also reveals the way that oppressions and their internalizations are layered and intertwined. Tamara advocates Black lesbian solidarity, yet she reveals her own sexism throughout the film. Tamara frequently encourages the single Cheryl to "cruise" for "cute girls" and declares that she hopes to "get some" from her girlfriend Stacy on an upcoming date. When Tamara criticizes Cheryl at the video store, telling her "All you do since you don't have a girlfriend is watch those boring old films," Cheryl retorts, "I'd rather watch films than black porn like you." In this way, the internalized sexism of some lesbian women is presented through the character of Tamara, who views women as sexual objects. As always, this portrayal is presented with humor. For instance, one of the films Tamara orders from the video store is called *Bad Black Ballbusters*; Tamara justifies her film choice to Cheryl: "I was curious to see what they look like without hair."

Cheryl is caught in the crossfire of the various vectors that pressure her identity. She is not a typical lesbian in Tamara's eyes because she is not obsessed with finding a girlfriend and because she does not visually objectify women. Tamara sees an inevitable connection between a lesbian identity and chasing women: "We're lesbians—remember, Cheryl? We're *into* female-to-female attraction. Anyway, you're the one who's supposed to be clocking all the girls—how long has it been since you've been with one, anyway?" Cheryl's lack of preoccupation with women is evidence to Tamara that Cheryl is not behaving authentically as a lesbian. Cheryl has other struggles as a lesbian. She feels "set up" by Diana, who invites her to dinner and then seduces her. After she sleeps with Diana, Cheryl tells us in a voiceover, "I'm still in shock over the whole having-sex-with-Diana thing. I've never done anything else like that before, *let me assure you*. The hip, swinging lesbian style isn't my forte. . . . I'm just an old-fashioned girl trying to keep up with the times." For many viewers, the idea that all lesbians are alike will be shattered by these depictions.

The film also reveals the instability of racial subjectivity. Bob, the owner of the video store, is a Black man who oozes sexism—and heterosexism—in his mistreatment of the women who work for him, Black and white. Lee Edwards, the Black gay race film expert, knows nothing about the Watermelon Woman or Martha Page. He excuses his ignorance of these two women, telling Cheryl and Tamara, "Women are not my specialty." And Black

feminist essentialism is likewise critiqued in this film. Tamara, Cheryl, and Annie film a poetry reading by "Sistah Sound" at the local women's community center. With African drum-
ming for background rhythm, a Black woman performs a poem that repeats "I am Black
woman, Black woman, yes," in a scene that both celebrates and pokes fun at such gatherings.

Racial politics also influence the relationship between Tamara and Cheryl, which becomes increasingly conflicted as the film's narrative progresses. Tamara's opinion of Diana
is predicated on her wariness of white women. Tamara sees Diana as trying to usurp the
Black lesbian's place in the world, calling her Cheryl's "wannabe Black girlfriend." Tamara
questions Cheryl's alliance to Black women once she begins dating Diana, telling Cheryl, "I
see that once again you're going out with a white girl acting like she wants to be Black, and
you're being a Black girl acting like she wants to be white. What's up with you, Cheryl?
Don't you like the color of your skin?" While Cheryl defends herself to Tamara—defen-
sively asking, "Who's to say that dating somebody white doesn't make me Black?"—she is
clearly uncomfortable when Diana reveals that she was born in Jamaica, and even more
disturbed by Diana's revelations that she has had Black boyfriends in the past and that her
"father's sister's first husband was an ex-Panther" whose name was "Tyrone Washington."[2]
Moreover, both the white lesbian archivist and the white sister of Martha Page, with whom
Diana has arranged an interview, treat Cheryl condescendingly. When Diana does not
stand up to Mrs. Page-Fletcher when she refers to "all those coloreds" that Martha Page
employed and when she denies her sister's lesbianism, Cheryl has had enough. Thus, while
Cheryl rejects Tamara's essentialist view of Black lesbian identity, she struggles with race
dynamics in her relationship nonetheless.

Likewise, Cheryl argues against June Walker's call for Cheryl to eliminate Martha Page
from her film. In a letter to Cheryl, the woman who was Fae Richards's lover for the last
twenty years of her life says,

> I was so mad that you mentioned the name of Martha Page. Why do you even want to include
> a white woman in a movie on Fae's life? Don't you know she had nothing to do with how peo-
> ple should remember Fae? I think it troubled her soul for the world to see her in those mammy
> pictures. . . . If you really are in "the family," you better understand that our family will only
> have each other.[3]

Cheryl responds to June's letter in her last monologue, insisting that there is no one Black
lesbian subject position, and declaring that she might make different choices about the
meaning of this Black actress's legacy. Cheryl tells June, "I know she meant the world to
you, but she also meant the world to me, and those worlds are different." She refuses to
erase the history of Fae's romance with the white woman director from her film: "The
moments she shared with you—the life she had with Martha, on and off the screen—those
are precious moments, and nobody can change that." She then points to the generational
differences in operation in this debate, "But what she means to *me*—a twenty-five-year-old
Black woman, means something else," explaining how this figure inspires her as a Black,
lesbian filmmaker.

This film calls into question the idea of "difference" itself. The character Annie, the
young, white lesbian who works with Cheryl and Tamara in the video store, has blond
streaks in her black hair and wears a dog collar. Cheryl and Annie get along well, but

Tamara bristles at the girl's street style and sense of self-confidence. When Cheryl asks her why she so dislikes Annie, Tamara retorts, "She gets on my last Black lesbian nerve with all that piercing and hair dye business." When Cheryl reminds her that they also share a marginalized status—"Tamara, you know we're different, too"—Tamara reverts to segregationist and classist arguments to justify her denigration of Annie: "Yeah, but see we're not different amongst a group of ritzy Black folk. I mean, we were there to get their business and to be professional. We weren't there to look like a bunch of hip-hop multicultural mess." She says that she is disgusted by Annie's way of dressing and by her dog collar. Later in the video store back room, Tamara tells Annie, "You're so helpful—you probably know a place to get a good clit piercing, don't you?" Annie responds, "Look Tamara, just because you and I are different doesn't mean you have to treat me like shit all the time." The conflict between these two women highlights the fragmentation and multiplicity in lesbian subject positions, as well as the way that different aspects of identity are sometimes at cross purposes with one another. This film undercuts the essentialist assumptions of both oppressive and liberatory positions, undermining a heterosexist view that lumps together all gay people, as well as an antiracist view that would promote an essentialist view of all white people. In this way, the film moves beyond what hooks calls the "de-center[ing] of the white patriarchal gaze" (Dash and hooks 40) to question the racist heterosexist gaze, including the potentially homophobic gaze of nonwhite straight viewers, as well as the potentially racist gaze of white lesbian viewers. The film enacts this decentering both visually, as interracial lesbian romances are prominently pictured, and diegetically, through the conflicts of its characters. Revealing its racist and heterosexist agenda, the American Family Association labeled the film's depictions of lesbian sex "smut" (McAlister). However, the film forces even those viewers who are not on the "right wing" end of the political spectrum to confront their own prejudices.

The film also contains a complex presentation of class identity. The video store owner, Bob, wields power over his three female employees, incessantly berating them for not being familiar enough with what he calls "the Bob system," although they clearly know how to perform their jobs well. While Tamara and Cheryl barely make ends meet, and while Cheryl must work hard at two jobs in order to finance her film project, Diana is well-off financially, as indicated by the credit cards she flashes at the video store, by the spacious apartment she rents while she takes time off from school, and by the fact that she does not work during the time of the film, but volunteers with homeless children of color (a race dynamic that does not go unremarked upon by Tamara). In contrast to Diana's life of leisure, Cheryl and Tamara have had to resort to a "tape scam" at work in order to secure videos for themselves, films for Cheryl's research and porn movies for Tamara's enjoyment. They rent tapes under customers' names, preview them, and return them, as Cheryl explains to Diana. Finally, we learn that Annie is a Bryn Mawr college graduate, yet she needs the job at the video store, pointing to the way that college degrees no longer guarantee security in the workforce. Even the parodied lesbian archives (in the film called C.L.I.T.—the Center for Lesbian Information and Technology) struggle financially, relying on volunteer help and not having a catalogued organization yet in place. The documentary portions similarly present class dimensions of the characters' experiences. Fae Richards, we learn, was a maid before she became an actress. Black cast films eventually became passé in part because even Black audiences wanted to see Hollywood films instead, as Lee Edwards explains to Cheryl and Tamara. Although Tamara points to the real connection between race, power, and wealth when she refers to "the white folks at the bank" at the film's outset, in this film, there are no clear correlations between race, gender, sexual orientation, and class status. The film does not undertake an explicit class critique, but it does convey the oppressive elements of class and the way that class position meshes with and influences other types of identity formation.

(RE)WRITING HISTORY

The Watermelon Woman draws upon "pseudo-realism, borrowing heavily from the documentary format" (Turoff). The viewer's relationship to the film's presentation of "truth"—that is, whether or not the viewer is aware that the Watermelon Woman is a fictionalized construction—pivotally influences the viewing experience. For example, I first viewed this film at a local cinema in the spring of 1997. During the entire film, I was unaware that Fae "The Watermelon Woman" Richards was a fictional creation of Dunye's; I was shocked to read in the credits an acknowledgment of the fictionality of this character. At the time, I believed that Dunye's inclusion of this information in the credits revealed that the filmmaker did not anticipate that viewers would necessarily realize that the Black actress named Fae Richards never existed. For while Dunye deconstructs and satirizes the documentary form throughout the film, she also replicates it in a way that leads viewers not to question its verisimilitude. In fact, the Internet Movie Database even goes so far as to list the film's genre as "Documentary."

Since the time of my initial viewing of the film, I have learned that when the film was first screened, it did not contain any reference to the fictional status of Fae Richards, so the film's first viewers were not aware of this dimension of the film (Jackson and Moore 500). Conversely, some viewers do not have the privilege of seeing the film and sorting through this issue of the actress's fictionality for themselves. I saw the film a second time while in London in August of 1998. Although I was thrilled that such a film was being shown on British television (as part of Channel 4's *Queer Street* series), and although I was prepared to watch the film again from a position of already knowing its "secret," I was dismayed to see that the British weekly magazine *Time Out* directly indicated that Fae Richards was not a real person in its description of the film. I knew that British first-time viewers would approach the film much differently because they already were aware that its documentary was staged.

Thus, there are three possible viewing positions of the film: never learning that the documentary portions record a fictional subject's life; realizing while viewing the film, or learning during the film's credits that Dunye created the character of Fae Richards; and knowing about the actress's fictional status at the film's outset, for example, after having read a review of the film. (I am aware that this article itself, ironically, reproduces this last dynamic for readers who have not yet seen the film.) Another irony is that while the issue of secrecy and confession are typically associated with gay identity, this film does not conceal homosexuality, but instead contains a "secret" about the fictional nature of the subject of the central character's documentary. Having now watched the film for a third time on video, I am convinced that much of its power comes from the ambiguity of the figure of Fae Richards. Dunye leads the viewer to ask herself why she is unfamiliar with this actress, a questioning that has significant implications for thinking through the relationship among media texts, politics, and history. Watching the film from the position of not knowing that the documentary subject is fictional enables viewers to appreciate fully the way that this film "create[s] a certain tension between the social formation, subjectivity, and representation" (Kaplan 138).

Bobo reminds us that "Within the last several decades Black women have effectively written themselves back into history; they have retrieved their collective past for sustenance and encouragement for present-day protest movements" (36). In some ways, Dunye's film is situated within this tradition. However, Dunye's final remarks make clear that she was unable to retrieve this history she wanted to find; in the credits she tells viewers: "Sometimes you have to create your own history," explaining that "The Watermelon Woman is fiction." Yet although Dunye rewrites a history that is/was not there, she does so with a firm grounding in historical realities for black people, particularly Black women, in this century. For example, Cheryl's search for information on the Watermelon Woman leads her to interview her mother and others who were part of the vibrant Black club scene in Philadelphia in the interwar decades. Cheryl learns that Black films were played before the Hollywood features at the early twentieth-century black-owned cinemas from Lee Edwards, who tells her, "If they'd only played the Black cast films, they would've gone out of business during the Depression. Black folks [in the '20s and '30s] wanted to see the Hollywood stuff with the stars, the costumes—all that junk." In such segments of the film, Dunye informs viewers about lost pieces of African-American history through her construction of Fae Richards's history and her fictional account of Cheryl's investigation of it.

The film liberally uses photographs in its documentary portions. The photograph is a textual form that supposedly signifies "this really happened" to the viewer; it testifies to the existence of people and events. Yet, in this case, the photographs have been created for this film, and the history they purportedly record is fabricated. In a further irony, these photographs are now objects of textual analysis themselves. A journal published in West Germany, *Parkett*, contains an article titled "Watermelon Woman: The Fae Richards Photo Archives." The abstract for this article specifies that it contains "A selection of photographs from a series created for use in Cheryl Dunye's film *The Watermelon Woman*." The abstract goes on to tell us, "Created in collaboration with Zoe Leonard, the photographs depict scenes from the life of a fictional character, Fae Richards." So the constructed figure of this Black lesbian actress visually lives on, at least in the world of academic cultural criticism.

The feminist cultural critic Jeanie Forte, in the words of Jill Dolan, "suggests that because of its structural recognizability, or 'readability,' realism might be able to politicize spectators alienated by the more experimental conventions of non-realistic work" (43). This film draws upon this strategy of textual production. Both the film's narrative portions and the film's documentary segments contain realist aspects and are, as such, "readable" to the film's viewers. However, in the juxtaposition of these two "stories," the film enacts a postmodern deconstruction of both realist cinema and documentary forms. The film's metafictional elements, such as Cheryl's asides to the film's viewer, further serve to destabilize the film's realistic quality. And this critique of realism is also a critique of the racist politics often promoted by the mainstream mass media's realist presentations; as bell hooks explains, "one of the major problems facing Black filmmakers is the way both spectators and, often, the dominant culture want to reduce us to some narrow notion of 'real' or 'accurate'" (Dash and hooks 31). *The Watermelon Woman* seduces viewers with realist elements, only to make us question our naïveté at the film's end, and in this way the film disrupts the naturalizing function of realist discourse.

This film's technical qualities, such as the use of montage, talking-head interviews, segments that appear to be from early film news spots, and film footage with an archival look, lead viewers to perceive the text initially as based upon reality. They see all the film's characters as "ethnographic subjects" and believe the film to be "Dunye's casually taped, autobiographical video journal" (Jackson and Moore 500). This reading of the film goes against what film critic E. Ann Kaplan recommends for a "counter-cinema" such as feminist cinema (131). She argues that filmmakers

> must confront within their films the accepted representations of reality so as to expose their falseness. Realism as a style is unable to change consciousness because it does not depart from the forms that embody the old consciousness. Thus, prevailing realist codes—of camera, lighting, sound, editing, mise-en-scène—must be abandoned and the cinematic apparatus used in a new way so as to challenge audiences' expectations and assumptions about life. (131)

The Watermelon Woman confronts realism not by presenting a film that radically breaks from realist form; rather, this film reworks Kaplan's formulation so that the challenge to viewers comes at the film's end, when we are often shocked to see that the documentary subject matter within the film has been constructed and when we thus must confront our own ideological investments that led us to misinterpret this aspect of the film.

In contrast, viewers who read about the film's fictional elements in reviews or who have previously seen the film with the final disclaimer included are more able to appreciate the film's humor. In the words of Randy Turoff, the film is "savvy, wry, and self-consciously ironic." One way that the film employs humor is to enact a critique of what bell hooks calls "the Eurocentric biases that have informed our understanding of the African American experience" (Dash and hooks 39). Particularly through a scene featuring a mock interview of the white cultural scholar Camille Paglia, the film comments on the way that white scholars appropriate and treat condescendingly the work of nonwhite scholars. Paglia tells us,

> Well, actually, the mammy figure is a great favorite of mine, particularly Hattie McDaniel's brilliant performance in *Gone with the Wind*. I really am distressed with a lot of the tone of recent African American scholarship. [cut] It tries to say about the mammy that her largeness as a figure is de-sexualizing, degrading, and de-humanizing, and this seems to me utterly wrong. Where the large woman is a symbol of abundance and fertility, is a kind of goddess figure.

Demonstrating the way that white critics often falsely bring their own life histories and experiences to bear on those of the non-white objects of their investigations, Paglia continues:

> Even the presence of the mammy in the kitchen it seems to me has been misinterpreted: "Oh the woman in the kitchen is a slave, a subordinate—." Well, my grandmas, my Italian grandmothers, never left the kitchen. In fact this is why I dedicated my first book to them. And Hattie McDaniel in *Gone with the Wind* is the *spitting image* of my grandmother, in her style, in her attitude, in her ferocity. It brings tears to my eyes.

That I did not originally view this interview as a satire says a lot about my opinion of Camille Paglia as a feminist critic, but the fact that almost all of the film's other initial viewers, college students and art house audiences, missed the irreverent and exaggerated portrayal here also speaks to the power of the film's precise simulation of the documentary form, right down to the title at the bottom of the screen at this interview's outset, "Camille Paglia, Cultural Critic." Alexandra Juhasz emphasizes that "many of the codes of documentary label, categorize, and imply understandings of authority," revealing that documentary images are not merely recording nor undermining traditional power relations, but, rather, deepening them (98). Audiences have been taught to view the documentary's elements evidenced in *The Watermelon Woman* as indications of a person's credibility and expertise, and thus, initial audiences did not question this woman's authority. Additionally, because similar trends exist in academic criticism, where members of groups in power presume to speak for "marginalized" groups, Camille Paglia's monologue did not seem outside the realm of truth or possibility. As Bobo makes clear, there is "an unstated presumption that the only reliable information about [Black women] is that collected by white observers" (11). Camille Paglia's character romanticizes representations of African-American women in her commentary; for instance, she completely elides the impact of slavery or issues of unequal power relations, yet viewers seduced by the realist coding of her presentation miss the film's implicit critique of racism in this section.

In the last point that Paglia makes in her "interview," the white scholar's actions are carried to their greatest point of exaggeration. As before, Paglia continues to speak rapidly, rarely pausing for breath, and to gesture frequently with her hands, in a parody of the ludicrous connections that some scholars often make in their work:

> The watermelon, it seems to me, is another image that has been misinterpreted by a lot of Black commentary—the great extended family Italian get togethers that I remember as a child ended with the men bringing out a watermelon and ritualistically cutting it, distributing the pieces to everyone, almost like the communion service. [cut] And I really dislike these kinds of reductionism of a picture of, let's say, a small Black boy with a watermelon, him smiling broadly over it, looking at that as negative. Why is that not, instead, a symbol of joy? and pleasure, and fruitfulness? After all, a piece of watermelon has the colors of the Italian flag—red, white, and green—so I'm biased to that extent. I think that if the watermelon symbolizes African American culture, then rightly so, because look what white, middle-class feminism stands for—anorexia and bulimia—

In this way, the film shows us not only how women of color must go up against white control of signifying practices, but also demonstrates the oppressiveness of the racist interpretation of signs (as well as the ridiculousness of much of the esoteric ideas of contemporary criticism).

The Watermelon Woman again parallels *Daughters of the Dust* in that "part of what [the film] does is construct for us an imaginative universe around the question of Blackness and Black identity" in an examination that the director does "situate historically," as bell hooks comments to Julie Dash about her film (28). Dunye takes this imaginative creation and historical situating a step further, however, because she has had to create a history of a lesbian Black celebrity; these women, too, are invisible in our received history of popular culture. After the Paglia interview, we see Cheryl interviewing white (lesbian-looking) women on the street. One says that she has heard of Martha Page, but does not know the watermelon woman. Another adds, "If she's in anything after the 1960s, don't ask us, we haven't covered women and blaxploitation yet," again parodically pointing to the way that the institutionalization of women's studies and African-American studies have yet to transcend gendered and racialized stereotypes in their curriculums. The film then segues back to Camille Paglia, who tells Cheryl, "I'm stunned to hear that the director was lesbian or bi-sexual" and that "any kind of interracial relationship at this time [is] mind-boggling," remarks that reveal how heterosexism and racism often underlie the romanticization of the celebrated white creators of popular culture's representations. When Paglia tells Cheryl, "This is an astounding discovery that you've made," she seems jealous of the young Black woman, even though she then wishes her good luck. The competition amongst cultural scholars is invoked in this exchange.

At film's end, Cheryl addresses the viewer. She speaks to the concerns raised in June Walker's letter, explaining to Walker that they have different experiences of Fae Richards and thus she means different things to each of them, as described above. Cheryl then elaborates about what remembering this actress means to her:

> It means hope; it means inspiration; it means possibility. It means *history*. And most important what I understand is it means that I am gonna be the one who says, "I am a Black, lesbian film-maker," who's just beginning, but I'm gonna say a lot more and have a lot more work to do. Anyway—what you've all been waiting for—the biography of Fae Richards. Faith Richardson.

This monologue is followed by a series of images, including simulated filmstills and scenes from films, depicting the life of Fae Richards, in chronological order, narrated by Cheryl's voice-over. This "biography" is interspersed with titles giving the film's credits, and in the middle of this "documentary," the title that explains the fictionality of the character flashes by, rather quickly, I might add. Thus, we learn then that all of these "meanings" of Fae Richards to Cheryl—hope, inspiration, possibility, history—are, to some extent, illusions. Dunye had to make up a history of a Black lesbian actress; in other words, she had to create her own hope, inspiration, and possibility through the creation of a history that was not, but could have been, in some ways should have been, there. However, this undoing of the power of the influence of Fae Richards is not total. For Cheryl's ending statement, while spoken by a fictional character about, we soon learn, another fictional character, documents a real Black lesbian filmmaker, Cheryl Dunye, who has acted on hope, inspiration, and a sense of possibility through her (meta)fictional text. Thus Cheryl's declaration that she will be the one who says that she is a Black, lesbian filmmaker is found to be true in Dunye, and in the end we are left to ponder just what effort it took for her to realize that proclamation, to reflect upon the invisibility of Black lesbians in American popular culture.

NOTES

1. However, while the film breaks with convention in highlighting an interracial lesbian romance, its ultimate commentary on such relationships—especially between African-American and white women—is that they are unlikely to overcome the difficulties related to social dynamics that often plague such relationships. Class differences, including Diana's racist fetishization of the "Other," come between Cheryl and Diana in the end, and the film encourages us to speculate that racist social norms of the midcentury came between Fae Richards and Martha Page.

2. Scenes such as this only "work" in this film because they are exaggeratedly humorous and because they also ring true as well. It is likely that viewers are familiar with white women who fetishize people of color, and who date them in the spirit of this fetishization.

3. Here Walker invokes a phrase used throughout the film, "the family," slang for "homosexual," or, more specifically, "lesbian." In this passage, the character of June Walker makes it clear that "family" for her includes race and is limited to lesbians who are also women of color.

WORKS CITED

Bobo, Jacqueline. *Black Women as Cultural Readers.* New York: Columbia University Press, 1995.

Dash, Julie, and bell hooks. "Dialogue between bell hooks and Julie Dash." In *Daughters of the Dust: The Making of an African American Woman's Film.* New York: The New Press, 1992, 27–67.

Desert Hearts. Dir. Donna Deitch. Samuel Goldwyn, 1985.

Dolan, Jill. " 'Lesbian' Subjectivity in Realism: Dragging at the Margins of Structure and Ideology." *Performing Feminisms: Feminist Critical Theory and Theatre.* Ed. Sue-Ellen Case. Baltimore: Johns Hopkins University Press, 1990, 40–53.

Go Fish. Dir. Rose Troche. Samuel Goldwyn, 1994.

Gomez, Jewelle. "A Cultural Legacy Denied and Discovered: Black Lesbians in Fiction by Women." In *Home Girls: A Black Feminist Anthology.* Ed. Barbara Smith. New York: Kitchen Table: Women of Color Press, 1983, 110–23.

Gone with the Wind. Dir. Victor Fleming. MGM, 1939.

Jackson, Phyllis J., and Darrell Moore. "Fictional Seductions." (Film Review.) *GLQ* 4.3 (1998): 499–508.

Juhasz, Alexandra. *AIDS TV: Identity, Community, and Alternative Video.* Durham, N.C.: Duke University Press, 1995.

Jungle Fever. Dir. Spike Lee. Universal Pictures, 1991.

Kaplan, E. Ann. *Women & Film: Both Sides of the Camera.* New York: Routledge, 1983.

McAlister, Linda Lopez. "The Watermelon Woman." (June 28, 1997.) http://www.inform.umd.edu.EdRes/Topic/WomensStudies/FilmReviews/ watermelon. February 1, 1999.

Turoff, Randy. "Watermelon Woman." http://www.planetout.com/pno/popcornq/db/getfilm.html?2117&shop. February 1, 1999.

The Watermelon Woman (1996). The Internet Movie Database—http://us.imdb.com/ Title?Watermelon+Woman,+The+(1996) February 1, 1999.

When Night Is Falling. Dir. Patricia Rozema. Crucial Pictures, 1995.

16

DREADPATH/LOCKSPIRIT

Akasha Gloria Hull

QUESTION: Why did I cut off (or, in Rastafarian parlance, "trim") a set of perfectly beautiful nine-year-old dreads only to commence locking again just one year later? The trimming actually began before that, in October 1988, almost immediately after I had made a cross-country relocation and assumed a new job. I radically pruned my locks, but did not completely divest myself of them until 1989, shortly after my December 6th birthday. I suspect that the move and the midlife birthday both contributed to a deeply felt sense of shedding the old and beginning anew. I was also extricating myself from a love relationship that was heavily associated with my hair: off with the hair, out with the lover! In general, this seems to have been a time to discard old, "locked-in" energy in order to make fresh starts. Just as clearly, though, I was loathe to give up–in one fell swoop–so many years of cultivated beauty and my elder lockswoman status. Yet, despite its fineness, this head of hair had reached—for me—a static state that was very different from the ever-changing dynamism that had helped attract me to dreadlocks in the first place. I have an even better understanding now of why people play around with various hairstyles "simply" for the sake of change.

After that one in-between year of no locks, I was eager to grow them again. I had spent those twelve months in total dissatisfaction with everything I did and did not do with my hair. The basic problem was that I could not make myself either comb it or cut it. Using the comb or pick was a laborious ordeal, and cutting it felt like a bloody amputation. So many years of not doing these things—fueled by the philosophies behind it—had thoroughly "ruined" me. Grooming my hair with my bare hands sufficed for quite a while, but when it grew beyond the shorter lengths, my Black women friends wanted to know if I knew what I was doing with my hair, and one of them, Jamilah, volunteered to give me braids and a counseling session. This "neither fish nor fowl" state was obviously not working. With the well-earned relief of someone who has given an experiment a dogged try, I let my understanding son barber me a soft Afro from which I could neatly begin my second dread in December 1990.

By this time, I knew that I would be gridding in new growth and power and a transformed sense of self. One indication was my determination to lock exactly as I believed it

should be done. This meant following what "roots" people in the know had always coun-
seled: to simply stop combing the hair and let it go. That easy, that simple. Just put away the
paraphernalia and allow nature to take its course. No parting and twisting, no "glueing" and
not washing, none of those make-it-happen, hairstyling, hair management instructions that
currently pass as the correct information about how to have locks. If there is "kink" in the
genes and the hair is chemical-free, it will (eventually) ravel itself together in some way(s).
My first time, I had twisted a bit and had encouraged a pattern of small, symmetrical separations. This time, I would do nothing except keep the clumps divided into the aggregations
they themselves made so that I would not end up with huge "kungas" on my head. This possible outcome was the only thing that was not okay with me, and this management the only
manipulation that did not feel inconsistent with an extremely natural approach.

From my years of consciously absorbing dreads of all kinds (especially in Jamaica), I
had really come to see that the healthiest, most beautiful sets of locks were those which
evolved organically, growing out of the physicality and spirit of their individuals. I noticed
the startling but always pleasing variety, the inexplicable resemblances to trees, roots, and
other natural formations, the absolute rightness of each dread for its person—how the
arch of the hair echoed the arch of the brows, eyes, or nose, or the thickness of lock paralleled the body's musculature, or the way texture and tint complemented the skin's own
grain and tone. This, to me, was marvelous, magnificent–and I drank in these framed
Black faces with joy and appreciation. Yes, here was the way to truly have dreadlocks.

Unfortunately, preconceived notions about how a nice dread is supposed to look get in
the way of this natural, laissez-faire approach. Most people seem to want to have (and see)
locks that are thin and uniform, approximating as closely as possible the smooth regularity
of braided styles, rather than deal with thick and/or thin, unpredictable organicism. And
many prefer them long, still equating—for women—length with feminine attractiveness.
When my first locks reached my shoulders, my mother finally accepted them, but told me—
lovingly but baldly—that my new dread was "at that ugly stage." In similar fashion, Cheryl, a
nationalist-minded, midthirties friend, all but turned up her nose at my "stubby-looking"
hair even as she shared that she was contemplating letting her (thin and regular eight-inch)
plaits go into locks.

We are still being influenced by cosmetic—and commercial—standards of beauty, still
buying into the system in the ostensible act of repudiating it. How hard it is to shed this
programming! Defensive, a little hurt, a bit angry (but outwardly cool), I found myself explaining to Cheryl that the locks only looked stubby at the ends and would grow out with
a different appearance. As opposed to maintaining a centered, serenely immune attitude,
I was desiring her approval and positive response. This was the reversed version of the ambivalence I used to feel when accepting compliments for my locks from folks who said, "I
like *yours*"—*mine* being the exception to those other wild-looking things they had seen on
Bob Marley and MOVE members in Philadelphia. All of this is not to say that we lockswomen
do not receive clear-eyed admiration. We do—quite often and sometimes from unexpected
quarters—and it is immensely affirming.

Even though dreadlocks primarily assert a racial message and are basically free of stereotypical sex-role signification (although something could probably be made of a wild-irregular-
powerful-masculine versus thin-groomed-feminine equation), they yet make an emphatic,
gender-related statement. I wish I really knew, for instance, in what ways wearing long hair

reflects a Black man's self-concept and image projections. I do know that, for women, dreading is a rejection of a capitalistic, fetishized definition of female be-ing. Especially in the United States, strong, self-defining, and self-referenced women who have eschewed traditional notions of femininity—predominantly race/roots women and lesbians (often combined)—are the ones who dare to lock. Generally speaking, it still requires an ample measure of internal steadiness to walk this path of difference.

Dreading seems to also require at least a minimum level of comfort with the spiritual dimensions of existence. And, if one is going to lock in what I earlier described as the most natural way (though I am humble about prescriptiveness and the possible range of what is natural), spiritual issues become even more obvious: really, truly giving up control and "going with the flow"; trusting process/this process to yield what is appropriate and best; and having patience. I have learned the hard way (and am still learning—though with less hardness) that these three desiderata—faith, patience, and surrender—are major keystones of an evolving spiritual consciousness and approach to life. Having them on any level, in any arena is not easy. When trying to lock, one's patience is tested because it takes time, often a long time for the hair to aggregate and grow, not to mention its achieving full bloom. Faith waivers during those "ugly stages" and also when it looks as if what the hair is doing is headed in the wrong direction. Foregoing control is the hardest of all because one can so easily and summarily intervene (just reach up and twist or separate). The temptation to do so is also considerable, especially if one is susceptible to the ever-present pressure to always look "nice/good."

From this perspective, dreading can thus be viewed as a spiritual path/discipline. It can become a vehicle to enlightenment on an inner level comparable to the way it illuminates the external world via what we see/receive from wearing locks. If we are conscious and receptive, it functions as a full-time, built-in mirror that magnifies our realities. Having patience, faith, and the ability to surrender is an uplifting and liberating experience. Many of us women with locks say that we feel so "free." I believe this is not just because there is no combing, picking, teasing, styling, frying, fretting of our hair, but because there is likewise much less of that in our souls.

Related to this freedom is the opportunity that locking provides for a Black woman to learn how she really feels about herself, to get in touch with her own true reaction to herself as she is. Here I mean internal feeling and not externally driven judgment or evaluation. Being so different forces us to really look at ourselves and ask/answer, "Hmm, what have we here?" Since the standard templates do not apply, it encourages the development of authentic/natural/original response. Regardless of what anybody says, I feel empowered to have discovered that I genuinely *love* the soft clumpings of hair at the base of my locks, or the tensile waviness of these tough, skinny ones, or the untamed way they all spring out when I am energized by sex or other fierce emotions:

Sometimes, though, I cannot be sure of how I feel. Sometimes I have to admit that I do not always like everything I see. At one point, I was wrapping my locks with scarves. This is because I did not relate well to the flatness of my hair when it was freshly washed, to its bangs-and-skullcap silhouette that called up for me unpleasant images of men and wet-look curls. However, this was my own not liking, my own unique and private quirkiness, emanating from some personal aesthetic inside myself and not adopted from the outside/others. I was wrapping because *I* felt prettier with locks and scarf. Of course, the social aspect of this was that I wanted to look good in public. But I was the one deciding about that "good."

Finally, locking can be healing—for any African woman who has internalized a negative dismissal of herself as ugly, particularly as this relates to hair and color issues. The almost formulaic epithet "Black and nappy-headed" has inflicted many a wound, for generations. In my case, this general experience was exacerbated by growing up with a light-skinned, "good-haired" sister with whom I was paired and compared. It was further amplified by the traumatic baby girl ordeal of having all my hair shaved off for medical reasons and suffering from the resulting rejections at an age when I could only feel but not understand. Once, without even knowing this story, a chiropractic healer performing craniopathy on me said that I/my head had never gotten enough holding. The psychic, emotional, and physical embracing of my locks helps cure this long-standing deficiency. And its power is somehow so deep and complete that it withstands society's sometimes still negative appraisals. This mojo is stronger than their bad medicine.

17

IN THE YEAR 1915
D. W. Griffith and the Whitening of America

Cedric J. Robinson

The purpose of racism is to control the behaviour of white people, not black people. For blacks, guns and tanks are sufficient.
—Otis Madison[1]

ABSTRACT

The appearance of D. W. Griffith's film The Birth of a Nation, *in 1915 colluded with a host of powerful economic interests (industrial capitalism) and political initiatives (imperialism) in America. As well, it coincided with dramatic changes in the American population (immigration) and film production (the defeat of the Edison-led Trust). Providing a racial catechism that included a mythical national history of white sameness, Griffith appropriated narratives from coideologists Woodrow Wilson and Thomas Dixon Jr. to designate Black desire authoritatively as the recurring menace to Western civilization and a Christian Aryan nation. And by employing the epic genre, Griffith ensured that his imagined moral order would acquire a compelling authority, particularly for his immigrant audience. Griffith succeeded in his effort to pose national redemption in racial terms and established cinematic protocols and racial icons that would survive to the present.*

PATROLLING FILM HISTORIOGRAPHY
The 1970s usher in the beginnings of sustained research into the discursive and representational arts of Black imaging in American films. Among the pioneers of the endeavor, the two most enduring treatments of this material have been Donald Bogle's *Toms, Coons, Mulattoes, Mammies & Bucks*, published in 1973, and Thomas Cripps's *Slow Fade to Black*, which appeared in 1977.[2] But from the very outset, major interpretive differences erupted. Bogle had argued that Black cinematic iconography was concomitant with the appearance of moving pictures; while the more conventionally academic Cripps largely eschewed Bogle's approach, suggesting that not only was Bogle writing popular rather than formally canonized history, but in method and conceptualization his theory of an enduring quintuplet of Black representation could only be supported by a kind of primitive historiography.

Cripps found mystifying the speed and power with which Black icons infected early American film. Asserting that from the beginnings of moving pictures and for most of the first decade of the new century Black imaging was predominantly reportorial, Cripps postulated that as a concomitant to film editing something went terribly wrong. Nevertheless he was forced to concede that "it is difficult to attribute causes to the seeming decline in Black fortunes after 1910" (Cripps, 1977, 25–26).

For Bogle the mystery would have been the absence of devaluing Black images from an embryonic American film culture. He was persuaded that a natural history served to explain the appearance of these images:

> All were merely filmic reproductions of black stereotypes that had existed since the days of slavery and were already popularized in American life and arts. The movies . . . borrowed profusely from all the other popular art forms. (Bogle, 1995, 4)

This was not the case according to Cripps. For Cripps there had to be immediate causes that conspired to disrupt an otherwise racially benign form of entertainment. The causes, he mused, might be the racist southern (white) literati's migration into the fledgling movie industry; the approaching anniversary of the ending of the Civil War; and intersectional reconciliation coupled with a nostalgia among a recently urbanized America for an idealized rural past represented by the Old South (Cripps, 1977, 26).

Bogle, of course, was being intuitive and, unfortunately, historically mistaken. The images he identified have different histories: for examples, the buck long antedates the Atlantic slave trade (recall Shakespeare's Othello); and the mulatto (or more precisely the mulatta) would make her appearance in American popular culture in the first quarter of the nineteenth century. But Cripps, too, was intuitive and in error to presume that American motion pictures had some sort of period of innocence and that southern whites had been the authors of the racialization of film. These are not trivial matters. They are important to our present understanding of American cultural history for what they inadvertently conceal; and we can sense their importance to Cripps by the lengths to which he resorts to defend them.

From the 1890s into the early twentieth century, Edison and his contemporary filmmakers constructed what Cripps characterizes as "relatively benign, vaguely anthropological" shorts. While it is true that some of Edison's racial "vignettes" were entitled *A West Indian Woman Bathing a Baby* (1895), *Colored Troops Disembarking* (1898), *The Ninth Negro Cavalry Watering Horses* (1898), many more bore titles such as *Buck Dance* (1898), *Watermelon Contest* (1899), *The Edison Minstrels, Minstrels Battling in a Room, Sambo and Aunt Jemima: Comedians* (all of the latter series produced between 1897 and 1900) (Cripps, 1977, 393). Moreover, none of Edison's films, not even those which were reportorial, appeared to suggest the éxistence of Black men like Lewis H. Latimer. Latimer, while working with Alexander Graham Bell as a draftsman, had improved the latter's patent design for the telephone. Later, in 1881, he had added the carbon element to Edison's light bulb, and then had worked for Edison (Edison Electric, later General Electric) and Maxim-Weston (Westinghouse) as chief engineer. He supervised the installation of electric lighting systems in New York, Philadelphia, Montreal, and London, and authored the first textbook on lighting systems used by the Edison company (see Low and Cloft, 1981). Latimer's apparent intrusion into Edison's commercial world, as inventor, draftsman, patents arbitrator, and engineer, did not alter the transfer of selected Black images to film by his colleagues at Edison. In negating his existence and that of other Black intellectuals, their body of work can hardly be taken as a substantiation of Cripps's claims for a period in which film primarily recorded actual Black life.

A similar unease adheres to Cripps's other assertions about the silents: that the white racism in them emanated from the "South,"[3] and that the proximity of a Civil War observance triggered an imagined transformation of Black filmic representations. For some decades prior to the opening of the twentieth century, northern as well as southern and even European racist intellectuals had played an important part in the formation of American national culture, academic life, medicine, art, and popular culture (including high and low theatre).[4] Cripps, however, repeatedly constructed white racism as initially a regional impulse which eventually enveloped American society. And it is hard to credit any anniversary related to the Civil War as an inspiration for Woodrow Wilson to publish his Teutonic ode, the five-volume *A History of the American People*, in 1903. In its treatment of the Civil War, the Reconstruction, and the Ku Klux Klan, the work was so profoundly negative towards Blacks and solicitous of "white civilization" that Griffith would unabashedly borrow from it to structure *The Birth of a Nation* (see Rogin, 1985).

The continuity of the grotesque representations of Blacks between nineteenth-century dramatic and vaudevillian theatre, humor magazines, postcards, children's books, the new social sciences, historical works, and twentieth-century popular culture and scholarship is hard to ignore, but Cripps had largely erased it. He achieved this by presuming that the documentary film, the short, the vignette, sufficed as entertainment during the novelty period of movies, and thus had assumed the dominant form, and by the audacious assertion that immigrants, a large proportion of the new entertainment's audience, "not only carried no baggage of racial lore, but were insulated from Southern literary racism by their own illiteracy" (Cripps, 1977, 9). But the "vaguely anthropological" documentary shorts were merely an alternative and not the dominant form of the early silents; and the European immigrants were encrusted with racial lore both intra-European and otherwise consequent to several centuries of imperial wars, slavery and colonialism (Robinson, 1983). Cripps thus retrieved a recent past that was as fabulous as the long lost past invented by Marx.

Contrary to Cripps's constructions, neither Edison nor Ellis Island constituted proper historical markings for the defamatory cultural codes employed in early American film. On that score Bogle's observations were the more trenchant: an established racist iconography of Blacks merely acquired new visual techniques in early American film. What Cripps mistook for their supersession was largely reassertion of racial conventions. Thus, as Daniel Bernardi (1996) has observed, "racial meanings are a significant, omnipresent part of the birth of cinema." But even this realization masks a more profound emergence: through the intervention of film, a new American social order was naturalized. The new order differed radically from that of the early national period a century earlier. It required race discourse to function not to justify the early-nineteenth-century ideal of rural republicanism or to forgive its faltering achievement of social justice. At the beginnings of the twentieth century, America capital was no longer a middling mercantile player in a global economy commanded by imperial European powers. Now it was a robust industrial society voraciously appropriating a vast but disparate labor force that required cultural discipline, social habituation, and political regulation.

RE-WHITING HISTORY

Taking 1915 as a particularly auspicious moment in film history, the number of crucial historical events colluding with the appearance of Griffith's *The Birth of a Nation* suggests that it was a moment during which the mapping of American culture was reinscribed, when the contours of the social practices which came to characterize twentieth-century American society were fixed. Let us consider this possibility for a moment. Nineteen-fifteen, of course, marked the fiftieth anniversary of the ending of the American Civil War. It was also the second year of World War I, but the year that German submarines sank the *Lusitania*, and Hugo Junkers developed the first fighter plane. In that same year, and closer to our concerns, Leo Frank was lynched, the Second Klan was inaugurated, the United States invaded Haiti, and Jess Willard defeated the Black heavyweight boxing champion, Jack Johnson. Also implicated in our film history, in response to *The Birth of a Nation*, the six-year-old NAACP launched mass demonstrations, and the Association for the Study of Negro Life and History was initiated (see Cripps, 1977, and Aptheker, 1992). Finally, the phenomenal success of *The Birth of a Nation* (Neal Gabler, 1988, describes it as "the first block-buster") brought the independents to their definitive triumph over Edison's Trust, thus establishing the governing structure of the movie industry for the next decade.

On the screen, Griffith made several explicit claims for his film. At the beginning of *The Birth of a Nation*, before he introduced his "impersonators" and the roles they undertook, Griffith conflated in one title an alleged sensitivity for social etiquette, his resolve for a broad and clear moral binary, and a claim that his film was art:

> we have no wish to offend with improprieties or obscenities, but we do demand, as a right, the liberty to show the dark side of wrong, that we may illuminate the bright side of virtue—the same liberty that is conceded to the art of the written word—the art to which we owe the Bible and works of Shakespeare.[5]

A moment later, having privileged Lillian Gish (Elsie Stoneman), Mae Marsh (Flora Cameron), Henry Walthall (Col. Ben Cameron), Miriam Cooper (Margaret Cameron), and Mary Alden (*Lydia, Stoneman's mulatto housekeeper*), and then scrolled fourteen other players, Griffith inserted one more claim:

> *If in this work we have conveyed to the mind the ravages of war to the end that* war may be held in abhorrence, *this effort will not have been in vain.*

Griffith's film is thus marked by the colliding economic and cultural forces of its time: hegemonic Victorian moral values contending with the meteoric expansion of a culturally diverse working class; insurgent and enterprising businessmen in the new film industry, in order to justify their fragile economic position, became claimants to the status of artists; and movies were proposed as a site of moral instruction.

Huge financial, industrial, and commercial interests had already transformed the American economy from a primarily rural society engaged in agrarian and manufacturing activities into an urban industrial giant capable of superseding the machine production of Great Britain and Germany. And now with its vast industrial plantations ranging from the stark and brutal coal fields in the East and the silver mines of the West to the equally hazardous shipyards and the hard- and soft-good factories of the Northeast, the slaughterhouses of the Midwest, and the lumbermills of the South and Far West, in the production of steel, iron, railways, clothing, food, and the horizontal and vertical expansion of its cities, the economy appeared to possess an insatiable appetite for workers. They came in the millions: 5.5 million in the 1880s; 4 million in the 1890s; 14 million between 1900 and 1920 (Zinn, 1995). Some migrated from the American South, the Caribbean and Asia, but many more from Eastern and Southern Europe.

In the cities, the immigrants were clustered in squalid ghettoes, arranged as they had been recruited: by employment, language, culture, ethnicity, region, and nation of origin. Robert Sklar's (1975) assertion that the

> old American city, which had been a single community, became the new American city of many communities, separated from each other by social barriers,

was not historically true, but the sheer volume of the newcomers might have made it seem so. From colonial times, recruitment for American settlements had been characteristically diverse, homogeneity being the exception. In the countryside, where hundreds of thousands of immigrants were employed in mining and lumbering, and ordered "residentially" by a similar social calculus, they existed in company towns and camps regimented by company enforcers and servers. Numerically dominated by males, these immigrant and migrant assemblages exhibited in their recreational activities what polite society ascribed as the vices of the ignorant poor: alcoholism, drugs (ranging from cigarettes to opium), and rowdy combativeness. In order to relieve the sexual frustrations and loneliness which resulted from the separation from their families and native communities, their overt sexual impulses fostered prostitution and the transformation of the cheap burlesque theatre into female exhibitionism. And by 1910, it was discovered they constituted three-quarters of the 26 million who made up the movie audience (Brownlow, 1990).

For years, as Griffith implies in his foreword to *The Birth of a Nation*, the nickelodeons had been the object of elite and middle-class suspicion and revulsion. The reformers were intent to cleanse the form of its "obscenities and improprieties" in order to transform it into an instrument for moral and cultural education. Recognizing, as Mary Grey Peck of the Women's Clubs put it in 1917, that

> Motion pictures are going to save our civilization from the destruction which has successively overwhelmed every civilization of the past. They provide what every previous civilization has lacked—namely a means of relief, happiness and mental inspiration to the people at the bottom.

The World Today declared in 1908 that pictures were "the academy of the working man, his pulpit, his newspaper, his club." In his 1915 production, given the enormous financial stake, Griffith had attempted to appropriate the reformers' objectives, but earlier he had been less circumspect. Kevin Brownlow (1990) informs us that

> D. W. Griffith was particularly contemptuous of them. In 1913, he made an extraordinary film called *The Reformers, or the Lost Art of Minding One's Own Business* . . . Two of his reformers are obvious homosexuals, and Griffith goes so far as to show prostitutes, dressed as pious churchgoers, continuing to ply their trade. (xviii–xix)

Brownlow, a filmmaker and historian of the silent film era, assures us that the period before 1919 was the "richest source of social films," but that many of the directors of the genre, like George Nichols, Barry O'Neill, and Oscar Apfel, were subsequently forgotten (however, more occasional contributors like Raoul Walsh and King Vidor were more fortunate). And probably the most extraordinary of them was Lois Weber. Weber was not cynical about reform and she devoted her entire career to the cause. A Christian Scientist, in 1913 Weber directed *Suspense, Civilized and Savage,* and *The Jew's Christmas* (concerned with poverty, racism, and anti-Semitism, respectively); in 1914 she produced *The Hypocrites* exposing the corruption of churches, politicians, and big business; and later she filmed stories concerned with abortion and birth control (*Where Are My Children,* 1916), opium smuggling (*Hop, The Devil's Brew,* 1916), capital punishment (*The People vs John Doe,* 1916), and alcoholism (*Even As You and I,* 1917, xii–xxiii).

Griffith's foray into the moral realm in *The Birth of a Nation* was not then singular or unusual. But it did coincide with a profound structural change in the production and exhibition of motion pictures. From 1908 to 1914, motion picture production and exhibition had been dominated by Edison's cartel, the Motion Picture Patents Company ("The Trust," as Carl Laemmle termed it), the combination of Edison, Biograph, Vitagraph, Essanay, Kalem, Selig, Lubin, Pathe Freres and Méliès, and George Kleine (Sklar, 1975). The members of the near monopoly, based on the patents for cameras, projectors, etc., that were held by Edison's company, and American Mutoscope and Biograph, were

primarily older white Anglo-Saxon Protestants who had entered the film industry in its infancy by inventing, bankrolling, or tinkering with movie hardware.

But by 1912, the Trust had been effectively challenged by exhibitors and producers who were "largely ethnic Jews and Catholics" (Gabler, 1988, 58).

The Trust had signed an exclusive deal with Eastman Kodak, ensuring that raw film stock would only be available to filmmakers who operated under its licences. With these several instruments of control, the monopoly had determined that motion pictures would remain one-reel recreations for the poor, and had also embedded its own social ethics, including anti-Semitism, in film. In 1913, *Moving Picture World* had reported:

Whenever a producer wishes to depict a betrayer of public trust (ran the report of the Anti-Defamation League) a hard-boiled usurious money-lender, a crooked gambler, a grafter, a depraved fire bug, a white slaver or other villains of one kind or another, the actor was directed to represent himself as a Jew. (Brownlow, 1990, 376)

The independents like Adolph Zukor, Carl Laemmle with Robert Cochrane, William Fox, and Harry Aitkin successfully challenged the Trust by covertly filming while using Trust-patented equipment, raiding Trust companies for their most recognized screen personalities, lawsuits, introducing feature-length films, and importing films from Europe. And they secured financing primarily from Jewish investment houses like S. W. Strauss, Kuhn, Loeb, and Goldman, Sachs (Gabler, 1988, 117).[6] As a consequence, Brownlow observes, "direct references to Jewish criminals began to disappear from the screen, partly because more Jews were taking control of the picture business" (Brownlow, 1990, 337). But among their imports were features like the French film *Queen Elizabeth* (with Sarah Bernhardt) and the Italian epics *Quo Vadis?* and *Cabiria*. And when the war disrupted access to Europe, Aitkin's Mutual Company and Kuhn, Loeb (through Felix and Otto Kahn) took up the slack by backing Griffith's project to produce the first American-made epic (Schickel, 1996). It is also instructive to note that Louis B. Mayer, another of the future movie moguls, acquired his first big return in the business (some $500,000) by securing the New England distribution rights to *The Birth of a Nation* (Gabler, 1988, 90–91).

To return to the film itself, in the very next moment following Griffith's imposturing *Birth* as an antiwar film, he placed a marker for whiteness costumed in an Edenic metaphor: *the bringing of the African to America planted the first seed of disunion*. He ellipsed the brutality and wrenching pain of the slave trade, the tyranny of the mass appropriation of African life and labor by following the title with a scene portraying the benediction of a slave auction by a Christian minister. His next subject was the ordinary white abolitionists (thus erasing the Black abolitionists who dominated the movement from the 1840s (Quarles, 1969)) sentimentalized by their concern for a Black child; and then he installed the first antagonist of his melodramatic structure: *in 1860 a great parliamentary leader, whom we shall call Austin Stoneman, was rising to power in the National House of representatives*. Stoneman's ambitions for power would corrupt abolitionism; but for the moment, the only tension in his otherwise idyllic household was Elsie's discomfort in being excluded from her brothers' plan to visit friends (the Cameron brothers) in the South. Having established Stoneman's household, Griffith immediately herded his audience back to Edenic lore: *Piedmont, South Carolina, the home of the Camerons, where life runs in a quaintly way that is to be no more.*

The depiction of the Cameron household differs from Griffith's introduction of the Stonemans in two important markings: exteriors dominate interiors (an extended street scene fronting Cameron Hall visually confirming the easy, leisured, and stylized patriarchy of antebellum life); and the street and the household are decorated with amiable adult domestic slaves (*Mammy* and the tom role are played by white actors in blackface), the Black children performing amusements for white observers. The Stoneman boys arrive, and the two younger sons bond (*Chums*); Ben Cameron becomes enamored with a miniature portrait of Elsie while Phil Stoneman is infatuated with Margaret Cameron. The young Camerons and Stonemans visit a slave quarter and the slaves perform an impromptu dance, stomping their feet, clapping their hands. Griffith has evacuated fugitive slaves from history, vanquishing the Nat Turners, the David Walkers, and the very possibility of the hundreds of maroon communities that struck fear in the hearts of plantation owners, state officials, and their militia has vanished (Robinson, 1997).

Griffith now fuses *the gathering storm* (a southern newspaper announces the South's stake in the 1860 presidential election) with scenes depicting Stoneman's dual corruption: ambition for power and his apparently intimate relationship with his mulatto domestic, *Lydia: the great leader's weakness that is to blight a nation*. By associating Stoneman *pere* with mulattos such as Lydia and, later, Silas Lynch, Griffith has evaded another historical truth by grafting the *blight* of miscegenation to a powerful northern abolitionist! In fact, most of the nearly half a million mulattos in the country resided in the South at midcentury, the issue principally of slave owners and female slaves. Nevertheless, since Griffith will characterize his two mulatto roles with a neurotic sexuality necessitated by plot and ideology, disclosing their relation to the ruling plantocracy would risk an unseemly speculation as to the source of their sexual depravity. Meanwhile the Stoneman boys return north.

The remainder of the first part of the film takes up the Civil War itself. And here Griffith exhibits his extraordinary technical mastery of the medium, establishing the cinematic tropes that will come to dominate depictions of the war for decades: the tragic beauty of a Confederate ball interrupted by the call to assembly (powerfully imitated in *Santa Fe Trail*, 1940, a film indebted to Griffith cinematically and ideologically); the Confederate troops parading down the streets of Piedmont and led by mounted officers); the mass charges of the armies in battle, cutting to individualized acts of heroism (Ben Cameron leading his troops into a Union barrage; bringing water to a wounded Union soldier; a wounded Ben Cameron rescuing the Confederate flag in the midst of conflagration, etc.); and the severed fraternity (*true to their promise, the chums meet again*) as Tod Stoneman and Duke Cameron expire together. Griffith reenacts the burning of Atlanta (preceded by a marvellous shot of Sherman's army in serpentine march), and brings authenticating detail of Robert E. Lee's desperate attempt to break out of a Union encirclement at Petersburg. And true to the promise made to his audience, Griffith provides graphic scenes of the carnage of war.

Meanwhile, in Piedmont, Black irregulars invade (*the first negro regiments of the war were raised in South Carolina*), attempting to put Cameron Hall to the fire, but are frustrated by Confederate rescuers. In the actual war, approximately 189,000 Blacks fought in the Union Army, most of them volunteering from the slave states. They fought in some 449 engagements, absorbing 16 percent of the 360,222 killed on the Union side. Confederate troops, at first, murdered captured Union Blacks (at Fort Pillow and Poison Spring, for examples); but then when Black units pledged to take no prisoners, Lee and other Confederate officers insisted on, and then extended to Blacks, the rules of "civilized" warfare.[7] Once again, Griffith bends history to ideology, restricting his reconstruction of the work of Black troops to acts of marauding and victimizing the feeble and the female.

Wade Cameron is killed and Ben, wounded, ends up in a makeshift Union military hospital (where Elsie has volunteered), condemned to be hanged as an irregular. Elsie and Ben's mother reunite at Ben's hospital bed; and Mrs Cameron, learning of her son's plight, travels with Elsie to appeal to Lincoln for her son's life. Lincoln (*the Great Heart*) intercedes. Lee surrenders to Grant (Griffith reproduces Horace Porter's painting of Appomattox); and Ben, now recovered, returns to his beloved but ruined Cameron Hall. Five days following the Confederate surrender, Lincoln attends the performance of *Our American Cousin* at Ford's theatre and is assassinated by John Booth. In the Stoneman household, Lydia exults at the news, gloating to Stoneman: "*You are now the greatest power in America.*" At Cameron Hall, Cameron *pere* laments: "*Our best friend is gone. What is to become of us now!*" End of part one.

Griffith's portrayal of Reconstruction is foreworded by a claim he would recite until the end of his days: *this is an historical presentation of the Civil War and Reconstruction Period, and is not meant to reflect on any race or people of today*. And then in the sure embrace of language excerpted from Wilson's *A History of the American People*, Griffith assures his audience that the Ku Klux Klan arose to defend the *civilization of the South* from the depredations of congress and invading *adventurers* who sought *to cozen, beguile, and use the negroes . . .*

In his earlier films, Griffith's racism had assumed a sentimental, paternalistic form. Thus, as Jack Temple Kirby (1978) informs us, Griffith's stock Black characterizations in films like *In Old Kentucky* (1909), *Swords and Hearts, His Trust*, and *His Trust Fulfilled* (1911) were Uncle Ben and Mammy, "cheering, weeping, comforting and ever-loyal Negroes" shackled to the plantation aristocracy. Kirby is persuaded that "Griffith's greatest indulgence in the black-as-beast theme was in *The Birth of a Nation*." Thomas Dixon Jr. had collaborated with Griffith in constructing the earlier portions of the film, but now in the second part of *Birth* the brutal virulence of Dixon's race-hating, *The Clansman* (1905), became dominant (Cook, 1962). As Thomas Clark observed in the 1970 reissue of the novel:

> There is no comedy . . . in Dixon's characterization of the Negro. He recited every scurrilous thing that had been said about the race. In one passage after another he portrayed the Negro as a sensuous brute whose every physical feature was the mark of the jungle and the untamed animal. (Clark, 1970, 9)

And Dixon's Aryan characters, one after another, are nearly overcome by the "African odor" of black bestiality.

Understandably, Dixon's disaffection with mulattos was even more pronounced. Their mongrel existence is simultaneously alluring and repulsive. He more than once refers to Lydia as a woman of "animal beauty" with the temperament of a "leopardess," unnatural ambition, and the sexual seductiveness to ruin a nation. In the final pages of his novel, Dixon has Stoneman confess:

> Three forces moved me—party success, a vicious woman, and the quenchless desire for personal vengeance. When I first fell a victim to the wiles of the yellow vampire who kept my house, I dreamed of lifting her to my level.

And Dixon described Silas Lynch, Lydia's covert agent, as

> a man of charming features for a mulatto, who had evidently inherited the full physical characteristics of the Aryan race, while his dark yellowish eyes beneath his heavy brows glowed with the brightness of the African jungle . . . the primeval forest. (57, 53)

As Griffith himself revealed, he managed the difficult task of reconciling the affectionate portrayal of his earlier films with Thomas Dixon Jr.'s unrelievedly vicious construction of Blacks by the interposing of an evil master, the northern scallywag.

The second part of *The Birth of a Nation* is no more historical than its antecedent; and in its unadornedly manic representation of Dixon's race consciousness, it pursues the villainy of Blacks, mulattos, and their abolitionist Rasputin with melodramatic vitality. Under the leadership of Lieutenant Governor Silas Lynch, the Blacks appropriate power, the once safe streets of Piedmont, and the destruction of civilization and white women. In their nearly unintelligible imitation of the English language, they demand political and civil rights for which they have not the barest understanding: "*Ef I doan' get 'nuf franchise to fill mah bucket, I doan' want it nohow.*" Their corruption and greed are boundless: the law, the courts, the legislature (scenes of the Black-dominated State House are titled *The Riot in the Master's Hall*), the land and real property, social equality, and the most virtuous of white women. Fascinating for its unintended irony, Griffith's indictment of Blacks is constructed in a mirror image of the antebellum slave order: fraud and injustice at the polls (*all Blacks are given the ballot, while the leading whites are disfranchised*); racial dominion of the law ("*the case was tried before a negro magistrate and the verdict rendered against the whites by the negro jury*"); the forging of race privileges in legislation (*passage of a bill, providing for the intermarriage of Blacks and whites*); physical terror (*the town given over to crazed negroes brought in by Lynch and Stoneman to overawe the whites*), the routine and public displays of petty racial humiliation and insult, etc.

Meanwhile, as the white tragedies accumulate, Ben has fortuitously imagined (*The Inspiration*) the creation of an Invisible Empire: the Klan. This was Dixon's fabrication of the Klan's origins, but even as Woodrow Wilson's version contradicted that aspect of Dixon's fantasy, he shared with Dixon the rationale for the secret society:

> It threw the negroes into a very ecstasy of panic to see these sheeted "Ku Klux" move near them in the shrouded night; and their comic fear stimulated the lads who excited it to many an extravagant prank and mummery. (Wilson, 1908)

One such prank is the castration of Gus, the Black uniformed deviant who, in one of the film's most memorable sequences (the Gus chase), pursues Flora, the youngest Cameron daughter, to her suicide (Diawara, 1993, 212–13). But it is the specter of just such Black depravity that will reconcile Elsie and Phil Stoneman and Ben and Margaret Cameron in the embrace of the Klan: *the former enemies of the North and South are united again in common defense of their Aryan birthright.*

Maddened by an ambition which wreaks havoc on his own congenital instability, Lynch pursues Elsie ("*See! My people fill the streets. With them I will build a Black Empire and you as Queen shall sit at my side*") and eventually is forced to take both her and her father hostage. Elsewhere, frenzied by Klan raids and open confrontations, Black troops enforce a martial order: arresting whites indiscriminately; taking prisoner innocent white families; intimidating Blacks loyal to their former masters. The Klan routs the Black soldiers holding Piedmont; Ben and his Klansmen rescue the kidnapped Elsie, the besieged Phil, the Camerons and their loyal domestics; and the Klan disarms the blacks. Under the Klan's protection a second election is held, and the natural order is restored. And at the seaside, Phil and Margaret are united (interior); and Ben and Elsie, seated together on a bluff overlooking the sea, contemplate a miraculous vision:

> the figure of Christ, projected in the background, is mounted on a horse and with both hands is swinging his sword above his head. On the right, in front of him, lies a huge heap of bodies, and on the left a crowd writhes and pleads with him. The image of the God of War fades out. (Lang, 1994, 155)

The concluding images are magnificently costumed and apocalyptic but have also cleverly prepared the audience for Griffith's final nationalist message: '*Liberty and union, one and inseparable, now and forever!*.' The abrupt juxtaposition of these visual constructions fuses whiteness and a race theodicy, patriarchy and filopiety, historical destiny and Christian civilization on the mass consciousness.

In *The Birth of a Nation*, Griffith invoked structural and discursive oppositions to achieve the representations of good and evil, employing narrative conventions that were thoroughly familiar to the cultural elite and compelling to the popular imagination. As Plato had done in *The Republic* for his immediate audience at the Academy in ancient Athens, Griffith designated the site of his moral contestation as the metaphorical and ideological space occupied by two opposing families, one northern and one southern. Unlike Plato for whom the opposition between Athenian (Plato's brothers and the Sophist Socrates) and non-Athenian (Cephalus, his sons, and their Sophist, Thrasymachus) was immutable (Robinson, 1995), Griffith resolved the contradiction between the real (the South) and the unreal (the North) by transforming the conflict into racial constructions. The Stonemans and the Camerons were white, an Aryan racial fraternity, the imminent "nation."[8] Opposed to this racial utopia was the ubiquitous evil: the Blacks and *their* mongrel mulattos whose savage, anarchic, sexual desires poisoned the spiritual and biological life blood of the good. It was clear that for Griffith as for Dixon, "one of the main reasons for making the film was to help prevent the mixing of white and negro blood by intermarriage" (Lang, 1994, 17).

Rather than a contest between opposing factions of capital over the domination of millions of southern laborers (black and white), Griffith recast the American Civil War as a violent fratricidal confrontation between whites. And in the melodramatic genre he favored, the poignancy of the conflict was crystallized in the romantic and fated liaisons between the elder Stoneman and Cameron children. Griffith then reimagined Reconstruction as a temporary moment of mulatto political ascendancy and black triumph, rape, and anarchy. Interposed between the seeing (southern white plantocrats) and the unseeing (northern white abolitionists) were what Griffith had dramatically determined to be the *seed of disunion*, African slavery. Griffith instructed (or reminded) his audience that Abraham Lincoln (*the Great Heart*) had understood the evil in the white American paradise and had made preparations to expel blacks: "Lincoln's dream" was to return blacks to Africa, and only his assassination had frustrated his act of cleansing (Robinson, 1997, 70–71). It was a promise that only the death of the Christ-like patriarch had aborted. But Lincoln also had vowed of the white South "*I shall deal with them as though they had never been away.*" And Wilson, Dixon, and Griffith, each in his own way and now as collaborators, longed to realize that Aryan fraternity.

The film was privately premiered on February 8, 1915, in Los Angeles; and then began a seven-month showing at Cline's Auditorium. And from the first, movie reviewers in all the major newspapers and trade papers enthused over the spectacle.[9] There were some detractors, however, particularly the NAACP's Moorfield Storey, W. E. B. Du Bois and Oswald Garrison Villard, Rabbi Stephen Wise of the Jewish reform community, and Monroe Trotter of Boston's National Equal Rights League. Rather than Griffith, the critics discerned the mind of Dixon behind the film, and thus Jane Addams of Hull House in Chicago decried Dixon's film as "both unjust and untrue"; Rabbi Wise raged at the presentation of "the Negro of a generation ago as a foul and murderous beast"; and Francis Hackett, in the pages of the new journal *The New Republic*, wrote of Dixon:

> Dixon corresponds to the yellow journalist . . . he is a yellow clergyman. He is yellow because he recklessly distorts Negro crimes, gives them a disproportionate place in life and colors them dishonestly to inflame the ignorant and credulous. And he is especially yellow, and quite disgustingly and contemptibly yellow, because his perversions are cunningly calculated to flatter the white man and provoke hatred and contempt for the Negro.[10]

And Du Bois, still twenty years from publishing his definitive account of Reconstruction (1935), would add in his editorial in the May 1915 issue of *The Crisis*:

It is sufficient to add that the main incident in the "Clansman" turns on a thinly veiled charge that Thaddeus Stephens, the great abolition statesman, was induced to give the Negroes the right to vote and secretly rejoice in Lincoln's assassination because of his infatuation for a mulatto mistress. Small wonder that a man who can thus brutally falsify history has never been able to do a single piece of literary work that has brought the slightest attention, except when he seeks to capitalize burning race antagonisms.[11]

The critics sought to ban the film before its release in New York and elsewhere;[12] and short of total censure, they pursued cuts from the film of the most grotesque or frightening scenes

They cut out a quote from Lincoln opposing racial equality, though Lincoln had actually spoken the offending words. They censored "Lincoln's solution" at the end of the film, showing blacks deported to Africa. They eliminated some graphic black sexual assaults on white women. And they cut out Gus's castration. (Rogin, 1985, 174)[13]

with some success. Eventually, the detractors were to be overwhelmed by a most practical collaboration between Wilson, Dixon, and Griffith.[14]

In mid-February, Dixon wrote to President Wilson, requesting an audience with his former classmate at Johns Hopkins. Though Wilson was still in mourning at the death of his first wife, he responded positively. Receiving Dixon in the White House, and upon hearing Dixon's excitement about the potential propagandistic power of films, Wilson agreed to a showing of *Birth* in the East Room. On February 18, the film was displayed before the president, members of his family, and some of his cabinet; the next day, following a visit to another chum, Secretary of the Navy Josephus Daniels, Dixon obtained an interview with Edward D. White, the chief justice of the Supreme Court. White was contemptuous of a "moving picture" ("I never saw one in my life and I haven't the slightest curiosity [sic] to see one"), but when he learned the film championed the Klan, he confided to Dixon that he had been himself a Klansman in New Orleans. That evening, White, other members of the Supreme Court, and guests from the House of Representatives and Senate viewed Dixon's project. Dixon recorded his excitement as he "watched the effects of the picture on the crowd of cultured spectators."[15] Wilson, as we have been assured, proclaimed: "It is like writing history with lightning. And my only regret is that it is all so terribly true." And armed with the president's endorsement and the fact of the film's reception by the most eminent jurists and politicians in the country, Dixon (Griffith may have been at the February 19 screening) returned to New York to face off his critics. He succeeded, and on March 3 the film opened in New York. By the end of its first run, in 1917, Schickel estimates the film had grossed close to $60 million (Schickel, 1996, 1281).

BIRTHING A NEW AMERICA

The "reconstruction" with which The Birth of a Nation *is ultimately concerned is the reconstruction of America in 1915.*
                                    —James Chandler

What Griffith had inadvertently served as midwife for was the birth of a new, virile American whiteness, unencumbered by the historical memory of slavery, or being enslaved, undaunted by the spectacle of racial humiliation so suddenly manufactured by the shock of poor white immigrants in the cities, a European war that settled into a slaughter of a generation, and the taunts of the Black giant Jack Johnson. No force in the world was its equal. No moral claim would dare challenge the sovereignty of race right.[16]

The millions of immigrants, largely from what their "betters" thought of as the "inferior stocks" of Europe, had deserted the Old World. Like wild animals fleeing before some cataclysmic disaster, their infestation of America had anticipated the First World War. From its beginnings in August 1914, the scale of the impending disaster mounted: Howard Zinn observes (1995, 351), "In the first three months of the war, almost the entire original British army was wiped out." And by its end, some 10 million had been lost in battle, another 20 million—civilians—dead. If the Old World, the seat of Anglo-Saxon and Western civilization, had such a fragile hold on order and the dignity of life, what could be expected in America, plagued by Europe's genetic debris of Jews, Catholics, Italians, Slavs, etc., and its native-born mongrel races?

One answer was the unsettling specter of Jack Johnson. In 1908, Johnson had defeated Tommy Burns for the heavyweight boxing championship. "[Jack] London depicted the new champion as an 'Ethiopian colossus.' " In the most influential and widely quoted words of London's career, the writer concluded his account of the fight with a racial call to arms (Gilmore, 1975; Streible, 1996, 173). But over the next seven years, Johnson would substantiate his superior prowess by easily defeating the Great White Hope, Jim Jeffries, in 1910, and a string of lesser white opponents. Even more painful to white Americans, Johnson's mocking performances had been filmed.

In the Burns fight, Randy Roberts asserts that Johnson extended the bout into later rounds, aware that fight film audiences would hardly pay to see a short contest but also because he hated Burns (whose prowess was restricted to calling Johnson a "big dog," "cur," or "nigger"). Johnson punished Burns,

> But punishment was not enough. Johnson wanted also to humiliate Burns. He did this verbally. From the very first round Johnson insulted Burns, speaking with an affected English accent, so that "Tommy" became "Tahmy." Mostly what Johnson said was banal . . . In almost every taunt Johnson referred to Burns in the diminutive. It was always "Tommy Boy" or "little Tommy." And always a derisive smile accompanied the words. (Roberts, 1983, 63)

The film of Johnson's fight with Stanley Ketchel in 1909 showed Ketchel's apparent knockdown of the champion. Film audiences stood and cheered, and then:

> a deliberate Johnson lunged across the ring, smashing Ketchel squarely in the mouth and immediately rendering him unconscious. Johnson leaned casually on the ropes, hand on hip, as the referee counted out his victim. (Streible, 1996, 176).

The films were disturbing to representatives from all sectors of white society, particularly so the film of Johnson's defeat of Jeffries. In San Francisco, Mrs. James Crawford, vice president of the California Women's Clubs, wrote to the *Examiner*:

> The negroes are to some extent a childlike race, needing guidance, schooling, and encouragement. We deny them this by encouraging them to believe that they have gained anything by having one of their race as a champion fighter. (Gilmore, 1975, 81)

In Tennessee,

> the *Chattanooga Times* editorialized that it would do white men no good to see a motion pic-
> ture of "a powerful negro knocking a white man about the ring" and that the films would be a
> positive injury to blacks as they would "inspire the ignorant negro with false and pernicious
> ideas as to the physical prowess of his race." (83)

And identical sentiments voiced by governors, ministers, and civic leaders were to be heard
and read all over the country. At first municipal authorities imposed local bans on their exhibition (there were some exceptions, for example, New York, Philadelphia, and Toledo),
and then in 1912, with the encouragement of organizations like the United Society for
Christian Endeavor, the Women's Christian Temperance Society, the press, and such nota-
bles as Theodore Roosevelt, Congress banned fight films in America. Notwithstanding, as
Dan Streible recounts, "The 1910 film . . . became as widely discussed as any single production prior to *The Birth of a Nation*" (Streible, 1996, 193).

Worst of all, however, while his films inflamed the imaginations and aspirations of
Black audiences, Johnson openly consorted with white women. Indeed, he was to marry
four white women in succession. And though Randy Roberts maintains that Johnson's
love-hate relations with white women drove him to an association with white prostitutes,
it was his romantic relationships that brought him his first grief with the law. Johnson's
first white wife, Etta Duryea, committed suicide in 1912; and the mother of his second
white wife, Lucille Cameron (ironically an echo of Dixon's novel), brought charges of abduction against Johnson. Johnson married Lucille in December 1912 and their marriage
became fodder for editorials and letters to the editor in Black and white newspapers; the
cause for threats of lynching (one by Governor Cole Blease of South Carolina); the instigation for the introduction of an antimiscegenation amendment to the Constitution by Representative Seaborn Roddenberry of Georgia, supported by a score of governors; and
several successful state laws banning such marriages (Gilmore, 1975, 106). But a month before the marriage Johnson had been charged by federal authorities with violating a new
law, the Mann Act, for allegedly transporting women across state lines for immoral purposes. The woman in question was a third white woman, Belle Schreiber, a Chicago prosti-
tute and former mistress of Johnson (in his autobiography, *Jack Johnson Is a Dandy*, he
insisted she was his secretary/accountant). The uproar around Johnson now extended to
sports pages and escalated to mailed death threats and public calls for southern white
lynching parties to visit Johnson in New York or Chicago (Gilmore, 1975; Roberts, 1983).
Eventually, to avoid prosecution, Johnson and Lucille fled the United States. Johnson's display of racial insolence was disturbing because he seemed to be impervious by nature and
by his celebrity status to the discipline that controlled more ordinary Black brutes. He also
disturbed because, like Frankenstein's monster, he escaped the confines and purposes of
the original invention. The national myth of the Black rapist of innocent white women had
been employed to patrol Black men for generations and more important, of course, to
mask the reality of white rapists. Black men accused of white rape or even suspected to be
thinking of white rape were lynched or beaten to death. Mobs did the deed but with the as-
surance that numbers merely confirmed moral and social approbation. Their members
pretended to themselves that Black men were cowards and that the white mass of the lynch
crowd signified approbation not fear. Edison's early documentary silents had done their

part in confirming the tribal lore: "The myth of the 'spooked' black fighter, in fact, often appeared in accounts about the first moving pictures" (Streible, 1996, 170). Johnson ruptured whole fragments of the myth, and with a vengeance his fight films documented that terrible truth: he was not only uncowered but contemptuous of his white opponents. In life, moreover, legions of newspaper stories recited that Johnson confirmed the secret fear that white women were transfixed by a *desire* and *allure* of black men: his white wife and white mistresses fawned over him.[17]

While Johnson's challenge to white superiority was public, daunting, and counterintuitive in critical ways, other threats from the inferior races were stealthy and assuring. But Griffith would merge these dissimilar Others in his screenplay. One model for Flora's (*Lil' Sis*) suicide in *Birth* was the killing in 1913 of thirteen-year-old Mary Phagan. "The descendant of an established Piedmont farm family that had lost its land and been reduced first to tenancy and then to wage labor" (MacLean, 1991, 921), Phagan was murdered at the National Pencil Factory in Atlanta, on the day of the Confederate Memorial Day parade. She died, according to the lead prosecutor, "because she wouldn't yield her virtue to the demands of her superintendent" (930). The accused was Leo Frank, a manager in the factory and a northern-born Jew.

Originally there was another suspect: the black factory janitor, Jim Conley. Conley's role, however, was reduced to an accessory after the fact, as testifying against Frank he admitted on the stand that he had helped Frank move Mary's body. But despite a defense strategy that MacLean characterizes as "a virulent racist offence against the only other suspect . . . Jim Conley," class animosity and anti-Semitism superseded negrophobia:

> the concern of elites about the Frank case reflected profound fears about the stability of the social order over which they presided. Time and again, they complained about the spread of "anarchy" and "mob rule" as revealed in the case. "Class hatred was played on" by the prosecutors, Frank's attorney complained in court, "They played on the enmity the poor feel against the wealthy" and encouraged "discontent." A prominent Progressive supporter of Frank, the Reverend C. B. Wilmer, observed that "class prejudice" "was perfectly obvious" at every stage in the case and warned of the dangers of pandering to it. (924, 926)

And in his summation, the prosecutor Hugh Dorsey told the jury: "although he had never mentioned the word *Jew*, once it was introduced he would use it." The Jews "rise to heights sublime," he asserted, "but they also sink to the lowest depths of degradation."[18] Following a nationally publicized four-month trial, Frank was convicted, and sentenced to death. In June 1915, his sentence was commuted to life in prison by Governor Slaton (who then had to declare martial law for self-protection). But on August 16, 1915, Frank was abducted from the Georgia state farm by the "Knights of Mary Phagan," carried to Marietta, Phagan's home town, and lynched (*New York Times*, August 7, 1915).

Many of the cultural signifiers Griffith embedded in *The Birth of a Nation* closely resembled elements from the Phagan-Frank case. In terms of place, Griffith had reconstructed Mary Phagan's Georgia region into the fictive town of Piedmont, and in the process transformed it from a rural redneck region to a center of southern gentry. More strikingly, in his dramatization of Dixon's *The Clansman*, Griffith replaced the novel's double suicide of Mother Lenoir and her ravished daughter, Marion, with Flora's solitary leap. Yet Griffith's Flora, like Mary Phagan in the scenario imagined by Dorsey, had chosen death when faced with rape. And like Flora (impersonated by the attractive Mae Marsh) whom Griffith had fashioned to serve as an innocent icon for whiteness, Mary Phagan had been refashioned by the press for a similar purpose. As Nancy MacLean informs us, the published photographs of Mary Phagan were altered: Phagan's flat nose was Aryanized; her thick eyebrows thinned glamorously; her hair styled beyond the skill of hairdressers to which she had access. In actual life her appearance too closely resembled the notoriously incestuous white poor Appalachians whom eugenicists had campaigned to eliminate from the American gene pool (see Gould, 1981, chap. 5). But in death Phagan's modified self could serve as an emblem of the threat posed by Jews to the white American race; her manufactured innocence and prettiness a proof of race virtue.[19]

> In his film, Griffith had swapped Leo Frank with Gus, the black rapist. And with Gus standing in as Frank's substitute, Griffith imported Jim Conley, the murderer of choice for many of Frank's defenders, past and present.[20] As well, the renegade Gus, in his cowering posture and sneaky simian-like movements, could serve to erase Jack Johnson, the bold, graceful athlete, from the minds of the audience, and Flora's suicidal gesture put the lie to the intolerable ruse that white women would willingly submit to black men. And since a white actor, Walter Long, impersonated Gus in blackface, Griffith was assured of an interpretive mastery of Johnson not otherwise possible. Thus Long's Gus underscored Griffith's racial contempt. After all, Griffith had explained, "On careful weighing of every detail concerned, the decision was made to have no black blood among the principals." As such, Michael Rogin observes, Griffith's Negros [sic] were as bad as he painted them because he painted whites black . . . Griffith allowed a few blacks to act the nigger. But he did not want to let the representation of blackness go. (Rogin, 1985, 181–82)

The character of Gus, providing visual reality to the suppositions around Conley, thus debased Johnson and the threatening racial signature Johnson had come to represent.

Life, they say, does imitate art. And so it occurred on Thanksgiving night in 1915 when William Joseph Simmons and a group of friends met on Stone Mountain outside Atlanta, Georgia, and declared a new beginning, the new Knights of the Ku Klux Klan (MacLean, 1994, 5). Over the next ten years, particularly from 1920 to 1925, the Second Klan enrolled millions, frequently drawing recruits with a showing of *The Birth of a Nation.* To be sure, the Second Klan rode to the rescue of abused wives, communities preyed on by corrupt politicians and exploitative employers, impoverished families, and supporters of Prohibition; but its staple was hatred: blacks, Jews, Catholics, and immigrants.[21]

ARYAN-AMERICAN EXPANSIONISM

While Johnson and Frank were signatures of the presence of a troubling domestic enemy, a potentially degrading strain in the otherwise pure, white soul of the country, the nation's commercial, industrial, and political elites were simultaneously pursuing robustly expansive policies that might secure profit, a preferred national identity, and the American share of world power.

The war just begun in 1914 in Europe, of course, provided Griffith the opportunity to manufacture an allegoric counterpoint for the American Civil War. For Griffith, Europe was the place of origin for the mythical white civilization he held sacred, and just as the present war was proving to be catastrophic, the "war between the states" as white southerners referred to it, had overturned the natural order. And given the substantially European origins of much of his audience, the easy transfer from one war to the other encouraged Griffith to superimpose negrophobia onto antiwar sentiments. He could empirically, i.e., historically, demonstrate the evil of war by giving dramatic realization to its consequences. Moreover, his rhetorical strategy of maintaining that his epic was *not meant to reflect on any race or people of today* was cleverly employed to establish that even with the most delicately contrived fairness, history itself documented black inferiority.

The Birth of a Nation was conceived, realized, and exhibited two years before the American entry into World War I. While it is difficult to determine public opinion on involvement in the European war prior to 1917, Howard Zinn testifies, "The government had to work hard to create its consensus" for war:

> George Creel, a veteran newspaperman, became the government's official propagandist for the war; he set up a Committee on Public Information to persuade Americans the war was right. It sponsored 75,000 speakers, who gave 750,000 four-minute speeches in five thousand American cities and towns. It was a massive effort to excite a reluctant public. (Zinn, 1995, 355)

Notwithstanding, in need of a million enlistments and faced with a mere 73,000 six weeks after the declaration of war, the Congress enacted a draft. The sale of war and other materials to the Allies had transformed the United States—in the form of capital—from a debtor nation to the leading lender nation in the world (a position not relinquished until the War in Vietnam). This was reason enough for American interests to intervene on the side of their new debtors. And as Eric Hobsbawm reports, "Thanks to the flood of American reinforcements and equipment, the Allies recovered, but for a while it looked a close thing" (Hobsbawm, 1994, 29).

For a time, Griffith had been on the side of the angels, but by late 1915 or early 1916, he was preparing to exploit his new reputation as "the world's preeminent director of military spectacle" (Schickel, 1996, 342). Travelling to Britain for the premier of *Intolerance* (1916), Griffith was charmed by the British prime minister, Lloyd George, into producing a war spectacle, *Hearts of the World* (1918).

> Griffith had arrived at the very event that would undo the cultural consensus that had formed his sensibility and informed all his work. But he would emerge from this encounter essentially oblivious to the nature of the war and to the effect it was having on the young generation that bore its brunt. (343)

More and more taken up with his own growing legend, Griffith's resolve to exploit *the ravages of war to the end that war may be held in abhorrence*, evaporated.

Interestingly enough, the first U.S. military intervention on the part of the Allies was not the declaration of war in 1917, but the invasion of Haiti two years earlier. From 1915 to 1934, American marines would occupy Haiti, providing the repressive force necessary for the conversion of Haiti from a semiautonomous nation to an American colony by American financiers, businessmen, and State Department bureaucrats (Schmidt, 1971; Plummer, 1988, 1992). The official rationales for the U.S. invasion were the fear of German influence in Haiti; the security of the Panama Canal; and a concern for order and stability in that country (from 1888 to 1915, ten Haitian presidents had been killed or overthrown (Schmidt, 1971, 42)). On the surface, all of these issues were legitimate, but they could afford no closer scrutiny: for nearly all of Haiti's existence since 1804, the primary source of its destabilization had been the United States (Plummer, 1988, chap. 1). The Haitian Revolution for independence from France (and Britain) had been the second successful rebellion in the New World, but unlike its predecessor, the American Revolution, it had been achieved by slaves (James, 1989). Thus for the first half of the nineteenth century, Haiti was perceived as a threat to American slavery by the plantocrats and the national government they dominated; and in the second half, pliant Haitian governments headed by American-installed presidents had facilitated the conversion of the country into an American treasury.

Beneath the surface, it was American capital that was the central agent fuelling invasion. Roger Farnham was the vice president of the Rockefeller group's National City Bank; Farnham was also vice president of Haiti's central bank, the Banque Nationale, and Haiti's national railway. All these interlocking roles gave Farnham special interests in his additional identity as the principal advisor to the American secretary of state, William Jennings Bryan. Farnham's desire was that Haiti become an American colony, and Bryan's sophistication with respect to Haiti (in 1912 Bryan had commented to John Allen, another American officer to Haiti's Banque Nationale: "Dear me, think of it! Niggers speaking French" (Schmidt, 1971, 48)) forfeited the advantage to Farnham. Farnham was concerned that German (or French) bankers would outmaneuver National City Bank, and he orchestrated American businessmen (the United Fruit Company was advised to resist the lure of plantations until an occupation) and the government into actions that would ensure total American domination of Haiti's economy (the only significant missing element was American control of Haitian customs revenue).

President Wilson, Farnham, and the marines staged a mini-invasion in December 1914, securing $500,000 from the Haitian treasury that was duly installed in the vaults of National City Bank. And in July of 1915, a full-scale invasion took place. Over the next several years, nationalist resistance ("bandits," the American press assured its public) was extirpated; the Haitian military was reorganized into a colonial force; the country's transportation and communications systems were appropriated; and good government (dictatorship, of course) was established. It was all to the good, as in 1918 Robert Lansing (Bryan's successor) wrote to Rear Admiral J. H. Oliver, another American colonial officer (governor of the Virgin Islands):

> The experience of Liberia and Haiti show that the African race is devoid of any capacity for political organization and lack genius for government. Unquestionably there is in them an inherent tendency to revert to savagery and to cast aside the shackles of civilization which are irksome to their physical nature . . . It is that which makes the negro problem practically unsolvable [sic]. (62–63)

Lansing's knowledge of Blacks bears an uncanny resemblance to the written and cinematic images that Wilson, Dixon, and Griffith had transmitted into the new American culture in 1915. *The riot in the Master's Hall . . . a representative furtively takes a bottle of liquor from beneath a book and steals a mouthful . . . a representative with his feet on his desk takes off a shoe, as another, standing in front of him, eating a joint of meat, turns . . .* (Lang, 1994, 110–11). Wilson, Dixon and Griffith had not invented these myths, but they made them accessible to millions, and they made them unforgettable. Wilson, Dixon, and Griffith and their large fraternity of racist intellectuals had supplied a fabulous history, a white history, that portrayed the white as the forever normal, forever real, the race responsible for the order of the world, the race that was the destiny of the species, the true subject of world history and its civilizations.

REPRESSED CONSCIOUSNESS

In the June 1915 issue of *The Crisis*, the NAACP organ, it was reported that the *New York Evening Globe* complained that the very title *The Birth of a Nation* constituted an insult to the achievements of George Washington and Abraham Lincoln: Washington had contributed to the beginnings of the American nation in the Revolutionary War; Lincoln had fought against "the attempt to denationalize a nation."[22] There was, to be sure, some justification for challenging the peculiar chronology to which race hunger drove Dixon and Griffith. But, as we have seen, this criticism merely skimmed along the surface of the film's racial agenda. Griffith's historical memorial posed and deposed, invented and effaced to a purpose. His plots, his stagings, his choice of shots, his editing techniques, and his creation of archetypes were complex declaratives intended to flood the consciousness of his audience. He possessed a certain knowledge of what must be remembered and how, and what was required to make the intolerable past vanish.

In the *Mammy*, the dominant characterization of dark-skinned Black women in *Birth*, Griffith erased two or more centuries of what one Black spokesman decried as white "enforced debauchery." Countless slave women (and white indentured women) had, of course, been sexually used by their so-called masters and other males protected by race and class privilege. The documentation of this depravity, Ida B. Wells insisted, could be readily discovered in the large percentage of mulattos, and she recorded in her autobiography:

> I found that this rape of helpless Negro girls and women, which began in slavery days, still
> continued without let or hindrance, check or reproof from church, state, or press until there
> had been created this race within a race. (Wells, 1970, 70)

Indeed, though Griffith's asexual *Mammy* negated that very possibility, one rationale for the exploitation of black women had been their lewdness, their own sexual appetites, and seductiveness (Jordan, 1994, 56). For white males of the plantocracy and its support strata (overseers, militia, etc.), slave society had been a highly charged sexual hothouse, as Catherine Clinton maintained: "Flesh and blood were an explosive mix in the Old South" (1991, 52).

In Virginia, the heat of the sexual licence granted by slavery had eventually assumed a market function: slave breeding. The Founding fathers, most of them implicated in the slave trade, slave commodity production, or slave ownership, appropriated the American Revolution to gain a monopoly over the trade in slaves. Having already determined that in North America the slave population was uniquely capable of self-production through natural increase, by the end of the eighteenth century Virginian slave owners were engaged in breeding and a domestic commerce in slaves. As a consequence, Catherine Clinton reports, "The number of slaves grew at an annual rate of 2.5 per cent per year for almost sixty years, a phenomenal rate for any population but especially impressive when compared with the net natural decreases of other slave populations in the hemisphere" (53). And Ervin Jordan Jr. found indirect evidence in the 1860 census confirming the account that

> A Union soldier who visited the King William County, Virginia, plantation of a seventy-four-year-old farmer named Anderson Scott in 1864 described it as inhabited by over 150 slaves, many with blue eyes and straight hair . . . the children and grandchildren of Scott who felt little remorse about the incestuous fathering of mulatto children upon his Black daughters and granddaughters. (Jordan, 1994, 56)

Enforced debauchery was thus doubly profitable, producing labor and commodity. And in the 1930s, former slave women provided horrifying testimony of breeding practices and "breedin' niggers" in interviews to Works Progress Administration recorders who were documenting the last era of slavery (Clinton, 1991, 54–55).

Breeding, of course, as a practice and performance, lent greater strength to the proprietary rights of slave owners, eventually acquiring an articulated theory of rights. It was unapologetically Aristotelian. In 1858, J. P. Holcombe told the Virginia State Agricultural Society that the slave "scarcely labors under any personal disability to which we may not find a counterpart in those which attach to those incompetent classes—the minor, the lunatic, and the married woman"; in 1861, Reverend Joseph R. Wilson, of Augusta, Georgia, sermonized that:

> servitude is inherent in the human condition . . . that no household is perfect under the gospel which does not contain all the grades of authority and obedience, from that of husband and wife, down through that of father and son, to that of master and servant,

and James H. Hammond, of South Carolina, submitted to his diary: "I love my family, and they love me. It is my only earthly tie. It embraces my slaves, and there to me the world ends' (Genovese, 1991, 73). And it bespoke an extraordinarily perverse moral obligation:

> George Fitzhugh of Caroline County [Virginia] defended the sexual pursuit of black women as necessary to avoid infecting White womanhood with erotic degeneracy. He praised slavery for allowing slaveowners to "vent their lust harmlessly upon slave women" and contended that slavery protected black women from abuse by black men. (Jordan, 1994, 56)

But notwithstanding Fitzhugh's open conceit, much of white southern lore concerning antebellum society strove mightily to conceal the lure of, the lust for, and the rape of black women. The mammy achieved this masquerade, and the mammy, Cheryl Thurber assures us, was an imagined reality originating in white southern fiction.

> Several recent studies on slavery, notably those by Catherine Clinton, Deborah Gray White, Joan Cashin, Herbert Gutman, and Jacqueline Jones, have found little evidence for real mammies in the ante-bellum period and have even questioned the historical evidence for the existence of mammies in the period immediately after Emancipation. (Thurber, 1992, 88, 93)

On the contrary, in the slaveholders' households, domestic service was usually performed by young Black women. The compelling attractiveness of these Black women was memorialized by nineteenth-century American (and European) painters: Eastman Johnson recorded his father's slaves in Washington, D.C. (*Negro Life at the South*, 1859, later titled *Old Kentucky Home*) and during the Civil War witnessed the arrival of a "contraband" family at an army camp (*A Ride for Liberty—The Fugitive Slaves*, 1862); Richard Ansdell captured the haunting beauty of one Black woman in *Hunted Slaves* (1861); and Winslow Homer's *At the Cabin Door* (1865–66) depicted a handsome young Black woman forlornly watching the forced march of captured Union soldiers.[23] No matter. Griffith's *Mammy*, like her fictional predecessor, displaced the real. She became a stock character among similarly grotesque Black domestic servants in American films (and later television with characters like *Beulah*). And her important actuality in this mutilated historical memory was eventually confirmed when Hattie McDaniel received the first Oscar awarded to a Black for her *mammy* in *Gone with the Wind* (1939).

In the stead of his pretentious claims for *The Birth of a Nation*, Griffith had perfected a genre, what Ed Guerrero has termed the "plantation genre," which would dominate Holly-wood's representation of the Old South of the antebellum, American slavery and its ending, and Blacks for generations (Guerrero, 1993). In this fabulous narrative, the poor whites who had worked and sometimes fought alongside the slaves, and later the free Blacks, disappeared. Their historical complexity and ambiguous race loyalty could not be contained by the genre. In the plantation genre, only two classes were of any importance: the plantocrats and their childlike charges, the Blacks. Prominent white abolitionists, like the fictional Stoneman, were transfigured, as in *The Santa Fe Trail*, into megalomaniacal fanatics like John Brown (Raymond Massey) or Judases (Van Heflin's role as Rader). White southern aristocratic women were infrequently the responsible adults whom Margaret Sullavan constructed in *So Red the Rose* (1935) but more often the irresponsible, childlike, or egotistical materialists so brilliantly portrayed by Bette Davis in *Jezebel* (1938), Vivian Leigh in *Gone with the Wind* (1939), and the actual child, Shirley Temple.

With rare exceptions, the representation of Blacks in American films degraded even further from Griffith's oppositions between the loyal and the brute. Black actors with professional training as doctors (Rex Ingram) and lawyers (Paul Robeson, Clarence Muse) stood in for modern domestics, slaves, and colonized savages; most training themselves as Louise Beavers did for her role as Delilah in *Imitation of Life* (1934) to tie their articulate tongues to the cinematic Black pseudo-speech Griffith popularized in *Birth*. During the silent film era, only the Black independents filmmakers like George and Noble Johnson (Lincoln Motion Pictures), Oscar Micheaux, and a few non-Blacks producing Black-cast films like Norman Film resisted. But their art was largely restricted to the audiences congregated in the all-Black theatre circuit—approximately 500 theatres compared with the 12,000 or more available to the negrophobes in the 1920s.[24]

Griffith was fortunate: his maturing as a filmmaker coincided with that moment during which immigrant haberdashers, junk dealers, and garment kings took command of the movie industry. Their historical memory was of the ghettoes of Europe and the Pale of Settlement; about America they were largely ignorant. Griffith, whose moral and historical sensibility was borrowed from the rulers of the ancien régime of slavery, imagined the American past as the ideologists of slavery had intended it to be remembered, as a race hierarchy. This is precisely what it had not been—a wealthy landed aristocracy had ruled over Black, white, and indigenous labor—but this rule by an oligopoly could only be sustained with the support or indifference of those whose social and political privileges met a bare minimum. Griffith's advantage over his associates in the movie business was that he possessed *some* memory of America even if it was a fraudulent one.

Griffith was for most of his career a journeyman director.[25] Only twenty-five of the more than four hundred films he directed were produced after *Birth* and exceeded one or two reels. And only one or two of the later films (the drenchingly sentimental *Broken Blossoms*, 1919, and *Way Down East*, 1920) have warranted serious critical discussion and only then as the works of the director of *Birth of a Nation*.[26] Six years after completing *Birth*, Griffith was creating an omnibus-like *Orphans of the Storm*. In fact, he never matched the creativity of the great film directors of his era like Sergei Eisenstein or Jean Renoir. Schickel, his most sympathetic biographer, could muster only the following defense:

> Considering the pace of innovation from 1914 to the establishment of the first set of generic conventions for the sound film approximately twenty years later, it is ridiculous to ask one man, no matter how gifted, to partake of them all or even approve of them all, let alone take the lead in establishing them all. Griffith obviously had his limitations and if there are no masterpieces among his last eight films, little innovation and much imitation, only two or three are out-and-out disgraces. (1996, 510)

Mechanics and techniques, as Renoir pointedly remarked about Griffith, are not the issue (597). What had distinguished Griffith was that he extended a fantastic history of America into the most profoundly significant mass media art form prior to television. His timing was accidental but no less determinant since he offered his vision to an audience largely uninformed of America with the collaboration of producers, exhibitors, and financiers equally ignorant of America except as a market.

Together—Griffith (Dixon, Wilson, etc.), his industry cohorts, and his audience—they constituted the social and cultural platform for a robust economic and political agenda. An agenda in the process of seizing domestic and international labor, land, and capital. Under the imprimatur of race destiny, but irrespective of race, the lives and destinies of men and women all over the globe were dealt with as so many marketable assets, as human capital. White patrimony deceived some of the majority of Americans, patriotism and nationalism others, but the more fugitive reality for "white" Americans was the theft they themselves endured and the voracious expropriation of others they facilitated. The table scrap which was their reward was the installation of black inferiority into their shared national culture. It was a paltry dividend, but it still serves.

Cedric J. Robinson may be contacted at the Department of Black Studies, Division of Social Sciences, University of California at Santa Barbara, Santa Barbara, California 93106, USA, telephone +805 893 3800, facsimile +805 893 3597.

NOTES

1. "Confronting Racism," public lecture, Santa Barbara, Calif., January 20, 1997.

2. One earlier treatment was by the British film historian Peter Noble (1948), *The Negro in Film*, and the 1976 publication by Daniel Leab, *From Sambo to Superspade*.

3. In common with most American observers, Cripps employs the term *South* and its derivatives in a fashion that evacuates Blacks, all women, poor whites, and Native Americans from the region. For instance he writes: "The dominance of Southern themes in drama was matched by a Southern literary revival in New York. Even though the hothouse plant that was the Southern mystique could not survive in antique purity in Northern cities, its purveyors moved there." According to this usage, as a historical or social agent the *South* generally refers to a small fraction of the region's population: white ruling, class males, their activities, ideology, interests, and sympathizers.

4. For the academy, see Trumpbour (1989); for art and medicine, see Gilman (1985); for theatre, see Saxton (1990).

5. In the following section, italics are employed to mark titles taken from the continuity script constructed by Robert Lang as published in his (1994) edited volume.

6. Fox, the exception, raised capital from the gentile firm of Halsey, Stuart and Company.

7. See the accounts by the black Civil War veteran Joseph Wilson (1994, original 1887), and Dudley Cornish (1987).

8. The racial mythology of America was supported by eminent American anthropologists like Madison Grant (chair of the New York Zoological Society and a trustee of the American Museum of Natural History): "At the time of the Revolutionary War the settlers in the thirteen Colonies were not only purely Nordic, but also purely Teutonic, a very large majority being Anglo-Saxon in the most limited meaning of that term. The New England settlers in particular came from those counties of England where the blood was almost purely Saxon, Anglian, and Dane" (Grant, 1916, 74).

9. For a host of reviews from the *New York Times*; the *Christian Science Monitor*; Cripps (1977), chap. 2; and Schickel (1996), chap. 10.

10. For Addams and Wise, see "Opinions," in *The Crisis*, May 1915, 19; and for Addams again and Hackett, see Schickel (1996, 283–84).

11. Schickel claims the film, originally titled *The Clansman*, was retitled in early March after "Griffith dropped a love scene between Senator Stoneman and his mulatto mistress and a scene in which a black and a white engaged in a fight" (Schickel, 1996, 282).

12. Ida B. Wells (1970), in Chicago, condemned that city's branch of the NAACP for its failure to prepare properly to resist the exhibition of the film. Wells was a founder of the antilynching campaign in the late nineteenth century, perhaps its most important mobilizer. She was also a founding member of the NAACP in 1909. She left the organization for its lack of radical militancy in opposing lynching, becoming the head of the Negro Fellowship League and a member of Trotter's National Equal Rights League. Both organizations aggressively intervened on the behalf of potential lynch victims.

13. Lang does not believe that the deportation scenes were shot, but he did discover that 'The synopsis submitted to the U.S. Copyright Office on February 8, 1915, includes the comment, "Lincoln's plan of restoring the negroes to Africa was dreamed of only, never carried out," which lends credence to the hypothesis that the film once included at least

an intertitle to this effect' (Lang, 1994, 26). For a fuller discussion of the various alterations of the film, see Janet Staiger (1994).

14. The following tale of Dixon's activities in Washington, D.C., is taken from Rogin (1985, 154); Schickel (1996, 268); and Cook (1962, 529).

15. The three quotes in this paragraph are taken from Cook (1962, 531, 532, and 530, respectively). Wilson later disavowed his endorsement of *Birth* (Schickel, 1996, 298–99).

16. A year after the film's release, Madison Grant (1916, 73) wrote: "The negroes of the United States, while stationary, were not a serious drag on civilization until, in the last century, they were given the rights of citizenship and were incorporated in the body politic."

17. Roberts asserts: "In cartoons, [Johnson's] shaved head was sometimes pictured as the head of a snake, with all the sexual implications that reptile carried . . . Sexuality was the essence of Jack Johnson, the driving force behind his success, and this power was perceived by white females and males" (1983, 74).

18. Dinnerstein (1996). The next year Dorsey was elected governor, serving two terms.

19. Griffith had also considerably altered Dixon's feminist rendering of Elsie Stoneman. The Elsie who in an extended debate concerning slavery had declared to Ben, "I don't care to be absorbed by a mere man" (Dixon, 1905, 127) was transformed into a dependent, filopietic adolescent by Griffith and Lillian Gish.

20. For attempts to prove Conley's guilt, see Dinnerstein (1996); Stephen Goldfarb (1996); and Robert Seitz Frey and Nancy Thompson-Frey (1988).

21. For an apology of the Klan as typically "a social and civic organization, reinvigorating a sense of unity and cohesiveness in community life with its spectacular social events, civic activities and philanthropic works," see Leonard Moore (1990). MacLean responds to "the trend in recent historical writing about the Klan to de-emphasize the racial hatred of its politics and the violence of its practice," by suggesting that "false polarities" (whether the Klan was primarily rural or urban, concerned with local or national politics, consisted of civic crusaders or vigilantes, was populist or racist) conceal the fact that: "It was at once mainstream and extreme, hostile to big business and antagonistic to industrial unions, anti-elitist and hateful of blacks and immigrants, pro–law and order and prone to extralegal violence. If scholars have viewed these attributes as incompatible, Klansmen themselves did not" (MacLean, 1994, xiii).

22. "Opinion," *The Crisis* (June 1915, 70). In 1915, contrary to most recent commentary, much if not most of the criticism of the film targeted Dixon, the intellectual and novelist, and not Griffith, who seemed to be considered merely a moviemaker.

23. Hugh Honour (1989), chap. 3. In the first year or so of the war, Lincoln ordered his officers to treat fugitive blacks as contraband; and to return them to their masters when possible. See Ira Berlin et al. (1993).

24. See Cripps (1977), chap. 3; and Pearl Bowser and Jane Gaines (1993); and J. Ronald Green (1993). For the number of movie houses between 1912 and 1921, see Sklar (1975, 146).

25. Edward Wagenknecht (1975) deflated many of Griffith's claims to have "introduced" to filmmak-

ing "the large or close-up figure," distant views . . . the "switchback," sustained suspense, the "fade out," and restraint in expression. Much of this is not literally true: Griffith had himself been photographed in close-up in films made by others before he became a director (465).

26. Even William Johnson (1976), in his yeoman-like effort to appraise Griffith's Biograph films (some 450 between 1908 and 1913) is forced to acknowledge that Griffith's "basic syntax cannot be read without exceptional care; as to content, even the central diegetic events may be elusive" (Johnson admits to not seeing the "psychological implications" of *A Country Cupid* until his fourth viewing).

REFERENCES

Albright, A. (1993) "Micheaux, Baudeville and Black Cast Film," *Black Film Review*, 7 (4).

Aptheker, H. (1992) *Afro-American History*, New York: Carol.

Berlin, I., B. J. Fields, S. F. Miller, J. P. Reidy, and L. S. Rowland (1993) "The Destruction of Slavery," in I. Berlin, B. J. Fields, S. F. Miller, J. P. Reidy, and L. S. Rowland (eds.) *Slaves No More*, New York: Cambridge University Press.

Bernardi, D. (ed.) (1996) *The Birth of Whiteness: Race and the Emergence of US Cinema*, New Brunswick, N.J.: Rutgers University Press.

Bernhard, V., B. Brandon, E. Fox-Genovese, and T. Perdue (eds.) (1992) *Southern Women*, Columbia: University of Missouri Press.

Black Film Review (1993) "History of Black Film" issue, 7 (4).

Bleser, C. (ed.) (1991) *In Joy and in Sorrow: Women, Family, and Marriage in the Victorian South, 1830–1900*, New York: Oxford University Press.

Bogle, D. (1995) *Toms, Coons, Mulattoes, Mammies & Bucks*, New York: Continuum.

Bowser, P., and J. Gaines (1993) "New Finds/Old Films," *Black Film Review*, 7 (4).

Brownlow, K. (1990) *Behind the Mask of Innocence*, Berkeley: University of California Press.

Chandler, J. (1994) "The Historical Novel Goes to Hollywood: Scott, Griffith, Film Epic Today," in R. Lang (ed.) *The Birth of a Nation*, New Brunswick, N.J.: Rutgers University Press.

Clark, T. (1970) "Introduction," in Thomas Dixon Jr., *The Clansman*, Lexington: University of Kentucky.

Clinton, C. (1991) " 'Southern Dishonor' Flesh, Blood, Race, and Bondage," in C. Bleser (ed.), *In Joy and in Sorrow: Women, Family, and Marriage in the Victorian South, 1830–1900*, New York: Oxford University Press.

Cook, R. (1962) "The Man behind *The Birth of a Nation*," *North Carolina Historical Review*, 39 (October).

Cornish, D. (1987) *The Sable Arm*, Lawrence: University of Kansas.

Cripps, T. (1977) *Slow Fade to Black*, New York: Oxford University.

Diawara, M. (ed.) (1993) *Black American Cinema*, New York: Routledge.

Dinnerstein, L. (1996) "The Fate of Leo Frank," *American Heritage*, 47 (6, October).

Du Bois, W. E. B. (1935) *Black Reconstruction*, New York: S.A. Russell.

Frey, R. S., and N. Thompson-Frey (1988) *The Silent and the Damned*, Lanham: Madison.

Gabler, N. (1988) *An Empire of Their Own*, New York: Crown.

Genovese, E. (1991) " 'Our Family, White and Black': Family and Household in the Southern Slaveholders' World View," in C. Bleser (ed.) *In Joy and in Sorrow: Women, Family, and Marriage in the Victorian South, 1830–1900*, New York: Oxford University Press.

Gibson-Hudson, G. (1993) "The Norman Film Manufacturing Company," *Black Film Review*, 7 (4).

Gilman, S. (1985) "Black Bodies, White Bodies: Toward an Iconography of Female Sexuality in Late Nineteenth-Century Art, Medicine, and Literature," *Critical Inquiry*, 12 (Autumn).

Gilmore, A.-T. (1975) *Bad Nigger! The National Impact of Jack Johnson*, Port Washington: Kennikat.

Goldfarb, S. (1996) "Framed," *American Heritage*, 47 (6, October).

Gould, S. J. (1981) *The MisMeasure of Man*, New York: W.W. Norton.

Grant, M. (1916) *The Passing of the Great Race*, New York: Charles Scribner's Sons.

Green, J. R. (1993) "The Micheaux Style," *Black Film Review*, 7 (4).

Guerrero, E. (1993) *Framing Blackness: The African American Image in Film*, Philadelphia: Temple University Press.

Hobsbawm, E. (1994) *The Age of Extremes*, New York: Vintage.

Honour, H. (1989) *The Image of the Black in Western Art*, Part 1, Cambridge: Harvard University Press.

James, C.L.R. (1989) *The Black Jacobins*, London: Allison and Busby.

Johnson, W. (1976) "Early Griffith: A Wider View," *Film Quarterly*, XXIX (3, Spring).

Jones, E. (1965) *Othello and His Countrymen*, London: Oxford University.

Jordan, E. L., Jr. (1994) "Sleeping with the Enemy: Sex, Black Women, and the Civil War," *The Western Journal of Black Studies*, 18 (2, Summer).

Kirby, J. T. (1978) "D.W. Griffith's Racial Portraiture," *Phylon*, XXXIX (2, June).

Lang, R. (1994) *The Birth of a Nation*, New Brunswick, N.J.: Rutgers University Press.

Low, W. A. and V. Cloft (1981) *Encyclopedia of Black Americans*, New York: McGraw-Hill.

—— (1991) "The Leo Frank Case Reconsidered: Gender and Sexual Politics in the Making of Reactionary Populism," *Journal of American History*, 78 (December).

Moore, L. (1990) "Historical Interpretations of the 1920s Klan: the Traditional View and the Populist Revision," *Journal of Social History*, 24 (2, Winter).

Plummer, B. G. (1988) *Haiti and the Great Powers*, Baton Rouge: Louisiana State University.

—— (1992) *Haiti and the United States*, Athens: University of Georgia.

Quarles, B. (1969) *Black Abolitionists*, New York: Da Capo.

Roach, J. (1992) "Slave Spectacles and Tragic Octoroons: A Cultural Genealogy of Antebellum Performance," *Theatre Survey*, 33 (November).

Roberts, R. (1983) *Papa Jack: Jack Johnson and the Era of White Hopes*, New York: Free Press.

Robinson, C. J. (1997) *Black Movements in America*, New York: Routledge.

—— (1995) "Slavery and the Platonic Origins of Anti-Democracy," *National Political Science Review*, 5.

—— (1983) *Black Marxism*, London: Zed.

Rogin, M. (1985) "The Sword Became a Flashing Vision," in D. W. Griffith (ed.) *The Birth of a Nation, Representations*, 9 (winter).

Saxton, A. (1990) *The Rise and Fall of the White Republic*, London: Verso.

Schickel, R. (1996) *D. W. Griffith: An American Life*, New York: Limelight.

Schmidt, H. (1971) *The United States Occupation of Haiti, 1915–1934*, New Brunswick, N.J.: Rutgers University Press.

Sklar, R. (1975) *Movie-Made America*, New York: Random House.

Staiger, J. (1994) "*The Birth of a Nation*: Reconsidering Its Reception," in R. Lang (ed.) *The Birth of a Nation*, New Brunswick, N.J.: Rutgers University Press.

Streible, D. (1996) "Race and the Reception of Jack Johnson Fight Films," in D. Bernardi (ed.) (1996) *The Birth of Whiteness: Race and the Emergence of US Cinema*, New Brunswick, N.J.: Rutgers University Press.

Thurber, C. (1992) "The Development of the Mammy Image and Mythology," in V. Bernhard, B. Brandon, E. Fox-Genovese, and T. Perdue (eds.) *Southern Women*, Columbia: University of Missouri Press.

Trumpbour, J. (1989) "Binding Them with Science: Scientific Ideologies in the Ruling of the Modern World," in J. Trumpbour (ed.) *How Harvard Rules*, Boston: South End.

Wagenknecht, E. (1975) "Griffith's Biographs," *Films in Review*, XXVI (I, October).

Wells, I. B. (1970) *Crusade for Justice*, Chicago: University of Chicago.

Wilson, J. (1994) *The Black Phalanx*, New York: Da Capo.

Wilson, W. (1908) *A History of the American People*, New York: Harper and Brothers.

Zinn, H. (1995) *A People's History of the United States*, New York: Harper's Perennial.

18

WHAT IS THIS "BLACK" IN BLACK POPULAR CULTURE?

Stuart Hall

I BEGIN WITH A QUESTION: What sort of moment is this in which to pose the question of Black popular culture? These moments are always conjunctural. They have their historical specificity; and although they always exhibit similarities and continuities with the other moments in which we pose a question like this, they are never the same moment. And the combination of what is similar and what is different defines not only the specificity of the moment but the specificity of the question, and therefore the strategies of cultural politics with which we attempt to intervene in popular culture, and the form and style of cultural theory and criticizing that has to go along with such an intermatch. In his important essay "The New Cultural Politics of Difference,"[1] Cornel West offers a genealogy of what this moment is, a genealogy of the present that I find brilliantly concise and insightful. His genealogy follows, to some extent, positions I tried to outline in an article that has become somewhat notorious,[2] but it also usefully maps the moment into an American context and in relation to the cognitive and intellectual philosophical traditions with which it engages.

According to Cornel, the moment, this moment, has three general coordinates. The first is the displacement of European models of high culture, of Europe as the universal subject of culture, and of culture itself in its old Arnoldian reading as the last refuge . . . I nearly said of scoundrels, but I won't say who it is of. At least we know who it was against—culture against the barbarians, against the people rattling the gates as the deathless prose of anarchy flowed away from Arnold's pen. The second coordinate is the emergence of the United States as a world power and, consequently, as the center of global cultural production and circulation. This emergence is both a displacement and a hegemonic shift in the *definition* of culture—a movement from high culture to American mainstream popular culture and its mass-cultural, image-mediated, technological forms. The third coordinate is the decolonization of the third world, culturally marked by the emergence of the decolonized sensibilities. And I read the decolonization of the third world in Frantz Fanon's sense: I include in it the impact of civil rights and Black struggles on the decolonization of the minds of the peoples of the Black diaspora.

Let me add some qualifications to that general picture, qualifications that, in my view, make this present moment a very distinctive one in which to ask the question about Black popular culture. First, I remind you of the ambiguities of that shift from Europe to America, since it includes America's ambivalent relationship to European high culture and the ambiguity of America's relationship to its own internal ethnic hierarchies. Western Europe did not have, until recently, any ethnicity at all. Or didn't recognize it had any. America has always had a series of ethnicities, and consequently, the construction of ethnic hierarchies has always defined its cultural politics. And, of course, silenced and unacknowledged, the fact of American popular culture itself, which has always contained within it, whether silenced or not, Black American popular vernacular traditions. It may be hard to remember that, when viewed from outside of the United States, American mainstream popular culture has always involved certain traditions that could only be attributed to Black cultural vernacular traditions.

The second qualification concerns the nature of the period of cultural globalization in progress now. I hate the term "the global postmodern," so empty and sliding a signifier that it can be taken to mean virtually anything you like. And, certainly, Blacks are as ambiguously placed in relation to postmodernism as they were in relation to high modernism: even when denuded of its wide-European, disenchanted Marxist, French intellectual provenance and scaled down to a more modest descriptive status, postmodernism remains extremely unevenly developed as a phenomenon in which the old center/peripheries of high modernity consistently reappear. The only places where one can genuinely experience the postmodern ethnic cuisine are Manhattan and London, not Calcutta. And yet it is impossible to refuse "the global postmodern" entirely, insofar as it registers certain stylistic shifts in what I want to call the cultural dominant. Even if postmodernism is not a new cultural epoch, but only modernism in the streets, that, in itself, represents an important shifting of the terrain of culture toward the popular—toward popular practices, toward everyday practices, toward local narratives, toward the decentering of old hierarchies and the grand narratives. This decentering or displacement opens up new spaces of contestation and affects a momentous shift in the high culture of popular culture relations, thus presenting us with a strategic and important opportunity for intervention in the popular cultural field.

Third, we must bear in mind postmodernism's deep and ambivalent fascination with difference—sexual difference, cultural difference, racial difference, and, above all, ethnic difference. Quite in opposition to the blindness and hostility that European high culture evidenced on the whole toward ethnic difference—its inability even to speak ethnicity when it was so manifestly registering its effects—there's nothing that global postmodernism loves better than a certain kind of difference: a touch of ethnicity, a taste of the exotic, as we say in England, "a bit of the other" (which in the United Kingdom has a sexual as well as an ethnic connotation). Michele Wallace was quite right, in her seminal essay "Modernism, Postmodernism and the Problem of the Visual in Afro-American Culture,"[3] to ask whether this reappearance of a proliferation of difference, of a certain kind of ascent of the global postmodern, isn't a repeat of that "now you see it, now you don't" game that modernism once played with primitivism, to ask whether it is not once again achieved at the expense of the vast silencing about the West's fascination with the bodies of Black men and women of other ethnicities. And we must ask about that continuing silence within postmodernism's shifting terrain, about whether the forms of licensing of the gaze that this proliferation of difference invites and allows, at the same time as it disavows, is not really, along with Benetton and the mixed male models of the face, a kind of difference that doesn't make a difference of any kind.

Hal Foster writes—Wallace quotes him in her essay—"the primitive is a modern problem, a crisis in cultural identity"[4]—hence, the modernist construction of primitivism, the fetishistic recognition and disavowal of the primitive difference. But this resolution is only a repression; delayed into our political unconscious, the primitive returns uncannily at the moment of its apparent political eclipse. This rupture of primitivism, managed by modernism, becomes another postmodern event. That managing is certainly evident in the difference that may not make a difference, which marks the ambiguous appearance of ethnicity at the heart of global postmodernism. But it cannot be only that. For we cannot forget how cultural life, above all in the West, but elsewhere as well, has been transformed in our lifetimes by the voicing of the margins.

Within culture, marginality, though it remains peripheral to the broader mainstream, has never been such a productive space as it is now. And that is not simply the opening within the dominant of spaces that those outside it can occupy. It is also the result of the cultural politics of difference, of the struggles around difference, of the production of new identities, of the appearance of new subjects on the political and cultural stage. This is true not only in regard to race, but also for other marginalized ethnicities, as well as around feminism and around sexual politics in the gay and lesbian movement, as a result of a new kind of cultural politics. Of course, I don't want to suggest that we can counterpose some easy sense of victories won to the eternal story of our own marginalization—I'm tired of those two continuous grand counternarratives. To remain within them is to become trapped in that endless either/or, either total victory or total incorporation, which almost never happens in cultural politics, but with which cultural critics always put themselves to bed.

What we are talking about is the struggle over cultural hegemony, which is these days waged as much in popular culture as anywhere else. That high/popular distinction is precisely what the global postmodern is displacing. Cultural hegemony is never about pure victory or pure domination (that's not what the term means); it is never a zero-sum cultural game; it is always about shifting the balance of power in the relations of culture; it is always about changing the dispositions and the configurations of cultural power, not getting out of it. There is a kind of "nothing ever changes, the system always wins" attitude, which I read as the cynical protective shell that, I'm sorry to say, American cultural critics frequently wear, a shell that sometimes prevents them from developing cultural strategies that can make a difference. It is as if, in order to protect themselves against the occasional defeat, they have to pretend they can see right through everything—and it's just the same as it always was.

Now, cultural strategies that can make a difference, that's what I'm interested in—those that can make a difference and can shift the dispositions of power. I acknowledge that the spaces "won" for difference are few and far between, that they are very carefully policed and regulated. I believe they are limited. I know, to my cost, that they are grossly underfunded, that there is always a price of incorporation to be paid when the cutting edge of difference and transgression is blunted into spectacularization. I know that what replaces invisibility is a kind of carefully regulated, segregated visibility. But it does not help simply to name-call it "the same." That name-calling merely reflects the particular model of cultural politics to which we remain attached, precisely, the zero-sum game—our model replacing their model, our identities in place of their identities—what Antonio Gramsci called culture as a once and for all "war of maneuver," when, in fact, the only game in town worth playing is the game of cultural "wars of position."

Lest you think, to paraphrase Gramsci, my optimism of the will has now completely outstripped my pessimism of the intellect, let me add a fourth element that comments on the moment. For, if the global postmodern represents an ambiguous opening to difference and to the margins and makes a certain kind of decentering of the Western narrative a likely possibility, it is matched, from the very heartland of cultural politics, by the backlash: the aggressive resistance to difference; the attempt to restore the canon of Western civilization; the assault, direct and indirect, on multiculturalism; the return to grand narratives of history, language, and literature (the three great supporting pillars of national identity and national culture); the defense of ethnic absolutism, of a cultural racism that has marked the Thatcher and the Reagan eras; and the new xenophobias that are about to overwhelm fortress Europe. The last thing to do is read me as saying the cultural dialectic is finished. Part of the problem is that we have forgotten what sort of space the space of popular culture is. And Black popular culture is not exempt from that dialectic, which is historical, not a matter of bad faith. It is therefore necessary to deconstruct the popular once and for all. There is no going back to an innocent view of what it consists of.

Popular culture carries that affirmative ring because of the prominence of the word "popular." And, in one sense, popular culture always has its base in the experiences, the pleasures, the memories, the traditions of the people. It has connections with local hopes and local aspirations, local tragedies and local scenarios that are the everyday practices and the everyday experiences of ordinary folks. Hence, it links with what Mikhail Bakhtin calls "the vulgar"—the popular, the informal, the underside, the grotesque. That is why it has always been counterposed to elite or high culture, and is thus a site of alternative traditions. And that is why the dominant tradition has always been deeply suspicious of it, quite rightly. They suspect that they are about to be overtaken by what Bakhtin calls "the carnivalesque." This fundamental mapping of culture between the high and the low has been charted into four symbolic domains by Peter Stallybrass and Allon White in their important book *The Politics and Poetics of Transgression*. They talk about the mapping of high and low in psychic forms, in the human body, in space, and in the social order.[5] And they discuss the high/low distinction as a fundamental basis to the mechanisms of ordering and of sense making in European and other cultures despite the fact that the contents of what is high and what is low change from one historical moment to another.

The important point is the ordering of different aesthetic morals, social aesthetics, the orderings of culture that open up culture to the play of power, not an inventory of what is high versus what is low at any particular moment. That is why Gramsci, who has a side of common sense on which, above all, cultural hegemony is made, lost, and struggled over, gave the question of what he called "the national popular" such strategic importance. The role of the "popular" in popular culture is to fix the authenticity of popular forms, rooting them in the experiences of popular communities from which they draw their strength, allowing us to see them as expressive of a particular subordinate social life that resists its being constantly made over as low and outside.

However, as popular culture has historically become the dominant form of global culture, so it is at the same time the scene, par excellence, of commodification, of the industries where culture enters directly into the circuits of a dominant technology—the circuits of power and capital. It is the space of homogenization where stereotyping and the formulaic mercilessly process the material and experiences it draws into its web, where control over narratives and representations passes into the hands of the established cultural bureaucracies, sometimes without a murmur. It is rooted in popular experience and available for expropriation at one and the same time. I want to argue that this is necessarily and inevitably so. And this goes for Black popular culture as well. Black popular culture, like all popular cultures in the modern world, is bound to be contradictory, and this is not because we haven't fought the cultural battle well enough.

By definition, Black popular culture is a contradictory space. It is a sight of strategic contestation. But it can never be simplified or explained in terms of the simple binary oppositions that are still habitually used to map it out: high and low; resistance versus incorporation; authentic versus inauthentic; experiential versus formal; opposition versus homogenization. There are always positions to be won in popular culture, but no struggle can capture popular culture itself for our side or theirs. Why is that so? What consequences does this have for strategies of intervention in cultural politics? How does it shift the basis for black cultural criticism?

However deformed, incorporated, and inauthentic are the forms in which Black people and black communities and traditions appear and are represented in popular culture, we continue to see, in the figures and the repertoires on which popular culture draws, the experiences that stand behind them. In its expressivity, its musicality, its orality, in its rich, deep, and varied attention to speech, in its inflections toward the vernacular and the local, in its rich production of counternarratives, and above all, in its metaphorical use of the musical vocabulary, Black popular culture has enabled the surfacing, inside the mixed and contradictory modes even of some mainstream popular culture, of elements of a discourse that is different—other forms of life, other traditions of representation.

I do not propose to repeat the work of those who have devoted their scholarly, critical, and creative lives to identifying the distinctiveness of these diasporic traditions, to exploring their modes and the historical experiences and memories they encode. I say only three inadequate things about these traditions, since they are germane to the point I want to develop. First, I ask you to note how, within the Black repertoire, *style*—which mainstream cultural critics often believe to be the mere husk, the wrapping, the sugar coating on the pill—has become *itself* the subject of what is going on. Second, mark how, displaced from a logocentric world—where the direct mastery of cultural modes meant the mastery of writing, and hence, both of the criticism of writing (logocentric criticism) and the deconstruction of writing—the people of the Black diaspora have, in opposition to all of that, found the deep form, the deep structure of their cultural life in music. Third, think of how these cultures have used the body—as if it was, and it often was, the only cultural capital we had. We have worked on ourselves as the canvases of representation.

There are deep questions here of cultural transmission and inheritance, and of the complex relations between African origins and the irreversible scatterings of the diaspora, questions I cannot go into. But I do believe that these repertoires of Black popular culture, which, since we were excluded from the cultural mainstream, were often the only performative spaces we had left, were overdetermined from at least two directions: they were partly determined from their inheritances; but they were also critically determined by the diasporic conditions in which the connections were forged. Selective appropriation, incorporation, and rearticulation of European ideologies, cultures, and institutions, alongside an African heritage—this is Cornel West again—led to linguistic innovations in rhetorical stylization of the body, forms of occupying an alien social space, heightened expressions, hairstyles, ways of walking, standing, and talking, and a means of constituting and sustaining camaraderie and community.

The point of underlying overdetermination—Black cultural repertoires constituted from two directions at once—is perhaps more subversive than you think. It is to insist that in black popular culture, strictly speaking, ethnographically speaking, there are no pure forms at all. Always these forms are the product of partial synchronization, of engagement across cultural boundaries, of the confluence of more than one cultural tradition, of the negotiations of dominant and subordinate positions, of the subterranean strategies of recoding and transcoding, of critical signification, of signifying. Always these forms are impure, to some degree hybridized from a vernacular base. Thus, they must always be heard, not simply as the recovery of a lost dialogue bearing clues for the production of new musics (because there is never any going back to the old in a simple way), but as what they are—adaptations, molded to the mixed, contradictory, hybrid spaces of popular culture. They are not the recovery of something pure that we can, at last, live by. In what Kobena Mercer calls the necessity for a diaspora aesthetic, we are obliged to acknowledge they are what the modern is.

It is this mark of difference *inside* forms of popular culture—which are by definition contradictory and which therefore appear as impure, threatened by incorporation or exclusion—that is carried by the signifier "Black" in the term "Black popular culture." It has come to signify the Black community, where these traditions were kept, and whose struggles survive in the persistence of the Black experience (the historical experience of Black people in the diaspora), of the Black aesthetic (the distinctive cultural repertoires out of which popular representations were made), and of the Black counternarratives we have struggled to voice. Here, Black popular culture returns to the ground I defined earlier. "Good" Black popular culture can pass the test of authenticity—the reference to Black experience and to Black expressivity. These serve as the guarantees in the determination of which black popular culture is right on, which is ours and which is not.

I have the feeling that, historically, nothing could have been done to intervene in the dominated field of mainstream popular culture, to try to win some space there, without the strategies through which those dimensions were condensed onto the signifier "Black." Where would we be, as bell hooks once remarked, without a touch of essentialism? Or, what Gayatri Spivak calls strategic essentialism, a necessary moment? The question is whether we are any longer in that moment, whether that is still a sufficient basis for the strategies of new interventions. Let me try to set forth what seem to me to be the weaknesses of this essentializing moment and the strategies, creative and critical, that flow from it.

This moment essentializes differences in several senses. It sees difference as "their traditions versus ours," not in a positional way, but in a mutually exclusive, autonomous, and self-sufficient one. And it is therefore unable to grasp the dialogic strategies and hybrid forms essential to the diaspora aesthetic. A movement beyond this essentialism is not an aesthetic or critical strategy without a cultural politics, without a marking of difference. It is not simply rearticulation and reappropriation for the sake of it. What it evades is the essentializing of difference into two mutually opposed either/ors. What it does is to move us into a new kind of cultural positionality, a different logic of difference. To encapsulate what Paul Gilroy has so vividly put on the political and cultural agenda of Black politics in the United Kingdom: Blacks in the British diaspora must, at this historical moment, refuse the binary Black *or* British. They must refuse it because the "or" remains the site of *constant contestation* when the aim of the struggle must be, instead, to replace the "or" with the potentiality or the possibility of an "and." That is the logic of coupling rather than the logic of a binary opposition. You can be Black *and* British, not only because that is a necessary position to take in 1992, but because even those two terms, joined now by the coupler "and" instead of opposed to one another, do not exhaust all of our identities. Only some of our identities are sometimes caught in that particular struggle.

The essentializing moment is weak because it naturalizes and dehistoricizes difference, mistaking what is historical and cultural for what is natural, biological, and genetic. The moment the signifier "Black" is torn from its historical, cultural, and political embedding and lodged in a biologically constituted racial category, we valorize, by inversion, the very ground of the racism we are trying to deconstruct. In addition, as always happens when we naturalize historical categories (think about gender and sexuality), we fix that signifier outside of history, outside of change, outside of political intervention. And once it is fixed, we are tempted to use "Black" as sufficient in itself to guarantee the progressive character of the politics we fight under the banner—as if we don't have any other politics to argue about except whether something's Black or not. We are tempted to display that signifier as a device which can purify the impure, bring the straying brothers and sisters who don't know what they ought to be doing into line, and police the boundaries—which are of course political, symbolic, and positional boundaries—as if they were genetic. For which, I'm sorry to say, read "jungle fever"—as if we can translate from nature to politics using a racial category to warrant the politics of a cultural text and as a line against which to measure deviation.

Moreover, we tend to privilege experience itself, as if Black life is lived experience outside of representation. We have only, as it were, to express what we already know we are. Instead, it is only through the way in which we represent and imagine ourselves that we come to know how we are constituted and who we are. There is no escape from the politics of representation, and we cannot wield "how life really is out there" as a kind of test against which the political rightness or wrongness of a particular cultural strategy or text can be measured. It will not be a mystery to you that I think that "Black" is none of these things in reality. It is not a category of essence and, hence, this way of understanding the floating signifier in Black popular culture now will not do.

There is, of course, a very profound set of distinctive, historically defined Black experiences that contribute to those alternative repertoires I spoke about earlier. But it is to the diversity, not the homogeneity, of Black experience that we must now give our undivided creative attention. This is not simply to appreciate the historical and experiential differences within and between communities, regions, country and city, across national cultures, between diasporas, but also to recognize the other kinds of difference that place, position, and locate Black people. The point is not simply that, since our racial differences do not constitute all of us, we are always different, negotiating different kinds of differences—of gender, of sexuality, of class. It is also that these antagonisms refuse to be neatly aligned; they are simply not reducible to one another; they refuse to coalesce around a single axis of differentiation. We are always in negotiation, not with a single set of oppositions that place us always in the same relation to others, but with a series of different positionalities. Each has for us its point of profound subjective identification. And that is the most difficult thing about this proliferation of the field of identities and antagonisms: they are often dislocating in relation to one another.

Thus, to put it crudely, certain ways in which Black men continue to live out their counteridentities as Black masculinities and replay those fantasies of Black masculinities in the theaters of popular culture are, when viewed from along other axes of difference, the very masculine identities that are oppressive to women, that claim visibility for their hardness only at the expense of the vulnerability of Black women and the feminization of gay Black men. The way in which a transgressive politics in one domain is constantly sutured and stabilized by reactionary or unexamined politics in another is only to be explained by this continuous cross-dislocation of one identity by another, one structure by another. Dominant ethnicities are always underpinned by a particular sexual economy, a particular figured masculinity, a particular class identity. There is no guarantee, in reaching for an essentialized racial identity of which we think we can be certain, that it will always turn out to be mutually liberating and progressive on all the other dimensions. It *can* be won. There *is* a politics there to be struggled for. But the invocation of a guaranteed Black experience behind it will not produce that politics. Indeed, the plurality of antagonisms and differences that now seek to destroy the unity of Black politics, given the complexities of the structures of subordination that have been formed by the way in which we were inserted into the Black diaspora, is not at all surprising.

These are the thoughts that drove me to speak, in an unguarded moment, of the end of the innocence of the Black subject or the end of the innocent notion of an essential Black subject. And I want to end simply by reminding you that this end is also a beginning. As Isaac Julien said in an interview with bell hooks in which they discussed his new film, *Young Soul Rebels*, his attempt in his own work to portray a number of different racial bodies, to constitute a range of different Black subjectivities, and to engage with the positionalities of a number of different kinds of Black masculinities:

> . . . blackness as a sign is never enough. What does that black subject do, how does it act, how does it think politically . . . being black isn't really good enough for me: I want to know what your cultural politics are.[6]

I want to end with two thoughts that take the point back to the subject of popular culture. The first is to remind you that popular culture, commodified and stereotyped as it often is, is not at all, as we sometimes think of it, the arena where we find who we really are, the truth of our experience. It is an arena that is *profoundly* mythic. It is a theater of popular desires, a theater of popular fantasies. It is where we discover and play with the identifications of ourselves, where we are imagined, where we are represented, not only to the audiences out there who do not get the message, but to ourselves for the first time. As Freud said, sex (and representation) mainly takes place in the head. Second, though the terrain of the popular looks as if it is constructed with single binaries, it is not. I reminded you about the importance of the structuring of cultural space in terms of high and low, and the threat of the Bakhtinian carnivalesque. I think Bakhtin has been profoundly misread. The carnivalesque is not simply an upturning of two things which remain locked within their oppositional frameworks; it is also crosscut by what Bakhtin calls the dialogic.

I simply want to end with an account of what is involved in understanding popular culture, in a dialogic rather than in a strictly oppositional way, from *The Politics and Poetics of Transgression* by Stallybrass and White:

A recurrent pattern emerges: the "top" attempts to reject and eliminate the "bottom" for reasons of prestige and status, only to discover, not only that it is in some way frequently dependent upon the low-Other . . . but also that the top *includes* that low symbolically, as a primary eroticized constituent of its own fantasy life. The result is a mobile, conflictual fusion of power, fear, and desire in the construction of subjectivity: a psychological dependence upon precisely those others which are being rigorously opposed and excluded at the social level. It is for this reason that what is socially peripheral is so frequently *symbolically* central . . .[7]

NOTES

1. Cornel West, "The New Cultural Politics of Difference," in *Out There: Marginalization and Contemporary Cultures*, ed. Russell Ferguson et al. (Cambridge: MIT Press in association with the New Museum of Contemporary Art, 1990), 19–36.

2. Stuart Hall, "New Ethnicities," *Black Film/British Cinema, ICA Document 7*, ed. Kobena Mercer (London: Institute of Contemporary Arts, 1988), 27–31.

3. Michele Wallace, "Modernism, Postmodernism and the Problem of the Visual in Afro-American Culture," in *Out There: Marginalization and Contemporary Cultures*, 39–50.

4. Hal Foster, *Recodings: Art, Spectacle, and Cultural Politics* (Port Townsend, Wash.: Bay Press, 1985), 204.

5. Peter Stallybrass and Allon White, *The Politics and Poetics of Transgression* (Ithaca, N.Y.: Cornell University Press, 1986), 3.

6. bell hooks. "States of Desire" (interview with Isaac Julien), *Transition* 1, no. 3, 175.

7. Stallybrass and White, *The Politics and Poetics of Transgression*, 5.

19

DYES AND DOLLS

Multicultural Barbie and the Merchandising of Difference

Ann duCille

The white missionaries who came to Saint Aug's from New England were darling to us. They gave Bessie and me these beautiful china dolls that probably were very expensive. Those dolls were white, of course. You couldn't get a colored doll like that in those days. Well, I loved mine, just the way it was, but do you know what Bessie did? She took an artist's palette they had also given us and sat down and mixed the paints until she came up with a shade of brown that matched her skin. Then she painted that white doll's face! None of the white missionaries ever said a word about it. Mama and Papa just smiled.

—Sarah Delany

This is my doll story (because every black journalist who writes about race gets around to it sometime). Back when I started playing with Barbie, there were no Christies (Barbie's black friend, born in 1968) or black Barbies (born in 1980, brown plastic poured into blond Barbie's mold). I had two blonds, which I bought with Christmas money from girls at school. I cut off their hair and dressed them in African-print fabric. They lived together (polygamy, I guess) with a black G.I. Joe bartered from the Shepp boys, my downstairs neighbors. After an "incident" at school (where all of the girls looked like Barbie and none of them looked like me). I galloped down our stairs with one Barbie, her blond head hitting each spoke of the banister, thud, thud, thud. And galloped up the stairs, thud, thud, thud, until her head popped off, lost to the graveyard behind the stairwell. Then I tore off each limb, and sat on the stairs for a long time twirling the torso like a baton.

—Lisa Jones

Growing up in the 1950s, in the shadow of the Second World War, it was natural for children—including little Black children like my two brothers and me—to want to play war, to mimic what we heard on the radio, what we watched in black and white on our brand new floor model Motorola. In these war games, everyone wanted to be the Allied troops—the fearless, conquering white male heroes who had made the world safe for democracy, yet again, and saved us all from yellow peril. No one, of course, wanted to play the enemy—who most often was not the Germans or the Italians but the Japanese. So the enemy became or, more rightly, remained invisible, lurking in bushes we shot at with sticks we pretended were rifles and stabbed at with make-believe bayonets. "Take that," we shouted, liberally peppering our verbal assaults with racial epithets. "And that! And that!" It was all in fun—our venom and vigor. All's fair in wars of words. We understood little of what we said and nothing of how much our child's play reflected the sentiments of a nation that even in its finer, prewar moments had not embraced as citizens its Asian immigrants or claimed as countrymen and women their American-born offspring.

However naively imitative, our diatribe was interrupted forever one summer afternoon by the angry voice of our mother, chastising us through the open window. "Stop that," she said. "Stop that this minute. It's not nice. You're talking about the Japanese. *Japanese*, do you understand? And don't let me ever hear you call them anything else." In the lecture that accompanied dinner that evening, we were made to understand not the history of Japanese-Americans, the injustice of internment, or the horror of Hiroshima, but simply that there were real people behind the names we called; that name-calling always hurts somebody, always undermines someone's humanity. Our young minds were led on the short journey from "Jap" to "nigger"; and if we were too young then to understand the origins and fine points of all such pejoratives, we were old enough to know firsthand the pain of one of them.

I cannot claim that this early experience left me free of prejudice, but it did assist me in growing up at once aware of my own status as "different" and conscious of the exclusion of others so labeled. It is important to note, however, that my sense of my own difference was affirmed and confirmed not simply by parental intervention but also by the unrelenting sameness of the tiny, almost exclusively white town in which I was raised. There in the country confines of East Bridgewater, Massachusetts, the adults who surrounded me (except for my parents) were all white, as were the teachers who taught me, the authors who thrilled me (and instilled in me a love of literature), and the neighborhood children who called me nigger one moment and friend the next. And when my brothers and I went our separate ways into properly gendered spheres, the dolls I played with—like almost everything else about my environment—were also white: Betsy Wetsy, Tiny Tears, and Patty Play Pal.

It seems remarkable to me now, as I remember these childish things long since put away, that, for all the daily reminders of my Blackness, I did not take note of its absence among the rubber-skin pinkness of Betsy Wetsy, the bald-headed whiteness of Tiny Tears, and the blue-eyed blondness of Patty Play Pal. I was never tempted like Elizabeth Delany to paint the dolls I played with brown like me or to dress them in African-print fabric like Lisa Jones. (Indeed, I had no notion of such fabrics and little knowledge of the "dark continent" from which they came.) Caught up in fantasy, completely given over to the realm of make-believe, for most of my childhood I neither noticed nor cared that the dolls I played with did not look like me. The make-believe world to which I willingly surrendered more than just my disbelief was thoroughly and profoundly white. That is to say, the "me" I invented, the "I" I imagined, the Self I daydreamed in technicolor fantasies was no more Black like me than the dolls I played with. In the fifties and well into the sixties of my childhood, the Black Other who was my Self, much like the enemy Other who was the foreign body of our war games, could only be imagined as faceless, far away, and utterly unfamiliar.

As suggested by my title, I am going to use the figure of multicultural Barbie to talk about the commodification of race and gender difference. I wanted to back into the present topic, however, into what I have to say about Barbie as a gendered, racialized icon of contemporary commodity culture, by reaching into the past—into the admittedly contested terrain of the personal—to evoke the ideological work of child's play. More than simple instruments of pleasure and amusement, toys and games play crucial roles in helping children determine what is valuable in and around them. Dolls in particular invite children to replicate them, to imagine themselves in their dolls' images. What does it mean, then, when little girls are given dolls to play with that in no way resemble them? What did it mean for me that I was nowhere in the toys I played with?

If the Japan and the Africa of my youth were beyond the grasp (if not the reach) of my imagination, children today are granted instant global gratification in their play—immediate, hands-on access to both Self and Other. Or so we are told by many of the leading fantasy manufacturers—Disney, Hasbro, and Mattel, in particular—whose contributions to multicultural education include such playthings as Aladdin (movie, video, and dolls), G.I. Joe (male "action figures" in Black and white), and Barbie (now available in a variety of colors and ethnicities). Disneyland's river ride through different nations, like Mattel's Dolls of the World Collection, instructs us that "It's a Small World After All." Those once distant lands of Africa, Asia, Australia, and even the Arctic regions of the North Pole (yes, Virginia, there is an Eskimo Barbie) are now as close to home as the local Toys "R" Us and FAO Schwarz. And lo and behold, the inhabitants of these foreign lands—from Disney's Princess Jasmine to Mattel's Jamaican Barbie—are just like us, dye-dipped versions of archetypal white American beauty. It is not only a small world after all, but, as the Grammy award–winning theme from *Aladdin* informs us, "it's a whole new world."

Many of the major toy manufacturers have taken on a global perspective, a kind of nearsightedness that constructs this whole new world as small and cultural difference as consumable. Perhaps nowhere is this universalizing myopia more conspicuous than in the production, marketing, and consumption of Barbie dolls. By Mattel's reckoning, Barbie enjoys 100 percent brand-name recognition among girls ages three to ten, 96 percent of whom own at least one doll, with most owning an average of eight. Five years ago, as Barbie turned thirty, *Newsweek* noted that nearly 500 million Barbies had been sold, along with 200 million G.I. Joes—"enough for every man, woman, and child in the United States and Europe" (Kantrowitz 59–60). Those figures have increased dramatically in the past five years, bringing the current worldwide Barbie population to 800 million. In 1992 alone, $1 billion worth of Barbies and accessories were sold. Last year, Barbie dolls sold at an average of one million per week, with overall sales exceeding the $1 billion all-time high set the year before. As the *Boston Globe* reported on the occasion of Barbie's thirty-fifth birthday on March 9, 1994, nearly two Barbie dolls are sold every second somewhere in the world; about 50 percent of the dolls sold are purchased here in the United States (Dembner 16).

The current Barbie boom may be in part the result of new, multiculturally oriented developments both in the dolls and in their marketing. In the fall of 1990, Mattel, Inc. announced a new marketing strategy to boost its sales: the corporation would "go ethnic" in its advertising by launching an ad campaign for the Black and Hispanic versions of the already popular doll. Despite the existence of Black, Asian, and Latina Barbies, prior to the fall of 1990 Mattel's print and TV ads featured only white dolls. In what *Newsweek* described as an attempt to capitalize on ethnic spending power, Mattel began placing ads for multicultural

Barbies in such Afrocentric publications as *Essence* magazine and on such Latin-oriented shows as *Pepe Plata* after market research revealed that most Black and Hispanic consumers were unaware of the company's ethnic dolls. This targeted advertising was a smart move, according to the industry analysts cited by *Newsweek*, because "Hispanics buy about $170 billion worth of goods each year, [and] blacks spend even more." Indeed, sales of Black Barbie dolls reportedly doubled in the year following this new ethnically oriented ad campaign.[1] But determined to present itself as politically correct as well as financially savvy, Mattel was quick to point out that ethnic audiences, who are now able to purchase dolls who look like them, also have profited from the corporation's new marketing priorities. Barbie is a role model for all of her owners, according to product manager Deborah Mitchell, herself an African American. "Barbie allows little girls to dream," she asserted—to which the *Newsweek* reporter added (seemingly without irony): "now, ethnic Barbie lovers will be able to dream in their own image" (Berkwitz 48).

Dream in their own image? The *Newsweek* columnist inadvertently put his finger on precisely what is so troubling to many parents, feminist scholars, and cultural critics about Barbie and dolls like her. Such toys invite, inspire, and even demand a potentially damaging process not simply of imagining but of interpellation. When little girls fantasize themselves into the conspicuous consumption, glamour, perfection, and, some have argued, anorexia of Barbie's world, it is rarely, if ever, "in their own image that they dream."[2] Regardless of what color dyes the dolls are dipped in or what costumes they are adorned with, the image they present is of the same mythically thin, long-legged, luxuriously haired, buxom beauty. And while Mattel and other toy manufacturers may claim to have the best interests of ethnic audiences in mind in peddling their integrated wares, one does not have to be a cynic to suggest that profit remains the motivating factor behind this merchandising of difference.[3]

Far from simply playing with the sixty or so dolls I have acquired in the past year, then, I take them very seriously. In fact, I regard Barbie and similar dolls as Louis Althusser might have regarded them: as objects that do the dirty work of patriarchy and capitalism in the most insidious way—in the guise of child's play. But, as feminists have protested almost from the moment she hit the market, Barbie is not simply a child's toy or just a teenage fashion doll; she is an icon—perhaps *the* icon—of true white womanhood and femininity, a symbol of the far from innocent ideological stuff of which the (Miss) American dream and other mystiques of race and gender are made.

Invented by Ruth Handler, one of the founders of Mattel, and named after her daughter, Barbie dolls have been a very real force in the toy market since Mattel first introduced them at the American Toy Fair in 1959. In fact, despite the skepticism of toy store buyers—who at the time were primarily men—the first shipment of a half million dolls and a million costumes sold out immediately (Larcen A7). The first Barbies, which were modeled after a sexy German doll and comic strip character named Lilli, were all white, but in 1967 Mattel premiered a Black version of the doll called "Colored Francie." "Colored Francie," like white "Francie Fairchild" introduced the year before, was supposed to be Barbie's "MOD-'ern" younger cousin. As a white doll modeled and marketed in the image of Hollywood's Gidget, white Francie had been an international sensation, but Colored Francie was not destined to duplicate her prototype's success. Although the "Black is beautiful" theme of both the civil rights and Black power movements may have suggested a ready market for a beautiful Black doll, Colored Francie in fact did not sell well.

Evelyn Burkhalter, owner, operator, and curator of the Barbie Hall of Fame in Palo Alto, California—home to 16,000 Barbie dolls—attributes Colored Francie's commercial failure to the racial climate of the times. Doll purchasing patterns, it seems, reflected the same resistance to integration that was felt elsewhere in the nation. In her implied family ties to white Barbie, Colored Francie suggested more than simple integration. She implied miscegenation: a make-believe mixing of races that may have jeopardized the doll's real market value. Cynthia Roberts, author of *Barbie: Thirty Years of America's Doll* (1989), maintains that Colored Francie flopped because of her straight hair and Caucasian features (44), which seemingly were less acceptable then than now. No doubt Mattel's decision to call its first Black Barbie "Colored Francie" also contributed to the doll's demise. The use of the outmoded, even racist term "colored" in the midst of civil rights and Black power activism suggested that while Francie might be "MOD'ern," Mattel was still in the dark(y) ages. In any case, neither Black nor white audiences bought the idea of Barbie's colored relations, and Mattel promptly took the doll off the market, replacing her with a Black doll called Christie in 1968.

While a number of other Black dolls appeared throughout the late sixties and seventies—including the Julia doll, modeled after the TV character played by the Black singer and actress Diahann Carroll—it was not until 1980 that Mattel introduced Black dolls that were called Barbie like their white counterparts. Today, Barbie dolls come in a virtual rainbow coalition of colors, races, ethnicities, and nationalities—most of which look remarkably like the prototypical white Barbie, modified only by a dash of color and a change of costume. It is these would-be multicultural "dolls of the world"—Jamaican Barbie, Nigerian and Kenyan Barbie, Malaysian Barbie, Chinese Barbie, Mexican, Spanish, and Brazilian Barbie, et cetera, et cetera, et cetera—that interest me. For me these dolls are at once a symbol and a symptom of what multiculturalism has become at the hands of contemporary commodity culture: an easy and immensely profitable way off the hook of Eurocentrism that gives us the face of cultural diversity without the particulars of racial difference.

If I could line up across the page the ninety "different" colors, cultures, and other incarnations in which Barbie currently exists, the fact of her unrelenting sameness (or at least similarity) would become immediately apparent. Even two dolls might do the trick: "My First Barbie" in white and "My First Barbie" in Black, for example, or white "Western Fun Barbie" and Black "Western Fun Barbie." Except for their dye jobs, the dolls are identical: the same body, size, shape, and apparel. Or perhaps I should say *nearly* identical because in some instances—with Black and Asian dolls in particular—coloring and other subtle changes (stereotypically slanted eyes in the Asian dolls, thicker lips in the Black dolls) suggest differently coded facial features.

In other instances, when Barbie moves across cultural as opposed to racial lines, it is costume rather than color that distinguishes one ethnic group or nation from another. Nigeria and Jamaica, for instance, are represented by the same basic brown body, dolled up in different native garbs—or Mattel's interpretation thereof.[4] With other costume changes, this generic Black body becomes Western Fun Barbie or Marine Barbie or Desert Storm Barbie, and even Presidential Candidate Barbie, who, by the way, comes with a Nancy Reagan–red taking-care-of-business suit as well as a red, white, and blue inaugural ball gown. Much the same is true of the generic Asian doll—sometimes called Kira—who reappears in a variety of different dress-defined ethnicities. In other words, where Barbie is concerned, clothes not only make the woman, they mark the racial and/or cultural difference.

Such difference is marked as well by the cultural history and language lessons that accompany each doll in Mattel's international collection. The back of Jamaican Barbie's box tells us, for example, "*How-you-du* (Hello) from the land of Jamaica, a tropical paradise known for its exotic fruit, sugar cane, breathtaking beaches, and reggae beat!" The box goes on to explain that most Jamaicans have ancestors from Africa. Therefore, "even though our official language is English, we speak patois, a kind of '*Jamaica Talk*,' filled with English and African words." The lesson ends with a brief glossary (eight words) and a few more examples of this "Jamaica Talk," complete with translations: "*A hope yu wi come-a Jamaica!* (I hope you will come to Jamaica!)" and "*Teck care a yusself, mi fren!* (Take care of yourself, my friend!)" A nice idea, I suppose, but for me these quick-and-dirty ethnographies only enhance the extent to which these would-be multicultural dolls treat race and ethnic difference like collectibles, contributing more to commodity culture than to the intercultural awareness they claim to inspire.

Is the current fascination with the Black or colored body—especially the female body—a contemporary version of the primitivism of the 1920s? Is multiculturalism to postmodernism what primitivism was to modernism? It was while on my way to a roundtable discussion on precisely this question that I bought my first Black Barbie dolls in March of 1993. As carbon copies of an already problematic original, these colorized Mattel toys seemed to me the perfect tools with which to illustrate the point I wanted to make about the collapse of multiculturalism into an easy pluralism that simply adds what it constructs as the Other without upsetting the fundamental precepts and paradigms of Western culture or, in the case of Mattel, without changing the mold.

Not entirely immune to such critiques, Mattel sought expert advice from Black parents and early childhood specialists in the development and marketing of its newest line of Black Barbie dolls. Chief among the expert witnesses was the clinical psychologist Darlene Powell Hopson, who coauthored with her husband, Derek S. Hopson, a study of racism and child development titled *Different and Wonderful: Raising Black Children in a Race-Conscious Society* (1990). As part of their research for the book, the Hopsons repeated a groundbreaking study conducted by the Black psychologists Kenneth and Mamie Clark in the 1940s.

The Clarks used Black and white dolls to demonstrate the negative effects of racism and segregation on Black children. When given a choice between a white doll and a Black doll, nearly 70 percent of the Black children in the study chose the white doll. The Clarks' findings became an important factor in *Brown v. Board of Education of Topeka* in 1954. More recently, some scholars have called into question not necessarily the Clarks' findings but their interpretation: the assumption that, in the realm of make-believe, a Black child's choosing a white doll necessarily reflects a negative self-concept.[5] For the Hopsons, however, the Clarks' research remains compelling. In 1985 they repeated the Clarks' doll test and found that an alarming 65 percent of the Black children in their sample chose a white doll over a Black one. Moreover, 76 percent of the children interviewed said that the Black dolls "looked bad" to them (Hopson xix).

In addition to the clinical uses they make of dolls in their experiments, the Hopsons also give considerable attention to what they call "doll play" in their book, specifically mentioning Barbie. "If your daughter likes 'Barbie' dolls, by all means get her Barbie," they advise Black parents. "But also choose black characters from the Barbie world. *You do not want your child to grow up thinking that only White dolls, and by extension White people, are attractive and nice*" (Hopsons 127, emphasis original). (Note that "Barbie," unmodified in the preceding passage, seems to mean *white* Barbie dolls.) The Hopsons suggest that parents should not only provide their children with Black and other ethnic dolls but that they should get involved in their children's doll play. "Help them dress and groom the dolls while you compliment them both," they advise, offering the following suggested routine: " 'This is a beautiful doll. It looks just like you. Look at her hair. It's just like yours. Did you know your nose is as pretty as your doll's?' " (119). They also suggest that parents use "complimentary words such as *lovely, pretty, or nice* so that [the] child will learn to associate them with his or her own image" (124).

Certainly it is important to help children feel good about themselves. One might argue, however, that the "just like you" simile and the beautiful doll imagery so central to these suggestions for what the Hopsons call positive play run the risk of transmitting to the child a colorized version of the same old beauty myth. Like Barbie dolls themselves, they make beauty—and by implication worth—a matter of physical characteristics.

In spite of their own good intentions, the Hopsons, in linking play with "beautiful" dolls to positive self-imagining, echoed Mattel's own marketing campaign. It is not surprising, then, that the Hopsons' findings and the interventional strategies they designed for using dolls to instill ethnic pride caught the attention of Mattel. In 1990 Darlene Hopson was asked to consult with the corporation's product manager Deborah Mitchell and designer Kitty Black-Perkins—both African Americans—in the development of a new line of "realistically sculpted" Black fashion dolls. Hopson agreed and about a year later Shani and her friends Asha and Nichelle became the newest members of Barbie's ever-expanding family.

Shani means "marvelous" in Swahili, according to the dolls' press kit. But as the *Village Voice* columnist Lisa Jones has noted, the name has other meanings as well: "startling, a wonder, a novelty" (36). My own research indicates that while Shani is a Swahili female name meaning marvelous, the Kiswahili word "shani" translates as "an adventure, something unusual" (Stewart 120). So it seems that Mattel's new plaything is not just marvelous, too marvelous for words, but, as her name also suggests, she is difference incarnate—a novelty, a new enterprise or, perhaps, as the Black female Other so often is, an exotic. Mattel, it seems to me, both plays up and plays on what it presents as the doll's exotic Black-is-beautiful difference. As the back of her package reads:

> *Shani means marvelous in the Swahili language . . . and marvelous she is! With her friends Asha and Nichelle, Shani brings to life the special style and beauty of the African American woman. Each one is beautiful in her own way, with her own lovely skin shade and unique facial features. Each has a different hair color and texture, perfect for braiding, twisting and creating fabulous hair styles! Their clothes, too, reflect the vivid colors and ethnic accents that showcase their exotic looks and fashion flair!*
>
> *Shani, Asha and Nichelle invite you into their glamorous world to share the fun and excitement of being a top model. Imagine appearing on magazine covers, starring in fashion shows, and going to Hollywood parties as you, Shani, Asha and Nichelle live your dreams of beauty and success, loving every marvelous minute!* (emphasis added)

While these words attempt to convey a message of Black pride—after the fashion of the Hopsons' recommendations for positive play—that message is clearly tied to bountiful hair, lavish and exotic clothes, and other outward and visible signs not of brains but of beauty, wealth, and success. Shani may be a top fashion model, but don't look for her (or, if Mattel's own oft-articulated theory of Barbie as role model holds, yourself or your child) at M.I.T.

Like any other proud, well-to-do parents of a debutante, Mattel gave Shani her own coming-out party at the International Toy Fair in February of 1991. This gala event included a tribute to Black designers and an appearance by En Vogue singing the Negro National Anthem, "Lift Every Voice and Sing"—evidently the song of choice of the doll Mattel describes as "tomorrow's African American woman." Also making their debuts were Shani's friends Asha and Nichelle, notable for the different hues in which their black plastic skin comes—an innovation due in part to Darlene Hopson's influence. Shani, the signature doll of the line, is what we call in the culture "brown-skinned"; Asha is honey-colored (some would say "high-yella"); and Nichelle is deep mahogany. Their male friend Jamal, added in 1992, completes the collection.

For the un(make-)believing, the three-to-one ratio of the Shani quartet—three Black females to one Black male—may be the most realistic thing about these dolls. In the eyes and the advertising of Mattel, however, Shani and her friends are the most authentic Black female thing the mainstream toy market has yet produced. "Tomorrow's African American woman" (an appellation which, as Lisa Jones has noted, both riffs and one-ups *Essence*'s "Today's Black Woman") has broader hips, fuller lips, and a broader nose, according to product manager Deborah Mitchell. Principal designer Kitty Black-Perkins, who has dressed Black Barbies since their birth in 1980, adds that the Shani dolls are also distinguished by their unique, culturally specific clothes in "spice tones, [and] ethnic fabrics," rather than "fantasy colors like pink or lavender" (quoted in Jones 36)—evidently the colors of the faint of skin.

The notion that fuller lips, broader noses, wider hips, and higher derrières somehow make the Shani dolls more realistically African American raises many difficult questions about authenticity, truth, and the ever-problematic categories of the real and the symbolic, the typical and the stereotypical. Just what are we saying when we claim that a doll does or does not "look Black"? How does Black look? What would it take to make a doll look authentically African-American? What preconceived, prescriptive ideals of legitimate blackness are inscribed in such claims of authenticity? How can doll manufacturers or any other image makers—the film industry, for example—attend to cultural, racial, and phenotypical differences without merely engaging the same simplistic big-lips/broad-hips stereotypes that make so many of us—Blacks in particular—grit our (pearly white) teeth? What would it take to produce a line of dolls that more fully reflects the wide variety of sizes, shapes, colors, hairstyles, occupations, abilities, and disabilities that African Americans—like all people—come in? In other words: what price difference?

If such specificity—such ethnic "authenticity"—were possible to achieve in a doll, its purchase price, I suspect, would be much higher than a profit-driven corporation like Mattel would be willing to pay. Let me again invoke Shani to prove my point. On the one hand, Mattel was concerned enough about producing an ethnically correct Black doll to seek the advice of Black image specialists such as Darlene Hopson in the development and marketing of the Shani line. Ultimately, however, the company was not willing to follow the advice of such experts where doing so would cost the corporation more than the price of additional dyes and ethnic fabrics.

For example, Hopson reportedly argued not just for gradations in skin tones in the Shani dolls but also for variations in body type and lengths and styles of hair—for an Afro here or an asymmetrical cut there. But, while Mattel acknowledged both the legitimacy and the ubiquity of such arguments, profit motive mediated against the very realism the corporation set out to achieve in these dolls. "To be truly realistic, one [Shani doll] should have shorter hair." Deborah Mitchell confessed to Lisa Jones. "But little girls of all races love hair play. We added more texture. But we can't change the fact that long, combable hair is still a key seller" (Jones 36).

Mitchell, of course, has a point. It is after all the taste of consumers that is inscribed in Barbie's long, combable hair. In the process of my own archival research—poking around in the dusty aisles of Toys "R" Us—I encountered a Black teenage girl in search, like me, of the latest Black Barbie. During the impromptu interview that ensued, my subject confessed to me in gory, graphic details the many Barbie murders and mutilations she had committed over the years. "It's the hair," she said emphatically several times. "The hair, that hair; I want it. I want it." Her words recalled my own torturous childhood struggles with the straightening combs, curling irons, and relaxers that biweekly transformed my wooly, "just like a sponge" kinks into what the white kids at school marveled at as my "Cleopatra [read straight] hair." During one of those biweekly sessions with my mother and the straightening comb, I was foolish enough to say out loud what I had wished for a long time: that I had straight hair like the white girls at school. I still remember my mother's hurt, her sense of her daughter's racial heresy. Mitchell and Mattel indeed have a point. The difficult truth may just be that part of Shani's and Black Barbie's attraction for little Black girls in particular is the escape from their own often shorter, harder-to-comb hair that these dolls' lengthy straight locks represent.

Barbie's svelte figure, like her long combable hair, became Shani's body type as well. And here too marketability seems to have overruled professed attempts to capture the "unique facial features" and the "special style and beauty of the African American people." Even the reported subtle changes that are supposed to signify Shani's Black difference— her much-remarked broader hips and elevated buttocks, for example—are little more than optical illusions, according to the anthropologists Jacqueline Urla and Alan Swedlund of the University of Massachusetts at Amherst. Urla and Swedlund, who have been studying the anthropometry—the body measurements—of Barbie for some time, argue that, while Shani's hips may appear to be wider, they are actually smaller in both circumference and breadth than those of other Barbie dolls. It is essential, after all, that all the dolls be able to share the same clothes, thus making any dramatic alterations in body type unlikely. The effect of a higher buttocks is achieved, Urla and Swedlund maintain, by changing the angle of the doll's back. In other words, the Shani doll's buttocks may appear stereotypically higher, but she is not really dimensionally different from all the other eleven-and-a-half inch fashion dolls.

Lisa Jones concludes her *Village Voice* article on Barbie by noting that the women behind Shani—Black women like Hopson and Mitchell—want the doll to be more than just a Barbie in blackface. While Hopson, in particular, certainly hoped for—shall I say—*different* difference, she nevertheless maintains that the Shani dolls demonstrate "social consciousness on Mattel's part" (Jones 36). The British fashion designer and Barbie aficionado extraordinaire Billy Boy made a similar point in praising Mattel for integrating Barbie's family with first Colored Francie and then Christie in the late 1960s (Billy Boy 82). After nearly thirty years, I think we can forgive Mattel its Colored Francie faux pas and perhaps even applaud the attempt. But if Shani (who came out in a new scantily clad Soul Train edition in 1993) stands as Mattel's best effort to "go ethnic," as it were—to corner the contemporary mainstream market in "realistically sculpted" Black dolls that "bring to life" the "special style and beauty of the African-American people"—she stands on shaky ground.

And yet it may not be fair to single out Mattel as an example of what seems to be a national if not international phenomenon. Racial difference, like ethnic Barbie, is a hot commodity, and it isn't only Mattel who is making money. In the words of David Rieff, a contributing editor of *Harper's Magazine*:

> *Everything is commodifiable, even Afrocentrism (there is money being made on all the Kinte [sic] cloth and Kwanza [sic] paraphernalia that are the rage among certain segments of the black community, and not only the black community), bilingualism (currently the hottest growth market in publishing is Spanish-language children's books), and the other "multicultural" tendencies in American society that conservatives fear so desperately.*

Rieff goes so far as to call this newly globalized consumer economy multiculturalism's silent partner. I want to be careful in expressing my own concerns about the relationship between multiculturalism and the conspicuous consumption of difference, however, lest my critique appear complicit with that of the conservatives to whom Rieff refers, who fear the possibilities of a truly transformative social, cultural, and economic order, which I in fact would welcome.

All cultural commodities are not created equal. It seems to me that however profitable their production may be for the publishing industry, Spanish-language children's books serve a useful, educational function for their target audiences. On the other hand, even taking into account the argument that Black girls need Black dolls to play with, I have a difficult time locating the redeeming social value in Mattel's little plastic women, even—or perhaps especially—when they are tinted brown and decorated in Kente cloth and Kufi hats, as the new Soul Train Shani dolls are. And while I am certain that hordes of Black consumers are grateful for the Black haircare products and cosmetics marketed by mainstream corporations such as Clairol, Revlon, and Mary Kay, I am less convinced that JCPenney's target audience will really find much cultural enlightenment in the Kente cloth potholders, napkin rings, and dish towels that the store is currently marketing as "expressions of cultural pride."

In *Fashion Influences*, a catalog clearly intended to cater to what it takes to be the tastes of Black audiences, JCPenney advertises an assortment of housewares, ethnic artifacts, and exclusive designer fashions with "Afrocentric flair." Such specialty items as triple-woven cotton throws, which sell for $50 each, are available in four culturally edifying patterns: 01 Kwanzaa; 02 Kenté; 03 Martin Luther King; and 04 Malcolm X. For another $40, customers can complement their Kwanzaa-patterned throw with a Kwanzaa needlepoint pillow. (For the not quite multiculturally literate shopper, Penney's provides a cultural history lesson: "Kwanzaa means 'first fruits of the harvest' in Swahili," the catalog informs. "Created in 1966, Kwanzaa is a seven-day celebration synthesizing elements from many African harvest festivals.") And just so consumers know precisely how politically correct their Penney's purchases are, many of the catalog descriptions inform shoppers that these Afrocentric items are made in the U.S.A. The Ivory Coast Table Linens, for example, are billed as an "exuberantly colored interpretation of authentic African woven cloth . . . Made in the U.S.A." The

Kente-cloth pillows are made in the U.S.A. of fabric imported from Africa, but the MLK and Malcolm X throws are just plain made in the U.S.A. In other words, for not-so-modest prices, culturally and socially conscious American consumers can look for the union label as they shop for these and other interpretations-of-authentic-African-inspired-made-in-America goods.

Thus it is that from custom-designed bedroom coordinates inspired by mud cloth from Mali in West Africa to an embroidered metallic caftan or "Uwe (pronounced yoo-way, meaning dress)" inspired by "garments worn by the royal court on special occasions," what JCPenney is trading in and trading on in this blaxploitation catalog is cultural difference and, if you will, misspent racial pride. Although I doubt that Penney's cares who buys its Kufi hats, Black-on-Black dishware, and "In Search of Identity" games, it is also clear that the company does not waste such catalogs on just anybody. I, for example, have been a loyal Penney's catalog shopper for years; I receive the annual seasonal catalogs, as well as special fliers advertising queen-size fashions. I only happened upon Penney's blaxploitation catalog recently, however, when it was mailed not to me—faithful shopper—nor to my home but to the Center for African American Studies at Wesleyan University. While my shopping history identified me as larger-sized. there was evidently nothing about my purchasing pattern that identified me as Black. Penney's marketing division seems to have assumed—quite cleverly, I think—that a Center for African American Studies would be a likely place to find middle-class, culturally conscious Black consumers who might actually be able to afford the high-priced items in its Afrocentric catalog. (What a miscalculation in that last regard.)

I suspect that such catalogs are mailed not only to Black studies departments but also to Black beauty parlors (indeed I found a similar catalog from Spiegel at the shop where I get my hair cut) and Black churches, where there is sure to be a ready-made market for the Sunday-go-to-meetin' hats, high-heel shoes, and church-lady suits "with an Afrocentric flair" that fill their pages. Just to bring this discussion full circle, let me note that six Black Barbie dolls are available through this special catalog—Black Desert Storm Barbie and Ken and Soul Train Shani and her three friends Asha, Nichelle, and Jamal. Army Barbie and Ken are dressed in "authentic desert fatigues with authentic insignias for enlisted personnel," and the Shani dolls are decked out in "cool hip-hop fashions inspired by the hot T.V. dance show." But don't let these patriotic, all-American girls and boys fool you; they are all imported from Malaysia.

THE BODY POLITIC(S) OF BARBIE

> Barbie's body is a consumer object itself, a vehicle for the display of clothing and the spectacular trappings of a wealthy teenage fantasy life. Her extraordinary body exists not simply as an example of the fetishized female form typical of those offered up to the male gaze, but as a commodity vehicle itself whose form seduces the beholder and sells accessories, the real source of corporate profit. Like Lay's chips, no one can buy just one outfit for the doll. Barbie is the late capitalist girl incarnate.
>
> –Mel McCombie

In focusing thus far on the merchandising of racial, perhaps more so than gender, difference, I do not mean to imply that racial and gender identities are divisible, even in dolls.

Nor, in observing that most if not all of Mattel's "dolls of the world" look remarkably like what the company calls the "traditional, blond, blue-eyed Barbie," do I mean to suggest that the seemingly endless recapitulation of the white prototype is the only way in which these dolls are problematic. In fact, the most alarming thing about Barbie may well be the extent to which she functions as what M. G. Lord calls a teaching tool for femininity, whatever her race or ethnicity. Lord, the author of *Forever Barbie: The Unauthorized Biography of a Real Doll*, due out later this year, describes Barbie as a "space-age fertility icon. She looks like a modern woman, but she's a very primitive totem of female power" (quoted in Dembner 1).

Barbie has long had the eye and ire of feminists, who, for the most part, have reviled her as another manifestation of the damaging myths of female beauty and the feminine body that patriarchy perpetuates through such vehicles as popular and commodity culture. A counternarrative also exists, however, one in which Barbie is not an empty-headed, material girl bimbo, for whom math class is tough, but a feminist heroine, who has been first in war (a soldier who served in the Gulf, she has worn the colors of her country as well as the United Colors of Benetton), first in peace (she held her own summit in 1990 and she's a longtime friend of UNICEF, who "loves all the children of the world"), and always first in the hearts of her country (Americans buy her at the rate of one doll every second). While time does not allow me to reiterate or to assess here all the known critiques and defenses of Barbie, I do want to discuss briefly some of the gender ideals that I think are encoded in and transmitted by this larger-than-life little woman and what Barbie's escalating popularity says about contemporary American culture.

In *Touching Liberty: Abolition, Feminism, and the Politics of the Body* (1993), Karen Sanchez-Eppler argues that all dolls are intended to teach little girls about domesticity (133). If such tutelage is Barbie's not-so-secret mission, her methodology is far more complex and contradictory than that of the Betsy Wetsy and Tiny Tears baby dolls I played with thirty-five years ago. Those dolls invoked and evoked the maternal, as they and the baby bottles and diapers with which they were packaged invited us to nestle, nurse, and nurture. Barbie's curvaceous, big-busted, almost fully female body, on the other hand, summons not the maternal but the sexual, not the nurturant mother but the sensuous woman. As Mel McCombie has argued, rather than rehearsing parenting, as a baby doll does, Barbie's adult body encourages children to dress and redress a fashion doll that yields lessons about sexuality, consumption, and teenage life (3). To put it another way, we might say that Barbie is literally and figuratively a titillating toy.

Bodacious as they may be, however, Barbie's firm plastic breasts have no nipples—nothing that might offend, nothing that might suggest her own pleasure. And if her protruding plastic mounds signify a simmering sensuality, what are we to make of her missing genitalia? McCombie suggests that Barbie's genital ambiguity can be read as an "homage to 'good taste' " and as a "reflection of the regnant mores for teenage girls—to be both sexy and adult yet remain virginal" (4). I agree that her body invites such readings, but it also seems to me that there is nothing ambiguous about Barbie's crotch. It's missing in inaction. While male dolls like Ken and Jamal have bumps "down there" and in some instances simulated underwear etched into the plastic, most Barbies come neither with drawers nor with even a hint of anything that needs covering, even as "it" is already covered or erased. As an icon of idealized femininity, then, Barbie is locked into a never-never land in which she must be always already sexual without the possibility of sex. Conspicuously sensual on top but definitively nonsexual below, her plastic body indeed has inscribed within it the very contradictory, whore/madonna messages with which patriarchy taunts and even traumatizes young women in particular.

This kind of speculation about Barbie's breasts has led the doll's creator, Ruth Handler, to chide adults for their nasty minds. "In my opinion people make too much of breasts," Handler has complained. "They are just part of the body" (quoted in Billy Boy 26). Mrs. Handler has a point (or maybe two). I feel more than just a little ridiculous myself as I sit here contemplating the body parts and sex life of a piece of plastic. What is fascinating, however, what I think is worth studying, what both invites and resists theorizing, is not the lump of molded plastic that is Barbie, but the imaginary life that is not—that is *our* invention. Barbie as a cultural artifact may be able to tell us more about ourselves and our society—more about society's attitudes toward *its* women—than anything we might say about the doll her or, rather, *itself.*

In the nineteenth century, Alexis de Tocqueville and others argued that you could judge the character, quality, and degree of advancement of a civilization by the status and treatment of its women. What is the status of women in soon to be twenty-first-century America, and can Barbie serve as a barometer for measuring that status? Barbie, it seems to me, is a key player in the process of socialization—of engendering and racialization—that begins in infancy and is furthered by almost everything about our society, including the books children read, the toys they play with, and the cartoons they watch on television.

While changing channels one Saturday morning, I happened upon a cartoon, just a glimpse of which impelled me to watch on. At the point that I tuned in, a big, gray, menacingly male bulldog was barking furiously at a pretty, petite, light-colored cat, who simply batted her long lashes, meowed coquettishly, and rubbed her tiny feline body against his huge canine leg in response. The more the dog barked and growled, the softer the cat meowed, using her slinky feline body and her feminine wiles to win the dog over. Her strategy worked; before my eyes—and, I imagine, the eyes of millions of children, the ferocious beast was transformed into a lovesick puppy dog, who followed the cat everywhere, repeatedly saving her from all manner of evil and danger. Time and time again, the bulldog rescued the helpless, accident-prone pussy from falling girders, oncoming traffic, and other hazards to which she, in her innocent frailty, was entirely oblivious. By the end, the once ferocious bulldog was completely domesticated, as his no longer menacing body became a kind of bed for the cat to nestle in.

There are, of course, a number of ways to read the gender and racial politics of this cartoon. I suppose that the same thought process that theorizes Barbie as a feminist heroine for whom men are mere accessories might claim the kitty cat, too, as a kind of feminist feline, who uses her feminine wiles to get her way. What resonates for me in the cartoon, however, are its beauty and the beast, light/dark, good/evil, female/male, race and gender codes: light, bright, catlike femininity tames menacing Black male bestiality. Make no mistake, however; it is not wit that wins out over barbarism but a mindless, can't-take-care-of-herself femininity.

Interestingly enough, these are the kinds of messages of which fairy tales and children's stories are often made. White knights rescue fair damsels in distress from dark, forbidding evils of one kind or another. As Darlene and Derek Hopson argue: "Some of the most blatant and simplistic representations of white as good and black as evil are found in children's literature," where evil Black witches and good white fairies—heroes in white and villains in Black—abound (121).

What Barbie dolls, cartoons like the one outlined above, and even the seemingly innocent fairy tales we read to our children seem to me to have in common are the mythologies of race and gender that are encoded in them. Jacqueline Urla and Alan Swedlund maintain that Barbie's body type constructs the bodies of other women as deviant and perpetuates an impossible standard of beauty. Attempting to live up to the Barbie ideal, others argue, fosters eating and shopping disorders in teenage girls—nightmares instead of dreams. Billy Boy, one of Barbie's most ardent supporters, defends his heroine against such charges by insisting that there is nothing abnormal about the proportions of Barbie's body. Rather, he asserts, "she has the ideal that Western culture has insisted upon since the 1920s: long legs, long arms, small waist, high round bosom, and long neck" (22). The irony is that Billy Boy may be right. "Unrealistic" or not, Barbie's weight and measurements (which if proportionate to those of a woman 5'6" tall would be something like 110 pounds and a top-heavy 39–18–33) are not much different from those of the beauty queens to whom Bert Parks used to sing "Here she is, Miss America. Here she is, our ideal."[6] If Barbie is a monster, she is our monster, our ideal.

"But is Barbie bad?" Someone asked me the other day if a Black doll that looks like a white doll isn't better than no Black doll at all. I must admit that I have no ready answer for this and a number of other questions posed by my own critique. Although, as I acknowledged in the beginning, the dolls I played with as a child were white, I still remember the first time I saw a Black doll. To me, she was the most beautiful thing I had ever seen; I wanted her desperately, and I was never again satisfied with white Betsy Wetsy and blonde, blue-eyed Patty Play Pal. She was something else, something *Other*, like me, and that, I imagine, was the source of her charm and my desire.

If I did not consciously note my own absence in the toys I played with, that absence, I suspect, had a profound effect on me nevertheless. We have only to read Toni Morrison's chilling tale *The Bluest Eye* to see the effect of the white beauty myth on the Black child. And while they were by no means as dire for me as for Morrison's character Pecola Breedlove, I was not exempt from the consequences of growing up Black in a white world that barely acknowledged my existence. I grew up believing I was ugly: my kinky hair, my big hips, the gap between my teeth. I have spent half my life smiling with my hand over my mouth to hide that gap, a habit I only began to get over in graduate school when a couple of Nigerian men told me that in their culture, where my body type is prized much more than Barbie's, such gaps are a sign of great beauty. I wonder what it would have meant for me as a child to see a Black doll—or any doll—with big hips and a gap between her two front teeth.

Today, for $24.99, Mattel reaches halfway around the world and gives little girls—Black like me—Nigerian Barbies to play with. Through the wonders of plastic, dyes, and mass production, the company brings into the homes of African-American children a Nigeria that I as a young child did not even know existed. The problem is that Mattel's Nigeria does not exist either. The would-be ethnic dolls of the world Mattel sells, like their "traditional, blond, blue-eyed" all-American girl prototype, have no gaps, no big ears, no chubby thighs or other "imperfections." For a modest price, I can dream myself into Barbie's perfect world, so long as I dream myself in her image. It may be a small world, a whole new world, but there is still no place for me as *me* in it.

This, then, is my final doll story. Groucho Marx said that he wouldn't want to belong to a club that would have him as a member. In that same vein, I am not so sure that most of us would want to buy a doll that "looked like us." Indeed, efforts to produce and market such truer-to-life dolls have not met with much commercial success. Cultural critics like me can throw theoretical stones at her all we want, but part of Barbie's infinite appeal is her very perfection, the extent to which she is both product and purveyor of the dominant white Western ideal of beauty.

And what of Black beauty? If Colored Francie failed thirty years ago in part because of her Caucasian features, what are we to make of the current popularity and commercial success of Black Barbie and Shani, straight hair and all? Have we progressed to a point where "difference" makes no difference? Or have we regressed to such a degree that "difference" is only conceivable as similarity—as a mediated text that no matter what its dye job ultimately must be readable as white. Listen to our language: we "*tolerate* difference"; we practice "racial tolerance." Through the compound fractures of interpellation and universalization, the Other is reproduced not in her own image but in ours. If we have gotten away from "Us" and "Them," it may be only because Them R Us.

Is Barbie bad? Barbie is just a piece of plastic, but what she says about the economic base of our society—what she suggests about gender and race in our world—ain't good.

I am particularly pleased to be publishing this essay in *differences*, since its genesis was at a roundtable discussion on multiculturalism and postmodernism, sponsored by the Pembroke Center for Teaching and Research on Women at Brown University, in March of 1993. I wish to thank the many friends and colleagues who have encouraged this project, especially Indira Karamcheti and her four-year-old daughter Gita, who introduced me to the miniature Barbies that come with McDonald's "Happy Meals," and Erness Brody, who, with her daughter Jennifer Brody, is a veteran collector of vintage dolls. I owe a special debt to fellow "Barbiologists" M.G. Lord, Mel McCombie, Jacqueline Urla, and Eric Swedlund, who have so generously shared their research, and to Darlene Powell Hopson for talking with me about her work with Mattel. I wish to acknowledge as well the work of Erica Rand, an art historian at Bates College, who is also working on Barbie.

NOTES

1. Mattel introduced the Shani doll—a Black. Barbie-like doll—in 1991, which also may have contributed to the rise in sales, particularly since the company engaged the services of a PR firm that specializes in targeting ethnic audiences.

2. Of course, the notion of "dreaming in one's own image" is always problematic since dreams, by definition, engage something other than the "real."

3. Olmec Toys, a Black-owned company headed by an African-American woman named Yla Eason, markets a line of Black and Latina Barbie-like dolls called the Imani Collection. Billed on their boxes as "African American Princess" and "Latin American Fantasy," these dolls are also presented as having been designed with the self-images of Black children in mind. "We've got one thing in mind with all our products," the blurbs on the Imani boxes read: "let's build self-esteem. Our children gain a sense of self importance through toys. So we make them look like them." Given their obvious resemblance to Barbie

dolls—their long, straight hair and pencil-thin plastic bodies—Imani dolls look no more "like them," like "real" Black children, than their prototype. Eason, who we are told was devastated by her son's announcement that he couldn't be a superhero because he wasn't white, may indeed want to give Black children toys to play with that "look like them." Yet, in order to compete in a market long dominated by Mattel and Hasbro, her company, it seems, has little choice but to conform to the Barbie mold.

4. After many calls to the Jamaican Embassy in Washington, D.C., and to various cultural organizations in Jamaica, I have determined that Jamaican Barbie's costume—a floor-length granny-style dress with apron and headrag—bears some resemblance to what is considered the island's traditional folk costume. I am still left wondering about the decision-making process, however: why the doll representing Jamaica is figured as a maid, while the doll representing Great Britain, for example, is presented

as a lady—a blonde, blue-eyed Barbie doll dressed in a fancy riding habit with boots and hat.

5. See among others Morris Rosenburg's books *Conceiving the Self* (1979) and *Society and the Adolescent Self-Image* (1989) and William E. Cross's *Shades of Black: Diversity in African American Identity* (1991), all of which challenge the Clarks' findings. Cross argues, for example, that the Clarks confounded or conflated two different issues: attitude toward race in general and attitude toward the self in particular. How one feels about race is not necessarily an index of one's self-esteem.

6. In response to criticism from feminists in particular, the Miss America Pageant has attempted to transform itself from a beauty contest to a talent competition, whose real aim is to give college scholarships to smart, talented women (who just happen to look good in bathing suits and evening gowns). As part of its effort to appear more concerned with a woman's IQ than with her bra size, the pageant did away with its long-standing practice of broadcasting the chest, waist, and hip measurements, as well as the height and weight, of each contestant.

WORKS CITED

Berkwitz, David N. "Finally, Barbie Doll Ads Go Ethnic." *Newsweek*, August 13, 1990, 48.

Billy Boy. *Barbie: Her Life and Times.* New York: Crown, 1987.

Cross, William E., Jr. *Shades of Black: Diversity in African American Identity.* Philadelphia: Temple University Press, 1991.

Delany, Sarah, and A. Elizabeth Delany. *Having Our Say: The Delany Sisters' First 100 Years.* New York: Kodansha, 1993.

Dembner, Alice. "Thirty-five and Still a Doll." *Boston Globe*, March 9, 1994, 1+.

Hopson, Darlene Powell, and Derek S. Hopson. *Different and Wonderful: Raising Black Children in a Race-Conscious Society.* New York: Simon and Schuster, 1990.

Jones, Lisa. "A Doll Is Born." *Village Voice* March 26, 1991, 36.

Kantrowitz, Barbara. "Hot Date: Barbie and G.I. Joe." *Newsweek*, February 20, 1989, 59–60.

Larcen, Donna. "Barbie Bond Doesn't Diminish with Age." *Hartford Courant*, August 17, 1993, A6–7.

Lord, M. G. *Forever Barbie: The Unauthorized Biography of a Real Doll.* New York: Morrow, 1994.

McCombie, Mel. "Barbie: Toys Are Us." Unpublished essay.

Morrison, Toni. *The Bluest Eye.* New York: Washington Square, 1970.

Rieff, David. "Multiculturalism's Silent Partner." *Harper's*, August 1993, 62–72.

Roberts, Cynthia. *Barbie: Thirty Years of America's Doll.* Chicago: Contemporary, 1989.

Rosenberg, Morris. *Conceiving the Self.* New York: Basic, Books, 1979.

———. *Society and the Adolescent Self-Image.* Middletown, Conn.: Wesleyan University Press, 1989.

Sanchez-Eppler, Karen. *Touching Liberty: Abolition, Feminism, and the Politics of the Body.* Berkeley: University of California Press, 1993.

Stewart, Julia. *African Names.* New York: Carroll and Graf, 1993.

Urla, Jacqueline, and Alan Swedlund. "The Anthropometry of Barbie: Unsettling Ideals of the Feminine in Popular Culture." In *Deviant Bodies.* Ed. Jennifer Terry and Jacqueline Urla. Bloomington: Indiana University Press, 1995.

20

AFRICAN SIGNS AND SPIRIT WRITING

Harryette Mullen

The recording of an authentic black voice, a voice of deliverance from the deafening discursive silence which an "enlightened" Europe cited as proof of the absence of the African's humanity, was the millennial instrument of transformation through which the African would become the European, the slave become the ex-slave, the brute animal become the human being. So central was this idea to the birth of the black literary tradition that four of the first five eighteenth-century slave narratives drew upon the figure of the voice in the text as crucial "scenes of instruction" in the development of the slave on his road to freedom. James Gronniosaw in 1770, John Marrant in 1785, Ottobah Cuguano in 1787, Olaudah Equiano in 1789, and John Jea in 1815, all draw upon the figure of the voice in the text. . . . That the figure of the talking book recurs in these . . . black eighteenth-century texts says much about the degree of "intertextuality" in early black letters, more than we heretofore thought. Equally important, however, this figure itself underscores the established correlation between silence and blackness we have been tracing, as well as the urgent need to make the text speak, the process by which the slave marked his distance from the master.

–Charles T. Davis and
Henry L. Gates Jr., *The Slave's Narrative*

Much of Henry Louis Gates's influential scholarship argues that Black literary traditions privilege orality. This critical position has become something of a commonplace, in part because it is based on accurate observation. From the "talking book" featured in early slave narratives, to "dialect poetry" and the "speakerly text," the Afro-American tradition that Gates constructs and canonizes is that which seeks to "speak" to readers with an "authentic black voice." Presumably, for the African-American writer, there is no alternative to production of this "authentic black voice" but silence, invisibility, or self-effacement. This speech-based and racially inflected aesthetic that produces a "black poetic diction" requires that the writer acknowledge and reproduce in the text a significant difference between the spoken and written language of African Americans and that of other Americans. Without disputing, as George Schuyler did in his satiric novel *Black No More* that any such difference exists, I would like to argue that any theory of African-American literature that privileges a speech-based poetics, or the trope of orality, to the exclusion of more writerly texts will cost us some impoverishment of the tradition. While Gates includes in his canon a consummately writerly text, such as Ralph Ellison's *Invisible Man*, because it also functions brilliantly as a speakerly text, and while Gates appreciates Zora Neale Hurston and celebrates Sterling A. Brown, he cannot champion Jean Toomer's *Cane* with the same degree of enthusiasm.[1] I would not worry so much about the criteria Gates has set for inclusion in his canon, if it did not seem to me that the requirement that a Black text be "speakerly" will inevitably exclude certain African-American texts that draw more on the culture of books, writing, and print than they do on the culture of orality.

Another concern I have about Gates's argument is its seeming acceptance of an erroneous Eurocentric assumption that African cultures developed no indigenous writing or script systems. Although he is well aware of Job ben Solomon, a captive African sold into slavery in Maryland, and later ransomed and returned to Africa after it was discovered that he was literate in Arabic, Gates seems to overlook the possibility that non-Islamic slaves might also have been familiar with writing or indigenous script systems used for various religious purposes in their own cultural contexts. While the institutionalized illiteracy of African-American slaves born in the United States was enforced by laws forbidding anyone to teach them to read or write, the illiteracy of Africans cannot be accepted as given, although to speak of non-Islamic Africans as literate would require broader definitions of writing than Western scholars such as Walter J. Ong might find acceptable.

This essay is an attempt to explore connections between African signs and African-American spirit writing, traditions that may be traced more readily within a visual arts and art history context, where perhaps more continuity exists between African and African-American forms of visual expression, than within a canon of African-American literature or literary criticism, since the loss of African languages by African Americans constitutes a much more decisive rupture.

Another part of my project as a literary critic is to read the texts of ex-slave narratives and spiritual narratives as precursors of complementary traditions of African-American literacy, while at the same time keeping in mind that much of what is considered most authentically African in traditional African-American culture has been preserved and maintained through extraliterary forms, and has in fact often been the creation of illiterate or marginally literate African Americans whose aesthetic impact is all the more astonishing given their exclusion from the educational, cultural, and political institutions of the dominant bourgeois white culture of the United States. As I look at parallel traditions of African-American literacy, inaugurated by ex-slave narratives and visionary texts mainly produced in the 19th century for possible answers, the larger question I am asking is this: How has the Western view of writing as a rational technology historically been received and transformed by African Americans whose primary means of cultural transmission have been oral and visual rather than written, and for whom graphic systems have been associated not with instrumental human communication, but with techniques of spiritual power and spirit possession? In other words: How, historically, have African Americans' attitudes toward literacy as well as their own efforts to acquire, use, and interiorize the technologies of literacy been shaped by what art historian Robert Farris Thompson calls "the flash of the spirit of a certain people armed with improvisatory drive and brilliance"?[2]

The ex-slave narratives offer one possible answer to this question.[3] Another possibility and an alternative tradition are suggested when Thompson notes that in African-American folk culture the printed text may provide ritual protection, as newspapers are used by "back-home architects" who "papered the walls of their cabins with newsprint to confuse jealous spirits with an excess of information," and writing may be employed to enclose and confine evil presences, as in the spirit-script of visionary artist J. B. Murray.[4] In what looks like illiterate scribbling or a handwriting exercise, Murray's noncommunicative spirit-writing or "textual glossolalia," Thompson finds an African-American manifestation of what may be a surviving element of Kongo prophetic practices in which a unique illegible script produced in a trancelike state functions as a graphic representation of spirit possession, "a visual equivalent to speaking in tongues" (Adele 14). In order to construct a cultural and material history of African America's embrace and transmutation of writing technologies, one might ask how writing and text functioned in a folk milieu that valued a script for its cryptographic incomprehensibility and uniqueness, rather than its legibility or reproducibility. How was the uniformity of print received by a folk culture in which perfect symmetry and straight, unbroken lines were avoided, an aesthetic preference for irregularity and variation that folklorist Gladys-Marie Fry attributes to "the folk belief of plantation slaves that evil spirits follow straight lines" (67).[5]

Thompson imaginatively suggests that, just as in African and diasporic forms of oral expression, from the pygmy yodel to the field holler of the slave, from the blues wail to the gospel hum, from the bebopping scat of the jazz singer to the nonsense riffs erupting in the performance of the rap, dub, or reggae artist, it is apparent that the voice may be "unshackled" from meaningful words or from the pragmatic function of language as a conveyor of cognitive information, so the written text, as spirit-script, may be unshackled from any phonetic representation of human speech or graphic representation of language. "Music brings down the spirit upon a prepared point in traditional Kongo culture," Thompson states. I might add that a reading of 19th-century African-American spiritual narratives suggests that, like music, the act of reading or writing, or the process of acquiring literacy itself, may be a means for the visionary writer to attract a powerful presence to inhabit a spiritually focused imagination or a blank sheet of paper. Jarena Lee recalls the moment of her conversion, a flash of the spirit, inspired by hearing the Bible read aloud in church: "At the reading of the Psalms, a ray of renewed conviction darted into my soul" (Andrews 27). Zilpha Elaw, attending a camp meeting, experienced a "trance or ecstacy" that resulted in an unprecedented feeling of empowerment.

> [M]y heart and soul were rendered completely spotless—as clean as a sheet of white paper, and I felt as if I had never sinned in all my life . . . when the prayer meeting afterwards commenced the Lord opened my mouth in public prayer; and while I was thus engaged, it seemed as if I heard my God [Andrews 67] of the mulberry-trees. Oh how precious was this day to my soul! (Andrews 67)

An African-American tradition of literacy as a secular technology and a tool for [Andrews 67], through appropriation of public symbols and participation in mainstream cultural discourses, coexists with a parallel tradition of visionary literacy as a spiritual practice in which divine inspiration, associated with Judeo-Christian biblical tradition, is syncretically merged with African traditions of spirit possession, as in the "spirit-writing" of Gertrude Morgan (1900–1980) and J. B. Murray (1910–1988), African-American visionary folk artists who were, respectively, literate and illiterate practitioners of what Robert Farris Thompson calls "arts of defense and affirmation" and "arts of black yearning" for transcendence and freedom.

The tradition of secular literacy may be traced in African-American tradition to the ex-slave narratives, with the 1845 narrative of Frederick Douglass as the paradigmatic text of the genre. The alternative tradition of visionary literacy may be traced to narratives and journals of spiritual awakening and religious conversion written by freeborn and emancipated Africans and African Americans in the 18th and 19th centuries. Each of these traditions of literacy, the sacred and the secular, has a specific relation to African and diasporic orality as well as to the institutionalized illiteracy that resulted from the systematic exclusion of African Americans from equal educational opportunities. Both traditions have a common origin in the early narratives of African captives for whom emancipation had been associated with conversion to the equally potent religions of Christianity and literacy.[6] By the 19th century, the bonds linking religious conversion and legal emancipation had been broken as masters complained that it made no sense economically to free slaves simply because they had become fellow Christians. It remained for 19th-century ex-slave narrators, notably Douglass, to perceive the legal codes forbidding literacy and social mobility to slaves as a secular analogue of the threat of spiritual alienation that had motivated Olaudah Equiano and others to learn to read in order to "talk to" the Bible.

The texts of ex-slave narratives signal a decisive movement of literate African Americans toward self-empowerment through the tools and technologies of literacy that are productive of bourgeois subjectivity, and away from the degradation imposed by slavery and compulsory illiteracy. The zealous pursuit of literacy embodied by ex-slave narrators, particularly Douglass, is an astute response to the disastrous assault on the collective cultural identities of African captives whose orally transmitted forms of knowledge brought from their various ethnic groups had been submerged, fragmented, or rendered irrelevant within a dominant bourgeois white culture that characterized whatever remained within slave culture of coherent African traditional aesthetic and spiritual systems as superstitious beliefs of primitive people.

Alongside the largely secular and overtly political ex-slave narratives, which of necessity are concerned with what happens to the slave's body, an alternate tradition of visionary literacy exists in the tradition of African-American spiritual autobiography, which concerned itself not with the legal status of the material body but with the shackles placed on the soul and on the spiritual expressiveness of the freeborn or emancipated African American, whose religious conversion, sanctification, and worship were expected to conform to the stringent standards of the white Christian establishment. Until the founding of Black churches and the calling of Black preachers, and until the white clergy loosened its strictures against emotional displays of religious enthusiasm, African-American worship had been constrained in its expressive forms and rituals, which included communal dancing, the call and response by which the community and its leaders mutually affirmed one another, and the spontaneous vocalizations of the spirit-possessed. For African-American visionary writers and artists, the Bible as sacred text and sublime speech, as the written record of a divine voice inspiring its authors to write and its readers to speak holy words, mediates the historical and mythic dislocation from primarily oral cultures to one in which literacy has the power of a fetish.

Although equally zealous in their pursuit of freedom through literacy, spiritual autobiographers, unlike most ex-slave narrators, often forsake "bourgeois perception" of reality (Lowe) for "things unseen" or "signs in the heavens." Because of the stress they place on visionary experience, these texts have as much in common with the practice of literate and illiterate African-American visionary folk artists as with contemporaneous narratives written or dictated by emancipated or fugitive slaves in the eighteenth and nineteenth centuries. For visionary artists, as for these spiritual autobiographers, the artwork or text is an extension of their call to preach. It functions as a spiritual signature or divine imprimatur, superseding human authority. The writer as well as the artist can become "an inspired device for the subconscious spirit," the African ancestor-spirit whose Black yearning, unleashed as glossolalia, would be regarded in the dominant culture as mumbo jumbo. Through the visionary artist or writer who serves as a medium, it is possible for the surviving spirit of African cultural traditions "to manifest itself on the physical plane" through the artist's materials or the materiality of the writing process. The work of such individuals, while resonating with ancient traditions, "is conceived out of [a] deeply intuitive calling and spiritual need" (Nasisse).

In addition to stressing spiritual and personal over material and political forms of power, visionary writers were also much more likely to attribute their literacy to supernatural agency, rather than the realistically difficult and tedious work Douglass details in his attempt to "get hold of a book" and grasp the instrumentality of literacy (278). The secular ex-slave narrative tradition is exemplified by Douglass, who substituted abolitionist tracts for the Bible (Olaudah Equiano's "talking book")[7] as the text of desire motivating his acquisition of literacy, and who learned to write by copying the penmanship of his young master, literally "writing in the spaces" of the master's copybook.

> I got hold of a book entitled "The Columbian Orator." Every opportunity I got, I used to read this book. . . . During this time, my copy-book was the board fence, brick wall, and pavement; my pen and ink was a lump of chalk. With these, I learned mainly how to write. . . . By this time, my little Master Thomas had gone to school, and learned how to write, and had written over a number of copy-books. . . . When left thus [unsupervised in the master's house], I used to spend the time in writing in the spaces left in Master Thomas's copy-book, copying what he had written. I continued to do this until I could write a hand very similar to that of Master Thomas. Thus, after a long, tedious effort for years, I finally succeeded in learning how to write. (Douglass 278–81)[8]

Both through his emphasis on the quotidian, his naming of the mundane material objects employed in his campaign of disciplinary self-instruction, through his substitution of abolitionist writings where previous narratives had placed the Bible as the text of desire motivating the narrator to become literate, Douglass refigures and secularizes the trope of divine instruction employed in spiritual autobiographies of some freeborn or manumitted African Americans who claimed to have acquired literacy by supernatural means: through divine intervention after earnest prayer. The ethnographic and historical research that documents continuities between African and African-American aesthetic and spiritual practices now makes it possible to explore how, in the eighteenth and nineteenth centuries, Africans and African Americans converting to Anglo-American/Protestant as well as Latin/Catholic Christianity, and interiorizing Western-style literacy, may themselves have transformed and refigured indigenous African concepts of protective religious writing, as Maude Southwell Wahlman suggests:

> In Africa, among the Mande, Fon, Ejagham, and Kongo peoples, indigenous and imported writing is associated with knowledge, power, and intelligence, and thus is considered sacred and protective. African signs were sewn, dyed, painted or woven into cloth; and Central African artifacts were often read as aspects of a Kongo religious cosmogram. . . . In Nigeria, the Ejagham people are known for their 400-year-old writing system, called *Nsibidi* (Talbot, 1912). It was most likely invented by women since one sees it on their secret society buildings, fans, calabashes, skin-covered masks, textiles, and costumes made for secret societies. . . . In the New World various mixtures of West African (*Vai*) and Nigerian (*Nsibidi*) scripts and the Kongo cosmogram fused to create numerous new scripts. (29–30)

This phenomenon has been most extensively documented in the Latin/Catholic traditions in which religious syncretism thrives through the identification of Catholic saints with African deities, as well as through the church's hospitality to mysticism, and through incorporation of indigenous paganisms into elaborately layered and localized rites and rituals. Yet it can also be demonstrated that even the more austere traditions of Anglo-American/Protestant worship, particularly after the establishment of Black churches, produced African-American syncretisms of African, European, and indigenous Native American spiritual practices. African-American preaching styles, call and response, spirituals, gospel singing, baptism and funeral rites, and ritual possession by "the Holy Ghost" are examples of such Protestant syncretisms. Particularly in its insistence upon grassroots literacy training as an aspect of religious conversion and sanctification, so that the Holy Word might be transmitted directly to each individual through Bible reading, Protestantism fostered in African-American religious topologies the figuring of acquisition and interiorization of literacy as a Christian form of spirit-possession compatible with African mystical traditions.

The tradition of spiritual writers includes John Jea, Jerena Lee, Zilpha Elaw, Julia Foote, and Rebecca Cox Jackson, whose spirituality links them to that of the illiterate visionaries Harriet Tubman, Sojourner Truth, and Harriet Powers, to literate insurrectionists such as Nat Turner and Denmark Vesey, as well as to 20th-century visionary artists such as J. B. Murray and Gertrude Morgan. By comparing similarities in the imagery of visionary folk artists and the religious visions of nineteenth-century mystics, it is possible to see a continuum of syncretic survival of African spiritual traditions and aesthetic systems that could hide and thrive in the interstices of accepted Christian practices. According to Andy Nasisse, "The overwhelming evidence that certain images and religious ideas encoded in the work of Black American visions has verifiable trans-Atlantic connections to specific cultures in Africa . . . gives additional support to the notion that these images surface from a collective source. . . . Although many of these Africanisms could have been taught and otherwise handed down through generations, there are numerous signs of the presence of tribal elements which seem to have spontaneously generated in an individual's art" (11).

Maude Southwell Wahlman locates visionary African-American art in a "creolized" tradition that blends cultural and aesthetic traditions of Africans, Native Americans, and Europeans. Because the artists, some of them illiterate, "could not always articulate the African traditions that shaped their visions, dreams, and arts," they have seemed "idiosyncratic" to art critics and art historians schooled in European and Euro-American traditions (28–29). The creolized tradition of visionary folk artists, which has been "transmitted somewhat randomly through the generations, resulted in the retention of original African motifs although the symbolic meanings of the images were sometimes lost" (Adele 13).

This syncretic, or creolized, tradition is manifest in a most visually striking way in the work of African-American quilters. The narrative quilts of Harriet Powers offer a fascinating example of artifacts that incorporate African techniques and design elements, while also expressing the spiritual preoccupations of an artistically gifted individual. Powers, who could neither read nor write, was born into slavery in 1837 and died in 1911. According to the folklorist Gladys-Marie Fry, "Harriet Powers's quilt forms a direct link to the tapestries traditionally made by the Fon people of Abomey, the ancient capital of Dahomey, West Africa" (85). Sterling Brown asserts that both Dahomean and Bakongo traditions are evident in Powers's Bible story quilts.

> Missionaries failed to halt African religion in Georgia because it took forms they did not understand or even recognize. Dahomean influence was even greater than one would have suspected by combining the insights of Bremer and Herskovits; it also appeared in a form and a place in which whites would least expect African religious expression of any kind—in the quilts of slave women. Fashioned from throw-away cloth, slave quilts were used to clothe mysteries, to enfold those baptized with reinforcing symbols of their faith. Such quilts in Georgia bore a remarkable resemblance to Dahomean applique cloth. Harriet Powers's Bible quilt is a brilliant example both of that tradition and of Bakongo tradition, combining the two so naturally as to reflect the coming together of Dahomean and Bakongo people in American slavery. . . . Thus, her quilt is a symbol of the fusion of African ethnic traditions in slavery and later. . . . When asked about the meaning of her quilt, Harriet Powers responded at considerable length and in much detail, asserting that the quilt in every particular is Christian (91–92).

The two extant Powers quilts memorialize historical, celestial, mythic, and biblical events, all drawn into the composition through the artist's imaginative system of visual representation. Powers's beautifully executed pictographic quilts also form an interesting link between folk material culture and the culture of literacy. Combining the distinctive applique techniques of Dahomey textile art with the distinctly American narrative quilt, Powers constructed visual narratives that could almost be described as storyboards. In the quilts themselves, textile approaches textuality; and dictated notes record Powers's recital of local, biblical, and apocryphal stories that had inspired the series of narrative frames, which "read" from left to right and top to bottom in her two extent quilts, now held in the collections of the Smithsonian Institution and Boston Museum of Fine Arts.

While I reject Nasisse's speculation that there may be some "genetic" reason for the recurrent images found in visionary folk art and their continuity with similar imagery found in African art and artifacts (other than the inherited tendency of human beings to make and preserve cultural symbols), certainly the persistence of such "Africanisms" in the work of southern folk artists suggests that African cultural systems were not utterly destroyed by slavery, but rather survived in fragmentary, dispersed, and marginalized forms that continue to exist alongside dominant cultural traditions that also significantly influence African-American cultural production.

Sterling Stuckey, following Thompson's insight, argues that African-American culture was formed not only through the syncretism of African with European and indigenous native traditions, but also through the fusion of traditional practices that were familiar and comprehensible to individuals from different African ethnolinguistic groups. The slave community actually served to consolidate, reinforce, and preserve certain African customs that diverse cultural systems had shared in common, such as burial rituals that included decorating graves with sea shells, glass, or crockery.

> Slaves found objects in North America similar to the shells and close enough to the earthenware of West Africa to decorate the grave in an African manner. . . . Africans from different points of the continent shared this vision, which could have *strengthened* an African trait under the conditions of North American slavery. . . . Being on good terms with the ancestral spirits was an overarching conceptual concern for Africans everywhere in slavery. . . . No one has yet demonstrated that skilled slaves sought to cut themselves off from their spiritual base in the slave community. If skilled slaves did not remove themselves from that base they remained connected to the African heritage on the profoundest possible level. (Stuckey 42–43, emphasis in original)

What may seem to be the "spontaneous generation" of African symbols in the work of African-American folk artists may in fact indicate that the folk tradition has served as a repository of African spiritual practices since the arrival of the first captive Africans in this country. Such seemingly idiosyncratic imagery, which nevertheless alludes to dispersed and hidden fragments of coherent cultural systems, generally does not appear in the secular tradition initiated in the materially based ex-slave narratives that tend to distance the narrator from "slave superstition" or "heathen" African spirituality, while providing a rationale for African-American displays of emotion. While Christianity strongly influences African-American spirituality, it is also evident that the visionary tradition allows within its spiritual matrix a space for a syncretic African-based spirituality or diasporic consciousness that a secular narrator such as Frederick Douglass specifically rejects as slave "superstition."

In his recollection of an incident in which an African-born slave offers and Douglass accepts a special root to serve as a protective charm against being whipped by the overseer, Douglass progressively dissociates himself from this superstitious belief in the power of the ritual object, while self-consciously using his text to suggest that his increasing grasp of literacy allowed Douglass eventually to transfer his youthful belief in the power associated in African cultures with ritual objects to the power associated in bourgeois Western culture with writing. First the written pass, which the slaves, significantly, swallow after a failed escape attempt, and finally the text of the narrative itself take on this aura of power that Douglass associates with his interiorization of literacy and its technologies.

Douglass's text registers cultural hybridity even as the narrator rejects the devalued alternative consciousness of the African captive in his determined pursuit of bourgeois subjectivity, the basic prerequisite of citizenship. His ambivalent portrayal of his own youthful belief in a spiritual technique later displaced in his regard by a belief in the greater efficacy of literacy might be read as Douglass's gloss on the failure of slave insurrections led by Denmark Vesey and Nat Turner.[9] Vesey, a free Black, and Turner, a slave, sought to forge leadership at the interface of African orality/spirituality and an African-American visionary literacy founded on a prophetic reading of the Bible. Vesey's coconspirator Gullah Jack, known among slaves as "the little man who can't be killed, shot, or taken," was, according to slave testimony, "born a conjuror and a physician, in his own country [Angola]," and possessed "a charm which rendered him invulnerable." Turner's insurrection relied upon his reading of "signs in the heavens" and "hieroglyphic characters" he had "found on the leaves in the woods" that corresponded with "the figures [he] had seen in the heavens," as well as his application of biblical prophecy to the historical circumstance of slavery in the United States. Eric Foner, in *Nat Turner*, speculates that Turner "may have inherited some of his rebelliousness from his parents, for according to local tradition, his African-born mother had to be restrained from killing her infant son rather than see him a slave and his father escaped when Nat was a boy." In his dictated 1831 "confession," Turner notes that his family and the slave community had implicitly equated his predilection for prophetic vision with his precocious aptitude for literacy (*Nat Turner* 41–50). Although, like Douglass, he stressed his own extraordinary and individual brilliance, the leader of the most famous insurrection of slaves in the United States suggested that his uncanny knowledge of events that "had happened before I was born," quick intelligence, and easy acquisition of literacy were perceived by the African-American community as miraculous spiritual gifts, which signalled that "I surely would be a prophet."

> To a mind like mine, restless, inquisitive and observant of every thing that was passing, it is easy to suppose that religion was the subject to which it would be directed, and although this subject principally occupied my thoughts—there was nothing that I saw or heard to which my attention was not directed—The manner in which I learned to read and write, not only had great influence on my own mind, as I acquired it with the most perfect ease, so much so, that I have no recollection whatever of learning the alphabet—but to the astonishment of the family, one day, when a book was shewn to me to keep me from crying, I began spelling the names of different objects—this was a source of wonder to all in the neighborhood, particularly the blacks—and this learning was constantly improved at all opportunities. (*Nat Turner* 41–42)

While the Black community that nurtured Nat Turner viewed literacy as compatible and continuous with African spiritual practice, Douglass's text stresses the divergence of the letter from the spirit as African spiritual traditions are uprooted by bourgeois literacy. Douglass's loss of faith in African power/knowledge is also echoed in Henry Bibb's Story (1969) when as a young man Bibb tries but is disappointed by the inefficacy of charms procured from a slave conjuror. Given the stereotypical association of rational thought and behavior with masculinity as well as with humanity, there may have been an even greater sense of obligation on the part of men than on women to portray themselves in their narratives as rational rather than emotional or spiritual beings. Interestingly, at least two women who had been slaves, the illiterate Mary Prince and the literate Harriet Jacobs, included in their narratives tributes to the knowledge and skill of black women who practiced arts of traditional healing among the slaves.

Yet Robert Farris Thompson's insightful study of continuities between African and African-American art, drawing upon ethnographic research that regards cultural practices as coherent and comprehensible social "texts," suggests an alternate possibility of comprehensively "reading" African-American traditions of literacy. Rather than presuming that

Western knowledge and literacy simply displaced African ignorance and illiteracy, as Douglass seems to simply, the visionary tradition, which encompasses both literate and illiterate spiritual practitioners, suggests alternatively that African-American literacy might be continuous rather than discontinuous with African ways of knowing and with traditional systems of oral and visual communication that represent natural and supernatural forces as participants in an extralinguistic dialogue with human beings. Following the work of Melville Herskovits, as well as the folklorist Zora Neale Hurston, Robert Farris Thompson has emphasized that ritual objects are invested with communicative power through the association of the names or qualities of objects with other objects, qualities, or actions.

> Kongo ritual experts have always worked with visionary objects. They call such objects *minkisi* (*nkisi*, in the singular). . . . The powers of such experts also resided in the ability to read and write the *nkisi* language of visual astonishment. Such signs (*bidimbu*) include chalked ideographs, plus myriad symbolic objects linked to mystic actions, through puns, on the name of the object and the sound of a verb. For example, a priest might place a grain (*luzibu*) in an *nkisi* so that it might spiritually open (*zibula*) up an affair. But Kongo writing also sometimes included mysterious ciphers, received by a person in a state of spiritual possession. This was "writing in the spirit," sometimes referred to as "visual glossolalia," this was writing as if copied from "a billboard in the sky." (101)

Nat Turner's prophetic interpretation of "signs in the heavens" suggests that the members of slave communities found in the text of the Bible a resonance with aspects of African spiritual techniques (41–50). Douglass's secular interpretation of the visionary object may have overlooked the spiritual power of the *nkisi* "visual language," suggested in the multivalent significance of the *root*, which might have been used by the conjuror in ritual practice to indicate the strength that comes of being *rooted* in a coherent culture and kinship structure.[10] In the twisted appearance of the gnarled root may be found an analogue, within nature, of the mystic scribbling that represents for J. B. Murray the possibility of mediumistic communication with the supernatural.

> "High John the Conqueror" or "Johnny the Conqueroo" is a gnarled root sold for love and gambling. "When you see a twisted root within a charm," Nigerian elder Fu-Kiau Bunseki told Robert Farris Thompson, "you know like a tornado hidden in an egg, that this *nkisi* is very very strong." (*Flash of the Spirit*, 131). [Contemporary African-American artist Alison] Saar has adapted this idea to a political image of Black power, a continuation of the concept of the extraordinary buried in the ordinary.[11]

The root's purported "magic" might lie simply in the power of language to aid in visualization as a healing technique, or as a psychological tool for self-affirmation. The effectiveness of visualization and affirmation as techniques of mental and physical health have only recently begun to be demonstrated through scientific experiment. Surely the African-American root doctor's "arts of defense and affirmation" also served as arts of survival for slaves barred from access to political power who were reliant upon religion for institutional structure and upon their own visionary powers of imagination to "make a way out of no way" and thus conjure a better future for their descendants. Contemporary African Americans, armed with technical skill and tools of secular analysis, may equally rely upon the inspiration they derive from these African arts for "creative strategies of cohesion and survival" (Piper 19).

> The transmission of two important African religious concepts—religious writing and healing charms—provides important examples of the influence of African cultural traditions on Afro-American visionary arts. Arts preserve cultural traditions even though the social context of traditions may change. In Africa the deeper significance of religious symbolism was revealed to those who had earned the title of elder. When religious ideas reappeared in the New World, they took different forms and meanings and were transmitted in different ways. They survived because they were essential tools of survival, and thus were encoded in a multiplicity of forms: visual arts, songs, dance, and black speech. Afro-American visionary arts can perhaps be classified into those more influenced by African script traditions or those more influenced by African charm traditions. (Wahlman 29)

If it can be demonstrated that aspects of African religious practice, such as spirit possession, survive in contemporary worship in many Black churches, then it may not be too great a stretch to suppose that similar spiritual values, including even a "miniaturization" of spirit possession, might also survive in a compatible tradition of visionary writing. The ability to produce knowledge through "readings" of signs offered by the natural world, as well as the freedom African-American visionaries have found in submission to a spiritual force experienced as the interiorization of an external, self-validating power certainly have resonance with attributes Timothy Simone identifies with African cultural systems.

> In traditional African cultures, the surfaces, depths, and beyonds were barely distinguishable from each other. Oscillating the demarcations with his own movements, man was simultaneously located in every dimension. Imprecision, fuzziness, and incomprehension were the very conditions which made it possible to develop a viable knowledge of social relations. Instead of these conditions being a problem to solve by resolute knowledge, they were viewed as the necessary limits to knowledge itself, determined by the value in which such knowledge was held, and the attitudes taken toward it.
>
> There were choices among readings to be made. People looked for the best way to read things. That chosen as the best was not viewed as inherently the best to the exclusion of other readings. The best was one that added resiliency, validation, or sustenance to the *act* of reading. Africans did consider every surface as a surface to be read. Each reading was to add something else that could be said, neither to the detriment, exclusion, or undoing of any other reading. Not all surfaces were visible.
>
> The position of being an individual with a capacity to articulate freely is expressed by the Songhai of Mali as: "I am a voice from elsewhere free to say exactly what they want" . . . Because he voices the thoughts of others, the speaker is not implicated, constrained, or held back in the speaking. His freedom to speak is not contingent upon what he has to say. He can make something happen—invent, undermine, posit, play—without it seeming that he is the one doing it. The speaker is not to be located in the situation he represents or creates with his speech and its concomitant assumptions and ideas. Some part of the speaker is always some place else. Therefore, no matter what happens as a result of the speaking, he is never fully captured, analyzed, apprehended, or pinned down by the listeners. Although this notion sounds

> like a Western deconstructive position toward identity in general, the difference in the Song-hai context is that this notion is consciously recognized as the precondition for speaking in general and descriptive of the psychological orientation assumed toward speaking. (153–54)

Of course, the Greek and Semitic cultures on which classical Western civilization is founded, and which had carried on a dialogue with Africa through Egypt, both viewed the inspired writer as the instrument of a divine spirit; and outside of scientific or critical discourses, this view of the artist still pertains, at least residually, in discussions of creativity. Also sometimes overlooked in discussions of African-American syncretism is the extent to which African cultures themselves typically have little interest in purity or orthodoxy, but have frequently sought to mesh tradition with exogenous influences.[12]

> Modern Kongo prophets, restructuring Christianity with the tenets of their classical religion, also use such mystic writing. The prophet submits to trance, and in the spirit, he taps unseen potencies, deriving from The Holy Spirit. . . . Vibrations of the spirit [may] blur the letters into undulating hints of powers streaming from the ancestors, from the woods or from the water. . . . This is not writing as the secular world understands such things. This is spiritual oscillography. These texts themselves embody *mayembo* (spiritual ecstacy) or *zakama* (spiritual happiness). In actual Kongo spirit-possession, ecstacy trembles the shoulder-blades of the ritual authority. Here, they ripple the body in a similar fashion, only miniaturized to the compass of a single writing hand.
>   The spirit enters into the shaping of every single utterance. It leaves a unique impress . . . this is what ecstasy might read like in transcription. (Thompson 101)

The Kongo concepts, *mayembo* and *zakama*, spiritual ecstasy and spiritual happiness, are paramount in the mystical experiences of those African-American preachers Jarena Lee, Zilpha Elaw, and Julia Foote, whose spiritual autobiographies are collected by William L. Andrews in *Sisters of the Spirit*. Each of these women had been disciplined and silenced during a childhood spent as an indentured servant in a white household, and each uses literacy to prepare herself for the visitation of the spirit that will "unbridle" the tongue and allow the reader of the Word to speak in God's name. Jarena Lee, in a spiritual autobiography published in 1836, asserts that her ecstatic experiences (which include visual, aural, and tactile impressions she believes are personal communications with God) derive from her continual preoccupation with spiritual matters.

> As to the nature of uncommon impressions, which the reader cannot but have noticed, and possibly sneered at in the course of these pages, they may be accounted for in this way: It is known that the blind have the sense of hearing in a manner much more acute than those who can see: also their sense of feeling is exceedingly fine, and is found to detect any roughness on the smoothest surface, where those who can see can find none. So it may be with such as [I] am, who has never had more than three months schooling; and wishing to know much of the way and law of God, have therefore watched the more closely the operations of the spirit, and have in consequence been fed thereby. (Andrews 48)

For Julia Foote, the pursuit of literacy led to self-fulfillment through the fulfillment of her spiritual aspirations:

I was a poor reader and a poor writer; but the dear Holy Spirit helped me by quickening my mental faculties. The more my besetting sin troubled me, the more anxious I became for an education. I believed that, if I were educated, God could make me understand what I needed; for, in spite of what others said, it would come to me, now and then, that I needed something more than what I had, but what that something was I could not tell. (Andrews 182)

Against the prevailing association of Blackness with ignorance and sin, Zilpha Elaw, much like Nat Turner, boldly asserts her intellectual authority and her intimacy with spiritual power:

At the commencement of my religious course, I was deplorably ignorant and dark; but the Lord himself was graciously pleased to become my teacher, instructing me by his Holy Spirit, in the knowledge of the Holy Scriptures. It was not by the aid of human instruments that I was first drawn to Christ; and it was by the Lord alone that I was upheld, confirmed, instructed, sanctified, and directed. (Andrews 60)

These writers are less interested than Douglass or other ex-slave narrators in providing credible documentary evidence of their literacy than in establishing a claim to direct spiritual communication with the divine. Such claims authorized their spiritual literacy, and ranged from attributing rapid learning to an eagerness to read the Bible, to outright miracles of sudden comprehension, or instruction in the form of spiritual guides sent in dreams or visions. Jarena Lee experienced her call to preach in a vision "which was presented to [her] so plainly as if it had been a literal fact." This vision had as its sequel a dream in which she responds to the call:

In consequence of this, my mind became so exercised that during the night following, I took a text, and preached in my sleep. I thought there stood before me a great multitude, while I expounded to them the things of religion. So violent were my exertions, that I awoke from the sound of my own voice, which also awoke the family of the house where I resided. (Andrews 35)

Similar preoccupations with spiritual awakening pervade the journals of Rebecca Cox Jackson, founder of an African-American Shaker community. Jean Humez argues persuasively that the Shaker religion attracted Jackson in part because of its emphasis on sexual and racial equality. With the Shakers, who acknowledged her "gifts of power" as a "spirit-instrument," Jackson found support and encouragement of her desire to lead a self-sufficient Black community. It is also worth noting that, although the requirement of celibacy would have discouraged most African Americans from joining the Shakers, theirs was virtually the only Christian religion that incorporated ecstatic dance into its worship. Most Protestant sects absolutely prohibited dancing, and this forbidden pleasure was a temptation to more than one African-American convert.

Zilpha Elaw's parents made a vow to give up dancing and joined the Methodist church after a nearly fatal accident occurred on their way home from a frolic. Later, Elaw's older sister "would run away from home and go to dances—a place forbidden to us all," and Elaw herself, as a youthful Christian, "yielded to the persuasions of the old fiddler," but soon repented her supposed sin: "Had I persisted in dancing, I believe God would have smitten me dead on the spot. . . . What good is all this dissipation of the body and mind? Does dancing help to make you a better Christian?" (Andrews 178).

Among Rebecca Cox Jackson's gifts of power was the gift of literacy, which she explained as the result of divine instruction. Jackson wrote in her spiritual journal, kept from 1830 to 1864, that "the gift of literacy" came to her after praying to God when her literate brother, who was always too tired or too busy to teach her to read, failed to take accurate dictation of her spoken words when asked to write a letter. (The letter-writing sessions suggest to the reader of her journals the actual material site of her acquisition of literacy, as she alertly watches her brother write down her spoken words and then has him read them back to her.)

> After I received the blessing of God, I had a great desire to read the Bible. . . . And my brother so tired when he would come home that he had not power so to do, and it would grieve me. Then I would pray to God to give me power over my feelings that I might not think hard of my brother. Then I would be comforted. So I went to get my brother to write my letters and to read them. So he was a writing a letter in answer to one he had just read I told him what to put in. Then I asked him to read. He did. I said, "Thee has put in more than I told thee. This he done several times. I then said, "I don't want thee to *word* my letter. I only want thee to *write* it." Then he said, "Sister, thee is the hardest one I ever wrote for!" These words, together with the manner that he had wrote my letter, pierced my soul like a sword. . . . And these words were spoken in my heart, "Be faithful, and the time shall come when you can write.". . . One day I was sitting finishing a dress in haste and in prayer. This word was spoken in my mind, "Who learned the first man on earth?" "Why God." "He is unchangeable, and if He learned the first man to read, He can learn you." I laid down my dress, picked up my Bible, ran upstairs, opened it, and kneeled down with it pressed to my breast, prayed earnestly to Almighty God if it was consisting to His holy will, to learn me to read His holy word. And when I looked on the word, I began to read. (107–8)

In her "dream of three books and a holy one," Jackson, who acquired literacy after age thirty-five, recalled:

> A white man took me by my right hand and led me on the north side of the room, where sat a square table. On it lay a book open. And he said to me. "Thou shall be instructed in the book, from Genesis to Revelations." And he took me on the west side, where stood a table. And it was like the first. And said, "Yea, thou shall be instructed from the beginning of creation to the end of time." And then he took me on the east side of the room also, where stood a table and book like the two first, and said, "I will instruct thee—yea, thou shall be instructed from the beginning of all things to the end of all things. Yea, thou shall be well instructed, I will instruct." (146)

Jackson's image of the "holy one" who leads and instructs is sustained by the missionary efforts of white preachers as well as prevalent representations of the Christian deity and his angelic assistants. The association of literacy with white men (whose authority seems to be emphasized by the multiplication of books in Jackson's dream, and underlined by the symbolic significance of the square table and the right hand) is also common to early writings of African captives such as Equiano, who wrote in his 1792 narrative, "I had often seen my master and Dick employed in reading; and I had a great curiosity to talk to the books, as I thought they did; and so to learn how all things had a beginning" (43).

Yet Jackson differs from Equiano, and from Douglass, who, with the help of white boys and women, steals the thunder of white men. What distinguishes her representation of the acquisition of literacy is her belief that she learned to read not from any actual white person or persons in her community, nor even from her literate kindred, but from heavenly messengers (visualized as white and male) who appeared in dreams to instruct her. More often, Jackson's inspiration to acquire literacy is represented as encouraging "words spoken in [her] heart," and the extent to which both literacy and Christianity reinforced the authority of male speakers is suggested by the fact that even this inner voice of self-empowerment is described as words of "a tender father" (107–8). Thus the struggle for self-authorization is as dramatic for freeborn or emancipated visionary writers as it is for the ex-slave narrators. Yet it is striking to note that their reliance on visions, dreams, inner voices, and possession by the Holy Spirit, empowering them to speak and write, also may be seen as attempts of African Americans, in the process of acquiring literacy, to fuse the inspiriting techniques of Christian prayer and biblical textuality with African traditions of oral and visual expressiveness. Protestantism in particular seems to have reinforced certain African cultural uses of "spirit-writing," while fostering an African-American visionary literacy that values and legitimates the protective power of writing over the use of ritual objects. Such objects or charms are now more closely associated in African-American culture with the persistence of African spiritual practices, while the links connecting African-American visionary literacy to African script-systems have, until recently, been obscured. The secular tradition of the blues paradoxically has circulated certain spiritual knowledge concerning the use of the mojo, while the Protestant religious tradition, with its emphasis on textuality, has been quite instrumental in promoting secular literacy among African Americans.

African-American literature of the 19th century registers the emergence of a specifically African-American culture marked by a productive tension between individuality and collectivity, and between the sacred and secular, aspects of everyday life that African cultures had worked to integrate seamlessly through communal rituals that forged collective identities and assured human beings of their significance in the universe. Certainly the ex-slave narrators' entry into the public discourse on slavery and freedom was politically and historically crucial, and their writings continue to resonate in the "call and response" that Robert Stepto designated as the characteristic mode of African-American literary influence. Yet it is also thanks to the complementary traditions of folk and visionary artists and writers who have preserved aspects of African and diasporic cultural consciousness in their syncretically visual and visionary works that the secular and spiritual traditions of African-American literacy have begun once again to merge aesthetically, not in collective ritual, but in the work of contemporary visual and performance artists, such as Xenobia Bailey, Romare Bearden, John Biggers, Houston Conwill, Mel Edwards, David Hammons, Philip Jones, Ed Love, Robbie McCauley, Alison Saar, Betye Saar, Joyce Scott, Lorna Simpson, Renee Stout, Michael Cummings, Jawole Willa Jo Zollar, and others (whose works have been studied by art critics, curators, and art historians, including Mary Schmidt Campbell, Kellie Jones, Kinshasha Conwill, Judith McWillie, Lowery Sims, Alvia Wardlaw, and Judith Wilson) as well as in the work of contemporary African-American writers, such as Toni Cade Bambara, Octavia Butler, Randall Kenan, Ishmael Reed, Adrienne Kennedy, Nathaniel Mackey, Toni Morrison, Gloria Naylor, Ntozake Shange, and Alice Walker, in whose works and texts it is possible to read "the persistence of vision" (Mullen 10–13).

NOTES

1. See Henry Louis Gates's *Figures in Black.*

2. See Thompson's *Flash of the Spirit* and "The Song That Named the Land."

3. I have written more extensively about this tradition in "Gender and the Subjugated Body: Readings of Race, Subjectivity, and Difference in the Construction of Slave Narratives" (Ph.D. dissertation, University of California, Santa Cruz, 1990).

4. Similarly, the elaborately decorative, asymmetrically gridlike "devil houses" drawn in bichromatic red and blue colored pencil by illiterate prison artist Frank Jones were meant to confine and imprison the dangerous "spirits" that Jones had seen since childhood, as a result of having been "born with a veil over his left eye." Lynne Adele speculates, "Like the individuals Jones encountered in his physical world, the inhabitants of his spiritual world were often dangerous. The haints tormented and haunted Jones, but by capturing them on paper and enclosing them in the cell-like rooms of the houses, he could render them harmless" (42). Jones and Murray may share the African-American aesthetic of quiltmakers such as Pecolia Warner, whose work, according to Maude Southwell Wahlman, employs "multiple patterning, asymmetry, and unpredictable rhythms and tensions similar to those found in other Afro-American visual arts and in blues, jazz, Black English, and dance." Traditionally African-American tropes expressing tension between discontinuity/continuity, innovation/tradition, individuality/community, movement/stasis, passage/confinement and inclusion/exclusion are addressed not only in the literary canon, but also in the work of illiterate quilters and painters who improvise various, idiosyncratic, irregular rhythms upon the stable, containing structure of the grid. According to Wahlman, "Multiple patterning, and vestiges of script-like forms and designs, are especially evident in Afro-American [folk] paintings" (33).

5. See also Ruth Bass's "Mojo" and "The Little Man."

6. See Angelo Costanzo's *Surprizing Narrative: Olaudah Equiano and the Beginnings of Black Autobiography.*

7. See Gates's *The Signifying Monkey* (127–69).

8. Douglass's acquisition of literacy alienates him from the culture of plantation slaves, whose attempt to create culture and community is increasingly viewed by the narrator as mere accommodation to their enslavement. Recent scholarship has expanded to include a broader spectrum of the slave community in addition to extraordinary individuals, such as Douglass, whose literacy and public stature allowed his immediate entry into the historical record. With a more extensive set of scholarly tools, it has become possible to appreciate the cultural contributions of slaves who left transcribed oral accounts and visual records of their existence. While Douglass's "copy-book" literacy implied a white male model, despite his oppositional stance, the folklorist Gladys-Marie Fry shows that slave women making quilts for their own families rejected the patterns found in quilting copybooks they had followed when supervised by their mistresses. They used opportunities to make their own quilts as occasions for enjoying their own oral expressiveness, and preferred their own cultural aesthetic when it came to making quilts for their own use. My argument is that new insights into African-American literature emerge when texts are read in relation to a continuum of expressivity that includes forms which are oral, visual, tactile, kinesthetic, nonliterate, and extraliterate, as well as literate:

> [S]laves made two types of quilts: those for their personal use, made on their own time; and quilts for the big house, stitched under the supervision of the mistress.... The plantation mistress learned some traditional patterns from English copybooks.... Slave women, however, learned traditional quilting patterns not only from the mistress but also from each other.... Slave women also used original patterns for their personal quilts.... Slaves quilted during their "own time".... Often during more extended periods of free time, such as Sundays and holidays, authorized quilting parties were held in the quarters for slave women to pass the time making quilts while telling stories and passing along gossip about plantation events.... The glue that helped cement the fragile and uncertain existence of slave life was their oral lore. It was an ever-present force—sometimes the main event, as in the slave quilting party—and sometimes the background event while slaves sewed, mended, knitted, and such. But present it was. While the of-

ficial learning of the master's literate world was denied the slave, it was the slave's oral lore that taught moral lessons, values, attitudes, strategies for survival, rites of passage, and humor! Folklore helped to preserve the slaves' sense of identity, of knowing who they were and how they perceived the world. Folk traditions also served as a buffer between the slaves and a hostile world, both on and off the plantation. For it was in the slave quarters that African traditions first met and intersected with Euro-American cultural forms. What emerged were transformations, adaptations, and reinterpretations. (39, 45–49, 63–64)

9. Perhaps for similar reasons as Douglass, Arna Bontemps also rejects the models of leadership and resistance offered by Vesey and Turner. Desiring to write a novel based on one of the most significant historically documented slave insurrections, Bontemps chose the rebellion led by Gabriel Prosser over the equally doomed plots of Vesey and Turner. While all three conspiracies failed, Prosser's style of leadership seemed preferable to the author. Bontemps wrote in his introduction to the novel, "Gabriel had not opened his mind too fully and hence had not been betrayed as had Vesey. He had by his own dignity and by the esteem in which he was held inspired and maintained loyalty. He had not depended on trance-like mumbo jumbo" (xii, xiii). Yet Prosser's leadership was not devoid of a spiritual or religious component, since he was probably to some degree influenced by his brother Martin, a preacher and coleader of the insurrection. See also Sterling Stuckey's *Slave Culture* and Herbert Aptheker's *American Negro Slave Revolts*.

10. Slave traders and masters deliberately mixed together Africans from diverse ethnolinguistic groups in order to prevent organized escape and rebellion. This uprooting and fragmentation of language and culture indeed destroyed the traditional bonds of kinship (and the kinship-based authority of the African patriarch) that had organized the collective identities of Africans. Although the common experience of the Middle Passage forged bonds among recent captives, many individuals did not begin to identify themselves racially with black people of other "nations" until slaves had forged a common African-American culture, while trying to hold together their slave families in their harsh, new environment. Their traditional group identification shattered, such displaced individuals (often adolescents who, like Equiano, were captured before they would have been ritually initiated into their clans) were sometimes easily manipulated by their masters, resulting in the disunity and betrayal of slaves who attempted to escape in groups or conspired to incite insurrection. Douglass's retrospective skepticism about the potency of the phallic root is in part the result of his strong suspicion that his first escape attempt had been betrayed by Sandy, the African-born conjuror. See also *American Negro Slavery*.

11. See Plate 13 (between pages 88 and 90) in Lucy R. Lippard's *Mixed Blessings*.

12. Discussing contemporary race relations in the United States, Timothy M. Simone points hopefully to this imaginative ability of Black culture to embrace rather than repulse otherness: "Although there is great variation among African societies . . . what is common among them is their ability to make the Other an integral aspect of their cultural and psychological lives. . . . When I ask my students to describe the basic difference between whites and blacks, the most-often-cited factor is the degree to which blacks are willing to extend themselves to the outside, to incorporate new ideas and influences with a minimum of a priori judgement. Minister Neal Massoud of the Nation of Islam: 'Our power has been our ability to extend ourselves to that which seems implausible, to that which makes little sense. . . . We have extended ourselves to both the unseen and the visible, to the fruits of our labor and the graves we have dug for them'" (57–58).

WORKS CITED

Adele, Lynne. *Black History/Black Vision: The Visionary Image in Texas.* The Gallery. Austin: University of Texas Press, 1989.

American Negro Slavery. Ed. Michael Mullin. New York: Harper and Row, 1976.

Andrews, William L. *Sisters of the Spirit: Three Black Women's Autobiographies of the Nineteenth Century.* Bloomington: Indiana University Press, 1986.

Aptheker, Herbert. *American Negro Slave Revolts.* New York: International Publishers, 1983; first published, New York: Columbia University Press, 1943.

Bass, Ruth. "Mojo" and "The Little Man." In *Motherwit from the Laughing Barrel.* Ed. Alan Dundes. New York: Prentice Hall, 1973.

Bibb, Henry (1969). Narrative of the life and adventures of Henry Bibb: An American Slave. New York: Negro Universities Press.

Bontemps, Arna. *Black Thunder.* Boston: Beacon Press, 1968; first published by Macmillan, 1936.

Costanzo, Angelo. *Surprizing Narrative: Olaudah Equiano and the Beginnings of Black Autobiography.* New York: Greenwood Press, 1987.

Davis, Charles T., and Henry L. Gates Jr. *The Slaves' Narrative.* New York: Oxford University Press, 1985.

Douglass, Frederick. *Narrative: The Classic Slave Narratives.* Ed. Henry Louis Gates Jr. New York: New American Library, 1987.

Equiano, Olaudah. *Travels: The Classic Slave Narratives.* Ed. Henry Louis Gates Jr. New York: New American Library, 1987.

Fry, Gladys-Marie. *Stitched from the Soul: Slave Quilts from the Antebellum South.* New York: Dutton Studio Books/Museum of American Folk Art, 1990.

Gates, Henry Louis, Jr. *Figures in Black: Words, Signs, and the "Racial" Self.* New York: Oxford University Press, 1987.

———. *The Signifying Monkey.* New York: Oxford University Press, 1988.

Jackson, Rebecca Cox. *Gifts of Power: The Writings of Rebecca Jackson, Black Visionary, Shaker Eldress.* Ed. Jean McMahon Humez. Amherst: The University of Massachusetts Press, 1981.

Lippard, Lucy R. *Mixed Blessings: New Art in a Multicultural America.* New York: Pantheon Books, 1990.

Lowe, Donald. *History of Bourgeois Perception.* Chicago: University of Chicago Press, 1982.

Mullen, Kirsten. "The Persistence of Vision." In *Rambling on My Mind: Black Folk Art in the Southwest.* Dallas: Museum of African-American Life and Culture, 1987.

Nasisse, Andy. "Aspects of Visionary Art." *Baking in the Sun: Visionary Images from the South.* University Art Museum. Lafayette: University of Southwestern Louisiana, 1987.

Nat Turner. Ed. Eric Foner. Englewood Cliffs, N.J.: Prentice Hall, 1971.

Piper, Adrian. "The Triple Negation of Colored Women Artists." In *New Generation: Southern Black Aesthetic.* New York: Southeastern Center for Contemporary Art, 1990.

Simone, Timothy Maliqalim. *About Face: Race in Postmodern America.* Brooklyn: Autonomedia, 1989.

Stepto, Robert B. *From Behind the Veil: A Study of Afro-American Narrative.* Urbana: University of Illinois Press, 1979.

Stuckey, Sterling. *Slave Culture: Nationalist Theory and the Foundations of Black America.* New York: Oxford University Press, 1987.

Thompson, Robert Farris. "The Song That Named the Land: The Visionary Presence in African-American Art." In *Black Art: Ancestral Legacy.* Dallas Museum of Art. New York: Harry N. Abrams, Inc., 1989, 97–141.

———. *Flash of the Spirit.* New York: Vintage Books/Random House, 1983.

Wahlman, Maude Southwell. "Africanisms in Afro-American Visionary Arts." In *Baking in the Sun.* Ed. Herman Mhire. Lafayette: University Art Museum, University of Southwestern Louisiana, 1987.

PART III
SEXUALITY, EDUCATION, RELIGION

21

BLACK (W)HOLES AND THE GEOMETRY OF BLACK FEMALE SEXUALITY

Evelynn Hammonds

The female body in the West is not a unitary sign. Rather, like a coin, it has an obverse and a reverse: on the one side, it is white; on the other, not-white or, prototypically, black. The two bodies cannot be separated, nor can one body be understood in isolation from the other in the West's metaphoric construction of "woman." White is what woman is; not-white (and the stereotypes not-white gathers in) is what she had better not be. Even in an allegedly postmodern era, the not-white woman as well as the not-white man are symbolically and even theoretically excluded from sexual difference. Their function continues to be to cast the difference of white men and white women into sharper relief.
                                                            –Lorraine O'Grady

When asked to write for the second special issue of *differences* on queer theory I must admit I was at first hesitant even to entertain the idea. Though much of what is now called queer theory I find engaging and intellectually stimulating, I still found the idea of writing about it disturbing. When I am asked if I am queer I usually answer yes even though the ways in which I am queer have never been articulated in the body of work that is now called queer theory. Where should I begin? I asked myself. Do I have to start by adding another adjective to my already long list of self-chosen identities? I used to be a Black lesbian, feminist, writer, scientist, historian of science, and activist. Now would I be a Black, queer, feminist, writer, scientist, historian of science, and activist? Given the rapidity with which new appellations are created I wondered if my new list would still be up to date by the time the article came out. More important, does this change or any change I might make to my list convey to anyone the ways in which I am queer?

   Even a cursory reading of the first issue of *differences* on queer theory or a close reading of *The Lesbian and Gay Studies Reader* (Abelove, Barale, and Halperin)—by now biblical in status—would lead me to answer no. So what would be the point of my writing for a second issue on queer theory? Well, I could perform that by now familiar act taken by Black feminists and offer a critique of every white feminist for her failure to articulate a conception of a racialized sexuality. I could argue that while it has been acknowledged that race is not simply additive to or derivative of sexual difference, few white feminists have attempted to move beyond simply stating this point to describe the powerful effect that race has on the construction and representation of gender and sexuality. I could go further and note that even when race is mentioned it is a limited notion devoid of complexities. Sometimes it is reduced to biology and other times referred to as a social construction. Rarely is it used as a "global sign," a "metalanguage," as the "ultimate trope of difference, arbitrarily contrived to produce and maintain relations of power and subordination" (Higginbotham 255).

If I were to make this argument, I wonder under what subheading such an article would appear in *The Lesbian and Gay Studies Reader*. Assuming, of course, that they would want to include it in the second edition. How about "Politics and Sex"? Well, it would certainly be political, but what would anybody learn about sex from it? As I look at my choices I see that I would want my article to appear in the section "Subjectivity, Discipline, Resistance." But where would I situate myself in the group of essays that discuss "lesbian experience," "lesbian identity," "gender insubordination," and "Butch-Femme Aesthetic"? Perhaps they wouldn't want a reprint after all and I'd be off the hook. Maybe I've just hit one of those "constructed silences" that Teresa de Lauretis wrote about as one of the problems in lesbian and gay studies ("Queer" viii).

When *The Lesbian and Gay Studies Reader* was published, I followed my usual practice and searched for the articles on Black women's sexuality. This reading practice has become such a commonplace in my life I have forgotten how and when I began it. I never open a book about lesbians or gays with the expectation that I will find some essay that will address the concerns of my life. Given that on the average most collections don't include writers of color, just the appearance of essays by African Americans, Latinos, and Native Americans in this volume was welcome. The work of Barbara Smith, Stuart Hall, Phillip Brian Harper, Gloria Hall, Deborah McDowell, and, of course, Audre Lorde has deeply influenced my intellectual and political work for many years as has the work of many of the other writers in this volume.

Yet, despite the presence of these writers, this text displays the consistently exclusionary practices of lesbian and gay studies in general. In my reading, the canonical terms and categories of the field: "lesbian," "gay," "butch," "femme," "sexuality," and "subjectivity" are stripped of context in the works of those theorizing about these very categories, identities, and subject positions. Each of these terms is defined with white as the normative state of existence. This is an obvious criticism which many have expressed since the appearance of this volume. More interesting is the question of whether the essays engaging with the canonical terms have been in any way informed by the work of the writers of color that do appear in the volume. The essays by Hull and McDowell both address the point I am trying to make. Hull describes the life of Angelina Weld Grimké, a poet of the Harlem Renaissance whose poetry expressed desire for women. This desire is circumscribed, underwritten, and unspoken in her poetry. McDowell's critical reading of Nella Larsen's *Passing* also points to the submersion of sexuality and same-sex desire among Black women. In addition, Harper's essay on the death of Max Robinson, one of the most visible African Americans of his generation, foregrounds the silence in Black communities on the issue of sexuality and AIDS. "Silence" is emphasized as well in the essay by Ana Maria Alonso and Maria Teresa Koreck on the AIDS crisis in "Hispanic" communities. But the issue of silence about so-called deviant sexuality in public discourse and its submersion in private spaces for people of color is never addressed in theorizing about the canonical categories of lesbian and gay studies in the reader. More important, public discourse on the sexuality of particular racial and ethnic groups is shaped by processes that pathologize those groups, which in turn produce the submersion of sexuality and the attendant silence(s). Lesbian and gay theory fails to acknowledge that these very processes are connected to the construction of the sexualities of whites, historically and contemporaneously.

QUEER WORDS AND QUEER PRACTICES

I am not by nature an optimist, although I do believe that change is possible and necessary. Does a shift from lesbian to queer relieve my sense of anxiety over whether the exclusionary practices of lesbian and gay studies can be resolved? If queer theory is, as de Lauretis notes in her introduction to the first special issue of *differences*, the place where "we [would] be willing to examine, make explicit, compare, or confront the respective histories, assumptions, and conceptual frameworks that have characterized the self-representations of North American lesbians and gay men, of color and white," and if it is "from there, [that] we could then go on to recast or reinvent the terms of our sexualities, to construct another discursive horizon, another way of thinking the sexual," then maybe I had found a place to explore the ways in which queer, Black, and female subjectivities are produced (iv–v). Of course, I first had to gather more evidence about this shift before I jumped into the fray.

In her genealogy of queer theory, de Lauretis argues that the term was arrived at in the effort to avoid all the distinctions in the discursive protocols that emerged from the standard usage of the terms *lesbian* and *gay*. The kind of distinctions she notes include the need to add qualifiers of race or national affiliation to the labels "lesbian" and "gay." De Lauretis goes on to address my central concern. She writes:

> The fact of the matter is, most of us, lesbians and gay men, do not know much about one another's sexual history, experiences, fantasies, desire, or modes of theorizing. And we do not know enough about ourselves, as well, when it comes to differences between and within lesbians, and between and within gay men, in relation to race and its attendant differences of class or ethnic culture, generational, geographical, and socio-political location. *We do not know enough to theorize those differences.* (viii; emphasis added)

She continues:

> Thus an equally troubling question in the burgeoning field of "gay and lesbian studies" concerns the discursive constructions and constructed silences around the relations of race to identity and subjectivity in the practices of homosexualities and the representations of same sex desire. (viii)

In my reading of her essay, de Lauretis then goes on to attribute the problem of the lack of knowledge of the experiences of gays and lesbians of color to gays and lesbians of color. While noting the problems of their restricted access to publishing venues or academic positions, she concludes that "perhaps, to a gay writer and critic of color, defining himself gay is not of the utmost importance; he may have other more pressing priorities in his work and life" (ix). This is a woefully inadequate characterization of the problem of the visibility of gays and lesbians of color. Certainly institutional racism, homophobia, and the general structural inequalities in American society have a great deal more to do with this invisibility than personal choices. I have reported de Lauretis's words at length because her work is symptomatic of the disjuncture I see between the stated goals of the volume she edited and what it actually enacts.

Despite the presence of writers of color, the authors of the essays in the *differences* volume avoid interrogating their own practices with respect to the issue of difference. That is to say to differences of race, ethnicity, and representation in analyzing subjectivity, desire, and the use of the psychoanalytic in gay and lesbian theory. Only Ekua Omosupe explicitly addresses the issue of Black female subjectivity, and her essay foregrounds the very issue that queer theory ostensibly is committed to addressing. Omosupe still sees the need to announce her skepticism at the use of the term *lesbian* without the qualifier "Black" and addresses the lack of attention to race in gay and lesbian studies in her analysis of Adrienne Rich's work (108). For her, the term "lesbian" without the racial qualifier is simply to be read as "white" lesbian. Despite her criticism, however, she too avoids confronting difference within the category of Black lesbian, speaking of "the" Black lesbian without attention to or acknowledgment of a multiplicity of identities or subject positions for Black women. She notes that the title of Audre Lorde's collected essays is *Sister Outsider*, which she argues is "an apt metaphor for the Black lesbian's position in relation to the white dominant political cultures and to her own Black community as well" (106). But metaphors reveal as much as they conceal and Omosupe cannot tell us what kind of outsider Lorde is, that is to say what sexual practices, discourses, and subject positions within her Black community she was rebelling against. As with the Hull and McDowell essays, Omosupe's article acknowledges silence, erasure, and invisibility as crucial issues in the dominant discourses about black female sexuality, while the essay and the volume as a whole continue to enact this silence.

Thus, queer theory as reflected in this volume has so far failed to theorize the very questions de Lauretis announces that the term "queer" will address. I disagree with her assertion that we do not know enough about one another's differences to theorize differences between and within gays and lesbians in relation to race. This kind of theorizing of difference, after all, isn't simply a matter of empirical examples. And we do know enough to delineate what queer theorists should want to know. For me it is a question of knowing specifically about the production of Black female queer sexualities: if the sexualities of Black women have been shaped by silence, erasure, and invisibility in dominant discourses, then are Black lesbian sexualities doubly silenced? What methodologies are available to read and understand this perceived void and gauge its direct and indirect effects on that which is visible? Conversely, how does the structure of what is visible, namely white female sexualities, shape those not-absent-though-not-present Black female sexualities which, as O'Grady argues, cannot be separated or understood in isolation from one another? And, finally, how do these racialized sexualities shaped by silence, erasure, and invisibility coexist with other sexualities, the closeted sexualities of white queers, for example? It seems to me that there are two projects here that need to be worked out. White feminists must refigure (white) female sexualities so that they are not theoretically dependent upon an absent yet-ever-present pathologized Black female sexuality. I am not arguing that this figuration of (white) female sexuality must try to encompass completely the experiences of Black women, but that it must include a conception of the power relations between white and Black women as expressed in the representations of sexuality (Higginbotham 252).[1] This model of power, as Judith Butler has argued, must avoid setting up "racism and homophobia and misogyny as parallel or analogical relations," while recognizing that "what has to be thought through, is the ways in which these vectors of power require and deploy each other for the purpose of their own articulation" (18).

Black feminist theorists must reclaim sexuality through the creation of a counternarrative that can reconstitute a present Black female subjectivity and that includes an analysis of power relations between white and Black women and among different groups of Black women. In both cases I am arguing for the development of a complex, relational but not necessarily analogous, conception of racialized sexualities (JanMohamed 94). In order to describe more fully what I see as the project for Black feminist theorists, I want to turn now to a review of some of the current discussions of Black women's sexuality.

THE PROBLEMATIC OF SILENCE

To name ourselves rather than be named we must first see ourselves. For some of us this will not be easy. So long unmirrored, we may have forgotten how we look. Nevertheless, we can't theorize in a void; we must have evidence.
                                    –Lorraine O'Grady

Black feminist theorists have almost universally described Black women's sexuality, when viewed from the vantage of the dominant discourses, as an absence. In one of the earliest and most compelling discussions of Black women's sexuality, the literary critic Hortense Spillers wrote: "black women are the beached whales of the sexual universe, unvoiced, misseen, not doing, awaiting their verb" ("Interstices" 74). For writer Toni Morrison, Black women's sexuality is one of the "unspeakable things unspoken" of the African-American experience. Black women's sexuality is often described in metaphors of speechlessness, space, or vision, as a "void" or empty space that is simultaneously ever visible (exposed) and invisible and where Black women's bodies are always already colonized. In addition, this always already colonized Black female body has so much sexual potential that it has none at all ("Interstices" 85). Historically, Black women have reacted to this repressive force of the hegemonic discourses on race and sex with silence, secrecy, and a partially self-chosen invisibility.

Black feminist theorists, historians, literary critics, sociologists, lawyers, and cultural critics have drawn upon a specific historical narrative that purportedly describes the factors that have produced and maintained perceptions of Black women's sexuality (including their own). Three themes emerge in this history: first, the construction of the Black female as the embodiment of sex and the attendant invisibility of Black women as the unvoiced, unseen everything that is not white; second, the resistance of Black women both to negative stereotypes of their sexuality and to the material effects of those stereotypes on their lives; and finally, the evolution of a "culture of dissemblance" and a "politics of silence" by Black women on the issue of their sexuality. The historical narrative begins with the production of the image of a pathologized Black female "other" in the eighteenth century by European colonial elites and the new biological scientists. By the nineteenth century, with the increasing exploitation and abuse of Black women during and after slavery, U.S. Black women reformers began to develop strategies to counter negative stereotypes of their sexuality and their use as a justification for the rape, lynching, and other abuses of Black women by whites. Although some of the strategies used by Black women reformers might have initially been characterized as resistance to dominant and increasingly hegemonic constructions of their sexuality, by the early twentieth century Black women reformers promoted a public silence about sexuality that, it could be argued, continues to the present.[2] This "politics of silence," as described by the historian Evelyn Brooks Higginbotham, emerged as a political strategy by Black women reformers who hoped by their silence and by the promotion of proper Victorian morality to demonstrate the lie of the image of the sexually immoral Black woman (262). The historian Darlene Clark Hine argues that the "culture of dissemblance" that this politics engendered was seen as a way for Black women to "protect the sanctity of inner aspects of their lives" (915). She defines this culture as "the behavior and attitudes of Black women that created the appearance of openness and disclosure but actually shielded the truth of their inner lives and selves from their oppressors" (915). "Only with secrecy," Hine argues, "thus achieving a self-imposed invisibility, could ordinary Black women accrue the psychic space and harness the resources needed to hold their own" (915). And by the projection of the image of a "super-moral" Black woman, they hoped to garner greater respect, justice, and opportunity for all Black Americans (915). Of course, as Higginbotham notes, there were problems with this strategy. First, it did not achieve its goal of ending the negative stereotyping of Black women. And second, some middle-class Black women engaged in policing the behavior of poor and working-class women and any who deviated from a Victorian norm in the name of protecting the "race."[3] My interpretation of the conservatizing and policing aspect of the "politics of silence" is that Black women reformers were responding to the ways in which any Black women could find herself "exposed" and characterized in racist sexual terms no matter what the truth of her individual life, and that they saw this so-called deviant individual behavior as a threat to the race as a whole. Finally, one of the most enduring and problematic aspects of the "politics of silence" is that in choosing silence Black women also lost the ability to articulate any conception of their sexuality.

Without more detailed historical studies we will not know the extent of this "culture of dissemblance," and many questions will remain to be answered.[4] Was it expressed differently in rural and in urban areas; in the North, West, or South? How was it maintained? Where and how was it resisted? How was it shaped by class? And, furthermore, how did it change over time? How did something that was initially adopted as a political strategy in a specific historical period become so ingrained in Black life as to be recognizable as a culture? Or did it? What emerges from the very incomplete history we have is a situation in which Black women's sexuality is ideologically located in a nexus between race and gender, where the Black female subject is not seen and has no voice. Methodologically, Black feminists have found it difficult even to fully characterize this juncture, this point of erasure where African-American women are located. As the legal scholar Kimberlé Crenshaw puts it, "Existing within the overlapping margins of race and gender discourse and the empty spaces between, it is a location whose very nature resists telling" (403). And this silence about sexuality is enacted individually and collectively by Black women and by Black feminist theorists writing about Black women.

It should not surprise us that Black women are silent about sexuality. The imposed production of silence and the removal of any alternative to the production of silence reflect the deployment of power against racialized subjects, "wherein those who could speak did not want to and those who did want to speak were prevented from doing so" (JanMohamed 105). It is this deployment of power at the level of the social and the individual which has to be historicized. It seems clear that we need a methodology that allows us to contest rather than reproduce the ideological system that has up to now defined the terrain of Black women's sexuality. Spillers made this point over a decade ago when she wrote: "Because black American women do not participate, as a category of social and cultural agents, in the legacies of symbolic power, they maintain no allegiances to a strategic formation of texts, or ways of talking about sexual experience, that even remotely resemble the paradigm of symbolic domination, except that such a paradigm has been their concrete disaster" ("Interstices" 80). To date, through the work of Black feminist literary critics, we know more about the elision of sexuality by Black women than we do about the possible varieties of expression of sexual desire.[5] Thus what we have is a very narrow view of Black women's sexuality. Certainly it is true, as Crenshaw notes, that "in feminist contexts, sexuality represents a central site of the oppression of women; rape and the rape trial are its dominant narrative trope. In antiracist discourse, sexuality is also a central site upon which the repression of Blacks has been premised; the lynching narrative is embodied as its trope" (405). Sexuality is also, as Carol Vance defines it, "simultaneously a domain of restriction, repression, and danger as well as a domain of exploration, pleasure, and agency" (1). The restrictive, repressive, and dangerous aspects of Black female sexuality have been emphasized by Black feminist writers while pleasure, exploration, and agency have gone underanalyzed.

I want to suggest that Black feminist theorists have not taken up this project in part because of their own status in the academy. Reclaiming the body as well as subjectivity is a process that Black feminist theorists in the academy must go through themselves while they are doing the work of producing theory. Black feminist theorists are themselves engaged in a process of fighting to reclaim the body—the maimed immoral Black female body—which can be and still is used by others to discredit them as producers of knowledge and as speaking subjects. The legal scholar Patricia Williams illuminates my point: "no matter what degree of professional I am, people will greet and dismiss my Black femaleness as unreliable, untrustworthy, hostile, angry, powerless, irrational, and probably destitute" (95). When reading student evaluations, she finds comments about her teaching and her body: "I marvel, in a moment of genuine bitterness, that anonymous student evaluations speculating on dimensions of my anatomy are nevertheless counted into the statistical measurement of my teaching proficiency" (95). The hypervisibility of Black women academics and the contemporary fascination with what bell hooks calls the "commodification of Otherness" (61) means that Black women today find themselves precariously perched in the academy. Ann duCille notes:

> Mass culture, as hooks argues, produces, promotes, and perpetuates the commodification of Otherness through the exploitation of the black female body. In the 1990s, however, the principal sites of exploitation are not simply the cabaret, the speakeasy, the music video, the glamour magazine; they are also the academy, the publishing industry, the intellectual community. (592)

In tandem with the notion of silence, Black women writers have repeatedly drawn on the notion of the "invisible" to describe aspects of Black women's lives in general and sexuality in particular. Lorde writes that "within this country where racial difference creates a constant, if unspoken distortion of vision, Black women have on the one hand always been highly visible, and on the other hand, have been rendered invisible through the depersonalization of racism" (91). The hypervisibility of Black women academics means that visibility too can be used to control the intellectual issues that Black women can and cannot speak about. As they are already threatened with being sexualized and rendered inauthentic as knowledge producers in the academy by students and colleagues alike, this avoidance of theorizing about sexuality can be read as one contemporary manifestation of their structured silence. I want to stress here that the silence about sexuality on the part of Black women academics is no more a "choice" than was the silence practiced by early-twentieth-century Black women. This production of silence instead of speech is an effect of the institutions such as the academy that are engaged in the commodification of Otherness. While hypervisibility can be used to silence Black women academics, it can also serve them. Lorde has argued that the "visibility which makes us most vulnerable," that of being Black, "is that which is the source of our greatest strength." Patricia Hill Collins's interpretation of Lorde's comment is that "paradoxically, being treated as an invisible Other gives black women a peculiar angle of vision, the outsider-within stance that has served so many African-American women intellectuals as a source of tremendous strength" (*Sister Outsider* 94).

Yet, while invisibility may be somewhat useful for academicians, the practice of a politics of silence belies the power of such a stance for social change. Most important, the outsider-within stance does not allow space for addressing the question of other outsiders, namely Black lesbians. Black feminist theorizing about Black female sexuality, with a few exceptions—Cheryl Clarke, Jewelle Gomez, Barbara Smith, and Audre Lorde—has been relentlessly focused on heterosexuality. The historical narrative that dominates discussion of Black female sexuality does not address even the possibility of a Black lesbian sexuality, or of a lesbian or queer subject. Spillers confirms this point when she notes that "the sexual realities of black American women across the spectrum of sexual preference and widened sexual styles tend to be a missing dialectical feature of the entire discussion" ("Interstices" 91).

At this juncture, then, I cannot cast blame for a lack of attention to Black lesbian sexuality solely on white feminist theorists. De Lauretis argues that female homosexualities may be conceptualized as social and cultural forms in their own right, which are undercoded or discursively dependent upon more established forms. They (and male homosexualities) therefore act as "an agency of social process whose mode of functioning is both interactive and yet resistant, both participatory and yet distinct, claiming at once equality and difference, and demanding political and historical representation while insisting on its material and historical specificity" ("Queer" iii). If this is true, then theorizing about Black lesbian sexuality is crucially dependent upon the existence of a conception of Black women's sexuality in general. I am not arguing that Black lesbian sexualities are derivative of Black female heterosexualities, but only that we cannot understand the latter without understanding it in relation to the former. In particular, since discussions of Black female sexuality often turn to the issue of the devastating effects of rape, incest, and sexual abuse, I want to argue that Black queer female sexualities should be seen as one of the sites where Black female desire is expressed.

Discussions of Black lesbian sexuality have most often focused on differences from or equivalencies with white lesbian sexualities, with "Black" added to delimit the fact that Black lesbians share a history with other Black women. However, this addition tends to obfuscate rather than illuminate the subject position of Black lesbians. One obvious example of distortion is that Black lesbians do not experience homophobia in the same way as do white lesbians. Here, as with other oppressions, the homophobia experienced by Black women is always shaped by racism. What has to be explored and historicized is the specificity of Black lesbian experience. I want to understand in what way Black lesbians are "outsiders" within Black communities. This, I think, would force us to examine the construction of the "closet" by Black lesbians. Although this is the topic for another essay, I want to argue here that if we accept the existence of the "politics of silence" as a historical legacy shared by all Black women, then certain expressions of Black female sexuality will be rendered as dangerous, for individuals and for the collectivity. From this it follows then that the culture of dissemblance makes it acceptable for some heterosexual Black women to cast Black lesbians as proverbial traitors to the race.[6] And this in turn explains why Black lesbians who would announce or act out desire for women—whose deviant sexuality exists within an already preexisting deviant sexuality—have been wary of embracing the status of "traitor" and the attendant loss of community such an embrace engenders.[7] Of course, while some Black lesbians have hidden the truth of their lives, there have been many forms of resistance to the conception of lesbian as traitor within Black communities. Audre Lorde is one obvious example. Lorde's claiming of her Black and lesbian difference "forced both her white and Black lesbian friends to contend with her historical agency in the face of [this] larger racial/sexual history that would reinvent her as dead" (Karla Scott, quoted in de Lauretis, *Practice* 36). I would also argue that Lorde's writing, with its focus on the erotic, on passion and desire, suggests that Black lesbian sexualities can be read as one expression of the reclamation of the despised Black female body. Therefore, the works of Lorde and other Black lesbian writers, because they foreground the very aspects of Black female sexuality that are submerged—that is, female desire and agency—are critical to our theorizing of Black female sexualities. Since silence about sexuality is being produced by Black women and Black feminist theorists, that silence itself suggests that Black women do have some degree of agency. A focus on Black lesbian sexualities, I suggest, implies that another discourse—other than silence—can be produced.

I also suggest that the project of theorizing Black female sexualities must confront psychoanalysis. Given that the Freudian paradigm is the dominant discourse that defines how sexuality is understood in this postmodern time, Black feminist theorists have to answer the question posed by Michele Wallace: "is the Freudian drama transformed by race in a way that would render it altered but usable?" (*Invisibility* 231). While some Black feminists have called the psychoanalytic approach racist, others such as Spillers, Mae Henderson, and Valerie Smith have shown its usefulness in analyzing the texts of Black women writers. As I am not a student of psychoanalytic theory, my suggested response to Wallace's question can only be tentative at best. Though I do not accept all aspects of the Freudian paradigm, I do see the need for exploring its strengths and limitations in developing a theory of Black female sexualities.

It can readily be acknowledged that the collective history of Black women has in some ways put them in a different relationship to the canonical categories of the Freudian paradigm, that is, to the father, the maternal body, to the female-sexed body (Spillers, "Mama's"). On the level of the symbolic, however, Black women have created whole worlds of sexual signs and signifiers, some of which align with those of whites and some of which do not. Nonetheless, they are worlds that always have to contend with the power that the white world has to invade, pathologize, and disrupt those worlds. In many ways the Freudian paradigm implicitly depends on the presence of the Black female other. One of its more problematic aspects is that in doing so it relegates Black women's sexuality to the irreducibly abnormal category in which there are no distinctions between homosexual and heterosexual women. By virtue of this lack of distinction, there is a need for Black women, both lesbian and heterosexual, to, as de Lauretis describes it, "reconstitute a female-sexed body as a body for the subject and for her desire" (*Practice* 200). This is a need that is perhaps expressed differently by black women than by white women, whose sexualities have not been subjected to the same forces of repression and domination. And this seems to me to be a critical place where the work of articulating Black female sexualities must begin. Disavowing the designation of Black female sexualities as inherently abnormal, while acknowledging the material and symbolic effects of the appellation, we could begin the project of understanding how differently located Black women engage in reclaiming the body and expressing desire.

What I want to propose requires me to don one of my other hats, that of a student of physics. As I struggled with the ideas I cover in this essay, over and over again I found myself wrestling with the juxtaposed images of "white" (read normal) and "Black" (read not white and abnormal) sexuality. In her essay, "Variations on Negation," Michele Wallace invokes the idea of the Black hole as a trope that can be used to describe the invisibility of Black creativity in general and Black female creativity specifically (*Invisibility* 218). As a former physics student, I was immediately drawn to this image. Yet it also troubled me.[8] As Wallace rightfully notes, the observer outside of the hole sees it as a void, an empty place in space. However, it is not empty; it is a dense and full place in space. There seemed to me to be two problems: one, the astrophysics of black holes, i.e., how do you deduce the presence of a black hole? And second, what is it like inside of a black hole? I don't want to stretch this analogy too far, so here are my responses. To the first question, I suggest that we can detect the presence of a black hole by its effects on the region of space where it is located. One way that physicists do this is by observing binary star systems. A binary star system is one that contains two bodies which orbit around each other under mutual gravitational attraction. Typically, in these systems one finds a visible apparently "normal" star in close orbit with another body such as a black hole, which is not seen optically. The existence of the black hole is inferred from the fact that the visible star is in orbit and its shape is distorted in some way or it is detected by the energy emanating from the region in space around the visible star that could not be produced by the visible star alone.[9] Therefore, the identification of a black hole requires the use of sensitive detectors of energy and distortion. In the case of Black female sexualities, this implies that we need to develop reading strategies that allow us to make visible the distorting and productive effects these sexualities produce in relation to more visible sexualities. To the second question—what is it like inside of a black hole?—the answer is that we must think in terms of a different geometry. Rather than assuming that Black female sexualities are structured along an axis of normal and perverse paralleling that of white women, we might find that for Black women a different geometry operates. For example, acknowledging this difference I could read the relationship between Shug and Celie in Alice Walker's *The Color Purple* as one that depicts desire between women and men simultaneously, in dynamic relationship rather than in opposition. This mapping of the geometry of Black female sexualities will perhaps require Black feminist theorists to engage the Freudian paradigm more rigorously, or it may cause us to disrupt it.

CAN I GET HOME FROM HERE?

I see my lesbian poetics as a way of entering into a dialogue—from the margins—with Black feminist critics, theorists and writers. My work has been to imagine an historical Black woman-to-woman eroticism and living—overt, discrete, coded, or latent as it might be. To imagine Black women's sexuality as a polymorphous erotic that does not exclude desire for men but also does not privilege it. To imagine, without apology, voluptuous Black women's sexualities.
                        –Cheryl Clarke

So where has my search taken me? And why does the journey matter? I want to give a partial answer to the question I posed at the beginning of this essay. At this juncture queer theory has allowed me to break open the category of gay and lesbian and begin to question how sexualities and sexual subjects are produced by dominant discourses and then to interrogate the reactions and resistances to those discourses. However, interrogating sites of resistance and reaction did not take me beyond what is generally done in gay and lesbian studies. The turn to queer should allow me to explore, in Clarke's words, the "overt, discrete, coded, or latent" and "polymorphous" eroticism of differently located Black women. It is still not clear to me, however, that other queer theorists will resist the urge to engage in a reranking, erasure, or appropriation of sexual subjects who are at the margins of dominant discourses.

Why does my search for Black women's sexuality matter? Wallace once wrote that she feared being called elitist when she acted as though cultural criticism was as crucial to the condition of Black women as health, the law, politics, economics, and the family. "But," she continued, "I am convinced that the major battle for the 'other' of the 'other' [Black women] will be to find voice, transforming the construction of dominant discourse in the process" (*Invisibility* 236). It is my belief that what is desperately needed is more rigorous cultural criticism detailing how power is deployed through issues like sexuality and the alternative forms that even an oppressed subject's power can take. Since 1987, a major part of my intellectual work as a historian of U.S. science and medicine has addressed the AIDS crisis in African-American communities. The AIDS epidemic is being used, as Simon Watney has said, to "inflect, condense and rearticulate the ideological meanings of race, sexuality, gender, childhood, privacy, morality and nationalism" (ix). The position of Black women in this epidemic was dire from the beginning and worsens with each passing day. Silence, erasure, and the use of images of immoral sexuality abound in narratives about the experiences of Black women with AIDS. Their voices are not heard in discussions of AIDS, while intimate details of their lives are exposed to justify their victimization. In the "war of representation" that is being waged through this epidemic, Black women are victims that are once again the "other" of the "other," the deviants of the deviants, regardless of their sexual identities or practices. While white gay male activists are using the ideological space framed by this epidemic to contest the notion that homosexuality is "abnormal" and to preserve the right to live out their homosexual desires, Black women are rendered silent.

The gains made by queer activists will do nothing for Black women if the stigma continues to be attached to their sexuality.

The work of Black feminist critics is to find ways to contest the historical construction of Black female sexualities by illuminating how the dominant view was established and maintained and how it can be disrupted. This work might very well save some Black women's lives. I want this epidemic to be used to foment the sexual revolution that Black Americans never had (Giddings 462). *I want it to be used to make visible Black women's self-defined sexualities.*

Visibility in and of itself, however, is not my only goal. Several writers, including bell hooks, have argued that one answer to the silence now being produced on the issue of Black female sexuality is for Black women to see themselves, to mirror themselves (61). The appeal to the visual and the visible is deployed as an answer to the legacy of silence and repression. As theorists, we have to ask what we assume such reflections would show. Would the mirror Black women hold up to themselves and to each other provide access to the alternative sexual universe within the metaphorical black hole? Mirroring as a way of negating a legacy of silence needs to be explored in much greater depth than it has been to date by Black feminist theorists. An appeal to the visual is not uncomplicated or innocent. As theorists we have to ask how vision is structured, and, following that, we have to explore how difference is established, how it operates, how and in what ways it constitutes subjects who *see* and *speak* in the world (Haraway, "Promises" 313). This we must apply to the ways in which Black women are seen and not seen by the dominant society and to how they see themselves in a different landscape. But in overturning the "polities of silence" the goal cannot be merely to be seen: visibility in and of itself does not erase a history of silence nor does it challenge the structure of power and domination, symbolic and material, that determines what can and cannot be seen. The goal should be to develop a "politics of articulation." This politics would build on the interrogation of what makes it possible for Black women to speak and act.

Finally, my search for Black women's sexuality through queer theory has taught me that I need not simply add the label queer to my list as another naturalized identity. As I have argued, there is no need to reproduce Black women's sexualities as a silent void. Nor are Black queer female sexualities simply identities. Rather, they represent discursive and material terrains where there exists the possibility for the active production of *speech, desire,* and *agency.*

NOTES

1. Here I am referring to the work of Stuart Hall and especially Hazel Carby: "We need to recognize that we live in a society in which dominance and subordination are structured through processes of racialization that continuously interact with other forces of socialization. . . . But processes of racialization, when they are mentioned at all in multicultural debates are discussed as if they were the sole concern of those particular groups perceived to be racialized subjects. Because the politics of difference work with concepts of individual identity, rather than structures of inequality and exploitation, processes of racialization are marginalized and given symbolic meaning only when subjects are black" (Carby, "Multicultural" 193).

2. See Higginbotham; Hine; Giddings; Carby (*Reconstructing*); and Brown ("What").

3. See Carby, "Policing." Elsa Barkley Brown argues that the desexualization of Black women was not just a middle-class phenomenon imposed on working-class women. Though many working-class women resisted Victorian notions of womanhood

and developed their own notions of sexuality and re-spectability, some also, from their own experiences, embraced a desexualized image ("Negotiating" 144).

4. The historical narrative discussed here is very incomplete. To date there are no detailed historical studies of Black women's sexuality.

5. See analyses of novels by Nella Larsen and Jessie Fauset in Carby (*Reconstructing*); McDowell; and others.

6. I participated in a group discussion of two novels written by black women, Jill Nelson's *Volunteer Slavery* and Audre Lorde's *Zami*, where one Black woman remarked that while she thought Lorde's book was better written than Nelson's, she was disturbed that Lorde spoke so much about sex and "aired all of her dirty linen in public." She held to this even after it was pointed out to her that Nelson's book also included descriptions of her sexual encounters.

7. I am reminded of my mother's response when I "came out" to her. She asked me why, given that I was already Black and that I had a nontraditional profession for a woman, I would want to take on one more thing that would make my life difficult. My mother's point, which is echoed by many Black women, is that in announcing my homosexuality I was choosing to alienate myself from the Black community.

8. I was disturbed by the fact that the use of the image of a black hole could also evoke a negative image of Black female sexuality reduced to the lowest possible denominator, i.e., just a "hole."

9. The existence of the second body in a binary system is inferred from the periodic Doppler shift of the spectral lines of the visible star, which shows that it is in orbit, and by the production of X-ray radiation. My points are taken from the discussion of the astrophysics of black holes in Wald, chapters 8 and 9.

WORKS CITED

Abelove, Henry, Michèle Barale, and David Halperin, eds. *The Lesbian and Gay Studies Reader.* New York: Routledge, 1993.

Alonso, Ana Maria, and Maria Teresa Koreck. "Silences, 'Hispanics,' AIDS, and Sexual Practices." In Abelove, Barale, and Halperin, 110–26.

Brown, Elsa Barkley. "Negotiating and Transforming the Public Sphere: African American Political Life in the Transition from Slavery to Freedom." *Public Culture* 7.1 (1994): 117–46.

———. " 'What Has Happened Here'; The Politics of Difference in Women's History and Feminist Politics." *Feminist Studies* 18.2 (1992): 295–312.

Butler, Judith. *Bodies That Matter: On the Discursive Limits of "Sex."* New York: Routledge, 1993.

Carby, Hazel. "The Multicultural Wars." In Wallace and Dent, 187–99.

———. "Policing the Black Woman's Body in the Urban Context." *Critical Inquiry* 18 (1992): 738–55.

———. *Reconstructing Womanhood: The Emergence of the Afro-American Woman Novelist.* New York: Oxford University Press, 1987.

Clarke, Cheryl. "Living the Texts Out: Lesbians and the Uses of Black Women's Traditions." In Busia and James, 214–27.

Collins, Patricia Hill. *Black Feminist Thought, Knowledge, Consciousness, and the Politics of Empowerment.* Cambridge: Unwin Hyman, 1990.

Crenshaw, Kimberlé. "Whose Story Is It Anyway?: Feminist and Antiracist Appropriations of Anita Hill." In Morrison, 402–40.

de Lauretis, Teresa. *The Practice of Love: Lesbian Sexuality and Perverse Desire.* Bloomington: Indiana University Press, 1994.

———. "Queer Theory: Lesbian and Gay Sexualities: An Introduction." *differences: A Journal of Feminist Cultural Studies* 3.2 (1991): iii–xviii.

duCille, Ann. "The Occult of True Black Womanhood: Critical Demeanor and Black Feminist Studies." *Signs* 19.3 (1994): 591–629.

Giddings, Paula. "The Last Taboo." In Morrison, 441–65.

Gomez, Jewelle. "A Cultural Legacy Denied and Discovered: Black Lesbians in Fiction by Women." In B. Smith, *Home Girls*, 110–23.

Haraway, Donna. "The Promises of Monsters: A Regenerative Politics for Inappropriate/d Others." In *Cultural Studies*. Ed. Laurence Grossberg, Cary Nelson, and Paula Treichler. New York: Routledge, 1992, 295–337.

———. "Situated Knowledges: The Science Question in Feminism and the Privilege of Partial Perspective." In *Simians, Cyborgs, and Women: The Reinvention of Nature.* New York: Routledge, 1991.

Henderson, Mae Gwendolyn. "Speaking in Tongues: Dialogics, Dialectics, and the Black Woman Writer's Literary Tradition." In Wall, 16–37.

Higginbotham, Evelyn Brooks. "African-American Women's History and the Metalanguage of Race." *Signs* 17.2 (1992): 251–74.

Hine, Darlene Clark. "Rape and the Inner Lives of Black Women in the Middle West: Preliminary Thoughts on the Culture of Dissemblance." *Signs* 14.4 (1989): 915–20.

hooks, bell. "Selling Hot Pussy: Representations of Black Female Sexuality in the Cultural Marketplace." *Black Looks: Race and Representation.* Boston: South End, 1992, 61–76.

Hull, Gloria T. " 'Lines She Did Not Dare': Angela Weld Grimké, Harlem Renaissance Poet." In Abelove, Barale, and Halperin, 453–66.

James, Stanlie, and Abena Busia, eds. *Theorizing Black Feminisms: The Visionary Pragmatism of Black Women.* New York: Routledge, 1993.

JanMohamed, Abdul. "Sexuality on/of the Racial Border: Foucault, Wright, and the Articulation of 'Racialized Sexuality.' " In *Discourses of Sexuality: From Aristotle to AIDS.* Ed. Domna Stanton. Ann Arbor: University of Michigan Press, 1992. 94–116.

Lorde, Audre. *Sister Outsider, Essays and Speeches.* Trumansburg, N.Y.: Crossing, 1984.

———. *Zami: A New Spelling of My Name.* Trumansburg, N.Y.: Crossing, 1982.

McDowell, Deborah E. " 'It's Not Safe. Not Safe at All': Sexuality in Nella Larsen's *Passing.*" In Abelove, Barale, and Halperin, 616–25.

Morrison, Toni, ed. *Race-ing Justice, En-gendering Power: Essays on Anita Hill, Clarence Thomas and the Construction of Social Reality.* New York: Pantheon, 1992.

Nelson, Jill. *Volunteer Slavery: My Authentic Negro Experience.* Chicago: Noble, 1993.

O'Grady, Lorraine. "Olympia's Maid: Reclaiming Black Female Subjectivity." *Afterimage* (1992): 14–23.

Omosupe, Ekus. "Black/Lesbian/Bulldagger." *differences: A Journal of Feminist Cultural Studies* 3.2 (1991): 101–11.

Smith, Barbara. "Toward a Black Feminist Criticism." *Conditions* 2 (1977): 25–44.

———, ed. *Home Girls: A Black Feminist Anthology.* New York: Kitchen Table, 1983.

Smith, Valerie. "Black Feminist Theory and the Representation of the 'Other.' " In Wall, 38–57.

Spillers, Hortense. "Interstices: A Small Drama of Words." In Vance, *Pleasure,* 73–100.

———. "Mama's Baby, Papa's Maybe: An American Grammar Book." *Diacritics* 17.2 (summer 1987): 65–81.

Vance, Carole, ed. *Pleasure and Danger: Exploring Female Sexuality.* London: Pandora, 1989.

———. "Pleasure and Danger; Toward a Politics of Sexuality." In Vance, *Pleasure* 1–24.

Wald, Robert. *Space, Time, and Gravity: The Theory of the Big Bang and Black Holes.* 2nd ed. Chicago: University of Chicago Press, 1992.

Wall, Cheryl, ed. *Changing Our Own Words: Essays on Criticism, Theory, and Writing by Black Women.* New Brunswick, N.J.: Rutgers University Press, 1989.

Wallace, Michele. *Invisibility Blues: From Pop to Theory.* New York: Verso, 1990.

Wallace, Michele, and Gina Dent, eds. *Black Popular Culture.* Seattle: Bay, 1992.

Walker, Alice. *The Color Purple.* New York: Harcourt, 1982.

Watney, Simon. *Policing Desire: Pornography, AIDS, and the Media.* Minneapolis: University of Minnesota Press, 1989.

Williams, Patricia J. *The Alchemy of Race and Rights: Diary of a Law Professor.* Cambridge: Harvard University Press, 1991.

22

BLACK BODIES/GAY BODIES
The Politics of Race in the Gay/Military Battle

Alycee J. Lane

NOW THAT THE SMOKE has begun to clear from the battle over the military's ban on lesbian and gay service personnel, it has become obvious that the way in which the issue of race was debated throughout this battle contributed to the failure to overturn the ban. Race was frequently evoked as an issue that determined the viability of gay and lesbian civil rights, for these were measured by the extent to which they could be equated with Black people's struggles to overcome racial discrimination in the armed forces. The evocation of race was initiated by gays and lesbians themselves, many of whom offered problematic analysis of the similarities between Black and gay experiences in the military. David M. Smith, for instance, spokesperson for the Campaign for Military Service, a coalition of gay and civil rights groups that oppose the ban, claimed that the arguments forwarded "50 years ago" by "opponents of integration" are the "same arguments being heard today" to rationalize the military's ban. As far as Smith was concerned, one just had to "[s]ubstitute [the words] 'gay' and 'lesbian' " for the word "Negro" (Reza A3). That this trivializes how the politics of race determined the language the military used fifty years ago, and as well sheds no light whatsoever on the complexities with which the antigay policy is constructed, is certainly an understatement. Such arguments proved to be an annoying distraction in an important political moment.

Those who opposed lifting the ban (as well as many blacks who were otherwise supportive of lifting it)[1] countered that comparisons such as Smith's were not only disingenuous but also, as the retired army lieutenant general Julius W. Becton claimed, patently "offensive" (Duke A9). Of course most of the arguments against the gay/Black comparison proved just as ridiculous as the comparisons forwarded by lesbians and gays. In spite of the obvious parallel that the military uses insidious stereotypes with gays, as they did (and *do*) with Blacks, to justify its discriminatory policies, many people chose to dismiss the obvious by, for instance, staking out the righteous position that one's history proved that one's oppression was greater. "I consider [the gay/Black comparison] offensively disrespectful of the recorded and unchronicled sufferings of millions of my people who were kidnapped, chained, shipped and sold like livestock," asserted Vernon Jarret, columnist for the *Chicago Sun-Times* (Williams A12). This appeal to history doesn't prove that there are no similarities;

it does, however, suggest the level of Jarret's homophobia and reveals his curious desire for the authority to determine whose oppression is authentic (this posturing I will critique later in my essay).

The opposition to gay and lesbian efforts took advantage of the tensions generated by Black/gay comparisons and paraded before the Senate Armed Services Committee one "expert" after another who would testify that the analogy was without merit and who would assert, as did the former joint chiefs of staff chairman Colin L. Powell in his address at the U.S. Naval Academy in Annapolis, that unlike race, "homosexuality is not a benign . . . characteristic" (Duke A9). Gays and lesbians, they argued, could not make any civil rights claims in regard to the military precisely because race and homosexuality are not the "same."

Not to be outdone, gay rights activists provided their own witnesses to argue the contrary and to offer "evidence" that "homosexuality is determined by biological factors rather than by choice" (Pine A20). This evidence indeed, argued the experts, makes the military's discriminatory policies against Blacks and gays the same because the policies regarding both are based on "immutable" characteristics. Gays and lesbians can then also assert, as did Lieutenant General Calvin Waller, the highest-ranking Black officer in the Gulf War, that they "had no choice" about what they were when "delivered from" their mothers' wombs (Gates 42).

Yet advocates were outmaneuvered, and the issue of race was critical to this outcome. By collapsing Black and gay struggles and denying their fundamental differences, advocates not only decontextualized the specificity of both struggles but also effectively rendered race expendable. Thus, how race continues to be central to the operations and organizational structure of the military; how it is implicated in gay and lesbian politics; and how the opposition, in its offensive against gay rights advocates, relied on what has been the conservative and far right's use of race over the past thirty years to dismantle civil rights as a whole, were rendered virtually unspeakable throughout the entire battle. Race mattered only insofar as it could legitimize gay rights.

While the expendability of race may have been viewed as strategic because it allowed gay rights advocates to mask the contradictions that plague their own movement, it actually served to empower even more the opposition. Appearing to champion Black claims because it framed these as authentic, the opposition could effectively mask how its arguments were grounded in the intersection of racism and homophobia, which are of course incompatible with support for civil rights.

In this essay I will examine how the conflation of Black and gay struggles operated within the gay/military battle. I will specifically challenge the terms by which the issue of race was framed by exploring the intersection[2] of race and sexuality, an important element that needed to be brought into the debates yet was completely and conspicuously ignored. It is my belief that the intersection exposes the gaps, failures, and privileges that structured the politics from which all sides of the debates operated; in so doing, it provides a basis from which to rethink the entire battle.

DECONTEXTUALIZATION

It is not my intent here to provide an overview of the historical context of Black struggles and gay struggles with the military, but to instead focus on some of the things that the decontextualization of both effected. And I want to begin this by focusing on David M.

Smith's assertion, previously quoted, that one simply needs to replace the word "Negro" with "gay" and "lesbian" in the military's past policies of segregation and discrimination against Black people. Smith's claim exposes the arguments forwarded by gay rights advocates as fundamentally flawed, for it presupposes that the intent and context within which the military's language of discrimination was and is constructed has nothing to do with the language itself; that the context is not "in" the content; that by replacing the word "Negro" one has established the basis for claiming "equivalent victimization"[3]; and, finally, that the substitution adequately addresses the nuances of gay rights claims.

Thus, when Smith in his argument uses as his examples the military's policy that "[w]hite soldiers will not shower or sleep in the same barracks" as Blacks and its claim that race mixing "weakens a unit's cohesion" (Reza A3), he nullifies the racial opposition by which these dictums were constructed. Consequently, Smith erases the history and institutionalization of white supremacy that the opposition narrates. For example, at the time that these policies were in place, the refusal to allow Blacks and whites to "shower or sleep" together was determined not by the fear that Black men would "cruise" white men (and those who opposed lifting the ban specifically evoked cruising in order to discredit the efforts of gay rights advocates), but instead by the stereotypes that define white people as "clean" against Black people as "unclean." In other words, the policy emerged from discourses that defined Black bodies as filthy and, more broadly, as inherently inferior to white bodies, heterosexual or otherwise.

In addition, the military's claim regarding "unit cohesion" articulated white separatism and shared notions of white superiority, both of which not only structured the military but were also (and continue to be) what the military *militarily* upholds. Thus, integrating units meant incorporating Black men on an equal basis; meant acknowledging Black men as equal to whites; meant challenging the entire logic of white supremacy. "Unit cohesion" as articulated in the context of the gay/military debates, however, is grounded in a different set of discourses, those which construct and are structured by the opposition between heterosexuality and homosexuality. Certainly this opposition is itself racialized, but in ways that disarticulate race because of how homosexuality has been theorized historically from white bodies (and this in turn has effectively disarticulated the intersection of Blackness and homosexuality).

Replacing the word "Negro" with "gay" and "lesbian" is a move that actually continues this trajectory, for it denies that a "Negro" could in fact be "gay" or "lesbian" as it also assumes that whiteness is the defining characteristic of homosexuals. These issues I will discuss later, but what I want to point out is that this silences critique of how homophobia and racism come together, and how intersections such as these are embedded in the military's discriminatory policies. The same can be said about replacing the word "white" with the word "heterosexual," which is implied in Smith's discourse. How does the intersection of whiteness and heterosexual privilege get played out?

While Smith and others might have believed that decontextualization helped them to establish the basis for claiming equivalent victimization, it actually demonstrated the extent to which white (male) privilege structured their position. In other words, the attempts to erase race only made more poignant the fact that some people had the privilege to do so. And that is precisely what makes insidious the easy conflation of Black and gay struggles. Moreover, it did nothing to illuminate the military's particular policies regarding gay and lesbian people. How, for example, is the language of antigay and lesbian policy structured?

What was/is the context for the military's policy? What assumptions does it articulate? How has the language affected and/or determined antidiscrimination strategies? How has the language been subverted, or has subversion of the military's discriminatory policies been in any way enabled by the language? Finally, what are the ways that the military's discriminatory practices intersect, what are the effects, and how might this challenge gay rights efforts?

Because advocates decontextualized Black and gay struggles, they predictably left these questions unanswered. Just as troubling, however, is the fact that through their flawed reasoning gay rights advocates also excised the military from its own history and present, such that it and others opposed to lifting the ban could evoke desegregation as paradigmatic of the military's recognition of "legitimate" civil rights claims. The result was that the opposition in total more often than not escaped relentless scrutiny for its reification of white male heterosexual privilege and of the military's efforts to rationalize demands for equality while not at all surrendering its investment in and support for a status quo defined by that privilege.

THE EXPENDABILITY OF RACE

The most important outcome of many gay advocates' strategies is that they neutralized race as a real issue of concern. This in turn opened up a space in which all sides of the struggle could perform as if racism in the military—and perhaps racism generally—was a thing of the past. Thus, while gay rights advocates, on the one hand, made their comparisons without ever engaging how racial discrimination structures the military lives of Black (and white) soldiers today, and particularly in ways that intersect with other forms of discrimination (including homophobia), the opposition, on the other hand, was busy constructing desegregation as an "end" to the military's practices of racial discrimination (and advocates certainly played their part in constructing this fiction as well). General Colin Powell, for instance, was always quick to credit "Black veterans of World War II for dismantling military racism and making his ascent possible," thereby using his own "success" to mask and forestall any critique of continued racial inequities within the military (Reza A3).

Additionally, advocates rationalized the construction of race and racism as issues separate from gay and lesbian identity and politics. The consequences of this are telling. First of all, it reinscribed whiteness as the norm of gay and lesbian identity and politics. Thus, as we saw throughout the battle, white gay men's experiences of discrimination were presented as the paradigmatic experiences, the ones that fully articulated what it means to be a gay or lesbian person in the military.

Second, it enabled the polarization of Blacks and gays into "separate and competing political camps" (Crenshaw 403) such that the battle too often evolved, and was represented in the media as, a competition between Blacks and gays over civil rights claims and legitimacy instead of as a battle with the military over its discriminatory policies. This is reflected, for instance, in such newspaper headlines as "Gay Issue Quietly Spreads Rifts through Civil Rights Groups," the subheading of which claims that "High-profile black and Latino groups are on sidelines in battle to end military's ban on homosexuals. Some say '60s coalition is fracturing" (Pine A20). Reports such as these only fueled the tensions that the comparisons of Black and gay struggles generated.

Finally, because gay rights advocates severed race and racism from the entire gays-in-the-military issue yet *simultaneously evoked Black bodies as a means to legitimize their civil rights claims*, they ultimately rationalized what has constituted the far right's tactics over the last thirty years to dismantle civil rights as a whole. Those tactics, which have been executed primarily through the auspices of the Republican Party, have included "fusing" race and racialized Others, e.g., Black people, with "almost every social and economic issue on the domestic agenda" and more specifically with the "expanding rights revolution" of which gay rights is a part, and in such a way that renders racism a nonissue (Edsall 55).[4] This tactic was and is used to tap into white voter resentment regarding the rights revolution and to persuade "white working and lower-middle-class voters to join in an alliance with business interests and the affluent" (13). And, in rationalizing this strategy, gay rights advocates consequently legitimated the opposition's reliance on fusion as a means to further its antigay agenda.

The reification of whiteness as the "norm" by which to measure gay and lesbian experiences in the military not only marks the extent to which white privilege determines, to a great extent, the articulation and practice of gay and lesbian politics, but also reveals the fact that many advocates erroneously presuppose that a "discriminator treats all people" within a particular category of identity "similarly" (Crenshaw 150).[5] During the gay/military battle, whiteness was treated as if it is a "neutral" quality, as if it is the space where "fairness" for gay and lesbian soldiers resides. Consequently, the military's antigay policy was defined as unfair only insofar as sexuality was concerned. Such a configuration reflects what UCLA law professor Kimberle Crenshaw defines as "dominant ways of thinking about discrimination" (150), for it does not take into account how the "compoundedness" of race, sexuality, gender, and class makes for very different experiences of discrimination among gays and lesbians.

In addition, the reification masked the ways whiteness was brought to bear on, or how it was negotiated in, the battle to lift the ban.[6] The comparisons that gay rights advocates made of Black and gay struggles enabled this camouflaging, for having measured gay rights in relation to Black (presumably heterosexual) people instead of in relation to white heterosexuals or Black gays and lesbians, advocates were able to evoke homosexual disadvantage while at the same time distancing white gays and lesbians from white privilege. In other words, Black (heterosexual) bodies were used to create an artificial racialized distance between (or difference from?) white gays and lesbians and their heterosexual counterparts, and in a way that left white power unchallenged.

This inevitably contributed to the polarization, encouraged by the opposition and the media, of Blacks and gays into competing political camps. Many Black people who resisted the Black/gay comparisons recognized the bias embedded in gay rights advocates' discourse, called them out for their refusal to acknowledge white privilege, and chastised them for their timidity in confronting racism generally and in gay communities. And rightly so. But one of the other effects of gay rights advocates' position was that it set in motion a dynamic in which some Blacks could then use the gay/military battle as a means to reinscribe both Black people as the "norm" by which the rights of all others are determined and the hierarchies by which this norm is constituted. That is, many Blacks would also engage the military issue in terms that reflected "dominant ways of thinking about discrimination."

Such is clear in Vernon Jarret's chronicle of the "sufferings" of Black people which I quoted earlier and which typifies the rhetoric by which Black "ownership" of civil rights is articulated.[7] Jarret challenges gays to prove that their historical experiences of suffering are similar to, if not greater than, Black suffering. Gays are unable to rise to such a challenge, as far as Jarret is concerned, because they "were never declared three-fifths human by the Constitution." Besides, unlike gays, Blacks cannot "hang [their] race" in the "closet . . . when it's convenient." Gays "still have the advantage of not being black" (Williams A12).

Jarret certainly relies on his being able to deny that there are gays and lesbians who do have the advantage of "being black" and that the intersection of Blackness, desire for someone of the same sex, *and* gender might have compounded the "sufferings" of some Black people throughout U.S. history. He also proceeds as if constructing a normative of civil rights claims, specifically through the intersection of Blackness, heterosexuality (and implicitly masculinity), is unproblematic.[8] Such gestures were not at all unusual during the debates, yet they somehow escaped critique and, as a consequence, no questions were raised at all to address how the interplay of heterosexual and male hegemony in Black communities was brought to bear on the contestation over Black/gay comparisons and how it bears on civil rights generally.

Those who opposed lifting the ban were served well by all of this. Yet they particularly benefitted from the fact that gay rights advocates inadvertently rationalized the far right's strategy of fusion upon which the opposition relied. This reliance is certainly not surprising, given that much of the opposition embraced right-wing politics.

Advocates rationalized the strategy when they discursively "freed up" Black people from the specificity of their material and social context, a context that narrates racism and racist practices and that demands, more often than not, that the issues within which Black people are referred be scrutinized for how they are structured or informed by the politics of race. This is exemplified, for instance, by gay rights advocates' rhetoric regarding "past" discrimination. In so "liberating" Black people, advocates were able to use them to narrate a text that would further the gay rights agenda, to narrate in fact the *meaning* of gay experiences of discrimination within the armed forces. Many gay rights advocates, then, simultaneously freed themselves from having to contend with how race and racism bear upon the gay/military issue.

The right's strategy of fusion accomplishes the same thing, but for different purposes. In giving "new meaning to the coded language of politics" (Edsall 213), meaning created when the right implicitly associates the language with—among other things—racialized bodies and the broader politics of race, the right ensures through decontextualization that it can communicate this meaning without evoking at the same time the material and social context within which racialized bodies are situated, a context that, as I have said, narrates racism. The right, then, guarantees that the narrative of racism and racist practices is never articulated in their discourse.

To illustrate, former president George Bush in his 1988 presidential campaign used Willie Horton as a means to stake out a position against Michael Dukakis on the issue of crime, and specifically to demonstrate that he would counter how the liberal politics Dukakis embraced "coddled" criminals. By choosing Horton, Bush associated him (and, by extension, all Black people) with the issue of crime as well as with liberal penal reform. In turn, his reference to "crime" as a "shorthand *signal*" or code word not only evoked the specter of Horton (and Black people generally), but also suggested "broader issues of social disorder" which tapped into racist sentiments that framed "ideas about authority, status, morality, self-control, and race" (Edsall 224).

Bush of course did not originate the conflation of crime with Black bodies and, more broadly, with racial politics, but it is important to note his reiteration of the right's political

strategies. By decontextualizing Horton and, more broadly, Black people from their material conditions (particularly the conditions of those in the inner cities who have been ravaged by the effects of deindustrialization), Bush was able to use Black people to narrate a
text that elided any engagement with the intersections of racism, crime, and justice. This
strategy was critical to his being elected and has been central in the right's galvanization of
white voters as a means to attain hegemony in the political arena.

Those who opposed lifting the military's ban on gays and lesbians relied on being able
to fuse race to the gay/military issue, and they ensured this through their decontextualization of Black bodies, exemplified by *their* references to the "end" of racism in the military.
This reliance becomes clear when one recognizes the extent to which the opposition employed the coded language that has become a staple of right-wing racial politics. For instance,
the opposition frequently argued that efforts to lift the ban were "special interest" demands
that constituted a "cultural war" directed against U.S. soldiers ("Worse than a Crime" 19); in
addition, it asserted that lifting the ban would threaten the "safety" of all Americans because
it would result in the creation of a "second class" military.

The term "special interest" has been persistently articulated in right-wing rhetoric in relation to "minority" concerns. While the term certainly is not used only to characterize the
interests of people of color, it has become one of the means by which those who so evoke
it align a variety of domestic issues with racialized Others.[9] "Cultural war," on the other
hand, is often used by the right to characterize multiculturalism as a war against the "sanctity" of Western culture, and the reference to "safety" conjures the right's law and order discourse within which Black bodies have figured most prominently. Finally, the idea of a
"second class" military echos the right's references to the effects of affirmative action which,
as far as the right is concerned, creates a second-class educational system, a second-class
workforce, etc.

What these terms do is circumscribe the gay/military issue within an ideology that insists that American society is "victimized already" by racialized "unfairness," an unfairness
that evolved from the challenges posed by the rights revolution.[10] Although this at first appears to contradict the opposition's insistence that Black and gay demands are entirely unrelated, it actually reinforced its efforts to maintain the ban on gay and lesbian service
personnel. On the one hand, the opposition could, through code words, subtly tap into
"voter . . . anxieties and resentments about race" and therefore use these to discredit gay
demands (Edsall 180). On the other hand, the opposition could explicitly evoke Black bodies
to define "legitimate" rights against the "illegitimacy" of gay claims, and thus appear supportive of the civil rights agenda. Gay rights advocates failed to scrutinize the meaning of
this contradiction, and this failure proved to be critical; for what the contradiction ultimately signifies is not a problem of logic, but instead how those who opposed lifting the
ban structured their resistance upon the intersection of racism and homphobia.[11]

The Gay Agenda, a video distributed to members of Congress, the joint chiefs of staff
and other members of the military, and whoever else would listen during the course of the
gay-military battle, provides a clear illustration of how this intersection works in antigay
efforts. Produced by the Antelope Valley Springs of Life Ministries, a fundamentalist
church in California, the video's purpose was to inform Congress and the "American people" about what the "homosexual lifestyle really involves," and part of what it involves, according to the producers, is a "quest for the special advantages of minority status in all fifty
states" (*The Gay Agenda*). One "two-star Army general" even claimed, prior to President

Clinton's issuing his "don't ask, don't tell," no-win policy, that the video was "a splendid teaching vehicle" that demonstrated the stakes involved in lifting the ban (Colker A16).

The idea of a "quest" for minority status determines the structure of the video and reflects how race functions as the backdrop of this example of antigay propaganda. In the opening scene, gay activists (almost all of whom are white) are shown rioting after Governor Pete Wilson of California vetoed Assembly Bill (AB) 101, which, according to the voice-over, would have granted "special minority rights" to homosexuals.[12] This event takes place in the evening: protesters burn buildings, break windows of businesses and loot; other protesters chant slogans or angrily confront the police. From these scenes of violence the camera fades to a daytime protest at the State Capitol in Sacramento. The voice-over claims that what the audience sees is an "aggressive nationwide offensive aimed at every segment of society." In addition, those protesting are attempting to secure, and violently, the "special" (and implicitly unfair) "advantages" of "minority status."

The effect created by the combination of the riot scene, the protest scene, and the narrative is a fusing of race and the gay and lesbian protests. This is because the narrative is structured, on the one hand, by racialized codes ("minority rights," "special advantages") similar to those that I have discussed; on the other hand, the narrative evokes the rhetoric of law and order ("an aggressive nationwide offensive aimed at every segment of society") that, again, has been used so often in relation to Black bodies. The latter aspect of this narrative (law and order) is accentuated by the decontextualized images of gay protest, in which one can only see the "violation" of law and order. One is never made privy to the specific social and political context (antigay discrimination) that neccessitated the protests in the first place.

Furthermore, since riot scenes generally have become tropes in the mass media to signify all that is wrong with the rights revolution, and particularly as defined by Black protest demands, this scene situates gay protest within this trope.[13] It suggests, in other words, that the gay and lesbian movement is part of this revolution and that its demands, like those of Blacks and other people of color, also cost the American public, costs which can be clearly measured here in terms of domestic tranquility and property loss. (This framework of course reasserted itself during the 1992 Los Angeles riots; both politicians and the media decontextualized those protesting and then proceeded to construct them as "thugs." And, in spite of the multicultural character of the Los Angeles riots, the bodies that dominated the media frame were those of Black men.)[14]

In a later segment of the video, wherein the audience is presented with an explanation by David Llewellyn, president of the Western Center for Law and Religious Freedom, of the "true" intent of "minority status" and what it means in terms of gay rights, the fusion is more explicit. Says Llewellyn:

> The purpose of "minority status under the law" is to protect people from prejudice on the basis of truly neutral qualities which ought not to affect anybody's reasonable judgement. Gay activities, the homosexual activities, the sexual activities that gays engage in are not neutral. They have public health consequences, they have financial and economic consequences. They are not to be equated with the truly morally neutral condition of particular racial or national origin or other status [sic].

Llewellyn's comments here can be dismantled in a number of ways, but what I want to focus on is how, through his juxtaposition of "gay activities" and "neutral qualities,"

Llewellyn renders inoperative the fact that these might intersect; that is, he suggests that gay activities are not performed by those who embody neutral qualities. And if this is the case, then those who perform gay activities are white people and those who are neutral are the "Others," the (racialized) bodies that Llewellyn evokes in order to discredit (white) gay rights and simultaneously to appear as if he considers legitimate "special minority status" that is based on race.

Yet this appearance of his is undercut by the narrative that precedes him, for it had already characterized minority status as creating "special advantages." Thus, race is hardly considered "neutral" in this video; it is actually galvanized, in very subtle ways, to illustrate the extremes to which the rights revolution can go. In other words, not only can one gain special advantages by being a racial Other, but one can also acquire these because of one's performances. (This explains in part why Llewellyn's juxtaposition is one that sets the body [race] against activities [gay].) Thus, he constructs gay rights as an integral aspect of the "racialized unfairness" with which America is already victimized.

The video ends by "revealing" what special minority status will "mean." Not only will it elevate gays and lesbians, but it will also enable them to perform in ways that will "force" society "to give up its standards." The closing scene, which remarkably mirrors the first, shows gays and lesbians (again, overwhelmingly white) partying during a San Francisco Gay Pride parade. They're kissing and hugging; some lesbians walk around topless, some gay men are in drag. The camera's eye clearly looks for the "outrageous": the Club Fuck float, upon which men and women dance practically nude, a gay man donning a three-foot dildo, etc. The voice-over describes this party as a celebration of the passage of California AB2601,[15] a bill referred to as a "gay victory" because gays have "forced" Governor Pete Wilson to give them the "special advantages of minority status." It represents just one more loss "American society" has suffered as a result of the rights revolution.[16] Race has thus been firmly integrated in this critique of gay rights, and in a way that camouflages the video's grounding in both homophobia *and* racism.

Yet what is striking about this video is not only that it demonstrates clearly the strategy of fusion, but also that it reveals quite candidly what was shared among all participants in the gay/military battle: their absolute silence regarding intersectionality. Black gays and lesbians were virtually banished to "a political vacuum of erasure and contradiction," a space "whose very nature resists telling" because Black gays and lesbians were put in the position of having to choose between speaking as Black and speaking as gay or lesbian people (Crenshaw 403). Yet considering the increasing numbers of Black people who have entered the ranks of the military since the Vietnam era, and that many of them may be lesbian and gay, marginalizing Black gays and lesbians is problematic indeed. In fact, once intersectionality is brought to bear on the debates, it becomes clear that the arguments of gay rights advocates, Blacks opposed to the comparisons between Black and gay struggles, and those opposed to lifting the ban were not only fraught with contradictions but also structured by privilege and the reaffirmation of the status quo.

BLACK BODIES/GAY BODIES

The deliberate refusal of gay rights advocates to engage intersectionality is aptly illustrated by the way in which the former army sergeant Perry Watkins figured in (or didn't figure in) the debates. Watkins, a Black soldier who was the only "openly gay serviceman to have successfully challenged the military's anti-gay policy" and to have "won a landmark lawsuit [1991] against the Army that resulted in his reinstatement, a promotion and his retiring with credit for 21 years of service," was not, according to his own assertions, asked by the "'leadership' within the gay movement to lend his voice" in the gay/military battle (Williams A12). Instead, the "leadership" chose to parade the Keith Meinholds as the models for gay experiences in the military.

I am not suggesting that Watkins should have been paraded, or that such parading would have signified the leadership's willingness to contend with how the compoundedness of race, sexuality, and gender complicated the "speaking for" position of white gays and lesbians, or even that the court's decision in Watkins's case reflected any concern for how the intersection of his Blackness, gayness, and maleness determined his experiences of discrimination. I am asserting, however, that the choice between Watkins and Meinhold was one between the nonuniversality of Blackness and the universality of whiteness, between that which could not represent and the representative. How could advocates assert, for instance, that gays and lesbians were just "like everybody else"—a phrase unbearably repeated during the gay/military battle—when whiteness is always implicated in "everybody" and Blackness is always that which makes one *not* like everybody else (and especially in regard to sexuality)?

For Black gays and lesbians to have been considered representative would have necessarily challenged advocates to attend to how race, class, and gender issues are both implicated in the military's policies and in advocates' own strategies. It would have also revealed that by positing the white homosexual male as the norm, advocates were both obfuscating the complex means by which the military discriminates against lesbians and gays and constructing gay rights from the position of the most privileged.

Blacks who were opposed to the Black/gay comparisons, on the other hand, were continuing to rationalize the fiction that homosexuality is something that white people "do," a fiction that has been circulated and reified in Black communities at least since the 1960s. In so doing, they were also legitimizing the ways in which hegemonies within Black communities, particularly those regarding certain race, sexuality, and gender norms, are regulated and policed, such that the Black heterosexual male functions as the communal paradigm of Black *being* and consequently as the norm by which to articulate "Black interests." Homosexuality, however, is not something only white people "do," and the silence regarding Black gays and lesbians, the insistence that the gay/military issue is not a "Black issue," only illuminates the fundamental inequalities that structure and are perpetuated in Black communities.

One cannot help concluding that the arguments specifically between gay rights advocates and many Blacks who contested the comparisons ultimately constituted a drama among the most privileged of both claimant groups who, far from seeking to undermine the status quo and to challenge the distribution of power within the military apparatus and in their own communities—particularly in terms of compounded identities—were simply securing their own set of privileges, their own rank in the hierarchical ordering of American society. Neither's position was "grounded in a bottom-up commitment to improve the substantive conditions for those who are victimized by the interplay of numerous factors"; instead, each side defined rights "in terms of the experiences of those who are privileged *but for*" specific characteristics (Crenshaw 150–51). Their debates on race, then, rationalized a "normative view of society that reinforces the status quo" (167).[17]

Considering this investment in the status quo, it is not surprising that their refusal to engage intersectionality was shared by the opposition, a fact that is, again, illustrated in *The Gay Agenda*. For example, the video is peopled by a virtually all white gay and lesbian community (something I found at least curious since I myself, along with a sizeable contingent of Black and other people of color, attended the Sacramento protest that was filmed). Periodically, a Black body does enter one of the video's frames, but it is never interrogated by the camera as closely and as relentlessly as are white bodies.[18] In fact, the camera's eye appears to be specifically interested in white men who perform the "outrageous."

This virtual whiteness accomplishes several things: it reinscribes whiteness as the normative of gay rights and therefore enables the producers to avoid the sticky question of how racism intersects with antigay politics, and it legitimizes white privilege in the sense that the producers define the meaning of the protests for gay and lesbian rights as demands for white privilege *in excess of the reasonable amount* to which (white) gays and lesbians are entitled. The idea that gays demand more than their fair share of white privilege is conveyed not only in code words such as "special advantages" but is also communicated in the voice-over's assertion that gays and lesbians command a "high income," one "twice" that of "you and I" (a fact that could only be ascribed to middle- and upper-class gays and lesbians who are, without a doubt, predominantly white. To make this claim requires, then, that white gays and lesbians be the featured performers in this video since Black bodies might cast doubt on this assertion).[19] The (white) gay and lesbian movement, then, is constructed as endangering an already decreasing supply of white privilege that has already been diminished by Black civil rights demands.

The opposition's use of the fiction created political and discursive effects that were practically indistinguishable from those produced by gay rights advocates and Blacks contesting comparisons of gay and black struggles. That is, it enabled the opposition, just as it did for the others, to avoid addressing the compoundedness of discrimination. Thus, by banishing Black gays and lesbians to the regions of silence, all sides could ignore the fundamental inequalities that structure the status quo.

Intersectionality calls into question the construction of monolithic identities and forces one to consider how one is positioned by the intersecting and multiple hegemonies that structure American culture. It reveals, in other words, the extent to which "the individual" is implicated "in contradictory ways" in relation to power and to a broad spectrum of political and social issues (Martin and Mohanty 209–10). In so doing, it renders problematic how antidiscrimination strategies are formulated, and specifically from the "top-down" approach that situates the most privileged as the norm that addresses the interests of many.

At the same time, intersectionality exposes the inequities that are produced by the top-down character of American politics generally; in the same ways that it implicates the individual in contradictory ways, intersectionality simultaneously exposes the contradictions of American life, the compoundedness of inequality and privilege from which its democracy operates.

That intersectionality exposes these contradictions means, however, that it also opens a space for the creation of what Biddy Martin and Chandra Talpade Mohanty define as "political community," an arrangement of activism that is determined not by "essential connections" that are based on monolithic constructs of identity or only by "political urgency or necessity," but instead by the constant recontextualization of "the relationship between personal/group history and political priorities" (210), by the negotiations one makes, in other words, with one's positionality. Creating political community forces to the surface the contradictions of one's multiple locations and creates, for those who have been banished to places that resist telling, spaces in which they can speak.

Yet it is ultimately critical in the struggle to overcome right-wing politics, for what these rely on is the construction of a monolithic white American "we" that must defend itself against "them." White gay rights advocates would have truly presented a challenge had they articulated their whiteness against this monolith instead of hiding it behind Black bodies; for if there is any "sameness" in the military's discriminatory policies, it is that their intent is and has been the reification of a particular *kind* of whiteness and white privilege, both of which are defined against all Black people and which have been used to victimize white gays and lesbians as well.

"The reason gays are making parallels," exclaimed Reverend Lou Sheldon, chairman of the Traditional Values Coalition that actively seeks to deny gay and lesbian civil rights, "is that it may bring empathy from white men like me, who feel a collective sense of guilt about the way Blacks have been treated. The fact remains that this is not a civil rights issue but a moral issue."[20]

NOTES

1. I am not suggesting that some Blacks did not embrace the sameness argument. Roger Wilkins, for instance, considered the comparisons legitimate and claimed that "[i]f any people should understand another group's desire, drive, and thirst for full citizenship, it should be us" (Duke A8). But these voices were few and far between, such that those who were making the Black/gay comparisons were primarily white gays and lesbians, who for this reason are the focus of my critique. I should also point out that those Black people who did embrace the sameness argument ended up, I believe, reifying the very problematic assumptions, which I explore here, that structured the position of white gay rights advocates.

2. I am borrowing here from the concept of "intersectionality" as conceived by the law professor Kimberle Crenshaw in "Demarginalizing the Intersection of Race and Sex" (Crenshaw 1989). This concept is predicated on the assumption that identities are not "mutually exclusive categories of experience"; rather, identities "intersect."

3. I am borrowing this term from footnote 46 of Adolph Reed Jr.'s important essay "The 'Black Revolution' and the Reconstitution of Domination" in *Race, Politics and Culture: Critical Essays on the Radicalism of the 1960s*, ed. Adolph Reed Jr. (New York: Greenwood Press, 1986), 90–91.

4. The idea of fusion is explored by Thomas Byrne Edsall and Mary D. Edsall in their work entitled *Chain Reaction*. However, not only are the Edsalls "so locked into an image of black demands as the root of all evil that they do not bother to consider why, after all, there was ever a need for aggressive anti-discrimination efforts in the first place" (734), as Adolph Reed Jr., and Julian Bond note, but they

also "identify race rather than racism as the pivotal issue" in American politics (736). In my essay I attempt to center racism, by specifically referring to racialized Others, as that which structures the far right's strategy of fusion. See pp. 000–000 in particular. (My thanks to Herman Gray for pointing this source out to me.)

5. This assumption, as Crenshaw argues, structures much of antidiscrimination doctrine (1989).

6. Negotiating whiteness is central to white gay and lesbian politics generally, even as this remains unspoken.

7. It makes sense, of course, that Black people express ownership of civil rights, especially since antidiscrimination doctrine emerged from their particular struggles. It is equally understandable that Black people would serve as the referent for the struggles of others. Nevertheless, civil rights laws opened a space, as they should have, in which many oppressed groups could seek relief from discrimination. This *theoretically* should not be threatening, but it is, and precisely because very powerful forces do not consider democracy something that is in this nation's best interests. Hence, relief from oppressive practices has too often evolved into a competition for rights treated as if "scarce."

8. Although he doesn't directly mention heterosexuality, it nevertheless dictates his ability to juxtapose sexuality to race.

9. " 'Special interests' [are perceived as] pressing the claims of minorities, including trade unionists, blacks, Hispanics, feminists, homosexuals, AIDS victims, etc., for government special preferences. These special preferences, in turn, were potentially damaging, in the minds of a significant number of [white] voters, not only to America's overall inter-

national competitive position, but detrimental as well to the moral fibre, the personal well-being, and the security of individual 'ordinary' citizens" (Edsall 203).

10. "[T]he GOP portrayed *opposition* to central elements of civil rights enforcement . . . as deriving from a principled concern for fairness: as a form of populist opposition to the granting of special privilege" (Edsall 144).

11. This is what was so ironic about the use of the "special rights" argument by General Powell and other Blacks who supposedly champion civil rights. By distinguishing Black and gay demands in the framework that they used, they ultimately reinscribed the language by which civil rights has been aggressively dismantled.

12. Assembly Bill 101 was designed to "ban employment discrimination against" gays and lesbians. The state Republican Party "went on record against the measure, calling it 'anti-family' and an 'insult to *legitimate* minorities' " (Decker A3, my emphasis).

13. "For the Republican Party, the [Black urban riots of the 1960s] provided the opportunity to change the direction of the national debate by initiating a full-scale assault on liberal social policies. 'How long are we going to abdicate law and order—the backbone of any civilization in favor of a soft social theory that the man who heaves a brick through your window or tosses a fire-bomb into your car is simply the misunderstood and under-privileged product of a broken home?' House Republican Leader—and future president—Gerald Ford of Michigan asked" (Edsall 51).

14. One must recall that former president Bush asserted that the Los Angeles riots were "not about civil rights" but instead reflected "the brutality of a mob," thereby refusing the context of racial and class injustice.

15. Assembly Bill 2601 bans "workplace discrimination based on sexual preference" ("Building a Just Society" B7).

16. It is important to note how the producers of this video reinterpret the California Assembly bills. The ban on discrimination in the workplace is defined as an "advantage" enjoyed by "legitimate" minorities. That such a law is defined as an advantage speaks to the extent to which the producers consider civil rights unfair. Answering the question "advantage over whom?" clarifies the racial politics underlying this discourse.

17. Of course the gay/military issue has always been a status quo issue. As Barbara Smith has argued, a truly "radical lesbian and gay movement" would have been "working to dismantle the military completely" (Smith 16). This, however, was not such a struggle; it neither called into question the hierarchies within the military nor those throughout society which the military is organized to protect.

18. This is not a complaint, of course.

19. It is important to note how the producers conflate money and whiteness. See Cheryl I. Harris's brilliant critique of how whiteness has been and is treated in American jurisprudence as "property," as something that has—among other things—monetary value ("Whiteness as Property").

20. Available at http://www.traditionalvaluescoalition.org.

WORKS CITED

"Building a Just Society." *Los Angeles Times*, September 26, 1992, B7.

Colker, David. "Anti-Gay Video Highlights Church's Agenda." *Los Angeles Times*, February 22, 1993, A1, A16.

Crenshaw, Kimberle. "Demarginalizing the Intersection of Race and Sex: A Black Feminist Critique of Antidiscrimination Doctrine, Feminist Theory and Antiracist Politics." *The University of Chicago Forum* (1989): 139–67.

———. "Whose Story Is It, Anyway? Feminist and Antiracist Appropriations of Anita Hill." In *Race-ing Justice, En-gendering Power*. Ed. Toni Morrison. New York: Pantheon Books, 1992, 402–40.

Decker, Cathleen. "Seymour Opposes State Gay Rights Bill." *Los Angeles Times*, September 29, 1991, A3, A31.

Duke, Lynne. "Drawing Parallels—Gays and Blacks." *Washington Post*, February 13, 1993, A1, A8–9.

Edsall, Thomas Byrne, and Mary D. Edsall. *Chain Reaction: The Impact of Race, Rights, and Taxes on American Politics*. New York: W.W. Norton and Company, 1992.

Gates, Henry Louis, Jr. "Blacklash?" *The New Yorker*, May 17, 1993, 42–44.

Gay Agenda, The. Produced by the Antelope Valley Springs of Life Ministries. 20 min. Videocassette. 1992.

Harris, Cheryl I. "Whiteness as Property." *Harvard Law Review* 106 (1993): 1709–91.

Martin, Biddy, and Chandra Talpade Mohanty. "Feminist Politics: What's Home Got to Do with It?" *Feminist Studies, Critical Studies*. Ed. Teresa de Lauretis. Bloomington: Indiana University Press, 1986, 191–212.

Pine, Art. "Gay Issue Quietly Spreads Rifts through Civil Rights Groups." *Los Angeles Times*, January 29, 1993, A20.

Reed, Adolph, Jr. "The 'Black Revolution' and the Reconstitution of Domination." *Race, Politics and Culture: Critical Essays on the Radicalism of the 1960s.* Ed. Adolph Reed, Jr. New York: Greenwood Press, 1986.

Reed, Adolph, Jr., and Julian Bond. "Equality: Why We Can't Wait." *The Nation*, December 9, 1991, 733–37.

Reza, H. G. "Blacks' Battle in Military Likened to Gays." *Los Angeles Times*, June 14, 1993, A3, A18–19.

Smith, Barbara. "Where's the Revolution?" *The Nation*, July 5, 1993, 12–16.

Williams, Lena. "Blacks Reject Gay Rights Fight as Equal to Theirs." *New York Times* June 28, 1993, A1, A12.

"Worse than a Crime." *National Review*, December 14, 1992, 18–19.

I'd like to thank the following people for sharing their critique and ideas at various stages of this paper: Kimberle Crenshaw, Mary Pat Brady, Jeanne Stanford, Alana Bowman, Teresa Conrow, and those who attended "Intersectionalities: Theorizing Identities/Reconstructing Politics," a Humanities Research Institute Colloquium held at the University of California, Irvine, 1993.

23

HORMONES AND MELANIN

The Dimensions of "Race," Sex, and Gender in Africology; Reflexive Journeys

Patrick Bellegarde-Smith

> *"a colonial rage . . . a rage with the people who had allowed themselves to be corralled into a foreign fantasy."*
>
> –V. S. Naipaul, *A' Bend in the River*

There are ancestral and spiritual journeys taken with the strength of those who struggled before me, whose anchors reside in my (physical) ancestry, Vodun religion, languages, sexuality—all cultural vectors in which one acts and is acted upon. These are the core, the center, the parameters and "*la source* (the river)." I salute my mother, her mother, all those before her until we reach Ezili Danto (Yemoja, Lasirenn, Mammy Wata), the broad elements described above and all their subsets, would warrant considerable expansion elsewhere. But suffices to say that in my view, they both tended to reinforce an argument for an incipient and evolving cultural unity writ large—a universality of sorts within particularities. An illustration of that process might be the detribalization of South Africa before and under Apartheid in the United States and the Caribbean, and the (re)constitution of these populations into Africans, Blacks or West Indians over historical time; or, as argued by some anthropologists, for instance, the overarching cultural unity of the Caribbean archipelago under the process of creolization, from similar historical conditions though the masters were not the same.

In her book, *Reinventing Africa*, Ifi Amadiume challenged Western anthropologists that seemed to have rendered Africa into a pale (perhaps a dark) vision/version of Europe, the first becoming a reflection or an extension of Western thought and desiderata. Based on forms of dichotomous thinking, Africa would become (for liberals) a worldwide extension of humanity on the Western (social) scientific model, a carbon copy of Europe in its infancy or (for conservatives) the "reverse" image, that of a Dark Continent without the possibility of enlightenment. Humanity in its infancy. Both Amadiume and Oyewumi addressed the issue of the masculinization of African religions alongside the larger Western project of (re)inventing Africa—we shall return to this later. These are some of the crucial issues that need to be addressed elsewhere; our scope is more limited.

Race was a reality well before the advent of modern science, though through it, it gathered certain patterns, getting—according to L.C. Dunn, "its character from the commonness within it of hereditary characters, and upon the habit of marrying within the race rather than outside it." L. C. Dunn continued, race then, "is a group of related intermarrying individuals, a population, which differs from other populations in the relative commonness of certain hereditary traits" (Dunn 1961: 273). That definition harks back to a primordial and simpler stage where family, lineage, clan and tribe did indeed define "race" as a group of intermarrying individuals living and *loving* in relative isolation. This gave us the basis for racism and anti-Semitism. Previous generations of Western scholars and policy makers had argued convincingly to their audience for theories of racial superiority and inferiority based on psychosomatic attributes, such as brain or penile size, leading invariably to congenital mental deficiencies for all groups of color (Comas 1961: 30). Geographical isolation, adaptation to the physical environment and the available marriage pool accounted for differences though we, in fact, form one large gene pool, one species, in which there never were any "pure" races Dunn 1961: 271–273 The mule, the offspring of an ass and a horse, is sterile; not so its human counterpart, the mulatto. Faced with the evidence of its reproductive capacity, the mulatto then becomes officially "oversexed."

In reality the scientific definition of race would seem to be a generous expansion of the idea of clan and tribe. When the Haitian says, "*lo ou marye, ou marye ak tout ras moun nan,*" (as you marry, you take on that person's "race," his/her extended family, its history, its obligations), in a country where *everyone* is of African descent. Hispanics in archetype, in whose blood, amniotic waters and tears I wallowed.

One approaches the topic of "race," sex and gender with awe and some humility, overwhelmed by the (mis)use scientists and social scientists and policy makers have made of them and of the subject of difference in general. Differences, in fact, become crucial in "meting out" judgments against persons and communities. Thus these become the bases upon which one dominates over others and discriminates against others. My humility is sustained by fear. Out there, there is a "trained" world—from anthropologists to zoologists—that will take exceptions to my remarks and, of course, dismiss them out of hand, accepting not at all challenges from the "outside." Africology (and Black studies) is outside the realm of polite discourse, reflecting its peripheral nature in academe and that of peoples of primary African descent in a planetary context.

These comments are anchored on reflections upon the subject matter phenomena of "race," sex and gender as they occur in varied cultural contexts. Each assertion made raises further issues and questions whose function is to maintain a dialogue and a conversation. In each statement, please read a question that begs further development. My comments hope to distill an accumulated wisdom, if I am able and worthy. The work acknowledges that of intellectual ancestors and more recent writers. But that work I now write is never done. We bend to working-class realities which assert, "men work from sun-up to sundown; women's work is never done." Indeed. The remarks are scrambled blocs to be reassembled many times by wiser children who later will form complete sentences and give the discipline of africology its voice. And that voice will have explanatory value for the Afroworld as well as for others.

Of primary concern are the concepts of "race," sex and gender and the ascriptive roles they play in "reality," and their reality as culturally constructed phenomena that sustain a social order and its status quo. Once this is understood, one will need to formulate the necessary correctives one may desire. I would call, as others have done, for a reconceptualization of these phenomena as they occur in world cultures. The creation of reality is a process controlled largely by societies and the powerful groups within them. I would assert, moreover, that the hierarchical and dichotomous thinking one finds in Positivist frameworks could be construed as "unnatural" in some other cultural and philosophical systems, those systems that remain largely unfamiliar outside our daily realms that are lived as Westerners or near-Westerners. The evidence may in fact change over time, accommodating new conditions/dimensions and new research (though not necessarily a new reality), while our obsessions may remain static. But power, implying besides intricate relationships between persons and groups, remains true to itself.

Race, sex and gender are rendered archetypes in a dichotomous worldview, with sex likely to be the prototype. It is in this sense of that worldview, perhaps, that the idea of "miscegenation" and homosexuality were abhorrent as entities sui generis or as discrete categories. They may not "fit" the framework established by certain kinds of Western religion, philosophical schools or science since their existence may be a reminder of an "imperfect" world or a nondichotomous universe. Points on a spectrum are more intractable than an either/or proposition. Oftentimes data collected will bend to preconceived notions, when sincere beliefs find it rough to entertain alternative or contradictory propositions. Centuries of arrogance buttressed by a large measure of success in the Western civilizational process resulted in yet more arrogance. Of course, there is an obvious relationship between holding forth a notion and the questions one might ask. Is "race" immutable? Are we certain that Homo Sapiens is merely subdivided between males and females? Is the evidence self-evident?

Deeply concerned with that arrogance and the blinders that ensue, the Nigerian scholar Oyeronke Oyewumi responded with anguish and measured anger, demanding a corrective to Western feminist thought that seemed established on a dichotomous principle. She argued that that thought was an imposition of Western gender categories on an [African] discourse. In a "nod" to history's dynamic course and the interaction between dominant and subaltern societies, she continued: "The woman question is a Western-derived issue—a legacy of the age-old somatocentricity in Western thought. It is an imported problem, and it is not indigenous to the Yoruba. If it has become relevant in Yoruba studies, the history of that process needs to be told." She concluded, "the cultural logic of Western social categories is based on an ideology of biological determinism" (Oyewumi 1997: ix). Though she is concerned about sex and gender, her analysis is in my estimation, equally valid with the social construction of race. To these thoughts, I add, and the arrogance of a culture that fancied its systems universal, representing "Man" in all his glory. Universality becomes central to my analysis, particularly when dealing with peoples that lived lives in relative isolation and had kept their own agency. Peoples are not just people, but are different based on the ethos of cultural groups evolving apart.

Concepts of sex and gender (with race distantly following) are shared notions that predated scientific analyses in a given culture. These prescientific analyses, through systematic and methodical simple-mindedness, created and maintained a reality defined a priori. They become systemic. A subaltern population tends to conceive of some of these phenomena somewhat differently than the dominant group though it lacks, by definitional necessity, the necessary power to impose its definitions no matter how well thought out these may be. That reality remains hidden. It is in this sense that the Native American institution of "*berdache*," or the African-American concept of "*nationality*," may in fact differ in essence from the (Euro) American perspective on these same matters. The latter example may join, in its essential lines, broad, observable similarities in the construction of the definition of *ethnos* found in other peoples of African descent, despite distances of time and space. For instance, at its independence in 1804, Haiti made "race" coterminous with nationality and established a "law of the return" for all of Africa's children who landed in the new republic. That broad similarity hinged on two distinct but overlapping elements. The first, an autochthonous element, concerns what scholars have seen as some striking cultural unity as a part of an African civilizational process. The second, recent in historical derivation, concerns the 500-years-old impact of Western civilization upon peoples of the world generally, and upon peoples of African descent specifically. In a much larger study, one would have to refer to European capitalist development as it is translated in imperialism, colonialism and neocolonialism and racism. Each of the two

If Africology can be defined as an academic discipline emanating from the lifeworlds, the "worldsense"—to use the felicitous phrasing of Oyewumi—experiences and behaviors of peoples of primary African origin, then its rationale and justification hinge largely on an argument that these peoples represent variants from a fairly constant source, a source from which all are fairly equidistant despite the ravages of time and milieu. That source then is the cultural systems, the structures and the institutions as well as the worldsense devised autonomously by these peoples during times of relative isolation and during the time of equal and unequal interaction between varied civilizations in the last half millennium. The ethnonational and language groups we observe in Africa and the languages and dialects we speak in the West, in their deep structure and resonance, bear more than passing resemblance to West and Central African grammatical and syntactical patterns; bloodlines are established similarly. The religions we practice, adapted to locale and whose culturally appropriate rituals are of a transcendent spirituality, are a part of that "élan vital," the *ase* that suffuse the structures and institutions spoken of earlier. Language and religion, then, become "keys" in understanding race, sex and gender, all dripping of the kind of symbolism that generates worlds and the framework for meaning, merging theory and practice.

Though discrete entities in academic study, language and religion are part of living and ailing cultures, and it is only through intellectual subterfuge that the one is separated from the other. It is in this context, for instance, that Haitian (Creole) can partly reveal the worlds of sex and gender and race through grammatical construction and vocabulary; or through Vodun, la Regla de Ocha (Lukumi), Candomble, Umbanda, Obeah and Shango that one may glance at the idealized societies concocted through religion for a refined understanding of actual phenomena. At home, in Haitian, the vocable "*neg*" (*negre*/someone) is as likely to refer to "person/individual" as "*moun*." The pronouns are desexed, and male/female-ness is deduced from context.

Before unequal cultural penetration, each element was designed to complement all others in a fairly closed sociocultural system, open only insofar as one chose to indulge freely in cultural borrowing and exchange. The obverse of that medal is a "breached citadel" where imposition of alien modes of thought and ways of being made specific elements incomprehensible in the absence of their original overall superstructure. Religion is thus divorced from its universal "tribal" origin where it remained unnamed, to a new situation where it competed with imported religions. Each had to be named. Haitians resisted as best they could, and *technically* their national religion remains unnamed, defining itself as "*those who serve the Spirits*," rather than "Vodun (voodoo)" by which it becomes known abroad and at home. Typically though not always, creation based on choice(s); slavery on certain coercion. At the personal, interpersonal and societal levels, that situation translated into identity crises yet to be resolved.

The idea of universality in Western science and religion becomes problematic. That universality is indeed said to be the basis of all science, philosophy and religion as spoken about in the West for the past five centuries as the planet became ensconced in one overarching and overwhelming economic system. An ethnotribal conception was given both a planetary dimension and eternal validity, while a truly universal culture, perhaps of the kind Leopold Sedar Senghor called "*la civilisation de l'universel*," built on free participation, would remain wanting. And because collected data are predicated on questions asked, the africologist imbued by different visions that allow for differing possibilities, asks unasked questions whose answers perform a corrective act at least, or set in motion a potential for renewal, an approximation of other truths at most.

Male and female hormones and melanin have a tangible existence in all individuals. How one chooses to interpret and qualify that reality, however, has more to do with a social construction which becomes a reality that undergirds any given social system. Melanin and hormones symptomatically lift and separate rather than unite, which they may have done. Differences are emphasized rather than commonalities and a fear of difference rather than acceptance fueled and circumscribed the debate. Sex and gender are as race and ethnicity, concepts that seem to exhibit the same distance one from the other, and at every phase, illustrate the difficulty of extricating the intricacies and more meaningful meanings from biology and culture. As argued earlier, they become cultural archetypes rooted in androcentric "objectivity," as they find their intersection away from biology but within ethnicity, kinship and family. Methods, criteria, measurements have their echoes in premises, in group self-interest that coincides with a particular social system as it sets its priorities. In the West, dichotomies rather than points on a spectrum have tended to define reality, but have they illustrated or defined nature?

RACE, CLASS AND COLOR: PRELIMINARY NOTES

One is tempted to surround the word "race" with quotation marks each time one uses it, because it provides us with little scientific information. "Race" developed into a social rather than scientific concept within ever-present hierarchical patterns. As expressed in the Western popular mind, it gathered strength initially from a sort of Pan-European tribal understanding whereby olden concepts of kinship exploded narrow historical confines for a more modern, yet still conventional definition, starting in the *Age of Exploitation*, (the Age of Exploration). Race has remained *essentially* a tribal concept. The universalization of that concept occurred from an inadequate base, as perhaps the Aztec, Greek and Roman religions (and perhaps even Christianity) never quite transcended their tribal origins, seemingly ill suited for the requirements for their far-flung empires. "Race" parallels other words expressing a "we-feeling," extending them, and at times was used interchangeably with family and kinship, revealed in the antiquated juxtaposition with nationality (e.g., the Irish "race"). One finds that the meaning of the word in the current Black American vocable that equates the two, denoting "race" as ethnic culture and nationality.

Though there are differences between the popular and scientific conception of race, there are nonetheless profound connections between the two as well, connections in which the latter originally derives from the former, as European folk dance led to Marius Petipa's brilliant ballet choreography, from blues to jazz, or as gender constructions are related to an a priori belief of a rigid sexual division of humanity. Anything but flaccid, that division creates man-ness and woman-ness; masculinity and femininity where only "male" and "female" may have existed (barely).

Because permutations seem endless, races are either said to be increasing, from three to thirty, or decreasing as evidenced by "miscegenation." Gene and blood type frequencies and other more mundane criteria ostensibly form the basis for categorization. (In neo-colonial terms and in the psychology of mentalities, one found the basis for instituting categories of whiteness versus blackness, good hair versus bad hair—the dominant groups forming the "norm.") Yet, no "race" is uniform with reference to any of these criteria that would define them in the first place. Individual heredity showed as widespread a pattern "intra" as "inter" group. Anthropologists as late as the 1950s and 1960s could see still new groups in the offing as the Latin American "mulatto" and the South African "Coloured." Hurting from an invasive and all-pervasive form of westernism, Mexico would give us *la raza cosmica* of Jose Vasconcelos in self-defense and in defiance, and the Brazil its "ideal" of a fondue pot in which an enlightened nation strove for a lighter complexion with the addition of further *queijo branco* (white cheese). At a deeper level, it is not a coincidence that Coloureds were given preferential treatment in South Africa or that white homes in the United States who seek Black children for adoption use the legitimizing newly devised status of biracial babies, in a marked departure from Anglo-Saxon tradition. The American definition of Black and white had been remarkably consistent and the most rigid in the world, especially when contrasted with the Latin American and Afrikaner versions of the concepts. The United States of all colors and complexions celebrate "*el dia de la raza*," the day of the "race," a celebration of Spanish (colonial)-derived cultures worldwide. Both colonizer and colonized are allowed to wallow in their similitude. Arising from a narrow gene pool because of endogamy, European royal families could be judged to be an extreme (and absurd) illustration of a race in the making, warts and all. The issue of a marriage pool, as it occurs along the parameters of class, color, sex and gender taboos, refocuses race—once again—as a social construct.

W. E. B. Du Bois argued early last century that the problem of the 20th century was that of the color line. His prescient statement had taken race in all its dimensions, as economic exploitation of the "dark" races and the ideologies that sustained racism, including the precursor of modern social science, Positivism. In his thought, Du Bois foreshadowed the Third World and the North/South conflict, as had later this other African-American/Trinidadian scholar, Oliver C. Cox. Inherent in the times in which these men wrote was the overwhelming presence of Western tradition as it evolved over time and Western conceptual definitions with the marked absence from the debate of other cultural traditions in this regard. Instead of a profusion of new racial groupings—in contradistinction to the arguments advanced by the likes of Coon, Garn and Birdsell—one could see occurring, instead, both a narrowing and a polarization in the international arena between peoples of color and peoples of primary European descent, setting once more race in a social, economic, political and cultural rather than in a "scientific" context. It is by no means an accident that many (East) Indians and Coloureds in South Africa had opted for the political label "Black" in opposition to Apartheid, or that (East) Indians, Pakistanis and West Indians in Great Britain, are called "Black." This becomes an echo of a Haitian 1805 policy where all citizens of the country, whether white, *mulatre* or Black, assumed by governmental fiat the generic and revolutionary name of "*noirs* (Blacks)."

That the ancient Greeks used the word "barbarian" for all non-Greeks or that African ethnonational groups referred to themselves as humans, at times seeing others as ghosts or apparitions or figments of one's imagination, merely told us something about a process, one in which ethnocentrism (but not necessarily racism) played a dominant part. Racism, to proceed harmoniously, needed to incorporate the power to name as an adjunct to the power to define. And this can be accomplished more easily in a worldwide capitalist context. Ethnocentrism, on the other hand, defines within the context of an integral culture and its language, *une culture integrale, integrante et integree.* This indicated a worldview/worldsense still relatively whole, systems, structures and institutions where each element reinforced the others. If colonialism as the "*force motrice*" of colonization was to be successful, one of its functions was to forcibly undermine that cultural wholeness by radical and incremental cultural shifts, particularly in language and religion, in an effort to sap the legitimacy of the social contract, of the legitimization of the political contract between the rulers and the ruled, reorienting societies in its wake towards a new purpose. Once the core was gone, a far-reaching identity crisis could ensue with little hope for a resolution in the short or medium range. The new (postcolonial) states arising from old (precolonial) nations would have to negotiate a difficult modus vivendi for state and nation to coexist and find a modicum of harmony. In March 1987, Haiti adopted a new constitution in which the Haitian language was adopted as one of two official languages and the national religion Vodun could coexist with Christianity for the first time.

Physical miscegenation had its cultural and psychological counterpart, and together with social class rendered the prospect for an integrated culture and the resolution of crises of identity more arduous. This argument is not meant to be read as argument for essentializing identity, but as being about the reality of time-honored cultural processes in which cultural shifts are unsettling at first and for a long time. Roman Catholicism and the Spanish language survived the Moorish occupation of Spain. Spain survived, altered. The imposition of a given worldview upon militarily weaker populations, the desire to impose one's worldview and the struggle that ensued in order to survive, did ensure the broad success of colonialism at the dawn of the modern (European) era. Power and powerlessness and all points that lay in between become a part of the equation. In the final analysis, racism became far more significant than race.

SEX, GENDER AND SEXUALITY *IN* CULTURE

There is more than a passing resemblance between race—however defined—and sex and gender, either in the construction of these varied concepts, their impact or their use. Moreover, definitions of family and kinship are linked to ethnicity, culture, sex and gender, but not "race." The data reveal that while women represent 52 percent of "the world's population, and one-third of the official labor force, they [account] for nearly two-thirds of all working hours, receive only one-tenth of world income and own less than one percent of world property" (Boulding 1979). Sex as "class." The statistics appear to remain consistent over time. When studied in reference to Africa, that kind of situation arose largely from the incorporation of that continent into the world capitalist economy, which resulted in economic decline in many societies, a loss in the standard of living, increased social stratification, and, in some instances, a deterioration of the status of women. These were sociopolitical processes at the service of an economic system.

Since political independence in the mid-1960s in Africa and the West Indies, the continuation of the Western model of economic development, euphemistically labeled modernization in the early development literature, with much of what it entailed—legal codes, religious (Christian) and secular ideologies, new land tenure patterns with private ownership—occurred in a patriarchal context in which women had no "official role" and very little actual control over their lives.

The linkage between sex and gender and the economic system have now become obvious, but by no means do they explain the totality of the interaction between male and female. Discriminatory structures were already institutionalized in many precolonial African societies as social stratifications arose. Acquiring a life of their own, discriminatory practices against women could and would crystallize under the weight of "tradition," particularly in agricultural—those using the plow—and in pastoral societies, such as in parts of East Africa. Hunting and gathering and horticultural societies, the latter using the hoe, seemed more egalitarian in their social relations, sometimes showing a low level of stratification. The necessity for all "citizens" to contribute to group survival, the (physical) reproduction of the body politic—coupled with widely differing spheres of activity for males and females, in both the public and private domain—became significant when such distinctions were made. Societies were/are never purely of one type or another, but the generalization held/holds. Many of these societies, particularly in West and Central Africa, populated the Caribbean countries where some of the arrangements seemed to have survived with ample adjustments and modifications.

The material basis of African societies would seem to explain in part the particular communal thrust expressed in the ideological superstructure, including the somewhat separate and rigid spheres of activity between male and female, and the ascribed positions (in the plural) of individuals that gave these cultures their self-definition and their intrinsic worth. Whether a mother, aunt, daughter and wife or a father, uncle, son and husband, persons (rather than individuals) were locked into a web of obligations whose duties and privileges *shifted* with the nature of the relationship and the particular interaction at the *moment, within* an ever-expanding chronological scale that extended/extends from birth and beyond the grave. These obligations imposed constraints on males and females both, based on "needs" defined communally. But these obligations and constraints were mediated by the very multiplicity of the relationships and roles one entertained simultaneously. For instance, the respect a son showed his mother versus the deference she showed her husband or her husband's sister. Additionally one may need to take into account the (metaphysical) principle of reincarnation and the vaunted status of elder and ancestor, where reincarnation is a facet to understanding social reality.

The inherently sophisticated social systems created in much of Africa to sustain these social arrangements were elaborate and *integrated* from the household unit, to the family, to the clan and the tribe, within metaphysical concepts, giving these institutions and structures validity and legitimacy. In combinations—matrilineal, patrilineal, matrifocal, patrifocal, matrilocal, patrilocal—much energy is expended in mastering social relations. As could be expected, women could indeed be in a relatively advantageous situation in societies that favored their lineage over that of their mates. It may be interesting to argue that reaching a compromise with extant capitalism, African-American families and Blacks elsewhere in the Western Hemisphere have exhibited, as an adaptive mechanism, matrilineal or matrilocal patterns. Marriage through the practice of bridewealth, was/is a socioeconomic institution crafted carefully to delineate obligations of partnership in sexualized divisions of labor, though women need not lose their lineage or their self-identity.

Generally plentiful land and a population characterized by low density aggravated by the history of European slavery made women's contributions in the productive and reproductive areas the sine qua non of wealth as societally defined. African women contribute about 60 to 80 percent of agricultural work. The major questions one must raise in the contexts of each pre- and postcolonial society concern access to land, retention of income from production, inheritance, and the more elusive matter of autonomy which, of course, have economic and political dimensions. Closer analysis, ethnic group by ethnic group, class by class, country by country is crucial.

Polygyny and, in some societies, woman-to-woman marriage—in which one woman assumed the "male" social (but not usually sexual) role—were institutionalized arrangements that tend to strengthen the analysis of marriage as a socioeconomic and political institution. (Some of these arrangements could provide a safe space for African lesbians within a traditional structure and mothering.) Some of this survived the Middle Passage and is, for instance, found in Haiti where the sexual division of labor can be a formalized understanding between a brother and a sister, a mother and a son. Haitian women refer to their genitalia as "my assets" or "my capital," reflecting a proverb that illustrates sex as an important economic resource, "*chak fanm fet ak yon karo te nan mitan janm-li* (all women are born with an acre of land at the meeting of her thighs)."

Despite present-day societal constraints one could conclude, as some scholars do, that African "women often had substantial independence, influence, decision-making authority, and even [sic] institutionally sanctioned power over men. Women assumed more varied and significant public roles in African societies than in most other cultures, and were important as farmers, traders, spirit mediums, chiefs, in at least one society, warriors" (Morrow 290). The ideological underpinnings, described by many as similar though not identical throughout sub-Saharan Africa, may yet provide a different kind of explanation for African social relations as distinct from those of Europe, whose explanations, nevertheless, are universalized across the globe by Western scholarship. Reflecting the ideal, religions present to our gaze an array of deities—male and female, androgynous, bisexual and homosexual—that sit below a supreme entity but atop ancestors. Their respective powers are tempered by obligations in ascending and descending order, the obligations of the Gods toward their worshippers, that of the latter to the former. After a sequence of reincarnations and with the assistance of progeny, ancestors ascend to the realm of divine principle, from *iku* to *Orisa*, from *mo* to *Lwa*—hence the absolute necessity for children and their place in African societies.

This (trans)generational imperative defining one's place/space in the cosmos, the economic structures and gendered division of labor, have resulted in African homosexuals commonly marrying while retaining fluidity in their natural affinity for same-sex relationships. African homosexual behavior—and the varying roles found for them in various societies—seldom translated into a homosexual identity as in the West, starting in the 19th century. Finding its "niche" in all African societies, the meaning attached to homosexuality varied based on differing cosmological and religious systems. Homophobia as now found in African and African-derived societies can be largely attributed to the European colonial impact and the Judeo-Christian ethic. A gay "identity" will prove a challenge to more traditional social systems.

If God is made in "man's" image, Gods that are materialized and gendered as female and homosexual come to reflect the order found in nature. And though the existence of female deities is not a sufficient cause or condition for a comfortable female status—Greece and Rome come to mind—field observations since the late 1960s and in the 1970s do lead to some interesting correlations and conclusions. The unifying elements between the dead, the living and those in the process of (re)birth, the awesome significance of a long past and of a short present in the process of becoming a past, the intersection of the temporal and the spiritual planes at right angles, mimic society. Harmony and a modicum of unity (not to be mistaken for unanimity) are sought in political consensus. Socially that unity is realized by "forging" mythical relationships out of struggle. Not by accident, the Maroons of the Jamaican Cockpit country find a common ancestor as *yoyo* (children) in Grundy Nanny—an Akan Ashanti born priest. Her sister's children, Sekesu—who remained a plantation slave—gave birth to all other Jamaicans. The frequency of populations practicing African-derived religions in the Americas not only sustains an ideological link between parts of the African world, but implies that much in terms of norms and values, its "world sense," survived. Additional research is necessary in the languages and dialects of that world with the issue of words and concepts on genderization—in brief, closer reflection in the field of metalinguistics.

Much of what precedes, a painting in broad brush strokes, does little perhaps to answer directly the question raised by or the definitions of sex and gender, though it does so by indirection. As with religion with which much is shared in the social sciences, science is not apolitical nor is it objective. It reflects, helps shape, directs and sustains the integrity of the other parts of the societal enterprise, and thus has an integrating function. And though, like religion, it has powers of transcendence, the appropriate answer is always formulated by the questioner and the question. It is in this sense that the role and status of African women—role and status different from women elsewhere—remained a "secret" until the last thirty years.

I argued earlier that sex might have been the prototype in the West for the dichotomous vision expressed in European societies and cultures, particularly as amended by gender. Race, replacing an earlier concept of peoplehood, may have followed. Sex and race are also metaphorical inside each culture, since there are in fact no universal sexual behaviors and no universal agreement on "race." Galloping globalization and white supremacy may make them so. And what does exist within each particular society is in constant flux. Context and locale then establish sexual behaviors and perhaps sexuality. In fact, sex itself eludes a simple definition since the scientific record—chromosomes and hormones—can easily mislead unless one relies on simple gender attribution and assignment. Chromosomes and hormonal levels are, in fact, inconclusive and are not prima facie evidence, but developed ex post facto: a process in which questions to preestablished answers were asked. We "know" about male and female before we find the evidence. So too with gene and blood type frequencies: race definition followed more mundane criteria and the record on race is inconclusive as well/hell despite our best efforts.

As with the establishment of sex, gender identity and gender role followed and, cross-cultural research shows, they vary. Even the constructs women and men (gender), as distinct from male and female, limited as these biological concepts are, are inherently suspect. Though a sexualized division of labor is well advanced in many African societies, one needs to elicit the primordial "biological" belief of sex *as a series of facts, but not opposites.* Thus from that base one may further elicit gender roles and gender identity less apposite with their retinue of ascribed and proscribed behaviors. Gender roles and identity are not static or identical everywhere. They respond to considerations of biology, environmental condition, economic necessity and, most essentially, to historical processes, all categories subsumed by culture. In this light, the reality of gender is merely a social reality, and the belief in the existence of "two" genders fosters an acceptance of the existence of "two" sexes. Both biological sex and gender are social constructions on the road to defining culture-specific realities. So-called feminine and masculine characteristics are likely to be a part of a spectrum as are hormones (estrogen and testosterone) and melanin. Cultural identities need not be attached to behaviors or physical characteristics though they usually are.

EPILOGUE

Many of the thoughts that appear above are distilled from five decades of living in an ostensibly westernized and feminist *extended* family of the Haitian aristocracy. I cannot but stress the significance of the crystallization of daily conversations with ever-present mother, three older female cousins, five aunts and a plethora of family friends called "*tantes.*" In this family compound, the *lakou*, there were some men—dismally few—who had married one of these *dames.* Two of my biological aunts had created the Haitian women's movement in the 1930s, and had gone as far as women of their class could go educationally in the first two decades of the 20th century. My mother had traveled alone in the segregationist United States in the 1930s and '40s before her marriage, on a diplomatic passport. My grandfather's model was his 19th century aunt who was arguably the country's best-known *educatrice* of her time or of any time. He chided the men of the upper and middle classes into granting women the right to vote when he presided over Haiti's constitutional assembly in 1950. Names are not important. All have become ancestors. To these people, I add those numerous female schoolteachers and professors I had over my life as a student.

There was a serious case of "disconnect" in my mind. The values extolled by the westernizing elite clashed with the realities I observed in which Haitian women of the upper class were strong and seemingly in charge, despite the laws of the Napoleonic code. I had yet to venture into the countryside. The face and the front presented to the foreigner, *le blanc*, the outside world, accorded with the prevailing status quo in Western Europe and the United States. One's status as civilized hung in the balance. In the bosom of the family, we were aware not to act "niggerishly" in the presence of whites, even if this was our preferred option. Feminism, then, was in the blood. Since then I have tried to become familiar with the extant literature, thus acquiring additional intellectual ancestors in the process. I was aware, dimly at first, of a further disconnect between Western and Caribbean perspectives *pris sur le vif*, while realizing early that Haitian scholars and scholarship were/are intensely Western, "*plus royaliste que le roi.*" Many of us are still in denial.

We were at once creole and African. Western African societies, shortly after the Berlin Conference of 1889, suffered the brunt of European ideals, ideas and categories. Some of these were forced, some were adopted for survival's sake, some adapted as desirable. But there are limits to the process of assimilation. We are no longer what we once were and we often aspire to be the other: we want good hair, not here or there, but everywhere! In an intensely complex African world which then becomes the world's most variegated laboratory, one senses the enormity of the Haitian proverb, "*zafe neg pa janm piti* (the black's thing is never small)." Our situation and the conditions in which we live force us to recognize an opportunity to raise different questions, to study alternatives modes of reality, to (re)construct cultures and lives, and to move away from the idea that all deviation from Western paradigms and normativity is pathological.

The "metalanguages" found in language and religion—the framing of one's thoughts through word/concepts and the prescripted idealized society—are as often as not untranslatable from one civilization to the next without enormous work. As an example, the category "world's major/great religions" leads to (monu)mental assumptions about these prescriptive frameworks with nary a thought about imperialism, colonialism or capitalism. The last three formed the bedrock of our modern and contemporary lives. Cultures are never neutral or value-free and neither are academic disciplines though we need to maintain the pretense.

In the United States, the category "Black" is inclusive rather than exclusive of all those who do not "fit" other racial categories, irrespective of other components of that person's biological heritage, if touched slightly by the tar brush. These are "African Americans." Latin American racism, to the contrary, demands that any amount of European ancestry be recognized, playing in *favor* of someone who is able to deny his/her African ancestry. Only purity of blood, what white and Black Latin Americans call "*limpieza de sangre*," will hoist an individual closer into the realm of the angels. Gender, as defined in the West, followed a similar course in that normativity in the West, has meant "male," all Others labeled women and various categories of "queer." The vocable "Man" embodies the species and God is both white and male, by definitional necessity in the merging of superstructural language and religion. The feeble colonial mind denoted (male) effeminacy and (female) masculinization, and colonies were always construed as "feminine" by the colonizer. In much the same way that man and woman are essentialized in irreducible categories, within race, Black and white suffered the same fate. University students who were thought to think about the "opposite sex" (that which is not male, the "coeds" to the male's "ed") are now mouthing pieties in class about the "opposite race." That "opposite race" is never about Native Americans (a socially constructed formulation of English, American and Spanish colonialism), Asians or the amalgamation "Hispanic," but rather, derives from the European binaries Black/white, and good/evil.

Indeed one knows that "sin" and the "law" were always defined by (neo)colonial authority; it behooved the bereaved subaltern population to internalize its dependent status. In a book review in the *New York Times* (February 11, 2001), "There'll Always Be an England in India," Pankaj Mishra stated, "The English-speaking Indian elite Arjun [the protagonist] belongs to a carefully thought-out creation of the British. . . . In fact, the original British intention behind setting up Western-style schools and universities in India, as very pragmatically specified by Macauley, was to have a class of Indians 'who may be interpreters between us and the millions whom we govern; a class of Indians in blood and color, but English in taste, in opinions, in morals and intellect.' Half a century after the British left India, this middle class appears to be their most enduring legacy. It is now fully in charge . . . of that British romance called the Raj: a romance that depended on a real distance, both physical and psychological, between the ruler and the rule." An American anglophile responding in a letter to the *New York Times'* article "There Will Always Be an England" (February 7, 1999), stated, "there will always be an England as long as its institutions, core

culture and language spread with ever-greater influence around the globe. British influence may be expressed less visibly . . . but it could be more powerful for being less ostenta-
tious." This was about race and class within capitalism.

As concerns sex and gender, in a review of the book by Walter L. Williams *The Spirit and
the Flesh: Sexual Diversity in American Indian Culture* (*New York Times*, March 29, 1987),
Edgar Gregersen asserted that [some?] traditional American Indian societies [protected
the homosexual berdaches, seen as an "anomaly, who] . . . usually had high status and were
often believed to possess supernatural powers. The European conquerors found this astonishing and almost invariably loathsome. Contact with whites early taught Indians to protect and even hide their berdaches. Because the berdaches were often thought of as
guardians of the spirituality of their culture, attacks on these men constituted an attack on
the culture as a whole." The Malian scholar Malidoma Some argued similarly for the "gate-
keepers" of the earth's spiritual domain in the Dagara people of Mali. The priests who initiated him, though married with children, were all homosexuals.

In (re)structuring africology, one will need to go beyond what now obtains in Black and
Africana studies generally, to undertake building new paradigms from old. The paradigm
shift away from Western social science disciplines takes into account our histories and
experiences, our vision, our worldview and worldsense, to use Oyewumi's construction.
Western intellectual categories have never been sufficient. Gender no longer "cuts it," as it
flies in the face of worldwide realities. Neither does "race." The color line stretches in fila-
ments in microseconds, yet expands in broad bands that invade all realms. Ours.

NOTES

These updated thoughts were drafted originally in
the summer of 1986 for delivery at the first international "Symposium on Africology," held at the University of Wisconsin-Milwaukee in Fall 1986. The
objective of this and subsequent symposia was to establish the bases for the discipline of africology.

1. Oyeronke Oyewumi, *The Invention of Women:
Making an African Sense of Western Gender Dis-
course* (Minneapolis: University of Minnesota
Press, 1997), page ix.

2. Oyewumi, Op Cit, page 63.

3. Cherrie Moraga and Gloria Anzaldua, eds. *This
Bridge Called My Back: Writings by Radical Women
of Color* (New York: Kitchen Table Press, 1983),
page 23.

4. Gloria Wekker, "Mat-ism and Black Lesbian-
ism," in *The Greatest Taboo: Homosexuality in Black
Communities*, Delroy Constantine-Sims, ed. (Los
Angeles: Alyson Books, 2001), page 155–156.

5. L. C. Dunn, "Race and Biology," in UNESCO,
*Race and Class: The Race Question in Modern Sci-

ence* (New York: Columbia University Press, 1961),
page 273.

6. Juan Comas, "racial Myths," in UNESCO, Op.
Cit, page 30.

7. Dunn, Op. Cit., pages 271–273.

8. Morrow, cited in L.C. Dunn, Op. Cit., page 290.

9. See the works by Constantine-Simms, *The Greatest Taboo*, Op. Cit., and Stephan O. Murray, *Homosexualities*, (Chicago: University of Chicago Press, 2000).

10. See Patrick Bellegarde-Smith and Claudine
Michel, eds. *Haitian Vodou: Spirit, Myth and Reality*
(Gainesville, FL: University Press of Florida), in
press and Patrick Bellegarde-Smith, ed. *Fragments
of Bone: Neo-African Religions in a New World* manuscript in preparation.

11. Patrick Bellegarde-Smith, *In the Shadow of
Powers: Dantes Bellegarde in Haitian Social Thought*
(Atlantic Highlands, NJ: Humanities Press Interna-
tional, 1985), page 148.

12. *In the Shadow of Powers*, Op. Cit., page 185,
February 18, 1976.

24

CAN THE QUEEN SPEAK?
Racial Essentialism, Sexuality, and the Problem of Authority

Dwight A. McBride

The gay people we knew then did not live in separate subcultures, not in the small, segregated black community where work was ifficult to find, where many of us were poor. . . . Sheer economic necessity and fierce white racism, as well as the joy of being there with black folks known and loved, compelled many gay blacks to live close to home and family. That meant however that gay people created a way to live out sexual preferences within the boundaries of circumstances that were rarely ideal no matter how affirming. In some cases, this meant a closeted sexual life. In other families, an individual could be openly expressive, quite out.

. . . Unfortunately, there are very few oral histories and autobiographies which explore the lives of black gay people in diverse black communities. This is a research project that must be carried out if we are to fully understand the complex experience of being black and gay in this white-supremacist, patriarchal, capitalist society. Often we hear more from black gay people who have chosen to live in predominately white communities, whose choices may have been affected by undue harassment in black communities. We hear hardly anything from black gay people who live contentedly in black communities.
–bell hooks[1]

I speak for the thousands, perhaps hundreds of thousands of men who live and die in the shadows of secrets, unable to speak of the love that helps them endure and contribute to the race. Their ordinary kisses of sweet spit and loyalty are scrubbed away by the propaganda makers of the race, the "Talented Tenth.". . .

The Black homosexual is hard pressed to gain audience among his heterosexual brothers; even if he is more talented, he is inhibited by his silence or his admissions. This is what the race has depended on in being able to erase homosexuality from our recorded history. The "chosen" history. But the sacred constructions of silence are futile exercises in denial. We will not go away with our issues of sexuality. We are coming home.

It is not enough to tell us that one was a brilliant poet, scientist, educator, or rebel. Whom did he love? It makes a difference. I can't become a whole man simply on what is fed to me: watered-down versions of Black life in America. I need the ass-splitting truth to be told, so I will have something pure to emulate, a reason to remain loyal.

–Essex Hemphill[2]

The fundamental question driving this essay is, who speaks for "the race," and on what authority? In partial answer to this query, I have argued elsewhere[3] that African-American intellectuals participate, even if out of political necessity, in forms of racial essentialism to authorize and legitimate their positions in speaking for or representing "the race." This essay is in some ways the culmination of a tripartite discussion of that argument. Of course, the arguments made here and in those earlier essays need not be limited solely to the field of African-American intellectuals. Indeed, the discursive practices described in these essays are more widely disseminated. Nevertheless, because I am quite familiar with African-American intellectualism and am actively invested in addressing that body of discourse, it makes sense that I locate my analysis of racial essentialism in the context of a broader discussion of how we have come to understand what "Black" is.

My essay moves from an examination of African-American intellectuals' efforts to problematize racial subjectivity through Black antiracist discourse to a critique of their representation, or lack thereof, of gays and lesbians in that process. I will further have occasion to observe the political process that legitimates and qualifies certain racial subjects to speak for (represent) "the race" and excludes others from that very possibility. I use three exemplary reading sites to formulate this analysis. First, I examine bell hooks's essay "Homophobia in Black Communities." I then move to an exchange, of sorts, between essays by the controversial Black psychiatrist Frances Cress Welsing and the late Black gay poet, essayist, and activist Essex Hemphill, "The Politics behind Black Male Passivity, Effeminization, Bisexuality, and Homosexuality" and "If Freud Had Been a Neurotic Colored Woman: Reading Dr. Frances Cress Welsing," respectively. Finally, I consider two moments from the documentary on the life and art of James Baldwin titled *James Baldwin: The Price of the Ticket.*

In her now oft-cited intervention into the 2 Live Crew controversy of a few years ago, "Beyond Racism and Misogyny: Black Feminism and 2 Live Crew,"[4] Kimberlé Williams Crenshaw asserts that the danger in the misogyny of the group's lyrics cannot simply be read as an elaborate form of cultural signifying as Henry Louis Gates Jr. argues in his defense of 2 Live Crew. On the contrary, Crenshaw maintains that such language is no mere braggadocio. Those of us who are concerned about the high rates of gender violence in our communities must be troubled by the possible connections between such images and violence against women. Children and teenagers are listening to this music, and I am concerned that the range of acceptable behavior is being broadened by the constant propagation of antiwoman imagery. I'm concerned, too, about young Black women who, together with men, are learning that their value lies between their legs. Unlike that of men, however, women's sexual value is portrayed as a depletable commodity: by expending it, girls become whores and boys become men.

My concerns are similar in kind to those of Crenshaw. Having come of age in a small rural Black community where any open expression of gay or lesbian sexuality was met with derision at best and violence at worst; having been socialized in a Black Baptist church that preached the damnation of "homosexuals"; having been trained in an African-American Studies curriculum that provided no serious or sustained discussion of the specificity of African-American lesbian and gay folk; and still feeling—even at the moment of this present writing—the overwhelming weight and frustration of having to speak in a race discourse that seems to have grown all too comfortable with the routine practice of speaking about a "Black community" as a discursive unit wholly separate from Black lesbians and gay men (evidenced by the way we always speak in terms of the relationship of Black gays and lesbians to the Black community or to how we speak of the homophobia of the Black community); all of this has led to the conclusion that, as a community of scholars who are serious about political change, healing Black people, and speaking truth to Black people, we must begin the important process of undertaking a truly more inclusive vision of "Black community" and of race discourse. As far as I am concerned, any treatment of African-American politics and culture, and any theorizing of the future of Black America, indeed, any Black religious practice or critique of Black religion that does not take seriously the lives, contributions, and presence of Black gays and lesbians (just as we take seriously the lives of Black women, the Black poor, Black men, the Black middle class) or any critique that does no more than render token lip service to Black gay and lesbian experience is a critique that not only denies the complexity of who we are as a representationally "whole people" but denies the very "ass-splitting truth" that Essex Hemphill referred to so eloquently and so very appropriately in *Ceremonies*.

I mean this critique quite specifically. Too often, African-American cultural critique finds itself positing an essential Black community that serves as a point of departure for commentary. In other cases, it assumes a kind of monolith in general when it calls upon the term "Black community" at all. Insofar as the position of such a construct might be deemed essential to the critical project, it is not that gesture to which I object. Rather, it is the narrowness of the vision for what is constitutive of that community that is most problematic. If we accept the fact that the term "community," regardless of the modifier that precedes it, is always a term in danger of presuming too much, I favor making sure that our use of the term accounts for as much of what it presumes as possible.

At present, the phrase "the Black community" functions as a shifter or floating signifier. That is, it is a term whose meaning shifts in accordance with the context in which it is articulated. But, at the same time, the phrase is also most often deployed in a manner that presumes a cultural specificity that works as much on a politics of exclusion as it does on a politics of inclusion. There are many visions and versions of the Black community that get posited in scholarly discourse, in popular cultural forms, and in political discourse. Rarely do any of these visions include lesbians and gay men, except perhaps as an afterthought. I want to see a Black antiracist discourse that does not need to maintain such exclusions in order to be efficacious.

Insofar as there is a need to articulate a Black antiracist discourse to address and to respond to the real and present dangers and vicissitudes of racism, essential to that discourse is the use of the rhetoric of community. Perhaps in the long term it would be best to explode all of the categories having to do with the very notion of "Black community" and all of the inclusions and exclusions that come along with it. That is a project the advent of which I will be among the first to applaud. However, in the political meantime, my aim here is to take seriously the state of racial discourse, especially Black antiracist discourse and the accompanying construct of "the Black community," on the very irksome terms in which I have inherited it.

As I think again on the example of the exchange between Crenshaw and Gates over the misogyny charges against 2 Live Crew, it also occurs to me that similar charges of homophobia or heterosexism could be waged against any number of rap or hip-hop artists, though this is a critique that seems to have been given very little attention.[5] If similar charges could be made, could not, then, similar defenses of heterosexism be mounted as well? The argument would go something like this: what appears to be open homophobia on the part of black rap and hip-hop artists is really a complicated form of cultural signifying that needs to be read not as homophobia but in the context of a history of derisive assaults on Black manhood. This being the case, what we really witness when we see and hear these artists participate in what appears to be homophobia is an act involved in the project of the reclamation of Black manhood that does not really mean the literal violence that it performs. This is, in fact, similar to the logic used by bell hooks in her essay "Homophobia in Black Communities" when she speaks of the contradiction that is openly expressed homophobia among Blacks:

> Black communities may be perceived as more homophobic than other communities because there is a tendency for individuals in black communities to verbally express in an outspoken way antigay sentiments. I talked with a straight black male in a California community who acknowledged that though he has often made jokes poking fun at gays or expressing contempt, as a means of bonding in group settings, in his private life he was a central support person for a gay sister. Such contradictory behavior seems pervasive in black communities. It speaks to ambivalence about sexuality in general, about sex as a subject of conversation, and to ambivalent feelings and attitudes toward homosexuality. Various structures of emotional and economic dependence create gaps between attitudes and actions. Yet a distinction must be made between black people overtly expressing prejudice toward homosexuals and homophobic white people who never make homophobic comments but who have the power to actively exploit and oppress gay people in areas of housing, employment, etc.[6]

hooks's rhetoric here is at once to be commended for its critique of the claims by many that Blacks are more homophobic than other racial or ethnic groups and to be critiqued as an apology for Black homophobia. For hooks to offer as a rationale for Black homophobia, as in her anecdote of the "straight black male in a California community," the fact that "bonding" (since it is unspecified, we can assume both male and racial bonding here) is the reason he participates in homophobic "play" is both revealing and inexcusable. This is precisely the kind of play that, following again the logic of Crenshaw, we cannot abide, given the real threats that still exist in the form of discrimination and violence to gays and lesbians. While hooks may want to relegate systemic discrimination against gays and lesbians to the domain of hegemonic whites, antigay violence takes many forms—emotional, representational, and physical—and is not a practice exclusive to those of any particular race. Furthermore, it seems disingenuous and naive to suggest that what we say about gays and lesbians and the cultural representations of gays and lesbians do not, at least in part, legitimate—if not engender—discrimination and violence against gays and lesbians.

The rhetorical strategy she employs here is a very old one, indeed, wherein Blacks are blameless because "powerless." The logic implied by such thinking is that because whites constitute a racial hegemonic block in American society that oppresses Blacks and other people of color, Blacks can never be held wholly accountable for their own sociopolitical transgressions. Since this is sensitive and volatile territory upon which I am treading, let me take some extra care to make sure that I am properly understood. I do not mean to suggest that there is not a grain of truth in the reality of the racial claims made by hooks and sustained by a history of Black protest. However, it is only a grain. And the grain is, after all, but a minute particle on the vast shores of discursive truth. For me, any understanding of Black oppression that makes it possible and, worse, permissible to endorse at any level sexism, elitism, or heterosexism is a vision of Black culture that is finally not politically consistent with liberation. We can no more excuse Black homophobia than Black sexism. One is as politically and, dare I say, morally suspect as the other. This is a particularly surprising move on the part of hooks when we consider that, in so many other contexts, her work on gender is so unrelenting and hard-hitting.[7] So much is this the case that it is almost unimaginable that hooks would allow for a space in which tolerance for Black sexism would ever be tenable. This makes me all the more suspect of her willingness not just to tolerate but to apologize for Black homophobia.

There is still one aspect of hooks's argument that I want to address here, which is her creation of a dichotomy between Black gays and lesbians who live in Black communities and those who live in predominately white communities. It is raised most clearly in the epigraph with which I began this essay. She laments that "often we hear more from black gay people who have chosen to live in predominately white communities, whose choices may have been affected by undue harassment in black communities. We hear hardly anything from Black gay people who live contentedly in black communities."[8] This claim about the removal of Black gays and lesbians from the "authentic" Black community is quite bizarre for any number of reasons. Is it to say that those who remain in Black communities are not "unduly harassed"? Or is it that they can take it? And is undue harassment the only factor in moves by Black gays and lesbians to other communities? Still, the statement is problematic even beyond these more obvious curiosities in that it plays on the kind of authenticity politics that are under critique here. hooks faults many Black middle-class gays and lesbians, and I dare say many of her colleagues in the academy, who live in "white communities" in a way that suggests that they are unable to give us the "real" story of Black gays and lesbians. What of those experiences of "undue harassment" that she posits as potentially responsible for their exodus from the Black community? Are those narratives, taking place as they do in hooks's "authentic" Black community, not an important part of the story of Black gay and lesbian experience, or are those gays and lesbians unqualified because of the geographical locations from which they speak? It appears that the standard hooks ultimately establishes for "real" Black gay commentary here is a standard that few Black intellectuals could comfortably meet anymore—a by-product of the class structure in which we live. In most cases, the more upwardly mobile one becomes, the whiter the circles in which one inevitably finds oneself circulating—one of the more unfortunate realities of American society.[9]

The logic used by hooks on Black homophobia is dangerous not only for the reasons I have already articulated but because it exists on a continuum with thinkers like Frances Cress Welsing. They are not, of course, the same, but each does exist in a discursive field that makes the other possible. Therefore, hooks's implied logic of apology played out to its fullest conclusion bears a great deal of resemblance to Welsing's own heterosexist text.

Welsing's[10] sentiments are exemplary of and grow out of a Black cultural nationalist response to gay and lesbian sexuality, which has most often read homosexuality as "counterrevolutionary."[11] She begins first by dismissing the entirety of the psychoanalytic community that takes its lead from Freud. Freud is dismissed immediately by Welsing because he was unable to deliver his own people from the devastation of Nazi Germany. This "racial" ineffectualness for Welsing renders moot anything that Freud (or any of his devotees) might have to say on the subject of sexuality. The logic is this: since the most important political element for Black culture is that of survival and Freud didn't know how to do that for his people, nothing that Freud or his devotees could tell us about homosexuality should be applied to Black people. The idea of holding Freud responsible for not preventing the Holocaust is not only laughable, but it denies the specific history giving rise to that event. Furthermore, if we use this logic of victim blaming in the case of the Jews and Freud, would it not also follow that we would have to make the same critique of slavery? Are Black Africans and the tribal leaders of West Africa, then, not also responsible for not preventing the enslavement of Blacks? It is precisely this sort of specious logic that makes a very articulate Welsing difficult and frustrating when one tries to take her seriously.

But take her seriously we must. Welsing continues to speak and to command quite a following among Black cultural nationalists.[12] We have to be concerned, then, about the degree to which Welsing's heterosexist authentication of Blackness contributes to the marginalization of Black gays and lesbians. For Welsing, Black Africa is the site of an "originary" or "authentic" Blackness. At the beginning of her essay, Welsing makes the following statement:

> Black male passivity, effeminization, bisexuality and homosexuality are being encountered increasingly by Black psychiatrists working with Black patient populations. These issues are being presented by family members, personnel working in schools and other social institutions or by Black men themselves. Many in the Black population are reaching the conclusion that such issues have become a problem of epidemic proportion amongst Black people in the U.S., although it was an almost non-existent behavioral phenomenon amongst indigenous Blacks in Africa.[13]

From the beginning, Welsing describes homosexuality in a language associated with disease. It is a "problem of epidemic proportion" that seems to be spreading among Black people. This rehearses a rhetorical gesture I mentioned earlier by speaking of the Black community as an entity wholly separate from homosexuals who infect its sacrosanct authenticity. Of course, it goes without saying that Welsing's claim that homosexuality "was an almost non-existent behavioral phenomenon amongst indigenous Blacks in Africa" is not only unsupported by anthropological study,[14] but it also suggests the biological or genetic, to use her language, link which nonindigenous Blacks have to indigenous Black Africans. Welsing more than adopts an Afrocentric worldview in this essay by positing Africa as the seat of all real, unsullied, originary blackness. In this way she casts her lot with much of Black cultural nationalist discourse, which is heavily invested in Afrocentrism. For further evidence of this, we need look no further than Welsing's own definition of "Black mental health":

The practice of those unit patterns of behavior (i.e., logic, thought, speech, action and emotional response) in all areas of people activity: economics, education, entertainment, labor, law, politics, religion, sex and war—which are simultaneously self- and group-supporting under the social and political conditions of worldwide white supremacy domination (racism). In brief, this means Black behavioral practice which resists self- and group-negation and destruction.[15]

Here, as elsewhere, Welsing prides herself on being outside the conceptual mainstream of any currently held psychiatric definitions of mental illness. She labels those the " 'European' psychoanalytic theories of Sigmund Freud."[16] She seems here to want to be recognized for taking a bold, brazen position as solidly outside any "mainstream" logic. This is because all such logic is necessarily bad because it is mainstream, which is to say, white. One, then, gets the sense that homosexuality too is a by-product of white supremacy—and, further, that, if there were no white supremacy, homosexuality would not at best exist or at worst be somehow okay if it did. The overriding logic of her argument is the connection between white supremacy and homosexuality. The former produces the latter as a way to control Black people. Hence, it follows that the only way to be really black is to resist homosexuality.

From this point on, Welsing's essay spirals into an ever-deepening chasm from which it never manages to return. For example, she argues that it is "male muscle mass" that oppresses a people. Since white men understand this fact and the related fact of their genetic weakness in relation to the majority of the world's women (women of color), they are invested in the effeminization and homosexualization of Black men.[17] She also states that the white women's liberation movement—white women's response to the white male's need to be superior at least over them—has further served to weaken the white male's sense of power, "helping to push him to a *weakened* and *homosexual* stance" (my emphasis—the two are synonymous for Welsing). Feminism, then, according to Welsing, leads to further "white male/female alienation, pushing white males further into the homosexual position and . . . white females in that direction also."[18] Finally, she suggests that it is Black manhood that is the primary target of racism, since Black men, of course, are the genetically superior beings who can not only reproduce with Black women but can also reproduce with white women. And since the offspring of such unions, according to Welsing's logic, are always Black (the exact opposite of the result of such sexual pairings for white men and Black women), Black manhood is the primary target of a white supremacist system. Welsing's words are significant enough here that I quote her at some length:

. . . Racism (white supremacy) is the dominant social system in today's world. Its fundamental dynamic is predicated upon the genetic recessive deficiency state of albinism, which is responsible for skin whiteness and thus the so-called "white race." This genetic recessive trait is dominated by the genetic capacity to produce any of the various degrees of skin melanation—whether black, brown, red or yellow. In other words, it can be annihilated as a phenotypic condition. Control of this potential for genetic domination and annihilation throughout the world is absolutely essential if the condition of skin whiteness is to survive. "White" survival is predicated upon aggressiveness and muscle mass in the form of technology directed against the "non-white" melanated men on the planet Earth who constitute the numerical majority. Therefore, white survival and white power are dependent upon the various methodologies, tactics and strategies developed to control all "non-white" men, as well as bring them into cooperative submission. This is especially important in the case of Black men because they have the great-est capacity to produce melanin and, in turn, the greatest genetic potential for the annihilation of skin albinism or skin whiteness.[19]

This passage demonstrates, to my mind, the critical hazards of privileging the category of race in any discussion of Black people. When we give "race," with its retinue of historical and discursive investments, primacy over other signifiers of difference, the result is a net-work of critical blindnesses that prevents us from perceiving the ways in which the conven-tions of race discourse get naturalized and normativized. These conventions often include, especially in cases involving—though not exclusive to—Black cultural nationalism, the denigration of homosexuality and the accompanying peripheralization of women. Under-lying much of race discourse, then, is always the implication that all "real" Black subjects are male and heterosexual. Therefore, in partial response to the query with which I began this essay, only these such subjects are best qualified to speak for or to represent the race.

Unfortunately, Welsing does not stop there. She continues her discussion of Black man-hood to a point where what she means by the appellation far and above exceeds her mere genetic definition. Though she never clearly defines what she intends by Black manhood, we can construct a pretty clear idea from the ways that she uses the term in her argument. "The dearth of Black males in the homes, schools and neighborhoods," Welsing proclaims,

> leaves Black male children no alternative models. Blindly they seek out one another as models, and in their blindness end up in trouble—in juvenile homes or prisons. But fate and the dy-namics of racism again play a vicious trick because the young males only become more alien-ated from their manhood and more feminized in such settings.[20]

It is clear from this statement that Black manhood is set in opposition to femininity and is something that is retarded by the influence of women, especially in female-headed house-holds. She describes the effect of effeminizing influences on Black men as the achievement of racist programming. This achievement is, in part, possible because of the clothing in-dustry as well, according to Welsing: "The white run clothing industry is all too pleased to provide the costumes of feminine disguise for Black male escape. However, they never would provide uniforms or combat gear if customers were willing to pay $1000 per out-fit."[21] She also faults television as "an important programmer of behavior in this social sys-tem" that "plays a further major role in alienating Black males (especially children) from Black manhood."[22] The examples she cites are Flip Wilson's persona Geraldine and Jimmy Walker's character, J. J., on the 1970s television series *Good Times*. "These weekly insults," she maintains, "to Black manhood that we have been programmed to believe are entertain-ment and not direct racist warfare, further reinforce, perhaps in the unconscious thinking of Black people, a loss of respect for Black manhood while carrying that loss to even deeper levels."[23] Most telling, perhaps, is that the clinical method she endorses for "disorders" of "passivity, effeminization, bisexuality, homosexuality" is to have the patients "relax and en-vision themselves approaching and opposing, in actual combat, the collective of white males and females (without apology or giving up in the crunch)."[24] Again, there is an essence to what Black manhood is that never receives full articulation except implicitly. But what is implied could be described as monstrous, combative, and even primitive. There is certainly no room for a nurturing view of manhood here. To be a man is to be strong. And strength, in Welsing's logic, is the opposite of weakness, which can only signify at best as effeminacy or passivity and at worst as bisexuality or homosexuality. Still another of the vexatious implications of this logic is that, in a world devoid of racism or white supremacy, there would be no Black male homosexuality. The result is that Black male homosexuality is reducible to being a by-product of racist programming. Once again, this is the function of an argument that privileges race discourse over other forms of difference in its analysis of Black oppression.

Let me turn my attention for a moment to Essex Hemphill's response to Welsing's troublesome essay. Hemphill's rhetoric demonstrates how even in a very astute and well-wrought "reading" of Welsing—and it is fair to say that Hemphill "reads" her in both the critical and the more campy sense of the word—the move is never made to critique the structure (and by "structure" here I mean the implied rules governing the use of) and function of race discourse itself. It is clear to me, as I have tried to demonstrate, that this is precisely what is missing from hooks's logic, which undergirds her discussion of homophobia in Black communities as well. Hemphill's response to Welsing is thoughtful and engaging and identifies the faulty premises upon which Welsing bases her arguments. Still, Hemphill's own essay and rhetoric falls prey to the conventions of race discourse in two very important ways. First, in order to combat Welsing's homophobia/heterosexism, Hemphill himself feels the pressure to legitimize and authorize himself as a speaker on race matters by telling his own authenticating anecdote of Black/gay experience at the beginning of his essay:[25]

> In 1974, the year that Dr. Frances Cress Welsing wrote "The Politics behind Black Male Passivity, Effeminization, Bisexuality, and Homosexuality," I entered my final year of senior high school.
>
> By that time, I had arrived at a very clear understanding of how dangerous it was to be a homosexual in my Black neighborhood and in society. . . . Facing this then-limited perception of homosexual life, I could only wonder, where did I fit in? . . .
>
> Conversely, I was perfecting my heterosexual disguise; I was practicing the necessary use of masks for survival; I was calculating the distance between the first day of class and graduation, the distance between graduation from high school and departure for college—and ultimately, the arrival of my freedom from home, community, and my immediate peers. . . .
>
> During the course of the next sixteen years I would articulate and politicize my sexuality. I would discover that homo sex did not constitute a whole life nor did it negate my racial identity or constitute a substantive reason to be estranged from my family and Black culture. I discovered, too, that the work ahead for me included, most importantly, being able to integrate all of my identities into a functioning self, instead of accepting a dysfunctional existence as a consequence of my homosexual desires.[26]

While Hemphill's personal anecdote demonstrates his access to the various categories of identity he claims, it is not a critique of the very idea of the categories themselves. In fact, he plays the "race/sexuality" card in a way that is similar to the way in which Welsing plays the "race" card.

And, second, while his critique of Welsing is thorough and extremely insightful, it does not move to critique the methodological fault Welsing makes in her analysis—that is, the fact that much of what is wrong with Welsing's argument is a result of the privileging of "race" over other critical categories of difference. Instead, Hemphill treats Welsing's heterosexism itself as the critical disease, instead of as symptomatic of a far more systemic critical illness.

One of the most noteworthy things about Hemphill's anecdotal testimony is that, while it insists, and rightly so, upon the integration of what Welsing has established as the dichotomous identities of race and homosexuality, it also participates in a familiar structural convention of race discourse in its necessity to claim the racial identification as a position from which even the Black homosexual speaks. In other words, part of the rhetorical strategy enacted by Hemphill in this moment is that of claiming the category of racial authenticity for himself as part of what legitimizes and authorizes the articulation of his corrective to Welsing's homophobic race logic. The net result is the substitution of heterosexist race logic with a homo-positive or homo-inclusive race logic. Still the common denominator of both positions is the persistence of race as the privileged category in discussions of Black identity.

The first clue we get of Hemphill's failure to identify the larger systemic problem of Welsing's argument is his comparison of Welsing and Shahrazad Ali:

> Dr. Welsing is not as easily dismissable as Shahrazad Ali, author of the notorious book of internal strife, *The Black Man's Guide to Understanding the Black Woman* (Philadelphia: Civilized Publications, 1989). . . . By dismissing the lives of Black lesbians and gay men, Ali is clearly not advocating the necessary healing Black communities require; she is advocating further factionalization. Her virulently homophobic ideas lack credibility and are easily dismissed as incendiary.
>
> Dr. Welsing is much more dangerous because she attempts to justify *her* homophobia and heterosexism precisely by grounding it in an acute understanding of African-American history and an analysis of the psychological effects of centuries of racist oppression and violence.[27]

Hemphill is right in his reading of Welsing, though his reading does not go far enough: Ali is not more easily dismissable than Welsing. In fact, Ali's ideas are rooted in a history of sorts as well, a history shared by Welsing's arguments—that is, the history of race discourse itself, which, in its privileging of the dominant category of analysis, has always sustained the derision or exclusion of black gays and lesbians.

Another such moment in Hemphill's essay comes when he identifies what he seems to understand as the central problem of Welsing's text. He writes:

> Welsing refutes any logical understanding of sexuality. By espousing Black homophobia and heterosexism—imitations of the very oppressive forces of hegemonic white male heterosexuality she attempts to challenge—she places herself in direct collusion with the forces that continually move against Blacks, gays, lesbians, and all people of color. Thus, every time a gay man or lesbian is violently attacked, blood *is* figuratively on Dr. Welsing's hands as surely as blood is on the hands of the attackers. Her ideas reinforce the belief on that gay and lesbian lives are expendable, and her views also provide a clue as to why the Black community has failed to intelligently and coherently address critical, life-threatening issues such as AIDS.[28]

Hemphill's statement is true. Welsing's logic does imitate that of the oppressive forces of white male heterosexuality which she tries to refute. The difference is that Welsing does not view the latter category as crucial to her analysis. The problem with Welsing's argument does not end where Hemphill supposes it does. Much of race discourse, even the discourse of racial liberation, participates in a similar relationship with hegemonic antigay forces. This is especially the case, and some might even argue that it is inevitable, when we consider the history and development of Black liberationist or antiracist discourse with its insistence on the centrality of Black masculinity (in the narrowest sense of the term) as the essential element of any form of Black liberation. If racial liberationist discourse suggests at best the invisibility of homosexuality and at worst understands homosexuality as racially antagonistic, Dr. Welsing radically manifests one of the more unseemly truths of race discourse for Blacks—the demonization of homosexuality.

The critical blindness demonstrated by Hemphill does not alone express the extent of what happens when a gay Black man takes up the mantle of race discourse. Another example worth exploring is that of James Baldwin. In the documentary of his life done in 1989, *James Baldwin: The Price of the Ticket*, there are at least two moments to which I want to call attention. The first is a statement made by Amiri Baraka, and the second is a statement made by Baldwin himself from interview footage from *The Dick Cavett Show*. I turn to these less literally textual examples to demonstrate that in our more casual or less scripted moments, our subconscious understanding of the realities of race discourse is laid bare even more clearly.

Baraka's regard for Baldwin is well documented by the film. He talks about how Baldwin was "in the tradition" and how his early writings, specifically *Notes of a Native Son*, really impacted him and spoke to a whole generation. In an attempt to describe or to account for Baldwin's homosexuality, however, Baraka falters in his efforts to unite the racially significant image of Baldwin that he clings to with the homosexual Baldwin with whom he seems less comfortable. Baraka states the following:

> Jimmy Baldwin was neither in the closet about his homosexuality, nor was he running around proclaiming homosexuality. I mean, he was what he was. And you either had to buy that or, you know, *mea culpa*, go somewhere else.

The poles of the rhetorical continuum that Baraka sets up here for his understanding of homosexuality are very telling and should remind us of the earlier dichotomy set up by bell hooks between homosexuals who live somewhat closeted existences in Black communities and those who do not. To Baraka's mind, one can either be in the closet or "running around proclaiming homosexuality" (the image of the effete gay man or the gay activist collide here, it would seem). What makes Baldwin acceptable to enter the pantheon of race men for Baraka is the fact that his sexual identity is unlocatable. It is neither here nor there, or perhaps it is everywhere at once, leaving the entire question an undecided and undecidable one. And if Baldwin is undecided about his sexual identity, the one identity to which he is firmly committed is his racial identity. The rhetorical ambiguity around his sexual identity, according to Baraka, is what makes it possible for Baldwin to be a race man who was "in the tradition."

Baldwin himself, it seems, was well aware of the dangers of, indeed, the "price of the ticket" for trying to synthesize his racial and sexual identities. He understood that his efficacy as race man was, in part at least, owing to his limiting his activism to his racial politics. The frame of the documentary certainly confirms this in the way it represents Baldwin's own response to his sexuality. In one interview, he makes the following statement:

> I think the trick is to say yes to life. . . . It is only we of the twentieth century who are so ob-
> sessed with the particular details of anybody's sex life. I don't think those details make a differ-
> ence. And I will never be able to deny a certain power that I have had to deal with, which has
> dealt with me, which is called love; and love comes in very strange packages. I've loved a few
> men; I've loved a few women; and a few people have loved me. That's . . . I suppose that's all
> that's saved my life.

It may be of interest to note that while Baldwin is making this statement, the camera pans
down to his hands, which are fidgeting with the cigarette and cigarette holder. This move
on the part of the camera undercuts the veracity of Baldwin's statement here. In fact, it
suggests what I think of as a fair conclusion about this statement. That is, Baldwin himself
does not quite believe all of what he is saying in this moment. From the 1949 essay "The
Preservation of Innocence,"[29] which he wrote and published in *Zero*, a small Moroccan
journal, Baldwin knows just how profoundly important sexuality is to discussions of race.
But the desire registered here for sexuality not to make a difference is important to recognize. When we understand this statement as spoken in a prophetic mode, it imagines a
world in which the details of a person's sex life can "matter" as part of a person's humanity
but not have to usurp their authority or legitimacy to represent the race.

If Baldwin's statement raises the complications of speaking from a complex racial/
sexual identity location, the following excerpt from his interview on *The Dick Cavett Show*
illustrates this point all the more clearly:

> I don't know what most white people in this country feel, but I can only conclude what they
> feel from the state of their institutions. I don't know if white Christians hate Negroes or not,
> but I know that we have a Christian church which is white and a Christian church which is
> black. I know, as Malcolm X once put it, "The most segregated hour in America is high noon
> on Sunday." That says a great deal to me about a Christian nation. It means that I can't afford
> to trust most white Christians and certainly cannot trust the Christian church. I don't know
> whether the labor unions and their bosses really hate me. That doesn't matter. But I know that
> I'm not in their unions. I don't know if the real estate lobby has anything against black people,
> but I know the real estate lobby keeps me in the ghetto. I don't know if the board of education
> hates black people, but I know the textbooks they give my children to read and the schools that
> we go to. Now this is the evidence! *You want me to make an act of faith risking myself, my wife,
> my woman, my sister, my children on some idealism which you assure me exists in America which
> I have never seen.* [emphasis added]

Interesting for both the rich sermonic quality and the vehement tone for which Baldwin
was famous, this passage is also conspicuous for the manner in which Baldwin assumes the
voice of representative race man. In the very last sentence, when Baldwin affects the position of race man, part of the performance includes the masking of his specificity, his sexuality, his difference. And in race discourse when all difference is concealed what emerges is
the heterosexual Black man "risking [himself], [his] wife, [his] woman, [his] children." The
image of the Black man as protector, progenitor, and defender of the race—which sounds
suspiciously similar to the image fostered by Welsing and much of Black cultural nationalism—is what Baldwin assumes here. The truth of this rhetorical transformation—the hard,

difficult, worrisome truth—is that in order to be representative race man, one must be het-erosexual. And what of women? They appear, in the confines of race discourse, to be ever the passive players. They are rhetorically useful in that they lend legitimacy to the Black male's responsibility for their care and protection, but they cannot speak, any more than the gay or lesbian brother or sister can. If these are part of the structural demands of race discourse, the erasure of subtlety and Black difference, it is time to own up to that truth. As Black intellectuals and cultural workers, we have to demand, insist upon, and be about the business of helping to create new and more inclusive ways of speaking about race that do not cause even good, thorough thinkers like hooks, Hemphill, and Baldwin (and there are many others) to compromise their/our own critical veracity by participating in the form of race discourse that has been hegemonic for so long. Race is, indeed, a fiction, an allegory, if you will, with an elaborate linguistic court. With that known, more needs to be done to reimagine race; to create new and inclusive mythologies to replace the old, weatherworn, heterosexual, masculinity-centered ones; to reconstitute "the Black community" as one that includes our various differences as opposed to the monolith to which we inevitably seem to return.

For far too long the field of African-American/Afro-American/Black Studies has thought about race as the primary category of analysis for the work that proceeds from the field. The problem with such work has always been, and continues to be, that African Americans and African-American experience are far more complicated than this. And it is time that we begin to understand what that means in the form of an everyday critical and political practice. Race is not simple. It has never been simple. It does not have the history that would make it so, no matter how much we may yearn for that degree of clarity. This is a point I have argued in a variety of venues. The point is that if I am thinking about race, I should already be thinking about gender, class, and sexuality. This statement, I think, as-sumes the very impossibility of a hierarchy or chronology of categories of identity. The point is not just one of intersection—as we have thought of it for so long—it is one of re-constitution. That is, race is already more than just race. Or, put another way, race is always already everything that it ever was, though some of its constitutive aspects may have been repressed for various nefarious purposes and/or for other strategic ones. Either way, it is never simple, never to be taken for granted. What I say is not revolutionary or revelatory. The theory, in this way, has gotten ahead of the critical practice. Almost all good race theorists these days will recognize the merit of this approach; the point is that the work we produce has not fully caught up. That explains why it is still possible today to query: What does a race theory, of which all of these categories of identity are constitutive, look like? And, more important, how do the critiques, the work informed by such theory, look differ-ent from what we now see dominating the field? I have great hope in the future for the work of scholars like Lindon Barrett, who are beginning to theorize racial Blackness in re-lationship to the category of value, with all the trappings of desire, commodification and exchange inherent in that operation. This may be just the kind of critical innovation needed to help us reconstitute our ideas about "race" and race discourse.[30]

Of course, it is not my intention in these reflections to suggest that there are not good heterosexual "race men" and "race women" on the scene who have progressive views about sexuality and are "down" with their gay and lesbian brothers and sisters. In fact, quite the contrary. In many instances, it adds an extra dimension of cachet and progressivism to hear such heterosexual speakers be sympathetic to gays and lesbians. So long as they are not themselves gay or lesbian, it would appear on the open market to enhance their "coolness" quotient. The issue that needs more attention exists at the level at which we authenticate our authority and legitimacy to speak for the race as representational subjects. In other words, there are any number of narratives that African-American intellectuals employ to qualify themselves in the terms of race discourse to speak for the race. And, while one routinely witnesses the use of narratives of racial discrimination, narratives of growing up poor and Black and elevating oneself through education and hard work, narratives about how connected middle-class Black intellectuals are to "the Black community" or "the hood," we could scarcely imagine an instance in which narrating or even claiming one's gay or lesbian identity would authenticate or legitimate oneself as a racial representative. And, as we see in the case of James Baldwin, when Black gays and lesbians do don the racial representational mask, they often do so at the expense of effacing (even if only temporarily) their sexual identities.

Given the current state of Black antiracist discourse, it is no wonder that even now there is only one book-length critical, literary investigation of the work of James Baldwin, by Trudier Harris;[31] it is no wonder that Langston Hughes's biographer, even in 1986, felt the need to defend him against the "speculation" surrounding his homosexuality; it is no wonder that, even to this day, we can still say, with Cheryl Clark and bell hooks, that there exists no sustained sociological study of Black lesbians and gays; and it is no wonder that among the vanguard of so-called Black public intellectuals there is the notable near absence of openly gay and lesbian voices. Lamentable though this state of affairs may be, we cannot deny that part of the responsibility for it has much to do with the limits of Black antiracist discourse, that is, what it is still considered appropriate to say about race, and the policing of who speaks for the race.

NOTES

1. bell hooks, "Homophobia in Black Communities," in *Talking Back* (Boston: South End, 1989), 120–26.

2. Essex Hemphill, "If Freud Had Been a Neurotic Colored Woman: Reading Dr. Frances Cress Welsing," in *Ceremonies: Prose and Poetry* (New York: Plume, 1992), 52–62.

3. See my two essays "Speaking the Unspeakable: On Toni Morrison, African American Intellectuals and the Uses of Essentialist Rhetoric," *Modern Fiction Studies* (fall/winter 1993): 755–76, and "Transdisciplinary Intellectual Practice: Cornel West and the Rhetoric of Race Transcending," *Harvard Black Letter Law Journal* (spring 1994): 155–68.

4. Kimberlé Williams Crenshaw, "Beyond Racism and Misogyny: Black Feminism and 2 Live Crew," *Boston Review* 16, 6 (December 1991): 6, 30.

5. Thinkers like Kobena Mercer at the Black Nations/Queer Nations Conference in 1995 represent a few of the exceptions to this claim. Still, such critique of homophobia has not been a part of the

more public debates about the objectionable qualities of rap and hip-hop.

6. bell hooks, see note 1, at 122.

7. See, for example, any number of hooks's essays in *Yearning: Race, Gender, and Cultural Politics* (Boston: South End, 1990) and *Black Looks: Race and Representation* (Boston: South End, 1992).

8. bell hooks, see note 6.

9. This is not to say that those of us who exist (at least professionally) in predominately white circles do not interact with the "Black community." It is to suggest that our interaction is, in a sense, constructed.

10. For a fuller discussion of how homosexuality is counterrevolutionary, see Eldridge Cleaver's *Soul on Ice* (New York: McGraw-Hill, 1968). The chapters entitled "The Allegory of the Black Eunuchs" and "The Primeval Mitosis" are especially noteworthy. In order to relate this to the earlier discussion of Crenshaw and Gates's exchange over 2 Live Crew, it is interesting to note the point made by Essex

Hemphill in his essay on Welsing, that she has been a highly "sought-after public speaker, and in recent years, her ideas have been embraced in the re-emergence of Black cultural nationalism, particularly by rap groups such as Public Enemy" (53–54).

11. Welsing herself is no exception to this rule. The last sentence of her essay reads as follows: "Black male bisexuality and homosexuality has [*sic*] been used by the white collective in its effort to survive genetically in a world dominated by colored people, and Black acceptance of this position does not solve the major problem of our oppression [read here the race problem] but only further retards its ultimate solution." Frances Cress Welsing, "The Politics behind Black Male Passivity, Effeminization, Bisexuality, and Homosexuality," in *The Isis Papers: The Keys to the Colors* (Chicago: Third World, 1991), 92.

12. Even as recently as a few weeks ago at the time of this writing, Welsing appeared on National Public Radio speaking about her famous Cress Theory of race. The theory is based on the genetic inferiority of whites to Blacks. Since whites have knowledge of this, they fear genetic annihilation. This fear, according to Welsing, has been the cause of the history of racism as we know it.

13. Welsing, see note 11, at 81.

14. For some preliminary discussion of anthropological evidence of the existence of homosexual practices among certain African cultures and other peoples of color, see Pat Caplan, ed., *The Cultural Construction of Sexuality* (London and New York: Tavistock, 1987).

15. Welsing, see note 11, at 82.

16. Ibid.

17. Welsing, see note 11, at 83–84.

18. Welsing, see note 11, at 85–86.

19. Welsing, see note 11, at 83.

20. Welsing, see note 11, at 89.

21. Ibid.

22. Ibid.

23. Welsing, see note 11, at 90.

24. Welsing, see note 11, at 91–92.

25. See my essay "Transdisciplinary Intellectual Practice: Cornel West and the Rhetoric of Race Transcending," where I argue that one of the essentializing gestures in which African-American intellectuals participate in order to legitimate themselves as speakers for the race is to relate racially affirming anecdotes from their own experience. Also, in fairness to Hemphill, his use of the anecdotal gesture of self-authorization is somewhat different from the usual race-based model. His narrative authority derives from the simultaneity of his gay and his Black experience. He insists upon them both. Still, the need to narrate the two side by side, indeed, to narrate his story at all, is interesting to note as a response to Welsing's very problematic position.

26. Hemphill, see note 2, at 52–53.

27. Hemphill, see note 2, at 54.

28. Hemphill, see note 2, at 55.

29. James Baldwin, "Preservation of Innocence," *OUT/LOOK* 2, 2 (fall 1989): 40–45.

30. See Lindon Barrett's forthcoming book, *Seeing Double: Blackness and Value* (Cambridge University Press).

31. I am also aware of the work-in-progress of Maurice Wallace at Yale titled *Hostile Witness: Baldwin as Artist and Outlaw.*

25

HOME-SCHOOL PARTNERSHIPS
THROUGH THE EYES OF PARENTS

Cynthia Hudley and Rhoda Barnes

ABSTRACT

This study was conducted to understand parents' beliefs about their relationships with their children's schools. The research surveyed parents of African-American children enrolled in public school in grades K–12. These children represent a small minority in a school district of Latino and Anglo students. We were interested in understanding how these parents perceived their roles as partners, how satisfied they were with both their own and the school's efforts to build partnerships, and how they believed their efforts related to their children's school achievement and adjustment. Based on a content analysis of interview protocols, responses were classified according to three broad themes: parents' beliefs about home-school relationships, parents' perceptions of their children's school experiences, and parents' satisfaction with the schools' performance in educating their child. The need for improved home-school communication was one of two major themes to emerge from these data; the second major theme was the need for cultural awareness and sensitivity at the school site. The data suggest that respondents, while endorsing the ideal of school site involvement, are much more likely to actually engage in home-based activities than to participate at the school site. These findings are discussed relative to various models of parental involvement that have been put forth in the literature.

INTRODUCTION

The evidence is beyond dispute that strong home-school relationships translate into higher academic achievement for students, more positive feelings about their profession for teachers, a nurturing, orderly climate for schools, and a greater sense of confidence for parents (Swap, 1993). However, conflicting beliefs about rights, expertise, abilities, and cultural stereotypes may cast teachers and parents into adversarial rather than cooperative relationships (Fine, 1993).

Often, teachers develop opinions about a child's home life based on the child's classroom behavior. Conversely, the parent may develop beliefs about the efficacy of the teacher and the school based on the child's report of classroom experiences (Power, 1985). Thus the parent-teacher relationship may be shaped by perceptions drawn from incomplete or inconsistent information and mediated by an underlying, competitive force to prove which of the adults knows what is "best" for children (Power, 1985). This competition to demonstrate competence may be especially problematic when parents and teachers are communicating over the gulf of ethnic or cultural differences (Boutte, 1992).

There is a consistent theme throughout the parent involvement literature that parents of poor and/or minority children are unlikely to participate in their children's schooling and are rarely if ever present in schools (Liontos, 1992). However, the majority of the data comes from the perspective of the school (Fine, 1993). Conversely, parent survey data report that almost all parents, irrespective of ethnicity, income, or education, desire educational success for their children and want to work with schools to achieve that goal (Epstein, 1990). For example, a recent survey (Powell and Peete, 1992) from an urban, Midwest sample with 50 percent ethnic minority respondents indicated that 95 percent of parents think about their child's future success and 67 percent of them expected their child to earn a college degree or complete graduate studies. African Americans in particular have historically used education as a shield against oppression and poverty (Anderson, 1988). However, empirical data from families of color are sparse and tend to confound ethnicity and class variables (Liontos, 1992).

The present study was conducted to ascertain parents' beliefs and concerns about their relationships with their children's schools. The research was conducted with parents of African-American children who are a small minority (3 percent of enrolled students) in a suburban public school district composed of Latino and Anglo students. Thus the research presented here sought to depict an extremely understudied population: employed African-American families with at least one child in public school. We were interested in understanding how these parents perceived their roles as partners, how satisfied they were with both their own and the school's efforts to build partnerships, and how they believed their efforts related to their children's school achievement and adjustment.

CONCEPTUAL FRAMEWORK

Constructing knowledge of home-school relations requires an understanding of how power and responsibility are parceled out to the various groups. A number of models have been proposed to describe the relationship between schools and parents. The protective model (Swap, 1993), still perhaps ascendant in American public education (Davies, 1992), assumes that schools have the primary responsibility for educating students and parents' efforts should be confined to school rituals such as open house. The goal is to protect the professionals from the unwanted intrusion of less competent parents (Power, 1985). The school-focused model assumes that the role of parents is to endorse and support the values and objectives identified as significant by the school (Irvine, 1992). The goal of this model, prominent in the education of minority and other "at-risk" children, is the remediation of students' deficient home environments. The multicultural model assumes that students learn best when the classroom curriculum reflects the history and culture of the students (Ogbu, 1990). The goal of this model is to enlist the expertise of parents in expanding the curricular offerings. The partnership model (Comer, 1990) assumes that schools must radically restructure the roles and relationships of all adults who are involved in the schooling of children. The goal is to join educators, parents, and community members in the common mission of overseeing the education and development of all children.

Each of these models presents advantages and disadvantages to both parents and school personnel. We are concerned here with how one group of parents perceived the structure of their own relationships with schools, and how that relationship affected their child's schooling.

METHOD
Sample

Participants were 147 parents of African-American children residing within the boundaries of a unified school district in a resort community in Southern California. Parents were recruited through phone contacts. Volunteers in a local, community-based organization contacted every household that school records identified as enrolling at least one African-American child in public school in grades K–12 (N=552) and invited them to participate. Only one parent per household served as a respondent.

The majority of respondents were female (88 percent) and the biological mother (83 percent) of the target child or children in the household. Two-thirds of the sample had resided in the local community for more than ten years. To preserve confidentiality, respondents were not required to specify the gender of the children. However, 29 percent of respondents voluntarily identified a child in the household as female, and 35 percent identified a child as male.

Procedures

Those who initially agreed to participate were interviewed by one of five trained, African-American female graduate students. Interviews occurred over a two-month period during the winter of 1993; they were conducted by phone, each lasting from thirty-five to sixty minutes. The semistructured interview protocol consisted of twenty-four questions. Three questions elicited demographic information and the balance assessed perceptions of respondent's roles in their children's education (e.g., In what ways do you think parents should help with the schooling of their children?).

DATA ANALYSIS

A content analysis of interview protocols was initially conducted by each of the experimenters for her own respondents. Analyses were subsequently integrated into a set of core categories representing the full data set in a series of research team meetings. Using Strauss's (1987) guidelines, the analysis employed a concept-indicator model, which derives conceptual categories directly from the data. Attributes are first deduced around which specific responses are seen to cluster (e.g., conditions, consequences); next the clusters are analyzed to assess the relationships among them. Those which coalesce into an emergent concept are assigned a conceptual code. The data, or indicators, are then compared to the emergent category to fully saturate, or define the properties of the conceptual category. Thus each protocol was read and coded by at least two researchers. Disagreements were resolved by the input of a third researcher.

RESULTS

Interview protocol items were classified according to three broad themes: parents' beliefs about home-school relationships, parents' perceptions of their children's school experiences, and parents' satisfaction with the schools' performance in educating their child.

Home-School Relationships

The majority (62 percent) of respondents stated that ideally, parents should take the initiative to communicate with the school, and 59 percent stated that parents should become involved at the school site ("take a prominent role," "help teachers in the class; they are overworked"). Of those endorsing an active partnership, 45 percent felt parents must serve as advocates for their children's interests. Another 20 percent identified themselves as role models for all children, a necessary means to enhance ethnic understanding ("These kids have all white teachers"). A majority of parents (66 percent) also urged schools to be more proactive in their efforts to communicate with parents. There was repeated mention of the need for two-way communication ("teachers need to listen, not just tell parents what to do").

Over half of the respondents (61 percent) reported attending at least the primary school ritual, open house, in the past year. Only 12 percent reported spending time in the classroom setting (e.g., room volunteer, career day speaker), and the majority of these responses came from parents of elementary school students. When asked what specific activities parents wanted initiated at the school site, a plurality of respondents (30 percent) did not see the need for more school-based events. Parents who identified a need for more school events identified a wide variety of activities including multicultural events, PTA meetings, parent education, and student education activities.

It is of note that half of the respondents specified a number of activities that should take place within the home to facilitate their children's education. They felt that their children's education should be comprised of learning experiences beyond those provided by the school. Cultural events (museum visits), ethnic awareness activities (African-American history lessons), and career exploration projects (visiting a friend's workplace) were frequently mentioned home-based efforts that parents felt to be their responsibility.

The data suggest that respondents do not endorse a protective model of home-school relations. Rather, specific responses support school-focused, multicultural, and partnership models, with no one of these models seemingly able to adequately characterize the data. In evaluating the data as a function of grade level, parents of elementary school children most often responded consistent with a school-focused model. They were more likely to show an interest in parent education activities at the school, to serve as parent volunteers in the classroom, and attend open house at the school. However, consistent with a partnership model, all of the responses expressing an interest in participating in school governance ($n = 9$) came from parents of elementary school students.

Perceptions of Adjustment

Children are perceived as performing well in school; over half of the responses concerning school performance were either "excellent" or "above average." The proportion of responses in the excellent category declined from elementary to high school, while responses in the below-average category increased with level of schooling. This pattern was duplicated for parental perceptions of their child(ren)'s satisfaction with school. Although a majority of respondents felt their child liked school, this proportion declined from elementary to secondary school. Parents of high school students were most likely to report that their children do not like school. However, parents of students at all three levels of education were equally likely to report that their children had many or some friends at school.

The definite decline in parents' perceptions of their children's school adjustment across the grade levels is not seen as a function of peer rejection. One possible explanation may rest with perceptions of teacher-student relationships. When asked if teachers generally had positive interactions with their children, 77 percent of elementary parents responded yes, while 67 percent of high school parents responded affirmatively. Further, 80 percent of elementary parents and only 48 percent of high school parents reported that teachers seemed to be interested in their children's educational progress.

Satisfaction with Schools' Efforts

Parental satisfaction overall appears mixed. Approximately one in four parents responded that they have no concerns (question #4) and no problems (question #18) regarding their children's schools. Among the concerns and problems that were identified, lack of academic help, lack of ethnic sensitivity and awareness, and poor home-school communication were cited repeatedly by respondents. Moreover, when specifically asked, fully 90 percent of the respondents could suggest changes in the schools that would be desirable. Suggested changes included greater diversity in the staff, curriculum, and student population, as well as improvements in site staff performance and responsiveness to both students and parents. Although 63 percent of respondents felt that their opinions were valued and respected by the schools, very few parents (18 percent) reported that the school solicited their opinions and input. The quality of academic instruction is considered satisfactory by a clear majority (60 percent) of respondents; however, this category of responses declined substantially from elementary to high school.

DISCUSSION

This group of parents espouses the importance of active participation, yet their self-reported levels of involvement at the school site do not mirror that belief. However, the majority of parents also supported providing educational enrichment activities in the home. Apparently, these parents are more likely to engage in activities outside of the traditional school-defined boundaries of parent involvement. Prior data from parents of ethnically diverse samples also report that parental involvement activities are more likely to occur outside of school (Stallworth & Williams, 1982). The data reported here suggest that respondents, while endorsing the ideal of school site involvement, are much more likely to actually engage in home-based activities than to participate at the school site.

The single exception to this trend is attendance at school open house. The need for improved home-school communication is one of two major themes to emerge from these data, and that venerable tradition may be a vital conduit of communication between home and school. The partnership model of parent involvement (Comer, 1990) relies on authentic, two-way communication to incorporate parents as full partners in the education of their children. All too often, communication from school is information (Epstein, 1986), a one-way set of directives telling parents where to be and when to arrive to participate in activities dictated by the schools. However, the parents surveyed here are clearly looking for communication as defined by a partnership model of involvement. Perhaps the face-to-face interaction available at open house is the least restricted channel of communication now in place.

The second major theme to emerge was the need for cultural awareness and sensitivity at the school site. The data suggest that parents desire changes in patterns of interaction and instruction in the schools to better accommodate the unique needs of African-American children. Such changes might be implemented by enhancing curriculum offerings and intensifying recruitment practices. These appear to be goals that can be addressed given sufficient commitment and will on the part of school district officials. The data suggest favorable opportunities for change are now present. These parents perceive their input to be valued in general by the schools, indicating that the door for authentic communication around these important issues may yet be open. What may now be needed is concerted community action to bring these issues to the forefront of the debate on education.

These respondents do not perceive themselves to be shut out by a protective model of parent involvement. Rather, school-focused and multicultural efforts predominate. These parents support a multicultural model of parent involvement; perhaps this is a reflection of their extremely small numbers in the total population. However, the germ of full partnership is present in such expressed desires as increased cultural awareness activities for staff and a more visible presence for minorities in the ranks of the district's educators. The next question is: What can be done to foster among all parties a belief in shared and overlapping responsibility for the education and optimal development of every child?

Note

This research was supported in part by the UCSB Center for Black Studies. Appreciation is extended to the parents who participated in this study. We would also like to thank LaTonya Evans, Toks Fashola, Gloria Howard, Sharon Woodley, Tonya Bunts, and Faleeta Charles for their assistance in data collection and analysis.

Address all correspondence to Cynthia A. Hudley, Graduate School of Education, 2220 Phelps Hall, University of California, Santa Barbara, CA 93106

REFERENCES

Anderson, J. (1988). *The education of Blacks in the South, 1860–1935.* Chapel Hill: University of North Carolina Press.

Becker, H. J. & Epstein, J. L. (1982). Parent involvement: A survey of teacher practices. *The Elementary School Journal, 83,* 85–102.

Berger, E. H. (1991). Parent involvement: Yesterday and today. *The Elementary School Journal, 91,* 209–19.

Boutte, G. (1992). Frustrations of an African-American parent: A personal and professional account. *Phi Delta Kappan, 74,* 786–788.

Boykin, A. W. (1986). The triple quandary and the schooling of Afro-American children. In U. Neisser (Ed.) *The school achievement of minority children* (pp. 57–92). Hillsdale, N.J.: Lawrence Erlbaum.

Brice-Heath, S. (1989). Oral and literate traditions among Black Americans living in poverty. *American Psychologists, 44,* 367–73.

Clark, R. (1983). *Family life and school achievement: Why poor Black children succeed or fail.* Chicago: University of Chicago Press.

Comer, J. (1990). *School power.* New York: Free Press.

Comer, J. P. & Haynes, N. M. (1991). Parent involvement in schools: An ecological approach. *The Elementary School Journal, 91,* 271–77.

Dauber, S. L. & Epstein, J. L. (1989). Parents' attitudes and practices of involvement in inner-city elementary and middle schools. *Paper presented at the annual meetings of the American Educational Research Association,* San Francisco.

Davies, D. (1992). Foreword. In L. Liontos, *At-risk families and schools: Becoming partners.* Eugene, Oreg.: ERIC Clearinghouse on Educational Management.

Epstein, J. (1984). Effects on parents of teacher practices in parent involvement. Baltimore: Johns Hopkins University, Center for Social Organization of Schools.

———. (1986). Parents reactions to teacher practices of parent involvement. *Elementary Researcher, 14,* 3–10.

Epstein, J. (1986). Parents' reactions to teacher practices of parent involvement. *Elementary School Journal, 86,* 277–94.

———. (1990). School and family connections: Theory, research, and implications for integrating sociologies of education and family. In D. Unger and M. Sussman (Eds.), *Families in community settings: Interdisciplinary perspectives* (pp. 99–126). New York: Haworth Press.

Epstein, J. L. & Becker, H. J. (1982). Teachers' reported practices of parent involvement: Problems and possibilities. *The Elementary School Journal, 91,* 279–88.

Epstein, J. L. & Dauber, S. L. (1991). School programs and teacher practices of parent involvement in inner-city elementary and middle schools. *The Elementary School Journal, 91,* 289–305.

Fine, M. (1993). [Ap]parent involvement: Reflections on parents, power, and urban public schools. *Teachers College Record, 94,* 682–710.

Gordon, I. R. (1977). Parent education and parent involvement: Retrospect and prospect. *Childhood Education, 54,* 71–79.

Greenwood, G. E. & Hickman, C. W. (1991). Research and practices in parent involvement: Implications for teacher education. *The Elementary School Journal, 83,* 103–13.

Hale-Benson, J. E. (1986). *Black children: Their roots, culture, and learning styles* (2nd ed.). Baltimore: Johns Hopkins University Press.

Henderson, A. T., Marbuger, C. L., & Ooms, T. (1986). *Beyond the bake sale: An educator's guide to working with parents.* Columbia, Md.: National Committee for Citizens in Education.

Herman, J. L. & Yeh, J. P. (1983). Some effects of parent involvement in school. *The Urban Review, 15,* 11–17.

Hester, H. (1989). Start at home to improve home-school relations. *NASSP Bulletin, 73,* 23–27.

Irvine, J. J. (1990). *Black students and school failure. Policies, practices, and prescriptions.* New York: Greenwood.

———. (1992). *Black Students and school failure.* New York: Praeger.

Leler, H. (1983). Parent education and involvement in relation to the schools and to parents of school-aged children. In R. Haskins & D. Adams (Eds.), *Parents education and public policy* (pp. 144–180). Norwood, N.J.: Ablex.

Lightfoot, S. L. (1981). Toward conflicts and resolutions: Relationship between families and schools. *Theory into Practice, 20,* 97–104.

Lindel, J. C. (1989). What do parents want from principals and teachers? *Educational Leadership, 47,* 12–14.

Liontos, L. (1992). *At-risk families and schools: Becoming partners.* Eugene, Oreg.: ERIC Clearinghouse on Educational Management.

Ogbu, J. (1990). Overcoming racial barriers to equal access. In J. Goodlad (Ed.), *Access to knowledge* (pp. 59–90). New York: College Entrance Examination Board.

Powell, D. & Peete, S. (1992). *Making it in today's world: Options for strengthening parents' contributions to children's learning.* West Lafayette, Ind.: Purdue University Department of Child Development and Family Studies.

Power, T. (1985). Perceptions of competence: How parents and teachers view each other. *Psychology in the Schools, 22,* 68–78.

Rich, D. (1988). Bridging the gap in education reform. *Educational Horizons, 66,* 90–92.

Stallworth, J. & Williams, D. (1982). *A Survey of Parents regarding Parent Involvement in Schools.* (Report No. PS013342). Austin, Tex.: Southwest Educational Development Laboratory (ERIC Document Reproduction Service No. ED 225 682).

Strauss, A. (1987). *Qualitative Analysis for Solid Scientists.* Cambridge: Cambridge University Press.

BIB:Steven, D. L. & Baker, D. P. (1987). The family-school relation and the child's school performance. *Child Development, 58,* 1348–1357.

Swap, S. (1993). *Developing home-school partnerships.* New York: Teachers College Press.

Taylor, A. R. (1991). Social competence and the early school transition: Risk and protective factors for African-American children. *Education and Urban Society, 24,* 1, 15–26.

William, D. L. & Chavkin, N. F. (1989). Essential elements of strong parent involvement programs. *Educational Leadership, 47,* 18–20.

26

DESEGREGATION EXPERIENCES OF MINORITY STUDENTS
Adolescent Coping Strategies in Five Connecticut High Schools

Randi L. Miller

Few studies have explored the adolescent subculture of minority students in desegregated schools. While it is well known that desegregated schools are not integrated environments, the question whether some schools foster more positive desegregation experiences than others remains largely unanswered. This study of minority students participating in a voluntary busing program, Project Concern, examines whether bused minority adolescents are assimilated into their white high schools. Data were collected using nonparticipant observation at five schools and through structured interviews with 69 Project Concern students. The findings first identify a number of coping strategies used by minority students and then show that desegregation has different effects for students at each school. Students bused to some communities reported more positive desegregation experiences than did students bused to others. This finding contradicts one prevailing assumption of desegregation, that busing to White schools necessarily fosters positive race relations.

Few studies have actually explored the adolescent subculture of minority students. In fact, most youth subculture research has given little attention to Black adolescents in general and to Black high school students in particular. Generally desegregation studies have also failed to investigate the nature of minority high school youth culture and whether Black children are integrated into the larger social world of desegregated schools. This study explores these questions by describing the youth culture of Black adolescents attending desegregated high schools and identifying the ways in which these students cope with their desegregation experience. The present article begins with a review of the existing literature, first on minority group students and adolescent society and then on the effects of busing on race relations. It then introduces data from a study of five Connecticut high schools participating in a voluntary desegregation program. The findings describe a variety of strategies used by minority students as they come to terms with the dominant youth culture of their predominantly White high schools. Finally, this study addresses itself to variation among schools in terms of student coping styles, and speculates on the effects that local school culture can have on the desegregation experiences of minority students.

MINORITY GROUP STUDENTS AND ADOLESCENT SOCIETY

Little of the research on high school adolescent subcultures, or what Coleman (1961) termed "adolescent society," has dealt extensively with minority students. In their concern with youth socialization and the emergence of adolescent subcultures, investigators have generally relied on a traditional set of independent variables, including family organization, social class, religion, parental education, and community structure. Race, as an independent variable, although not completely neglected, has not been used systematically. Gottlieb and TenHouten (1965) concluded that "in studies of youths within the formal setting of the high school, Negroes tend to be either 'lumped' together with other students or excluded from the analysis with the explanation that their presence would distort the findings" (p. 203). Twenty years after this observation, the literature on youth subcultures still retains much of this methodological segregation.

Perhaps the most successful recent attempt to explore the effect of race on the development of adolescent subcultures has been the qualitative work of Rist and colleagues (1979). The articles in Rist's volume offered considerable insight into the normative aspects of race relations and student networks and activities. The collection showed that while desegregation has resulted in the de facto mix of particular student bodies, integration was not ipso facto achieved. Moreover, it appeared that the issue of quality of interracial interaction had a large impact on the success of the desegregation process in general, and more specifically on intergroup contact between adolescents.

Nonetheless, it becomes clear from a review of the literature that insufficient attention has been paid to factors affecting the assimilation of minority students. This is in part the case because most scholars writing on adolescent society have assumed that a similar socialization/enculturation process occurs for all students, regardless of race. Most studies have inferred that the goal of schooling, in general, is to assimilate culturally divergent populations that have been segregated from dominant society (Iadicola & Moore, 1979). Yet there is clearly a need to explore the *quality* of the contacts between Black and White students in racially mixed schools. As the reader will next see, the desegregation literature has, to some degree, attempted to address this very issue.

EFFECTS OF BUSING ON RACE RELATIONS

Proponents of busing have argued that segregation both encourages stereotyping and prejudice and discourages interethnic friendships. But whether desegregation, by increasing interethnic contact, leads to deeper, more involved interactions, or to what is commonly referred to as "true integration," remains unresolved. Recent reviews of the research on the effects of desegregation on the ability of students of differing races to interact effectively yield a plethora of often contradictory conclusions (e.g., Braddock, Crain, & McPartland, 1984; Mercer, Iadicola, & Moore, 1979; St. John, 1975).

Does school desegregation actually improve race relations? Over 30 years ago Allport (1954) acknowledged that intergroup contact in and of itself was not an instant panacea for interracial hostilities. Instead, he cautioned that direct contact in the schools was merely a prerequisite for both acquaintance and contact. Nonetheless, opinion still holds that interaction between people is enough to alter positively their feelings toward one another, which at least in part explains why most desegregation studies have continued to speculate on which factors produce successful integration. For instance, Cook (1969) argued that acquaintance potential, which he defined as "the extent to which the situation provides opportunities for getting to know the other race as individuals" (p. 211), had an important impact on the outcome of contact between groups. Several factors influenced the acquaintance potential of a given situation, including physical proximity, sustained and varied contact with others, and opportunity for interaction. As further argued by Patchen (1982): "Greater proximity to schoolmates of another race may lead to frequent stimuli for friendly behavior, to acquiring positive information about the other group, to pleasant experiences which increase liking, to being rewarded for friendly behavior" (pp. 138–39). Thus desegregated classrooms have had an important impact on integration by cultivating a student's willingness to develop positive attitudes toward interaction with others from different backgrounds (Amir & Sharon, 1984).

Simply putting Black and white children in the same classrooms does not, however, ensure positive social learning. Evidence has shown that superficial intergroup contact does not necessarily produce changes in intergroup relations. For instance, Silverman and Shaw (1973) reported that the number of interracial interactions of high school students did not change over three observation periods during the first term of school desegregation and that the absolute percentage of such interracial contacts was low. Schofield and Sagar (1979) found that in desegregated schools there was more same-race seating than could be expected by chance alone. Clement, Eisenhart, and Harding (1979) reported that with few exceptions students, when free to do so, sat with others of the same racial group, and that when participation in special activities was voluntary, the activities were each dominated by one racial group. Other studies have also indicated that most extracurricular activities follow racial and ethnic boundaries (see Rist, 1979; Shaw, 1973). Some have argued that intimate contact, rather than merely increased contact, is the most potent agent for attitude change. For instance, Ashmore (1970) contended that casual intergroup contact generally had little or no effect on basic attitudes but, on the other hand, intimate friendships could bring about the reduction of prejudice. However, other studies have suggested that little interracial intimacy occurs among Black and white students (Dickinson, 1975; Petroni, 1971).

The social results of desegregation, and the quality of racial contact among high school students, have been largely ignored by researchers, with the exception of case studies. While descriptive case studies have enhanced our understanding of the factors affecting social integration in desegregated schools, these studies are generally of only one site, thus prohibiting systematic comparisons among schools. It is, for instance, quite possible that even students in different schools under the same desegregation plan may develop very different interracial attitudes and behaviors based largely on school effects (Cohen, 1975).

Since data for this study were collected from more than one site, it was possible to compare how minority high school students at different schools viewed their desegregation experience. In addition, alternative strategies used by minority students to cope in a variety of white schools were explored. To reiterate, this article will identify and describe the ways in which minority students cope with their desegregation experience and will determine whether their coping strategies vary from school to school. While the literature remains rather silent on these issues, this article speculates that minority students at desegregated schools will develop several different strategies to cope with their desegregation experience and that the style they choose will depend, in part, on the particular school they attend.

METHOD
Data Collection
The data on which this study was based were collected in five high schools in Connecticut participating in a voluntary metropolitan desegregation plan, Project Concern, that buses minority students from Hartford to thirteen suburban school districts. When this study was conducted, approximately 800 students were enrolled in the program in grades K–12. Because program size may have an effect on the extent of integration, five schools with different numbers of Project Concern students in attendance were chosen for this study. An attempt was also made to choose suburban communities representing a variety of income brackets.[1]

Data for this study were collected using several procedures. Fieldwork, employing non-participant observation techniques, was conducted at all five suburban high schools. In addition, 69 Project Concern students were interviewed using structured interview schedules. Originally every Project Concern student at each of the five schools was to be interviewed. This "saturation" method seemed feasible because the total number of Project Concern students in each school was small. Saturation of the sample was reached in all schools but one; the response rate for these four schools was 91 percent. The students not interviewed at these schools were absent when the interviews were conducted and their exclusion from the final sample can be interpreted as one would any other nonresponse bias. Sampling problems at one school meant that only eighteen out of 52 students were interviewed, chosen through a snowball sampling technique. Including all five schools, the response rate was 64 percent. While the sample is not random, it is likely representative of all Project Concern students at these five schools and of most students in the program.

The final sample consisted of 69 students in five schools. A total of 45 out of 69, or 65 percent, were female. Second, most respondents were Black (97 percent), although some (3 percent) were of Puerto Rican ancestry. Most students in the study were either sophomores (22 percent), juniors (26 percent), or seniors (35 percent). The smaller number of freshmen (17 percent) is because ninth graders at two of the schools did not attend the high school but went to the junior high and were therefore not interviewed for this study.

Analysis
Using both Guttman scaling and factor analysis, four meaningful themes were identified that described a variety of strategies employed by Project Concern students to cope with attending largely White high schools. The four factors, *Being a "Model" Student, Interracial Attraction, School Involvement,* and *Integration Conviction* will be described in detail and include qualitative assessments of those students with either high or low scores on particular factors.

Measuring Assimilation: Four Coping Strategies
The respondents were asked several questions related to their social lives; friends; integration into the school environment; extracurricular activities; dating, feelings about school life, and Project Concern; and future plans. A multistage scaling procedure then reduced the questionnaire answers to a manageable set of variables. First, 33 questionnaire items were Guttman-scaled into 9 scales. In addition, 9 variables that did not scale were retained. Then scale scores were produced for the 9 Guttman scales, using a weighting procedure whereby respondents who passed a particular item were given a score on that item that

equaled the complement of the frequency of those respondents passing each item, multiplied by 10 (see Abrahamson, 1969). Then the Guttman scales and additional dependent variables were correlated to determine the relationships of the dependent variables with each other. The resulting 18 × 18 correlation matrix revealed that those variables with consistently low correlations should be dropped from further analysis. Three single-item variables were eliminated at this point.

In an attempt at clarifying the remaining fifteen categories, the findings are described in terms of themes or patterns. In order to uncover these themes, a principal-component method of factor analysis was performed on the nine scales plus six other individual questionnaire items, producing four factors with eigenvalues of more than one. These four factors together explained 57 percent of the total variance, thus describing slightly more than one-half of the total variation of assimilation themes or coping strategies. For each Guttman scale or individual item, the factor loading is given, and for every item, the percentage *yes* on that item is shown. In order to interpret more precisely the rotated factor structure, categories with loadings of less than .30 were omitted. Four factor scores (one for each factor) were then computed for each individual. What follows is a descriptive interpretation and discussion of the four factors.

RESULTS

Factor I: Being a "Model" Student

One route to high involvement was simply to be a good student. The students who were high scorers on this particular factor made good grades, planned to go to college, had not been suspended, and were active in school activities. On the positive side, these categories represent the epitome of assimilation. On the negative side, Project Concern students who were best assimilated into the school environment reported negative reactions from their Hartford and fellow Project Concern friends, who resented the fact that model students went places after school with White students. Students who adopted other strategies that integrated them into the school did not feel this same pressure to avoid whites. For this group of model students, associating with Whites was perceived by other Blacks as part of academic "rate-busting"; they earned the hostility of their Black friends by being too good—cooperating too well with the White school, embarrassing their brothers and sisters with their good grades. To highlight this orientation, let me quote from a model student:

> I don't consider myself to be a minority because my [white] friends, they don't consider or even look at it as me being a different color, just being regular, being just like them. They [Project Concern students] prefer to be Black, they want to just hang around with the Blacks, they don't want nothing to do with the Whites. . . . I'm not like that. . . . I attended the ski club and I asked if anyone else wanted to get into it, and you should have seen their faces, it was hysterical. What is this kid talking about, the ski club? It's a bunch of "honkies" gonna be there.

In contrast to this approach, students alienated from school received a low factor score on this dimension. One such student told of the things he did not like about school:

> We be watched all the time. They trying to bust us for some kind of thing. Like one time somebody stole $100 and I was called down and my friend was called down. And when I asked the assistant principal why he do that he said 'cause you're suspicious.

Factor II: Interracial Attraction

The second factor identified a group of students whose path to involvement in school was interracial socializing. This factor is a composite of types of social activity that all bear on the degree to which the respondents were considered "popular" and had opportunities to interact with the opposite sex.

The Project Concern student who received the highest factor score on this dimension was a Black male who was dating a white girl from school. In addition, he reported that he was part of the leading crowd at school, participated in both varsity and nonvarsity sports, and attended numerous school events. He typified those best integrated into the social life of the high school culture. When this student was asked whether the social life of Project Concern students differed from students living in the community, he replied:

> No, not really. Well, some of the time you wouldn't really see the girl you're dating as often as you would like, not unless you came out here every day. . . . But you can do the same things that any other students do that live out here.

A more typical student was one with a low factor score on this dimension, characterized by the case of a Black female who never dated or went steady with whites, typically spent her Saturday nights with friends from her neighborhood, and attended few school events. By her own account, she did not have a group of friends with whom she "hangs out" after school, and she reported that she was not part of the leading crowd in school. When asked whether white and Black students did similar things on dates, she replied, "I don't know." Clearly her high negative factor score reflected both limited knowledge and experience regarding social activities at school.

Factor III: School Involvement

The third factor measured what is often called "school spirit." Without dating, students high on this scale nevertheless participated in a wide range of school activities, but, interestingly, this group of students, who were so highly involved in the school, were also ones who were most likely to complain that school rules were unfair. Perhaps because they were so involved, these students knew from personal experience about school regulations. It may have been also that well-integrated students felt less threatened when expressing negative opinions about school. Since they themselves were integrated, they could complain without raising the cognitively dissonant feelings they might have felt if they were displeased with their social experiences (If this school is so bad, what am I doing here?).

Students with high scores on this factor said that problems with school rules existed due to a lack of equitable enforcement; the reason Project Concern students experienced difficulty at school was that the *school* (including administrators, teachers, and white students) was prejudiced. Blacks were picked on, the rules were made for and applied only to the white students, and Black students often had difficulty conforming to those rules. The following quote from a student with a high score on this factor was enlightening:

> Some of them's prejudiced—some students and some teachers. . . . Like I had this teacher last year, she was prejudiced. If I talked I'd get in trouble, if a white student talked she'd just tell them to lower their voice.

Students with low factor scores on this dimension can be described as apathetic. One such student reported that he did not care at all if the school won in any type of competition, he had few friends at school, and he did not go to school social events. He did not consider himself part of the leading crowd, nor did he want to be. None of his best friends at school were White. As can be expected, he did not feel as if he belonged at school. In response to a question asking what the good things were about Project Concern, he replied, "There ain't none." When asked why he came to school in the suburbs, he replied, "My mother, she thinks I can get a better education here." Yet this student thought the rules at school were fair.

Factor IV: Integration Conviction

Finally, the fourth factor showed that it was possible for students to hold positive feelings about school without being involved directly in its social life. These were students who had an ideological and impersonal commitment to desegregation. Rather than speaking of how they themselves benefited from desegregation, they talked in terms of how minorities in general benefited. Those with high scores on this factor thought Blacks were an integral part of the school environment, but were less likely *themselves* to participate in many school activities. Perhaps because these students were in actuality less involved, they could afford to be more positive in their attitudes, which were based on an ideological rather than a de facto commitment to desegregation.

One student with a high score on Factor IV reflected this discontinuity between attitude and behavior as evidenced by her response to a question concerning the good things about Project Concern:

> It's good that we get to come to school here. That we get bused out to different schools other than inner Hartford. . . . They have more opportunities out here than they do in Hartford. I know I won't get along if I went to school with my own color. . . . I think when I'm around my own color it's more problems. Because there's a lot of fighting. We don't have that here. *When I'm by myself I can do my work, but not when I'm with my friends. And out here you don't get to see your friends.*

Clearly, she saw busing as offering her the opportunity to get a better education in an environment that was conducive to learning. Yet the last three lines of her statement illustrate her lack of actual involvement in school social life.

Conversely, students with a negative score on this factor claimed that there were serious problems between Black and white students, and they graded their schools low, thought the school rules were not fair, and did not like their principals. Yet they participated in several extracurricular activities and had personal contact with White students. The remarks made by one such student typified those with high negative factor scores on this dimension:

> I think this school is prejudiced. I didn't want to come out here. . . . It seems that some things are unfair. Like for example, two girls were being late for class. They're Black, and it was a hallway full of other kids, and the principal didn't say anything to anyone else. He singled them out, which I don't think is fair. . . . It's like the principal picks on us. . . . And this school does not do things that Black people can get into. Like at our prom, we wanted to have a D.J. that could play White music and Black music. But no, they [white students] didn't want that. They wanted a band, which we can't comprehend.

Yet this same student mentioned several positive aspects of Project Concern:

> I think it's good because it gives us an opportunity to get into a different environment. I think that by going out here it better prepares us for the outside world.

Differences among Schools

This assessment of the 69 Project Concern students in the study provided the dependent variables used to determine whether certain desegregation experiences were more common in particular schools. In comparing the average factor scores of the five schools using a one-way analysis of variance, certain factors discriminated between schools better than did others. In fact, Being a "Model" Student appeared to be little affected by school differences ($F = 1.05$, $p = $ ns, $Eta^2 = .06$). This may be so because all schools have some students who seem to excel, both scholastically and socially, regardless of the advantages and/or disadvantages associated with particular schools. Being a "Model" Student likely is affected more by a different set of criteria, specifically, familial influences such as SES, aspirations, transmission of values, and the like (see for example, Blau, 1977). In terms of the other three factors, the result showed that students at H.S. 3 were most likely to engage in interracial social activities and dating whereas those at H.S. 1 were least likely to do so. Differences among the five schools explained 12 percent of the variation in Project Concern students' Interracial Attraction scores ($F = 2.17$, $p < .10$, $Eta^2 = .12$). Students at H.S. 3 were also more involved in school activities than were their peers at the other four schools. Students at H.S. 2 were least involved. Differences among the schools accounted for 28 percent of the variation in School Involvement scores ($F = 6.09$, $p < .001$, $Eta^2 = .28$). Last, students at H.S. 5 had the strongest Integration Conviction whereas students at H.S. 4 were the least ideological in this regard. Differences among the five schools explained 38 percent of the variation in Project Concern students' ideological commitment ($F = 9.83$, $p < .0001$, $Eta^2 = .38$).

DISCUSSION

Minority students used four distinct strategies to cope with racial antagonisms in school. The strategies should not be viewed as composites of individual personality traits. Instead, they are derived, in large part, from situational factors at school and should be viewed as four alternative ways for minorities to cope in white suburban school settings. In general, students specialized in one or another of these coping strategies. If they excelled at Being a Model Student, then they were likely to abstain from Interracial Attraction. If they were preoccupied with School Involvement, then they did not bother with Integration Conviction. The analysis of variance showed significant differences among schools in three of these coping strategies. Therefore, differences among schools did affect the way in which Project Concern students coped with their desegregation experience. Specifically, students at H.S. 3 scored highest on both factors related to integration into the school community, Interracial Attraction and School Involvement. This finding was not surprising, given descriptive data reported elsewhere by Miller (1986) that showed a fairly high degree of assimilation of Project Concern students at H.S. 3. Further, it would be expected that students at schools with high scores on Interracial Attraction and School Involvement would score low on Factor IV: Integration Conviction. Students with high scores on Factor IV were not personally integrated into the social environment of their schools; their commitment to integration was ideological. Students at H.S. 5, who scored on the low end on

Factors II and III, scored highest on Factor IV. At H.S. 5 there was support for the Project Concern program among students and staff, and respondents had generally positive perceptions of race relations, yet most of the Project Concern students reported only marginal involvement in school activities. Unfortunately, it could not be determined from the analysis of variance what characteristics of the schools accounted for these reported differences. While schools had different effects on coping strategies, this finding leaves undetermined what it is about schools that caused the observed differences. While we can speculate that schools, school districts, community characteristics, and other situation-specific variables may all affect the desegregation experiences of minority students, the data presented here are insufficient to explain such differences.

CONCLUSION

Little attention has been devoted to the experiences of minority high school students in largely white schools. This study showed that, in fact, minority students have deep feelings about their position and travails as students in an alien white school environment. The emergent picture is one where, in addition to dealing with general concerns associated with adolescent development, Project Concern students must also struggle with the problem of race. Even if opportunities for contact were created within the school, a recommendation of most desegregation advocates, this research suggests that such an approach, at best, would yield mixed results. Such is likely the case because student experiences in school are not only products of social and structural forces within the school but also reflect status and power relationships in the larger society. Most school structures do not present many opportunities for interracial interaction within school. Outside of school, students live in segregated, status-unequal communities where there is little or no opportunity for interracial contact.

Most desegregation policies generally assume that by mixing students of different races, a "melting-pot" effect will ensue, encouraging interethnic acquaintances initially and genuine friendships ultimately. The goal of offering minority students equal educational opportunities is in part based on the belief that bused minority students can and will assimilate White middle-class values, but the process did not seem to occur uniformly for the Project Concern students studied. In fact, this research found that offering minorities access to the same educational opportunities as majority students did not ensure high levels of interracial contact or guarantee the quality of race relations. There were nevertheless some differences in this respect among particular schools. Some schools appeared to be far better equipped or willing to foster positive race relations between minority and majority groups. Clearly, differences among schools, their principals, teachers, and perhaps community culture had some effect on both encouraging and reinforcing intergroup contacts.

As this research showed, students at some of the schools participating in Project Concern were more integrated than were others and schools do make a difference in the degree to which minority students successfully integrate. While this study identified what Blalock (1986) has called the "micro-level process" of social integration, in the final analysis desegregation research must equally focus on the impact of "macro-level" variables within the school and the community. Such an approach has been termed "situational analysis" by its proponents (see Prager, Longshore, & Seeman, 1986), because it suggests that desegregation research must give more emphasis to the specific schooling situation. Following this approach, the next step, then, is to identify key situation-specific factors that may aid in providing positive desegregation experiences for minority students. By identifying some of these context variables, we will enhance our understanding of how students, teachers, administrators, school boards, public officials, and parents can foster more positive desegregation experiences. In so doing, we can hope to improve the position of minorities in the school setting initially, and ultimately in the larger society.

NOTE

1. Anonymous in the study, the schools are H.S. 1 (13 Project Concern students enrolled in high school, representing. 7 percent of the student body, 1979 per capita community income $8,500, per pupil school district expenditure $2,460); H.S. 2 (8 Project Concern students[.7 percent], per capital income $9,500, per pupil expenditure $3,000); H.S. 3 (17 Project Concern students [1.7 percent], per capita income $7,800, per pupil expenditure $2,340); H.S. 4 (52 Project Concern students [6 percent], per capita income $11,200, per pupil expenditure $3,230); H.S. 5 (31 Project Concern students [4.1 percent], per capital income $9,200, per pupil expenditure $2,560). The high school data were obtained from school administrators whereas the community data were obtained from the Board of Education, State of Connecticut. Further information on the five districts represented in the sample is available from the author.

REFERENCES

Abrahamson, M. (1969). The correlates of political complexity. *American Sociological Review, 5,* 690–701.

Allport, G. W. (1954). *The nature of prejudice.* Reading, Mass.: Addison-Wesley.

Amir, Y., & Sharon, S. (1984). *School desegregation.* Hillsdale, N.J.: Lawrence Erlbaum.

Ashmore, R. D. (1970). Solving the problem of prejudice. In B. E. Collins (Ed.), *Social psychology: Social influence, attitude change, group processes and prejudice* (pp. 298–339). Reading, Mass.: Addison-Wesley.

Blalock, H. M. (1986). A model for racial contact in schools. In J. Prager, D. Longshore, & M. Seeman (Eds.), *Desegregation research. New directions in situational analysis* (pp. 111–41). New York: Plenum.

Blau, P. (1977). *Inequality and heterogeneity: A primitive theory of social structure.* New York: Free Press.

Braddock, J. H., Crain, R. L., & McPartland, J. M. (1984). A long-term view of school desegregation: Some recent studies of graduates as adults. *Phi Delta Kappan, 66,* 259–64.

Clement, D. C., Eisenhart, M., & Harding, J. R. (1979). The veneer of harmony: Social-race relations in a southern desegregated school. In R. Rist (Ed.), *Desegregated schools. Appraisals of an American experiment* (pp. 15–64). New York: Academic Press.

Cohen, E. (1975). The effect of desegregation on race relations. *Law and Contemporary Problems, 39,* 271–99.

Coleman, J. (1961). *The adolescent society.* Glencoe, Ill.: Free Press.

Cook, S. W. (1969). Motives in a conceptual analysis of attitude-related behavior. In W. Arnold & D. Levine (Eds.), *Nebraska Symposium on Motivation* (pp. 179–285). Lincoln: University of Nebraska.

Dickinson, G. E. (1975). Dating behavior of Black and White adolescents before and after desegregation. *Journal of Marriage and the Family, 37,* 602–8.

Gottlieb, D., & TenHouten, W. D. (1965). Racial composition and the social systems of three high schools. *Journal of Marriage and the Family, 27,* 204–17.

Iadicola, P., & Moore, H. (1979). *The desegregated school and status relations among Anglo and minority students: The dilemma of school desegregation.* Public Health Service Research Grant No. MH 26607–03. Washington, D.C.: National Institute of Mental Health.

Mercer, J. R., Iadicola, P., & Moore, H. (1979). Building effective multi-ethnic schools: Evolving models and paradigms. In W. G. Stephan & J. R. Faegen (Eds.), *School desegregation, past, present, and future* (pp. 281–307). New York: Plenum.

Miller, R. L. (1986). The impact of voluntary busing on the desegregation experiences of minority students in five Connecticut suburban communities. Unpublished doctoral dissertation, University of Connecticut, Storrs.

Patchen, M. (1982). *Black-White contact in schools: Its social and academic effects.* West Lafayette, Ind.: Purdue University.

Petroni, F. A. (1971). Interracial dating: The price is high. *Transaction*, September, 54–59.

Prager, J., Longshore, D., & Seeman, M. (Eds.). (1986). *Desegregation research. New directions in situational analysis.* New York: Plenum.

Rist, R. C. (Ed.). (1979). *Desegregated schools. Appraisals of an American experiment.* New York: Academic Press.

Schofield, J. W., & Sagar, H. A. (1979). The social context of learning in an interracial school. In R. Rist (Ed.), *Desegregated schools. Appraisals of an American experiment* (pp. 155–200). New York: Academic Press.

Shaw, M. E. (1973). Changes in sociometric choices following forced integration of an elementary school. *Journal of Social Issues, 2,* 143–57.

Silverman, I., & Shaw, M. E. (1973). Effects of sudden mass school desegregation on interracial interaction and attitudes in one southern city. *Journal of Social Issues, 29,* 133–42.

St. John, N. H. (1975). *School desegregation: Outcomes for children.* New York: Wiley.

The research reported in this article was conducted while the author was a graduate student at the University of Connecticut. The research was supported by the University of Connecticut Graduate School and Research Foundation, and the RAND Corporation, Santa Monica, California. The author would like to thank Mark Abrahamson, Robert L. Crain, David Decker, Michael Gordon, J. Zvi Namenwirth, Cedric J. Robinson, Ronald L. Taylor, and Robin Thompson for their advice on this project.

27

RACIAL SOCIALIZATION STRATEGIES OF PARENTS IN THREE BLACK PRIVATE SCHOOLS

Deborah J. Johnson

THE INTERDEPENDENT ROLES OF PARENTS and schools are crucial to the issue of social mobility and the future of Black children. The way in which these roles influence each other are important to the development of the child's self-perception and the ultimate shaping of a viable coping style. Many researchers view Black parents as effective socializers of their children, particularly in their ability to successfully prepare the children to cope with the exigencies of our society while maintaining a positive sense of self.[1]

Achieving the delicate balance between creating an awareness of racial discrimination and prejudice, which are stressful, and encouraging racial coping strategies that protect the child's positive sense of self, is the challenge of Black parenthood.[2] The literature on children's group identity and personal self-esteem shows that many Black parents have been successful in achieving this goal.[3] Many Black children have a positive sense of self-worth and highly value the Black community to which they belong.[4] How is this achieved? One way is through the positive racial coping and socialization strategies of parents. This chapter describes the racial socialization strategies of parents whose children attend three different Black private schools.

BACKGROUND

Black families are particularly vulnerable to the ecological stress factor of race.[5] Within the ecology of the Black existence, all Black families develop strategies to cope with the exigencies of racism and discrimination.[6] Moreover, Black parents face the daily dilemma of simultaneously protecting their children's sense of self and preparing them to cope successfully with issues of race which they anticipate will occur in the child's future experiences.

Diana T. Slaughter and Barbara L. Schneider conducted a study that investigated Black parental educational goals, school type, and the experiences of Black children in four desegregated private school settings.[7] The authors concluded that the schools and Black families work together to affirm the overall private school community's sense of educational purpose, mission, and identity. The ensuing socialization context was educationally beneficial to Black children. However, the authors also found that many Black parents were concerned about the positive racial identity development of their children.

Since the most recent body of research suggests that self-esteem and group identity operate independently, parental emphasis on the one may result in no effect or a deleterious effect on the other.[8] A study by Margaret Beale Spencer demonstrated this point.[9] Spencer reported that preference patterns of children aged 3–9 years old were related to the cultural childrearing strategies of their parents. Specifically, the Eurocentric racial attitudes of Black children were negatively related to parents' teachings about civil rights, the child's knowledge of Black history, and discussions about racial discrimination. Spencer concluded that the "lack of direct teaching of specific cultural values resulted in the learning of Eurocentric racial attitudes/preferences."[10]

Harriette Pipes McAdoo studied stress and coping in middle-class Black families.[11] Like poor Black families, they suffer the effects and stresses of racism, discrimination, and economic isolation. Black families attain and maintain middle-class incomes through dual careers. Her findings indicate that middle-class Black families also utilize extended kin networks to abate the impact of ecological stress factors.

In an environmental ecology presupposing Black stress, the task of childrearing is a particular dilemma. Black parents are especially concerned with developing racial coping strategies (RCSs) in their children that will allow them to surmount blocked opportunity while simultaneously protecting their self-esteem. McAdoo explains that Black parents are acutely aware of the contradictions, particularly in the context of education, but push beyond them toward the ultimate goal of upward social mobility for their children.[12]

Positive affect to one's reference group has been shown to be related to effective racial coping and school success. Two studies of Black college students examined achievement and coping behavior.[13] These studies focused on the individual personality characteristics of high and low achievers. Specific coping strategies were conceptualized not in relation to race and culture, but in relation to whether, within a dominant cultural control ideology or a personal control ideology, a student operated from an internal or external control system.

Phillip J. Bowman and Cleopatra Howard extended the work of Patricia Gurin and Edgar Epps in a study of intergenerational race-related socialization.[14] Bowman and Howard found that intergenerational transmission of self-development orientations was related to adolescents' greater sense of personal efficacy, while emphasis on racial barrier awareness was associated with higher school grades. They concluded that the coping orientation transmitted by Black parents to their children is an important component of their motivation, achievement, and career aspirations.

Depending upon the school, parents can primarily either achieve insulation of the child's racial self, create coping opportunities (proactive, reactive), or work toward a balance between the two. From the point of view of Black parents, because education is so highly valued in the Black community and is the primary mechanism of social mobility, these racial coping strategies become intervening routes to upward social mobility.

Thus, by identifying which route a parent has chosen to protect the child's sense of self and understanding the parent's coping orientation, we may determine how the school environment complements or confounds parental racial socialization processes. The interaction of the parent with the school is a process that triangulates on the child. The child is at the apex of the triangle, with the school at one base angle and the parent(s)/home at the opposite base angle. The triangle itself is set within a circle of racial stress.

The research presented below is part of a larger study involving parents and children. However, in this chapter only parent data are reported. The strategies of Black parents who send their children to private schools were of particular interest because of the greater effort expended toward quality education for their children.

HYPOTHESES

These hypotheses follow from the question "What are the coping orientations of Black parents and how are different school settings reflected in their coping orientations?"

1. Parents whose proactive orientations require them to assert positives and/or minimize their child's contact with negative racial experiences will most often have children who attend an alternative school.

In one school there exists a strong Black ideology that emphasizes Black pride, political awareness, unity (communalism), and accountability to the larger Black community. Parents are encouraged to participate in the school and be a part of the school family and the school identity. The school is child-centered in its educational approach. It is especially concerned about who the child is as a person and how the school might enhance the child's racial identity development. Stresses that enter from the outside are discussed and interpreted within the context of a Black ideology.

2. Parents who have reactive coping orientations will primarily be found in traditional and parochial school settings.

It is assumed that these types of schools emphasize the basics of education. Such a school is focused on the child's acquisition of the basics and on eliminating those elements which might interfere with that acquisition. Parents emphasize the child's positive personal differences apart from the group.

METHOD

The design of this study uses qualitative and quantitative methods to explore these issues and identify their important elements. Given the socializing influence of the school and the objective of obtaining information on a wide range of possible RCSs, rather than have many schools participate, only three schools (representing particular types) were selected for participation in this study.

Subjects

At least one parent from each of forty-one families having a child aged 5–14 years old participated in the study. Parents had their children enrolled in one of three all-Black private schools. Two of the schools were located in Chicago and the third was in Washington, D.C. The schools were selected to be representative of small, stable, Black independent institutions for children. Among the institutions selected were a parochial school (fourteen families), a traditional school (seventeen families), and an alternative school (ten families). The alternative school in this study had a pan-African sociocultural orientation.

Within the three schools there was some variation in educational attainment and family income. Cross-tabulations of school with educational level resulted in significant differences in mother's education (X^2 (39) = 0.82, p = .00), but not in father's education (X^2 (32) = 0.38, p = .67). The annual family income in each school varied. At the alternative school, Watoto, 19 percent of parents reported incomes below $34,999, while 82 percent reported incomes above $35,000, and at the parochial school, St. Benedito, about 70 percent of parents reported an annual family income below $34,999 and 30 percent reported incomes above that figure.

School Selection

Five criteria were considered in the selection of schools for the study: diverse private school networks; 90–100 percent Black enrollment; fifty students or more; established for ten years or more; and location in metropolitan Chicago. All schools in the study met at least three of these criteria.

Racial Coping Interview—Parents

The interview schedule was adapted from the Slaughter and Schneider (1986) study of Blacks in private schools. The adult interview in their study was comprised of six sections (A thru F). Section F of their interview questioned parents about their expectations of problems of child racial coping as Black Americans and was used as the Racial Coping Interview in this study to identify parental RCSs. Racial coping strategies were coded from four questions in the parent interview:

1. What do you anticipate and how are you planning to protect your child (regarding the child's experiences as a Black American)?
2. How does your family go about ensuring that your child will have a positive Black identity?
3. What other day-to-day experiences in reference to being Black have you and your child talked about?
4. Describe any special features of your family's overall educational program for your child because (s)he is a Black American child.

Eighteen racial coping strategies (RCSs) were identified in an adult pilot study using the Slaughter and Schneider parent interview data.[15] Eleven new RCSs were identified in this study and eleven were either maintained or amplified from the pilot study.

Reliability

Reliability was calculated from the percent agreement between RCSs coded by two independent raters. If one rater coded strategies not coded by the second rater, those RCSs figured negatively into the percent agreement calculated. Both raters coded each of the forty-one cases. Using this conservative method, interrater reliability was established at .75 on this instrument.

PROCEDURES

Data Collection

The goals and procedures of the study were discussed with administrators, parents, students, and teachers in each school. Parents were generally interviewed in their homes.

Ten interviewers were trained in the following manner. Initially, they were given a tape of an adult interview, a packet of interview and test materials, and a manual of instruction. Two of the ten trainees were further required to observe an interview or were observed conducting an interview. The remaining eight interviewers were trained exclusively by taped interview (seven of these eight interviewers had prior interview experience through either clinical or research training).

Refusals

The rate of refusal at Watoto was about 33 percent and at St. Benedito about 50 percent. At Chaucer, of twenty contacts, only three parents refused. However, a complete parent list was not obtained from this school. The rate of refusals for parents in these schools brings into question the representativeness of this sample not only for Black families in general, but for the families in the particular schools studied. Caution is especially important in the context of the St. Benedito and Chaucer schools.

Decision Rules

The twenty-two RCSs were the basis for coding adult strategies from the parent Racial Coping Interview.[16] In the earlier pilot study of parental racial coping strategies, RCSs were categorized as proactive, reactive, or neutral prior to the data analysis.[17] Applying these categories to this study, examples of neutral RCSs (defined as a racial coping strategy having both negative and positive connotations or having neither connotation) are "persist and change or choice of environment." Examples of reactive RCSs (consistently used negatively) are "negate racial group" and "avoid or withdraw." Proactive RCSs (consistently used positively) "assert personal selfhood" and "strategic planning."

Many of the twenty-two RCSs identified in the study were not used frequently enough to warrant consideration in determining reactive, proactive, or neutral racial coping orientation(s). Therefore, in order to test the hypotheses, decision rules were instituted to eliminate those RCSs not used consistently across RCS instruments. Below is a brief description of those rules.

A dominant strategy list was developed from the preferred and overlapping RCSs of participants responding to the racial coping instruments. Five such strategies qualified; three were proactive ("defer to authority," "moral reasoning (nonracial)," "assert personal selfhood") and two were reactive ("ignore/do nothing," "superiority"). When one of the dominant RCSs was used in conjunction with a minor RCS, the pair was assessed with respect to the connotation of the dominant RCS. These pairings are referred to as combinations. Coping orientations were designated according to the predominant use of strategy combinations identified as proactive or reactive.

In order to enhance the reader's understanding of the findings in this section, examples of parents' proactive and reactive statements are presented below. Responses are to one of the four questions used, question #170, which asked, "How does your family go about ensuring that your child will have a positive Black identity?" Following each statement, the RCSs number(s) from table 16.1 (column 2) indicating the RCSs coded for each statement are listed in parentheses.

Proactive:

He has different role models. All the fellow police officers. The family is close. [We] meet and share every holiday, talk . . . (10, 11)

[We expose him to] artifacts and evidence of his cultural tradition.

If he understands where his roots are and they are in Africa, then he will have a positive Black identity (12)

Reactive:

We don't. We don't do nothing to ensure that he has a positive Black identity. (19)

Can't think of anything right now. (22)

RESULTS

Hypothesis Testing

Hypothesis 1 predicted that alternative school parents would have a predominantly proactive orientation. This hypothesis was upheld by data from the parent interview. Watoto parents were largely proactive (67 percent) in their RCSs. Hypothesis 2, however, was not upheld. Although Chaucer parents were mostly reactive (67 percent), parents at St. Benedito departed significantly from the hypothesis in that they were overwhelmingly proactive (83.3 percent).

The most highly preferred parental strategies were consistent across schools. The strategies "explore the problem" and "project racial pride" represented 26–47 percent of all parent RCSs. "Assert personal selfhood" was usually articulated as the third or fourth most frequently used RCS.

Chaucer's pattern emphasized "explore the problem" (26.8 percent), "project racial pride" (19.6 percent), and "project superiority" (8.9 percent). Watoto's emphasis on "project racial pride" (34.9 percent) far exceeded the articulation of the other RCSs, "explore the problem" (17.5 percent), "assert personal selfhood" (12.7 percent), and "change or choice of environment" (9.5 percent). Although St. Benedito parents also frequently identified racial pride, "explore the problem," and "assert personal selfhood" as RCSs, they were distinguished by their relatively high inarticulation of RCSs. As a result their configuration assumed the following pattern: "no racial coping indicated" (19.0 percent), "project racial pride" (14.3 percent), "explore the problem" (11.9 percent), "assert personal selfhood" (10.7 percent), and "moral reasoning (race-related)" (10.7 percent).

Overall, there were few differences in RCS usage between parents of boys and girls on the parent interview; parents were largely egalitarian in usage of preferred RCSs. However, sex of the child was important in the use of certain RCSs. For instance, "negate racial group" and "conform" were used exclusively by parents of boys. Conversely, "avoid or withdraw" was used exclusively by parents of girls. Parents of boys were twice as likely as parents of girls to articulate "persist," "project inferiority" (internalization), and "develop support systems" as prescribed ways of coping. Finally, parents of girls were twice as likely to articulate "moral reasoning" (race-related and nonracial).

Factor Analysis: Typologies

The basis for interpretation of factors (designated coping orientations) began far in advance of the statistical analysis. Prior to conducting the factor analysis, a detailed review of each child and adult case on each RCS measure was undertaken. Each protocol was categorized according to the RCS emphasized in the response. Each cluster of RCSs was labeled according to their apparent function. This made categorization more consistent. For each RCS measure, between five and eight patterns were distinguished. While not statistically sound, this procedure allowed the author to develop an intimate knowledge of how RCSs operated conceptually and functionally. Since RCSs were rarely used in isolation, it was important to understand how they might combine. The process described, then, was a critical step in interpreting the factors presumed to represent parental coping orientations.

In preparation for the factor analysis, the data from the racial coping measures were subjected to a natural log transformation in order to normalize the data. Within each RCS measure, a strategy was excluded from the variable list if its absolute frequency was less than or equal to one. Those RCSs remaining in the variable list were factor-analyzed separately for each measure.[18] Within each measure, three factors met the criterion set (eigen-value greater than 1.84). Individual RCSs having factor loadings greater than or equal to .46 were identified as significant contributors to a factor. After the factors had been identified, factor scores were generated and assigned using statistical software (SPSS, version 8).

Parent Interview

Adult prescriptions for and orientations toward child coping were reflected in responses to the parent interview. In this section, both quantitative and contextual information on parents' responses will be presented by school type. Quotes from individual parent interviews correspond by number to each of the four questions mentioned earlier:

1. What do you anticipate and how are you planning to protect your child (regarding the child's experiences as a Black American)?
2. How does your family go about ensuring that your child will have a positive Black identity?
3. What other day-to-day experiences in reference to being Black have you and your child talked about?
4. Describe any special features of your family's overall educational program for your child *because* (s)he is a Black American child.

Three factors accounted for nearly 50 percent of the variance.[19] Factor 1, described as insulatory (self-denying), explains 28.3 percent of the total variance and was a strongly reactive orientation composed of self-effacing and passive RCSs. The mean factor score was highest ($F(2,38) = 3.69$, $p = .03$) for parents at Benedito (M = .55), followed by Chaucer (M = -.27), and then Watoto (M = -.32).

The components of this coping orientation, consistent with several edicts of Christian ideology and ethics, include "ignore/do nothing," "avoid or withdraw," "moral reasoning race-related" (humanistic), and "moral reasoning—nonracial" (ethical). In combination with these RCSs, "persist" becomes both a reactive and a nonverbal strategy. This insulatory (self-denying) orientation deemphasizes and even rejects the racial self, both individually and as part of a devalued group, in favor of a global self which transcends race through humility and moralistic behavior and pursuits.

The following response of one parent to three of the four questions on the parent interview typifies the factor 1 coping orientation:

Question 1: No problems. I've always sacrificed and put him in private school—higher standards in private [school], I wouldn't pay for harassment. And most of the kids at school are Black.
Question 2: I just trained her to have self-respect and respect to others—not to regard people of their color or status. Not to feel low esteem because racist thing no bearing on ability to. We study Blacks who have made outstanding contributions—historians.
Question 3: Instilling in her that all she has to do is have faith in God. Never let anybody discourage her cause she's Black or brainwash her.

St. Benedito was significantly low, even of negative valence (M = -.67) on factor 2, described as competitive (assertive) orientation, in contrast to Chaucer's (M = .53) and

Watoto's (M = .03) relatively high mean factor scores (F(2,38) = 7.30, p = .002). The higher mean factor scores of Chaucer and Watoto parents on this proactive coping orientation indicated their attempts to foster competence in their children by emphasizing the superiority of Blacks either through historical or familial links. The children are encouraged to explore and understand the many facets of Black life. Often the children are guided through an interpretation and resolution of both child and adult events experienced as discriminatory or oppressive. This coping orientation is typified in the responses of the following parent:

> Question 1: The degree of education that he will receive if he is in a totally Black environment in High school—inferior education in the school system. By sending him to a school that will give him the tools I feel he needs as a Black person.
> Question 2: By discussing Blacks and their goals, what successful Blacks are doing, exposure to Black literature, not let Blackness become a product to make you feel inferior.

Contemporary-cultural versus global-historical characterizes the bipolar dimension of factor 3. Chaucer (M = .14) and, secondly, St. Benedito (M = .10) parents focused on the strength and solace of the contemporary Black community and family members (contemporary-cultural focus). Conversely, the projection of racial pride that links the broad historical context of African accomplishments to the present-day African-American potential and accomplishments (global-historical focus) was offered most often by Watoto parents (M = −.67). This coping orientation is illustrated by the following statements of one parent:

> Question 1: I expect that because she will express herself as being African—she will have strong discussion and may be intimidated . . . depending on strength or weakness of character, I don't know how she will deal with Euro-Americans . . . [I will] continue to emphasize the importance of who she is and what her role is in the community on this continent and on Africa. Identify with the role of the ancestors in history.
> Question 2: By reinforcing what the school has. Maintaining African frame of references in house and lifestyle. When she identifies with Africa as part of her past—then she will see it as part of her present and future.

Intercorrelations: Racial Coping Orientations and the Schools

Factor scores were generated that allowed adult coping orientations to be correlated among themselves and the schools. The schools were arrayed from high to low according to the degree of emphasis upon race in the school philosophy: Watoto, Chaucer, St. Benedito. School correlated significantly only with the second factor, competitive (assertive) (r = −.27, p <.05). Specifically, parents from St. Benedito, in contrast to Chaucer and Watoto parents, were least likely to be represented by the competitive (assertive) coping orientation.

SUMMARY AND CONCLUSIONS

Parents in the three independent, predominantly Black private schools reported that they used as many as seventeen of twenty-two possible different racial coping strategies, some proactive, some reactive, in socializing their children. In particular, "explore the problem," "project racial pride," and "assert personal selfhood" were popular strategies among parents at all schools. Overall, St. Benedito parents, followed by Watoto and Chaucer parents, respectively, were most likely to use a greater number of individual proactive racial coping strategies. When strategies were clustered using factor analysis techniques, three factors (designated coping orientations) accounted for nearly 50 percent of the variance: factor 1—insulatory (self-denying), factor 2—competitive (assertive), and factor 3—contemporary-cultural versus global-historical. On factor 1, St. Benedito parents, followed by Chaucer, and then Watoto, parents, scored highest. On factor 2, Chaucer and Watoto parents scored considerably higher then Benedito parents. On factor 3, Chaucer and St. Benedito parents tended to cluster toward the contemporary-cultural pole, while Watoto parents clustered toward global-historical.

The evidence presented demonstrates the varying approaches middle-income Black parents in three types of independent schools report teaching and modeling in preparing their children for school and beyond. The findings also indicate that the parents choose schools for their children that are certainly compatible, if not complementary, with the parent's racial socialization goals and strategies. However, some school environments were associated with a wider variety of coping options. Parents of boys were somewhat more likely than parents of girls to report encouraging primarily reactive racial coping strategies. Findings from the factor analyses and related analyses demonstrate the importance of both parents and schools as major socializing forces in children's lives.

This study underscores the partnership between parents and schools. Schools could potentially be involved and helpful in expanding parents' and children's options for coping. Future study in this area should focus on bringing mental health issues back into the classroom. In Black or predominantly Black schools, notwithstanding socioeconomic factors, identity diffusion is a primary concern.[20] The problem is balancing the goal of social mobility with the reality of blocked opportunity. Within a dominant American culture boasting of unlimited options, too often Black children, upon discovering their "Blackness," learn only about what they (and Black people generally) cannot do or become, Despite this dilemma, if Black children are to even survive into the next century, healthy identity-formation must be fostered. This responsibility should be jointly shared by parents and schools.

As one example of an effort to extend this research, this study has been expanded to include younger children who attend *public* elementary schools and their parents.[21] Hopefully, these data will aid in helping to determine those coping orientations which are effective and promote resilience in children. Another purpose of the new study is to identify and perhaps model those empowered parents whose children attend public schools.

The exigencies of racism cannot be ignored or pushed aside and Black families must be offered the resources to shape their approach to racial socialization with effective, proactive racial coping strategies and to eliminate or modify ineffective ones. More empirical work on racial socialization can be the foundation underlying and guiding this process.

NOTES

1. Virginia Young, "Family and childhood in a Negro Community," *American Anthropologist* 72 (April 1970): 269; John Ogbu, "Social Stratification and the Socialization of Competence," *Anthropology and Education Quarterly* 10 (1979): 3; Marie F. Peters and Grace C. Massey, "Mundane Extreme Environmental Stress in the Family: The Case of the Black Family in White America," in Hamilton L. McCubbin, Marvin B. Sussman, and Joan M. Patterson, eds., *Stress and the Family: Advances and Developments in Family Stress Theory and Research* (New York: Hayworth, 1983), 193; and Diane S. Pollard, "Perspectives of Black Parents Regarding the Socialization of Their Children" (manuscript).

2. Peters and Massey, "Mundane Extreme Environmental Stress"; Marie F. Peters, "Parenting in

Black Families with Young Children: A Historical Perspective," in Harriette Pipes McAdoo, ed., *Black Children: Social, Educational, and Parental Environments* (Beverly Hills, Calif.: Sage, 1981), 211.

3. William E. Cross, "Black Identity: Rediscovering the Distinction between Personal Identity and Reference Group Orientation," in Margaret B. Spencer, Geraldine K. Brookins, and Walter R. Allen, eds., *Beginnings: The Social and Affective Development of Black Children* (Hillsdale, N.J.: Erlbaum, 1985), 155; Margaret Beale Spencer, "Personal and Group Identity of Black Children: An Alternative Synthesis," *Genetic Psychology*, 106 (1982): 59; Margaret Beale Spencer, "Cultural Cognition and Social Cognition as Identity Correlates of Black Children's Personal Social Development," in Spencer et al., *Beginnings*, 215.

4. Robert Taylor, "Black Youth and Psychological Development," *Journal of Black Studies* 6 (1976): 353.

5. Chester Pierce, "The Mundane Extreme Environment and Its Effect on Learning," in S. G. Brainard, ed., *Learning Disabilities: Issues and Recommendations for Research* (Washington, D.C.: National Institute of Education, 1975). Jean Carew, "Effective Caregiving: The Child from Birth to Three," in M. D. Fantini and R. Cardenas, eds., *Parenting in a Multicultural Society* (New York: Longman, 1980). 170.

6. Diana T. Slaughter and Gerald A. McWorter, "Social Origins and Early Features of the Scientific Study of Black American Families and Children," in Spencer et al., *Beginnings*, 5; Peters and Massey, "Mundane Extreme Environmental Stress"; and Peters, "Parenting in Black Families."

7. Diana T. Slaughter and Barbara L. Schneider, *Newcomers: Blacks in Private Schools* ERIC, 1986 (ED 274 768 and ED 274 769).

8. Leachim Semaj, "Reconceptualizing the Development of Racial Preference in Children: A Socio-Cognitive Approach," *Journal of Black Psychology* 6 (1980): 59; Cross, "Black Identity"; Spencer, "Personal and Group Identity"; and Deborah J. Johnson, "Racial Preference and Biculturality in Interracial Preschoolers" (M.A. thesis, Cornell University, 1983).

9. Margaret Beale Spencer, "Children's Cultural Values and Parental Childrearing Strategies," *Developmental Review* 3 (1983): 351.

10. Ibid, 359.

11. Harriette Pipes McAdoo, "Stress Absorbing Systems in Black Families," *Family Relations* 31, (1982): 479.

12. Ibid.

13. Yvonne Abatso, "The Coping Personality: A Study of Black Community Students," in Spencer et al., *Beginnings*, 131; and Patricia Gurin and Edgar Epps, *Black Consciousness, Identity, and Achievement* (New York: John Wiley and Sons, 1975).

14. Phillip J. Bowman and Cleopatra Howard, "Race-Related Socialization, Motivation, and Academic Achievement: A Study of Black Youths in Three Generation Families," *Journal of the American Academy of Child Psychiatry* 24 (1985): 131.

15. Deborah J. Johnson, Diana T. Slaughter, and Barbara L. Schneider, "Parental Coping and Identity Formation in Black Children: Coding Manual IV," *Newcomers*. Contact the senior author for the most updated version of this manual.

16. Deborah J. Johnson, "Identity Formation and Racial Coping Strategies of Black Children and Their Parents: A Stress and Coping Paradigm," (Ph.D. dissertation, Northwestern University, 1987).

17. Johnson, Slaughter, and Schneider, "Coding Manual IV."

18. Norman H. Nie et al., *Statistical Package for the Social Sciences*, 2nd ed. (New York: McGraw-Hill, 1975); and John Scanzoni, "Sex Roles, Economic Factors, and Marital Solidarity in Black and White Marriages," *Journal of Marriage and the Family* 37 (1975): 130.

19. Factor 1 contained the following RCSs in highest to lowest order: avoid or withdraw (.82); legal reasoning (.80); negate racial group (.74); project inferiority (.71); moral reasoning (nonracial) (.61); ignore/do nothing (.53); strategic planning (.53); moral reasoning (race-related) (.52); persist (.51). Factor 2 contained the following RCSs in highest to lowest order: explore the problem (.75); project superiority (.61); no racial coping (−.75). Factor 3 contained the following RCSs in highest to lowest order: develop support systems (.59); strategic planning (.46); project racial pride (−.69).

20. Erik H. Erikson, *Identity: Youth and Crisis* (New York: W. W. Norton and Company, 1968).

21. Postdoctoral research was conducted under the auspices of the University of California at Berkeley, Department of Afro-American Studies.

28

TALKING ABOUT RACE, LEARNING ABOUT RACISM

The Application of Racial Identity Development Theory in the Classroom

Beverly Daniel Tatum

The inclusion of race-related content in college courses often generates emotional responses in students that range from guilt and shame to anger and despair. The discomfort associated with these emotions can lead students to resist the learning process. Based on her experience teaching a course on the psychology of racism and an application of racial identity development theory, Beverly Daniel Tatum identifies three major sources of student resistance to talking about race and learning about racism, as well as some strategies for overcoming this resistance.

As many educational institutions struggle to become more multicultural in terms of their students, faculty, and staff, they also begin to examine issues of cultural representation within their curriculum. This examination has evoked a growing number of courses that give specific consideration to the effect of variables such as race, class, and gender on human experience—an important trend that is reflected and supported by the increasing availability of resource manuals for the modification of course content (Bronstein & Quina, 1988; Hull, Scott, & Smith, 1982; Schuster & Van Dyne, 1985).

Unfortunately, less attention has been given to the issues of process that inevitably emerge in the classroom when attention is focused on race, class, and/or gender. It is very difficult to talk about these concepts in a meaningful way without also talking and learning about racism, classism, and sexism.[1] The introduction of these issues of oppression often generates powerful emotional responses in students that range from guilt and shame to anger and despair. If not addressed, these emotional responses can result in student resistance to oppression-related content areas. Such resistance can ultimately interfere with the cognitive understanding and mastery of the material. This resistance and potential interference is particularly common when specifically addressing issues of race and racism. Yet, when students are given the opportunity to explore race-related material in a classroom where both their affective and intellectual responses are acknowledged and addressed, their level of understanding is greatly enhanced.

This article seeks to provide a framework for understanding students' psychological responses to race-related content and the student resistance that can result, as well as some strategies for overcoming this resistance. It is informed by more than a decade of experience as an African-American woman engaged in teaching an undergraduate course on the psychology of racism, by thematic analyses of student journals and essays written for the racism class, and by an understanding and application of racial identity development theory (Helms, 1990).

SETTING THE CONTEXT

As a clinical psychologist with a research interest in racial identity development among African-American youth raised in predominantly white communities, I began teaching about racism quite fortuitously. In 1980, while I was a part-time lecturer in the Black Studies department of a large public university, I was invited to teach a course called Group Exploration of Racism (Black Studies 2). A requirement for Black Studies majors, the course had to be offered, yet the instructor who regularly taught the course was no longer affiliated with the institution. Armed with a folder full of handouts, old syllabi that the previous instructor left behind, a copy of *White Awareness: Handbook for Antiracism Training* (Katz, 1978), and my own clinical skills as a group facilitator, I constructed a course that seemed to meet the goals already outlined in the course catalogue. Designed "to provide students with an understanding of the psychological causes and emotional reality of racism as it appears in everyday life," the course incorporated the use of lectures, readings, simulation exercises, group research projects, and extensive class discussions to help students explore the psychological impact of racism on both the oppressed and the oppressed.

Though my first efforts were tentative, the results were powerful. The students in my class, most of whom were white, repeatedly described the course in the evaluations as one of the most valuable educational experiences of their college careers. I was convinced that helping students understand the ways in which racism operates in their own lives, and what they could do about it, was a social responsibility that I should accept. The freedom to institute the course in the curriculum of the psychology departments in which I would eventually teach became a personal condition of employment. I have successfully introduced the course in each new educational setting I have been in since leaving that university.

Since 1980, I have taught the course (now called the Psychology of Racism eighteen times, at three different institutions. Although each of these school is very different—a large public university, a small state college, and a private, elite women's college—the challenges of teaching about racism in each setting have been more similar than different.

In all of the settings, class size has been limited to thirty students (averaging twenty-four). Though typically predominantly white and female (even in coeducational settings), the class makeup has always been mixed in terms of both race and gender. The students of color who have taken the course include Asians and Latinos/as, but most frequently the students of color have been Black. Though most students have described themselves as middle class, all socioeconomic backgrounds (ranging from very poor to very wealthy) have been represented over the years.

The course has necessarily evolved in response to my own deepening awareness of the psychological legacy of racism and my expanding awareness of other forms of oppression, although the basic format has remained the same. Our weekly three-hour class meeting is held in a room with movable chairs, arranged in a circle. The physical structure communicates an important premise of the course—that I expect the students to speak with each other as well as with me.

My other expectations (timely completion of assignments, regular class attendance) are clearly communicated in our first class meeting, along with the assumptions and guidelines for discussion that I rely upon to guide our work together. Because the assumptions and guidelines are so central to the process of talking and learning about racism, it may be useful to outline them here.

WORKING ASSUMPTIONS

1. Racism, defined as a "system of advantage based on race" (see Wellman, 1977), is a pervasive aspect of U.S. socialization. It is virtually impossible to live in U.S. contemporary society and not be exposed to some aspect of the personal, cultural, and/or institutional manifestations of racism in our society. It is also assumed that as a result, all of us have received some misinformation about those groups disadvantaged by racism.

2. Prejudice, defined as a "preconceived judgment or opinion, often based on limited information," is clearly distinguished from racism (see Katz, 1978). I assume that all of us may have prejudices as a result of the various cultural stereotypes to which we have been exposed. Even when these preconceived ideas have positive associations (such as "Asian students are good in math"), they have negative effects because they deny a person's individuality. These attitudes may influence the individual behaviors of people of color as well as of whites, and may affect intergroup as well as intragroup interaction. However, a distinction must be made between the negative racial attitudes held by individuals of color and white individuals, because it is only the attitudes of whites that routinely carry with them the social power inherent in the systematic cultural reinforcement and institutionalization of those racial prejudices. To distinguish the prejudices of students of color from the racism of white students is *not* to say that the former is acceptable and the latter is not; both are clearly problematic. The distinction is important, however, to identify the power differential between members of dominant and subordinate groups.

3. In the context of U.S. society, the system of advantage clearly operates to benefit whites as a group. However, it is assumed that racism, like other forms of oppression, hurts members of the privileged group as well as those targeted by racism. While the impact of racism on whites is clearly different from its impact on people of color, racism has negative ramifications for everyone. For example, some white students might remember the pain of having lost important relationships because Black friends were not allowed to visit their homes. Others may express sadness at having been denied access to a broad range of experiences because of social segregation. These individuals often attribute the discomfort or fear they now experience in racially mixed settings to the cultural limitations of their youth.

4. Because of the prejudice and racism inherent in our environments when we were children, I assume that we cannot be blamed for learning what we were taught (intentionally or unintentionally). Yet as adults, we have a responsibility to try to identify and interrupt the cycle of oppression. When we recognize that we have been misinformed, we have a responsibility to seek out more accurate information and to adjust our behavior accordingly.

5. It is assumed that change, both individual and institutional, is possible. Understanding and unlearning prejudice and racism is a lifelong process that may have begun prior to enrolling in this class, and which will surely continue after the course is over. Each of us may be at a different point in that process, and I assume that we will have mutual respect for each other, regardless of where we perceive one another to be.

To facilitate further our work together, I ask students to honor the following guidelines for our discussion. Specifically, I ask students to demonstrate their respect for one another by honoring the confidentiality of the group. So that students may feel free to ask potentially awkward or embarrassing questions, or share race-related experiences, I ask that students refrain from making personal attributions when discussing the course content with their friends. I also discourage the use of "zaps," overt or covert put-downs often used as comic relief when someone is feeling anxious about the content of the discussion. Finally, students are asked to speak from their own experience, to say, for example, "I think . . ." or "In my experience, I have found . . ." rather than generalizing their experience to others, as in "People say . . ."

Many students are reassured by the climate of safety that is created by these guidelines and find comfort in the nonblaming assumptions I outline for the class. Nevertheless, my experience has been that most students, regardless of their class and ethnic background, still find racism a difficult topic to discuss, as is revealed by these journal comments written after the first class meeting (all names are pseudonyms):

> The class is called Psychology of Racism, the atmosphere is friendly and open, yet I feel very closed in. I feel guilt and doubt well up inside of me. (Tiffany, a White woman)
>
> Class has started on a good note thus far. The class seems rather large and disturbs me. In a class of this nature, I expect there will be many painful and emotional moments. (Linda, an Asian woman)
>
> I am a little nervous that as one of the few students of color in the class people are going to be looking at me for answers, or whatever other reasons. The thought of this inhibits me a great deal. (Louise, an African-American woman)
>
> I had never thought about my social position as being totally dominant. There wasn't one area in which I wasn't in the dominant group . . . I first felt embarrassed. . . . Through association alone I felt in many ways responsible for the unequal condition existing in the world. This made me feel like shrinking in a hole in a class where I was surrounded by 27 women and 2 men, one of whom was Black and the other was Jewish. I felt that all these people would be justified in venting their anger upon me. After a short period, I realized that no one in the room was attacking or even blaming me for the conditions that exist. (Carl, a white man)

Even though most of my students voluntarily enroll in the course as an elective, their anxiety and subsequent resistance to learning about racism quickly emerge.

SOURCES OF RESISTANCE

In predominantly white college classrooms, I have experienced at least three major sources of student resistance to talking and learning about race and racism. They can be readily identified as the following:

1. Race is considered a taboo topic for discussion, especially in racially mixed settings.
2. Many students, regardless of racial-group membership, have been socialized to think of the United States as a just society.
3. Many students, particularly white students, initially deny any personal prejudice, recognizing the impact of racism on other people's lives, but failing to acknowledge its impact on their own.

RACE AS TABOO TOPIC

The first source of resistance, race as a taboo topic, is an essential obstacle to overcome if class discussion is to begin at all. Although many students are interested in the topic, they are often most interested in hearing other people talk about it, afraid to break the taboo themselves.

One source of this self-consciousness can be seen in the early childhood experiences of many students. It is known that children as young as three notice racial differences (see Phinney & Rotheram, 1987). Certainly preschoolers talk about what they see. Unfortunately, they often do so in ways that make adults uncomfortable. Imagine the following scenario: A white child in a public place points to a dark-skinned African-American child and says loudly, "Why is that boy Black?" The embarrassed parent quickly responds, "Sh! Don't say that." The child is only attempting to make sense of a new observation (Derman-Sparks, Higa, & Sparks, 1980), yet the parent's attempt to silence the perplexed child sends a message that this observation is not okay to talk about. White children quickly become aware that their questions about race raise adult anxiety, and as a result, they learn not to ask the questions.

When asked to reflect on their earliest race-related memories and the feelings associated with them, both white students and students of color often report feelings of confusion, anxiety, and/or fear. Students of color often have early memories of name-calling or other negative interactions with other children, and sometimes with adults. They also report having had questions that went both unasked and unanswered. In addition, many students have had uncomfortable inter-changes around race-related topics as adults. When asked at the beginning of the semester, "How many of you have had difficult, perhaps heated conversations with someone on a race-related topic?", routinely almost everyone in the class raises his or her hand. It should come as no surprise then that students often approach the topic of race and/or racism with both curiosity and trepidation.

THE MYTH OF THE MERITOCRACY

The second source of student resistance to be discussed here is rooted in students' belief that the United States is a just society, a meritocracy where individual efforts are fairly rewarded. While some students (particularly students of color) may already have become disillusioned with that notion of the United States, the majority of my students who have experienced at least the personal success of college acceptance still have faith in this notion. To the extent that these students acknowledge that racism exists, they tend to view it as an individual phenomenon, rooted in the attitudes of the "Archie Bunkers" of the world or located only in particular parts of the country.

After several class meetings, Karen, a white woman, acknowledged this attitude in her journal:

> At one point in my life—the beginning of this class—I actually perceived America to be a relatively racist free society. I thought that the people who were racist or subjected to racist stereotypes were found only in small pockets of the U.S., such as the South. As I've come to realize, racism (or at least racially orientated stereotypes) is rampant.

An understanding of racism as a system of advantage presents a serious challenge to the notion of the United States as a just society where rewards are based solely on one's merit.

Such a challenge often creates discomfort in students. The old adage "ignorance is bliss" seems to hold true in this case; students are not necessarily eager to recognize the painful reality of racism.

One common response to the discomfort is to engage in denial of what they are learning. White students in particular may question the accuracy or currency of statistical information regarding the prevalence of discrimination (housing, employment, access to health care, and so on). More qualitative data, such as autobiographical accounts of experiences with racism, may be challenged on the basis of their subjectivity.

It should be pointed out that the basic assumption that the United States is a just society for all is only one of many basic assumptions that might be challenged in the learning process. Another example can be seen in an interchange between two white students following a discussion about cultural racism, in which the omission or distortion of historical information about people of color was offered as an example of the cultural transmission of racism.

"Yeah, I just found out that Cleopatra was actually a Black woman."

"What?"

The first student went on to explain her newly learned information. Finally, the second student exclaimed in disbelief, "That can't be true. Cleopatra was beautiful!" This new information and her own deeply ingrained assumptions about who is beautiful and who is not were too incongruous to allow her to assimilate the information at that moment.

If outright denial of information is not possible, then withdrawal may be. Physical withdrawal in the form of absenteeism is one possible result; it is for precisely this reason that class attendance is mandatory. The reduction in the completion of reading and/or written assignments is another form of withdrawal. I have found this response to be so common that I now alert students to this possibility at the beginning of the semester. Knowing that this response is a common one seems to help students stay engaged, even when they experience the desire to withdraw.

Following an absence in the fifth week of the semester, one white student wrote, "I think I've hit the point you talked about, the point where you don't want to hear any more about racism. I sometimes begin to get the feeling we are all hypersensitive." (Two weeks later she wrote, "Class is getting better. I think I am beginning to get over my hump.")

Perhaps not surprisingly, this response can be found in both white students and students of color. Students of color often enter a discussion of racism with some awareness of the issue, based on personal experiences. However, even these students find that they did not have a full understanding of the widespread impact of racism in our society. For students who are targeted by racism, an increased awareness of the impact in and on their lives is painful, and often generates anger.

Four weeks into the semester, Louise, an African-American woman, wrote in her journal about her own heightened sensitivity:

> Many times in class I feel uncomfortable when white students use the term Black because even if they aren't aware of it they say it with all or at least a lot of the negative connotations they've been taught goes along with Black. Sometimes it just causes a stinging feeling inside of me. Sometimes I get real tired of hearing white people talk about the conditions of Black people. I think it's an important thing for them to talk about, but still I don't always like being around when they do it. I also get tired of hearing them talk about how hard it is for them, though I

understand it, and most times I am very willing to listen and be open, but sometimes I can't. Right now I can't.

For white students, advantaged by racism, a heightened awareness of it often generates painful feelings of guilt. The following responses are typical:

> After reading the article about privilege, I felt very guilty. (Rachel, a White woman)
>
> Questions of racism are so full of anger and pain. When I think of all the pain White people have caused people of color, I get a feeling of guilt. How could someone like myself care so much about the color of someone's skin that they would do them harm? (Terri, a White woman)

White students also sometimes express a sense of betrayal when they realize the gaps in their own education about racism. After seeing the first episode of the documentary series *Eyes on the Prize*, Chris, a white man, wrote:

> I never knew it was really that bad just 35 years ago. Why didn't I learn this in elementary or high school? Could it be that the white people of America want to forget this injustice? . . . I will never forget that movie for as long as I live. It was like a big slap in the face.

Barbara, a white woman, also felt anger and embarrassment in response to her own previous lack of information about the internment of Japanese Americans during World War II. She wrote:

> I feel so stupid because I never even knew that these existed. I never knew that the Japanese were treated so poorly. I am becoming angry and upset about all of the things that I do not know. I have been so sheltered. My parents never wanted to let me know about the bad things that have happened in the world. After I saw the movie (*Mitsuye and Nellie*), I even called them up to ask them why they never told me this. . . . I am angry at them too for not teaching me and exposing me to the complete picture of my country.

Avoiding the subject matter is one way to avoid these uncomfortable feelings.

"I'M NOT RACIST, BUT . . ."

A third source of student resistance (particularly among white students) is the initial denial of any personal connection to racism. When asked why they have decided to enroll in a course on racism, White students typically explain their interest in the topic with such disclaimers as, "I'm not racist myself, but I know people who are, and I want to understand them better."

Because of their position as the targets of racism, students of color do not typically focus on their own prejudices or lack of them. Instead they usually express a desire to understand why racism exists, and how they have been affected by it.

However, as all students gain a better grasp of what racism is and its many manifestations in U.S. society, they inevitably start to recognize its legacy within themselves. Beliefs, attitudes, and actions based on racial stereotypes begin to be remembered and are newly observed by white students. Students of color as well often recognize negative attitudes they may have internalized about their own racial group or that they have believed about others. Those who previously thought themselves immune to the effects of growing up in a racist society often find themselves reliving uncomfortable feelings of guilt or anger.

After taping her own responses to a questionnaire on racial attitudes, Barbara, a white woman previously quoted, wrote:

> I always want to think of myself as open to all races. Yet when I did the interview to myself, I found that I did respond differently to the same questions about different races. No one could ever have told me that I would have. I would have denied it. But I found that I did respond differently even though I didn't want to. This really upset me. I was angry with myself because I thought I was not prejudiced and yet the stereotypes that I had created had an impact on the answers that I gave even though I didn't want it to happen.

The new self-awareness, represented here by Barbara's journal entry, changes the classroom dynamic. One common result is that some white students, once perhaps active participants in class discussion, now hesitate to continue their participation for fear that their newly recognized racism will be revealed to others.

> Today I did feel guilty, and like I had to watch what I was saying (make it good enough), I guess to prove I'm really *not* prejudiced. From the conversations the first day, I guess this is a normal enough reaction, but I certainly never expected it in me. (Joanne, a white woman)

This withdrawal on the part of white students is often paralleled by an increase in participation by students of color who are seeking an outlet for what are often feelings of anger. The withdrawal of some previously vocal white students from the classroom exchange, however, is sometimes interpreted by students of color as indifference. This perceived indifference often serves to fuel the anger and frustration that many students of color experience, as awareness of their own oppression is heightened. For example, Robert, an African-American man, wrote:

> I really wish the white students would talk more. When I read these articles, it makes me so mad and I really want to know what the white kids think. Don't they care?

Sonia, a Latina, described the classroom tension from another perspective:

> I would like to comment that at many points in the discussions I have felt uncomfortable and sometimes even angry with people. I guess I am at the stage where I am tired of listening to Whites feel guilty and watch their eyes fill up with tears. I do understand that everyone is at their own stage of development and I even tell myself every Tuesday that these people have come to this class by choice. Some days I am just more tolerant than others. . . . It takes courage to say things in that room with so many women of color present. It also takes courage for the women of color to say things about Whites.

What seems to be happening in the classroom at such moments is a collision of developmental processes that can be inherently useful for the racial identity development of the individuals involved. Nevertheless, the interaction may be perceived as problematic to instructors and students who are unfamiliar with the process. Although space does not allow for an exhaustive discussion of racial identity development theory, a brief explication of it here will provide additional clarity regarding the classroom dynamics when issues of race are discussed. It will also provide a theoretical framework for the strategies for dealing with student resistance that will be discussed at the conclusion of this article.

STAGES OF RACIAL IDENTITY DEVELOPMENT
Racial identity and racial identity development theory are defined by Janet Helms (1990) as

> a sense of group or collective identity based on one's *perception* that he or she shares a common racial heritage with a particular racial group . . . racial identity development theory concerns the psychological implications of racial-group membership, that is belief systems that evolve in reaction to perceived differential racial-group membership. (3)

It is assumed that in a society where racial-group membership is emphasized, the development of a racial identity will occur in some form in everyone. Given the dominant/subordinate relationship of whites and people of color in this society, however, it is not surprising that this developmental process will unfold in different ways. For purposes of this discussion, William Cross's (1971, 1978) model of Black identity development will be described along with Helms's (1990) model of white racial identity development theory. While the identity development of other students (Asian, Latino/a, Native American) is not included in this particular theoretical formulation, there is evidence to suggest that the process for these oppressed groups is similar to that described for African Americans (Highlen et al., 1988; Phinney, 1990).[2] In each case, it is assumed that a positive sense of one's self as a member of one's group (which is not based on any assumed superiority) is important for psychological health.

BLACK RACIAL IDENTITY DEVELOPMENT
According to Cross's (1971, 1978, 1991) model of Black racial identity development, there are five stages in the process, identified as Preencounter, Encounter, Immersion/Emersion, Internalization, and Internalization-Commitment. In the first stage of Preencounter, the African American has absorbed many of the beliefs and values of the dominant White culture, including the notion that "White is right" and "Black is wrong." Though the internalization of negative Black stereotypes may be outside of his or her conscious awareness, the individual seeks to assimilate and be accepted by whites, and actively or passively distances him/herself from other Blacks.[3]

Louise, an African-American woman previously quoted, captured the essence of this stage in the following description of herself at an earlier time:

> For a long time it seemed as if I didn't remember my background, and I guess in some ways I didn't. I was never taught to be proud of my African heritage. Like we talked about in class, I went through a very long stage of identifying with my oppressors. Wanting to be like, live like, and be accepted by them. Even to the point of hating my own race and myself for being a part of it. Now I am ashamed that I ever was ashamed. I lost so much of myself in my denial of and refusal to accept my people.

In order to maintain psychological comfort at this stage of development, Helms writes:

The person must maintain the fiction that race and racial indoctrination have nothing to do with how he or she lives life. It is probably the case that the Preen-counter person is bombarded on a regular basis with information that he or she cannot really be a member of the "in" racial group, but relies on denial to selectively screen such information from awareness. (1990, 23)

This deemphasis on one's racial-group membership may allow the individual to think that race has not been or will not be a relevant factor in one's own achievement, and may contribute to the belief in a U.S. meritocracy that is often a part of a Preencounter worldview.

Movement into the Encounter phase is typically precipitated by an event or series of events that forces the individual to acknowledge the impact of racism in one's life. For example, instances of social rejection by white friends or colleagues (or reading new personally relevant information about racism) may lead the individual to the conclusion that many whites will not view him or her as an equal. Faced with the reality that he or she cannot truly be white, the individual is forced to focus on his or her identity as a member of a group targeted by racism.

Brenda, a Korean-American student, described her own experience of this process as a result of her participation in the racism course:

I feel that because of this class, I have become much more aware of racism that exists around. Because of my awareness of racism, I am now bothered by acts and behaviors that might not have bothered me in the past. Before when racial comments were said around me I would somehow ignore it and pretend that nothing was said. By ignoring comments such as these, I was protecting myself. It became sort of a defense mechanism. I never realized I did this, until I was confronted with stories that were found in our reading, by other people of color, who also ignored comments that bothered them. In realizing that there is racism out in the world and that there are comments concerning race that are directed towards me, I feel as if I have reached the first step. I also think I have reached the second step, because I am now bothered and irritated by such comments. I no longer ignore them, but now confront them.

The Immersion/Emersion stage is characterized by the simultaneous desire to surround oneself with visible symbols of one's racial identity and an active avoidance of symbols of Whiteness. As Thomas Parham describes, "At this stage, everything of value in life must be Black or relevant to Blackness. This stage is also characterized by a tendency to denigrate White people, simultaneously glorifying Black people. . . ." (1989, 190). The previously described anger that emerges in class among African-American students and other students of color in the process of learning about racism may be seen as part of the transition through these stages.

As individuals enter the Immersion stage, they actively seek out opportunities to explore aspects of their own history and culture with the support of peers from their own racial background. Typically, white-focused anger dissipates during this phase because so much of the person's energy is directed toward his or her own group- and self-exploration. The result of this exploration is an emerging security in a newly defined and affirmed sense of self.

Sharon, another African-American woman, described herself at the beginning of the semester as angry, seemingly in the Encounter stage of development. She wrote after our class meeting:

Another point that I must put down is that before I entered class today I was angry about the way Black people have been treated in this country. I don't think I will easily overcome that and I basically feel justified in my feelings.

At the end of the semester, Sharon had joined with two other Black students in the class to work on their final class project. She observed that the three of them had planned their project to focus on Black people specifically, suggesting movement into the Immersion stage of racial identity development. She wrote:

We are concerned about the well-being of our own people. They cannot be well if they have this pinned-up hatred for their own people. This internalized racism is something that we all felt, at various times, needed to be talked about. This semester it has really been important to me, and I believe Gordon [a Black classmate], too.

The emergence from this stage marks the beginning of Internalization. Secure in one's own sense of racial identity, there is less need to assert the "Blacker than thou" attitude often characteristic of the Immersion stage (Parham, 1989). In general, "pro-Black attitudes become more expansive, open, and less defensive" (Cross, 1971, 24). While still maintaining his or her connections with Black peers, the internalized individual is willing to establish meaningful relationships with whites who acknowledge and are respectful of his or her self-definition. The individual is also ready to build coalitions with members of other oppressed groups. At the end of the semester, Brenda, a Korean American, concluded that she had in fact internalized a positive sense of racial identity. The process she described parallels the stages described by Cross:

I have been aware for a long time that I am Korean. But through this class I am beginning to really become aware of my race. I am beginning to find out that white people can be accepting of me and at the same time accept me as a Korean.

I grew up wanting to be accepted and ended up almost denying my race and culture. I don't think I did this consciously, but the denial did occur. As I grew older, I realized that I was different. I became for the first time, friends with other Koreans. I realized I had much in common with them. This was when I went through my "Korean friend" stage. I began to enjoy being friends with Koreans more than I did with Caucasians.

Well, ultimately, through many years of growing up, I am pretty much in focus about who I am and who my friends are. I knew before I took this class that there were people not of color that were understanding of my differences. In our class, I feel that everyone is trying to sincerely find the answer of abolishing racism. I knew people like this existed, but it's nice to meet with them weekly.

Cross suggests that there are few psychological differences between the fourth stage, Internalization, and the fifth stage, Internalization-Commitment. However, those at the fifth stage have found ways to translate their "personal sense of Blackness into a plan of action or a general sense of commitment" to the concerns of Blacks as a group, which is sustained over time (Cross, 1991, 220). Whether at the fourth or fifth stage, the process of Internalization allows the individual, anchored in a positive sense of racial identity, both to proactively perceive and to transcend race. Blackness becomes "the point of departure for discovering the universe of ideas, cultures and experiences beyond blackness in place of mistaking blackness as the universe itself" (Cross, Parham, & Helms, 1991, 330).

Though the process of racial identity development has been presented here in linear form, in fact it is probably more accurate to think of it in a spiral form. Often a person may move from one stage to the next, only to revisit an earlier stage as the result of new encounter experiences (Parham, 1989), though the later experience of the stage may be different from the original experience. The image that students often find helpful in understanding this concept of recycling through the stages is that of a spiral staircase. As a person ascends a spiral staircase, she may stop and look down at a spot below. When she reaches the next level, she may look down and see the same spot, but the vantage point has changed.[4]

WHITE RACIAL IDENTITY DEVELOPMENT

The transformations experienced by those targeted by racism are often paralleled by those of White students. Helms (1990) describes the evolution of a positive white racial identity as involving both the abandonment of racism and the development of a nonracist white identity. In order to do the latter,

> he or she must accept his or her own Whiteness, the cultural implications of being white, and define a view of Self as a racial being that does not depend on the perceived superiority of one racial group over another. (49)

She identifies six stages in her model of white racial identity development: Contact, Disintegration, Reintegration, Pseudo-Independent, Immersion/Emersion, and Autonomy.

The Contact stage is characterized by a lack of awareness of cultural and institutional racism, and of one's own white privilege. Peggy McIntosh (1989) writes eloquently about her own experience of this state of being:

> As a white person, I realized I had been taught about racism as something which puts others at a disadvantage, but had been taught not to see one of its corollary aspects, white privilege, which puts me at an advantage. . . . I was taught to see racism only in individual acts of meanness, not in invisible systems conferring dominance on my group. (10).

In addition, the Contact stage often includes naive curiosity about or fear of people of color, based on stereotypes learned from friends, family, or the media. These stereotypes represent the framework in use when a person at this stage of development makes a comment such as "You don't act like a Black person" (Helms, 1990, 57).

Those whites whose lives are structured so as to limit their interaction with people of color, as well as their awareness of racial issues, may remain at this stage indefinitely. However, certain kinds of experiences (increased interaction with people of color or exposure to new information about racism) may lead to a new understanding that cultural and institutional racism exist. This new understanding marks the beginning of the Disintegration stage.

At this stage, the bliss of ignorance or lack of awareness is replaced by the discomfort of guilt, shame, and sometimes anger at the recognition of one's own advantage because of being white and the acknowledgment of the role of whites in the maintenance of a racist system. Attempts to reduce discomfort may include denial (convincing oneself that racism doesn't really exist, or if it does, it is the fault of its victims).

For example, Tom, a white male student, responded with some frustration in his journal to a classmate's observation that the fact that she had never read any books by Black authors in any of her high school or college English classes was an example of cultural racism. He wrote, "It's not my fault that Blacks don't write books."

After viewing a film in which a psychologist used examples of Black children's drawings to illustrate the potentially damaging effect of negative cultural messages on a Black child's developing self-esteem, David, another white male student, wrote:

> I found it interesting the way Black children drew themselves without arms. The psychologist said this is saying that the child feels unable to control his environment. It can't be because the child has notions and beliefs already about being Black. It must be built in or hereditary due to the past history of the Blacks. I don't believe it's cognitive but more biological due to a long past history of repression and being put down.

Though Tom's and David's explanations seem quite problematic, they can be understood in the context of racial identity development theory as a way of reducing their cognitive dissonance upon learning this new race-related information. As was discussed earlier, withdrawal (accomplished by avoiding contact with people of color and the topic of racism) is another strategy for dealing with the discomfort experienced at this stage. Many of the previously described responses of white students to race-related content are characteristic of the transition from the Contact to the Disintegration stage of development.

Helms (1990) describes another response to the discomfort of Disintegration, which involves attempts to change significant others' attitudes toward African Americans and other people of color. However, as she points out,

> due to the racial naivete with which this approach may be undertaken and the person's ambivalent racial identification, this dissonance-reducing strategy is likely to be met with rejection by whites as well as Blacks. (59)

In fact, this response is also frequently observed among White students who have an opportunity to talk with friends and family during holiday visits. Suddenly they are noticing the racist content of jokes or comments of their friends and relatives and will try to confront them, often only to find that their efforts are, at best, ignored or dismissed as a "phase," or, at worst, greeted with open hostility.

Carl, a white male previously quoted, wrote at length about this dilemma:

> I realized that it was possible to simply go through life totally oblivious to the entire situation or, even if one realizes it, one can totally repress it. It is easy to fade into the woodwork, run with the rest of society, and never have to deal with these problems. So many people I know from home are like this. They have simply accepted what society has taught them with little, if any, question. My father is a prime example of this. . . . It has caused much friction in our relationship, and he often tells me as a father he has failed in raising me correctly. Most of my high school friends will never deal with these issues and propagate them on to their own children. It's easy to see how the cycle continues. I don't think I could ever justify within myself simply

turning my back on the problem. I finally realized that my position in all of these dominant groups gives me power to make change occur. . . . It is an unfortunate result often though that I feel alienated from friends and family. It's often played off as a mere stage that I'm going through. I obviously can't tell if it's merely a stage, but I know that they say this to take the attention off of the truth of what I'm saying. By belittling me, they take the power out of my argument. It's very depressing that being compassionate and considerate are seen as only phases that people go through. I don't want it to be a phase for me, but as obvious as this may sound, I look at my environment and often wonder how it will not be.

The societal pressure to accept the status quo may lead the individual from Disintegration to Reintegration. At this point the desire to be accepted by one's own racial group, in which the overt or covert belief in white superiority is so prevalent, may lead to a reshaping of the person's belief system to be more congruent with an acceptance of racism. The guilt and anxiety associated with Disintegration may be redirected in the form of fear and anger directed toward people of color (particularly Blacks), who are now blamed as the source of discomfort.

Connie, a white woman of Italian ancestry, in many ways exemplified the progression from the Contact stage to Reintegration, a process she herself described seven weeks into the semester. After reading about the stages of white identity development, she wrote:

I think mostly I can find myself in the disintegration stage of development. . . . There was a time when I never considered myself a color. I never described myself as a "white, Italian female" until I got to college and noticed that people of color always described themselves by their color/race. While taking this class, I have begun to understand that being white makes a difference. I never thought about it before but there are many privileges to being White. In my personal life, I cannot say that I have ever felt that I have had the advantage over a Black person, but I am aware that my race has the advantage.

I am feeling really guilty lately about that. I find myself thinking: "I didn't mean to be white, I really didn't mean it." I am starting to feel angry towards my race for ever using this advantage towards personal gains. But at the same time I resent the minority groups. I mean, it's not our fault that society has deemed us "superior." I don't feel any better than a Black person. But it really doesn't matter because I am a member of the dominant race. . . . I can't help it . . . and I sometimes get angry and feel like I'm being attacked.

I guess my anger toward a minority group would enter me into the next stage of Reintegration, where I am once again starting to blame the victim. This is all very trying for me and it has been on my mind a lot. I really would like to be able to reach the last stage, autonomy, where I can accept being White without hostility and anger. That is really hard to do.

Helms (1990) suggests that it is relatively easy for whites to become stuck at the Reintegration stage of development, particularly if avoidance of people of color is possible. However, if there is a catalyst for continued self-examination, the person "begins to question her or his previous definition of Whiteness and the justifiability of racism in any of its forms. . . ." (61). In my experience, continued participation in a course on racism provides the catalyst for this deeper self-examination.

This process was again exemplified by Connie. At the end of the semester, she listened to her own taped interview of her racial attitudes that she had recorded at the beginning of the semester. She wrote:

Oh wow! I could not believe some of the things that I said. I was obviously in different stages of the white identity development. As I listened and got more and more disgusted with myself when I was at the Reintegration stage, I tried to remind myself that these are stages that all (most) white people go through when dealing with notions of racism. I can remember clearly the resentment I had for people of color. I feel the one thing I enjoyed from listening to my interview was noticing how much I have changed. I think I am finally out of the Reintegration stage. I am beginning to make a conscious effort to seek out information about people of color and accept their criticism. . . . I still feel guilty about the feeling I had about people of color and I always feel bad about being privileged as a result of racism. But I am glad that I have reached what I feel is the Pseudo-Independent stage of White identity development.

The information-seeking that Connie describes often marks the onset of the Pseudo-Independent stage. At this stage, the individual is abandoning beliefs in white superiority, but may still behave in ways that unintentionally perpetuate the system. Looking to those targeted by racism to help him or her understand racism, the White person often tries to disavow his or her own whiteness through active affiliation with Blacks, for example. The individual experiences a sense of alienation from other whites who have not yet begun to examine their own racism, yet may also experience rejection from Blacks or other people of color who are suspicious of his or her motives. Students of color moving from the Encounter to the Immersion phase of their own racial identity development may be particularly unreceptive to the white person's attempts to connect with them.

Uncomfortable with his or her own whiteness, yet unable to be truly anything else, the individual may begin searching for a new, more comfortable way to be white. This search is characteristic of the Immersion/Emersion stage of development. Just as the Black student seeks to redefine positively what it means to be of African ancestry in the United States through immersion in accurate information about one's culture and history, the white individual seeks to replace racially related myths and stereotypes with accurate information about what it means and has meant to be white in U.S. society (Helms, 1990). Learning about whites who have been antiracist allies to people of color is a very important part of this process.

After reading articles written by antiracist activists describing their own process of unlearning racism, white students often comment on how helpful it is to know that others have experienced similar feelings and have found ways to resist the racism in their environments.[5] For example, Joanne, a white woman who initially experienced a lot of guilt, wrote:

This article helped me out in many ways. I've been feeling helpless and frustrated. I know there are all these terrible things going on and I want to be able to do something. . . . Anyway this article helped me realize, again, that others feel this way, and gave me some positive ideas to resolve my dominant class guilt and shame.

Finally, reading the biographies and autobiographies of white individuals who have embarked on a similar process of identity development (such as Barnard, 1987) provides white students with important models for change.

Learning about white antiracists can also provide students of color with a sense of hope that they can have white allies. After hearing a white antiracist activist address the class,

Sonia, a Latina who had written about her impatience with expressions of white guilt, wrote:

> I don't know when I have been more impressed by anyone. She filled me with hope for the future. She made me believe that there are good people in the world and that whites suffer too and want to change things.

For white students, the internalization of a newly defined sense of oneself as white is the primary task of the Autonomy stage. The positive feelings associated with this redefinition energize the person's efforts to confront racism and oppression in his or her daily life. Alliances with people of color can be more easily forged at this stage of development than previously because the person's antiracist behaviors and attitudes will be more consistently expressed. While Autonomy might be described as "racial self-actualization, . . . it is best to think of it as an ongoing process . . . wherein the person is continually open to new information and new ways of thinking about racial and cultural variables" (Helms, 1990, 66).

Annette, a White woman, described herself in the Autonomy stage, but talked at length about the circular process she felt she had been engaged in during the semester:

> If people as racist as C. P. Ellis (a former Klansman) can change, I think anyone can change. If that makes me idealistic, fine. I do not think my expecting society to change is naive anymore because I now *know* exactly what I want. To be naive means a lack of knowledge that allows me to accept myself both as a White person and as an idealist. This class showed me that these two are not mutually exclusive but are an integral part of me that I cannot deny. I realize now that through most of this class I was trying to deny both of them.
>
> While I was not accepting society's racism, I was accepting society's telling me as a white person, there was nothing I could do to change racism. So, I told myself I was being naive and tried to suppress my desire to change society. This is what made me so frustrated—while I saw society's racism through examples in the readings and the media, I kept telling myself there was nothing I could do. Listening to my tape, I think I was already in the Autonomy stage when I started this class. I then seemed to decide that being White, I also had to be racist which is when I became frustrated and went back to the Disintegration stage. I was frustrated because I was not only telling myself there was nothing I could do but I also was assuming society's racism was my own which made me feel like I did not want to be White. Actually, it was not being white that I was disavowing but being racist. I think I have now returned to the Autonomy stage and am much more secure in my position there. I accept my whiteness now as just a part of me as is my idealism. I will no longer disavow these characteristics as I have realized I can be proud of both of them. In turn, I can now truly accept other people for their unique characteristics and not by the labels society has given them as I can accept myself that way.
>
> While I thought the main ideas that I learned in this class were that white people need to be educated to end racism and everyone should be treated as human beings, I really had already incorporated these ideas into my thoughts. What I learned from this class is being White does not mean being racist and being idealistic does not mean being naive. I really did not have to form new ideas about people of color; I had to form them about myself—and I did.

IMPLICATION FOR CLASSROOM TEACHING

Although movement through all the stages of racial identity development will not necessarily occur for each student within the course of a semester (or even four years of college), it is certainly common to witness beginning transformations in classes with race-related content. An awareness of the existence of this process has helped me to implement strategies to facilitate positive student development, as well as to improve interracial dialogue within the classroom.

Four strategies for reducing student resistance and promoting student development that I have found useful are the following:

1. the creation of a safe classroom atmosphere by establishing clear guidelines for discussion;
2. the creation of opportunities for self-generated knowledge;
3. the provision of an appropriate developmental model that students can use as a framework for understanding their own process;
4. the exploration of strategies to empower students as change agents.

CREATING A SAFE CLIMATE

As was discussed earlier, making the classroom a safe space for discussion is essential for overcoming students' fears about breaking the race taboo, and will also reduce later anxieties about exposing one's own internalized racism. Establishing the guidelines of confidentiality, mutual respect, "no zaps," and speaking from one's own experience on the first day of class is a necessary step in the process.

Students respond very positively to these ground rules, and do try to honor them. While the rules do not totally eliminate anxiety, they clearly communicate to students that there is a safety net for the discussion. Students are also encouraged to direct their comments and questions to each other rather than always focusing their attention on me as the instructor, and to learn each other's names rather than referring to each other as "he," "she," or "the person in the red sweater" when responding to each other.[6]

THE POWER OF SELF-GENERATED KNOWLEDGE

The creation of opportunities for self-generated knowledge on the part of students is a powerful tool for reducing the initial stage of denial that many students experience. While it may seem easy for some students to challenge the validity of what they read or what the instructor says, it is harder to deny what they have seen with their own eyes. Students can be given hands-on assignments outside of class to facilitate this process.

For example, after reading *Portraits of White Racism* (Wellman, 1977), some students expressed the belief that the attitudes expressed by the white interviewees in the book were no longer commonly held attitudes. Students were then asked to use the same interview protocol used in the book (with some revision) to interview a white adult of their choice. When students reported on these interviews in class, their own observation of the similarity between those they had interviewed and those they had read about was more convincing than anything I might have said.

After doing her interview, Patty, a usually quiet white student, wrote:

I think I learned a lot from it and that I'm finally getting a better grip on the idea of racism. I think that was why I participated so much in class. I really felt like I knew what I was talking about.

Other examples of creating opportunities for self-generated knowledge include assigning students the task of visiting grocery stores in neighborhoods of differing racial composition to compare the cost and quality of goods and services available at the two locations, and to observe the interactions between the shoppers and the store personnel. For White students, one of the most powerful assignments of this type has been to go apartment hunting with an African-American student and to experience housing discrimination firsthand. While one concern with such an assignment is the effect it will have on the student(s) of color involved, I have found that those Black students who choose this assignment rather than another are typically eager to have their white classmates experience the reality of racism, and thus participate quite willingly in the process.

NAMING THE PROBLEM

The emotional responses that students have to talking and learning about racism are quite predictable and related to their own racial identity development. Unfortunately, students typically do not know this; thus they consider their own guilt, shame, embarrassment, or anger an uncomfortable experience that they alone are having. Informing students at the beginning of the semester that these feelings may be part of the learning process is ethically necessary (in the sense of informed consent) and helps to normalize the students' experience. Knowing in advance that a desire to withdraw from classroom discussion or not to complete assignments is a common response helps students to remain engaged when they reach that point. As Alice, a white woman, wrote at the end of the semester:

> You were so right in saying in the beginning how we would grow tired of racism (I did in October) but then it would get so good! I have *loved* the class once I passed that point.

In addition, sharing the model of racial identity development with students gives them a useful framework for understanding each other's processes as well as their own. This cognitive framework does not necessarily prevent the collision of developmental processes previously described, but it does allow students to be less frightened by it when it occurs. If, for example, white students understand the stages of racial identity development for students of color, they are less likely to personalize or feel threatened by an African-American student's anger.

Connie, a white student who initially expressed a lot of resentment at the way students of color tended to congregate in the college cafeteria, was much more understanding of this behavior after she learned about racial identity development theory. She wrote:

> I learned a lot from reading the article about the stages of development in the model of oppressed people. As a White person going through my stages of identity development, I do not take time to think about the struggle people of color go through to reach a stage of complete understanding. I am glad that I know about the stages because now I can understand people of color's behavior in certain situations. For example, when people of color stay to themselves and appear to be in a clique, it is not because they are being rude as I originally thought. Rather they are engaged perhaps in the Immersion stage.

Mary, another white student, wrote:

I found the entire Cross model of racial identity development very enlightening. I knew that there were stages of racial identity development before I entered this class. I did not know what they were, or what they really entailed. After reading through this article I found myself saying, "Oh. That explains why she reacted this way to this incident instead of how she would have a year ago." Clearly this person has entered a different stage and is working through different problems from a new viewpoint. Thankfully, the model provides a degree of hope that people will not always be angry, and will not always be separatists, etc. Although I'm not really sure about that.

Conversely, when students of color understand the stages of White racial identity development, they can be more tolerant or appreciative of a white student's struggle with guilt, for example. After reading about the stages of white identity development, Sonia, a Latina previously quoted, wrote:

This article was the one that made me feel that my own prejudices were showing. I never knew that Whites went through an identity development of their own.

She later told me outside of class that she found it much easier to listen to some of the things White students said because she could understand their potentially offensive comments as part of a developmental stage.

Sharon, an African-American woman, also found that an understanding of the respective stages of racial identity development helped her to understand some of the interactions she had had with white students since coming to college. She wrote:

There is a lot of clash that occurs between Black and White people at college which is best explained by their respective stages of development. Unfortunately schools have not helped to alleviate these problems earlier in life.

In a course on the psychology of racism, it is easy to build in the provision of this information as part of the course content. For instructors teaching courses with race-related content in other fields, it may seem less natural to do so. However, the inclusion of articles on racial identity development and/or class discussion of these issues in conjunction with the other strategies that have been suggested can improve student receptivity to the course content in important ways, making it a very useful investment of class time. Because the stages describe kinds of behavior that many people have commonly observed in themselves, as well as in their own intraracial and interracial interactions, my experience has been that most students grasp the basic conceptual framework fairly easily, even if they do not have a background in psychology.

EMPOWERING STUDENTS AS CHANGE AGENTS

Heightening students' awareness of racism without also developing an awareness of the possibility of change is a prescription for despair. I consider it unethical to do one without the other. Exploring strategies to empower students as change agents is thus a necessary part of the process of talking about race and learning about racism. As was previously mentioned, students find it very helpful to read about and hear from individuals who have been effective change agents. Newspaper and magazine articles, as well as biographical or autobiographical essays or book excerpts, are often important sources for this information.

I also ask students to work in small groups to develop an action plan of their own for interrupting racism. While I do not consider it appropriate to require students to engage in antiracist activity (since I believe this should be a personal choice the student makes for him/herself), students are required to think about the possibility. Guidelines are provided (see Katz, 1978), and the plans that they develop over several weeks are presented at the end of the semester. Students are generally impressed with each other's good ideas, and, in fact, they often do go on to implement their projects.

Joanne, a white student who initially struggled with feelings of guilt, wrote:

> I thought that hearing others' ideas for action plans was interesting and informative. It really helps me realize (reminds me) the many choices and avenues there are once I decided to be an ally. Not only did I develop my own concrete way to be an ally, I have found many other ways that I, as a college student, can be an active anti-racist. It was really empowering.

Another way all students can be empowered is by offering them the opportunity to consciously observe their own development. The taped exercise to which some of the previously quoted students have referred is an example of one way to provide this opportunity. At the beginning of the semester, students are given an interview guide with many open-ended questions concerning racial attitudes and opinions. They are asked to interview themselves on tape as a way of recording their own ideas for future reference. Though the tapes are collected, students are assured that no one (including me) will listen to them. The tapes are returned near the end of the semester, and students are asked to listen to their own tapes and use their understanding of racial identity development to discuss it in essay form.

The resulting essays are often remarkable and underscore the psychological importance of giving students the chance to examine racial issues in the classroom. The following was written by Elaine, a white woman:

> Another common theme that was apparent in the tape was that, for the most part, I was aware of my own ignorance and was embarrassed because of it. I wanted to know more about the oppression of people in the country so that I could do something about it. Since I have been here, I have begun to be actively resistant to racism. I have been able to confront my grandparents and some old friends from high school when they make racist comments. Taking this psychology of racism class is another step toward active resistance to racism. I am trying to educate myself so that I have a knowledge base to work from.
>
> When the tape was made, I was just beginning to be active and just beginning to be educated. I think I am now starting to move into the redefinition stage. I am starting to feel ok about being White. Some of my guilt is dissipating, and I do not feel as ignorant as I used to be. I think I have an understanding of racism; how it effects [*sic*] myself, and how it effects this country. Because of this I think I can be more active in doing something about it.

In the words of Louise, a Black female student:

> One of the greatest things I learned from this semester in general is that the world is not only Black and White, nor is the United States. I learned a lot about my own erasure of many Amer-

ican ethnic groups. . . . I am in the (immersion) stage of my identity development. I think I am also dangling a little in the (encounter) stage. I say this because a lot of my energies are still directed toward White people. I began writing a poem two days ago and it was directed to White racism. However, I have also become more Black-identified. I am reaching to the strength in Afro-American heritage. I am learning more about the heritage and history of Afro-American culture. Knowledge = strength and strength = power.

While some students are clearly more self-reflective and articulate about their own process than others, most students experience the opportunity to talk and learn about these issues as a transforming process. In my experience, even those students who are frustrated by aspects of the course find themselves changed by it. One such student wrote in her final journal entry:

What I felt to be a major hindrance to me was the amount of people. Despite the philosophy, I really never felt at ease enough to speak openly about the feelings I have and kind of watched the class pull farther and farther apart as the semester went on. . . . I think that it was your attitude that kept me intrigued by the topics we were studying despite my frustrations with the class time. I really feel as though I made some significant moves in my understanding of other people's positions in our world as well as of my feelings of racism, and I feel very good about them. I feel like this class has moved me in the right direction. I'm on a roll I think, because I've been introduced to so much.

Facilitating student development in this way is a challenging and complex task, but the results are clearly worth the effort.

IMPLICATIONS FOR THE INSTITUTION

What are the institutional implications for an understanding of racial identity development theory beyond the classroom? How can this framework be used to address the pressing issues of increasing diversity and decreasing racial tensions on college campuses? How can providing opportunities in the curriculum to talk about race and learn about racism affect the recruitment and retention of students of color specifically, especially when the majority of the students enrolled are White?

The fact is, educating white students about race and racism changes attitudes in ways that go beyond the classroom boundaries. As white students move through their own stages of identity development, they take their friends with them by engaging them in dialogue. They share the articles they have read with roommates, and involve them in their projects. An example of this involvement can be seen in the following journal entry, written by Larry, a white man:

Here it is our fifth week of class and more and more I am becoming aware of the racism around me. Our second project made things clearer, because while watching T.V. I picked up many kinds of discrimination and stereotyping. Since the project was over, I still find myself watching these shows and picking up bits and pieces every show I watch. Even my friends will be watching a show and they will say, "Hey, Larry, put that in your paper." Since they know I am taking this class, they are looking out for these things. They are also watching what they say around me for fear that I will use them as an example. For example, one of my friends has this fascination with making fun of Jewish people. Before I would listen to his comments and take them in stride, but now I confront him about his comments.

The heightened awareness of the white students enrolled in the class has a ripple effect in their peer group, which helps to create a climate in which students of color and other targeted groups (Jewish students, for example) might feel more comfortable. It is likely that White students who have had the opportunity to learn about racism in a supportive atmosphere will be better able to be allies to students of color in extracurricular settings, like student government meetings and other organizational settings, where students of color often feel isolated and unheard.

At the same time, students of color who have had the opportunity to examine the ways in which racism may have affected their own lives are able to give voice to their own experience and to validate it rather than be demoralized by it. An understanding of internalized oppression can help students of color recognize the ways in which they may have unknowingly participated in their own victimization, or the victimization of others. They may be able to move beyond victimization to empowerment, and share their learning with others, as Sharon, a previously quoted Black woman, planned to do.

Campus communities with an understanding of racial identity development could become more supportive of special-interest groups, such as the Black Student Union or the Asian Student Alliance, because they would recognize them not as "separatist" but as important outlets for students of color who may be at the Encounter or Immersion stage of racial identity development. Not only could speakers of color be sought out to add diversity to campus programming, but whites who had made a commitment to unlearning their own racism could be offered as models to those White students looking for new ways to understand their own whiteness, and to students of color looking for allies.

It has become painfully clear on many college campuses across the United States that we cannot have successfully multiracial campuses without talking about race and learning about racism. Providing a forum where this discussion can take place safely over a semester, a time period that allows personal and group development to unfold in ways that daylong or weekend programs do not, may be among the most proactive learning opportunities an institution can provide.

NOTES

1. A similar point could be made about other issues of oppression, such as anti-Semitism, homophobia and heterosexism, ageism, and so on.

2. While similar models of racial identity development exist, Cross and Helms are referenced here because they are among the most frequently cited writers on Black racial identity development and on white racial identity development, respectively. For a discussion of the commonalities between these and other identity development models, see Phinney (1989, 1990) and Helms (1990).

3. Both Parham (1989) and Phinney (1989) suggest that a preference for the dominant group is not always a characteristic of this stage. For example, children raised in households and communities

with explicitly positive Afrocentric attitudes may absorb a pro-Black perspective, which then serves as the starting point for their own exploration of racial identity.

4. After being introduced to this model and Helms's model of white identity development, students are encouraged to think about how the models might apply to their own experience or the experiences of people they know. As is reflected in the cited journal entries, some students resonate to the theories quite readily, easily seeing their own process of growth reflected in them. Other students are sometimes puzzled because they feel as though their own process varies from these models, and may ask if it is possible to "skip" a particular stage, for example. Such

questions provide a useful departure point for discussing the limitations of stage theories in general, and the potential variations in experience that make questions of racial identity development so complex.

5. Examples of useful articles include essays by McIntosh (1988), Lester (1987), and Braden (1987). Each of these combines autobiographical material with a conceptual framework for understanding some aspect of racism that students find very help-ful. Bowser & Hunt's (1981) edited book, *Impacts of Racism on Whites*, though less autobiographical in nature, is also a valuable resource.

6. Class size has a direct bearing on my ability to create safety in the classroom. Dividing the class into pairs or small groups of five or six students to discuss initial reactions to a particular article or film helps to increase participation, both in the small groups and later in the large group discussions.

REFERENCES

Barnard, H. F. (Ed.). (1987). *Outside the magic circle: The autobiography of Virginia Foster Durr.* New York: Simon & Schuster. (Originally published in 1985 by University of Alabama Press.)

Bowser, B. P., & Hunt, R. G. (1981). *Impacts of racism on whites.* Beverly Hills, Calif.: Sage.

Braden, A. (1987, April–May). Undoing racism: Lessons for the peace movement. *The Nonviolent Activist,* 3–6.

Bronstein, P. A., & Quina, K. (Eds.). (1988). *Teaching a psychology of people: Resources for gender and sociocultural awareness.* Washington, D.C.: American Psychological Association.

Cross, W. E., Jr. (1971). The Negro to black conversion experience: Toward a psychology of black liberation. *Black World, 20*(9), 13–27.

———. (1978). The Cross and Thomas models of psychological nigrescence. *Journal of Black Psychology, 5*(1), 13–19.

———. (1991). *Shades of black: Diversity in African-American identity.* Philadelphia: Temple University Press.

Cross, W. E., Jr., Parham, T. A., & Helms, J. E. (1991). The stages of black identity development: Nigrescence models. In R. Jones (Ed.), *Black psychology* (3rd ed., pp. 319–338). San Francisco: Cobb and Henry.

Derman-Sparks, L., Higa, C. T., & Sparks, B. (1980). Children, race and racism: How race awareness develops. *Interracial Books for Children Bulletin, 11*(3/4), 3–15.

Helms, J. E. (Ed.). (1990). *Black and white racial identity: Theory, research and practice.* Westport, Conn.: Greenwood Press.

Highlen, P. S., Reynolds, A. L., Adams, E. M., Hanley, T. C., Myers, L. J., Cox, C., & Speight, S. (1988, August 13). *Self-identity development model of oppressed people: Inclusive model for all?* Paper presented at the American Psychological Association Convention, Atlanta, Ga.

Hull, G. T., Scott, P. B., & Smith, B. (Eds.). (1982). *All the women are white, all the blacks are men, but some of us are brave: Black women's studies.* New York: Feminist Press at the City University of New York.

Katz, J. H. (1978). *White awareness: Handbook for anti-racism training.* Norman: University of Oklahoma Press.

Lester, J. (1987). "What happens to the mythmakers when the myths are found to be untrue?" Unpublished paper, Equity Institute, Emeryville, Calif.

McIntosh, P. (1988). *White privilege and male privilege: A personal account of coming to see correspondences through work in women's studies.* Working paper, Wellesley College Center for Research on Women, Wellesley, Mass.

———. (1989, July/August). White privilege: Unpacking the invisible knapsack. *Peace and Freedom,* 10–12.

Parham, T. A. (1989). Cycles of psychological nigrescence. *The Counseling Psychologist, 17*(2), 187–226.

Phinney, J. (1989). Stages of ethnic identity in minority group adolescents. *Journal of Early Adolescence, 9,* 34–39.

———. (1990). Ethnic identity in adolescents and adults: Review of research. *Psychological Bulletin, 108*(3), 499–514.

Phinney, J. S., & Rotheram, M. J. (Eds.). (1987). *Children's ethnic socialization: Pluralism and development.* Newbury Park, Calif.: Sage.

Schuster, M. R., & Van Dyne, S. R. (Eds.). (1985). *Women's place in the academy: Transforming the liberal arts curriculum.* Totowa, N.J.: Rowman & Littlefield.

Wellman, D. (1977). *Portraits of white racism.* New York: Cambridge University Press.

29

SLAVE IDEOLOGY AND BIBLICAL INTERPRETATION

Katie Geneva Cannon

SCHOLARS OF STATURE within mainline Christian denominations have produced immense literature on the Bible and slavery with very little unanimity. Some have written about the various types of antislavery arguments found in the Old and New Testaments. Others have engaged in rigorous historico-critical exegesis of selected Scriptures used to condone slavery. What is interesting in the analyses by liberationists is the direct correlation between apologetic selectivity and the exegetes' political-social commitments. Thus, my particular concern as a liberation ethicist is to unmask the hermeneutical distortions of white Christians, North and South, who lived quite comfortably with the institution of chattel slavery for the better part of 150 years. Slaveholders knew that in order to keep racial slavery viable, they needed—in addition to legal, economic, and political mechanisms—religious legitimation within the White society.

Apostles of slavery kept their eyes on the economic benefits and power relations at all times. Beneath their rhetoric and logic, the question of using the Bible to justify the subordination of Black people was fraught with their desire to maintain their dominance, to guarantee their continued social control. If the powerbrokers of the antebellum society were to continue benefitting from the privileges and opportunities the political economy provided, then the slaveholding aristocrats must, as a basic precondition, maintain their domination over the ideological sectors of society: religion, culture, education, and media.[1] The control of material, physical production required the control of the means of mental, symbolic production as well.

The practice of slaveholding was, therefore, largely unquestioned. The majority of white Christians engaged in a passive acceptance of the givenness of the main feature of slavocracy. Any questioning of the system or identification of contradictions to social practices within Christianity was undermined by the substratum of values and perceptions justified theologically by biblical hermeneutics determined from above. The rank and file of white church membership accepted the prevailing racist ideology, identifying with the slaveholders and copying their rationales, rituals, and values. They regarded slave ideology and Christian life as inseparable; they were integral parts of the same system. The defense of one appeared to require the defense of the other.

Admittedly, there were a few antislavery women and men in the mainline churches prior to the aggressive abolitionist movement of the 1830s, but as a whole the white church evaded responsibility and surrendered its prerogatives to slavocracy. For most of the years that chattel slavery existed, the mainline Protestant churches never legislated against slavery, seldom disciplined slaveholders, and at most gently apologized for the "peculiar institution."

Drawing principally upon socioethical sources of the late eighteenth and early nineteenth centuries, I investigate three intellectual, hierarchical constructs that lie at the center of the Christian antebellum society. (1) At what point and under what conditions did Americans of African descent lose their status as members of the moral universe? (2) What are the ethical grounds that make the formula for "heathen conversion" intrinsically wrong? and (3) What are the hermeneutical distortions that shaped the slavocracy's polemical patterns of biblical propaganda?

THE MYTHOLOGY OF BLACK INFERIORITY

The first ideological myth legitimizing the hermeneutical assumption of Christian slave apologists was the charge that Black people were not members of the human race. Most church governing boards, denominational missionary societies, local churches, and clergy held the position that human beings by nature were free and endowed with natural rights. Their basic concept of human relationships was equality of all people in the sight of God. No one was superior to another, none inferior. Black people had not forfeited their freedom nor relinquished their rights. This espoused oneness of humanity clashed directly with the perception that Black people must necessarily be possessed of low nature.[2]

To justify their enslavement, Black people had to be completely stripped of every privilege of humanity.[3] Their dignity and value as human beings born with natural rights had to be denied. Black Americans were divested so far as possible of all intellectual, cultural, and moral attributes. They had no socially recognized personhood. The institution of chattel slavery and its corollary, White supremacy and racial bigotry, excluded Black people from every normal human consideration. The humanity of Black people had to be denied, or the evil of the slave system would be evident.

In other words, hereditary slavery was irreconcilable with doctrines of inalienable rights.[4] So as not to contradict their avowed principles, legislatures enacted laws designating Black people as property and as less than human.[5] Black people were assigned a fixed place as an inferior species of humanity. The intellectual legacy of slavocracy was the development of certain white preconceptions about the irredeemable nature of Black women and Black men as "beings of an inferior order," a subpar species between animal and human. One of the many characterizations proposed was that Black people were irremediably different from Whites, as much as swine from dogs, "they are Baboons on two legs gifted with speech."[6]

Central to the whole hermeneutical approach was a rationalized biblical doctrine positing the innate and permanent inferiority of Blacks in the metonymical curse of Ham.[7] The Ham story in Genesis 9:25–27 was not only used to legitimize slavery in general, but it was also used by proslavery, pro-white supremacists to justify the enslavement of Blacks in particular. Ham became widely identified as the progenitor of the Black race, and the story of the curse that Noah pronounced against Canaan, the son of his son Ham, was symbolically linked to the institution of racial slavery. In a book entitled *Bible Defense of Slavery* Josiah

Priest took the position that the enslaving of Black people by the White race was a judicial act of God.

> The servitude of the race to Ham, to the latest era of mankind, is necessary to the veracity of God Himself, as by it is fulfilled one of the oldest of the decrees of the Scriptures, namely that of Noah, which placed the race as servants under other races.[8]

Christians caught in the obsessive duality of understanding Black people as property rather than as persons concurred with both faulty exegesis and social pressure that depicted people with black skin as demonic, unholy, infectious progenitors of sin, full of animality and matriarchal proclivities.

During the early part of the eighteenth century, state laws adopted the principle of *partus sequitur ventrem*—the child follows the condition of the mother regardless of the race of the father. Absolving all paternal responsibilities, this principle institutionalized and sanctioned sexual prerogatives of "stock breeding" with Black men and the rape of Black women by White men. What this means is that the Black woman's life was estimated in terms of money, property, and capital assets. She was a commodity to be bought and sold, traded for money, land, or other objects. Her monetary value was precisely calculated by her capacity to produce goods and services, combined with her capacity to reproduce "a herd of subhuman labor units."[9] Hence, the Black woman as the carrier of the hereditary legal status extended the status of slave to her children and her children's children, supposedly to the end of time. An entire race was condemned by the laws of a purportedly Christian people to perpetual, hereditary, unrequited servitude.[10]

The white antebellum church did not see the gross injustice of slavery. Outspoken supporters of slavery generally admitted that enslaved Blacks were mere property, a type of domesticated animal to serve as the white man's tool like any other beast of burden.[11] And as slaveholders, white Christian citizens must have the security that neither their property nor their privilege to own people as property would be taken from them. The church made every effort by admonition and legislation to see that the authority of slaveholders was not compromised. For them, the great truth written in law and God's decree was that subordination was the normal condition of African people and their descendants.[12]

Ideas and practices that favored equal rights of all people were classified as invalid and sinful because they conflicted with the divinely ordained structure that posited inequality between Whites and Blacks. The doctrine of biblical infallibility reinforced and was reinforced by the need for social legitimization of slavery. Thus, racial slavery was accepted as the necessary fulfillment of the curse of Ham. This had the effect of placing the truthfulness of God's self-revelation on the same level as Black slavery and White supremacy.[13] The institutional framework that required Black men, women, and children to be treated as chattel, as possessions rather than as human beings, was understood as being consistent with the spirit, genius, and precepts of the Christian faith.

THE MYTHOLOGIZING OF ENSLAVEMENT

The second ideological process that legitimated Christian slave apology was a reconstruction of history and divine action in it. It was claimed that God sent slavers to the wilds of Africa, a so-called depraved, savage, heathen world, in order to free Africans of ignorance, superstition, and corruption.[14] It is of more than passing significance that the proslavery writing portrayed Africa as the scene of unmitigated cannibalism, fetish worship, and licentiousness. Using gross caricatures, slave apologists mounted an ideological offensive in justification of the ravishing of the entire continent of Africa.[15] They argued that Africans by nature were framed and designed for subjection and obedience. Their preoccupation was that people designated by nature as "bestial savages" and "heathens" were destined by providence for slavery.[16]

Embracing false dogma of inherent African inferiority, beneficiaries of white supremacy described African character as the most depraved humanity imaginable. Africans were depicted as the epitome of heathenism, "wild, naked . . . man-eating savages," and "the great ethnological clown." White Christians had to be enabled to consider it an unspeakable privilege for Africans to be brought to the Americas as slaves.[17] Repeatedly, they claimed that slavery saved poor, degraded, and wretched African peoples from spiritual darkness.

North American Christians credited themselves with weaning Africans of savage barbarity.[18] Their joy in converting Africans was that they were giving to "heathens" elements of Christian civilization. Being enslaved in a Christian country was considered advantageous to Africans' physical, intellectual, and moral development. Slavery exposed Africans to Christianity, which made them better servants of God and better servants of men.

The popularity of "heathen conversion" was disclosed in the public reception of George Fitzhugh's *Cannibals All! or, Slaves without Masters*, who asserted Africans, like wild horses, had to be "caught, tamed and civilized."[19] Resting upon irrational antipathies, white Christians—prominent and common-bred alike—clearly distinguished their personhood from that of Africans. Many were convinced that African peoples were somehow irreparably inferior to and less worthy than Europeans. Fixated on the fetish of heathenism, they believed that the color of white skin proved sufficient justification to rob Africans by force and fraud of their liberty. The proper social hierarchy upon which the slave system rested—the putative inferiority of Africans and the alleged superiority of Europeans—had to remain safely intact.[20] The historian Winthrop Jordan declares:

> Heathenism was treated not so much as a specifically religious defect, but as one manifestation of a general refusal to measure up to proper standards, as a failure to be English or even civilized. . . . Being Christian was not merely a matter of subscribing to certain doctrines; it was a quality inherent in oneself and one's society. It was interconnected with all other attributes of normal and proper men.[21]

Entirely under the power of whites, against whom they dared not complain and whom they dared not resist, enslaved Africans were denied the right to possess property and deprived of the means of instruction and of every personal, social, civil, political, and religious mode of agency. If they asserted their personhood in defiance of oppressive authority, slaveholders punished them severely. Never before U.S. chattel slavery was a people so systematically deprived of their human rights and submerged in abject misery.[22]

The prevailing sentiment of American Christians—Presbyterians, Congregationalists, Roman Catholics, Quakers, Lutherans, Baptists, Methodists, and Anglicans—was that African peoples deserved imperial domination and needed social control.[23] Many churches preached a gospel that declared that Black people were indebted to white Christians and bound to spend their lives in the service of whites; any provisions for food, clothes, shelter, medicine, or any other means of preservation were perceived not as legal requirement but as an act of Christian charity. This "Christian feature" of Anglo-American enslavement was interpreted as an incalculable blessing to African peoples. Africans and their descendants were much better off bound in slavery with their souls free than vice versa.

These and similar judgments bolstered the belief that Anglo-Saxons, Spaniards, Danes, Portuguese, and Dutch had a divine right to defend themselves against the intolerable suffering and absolute despotism that they imposed so heavily on others. As long as the image of Africans as "heathens" was irrevocable, then the church's attempt to Christianize via enslavement could continue indefinitely, the exploitation of Africa's natural resources could proceed without hindrance, and white Christians could persist in enjoying a position of moral superiority. Ruthlessly exploiting African people was justifiable Christian action.

REMYTHOLOGIZING DIVINE WILL

The third ideological myth needed to legitimize the hermeneutical circle of Christian slave apologists was the understanding that the law of God and the law of the land gave them an extraordinary right to deprive Black people of liberty and to offer Blacks for sale in the market like any other articles of merchandise. For almost two centuries, slave apologists maintained that slavery was constantly spoken of in the Bible without any direct prohibition of it, no special law against it. And therefore, on the basis of the absence of condemnation, slavery could not be classified as sin. The presumptive evidence for many white Christians was that the absence of slaveholding from the catalogue of sins and disciplinary offenses in the Bible meant that slavery was not in violation of God's law.

Biblical scholars, along with distinguished scientists, lawyers, and politicians, produced a large quantity of exegetical data denying the arbitrariness of divinely ordained slavery.[24] The foundation of the scriptural case for slavery focused on an argument that neither Jesus of Nazareth, the apostles, nor the early church objected to the ownership of slaves. The fact that slavery was one of the cornerstones of the economic system of the Greco-Roman world was stressed and the conclusion reached that for the early church the only slavery that mattered was spiritual slavery to sin, to which all were bound. Physical slavery was spiritually meaningless under the all-embracing spiritualized hope of salvation. This line of reasoning was of central importance in reconciling the masses of white Christians to the existing social order. Instead of recognizing that slavery was ameliorated by early Christianity, slave apologists used their interpretative principle to characterize slavery as a sacred institution.[25]

To elicit white Christians' consent and approval of racial chattel slavery, which theologically contradicted a liberation reading of the Christian gospel, some of the leading antebellum churchmen—Robert Lewis Dabney, a Presbyterian theologian, Augustine Verot, the Catholic bishop of Georgia and East Florida, and John Leadley Dagg, Baptist layman who served as president of Mercer University—presented slavery as conforming to the divine principles revealed in the Bible. White clergy were trained to use the Bible to give credence to the legitimacy of racial chattelhood.[26] In other words, they adopted an implacable line of reasoning that made slavery an accepted fact of everyday life, not only in the entire Near East but also within normative biblical ethical teaching. Needless to say, the New Testament instruction that slaves should be obedient to their masters was interpreted as unqualified support for the modern institution of chattel slavery. The slave system was simply a part of the cosmos.[27]

Slave apologists such as George Fitzhugh, Thomas R. Dew, and William A. Smith used a hermeneutical principle that functioned to conceal and misrepresent the real conflicts of slave ideology and Christian life. Smith, the president of Randolph Macon College in Virginia, was quite candid:

> Slavery, *per se*, is right. . . . The great abstract principle of slavery is right, because it is a fundamental principle of the social state: and domestic slavery, as an *institution*, is fully justified by the condition and circumstances (essential and relative) of the African race in this country, and therefore equally right.[28]

Fitzhugh, a well-known essayist, and Dew, a prominent lawyer, concluded that since slavery was part of a natural order and hence in accord with the will of God, it could not be morally wrong.

Christian commentators, working largely to the advantage of wealthy aristocrats, used biblical and philosophical arguments to present slaveholders' interests and claims in the best possible light.[29] For example, scholars such as How, Ross, and Priest constructed "biblical facts" that permitted them to claim that the eradication of chattel slavery was inapplicable to Christian living. By using selective appeals to customary practices, they disseminated moral teachings to reinforce what counted as good Christian conduct. Clergy were condemned for preaching against slavery because abolition sermons were considered to be a part of a traitorous and diabolical scheme that would eventually lead to the denial of biblical authority, the unfolding of rationalism, deistic philanthropism, pantheism, atheism, socialism, or Jacobinism. Members of churches were warned against subscribing to antislavery books, pamphlets, and newspapers. The church condoned mob violence against anyone with abolitionist tendencies, which in turn, reassured that the existing social order would go unchallenged.

Having no desire to divorce themselves from the institution of slavery, church governing boards and agencies issued denominational pronouncements on behalf of the official platitudes of slave ideology. Denominational assemblies reinforced publicly their compliance with the assumed principle of human chattelhood. Black people were classified as moveable property, devoid of the minimum human rights that society conferred on others.

The vast majority of white clergy and laity alike appropriated this ideology to convince themselves that the human beings whom they violated or whose well-being they did not protect were unworthy of anything better. White Christians seemed to have been imbued with the permissive view that the enslavement of Black people was not too great a price to pay for a stable, viable labor system.[30] In a political economy built on labor-intensive agriculture, slave labor seemed wholly "natural." The security and prosperity of slavocracy evidently enabled white Christians, slaveholders and nonslaveholders alike, to feel secure with the fruits of the system.

Through a close analysis of slave ideology and biblical interpretation we can discern the many ways that chattel slavery maintained itself even after it was no longer the most economically profitable method of utilizing natural and technological resources. The majority of white Christians had learned well not to accept the equal coexistence of Whites and Blacks in the same society.[31] They believed that giving Black people civil parity with the white population would threaten the ease and luxury of White happiness, and perhaps dissolve the Union. For the sake of the public welfare, people with ancestors born in Europe, and not in Africa, needed to be relieved of degrading menial labor so that they could be free to pursue the highest cultural attainment. Slavery, sanctioned not just by civil law but by natural law as well, was considered the best foundation for a strong economy and for a superior society.

CONCLUDING ETHICAL REFLECTIONS

I have sketched three mythologizing processes that served as the foundational underpinnings for slave ideology in relation to white Christian life. I believe that it is important for us to trace the origin and expansion of these myths because the same general schemes of oppression and patterns of enslavement remain prevalent today and because the biblical hermeneutics of oppressive praxis is far from being dead among contemporary exegetes. As life-affirming moral agents we have a responsibility to study the ideological hegemony of the past so that we do not remain doomed to the recurring cyclical patterns of hermeneutical distortions in the present—i.e., violence against women, condemnation of homosexuality, spiritualizing Scripture to justify capitalism.

My analysis shows that slave apologists worked within an interpretative framework that represented the whole transcript of racial chattel slavery as ordained by God. They systematically blocked and refuted any discourse that presented contrary viewpoints. Using theoethical language, concepts, and categories White superordinates pressed their claims of the supposedly inherent inferiority of Black people by appealing to the normative ethical system expressed by the dominant slaveholders. The political and economic context incorporated a structure of discourse wherein the Bible was authoritatively interpreted to support the existing patterns of exploitation of Black people.

Antebellum Christians, abiding by the developing racial and cultural conceptions, resisted any threat to slavocracy or any challenge to the peace and permanency of the order of their own denomination. They conformed their ethics to the boundaries of slave management. It became their Christian duty to rule over African people who had been stricken from the human race and reclassified as a subhuman species.

Not surprisingly, denominations sprang officially to the defense of slave trading, slaveholding, and the Christianization of Africans with ingenious economic arguments. Wealthy slaveholders transmuted a portion of their disproportionate economic profit into modes of social control by public gestures that passed as generous voluntary acts of charity. They used revenue from slave labor to pay pastors, maintain church properties, support seminaries, and sustain overseas missionaries. Seduced by privilege and profit, white Christians of all economic strata were made, in effect, coconspirators in the victimization of Black people. In other words, slave apologists were successful in convincing at least five generations of white citizens that slavery, an essential and constitutionally protected institution, was consistent with the impulse of Christian charity.

NOTES

1. Antonio Gramsci, *Selections from the Prison Notebooks*, ed. and trans. Quinten Hoare and Geoffrey Norwell Smith (London: Lawrence & Wishart, 1971), 5–23; Cornel West, *Prophesy Deliverance! An Afro-American Revolutionary Christianity* (Philadelphia: Westminster, 1982), 9–127.

2. Winthrop D. Jordan, *White over Black: American Attitudes toward the Negro, 1550–1812* (Baltimore: Penguin Books, 1969), 3–98; Thomas F. Gossett, *Race: The History of an Idea in America* (Dallas: Southern Methodist University Press, 1963), 3–31.

3. H. Shelton Smith, *In His Image, But . . . : Racism in Southern Religion, 1780–1910* (Durham, N.C.: Duke University Press, 1972), 23–207.

4. E. S. Morgan, "Slavery and Freedom: The American Paradox," *Journal of American History* 59 (1972): 5–29; Carl N. Degler, "Slavery and the Genesis of American Race Prejudice," *Comparative Studies in Society and History* 2 (1959): 49–66.

5. Angela Y. Davis, *Women, Race and Class* (New York: Random House, 1981), 391–421.

6. J. William Harris, *Plain Folk and Gentry in a Slave Society* (Middletown, Conn.: Wesleyan University Press, 1985), 67.

7. Joseph R. Washington, Jr., *Anti-Blackness in English Religion, 1500–1800* (New York: Edwin Mellen, 1984), 231–320.

8. Josiah Priest, *Bible Defense of Slavery* (Glasgow, Ky.: W. S. Brown, 1851), 393.

9. Davis, *Women, Race and Class*, 3–29.

10. Oliver C. Cox, *Caste, Class, and Race: A Study in Social Dynamics* (New York: Doubleday, 1984), 353–91; Jordan, *White over Black*, 321–25.

11. Frederick A. Ross, *Slavery Ordained of God* (Philadelphia: J. B. Lippincott, 1857), 11–68.

12. William Sumner Jenkins, *Pro-Slavery Thought in the Old South* (Chapel Hill: University of North Carolina Press, 1935), 90–92.

13. L. R. Bradley, "The Curse of Canaan and the American Negro (Gen. 9:25–27)," *Concordia Theological Monthly* 42 (1971): 100–105.

14. Frederick Perry Noble, *The Redemption of Africa* (Chicago: Fleming H. Revell, 1899).

15. Walter Rodney, *How Europe Underdeveloped Africa* (London: Bogie l'Ouverture, 1972), 730.

16. Lester B. Scherer, *Slavery and the Churches in Early America 1619–1819* (Grand Rapids, Mich.: Wm. B. Eerdmans, 1975), 29–81.

17. Davis, *Women, Race and Class*, 165–96.

18. Washington, *Anti-Blackness in English Religion*, 103–39.

19. George Fitzhugh, *Cannibals All! or, Slaves without Masters*, ed. C. Van Woodward (Cambridge: Belknap Press of Harvard University, 1857, 1960).

20. Washington, *Anti-Blackness in English Religion*, 1–35.

21. *White over Black*, 24.

22. Orlando Patterson, *Slavery and Social Death: A Comparative Study* (Cambridge: Harvard University Press, 1982), 1–14.

23. C. Eric Lincoln, *Race, Religion and the Continuing American Dilemma* (New York: Hill and Wang, 1984), 23–31.

24. Samuel Blanchard How, *Slaveholding Not Sinful, the Punishment of Man's Sin, Its Remedy, the Gospel of Jesus Christ* (New Brunswick, N.J.: J. Terhune's Press, 1856), 63–133.

25. Thomas Virgil Peterson, *Ham and Japheth: The Mythic World of Whites in the Antebellum South* (Metuchen, N.J.: Scarecrow Press, 1978), 91–121.

26. Ibid., 12–26, 38–84.

27. Adam Gurowski, *Slavery in History* (New York: A. B. Burdick, 1860), 165–71.

28. Quoted in William A. Smith, *Lectures on the Philosophy and Practice of Slavery, as Exhibited in the Institution of Domestic Slavery in the United States: With the Duties of Masters and Slaves* (Nashville: Stevenson & Evans, 1856), 25.

29. Peterson, *Ham and Japheth*, 17–34.

30. Alfred Conrad and John Meyer, "The Economics of Slavery in the Antebellum South," *Journal of Political Economy* 66 (1958): 95–130, 442–34; Harold Woodman, "The Profitability of Slavery: A Historical Perennial," *Journal of Southern History* 29 (1963): 303–25.

31. Iveson L. Brookes, *A Defense of the South against the Reproaches and Incroachments of the North: in Which Slavery Is Shown to Be an Institution of God Intended to Form the Basis of the Best Social State and the Only Safeguard to the Permanence of a Republican Government* (Hamburg, S.C.: Republican Office, 1850), 45.

30

BLACK THEOLOGY AND
THE BLACK WOMAN

Jacquelyn Grant

LIBERATION THEOLOGIES HAVE ARISEN out of the contexts of the liberation struggles of Black Americans, Latin Americans, American women, Black South Africans, and Asians. These theologies represent a departure from traditional Christian theology. As a collective critique, liberation theologies raise serious questions about the normative use of Scripture, tradition, and experience in Christian theology. Liberation theologians assert that the reigning theologies of the West have been used to legitimate the established order. Those to whom the church has entrusted the task of interpreting the meaning of God's activity in the world have been too content to represent the ruling classes. For this reason, say the liberation theologians, theology has generally not spoken to those who are oppressed by the political establishment.

Ironically, the criticism that liberation theology makes against classical theology has been turned against liberation theology itself. Just as most European and American theologians have acquiesced with the oppression of the West, for which they have been taken to task by liberation theologians, some liberation theologians have acquiesced in one or more oppressive aspects of the liberation struggle itself. Where racism is rejected, sexism has been embraced. Where classicism is called into question, racism and sexism have been tolerated. And where sexism is repudiated, racism and classicism are often ignored.

Although there is a certain validity to the argument that any one analysis—race, class, or sex—is not sufficiently universal to embrace the needs of all oppressed peoples, these particular analyses, nonetheless, have all been well presented and are crucial for a comprehensive and authentic liberation theology. In order for liberation theology to be faithful to itself, it must hear the critique coming to it from the perspective of the Black woman—perhaps the most oppressed of all the oppressed.

I am concerned in this chapter with how the experience of the Black woman calls into question certain assumptions in liberation theology in general and Black theology in particular. In the Latin American context this has already been done by women such as Beatriz Melano Couch and Consuelo Urquiza. A few Latin American theologians have begun to respond. Beatriz Couch, for example, accepts the starting point of Latin American theologians, but criticizes them for their exclusivism with respect to race and sex. She says:

we in Latin America stress the importance of the starting point, the praxis, and the use of so-cial science to analyze our political, historical situation. In this I am in full agreement with my male colleagues . . . with one qualitative difference. I stress the need to give importance to the different cultural forms that express oppression; to the ideology that divides people not only according to class, but to race and sex. Racism and sexism are oppressive ideologies which de-serve a specific treatment in the theology of liberation.[1]

More recently, Consuelo Urquiza called for the unification of Hispanic-American women in struggling against their oppression in the church and society. In commenting on the con-tradiction in the Pauline Epistles, which undergird the oppression of the Hispanic-American woman, Urquiza said: "At the present time all Christians will agree with Paul in the first part of [Galatians 3:28] about freedom and slavery that there should not be slaves. However, the next part of this verse . . . has been ignored and the equality between man and woman is not accepted. They would rather skip that line and go to the epistle to Timothy [2:9–15]."[2] Women theologians of Latin background are beginning to do theology and to sensitize other women to the necessity of participating in decisions that affect their lives and the life of their communities. Latin American theology will gain from these inputs that women are making to the theological process.

Third World and Black women[3] in the United States will soon collaborate in an attack on another aspect of liberation theology—feminist theology. Black and Third World women have begun to articulate their differences and similarities with the feminist movement, which is dominated by white American women who until now have been the chief authors of feminist theology. It is my contention that the theological perspectives of Black and Third World women should reflect these differences and similarities with feminist theology. It is my purpose, however, to look critically at Black theology as a Black woman in an effort to determine how adequate is its conception of liberation for the total Black community. Pauli Murray and Theressa Hoover have in their own ways challenged Black theology.

I want to begin with the question: "Where are Black women in Black theology?" They are, in fact, invisible in Black theology and we need to know why this is the case. Because the Black church experience and Black experience in general are important sources for doing Black theology, we need to look at Bhe Black woman in relation to both in order to understand the way Black theology has applied its conception of liberation. Finally, in view of the status of the Black woman vis-à-vis Black theology, the Black church and the Black experience, a challenge needs to be presented to Black theology. This is how I propose to discuss this important question.

THE INVISIBILITY OF BLACK WOMEN IN BLACK THEOLOGY

In examining Black theology it is necessary to make one of two assumptions: (1) either Black women have no place in the enterprise, or (2) Black men are capable of speaking for us. Both of these assumptions are false and need to be discarded. They arise out of a male-dominated culture that restricts women to certain areas of the society. In such a culture, men are given the warrant to speak for women on all matters of significance. It is no acci-dent that all of the recognized Black theologians are men. This is what might be expected given the status and power accorded the discipline of theology. Professional theology is done by those who are highly trained. It requires, moreover, mastery of that power most accepted in the definition of manhood, the power or ability to "reason." This is supposedly what opens the door to participation in logical, philosophical debates and discussions presupposing rigorous intellectual training, for most of history, outside the "women's sphere." Whereas the nature of men has been defined in terms of reason and the intellect, that of women has to do with intuition and emotionalism. Women were limited to matters related to the home while men carried out the more important work, involving use of the rational faculties.[4] These distinctions were not as clear in the slave community.[5] Slaves and women were thought to share the characteristics of emotionality and irrationality. As we move further away from the slave culture, however, a dualism between Black men and women increasingly emerges. This means that Black males have gradually increased their power and participation in the male-dominated society, while Black females have continued to endure the stereotypes and oppressions of an earlier period.

When sexual dualism has finally run its course in the Black community (and I believe that it has), it will not be difficult to see why Black women are invisible in Black theology. Just as white women formerly had no place in white theology, except as the receptors of white men's theological interpretations, Black women have had no place in the development of Black theology. By self-appointment, or by the sinecure of a male-dominated society, Black men have deemed it proper to speak for the entire Black community, male and female.

In a sense, Black men's acceptance of the patriarchal model is logical and to be expected. Black male slaves were unable to reap the benefits of patriarchy. Before emancipation they were not given the opportunity to serve as protector and provider for Black women and children, as white men were able to do for their women and children. Much of what was considered "manhood" had to do with how well one could perform these functions. It seems only natural that the postemancipation Black men would view as of primary importance the reclaiming of their property—their women and their children. Moreover, it is natural that Black men would claim their "natural" right to the "man's world." But it should be emphasized that this is logical and natural only if one has accepted without question the terms and values of patriarchy: the concept of male control and supremacy.

Black men must ask themselves a difficult question. How can a white society characterized by Black enslavement, colonialism, and imperialism provide the normative conception of women for Black society? How can the sphere of the woman, as defined by white men, be free from the evils and oppressions that are found in the white society? The important point is that in matters relative to the relationship between the sexes, Black men have accepted without question the patriarchal structures of the white society as normative for the Black community. How can a Black minister preach in a way that advocates St. Paul's dictum concerning women while ignoring or repudiating his dictum concerning slaves? Many Black women are enraged as they listen to "liberated" Black men speak about the "place of women" in words and phrases similar to those of the very white oppressors they condemn.

Black women have been invisible in theology because theological scholarship has not been a part of the woman's sphere. The first of the above two assumptions results, therefore, from the historical orientation of the dominant culture. The second follows from the first. If women have no place in theology, it becomes the natural prerogative of men to monopolize theological concerns, including those relating specifically to women. Inasmuch as Black men have accepted the sexual dualisms of the dominant culture they presume to speak for Black women.

Before final dismissal of the two assumptions, a pertinent question should be raised. Does the absence of Black women in the circles producing Black theology necessarily mean that the resultant theology cannot be in the best interest of Black women? The answer is obvious. Feminist theologians during the past few years have shown how theology done by men in male-dominated cultures has served to undergird patriarchal structures in society.[6] If Black men have accepted those structures, is there any reason to believe that the theology written by Black men would be any more liberating of Black women than white theology was for white women? It would seem that in view of the oppression that Black people have suffered, Black men would be particularly sensitive to the oppression of others.[7]

James Cone has stated that the task of Black theology "is to analyze the nature of the gospel of Jesus Christ in the light of oppressed black people so they will see the gospel as inseparable from their humiliated condition, bestowing on them the necessary power to break the chains of oppression. This means that it is a theology of and for the black community, seeking to interpret the religious dimensions of the forces of liberation in that community."[8] What are the forces of liberation in the Black community and the Black church? Are they to be exclusively defined by the struggle against racism? My answer to that question is No. There are oppressive realities in the Black community that are related to, but independent of, the fact of racism. Sexism is one such reality. Black men seek to liberate themselves from racial stereotypes and the conditions of oppression without giving due attention to the stereotypes and oppressions against women that parallel those against Blacks. Blacks fight to be free of the stereotype that all Blacks are dirty and ugly, or that Black represents evil and darkness.[9] The slogan "Black Is Beautiful" was a counterattack on these stereotypes. The parallel for women is the history of women as "unclean," especially during menstruation and after childbirth. Because the model of beauty in the white male-dominated society is the "long-haired blonde," with all that goes along with that mystique, Black women have an additional problem with the Western idea of "ugliness," particularly as they encounter Black men who have adopted this white model of beauty. Similarly, the Christian teaching that woman is responsible for the fall of *mankind* and is, therefore, the source of evil has had a detrimental effect on the experience of Black women.

Like that of all oppressed peoples the self-image of Blacks has suffered damage. In addition they have not been in control of their own destiny. It is the goal of the Black liberation struggle to change radically the socioeconomic and political conditions of Black people by inculcating self-love, self-control, self-reliance, and political power. The concepts of self-love, self-control, self-reliance, and political participation certainly have broad significance for Black women, even though they were taught that, by virtue of their sex, they had to be completely dependent on *man*; yet while their historical situation reflected the need for dependence, the powerlessness of Black men made it necessary for them to seek those values for themselves.

Racism and sexism are interrelated just as all forms of oppression are interrelated. Sexism, however, has a reality and significance of its own because it represents that peculiar form of oppression suffered by Black women at the hands of Black men. It is important to examine this reality of sexism as it operated in both the Black community and the Black church. We will consider first the Black church and second the Black community to determine to what extent Black theology has measured up to its defined task with respect to the liberation of Black women.[10]

THE BLACK CHURCH AND THE BLACK WOMAN

I can agree with Karl Barth as he describes the peculiar function of theology as the church's "subjecting herself to a self-test." "She [the church] faces herself with the question of truth, i.e., she measures her action, her language about God, against her existence as a Church."[11]

On the one hand, Black theology must continue to criticize classical theology and the white church. But on the other hand, Black theology must subject the Black church to a "self-test." The task of the church, according to James Cone, is threefold: (1) "It proclaims the reality of divine liberation. . . . It is not possible to receive the good news of freedom and also keep it to ourselves; it must be told to the whole world . . .."; (2) "It actively shares in the liberation struggle"; (3) It "is a visible manifestation that the gospel is a reality. . . . If it [the church] lives according to the old order (as it actually has), then no one will believe its message."[12] It is clear that Black theology must ask whether or not the Black church is faithful to this task. Moreover, the language of the Black church about God must be consistent with its action.[13] These requirements of the church's faithfulness in the struggle for liberation have not been met as far as the issue of women is concerned.

If the liberation of women is not proclaimed, the church's proclamation cannot be about divine liberation. If the church does not share in the liberation struggle of Black women, its liberation struggle is not authentic. If women are oppressed, the church cannot possibly be "a visible manifestation that the gospel is a reality"—for the gospel cannot be real in that context. One can see the contradictions between the church's language or proclamation of liberation and its action by looking both at the status of Black women in the church as laity and Black women in the ordained ministry of the church.

It is often said that women are the "backbone" of the church. On the surface this may appear to be a compliment, especially when one considers the function to the backbone in the human anatomy. Theressa Hoover prefers to use the term "glue" to describe the function of women in the Black church. In any case, the telling portion of the word backbone is the word "back." It has become apparent to me that most of the ministers who use this term have reference to location rather than function. What they really mean is that women are in the "background" and should be kept there. They are merely support workers. This is borne out by my observation that in many churches women are consistently given responsibilities in the kitchen, while men are elected or appointed to the important boards and leadership positions. While decisions and policies may be discussed in the kitchen they are certainly not made there. Recently I conducted a study in one conference of the African Methodist Episcopal Church that indicated that women are accorded greater participation on the decision-making boards of smaller rather than larger churches.[14] This political maneuver helps to keep women "in their place" in the denomination as well as in the local congregations. The conspiracy to keep women relegated to the background is also aided by the continuous psychological and political strategizing that keeps women from realizing their own potential power in the church. Not only are they rewarded for performance in "backbone" or supportive positions, but they are penalized for trying to move from the backbone to the head position—the leadership of the church. It is by considering the distinction between prescribed support positions and the policy-making, leadership positions that the oppression of Black women in the Black church can be seen more clearly.

For the most part, men have monopolized the ministry as a profession. The ministry of women as fully ordained clergypersons has always been controversial. The Black church fathers were unable to see the injustices of their own practices, even when they paralleled the injustices in the white church against which they rebelled.

In the early nineteenth century, the Reverend Richard Allen perceived that it was unjust for Blacks, free and slaves, to be relegated to the balcony and restricted to a special time to pray and kneel at the communion table; for this he should be praised. Yet because of his acceptance of the patriarchal system Allen was unable to see the injustice in relegating women to one area of the church—the pews—by withholding ordination from women as he did in the case of Mrs. Jarena Lee.[15] Lee recorded Allen's response when she informed him of her call to "go preach the Gospel":

> He replied by asking in what sphere I wished to move in? I said, among the Methodists. He then replied, that a Mrs. Cook, a Methodist lady, had also some time before requested the same privilege; who it was believed, had done much good in the way of exhortation, and holding prayer meetings; and who had been permitted to do so by the verbal license of the preacher in charge at the time. But as to women preaching, he said that our Discipline knew nothing at all about it—that it did not call for women preachers.[16]

Because of this response, Jarena Lee's preaching ministry was delayed for eight years. She was not unaware of the sexist injustice in Allen's response.

> Oh how careful ought we be, lest through our by-laws of church government and discipline, we bring into disrepute even the word of life. For as unseemly as it may appear nowadays for a woman to preach, it should be remembered that nothing is impossible with God. And why should it be thought impossible, heterodox, or improper for a woman to preach, seeing the Saviour died for the woman as well as the man?[17]

Another "colored minister of the gospel," Elizabeth, was greatly troubled over her call to preach, or more accurately, over the response of men to her call to preach. She said:

> I often felt that I was unfit to assemble with the congregation with whom I had gathered, I felt that I was despised on account of this gracious calling, and was looked upon as a speckled bird by the ministers to whom I looked for instruction, some [of the ministers] would cry out, "you are an enthusiast," and others said, "the Discipline did not allow of any such division of work."[18]

Sometime later, when questioned about her authority to preach against slavery and her ordination status, she responded that she preached "not by the commission of men's hands: if the Lord had ordained me, I needed nothing better."[19] With this commitment to God rather than to a male-dominated church structure she led a fruitful ministry.

Mrs. Amanda Berry Smith, like Mrs. Jarena Lee, had to conduct her ministry outside the structure of the A.M.E. Church. Smith described herself as a "plain Christian woman" with "no money" and "no prominence."[20] But she was intrigued with the idea of attending the General Conference of 1872 in Nashville, Tennessee. Her inquiry into the cost of going to Nashville brought the following comments from some of the A.M.E. brethren:

> "I tell you, Sister, it will cost money to go down there; and if you ain't got plenty of it, it's no use to go"; another said:
>   "What does she want to go for?"
>   "Woman preacher; they want to be ordained," was they reply.
>   "I mean to fight that thing," said the other.
>   "Yes, indeed, so will I" said another.[21]

The oppression of women in the ministry took many forms. In addition to not being granted ordination, the authenticity of "the call" of women was frequently put to the test. Lee, Elizabeth, and Smith spoke of the many souls they had brought to Christ through their preaching and singing in local black congregations, as well as in white and mixed congregations. It was not until Bishop Richard Allen heard Jarena Lee preach that he was convinced that she was of the Spirit. He, however, still refused to ordain her. The "brethren," including some bishops of the 1872 General Conference of the A.M.E. Church, were convinced that Amanda Berry Smith was blessed with the Spirit of God after hearing her sing at a session held at Fisk University. Smith tells us that "the Spirit of the Lord seemed to fall on all the people. The preachers got happy." This experience brought invitations for her to preach at several churches, but it did not bring an appointment to a local congregation as pastor or the right of ordination. She summed up the experience in this way: "after that many of my brethren believed in me especially as the question of ordination of women never was mooted in the Conference."[22]

Several black denominations have since begun to ordain women.[23] But this matter of women preachers having the extra burden of proving their call to an extent not required of men still prevails in the Black church today. A study in which I participated at Union Theological Seminary in New York City bears this out. Interviews with Black ministers of different denominations revealed that their prejudices against women, and especially women in the ministry, resulted in unfair expectations and unjust treatment of women ministers whom they encountered.[24]

It is the unfair expectations placed upon women and blatant discrimination that keeps them "in the pew" and "out of the pulpit." This matter of keeping women in the pew has been carried to ridiculous extremes. At the 1971 Annual Convocation of the National Conference of Black Churchmen,[25] held at the Liberty Baptist Church in Chicago, I was slightly amused when, as I approached the pulpit to place my cassette tape recorder near the speaker, Walter Fauntroy, as several brothers had already done, I was stopped by a man who informed me that I could not enter the pulpit area. When I asked why not, he directed me to the pastor who told me that women were not permitted in the pulpit, but that he would have a man place the recorder there for me. Although I could not believe that explanation a serious one, I agreed to have a man place it on the pulpit for me and returned to my seat in the sanctuary for the continuation of the convocation. The seriousness of the pastor's statement became clear to me later at that meeting when Mary Jane Patterson, a Presbyterian Church executive, was refused the right to speak from the pulpit.[26] This was clearly a case of sex discrimination in a Black church—keeping women "in the pew" and "out of the pulpit."

As far as the issue of women is concerned, it is obvious that the Black church described by C. Eric Lincoln has not fared much better than the Negro church of E. Franklin Frazier.[27] The failure of the Black church and Black theology to proclaim explicitly the liberation of Black women indicates that they cannot claim to be agents of divine liberation. If the theology, like the church, has no word for Black women, its conception of liberation is inauthentic.

THE BLACK EXPERIENCE AND THE BLACK WOMAN

For the most part, Black churchmen have not dealt with the oppression of Black women in either the Black church or the Black community. Frederick Douglass was one notable exception in the nineteenth century. His active advocacy for women's rights was a demonstration against the contradiction between preaching "justice for all" and practicing the continued oppression of women. He, therefore, "dared not claim a right [for himself] which he would not concede to women."[28] These words describe the convictions of a man who was active both in the church and in the larger Black community. This is significant because there is usually a direct relationship between what goes on in the Black church and the Black secular community.

The status of Black women in the community parallels that of Black women in the church. Black theology considers the Black experience to be the context out of which its questions about God and human existence are formulated. This is assumed to be the context in which God's revelation is received and interpreted. Only from the perspective of the poor and the oppressed can theology be adequately done. Arising out of the Black power movement of the 1960s, Black theology purports to take seriously the experience of the larger community's struggle for liberation. But if this is, indeed, the case, Black theology must function in the secular community in the same way as it should function in the church community. It must serve as a "self-test" to see whether the rhetoric or proclamation of the Black community's struggle for liberation is consistent with its practices. How does the "self-test" principle operate among the poor and the oppressed? Certainly Black theology has spoken to some of the forms of oppression that exist within the community of the oppressed. Many of the injustices it has attacked are the same as those that gave rise to the prophets of the Old Testament. But the fact that Black theology does not include sexism specifically as one of those injustices is all too evident. It suggests that the theologians do not understand sexism to be one of the oppressive realities of the Black community. Silence on this specific issue can only mean conformity with the status quo. The most prominent Black theologian, James Cone, has recently broken this silence.

> The Black church, like all other churches, is a male-dominated church. The difficulty that Black male ministers have in supporting the equality of women in the church and society stems partly from the lack of a clear liberation-criterion rooted in the gospel and in the present struggles of oppressed peoples. . . . It is truly amazing that many black male ministers, young and old, can hear the message of liberation in the gospel when related to racism but remain deaf to a similar message in the context of sexism.[29]

It is difficult to understand how Black men manage to exclude the liberation of Black women from their interpretation of the liberating gospel. Any correct analysis of the poor and oppressed would reveal some interesting and inescapable facts about the situation of women within oppressed groups. Without succumbing to the long and fruitless debate of "who is more oppressed than whom?" I want to make some pointed suggestions to Black male theologians.

It would not be very difficult to argue that since Black women are the poorest of the poor, the most oppressed of the oppressed, their experience provides a more fruitful context for doing Black theology. The research of Jacquelyne Jackson attests to the extreme deprivation of Black women. Jackson supports her claim with statistical data that "in comparison with black males and white males and females black women yet constitute the most disadvantaged group in the United States, as evidenced especially by their largely unenviable educational occupational, employment and income levels, and availability of marital partners."[30] In other words, in spite of the "quite insignificant" educational advantage that Black women have over Black men, they have "had the greatest access to the worst jobs at the lowest earnings."[31] It is important to emphasize this fact in order to elevate to its rightful level of concern the condition of Black women, not only in the world at large, but in the Black community and the Black church. It is my contention that if Black theology speaks of the Black community as if the special problems of Black women do not exist, it is no different from the white theology it claims to reject precisely because of its inability to take account of the existence of Black people in its theological formulations.

It is instructive to note that the experience of Black women working in the Black power movement further accented the problem of the oppression of women in the Black community. Because of their invisibility in the leadership of the movement, they, like women of the church, provided the "support" segment of the movement. They filled the streets when numbers were needed for demonstrations. They stuffed the envelopes in the offices and performed other menial tasks. Kathleen Cleaver, in a *Black Scholar* interview, revealed some of the problems in the movement that caused her to become involved in women's liberation issues. While underscoring the crucial role played by women as Black power activists, Kathleen Cleaver, nonetheless, acknowledged the presence of sex discrimination.

> I viewed myself as assisting everything that was done. . . . The form of assistance that women give in political movements to men is just as crucial as the leadership that men give to those movements. And this is something that is never recognized and never dealt with. Because women are always relegated to assistance and this is where I became interested in the liberation of women. Conflicts, constant conflicts came up, conflicts that would rise as a result of the fact that I was married to a member of the Central Committee and was also an officer in the Party. Things that I would have suggested myself would be implemented. But if I suggested them the suggestion might be rejected. If they were suggested by a man the suggestion would be implemented.
>
> It seemed throughout the history of my working with the Party, I always had to struggle with this. The suggestion itself was never viewed objectively. The fact that the suggestion came from a woman gave it some lesser value. And it seemed that it had something to do with the egos of the men involved. I know that the first demonstration that we had at the courthouse for Huey Newton I was very instrumental in organizing; the first time we went out on the soundtracks, I was on the soundtracks; the first leaflet we put out, I wrote; the first demonstration, I made up the pamphlets. And the members of that demonstration for the most part were women. I've noticed that throughout my dealings in the black movement in the United States, that the most anxious, the most eager, the most active, the most quick to understand the problem and quick to move are women.[32]

Cleaver exposed the fact that even when leadership was given to women, sexism lurked in the wings. As executive secretary of the Student Nonviolent Coordinating Committee (SNCC), Ruby Doris Robinson was described as the "heart beat of SNCC." Yet there were the constant conflicts, the constant struggles that she was subjected to because she was a woman.[33]

Notwithstanding all the evidence to the contrary, some might want to argue that the central problem of Black women is related to their race and not their sex. Such an argument then presumes that the problem cannot be resolved apart from the Black struggle. I contend that as long as the Black struggle refuses to recognize and deal with its sexism, the idea that women will receive justice from that struggle alone will never work. It will not work because Black women will no longer allow Black men to ignore their unique problems and needs in the name of some distorted view of the "liberation of the total community." I would bring to the minds of the proponents of this argument the words of President Sekou Touré as he wrote about the role of African women in the revolution. He said, "if African women cannot possibly conduct their struggle in isolation from the struggle that our people wage for African liberation, African freedom, conversely, is not effective unless it brings about the liberation of African women."[34] Black men who have an investment in the patriarchal structure of white America and who intend to do Christian theology have yet to realize that if Jesus is liberator of the oppressed, all of the oppressed must be liberated. Perhaps the proponents of the argument that the case of Black women must be subsumed under a larger cause should look to the South African theologians Sabelo Ntwasa and Basil Moore. They affirm that "Black theology as it struggles to formulate a theology of liberation relevant to South Africa, cannot afford to perpetuate any form of domination, not even male domination. If its liberation is not human enough to include the liberation of women, it will not be liberation."[35]

A CHALLENGE TO BLACK THEOLOGY

My central argument is this: Black theology cannot continue to treat Black women as if they were invisible creatures who are on the outside looking into the Black experience, the Black church, and the Black theological enterprise. It will have to deal with the community of believers in all aspects as integral parts of the whole community. Black theology, therefore, must speak to the bishops who hide behind the statement "Women don't want women pastors." It must speak to the pastors who say, "My church isn't ready for women preachers yet." It must teach the seminarians who feel that "women have no place in the seminary." It must address the women in the church and community who are content and complacent with their oppression. It must challenge the educators who would reeducate the people on every issue except the issue of the dignity and equality of women.

Black women represent more than 50 percent of the Black community and more than 70 percent of the Black church. How then can an authentic theology of liberation arise out of these communities without specifically addressing the liberation of the women in both places? Does the fact that certain questions are raised by Black women make them any less Black concerns? If, as I contend, the liberation of Black men and women is inseparable, then a radical split cannot be made between racism and sexism. Black women are oppressed by racism and sexism. It is therefore necessary that Black men and women be actively involved in combating both evils.

Only as Black women in greater numbers make their way from the background to the forefront will the true strength of the Black community be fully realized. There is already a heritage of strong Black women and men upon which a stronger nation can be built. There is a tradition that declares that God is at work in the experience of the Black woman. This tradition, in the context of the total Black experience, can provide data for the development of a holistic Black theology. Such a theology will repudiate the God of classical theology who is presented as an absolute patriarch, a deserting father who created Black men and women and then "walked out" in the face of responsibility. Such a theology will look at the meaning of the total Jesus Christ Event; it will consider not only how God through Jesus Christ is related to the oppressed men, but to women as well. Such a theology will "allow" God through the Holy Spirit to work through persons without regard to race, sex, or class. This theology will exercise its prophetic function and serve as a "self-test" in a church characterized by the sins of racism, sexism, and other forms of oppression. Until Black women theologians are fully participating in the theological enterprise, it is important to keep Black male theologians and Black leaders cognizant of their dereliction. They must be made aware of the fact that Black women are needed not only as Christian educators but as theologians and church leaders. It is only when Black women and men share jointly the leadership in theology and in the church and community that the Black nation will become strong and liberated. Only then will there be the possibility that Black theology can become a theology of divine liberation.

One final word for those who argue that the issues of racism and sexism are too complicated and should not be confused. I agree that the issues should not be "confused." But the elimination of both racism and sexism is so crucial for the liberation of Black persons that we cannot shrink from facing them together. Sojourner Truth tells us why this is so. In 1867 she spoke out on the issue of suffrage and what she said at that time is still relevant to us as we deal with the liberation of Black women today.

> I feel that if I have to answer for the deeds done in my body just as much as a man, I have a right to have just as much as a man. There is a great stir about colored men getting their rights, but not a word about the colored women; and if colored men get their rights, and not colored women theirs, you see the colored men will be masters over the women, and it will be just as bad as it was before. So I am for keeping the thing going while things are stirring; because if we wait till it is still it will take a great while to get it going again.[36]

Black women have to keep the issue of sexism "going" in the Black community, in the Black church, and in Black theology until it has been eliminated. To do otherwise means that they will be pushed aside until eternity. Therefore, with Sojourner Truth, I'm for "keeping things going while things are stirring."

NOTES

1. Beatriz Melano Couch, remarks on the feminist panel of Theology in the Americas Conference in Detroit in August 1975, printed in *Theology in the Americas*, ed. Sergio Torres and John Eagleson (Maryknoll, N.Y.: Orbis Books, 1976), 375.

2. Consuelo Urquiza, "A Message from a Hispanic-American Woman," The Fifth Commission: A Monitor for Third World Concerns IV (June–July 1978) insert. The Fifth Commission is a commission of the National Council of the Churches of Christ in the USA (NCC), 475 Riverside Drive, New York, N.Y.

3. I agree with the Fifth Commission that "the Third World is not a geographical entity, but rather the world of oppressed peoples in their struggle for liberation." In this sense, Black women are included

in the term "Third World." However, in order to accent the peculiar identity, problems, and needs of Black women in the First World or the Third World contexts, I choose to make the distinction between Black and other Third World women.

4. For a discussion of sexual dualisms in our society, see Rosemary Ruether, *New Woman/New Earth* (New York: Seabury Press, 1975), chap. 1; and *Liberation Theology* (New York: Paulist Press, 1972), 16ff. Also for a discussion of sexual (social) dualisms as related to the brain hemispheres, see Sheila Collins, *A Different Heaven and Earth* (Valley Forge, Pa.: Judson Press, 1974), 169–70.

5. Angela Davis, "Reflections on the Black Woman's Role in the Community of Slaves," *The Black Scholar* 4, no. 3 (December 1971): 3–15. I do take issue with

Davis's point, however. The Black community may have experienced "equality in inequality," but this was forced on them from the dominant or enslaving community. She does not deal with the inequality within the community itself.

6. See Sheila Collins, *A Different Heaven and Earth*, Rosemary Ruether, *New Woman/New Earth*, Letty Russell, *Human Liberation in the Feminist Perspective* (Philadelphia: Westminster Press, 1974); and Mary Daly, *Beyond God the Father* (Boston: Beacon Press, 1973).

7. Surely the factor of race would be absent, but one would have to do an in-depth analysis to determine the possible side effect on the status of Black women.

8. James Cone, *A Black Theology of Liberation* (Philadelphia: J. B. Lippincott, 1970), 23.

9. Eulaho Baltazar discusses color symbolism (white is good; black is evil) as a reflection of racism in the white theology that perpetuates it. *The Dark Center: A Process Theology of Blackness* (New York: Paulist Press, 1973).

10. One may want to argue that Black theology is not concerned with sexism but with racism. I will argue in this chapter that such a theology could speak only half the truth, if truth at all.

11. Karl Barth, *Church Dynamics*, 1, part 1, 2.

12. Cone, *Black Theology*, 230–32.

13. James Cone and Albert Cleage do make this observation of the contemporary Black church and its response to the struggles against racism. See Cleage, *The Black Messiah* (New York: Sheed and Ward, 1969), passim; and Cone, *Black Theology*, passim.

14. A study that I conducted in the Philadelphia Conference of the African Methodist Episcopal Church, May 1976. It also included sporadic samplings of churches in other conferences in the First Episcopal District. As for example, a church of 1,660 members (500 men and 1,160 women) had a trustee board of 8 men and 1 woman and a steward board of 13 men and 6 women. A church of 100 members (35 men and 65 women) had a trustee board of 5 men and 4 women and a steward board of 5 men and 4 women.

15. Jarena Lee, *The Life and Religious Experience of Jarena Lee: A Colored Lady Giving an Account of Her Call to Preach the Gospel* (Philadelphia, 1836), printed in Dorothy Porter, ed., *Early Negro Writing 1760–1837* (Boston: Beacon Press, 1971), 49–514.

16. Jarena Lee, *The Life and Religious Experience of Jarena Lee*, 503. Carol George in *Segregated Sabbaths* (New York: Oxford University Press, 1973), presents a very positive picture of the relationship between Jarena Lee and Bishop Richard Allen. She feels that

by the time Lee approached Allen, he had "modified his views on woman's rights" (129). She contends that since Allen was free from the Methodist Church he was able to "determine his own policy" with respect to women under the auspices of the A.M.E. Church. It should be noted that Bishop Allen accepted the Rev. Jarena Lee as a woman preacher and not as an ordained preacher with full rights and privileges thereof. Even Carol George admitted that Lee traveled with Bishop Allen only "as an unofficial member of their delegation to conference sessions in New York and Baltimore," "to attend," not to participate in them. I agree that this does represent progress in Bishop Allen's view as compared to Lee's first approach; on the second approach, he was at least encouraging. Then he began "to promote her interests" (129). But he did not ordain her.

17. Jarena Lee, *The Life and Religious Experience of Jarena Lee*, 129.

18. "Elizabeth: A Colored Minister of the Gospel," printed in Bert James Loewenberg and Ruth Bogin, eds., *Black Women in Nineteenth-Century American Life* (University Park, Pa.: The Pennsylvania State University Press, 1976), 132. The denomination of Elizabeth is not known to this writer. Her parents were Methodists, but she was separated from her parents at the age of eleven. However, the master from whom she gained her freedom was Presbyterian. Her autobiography was published by the Philadelphia Quakers.

19. "Elizabeth: A Colored Minister of the Gospel," 133.

20. Amanda Berry Smith, *An Autobiography: The Story of the Lord's Dealings with Mrs. Amanda Smith, the Colored Evangelist* (Chicago: Meyer and Brother, 1893); printed in Loewenberg and Bogin, eds., *Black Women*, 157.

21. Amanda Berry Smith, *An Autobiography*, 158.

22. Amanda Berry Smith, *An Autobiography*, 159.

23. The African Methodist Episcopal Church started ordaining women in 1948, according to the Reverend William P. Foley of Bridgestreet A.M.E. Church in Brooklyn, New York. The first ordained woman was Martha J. Keys. The African Methodist Episcopal Zion Church ordained women as early as 1884. At that time, Mrs. Julia A. Foote was ordained deacon in the New York Annual Conference. In 1894, Mrs. Mary J. Small was ordained deacon, and in 1898, she was ordained elder. See David Henry Bradley Sr., *A History of the A.M.E. Zion Church*, vol. (part) II, 1872–1968 (Nashville: The Parthenon Press, 1970), 384, 393. The Christian Methodist Episcopal Church enacted legislation to ordain women in the 1970 General Conference. Since then

approximately seventy-five women have been ordained. See the Reverend N. Charles Thomas, general secretary of the C.M.E. Church and director of
the Department of the Ministry, Memphis, Tennessee. Many Baptist churches still do not ordain
women. Some churches in the Pentecostal tradition
do not ordain women. However, in some other
Pentecostal churches, women are founders, pastors,
elders, and bishops. In the case of the A.M.E.Z.
Church, where, women were ordained as early as
1884, the important question would be what happened to the women who were ordained? In addition, all of these churches (except for those that do
give leadership to women) should answer the following questions: Have women been assigned to
pastor "class A" churches? Have women been appointed as presiding elders? (There is currently one
woman presiding elder in the A.M.E. Church.)
Have women been elected to serve as bishop of any
of these churches? Have women served as presidents of conventions?

24. Yolande Herron, Jacquelyn Grant, Gwendolyn
Johnson, and Samuel Roberts, "Black Women and
the Field Education Experience at Union Theological Seminary: Problems and Prospects" (New York:
Union Theological Seminary, May 1978).

25. This organization continues to call itself the
National Conference of Black Churchmen despite
the protests of women members.

26. NCBC has since made the decision to examine
the policies of its host institutions (churches) to
avoid the reoccurrence of such incidents.

27. E. Franklin Frazier, *The Negro Church in America*; C. Eric Lincoln, *The Black Church since Frazier*
(New York: Schocken Books, 1974), passim.

28. Printed in Philip S. Foner, ed., *Frederick Douglass
on Women's Rights* (Westport, Conn.: Greenwood
Press), 51.

29. James Cone, "Black Ecumenism and the Liberation Struggle," delivered at Yale University, February
16–17, 1978, and Quinn Chapel A.M.E. Church,
May 22, 1978. In two other papers he has voiced concern on women's issues, relating them to the larger
question of liberation. These papers are: "New Roles
in the Ministry: A Theological Appraisal" and "Black
Theology and the Black Church: Where Do We Go
from Here?" Both papers appear in James Cone, *For
My People: Black Theology and the Black Church*
(Maryknoll, N.Y.: Orbis Books, 1984).

30. Jacquelyne Jackson, "But Where Are the Men?,"
The Black Scholar, 30.

31. Jacquelyne Jackson, "But Where Are the Men?,"

32. Kathleen Cleaver was interviewed by Sister Julia
Herve, 55–56.

33. Kathleen Cleaver was interviewed by Sister Julia
Herve, 55.

34. Sekou Touré, "The Role of Women in the Revolution," *The Black Scholar*, no. 6 (March 1975): 32.

35. Sabelo Ntwasa and Basil Moore, "The Concept
of God in Black Theology," in *The Challenge of Black
Theology in South Africa*, ed. Basil Moore (Atlanta,
Ga.: John Knox Press, 1974), 25–26.

36. Sojourner Truth, "Keeping the Things Going
While Things Are Stirring," printed in *Feminism: The
Essential Historical Writings*, ed. Miriam Schneir
(New York: Random House, 1972), 129–30.

An earlier version of this work appeared in *For My
People: Black Theology and the Black Church*, ed.
James Cone (Maryknoll, N.Y.: Orbis Books, 1984).

31

TEACHING HAITIAN VODOU

Claudine Michel

AN EARLY PORTUGUESE EXPLORER reported after a visit to the southern coast of Africa that the people had no religion. According to one commentator,

> . . . his mistake was understandable. After all, he was from Europe, where the presence of religion is manifested in church buildings, priests, and sacred scriptures . . . [In Africa] he saw no identifiable religious buildings, no distinctively religious functionaries, and certainly no scriptures. Therefore: [the statement] *"they have no religion."*[1]

African religions, and Vodou for that matter, are not necessarily recognizable as separate institutions with a book of law regimenting the moral life of its devotees. They pervade and permeate the whole society as their "theology, rituals and organizations intimately merged with the concepts and structure of secular institutions," a commentary originally made by Yang about China which, for similar reasons, has also been said to be *a country without religion.*[2]

It is, however, important to note that Booth's statement does not take into account the separate order of religion found among some European lower classes. He refers here to the phenomenology of Christianity (megalithic cathedrals, clergy, etc.) launched by medieval ruling classes (imperial aristocracies, papal empowerment, bureaucratic hierarchies), who conceived religion as a cosmic totality. To the extent that this phenomenology is used to "represent" Western theocracy, it conceals the religious folkways of the lower classes (the social movements of heresy and evangelicals, for example) that resisted the appropriation of religion by the upper classes. Therefore, Vodou as well as other non-Western religions are in opposition with the *church establishment*, not with Christian spirituality per se.

In Haiti, the ancestral religion is important not as a "separate institution," but because in its *diffused* form it performs a pervasive though organized function that regulates all aspects of the spiritual, social, and even economic and political life of Vodou adherents—an observation true also of other societies and religions outside the Western umbrella.[3]

FAMILY VODOU

The country continues to be an overwhelmingly rural society, and, as such, the cult of the ancestors is the guardian of peasant traditional values and is largely linked to rural family life and to matters of land. Haitian peasants *serve the spirits* daily in their home, on their land, as they work, and gather with members of their extended family and kin on special occasions for more elaborate ceremonies, which may range from the *birthday* of a *spirit* to a "*service*" for a particular event affecting the family or the land. In remote areas, people sometimes walk for days to partake in such ceremonies that may take place as often as several times a month, or as rarely as once or twice a year.

The Vodou religion is known to be closely tied not only to issues of division and administration of land, but also to matters of economy as it relates to the residential areas, the *lakous*.[4] It is concerned with conflict resolution and the overall well-being of its residents. This kind of *family* or *domestic* Vodou, practiced primarily within the context of the family network, is the type that the Haitian diaspora has taken with it overseas, using its African spirituality as frame of reference to help assure its collective survival in physical and social environments hostile, more often than not, to Haitian immigrants.

Throughout Haiti, in New York, in Paris, as in any other location where Vodou is practiced, the absence of a formal place of worship is noticeable. There is no Vodou church per se; instead, *all* places are sites of worships. The *hounfò*, the Vodou temple, is but one such place where the living gather to communicate with the spirits. It is usually (except if owned by an extremely rich family or by government officials) a very informal place, made of very simple material, not completely enclosed, with sometimes a dirt floor, and having no furniture (except for maybe a few chairs and drums, some flags, and pictures). The *hounfò* is quite different from typical places of worship related to other religions. In fact, it may not be readily identified as such, even during a ceremony, which an uninformed observer might mistakenly take for a social gathering with no specific goal.

In the Vodou world, among other sites, the cemetery as well as the *crossroads* are prominent and meaningful places of worship; the cemetery as repository of spirits and the crossroads, as points of access to the world of the invisible—the point where the mortal world crosses the metaphysical plane. Oceans, rivers, and chutes also have special significance in Vodou because important and demanding spirits, such as *Simbi*, Agwe, Maitresse dlo, *or* La Sirène *(the mermaid), reside in those large bodies of water. It is also believed that water has special powers, and that, for example, some individuals are initiated* anba dlo, *or under water.*[5]

Other places of remarkable religious importance include: various sites of pilgrimage, the parish church, as well as the fields, the markets, the compounds and households. Often, in a Vodou home the only recognizable religious items are some images of saints and a few candies with a rosary; in other homes, where people may more openly show their devotion to the *spirits*, noticeable items may include: an altar with Catholic deities and iconographies, rosaries, bottles, jars and rattles decorated or not, perfumes, oils, dolls, rags and a few other paraphernalia. This systematic absence of readily identifiable religious objects in "specifically designated sacred locations" is understandable for two reasons: (1) Vodou's continuous presence in all aspects of Haitian life and its overarching influence; (2) the fact that for so long Haitians had to practice their religion clandestinely. The lack of formal settings of worship reflects both the persistence and adaptiveness of the Haitian religion.

TEMPLE VODOU

Vodou in the more densely populated urban areas has been called "temple Vodou" where communal life revolves around the *hounfòs* and the head of the temples, the *manbos* and *houngans*, respectively priestesses and priests in the Vodou religion. Though, in most cases, few distinguishing marks identify these sites as places of worship, they remain the center of life in the cities. Through them, the devotees re-create the family and kin lost when they migrated to the city and continue their quest for religious and moral values. Vodou temples are often located near churches, yet another element of spatial juxtaposition of Haiti's complex religious traditions. It is not unusual, for example, for people to leave a Vodou ceremony early in the morning and to step right into the four o'clock Mass at a nearby Catholic church. In addition to the complex cosmological reasons behind such behavior, to be seen in church was traditionally a form of self-protection against possible persecutions and gossip. To be a faithful churchgoer is perceived as a sign of being a "good" Christian—someone who honors God and the saints, and who therefore, enjoys the respect of the Vodou community.

Although temples are mostly an urban phenomenon, this does not mean that *hounfòs* are not found in rural areas; neither does this mean that urbanites have abandoned domestic worshipping. Mostly, temple communities have common characteristics with the family cult though they sometimes exhibit differences, in particular in the areas of division of labor, spectators versus performers and greater hierarchization more visible in the temples than in families. Myths and rituals may differ from one *hounfò* to another, from one Vodou family to another, depending on the region, on the types of spirits who are served and invoked, on the style of worship chosen by a particular family, or on the specific issues facing a given community. However, they should mostly be viewed from the perspective of their commonness.

In the Vodou world where so many elements merge to form a diversified but always coherent whole, places of worship are not mutually exclusive, compartmentalized and categorized. Their functionality is what matters. This utilitarian characteristic is also what partly[6] explains the nonexistence of written dogma and the absence of specific instructional material in a context where teaching takes place *everywhere* and where *everything* represents an opportunity for growth and learning. More simply, Haitians have not developed written dogma and instructional material for the same reason that they have not built ostensibly recognizable and elaborate temples: they do not need them because they have no use for them. The proverb says, "Where there is a need, there is a way." In this particular instance, "There is no *way* because there is no *need*."

CHARACTERISTICS OF TEACHERS AND LEARNERS

Like everything else in Vodou, the issue of reachers and learners is quite complex. In Vodou society everyone continually plays the role of teacher and learner in a process of continuing exchanges and dialogues during ongoing interactions with family members, the community and the spirits. Elders, parents, members of the extended family, neighbors, priests and priestesses most often play the role of teachers and guides for the younger generations though they can also, at times, turn into learners among their peers and vis-à-vis the spirits. Senior members of the community may become learners, for example, in a situation where a young child may carry a message from an elder or from one of the spirits.

To be a good teacher one has to respect the *flow of nature*, Vodou's nonhierarchization as well as its functionality—all things that the learner also ought to master. Teachers and learners, in many ways, have the same agenda; they may just achieve these goals differently and at different moments of their human journey. Courlander wrote about Vodou's flexibility and limited directiveness:

> Vodou permeates the land, and, in a sense, it springs from the land. It is not a system imposed from above, but one which pushes out from below. It is a thing of the family, a rich and complex inheritance from a man's own ancestors. It is not the priests of Vodoun who control and direct its course. They, like the lowest peasant, simply move about within it and make use of its resources.[7]

For those who serve the spirits, life is about movement between people, movement between the living and the departed, and Vodou teaching and learning entail balancing commonalities and differences to create global harmony and peace. "Movement" refers here to sets of complex "interactions" among people, among people and the spirits, and reflects the different roles and functions involved in these rapports. In Haitian Creole, "balans" or "balanse" means to bring about equilibrium, to harmonize; it implies metaphysical elements not rendered by the English word "balance." These concepts also denote that teachers and learners play equally active roles in learning and teaching about the fluidity of the Vodou world and its ever-evolving cosmology. In that respect, Vodou's teaching approach is, in many ways, "learner-centered" with "teachers" serving primarily as guides and facilitators. This democratic foundation makes Vodou quite a progressive system compared to other more doctrinal world religions.

THE TEACHERS—THOSE WHO HAVE "KONESANS"
Everyone who has *konesans*[8] is typically a Vodou teacher, that is, a person who continuously participates in the propagation of the Vodou worldview and assists in clarifying choices for less experienced individuals. However, the "better" teachers perform in addition more complicated tasks. Seniority, experience, wisdom, accompanied with *konesans*, and always coupled with style, characterize these more effective teachers. They are truly skilled at helping others *balanse* their lives within the web of relationships of their community and deal with both symptomatic and asymptomatic disturbances of nature's harmony that they help restore. All Vodou adepts can be teachers, but clearly *houngans* and *manbos* hold specially designated teaching roles in the Haitian communities where they engage in sophisticated ministration and healing.

Though they do not wear a recognizable garb and do not attend formal theological centers for their training, these priests and priestesses are well-respected and powerful members of society. Having undergone the fourth and highest level of initiation that confirmed them as priests or priestesses and healers, *houngans* and *manbos* have leverage in the world of the spirits, a status that does not make them leaders in the most commonly used sense of the term but, one which allows them to "lead" their community.[9] In Vodou, the good leaders follow; the good teachers listen in order to "see things clearly" and help participants choose wisely among different possible paths. The functions that they perform are essential to the communal well-being: they minister, preside, heal, see and foresee. In other words, they restore equilibrium and keep things balanced through various forms of ritualizing and rituals. The skilled ritualizer—someone who knows how to orchestrate the arrival of the spirits and solicit their intervention in human affairs—is therefore a powerful technician of the sacred, a true moral leader and a teacher of distinction.

Furthermore, to the extent that some form of morals and ethics constitutes the essence of all religions, the life of the *houngans* and *manbos,* their deeds and tenets—as individuals and as people who orchestrate religious gatherings for the benefit of their Vodou family—tend to reflect the moral beliefs of those who serve the spirits. What emerges from their lives and ministrations represents a repository of *konesans,* of wisdom, and experience. They are teachers par excellence, not because they are necessarily moral exemplars, but because with the assistance of the spirits, they help the community find cohesion and teach Vodou adepts how to avoid the source of moral decay, imbalance. McCarthy Brown, explaining that in Vodou, the moral problem is not evil but imbalance, writes about the role of the moral leader:

> In the context of this pluralistic and conflict-centered description of life, the moral leader is not one who sets his or her own life up as a model of imitation. It is rather that person who, as a subtle and skilled technician of the sacred, can orchestrate ritual contexts in which each person discovers how to dance his or her own way through a process of dynamic balancing with others who dance in their own way.[10]

Most Vodou teachers officiate exclusively in their own communities whereas some of the more accomplished ones extend their ministrations further than their immediate world, accepting outsiders and sometimes foreigners into their Vodou family. Two such examples are Mathilda Beauvoir, who officiates in Paris, and Mama Lola, a renowned Vodou priestess who resides in Brooklyn; both have foreigners "eating at her table."[11] Though this may not be the rule, other cosmopolitan Vodou practitioners believe, like them, that race, color, or nationality should never be factors in making the decision to include or not a person in Vodou ritualizing or in a Vodou family. Mama Lola, for example, trusts that it is not for us to decide who the spirits call.[12]

Also, many famous Haitian painters and artists are Vodou initiates if not *houngans*[13] and, as such, they are important Vodou teachers in both the local context and in the international community. Through their paintings or iron cast work, they teach about Black aesthetics, the Haitian world and the Vodou worldview. The *Vodou Soul* and the *Haitian Spirit* are expressed in rather powerful ways in these pieces of artwork where signs and shapes become a message with a life of their own.

The *loas* and ancestral spirits are the other weighty Vodou teachers who harmonize specific aspects of life and serve as intermediaries between the humans and the ultimate self-existent *Bondye,* the *Grand Mèt,* the absolute and supreme Being, a concept that "shares much in common with Christian understandings of the deity."[14] To that effect, Mbiti wrote: "The God described in the Bible is none other than the God who is already known in the framework of traditional African religiosity."[15] In other words, there is a distinct monotheism in Vodou despite its henotheism and its pantheon of divinities and ancestral spirits. However, God is not the usual focus of worship in a Vodou service; people typically pray *Bondye* through the mediation of the spirits. In turn, *Bondye* does not get involved directly in the devotees' daily existence and in their personal relations with the spirits. Paris comments: "The deity's remoteness does not evidence any lack of concern for humanity. It rather connotes the reverse. By maintaining distance from nature and humanity the deity manifests divine care,"[16] although not in a direct tangible fashion like the other Vodou teachers. Zuesse offers an interesting summation of this African perspective which also applies to the Haitian experience:

> It is an expression of his continuing benevolence that [God] has withdrawn his overwhelming power and presence behind the intermediary beings he has appointed to govern the modulated realm of specific beings. God does not get involved himself too directly in the world that he sustains, for too particular and intense involvement might destroy the fabric of the divine order he sustains.[17]

Though Zuesse uses "he" to refer to the Supreme Deity it is, however, not absolutely clear that the Haitian concept of God is altogether masculine in that the Vodou religion strives to create harmony and maintain equilibrium, among other aspects, in the area of gender. Female and male spirits are, therefore, invoked frequently and served with equal deference, each one presiding over a specific, often "gendered" realm of human affairs. The power of the female *loas* represents an important lesson in itself, particularly for Haitian women who have endured such a long history of political and domestic oppression. In Vodou, women are priestesses, revered spirits, and fully participating members of their religious communities, which offers one of their rare sources of hope for a more egalitarian society. In this respect, the Haitian ancestral cult empowers women more than most other world religions.

The spirits most often served, and consequently, some of Vodou's most prominent teachers, include: *Dambala*, supreme, oldest, most respected, represented by a snake; *Aida Wedo*, his wife; *Legba*, the spirit of the crossroads who must be invoked to "open the gate" for the other *loas*; *Ogou*, who does not tolerate injustice and who controls power; *Erzili*, representing sexuality, lesbianism, motherhood; *Azaka*, the peasant, the worker, the one who controls money; *Baron Samedi* and *Gran Brigit*, guardians of the cemeteries; *Gédé*, the spirit of death and sexuality. Most of these divinities exhibit various personalities and characteristics depending on the names that they take. For example, *Ogou Badagri* behaves quite differently from *Ogou Ferraille*, *Erazili Freda* from *Erzili Férouge*, *Gédé Nimbo* from *Gédé Loray*, although the family relationship remains.

Each *loa* is an archetype of a moral principle that he or she represents although: "Virtue for both the *loa* and those who serve them is less an inherent character trait than a dynamic state of being that demands ongoing attention and care."[18] Like humans, they are whole, with strengths and weaknesses. McCarthy Brown says it well: "Vodou spirits are larger than *life* but not other than life." She further comments:

> The spirits talk with the faithful. They hug them, hold them, feed them, but also chastise them . . . The Vodou spirits are not models of the well-lived life; rather, they mirror the full range of, possibilities inherent in the particular slice of life over which they preside. Failure to understand this has led observers to portray the Vodou spirits as demonic or even to conclude that Vodou is a religion without morality—a serious misconception.[19]

Moreover, from Vodou's holistic conception of life derives the fundamental idea that the Vodou spirits are not saints because they are good but because they are all-encompassing, global, full, complex, and because, as such, they mirror human life, its poles and conflicts. Though these conflicts are manifestations of existing contradictions and of disturbances in the web of human relations, "the point is not to make conflict go away, but to make it work for, rather than against life."[20]

The Vodou spirits of the Haitian pantheon are teachers of distinction not because they guide by rigid examples or indoctrination but because they heighten the worshippers' vision of the world that they live in. *Loas* do not preach, nor do they typically advise per se. Through possession-performances, they help participants explore potentialities and choices by highlighting destructive and constructive aspects of particular situations. At times, they may appear disorganized, unfocused because they find it necessary to throw people off balance in order to help them find balance. They are, however, rarely off target: they always know what the issues are (sometimes, before the parties involved) and ceaselessly succeed in clarifying matters for the participants, helping them see what they may sometimes be oblivious to in their lives. The *loas* usually do not introduce what is not already there; their task is to show devotees how to see clearly in the midst of a multiplicity of truths.

THE LEARNERS—THE ENTIRE HAITIAN COMMUNITY

From its youngest members to its most acclaimed technicians of the sacred, all are lifelong learners in the Vodou faith. Adepts of the Haitian religious community continuously struggle to balance their lives in order to learn how to follow a moral path, ever guided by the overarching African ethos on which their religion is based. A "good" learner makes appropriate efforts according to age and status to incorporate the spirit of Vodou and its worldview in a relevant, lively and harmonized existence during which unrelenting, interconnected and responsible relationships are maintained for the benefit of the group.

Young children and youth are exposed to learning that involves mostly copying and imitating adults and elders. This informal type of education continues until children, youth and young adults become socialized into their society, until behavior and rituals have become habitual, until they have incorporated the traditional values of their culture into a harmonious blend of secular and religious activities. The very participation in the "regular" life of a Vodou family fosters this kind of informal learning and creates opportunities for informal education to occur, as with all other forms of Vodou teaching, outside the Haitian school system. Informal education is, in this case, the more deliberate and systematic ways used by servitors of the spirits, in particular those who have *konesans* to teach preplanned curricular items to those coming of age and those wishing to become "formally" initiated in Vodou.

The four levels of Vodou initiation (the specific steps taken to confer "ascending degrees of control" to humans in their relationships with the spirits), with the highest of these levels being the actual rising to the status of priesthood, fit, for example, into this category of informal education. Specific training is also undergone by other functionaries of a *hounfò*, such as, for example, the *Laplace* and the *Hounsis* who go through a long and formal apprenticeship with the head of the temples. Sustained and organized efforts are made during each stage of initiation to teach about particular rituals and reinforce character. Initiation is a complex, sophisticated, highly ritualistic and, sometimes, costly process.[21] Dunham made those revelations:

> We began the ritual of the crossed and recrossed handclasp, the bow with knees flexed, turn underarm, [those] of highest protocol guiding the other. Then, the turn to all four directions

of the compass, hand gripped tightly in hand, with sacred words spoken in each direction, the approach to the altar, the recognition of each grade of protocol by obeisance and work . . . It was up to my instructors to decide what to do, and I followed them, asking no questions . . . We danced, not as people in the houng-for, with the stress of possession or the escapism of hypnosis or for catharsis, but as I imagine dance when it must have been executed when body and being were more united, when form and flow and personal ecstasy became an exaltation of a superior state of things, not necessarily a ritual to any one superior being.[22]

Vodou cosmology emphasizes uniformity, conformity, group cohesion and support for one another. Initiation ceremonies are a primary conveyor of this worldview and initiates are rid of their will and desire to impose their ego on others. McCarthy Brown explains that it is "a spirituality that is more about empowerment than about gaining power over others."[23] During initiation, the neophytes are taught to liberate themselves from obstacles that may hinder their spiritual development: individuality, self-love, doubt, fears. During the days of seclusion, they become one with all other living creatures as well as with the four main forces of nature (air, fire, water, and earth). To be initiated, to *kouche* (literally to lie down), represents, in the most simplistic term, the death of the old self and the birth of a new self originating from a type of nonindividualistic collective consciousness. One is forced to regress into infancy and childhood—and, consequently, is treated as it is appropriate for these stages—only to be brought back, through rituals designed to overcome fear, pain, and selfishness, to a new state of adulthood and maturity. An initiate explains some of the feelings accompanying the initiation process:

> It was hard to become a child again, to let go of being in charge of myself, to give the care of myself over to another. Most difficult was letting go of words, of the appearance of control . . . I bit my tongue to stop the *How? and When? and Why?* . . . Entering the chamber was like dying . . . The drums were pounding as they had been for hours . . . Seven times I raised my hand and then darkness . . . I was thrown off-balance in order to learn to find balance . . . Ever so briefly I died . . .[24]

When the initiates leave the chamber where they are secluded, their heads are covered. It must remain so for forty days after initiation.[25] Clearly, the How, the exercise of the art of initiation, represents a moral message in itself: the forces of life and death are reckoned with, the limits of knowledge and power are challenged, truth and faith are revalorized through the initiation process—all this being, at the very least, an experience in humility and brotherhood.

All learn about Vodou starting from an early age in their home, in their extended family, in their community while attending Vodou ceremonies or participating in services at home or in a *hounfò*. However, with age comes not only increased privileges but additional responsibilities. The youth are expected to participate more and more in Vodou rituals, to guide younger children, to show increased respect for elders, to develop their sense of humanism and to learn to emphasize the common good over individual satisfactions. In other words, they are expected to systematically incorporate the Haitian secular and religious beliefs in a sustained effort to live a relevant and moral existence and to maintain equilibrium within their community.

However, as in other educational arenas, some learners are more perceptive and more talented than others. The good learner is a person who is receptive to the message communicated by the spirits, the elders, or even the group of peers, someone who is attentive to the aesthetic guiding every endeavor and encounter. The proficient learner is thus skilled at orchestrating the "reception of messages" and pays attention not only to content but also style, always striving to stay in touch with both the inner self and the outside world. The accomplished learner is open, honest, observant, vigilant, unblocked, extended; he or she is mindful of the traditions and values being passed down and loyal to the messages of the cosmic world.

Moreover, the consummated learner is often also a good *chwal* for the *loas*, that is, someone who easily and skillfully receives the spirits and their messages through possession or in their dreams. Someone who has been possessed by a god is said to be the *chwal*, the horse of the *loa*, someone whose *gro bonanj* (guardian angel/spirit/soul) has been displaced by that of the spirit who mounted her. The person possessed is in a state of trance. She is not conscious and is no longer herself but the incarnation of the *loa*. In particular, this is an area where *manbos* and *houngans* excel as students of the spirits and of the ancestors, making it possible for the gods to enter their bodies, becoming, by extension, gods themselves through spiritual and charnel communion.

The propagation of moral principles and educational values assumes many forms in Vodou communities. It happens during ceremonies, while interacting with the spirits or with other Vodou participants; in the homes and outside, while fulfilling one's daily activities around family members and in the larger community. In other words, one learns everywhere and at all times. More than actual "moral" principles, what is communicated inside and outside Vodou families is a worldview, a particular sensitivity and perspective on life—the *Vodou ethos* formed and informed by both African cosmological understandings and American and Creole realities.

NOTES

1. Newell S. Booth Jr., ed., "An Approach to African Religion," in *African Religions: A Symposium.* New York: Nok Publishers, 1977, 1.

2. Ch'ing Kum Yang, *Religion in Chinese Society: A Study of Contemporary Social Functions of Religions and Some Historical Factors.* Berkeley: University of California Press, 1970, 20.

3. Ibid. Yang made, for example, similar remarks about China. So did Booth: "There are interesting affinities between African and Chinese traditional religion." "An Approach to African Religion," 10.

4. Literally, *lakou* means "yard." The word *lakou* evokes the idea of many large extended families sharing a common compound and yard. It represents a residual structure of the African village.

5. *Anba dlo* literally means under water. Haitians believe that some people spend time "under water," down in *Ginen* (a Haitian appellation for Africa) as part of their initiation as priests and priestesses. This "inexpensive" type of initiation, unlike the more formal ones that may be somewhat costly, are considered a special "gift." Mathilda Beauvoir, who officiates primarily in Paris, may well be the most renowned *anba dlo* initiate. Also see: Harold Cour-

lander, *The Drum and the Hoe.* Berkeley: University of California Press, 1973, 19.

6. Other reasons include, by order of importance, (1) the essence of the Vodou worldview itself, (2) the orality that characterizes Haitian culture, (3) until recently, the lack of a standardized Creole spelling, (4) the unavailability of writers to produce such documents, (5) a clear lack of funding and resources to engage in such an activity.

7. Harold Courlander, *Hairi Singing.* New York: Cooper Square, 1973, 7.

8. *Konesans* means knowledge, but the Creole word is stronger than its English counterpart in that it encompasses the notions of experience mixed with wisdom, usually acquired with age. Typically, elders, *houngans* and *manbos*, the departed, the ancestors have a lot of *konesans*.

9. Especially during the Duvalier era, many such religious "leaders" were also members of the government.

10. Karen McCarthy Brown, "Alourdes: A Case Study of Moral Leadership in Haitian Vodou," in *Saints and Virtues*, J. S. Hawley, ed., Berkeley: University of California Press, 1987, 167.

11. In Haiti, eating is a life-sustaining activity in more ways than one. It is a means of maintaining ties; to say that someone eats at one's table or at one's place is a way of expressing the closeness of a relationship.

12. See: Karen McCarthy Brown, *Mama Lola: A Vodou Priestess in Brooklyn.* Berkeley: University of California Press, 1991. Mama Lola's reputation goes further than the boundaries of the Haitian community. Though many other technicians of the Vodou religion share her worldly approach, the international impact of her ministrations remains unusual.

13. Here I specifically refer to *houngans* and not *manbos.* Though Vodou is not a religion that differentiates between gender, there are still very few internationally renowned female painters and artists.

14. Peter Paris, *The Spirituality of African Peoples, The Search for a Common Moral Discourse.* Minneapolis: Fortress Press, 1995, 29.

15. Ibid. John Mibiti, in *The Spirituality of African People,* 29.

16. Ibid., 30.

17. Ibid., 31.

18. McCarthy Brown, *Mama Lola,* 6.

19. Ibid.

20. McCarthy Brown, "Alourdes: A Case Study," 166.

21. For more details on Vodou initiation, see McCarthy Brown, "Plenty Confidence in Myself: The Initiation of a White Woman Scholar into Haitian Vodou," *Journal of Feminist Studies in Religion,* vol. 3, no. 1 (spring 1987): 67–76; also, Katherine Dunham, *Island Possessed.* Chicago: The University of Chicago Press, 1969, reprinted 1994.

22. Dunham, *Island Possessed,* 108–9.

23. McCarthy Brown, "Plenty Confidence," 75.

24. Ibid., 73–75; McCarthy Brown wrote that although one is not allowed to reveal the secrets of Vodou initiation, she was permitted to write about her reactions to the process. She cautioned, however, not to "overinterpret" her "metaphoric speech."

25. Like a baby's skull, the new head, the new self, is believed to be vulnerable and as such must be protected.

32

ISLAM IN THE AFRICAN-AMERICAN EXPERIENCE

Richard Brent Turner

INTRODUCTION

Malcolm X and, more recently, Louis Farrakhan and the Million Man March are three of the more visible signs of Islam's influence in the lives and culture of African Americans. Yet, "Islam in the African-American Experience" shows, the involvement of Black Americans with Islam reaches back to the earliest days of the African presence in North America. Part I of the paper explores these roots in West Africa and antebellum America. Part II tells the story of the "Prophets of the City"—the leaders of the new urban-based African-American Muslim movements in the twentieth century. My work places the study of Islam in a historical context of racial, ethical, and political relations that influenced the reception of successive and varied presentations of Islam, including the West African Islam of African-American slaves, the multiracial Islam of the Ahmadiyya Movement from India, the orthodox Sunni practice of later immigrants, and the racial-separatist Nation of Islam and Moorish Science Temple of America.

Signification (the issue of naming and identity) is not only the interpretative thread that runs through the historical narrative of Islam in Black America, it is also the key to understanding that history in the context of global Islam. Signification became a central aspect of Islam in West Africa and the Middle East before modernity. In these contexts, Black peoples' signifying themselves as the people they wanted to be, through their embracing of Islam, was the result of the adaptation of the religion to local cultures that was integral to global Islam. In America, signification continued to be central in African-American Islam. There is a difference, of course, between a people who manage their own society and who themselves determine, on a selective basis, which aspects of an Arabian Islamic tradition they wish to practice and a religious organization of people, drawn from a numerical minority of a society who nominally declare themselves to be separate from that society. However, in both America and in West Africa, naming and renaming became controlling acts that documented Black peoples' struggles to define themselves separately in the context of global Islam.

I. ROOT SOURCES

African Muslim Slaves and Resistance

In the New World, African Muslim slaves were noteworthy for their sometimes violent resistance to the institution of slavery. In Brazil, hundreds of African Muslim slaves planned and executed a major slave uprising in Bahia, in 1835, fighting soldiers and civilians in the streets of Salvador. Moreover, at least one African Muslim participated in the revolt on the Spanish slave ship the *Amistad* in the Caribbean, in 1839. The slaves' knowledge of Arabic and of the religion of Islam were key factors in their identification as African Muslims. In other locations, African Muslims were noted for their bold efforts both to resist conversion to Christianity and to convert other Africans to Islam. Mohammed Sisei, an African Muslim in Trinidad in the early nineteenth century, noted that the Free Mandingo Society there was instrumental in converting a whole H.M. West Indian Regiment of Blacks to Islam. At the same time, prominent African Muslim slaves in Jamaica in the early 1800s circulated a letter urging other African Muslims in their communities to adhere to their religion. Muhammad, an African Muslim slave in Antigua, was manumitted by his master because of his stubborn adherence to Islam and returned to Africa in 1811.[1]

Resistance, then, was a global theme in New World Black Islam in the eighteenth and nineteenth centuries.[2] In the United States, however, African Muslims practiced more subtle forms of resistance to slavery. Some of them kept their African names, wrote in Arabic, and continued to practice their religion; others used the American Colonization Society to gain their freedom and return to Africa. All of this constituted intellectual resistance to slavery, as African Muslims, who had been members of the ruling elite in West Africa, used their literacy and professional skills to manipulate white Americans. This peculiar form of resistance accounts in part for the compelling and provocative nature of the life stories of the known African Muslim slaves in America.[3]

Even the slave community noted the compelling presence of African Muslims in its midst. Ex-slave Charles Ball, one of the first African Americans to publish an autobiography, was struck by the religious discipline and resistance to Christianity of a nineteenth-century African Muslim slave on a plantation in North Carolina. He wrote,

> At the time I first went to Carolina, there were a great many African slaves in the country . . .
> I became intimately acquainted with some of these men . . . I knew several, who must have
> been, from what I have since learned, Mohammedans; though at that time, I had never heard
> of the religion of Mohammed. There was one man on this plantation, who prayed five times
> every day always turning his face to the East, when in the performance of his devotions.[4]

Signification is the analytical key that explains resistance in the lives of the African Muslims noted previously and in the biographical sketches that follow, for African Muslim slaves preserved their Islamic identities by refusing to internalize the racist stereotypes that justified the system of exploitation. These were profound acts of resistance to an institution that, in setting the terms of pre-twentieth-century racial discourse in America, attempted to eradicate all aspects of African heritage in the slave quarters by stripping slaves of their culture, thus leaving them powerless. As African Muslims signified themselves as the people they wanted to be in America, they transformed Islam to meet the demands of survival and resistance in this "strange Christian land." Their signification turned their history, religion, and genealogies into "an instrument of identity and transformation."[5]

In this context, writing in Arabic, fasting, wearing Muslim clothing, and reciting and reflecting on the Quran were the keys to an inner struggle of liberation against Christian tyranny. Thus, for African Muslim slaves, their significations became "the ultimate test of their faith" in America and a "paradigm for the liberation struggles" of other oppressed Blacks in the New World. Their stories reveal that African slaves had ethnic and religious identities that could not be erased by the trauma of slavery[6]

Fascinating portraits of a few influential African Muslim slaves exist in the historical literature. Excerpts from two of their life stories follow.

Bilali and Salih Bilali were two of at least twenty Black Muslims who were reported to have lived and practiced their religion in Sapelo Island and St. Simon's Island during the antebellum period. The Georgia Sea Islands provided fertile ground for Islamic and other African retentions because of their relative isolation from Euro-American influences. Both Bilali and Salih Bilali remained steadfast in the struggle to maintain their Muslim identities in America. Both men were noted for their devotion to their religious obligations, for wearing Islamic clothing, and for their Muslim names, and one was noted for his ability to write and speak Arabic, which he passed on to his children. Moreover, available evidence suggests that they might have been the leaders of a small Black Muslim community in the Georgia Sea Islands.[7]

Georgia Conrad, a white American resident of one of the Sea Islands, met Bilah's family in the 1850s and was struck by their religion, dress, and ability to speak Arabic. She wrote:

> On Sapelo Island near Darcen, I used to know a family of Negroes who worshipped Mohamet. They were tall and well-formed, with good features. They conversed with us in English but in talking among themselves they used a foreign tongue that no one else understood. The head of the tribe was a very old man named Bilali. He always wore a cap that resembled a Turkish fez.[8]

Bilali, who was also known as Belali Mahomet, was a Muslim slave on the Thomas Spalding plantation on Sapelo Island, Georgia, from the early to the mid-1800s. His great grandchildren told his story to Works Progress Administration Writers in Georgia in the 1930s. Bilali maintained his identity by giving his nineteen children Muslim names and teaching them Muslim traditions. When he died, he left an Arabic manuscript he had composed, and had his prayer rug and Quran placed in his coffin.[9]

Only a few facts are known about Bilali's pre-American history. Although his surname is unknown, we do know that his first name represents the West African Muslim fascination with Bilal, the Prophet Muhammad's Black companion and the first muezzin. Bilali was born in Timbo, Futa Jallon. Like other Fulbe Muslim compatriots in America, he was probably raised in a prominent scholarly family, for the Arabic manuscript that he composed in America was undoubtedly the product of someone who wrote and read Arabic at an advanced level. The manuscript was a compilation of pieces from the Malikite legal text ar-Risala, which was originally written by Abu Muhammad "Abdullah ibn, Abi Zaid al-Qairawani." Bilali's work, "First Fruits of Happiness," attempts to reconcile the law of Islam with a wholesome daily life. It suggests that Bilali was struggling to uphold his faith in America.[10]

Bilah's leadership ability, reflecting his elite roots in West Africa, was legendary on Sapelo Island, He was the manager of his master's plantation, which included close to five hundred slaves. During the War of 1812, Bilali and approximately eighty slaves who had muskets prevented the British from invading their island. Some of these slaves were undoubtedly Muslim, since Bilali forewarned Thomas Spalding that, in battle, "I will answer for every Negro of the true facts, but not for the Christian dogs you own." Moreover, in 1824 during a hurricane, Bilali saved the slaves on Sapelo island by leading them into cotton and sugar shacks constructed of African tabby.[11]

Perhaps the most fascinating aspect of Bilali's Islamic legacy was that his descendants on Sapelo Island remembered him in the 1930s, when they were interviewed by the Savannah Unit of the Georgia Writers' Project. These interviews also brought to light other nineteenth-century Blacks who practiced Islam on the Georgia Sea Islands. Although they have been criticized for inaccuracy and contextual problems, these interviews are an invaluable source of information on Bilali and his descendants.[12]

According to Shadrack Hall, who was Bilali's great grandson, the African Muslim slave was brought to Georgia from the Bahamas with his wife, Phoebe, and maintained Islamic names and traditions in his family for at least three generations:

> Much gran wuz Hestah, Belali's daughter. She tell me Belali wuz coal Black, wid duh small feechuhs we hab, and he wuz very tall . . . Belali hab plenty daughtahs, Medina, Yaruba, Fatima, Bentoo, Hestah, Marget, and Chaalut.
>
> Ole Belali Smith wuz muh uncle. His son wuz George Smith's gran. He wuz much gran Hestah's son and muh muddduh Sally's brudduh. Hestah and all ub um sho pray on duh head. Dey weah duh string uh beads on duh neck. Dey pray at sun-up and face duh sun on duh knees an bow tuh it tree times, kneelin' on a lill mat.[13]

Finally, Katie Brown, another one of Bilah's great grandchildren, recalled her Muslim grandmother Margret who wore a Muslim head dress and made rice cakes for the children at the end of a fast day.[14]

Salih Bilali, born in Massina in 1765, was probably a member of a prominent Mandingo Fulbe clerical family. When he was twelve years old, he was taken into slavery while he was returning home from Jenne, one of the major Black Muslim intellectual centers of West Africa. In his African reminiscences, Salih Bilali remembered well the racial and cultural differences between the Black Muslims in his land and the white Arab Muslim traders who sold them goods in Jenne, Timbuktu, Kouna and Sego.[15]

Salih Bilali's odyssey in the New World brought him first to the Bahamas, where he was purchased by the Couper family around 1800. By 1816, he had become the overseer of the family's St. Simon's plantation, which had more than four hundred slaves. By all accounts, Salih Bilali was an impressive figure in the Georgia Sea Islands. His steadfast religiosity may have been the result of Islamic training under Bilali in the Bahamas and Georgia.[16] Together they formed the nucleus of a small Muslim community, of which the members can only be suggested by the interviews with Salih Bilah's grandchildren, conducted by the Georgia Writers' Project on the Georgia Sea Islands in the 1930s.[17]

Salih Bilali's grandson, Ben Sullivan, remembered that his father had received his Arabic name—Bilali—from his own father. Bilali was the butler on another Couper plantation until the end of the Civil War, when he chose the surname Sullivan. Bilali Sullivan made *saraka* (rice cakes) at certain times of the year. Ben Sullivan was one of several of Couper's slaves who practiced Islam. This group included Alex Boyd, his maternal grandfather, and two men named Daphne and Israel: "Ole Israel he pray a lot wid a boo he hab wit he hide and he take a lill mat and he say he prayuhs on it He pray wen duh sun go up and wen duh sun go down. He alluz tie he head up in a wite clawt."[18]

In the biographical sketches of Bilali and Salih Bilali, there is fragmentary evidence of a small African Muslim slave community that attempted to preserve Muslim identities and traditions in the nineteenth century. In these sketches, we also have evidence of how African Muslim women were involved in the struggle to preserve Muslim identities in America. It appears that they played a significant role in this struggle, for their preparation of Muslim foods, their Muslim clothing, and their disciplined devotion to their religion deeply impressed their children and grandchildren. And their families' memories of their Muslim identities have influenced the significations of nineteenth-century Islam that African Americans have preserved in their folklore in the twentieth century.

By the eve of the Civil War, the old Islam of the original African Muslim slaves was, for all practical purposes, defunct because these Muslims were unable in the nineteenth century to develop institutions that would perpetuate their religion. With no community of believers for them to connect with outside of the slave quarters, they were religious oddities, mavericks. When they died, their version of Islam, which was private and individually oriented, disappeared. Unfortunately, the historical record does not provide us with a holistic picture of their religious life. They were important, nevertheless, because they brought the religion of Islam to America.

Pan-Africanism and Black bitterness towards Christian racism were new seeds planted in the consciousness of nineteenth-century African Americans that in turn flowered into a new American Islam in the early twentieth century. This new American Islam in the African-American community was multicultural; and it developed a distinct missionary and internationalist political agenda. It was also part of a new era in American religious history as Eastern religions began to flourish in the United States. Noble Drew Ali's Moorish Science Temple of America was the first mass-based version of this new American Islam among African Americans in the early twentieth century.

II. PROPHETS OF THE CITY
Noble Drew Ali and the Moorish Science Temple of America

Booker T. Washington, an ex-slave and a conservative Black leader at the turn of the century, wrote that Black people in the South generally agreed upon two points when they were freed from slavery: "that they must change their names and that they must leave the old plantations for at least a few days or weeks in order that they might really feel sure they were free." Thus in 1913, when Noble Drew Ali, the flamboyant prophet and founder of the Moorish Science Temple of America, said "the name means everything," his words surely echoed the sentiments of the ex-slaves. Their children and grandchildren were part of the Great Migration of four to five million Blacks from the South to the northern and midwestern industrial cities in the early twentieth century. Some of them were Drew Ali's earliest followers.[19]

The Moorish Science Temple of America was the first mass religious movement in the history of Islam in America. It focused on the African-American community and embodied all the distinctive characteristics of this new religious tradition. It was urban, and multicultural, and it developed a distinct missionary and Pan-African political agenda. Its racial separation was due not only to Black nationalism but also to the historic patterns of racial separatism in Islam; Arab and Eastern European Muslims in America probably considered the Moorish Science Temple an embarrassing, peculiar, non-Islamic movement (because it created its own Quaran), and ignored it.

Noble Drew Ali was an intelligent and creative signifier, a self-styled prophet of the city who utilized eclectic religious, cultural, and political motifs to construct a new Black American cultural and political identity that involved changes in name, nationality, religion, diet, and dress. His initial inspiration came from Islam as a global religious, political, and cultural phenomenon. He was familiar with Indian philosophy and "central Quranic concepts such as justice, a purposeful creation of mankind, freedom of will, and humankind as the generator of personal action (both good and bad)." Thus the Indian subcontinent continued to be a source of information and inspiration for American Islam, as Drew Ali developed the tradition of the "jihad of words" by utilizing the written word to strive in the path of Allah. He also appropriated ideas and symbols about Islam from the Black Freemason movement to which he belonged. His Pan-African political inspiration and rhetoric came from Marcus Garvey's Universal Negro Improvement Association, which began and declined in Black America almost contemporaneously with the establishment and decline of the Moorish Science Temple. Marcus Garvey's movement and the Great Migration were two of the major social facts of Black America during the interwar period, both of which had a profound impact on the political thought, worldview, and demographics of modern American Islam.[20]

Martin Marty's *The Noise of Conflict, 1919–1941*, focused on the word "America" as central to an understanding of the political and cultural identity of the Moorish Science Temple of America. Noble Drew Ali was an important voice in the "conflict between peoples and among people" about the shape of American religion in the interwar period. He described the "noise of conflict," which concerned public religious and political power and influence in the United States. At stake were "the shape and destiny of America, the role of various religions and peoples in the nation, and the part faiths should play in personal destinies." In this context, as Jewish, Catholic, European, and Asian immigrants came to America in unprecedented numbers, and as millions of Black people moved into the cities, establishing scores of new religious and political movements, Anglo-Saxon Protestants who considered themselves "100 percent Americans" fought to maintain a racially homogeneous Christian America. Meanwhile, other Americans struggled to force their country to come to terms with its racial, cultural, political, and religious pluralism. Marty contends that because of its small numbers, Islam was "not in position to have public impact" in this conflict. But as we shall see, Noble Drew Ali, Mufti Muhammad Sadiq, W. D. Fard, Elijah Muhammad, and other Muslim leaders were all struggling to extend the political and cultural boundaries of white Protestant Christian America to include American Islam. Thus "conflict between whites and Blacks" was a central issue in this "war" over religious and political hegemony in the cities of the United States.[21]

Noble Drew Ali was born in North Carolina on January 8, 1886. His birth name was Timothy Drew. Diverse legends have developed around his identity and activities before

1913. Some of his first followers claimed that "he was a child of exslaves raised among the Cherokee Indians." He spent his early childhood as an orphan, wandering with a gypsy group. At the age of sixteen he was spotted by a gypsy woman who took him to Egypt, where he studied in the Essene Schools. As a young man, he then returned to America and became a merchant seaman in Newark, New Jersey. Another legend claimed that Ali went back to Egypt in the early twentieth century and met the last priest of an ancient cult of high magic. He proved that he was a prophet by finding his way out of the pyramids. He was also thought to have traveled to Morocco and Saudi Arabia, where he obtained a char- ter from the sheiks to teach Islam in America and received the name Ali from Sultan Abdul Ibn Said in Mecca. In 1910, he returned to the United States, where he worked as a train ex- pressman and joined the Prince Hall Masons. The final legend concerning his early years was that Noble Drew Ali went to Washington, D.C., in 1912 to ask President Woodrow Wil- son for the authority to teach his people Islam, the religion of their "ancient forefathers." He also asked that the nationality "Moorish American," the names "Ali, Bey, and El," and the flag of Morocco, which were taken away from his people in the colonial era, be given back. Closer to the truth than these legends is the Associated Negro Press's report that "he [Ali] was accompanying a Hindu Fakir in circus shows when he decided to start a little order of his own."[22]

In 1913, Noble Drew Ali, calling himself the second prophet of Islam, founded the order—the first Moorish Science Temple of America—in Newark, New Jersey. Over the next decade, his movement grew to an estimated membership of thirty thousand, and he established temples in Detroit, Pittsburgh, and Chicago. In 1914, Ali's leadership was unsuccessfully challenged in Newark by Abdul Wali Farad Muhammad Ali, a mysterious teacher of Islam from the East about whose origins and early years at his Newark mission little is known. At any rate, in 1923 Drew Ali moved to Chicago, and in 1925, he set up the permanent headquarters of his movement there.[23]

In their quest for an alternate signification and identity, the Moorish Americans wore Black fezzes and white turbans. They carried nationality cards and used as their symbol a red flag with a five-pointed star in the center, recalling the flag of Morocco. They claimed that they were not Negroes, Blacks, or colored people, but instead an olive-skinned Asiatic people who were the descendants of Moroccans. According to their teachings, the Moorish Science Temple of America had been founded so that the prophet Noble Drew Ali could lift the fallen "Asiatic nation of North America" by teaching its members their true religion (Islam), their true nationality, and their true genealogy. Noble Drew Ali taught his follow- ers that they could trace their genealogy directly to Jesus, who was a descendant of "the an- cient Canaanites, the Moabites, and the inhabitants of Africa." The sacred text of the Moorish Science Temple of America, a so-called *Holy Koran*, was written by Ali in 1927; but it was rejected by other Islamic groups because it replaces the original Quran, which Muslims believed was revealed to the Prophet Muhammad by Allah in the seventh century. Noble Drew Ali wrote several versions of this sixty-four-page book compiling his informa- tion from four sources: *The Aquarian Gospels of Jesus Christ* (an occult version of the New Testament), *Unto Thee I Grant* (literature of the Rosicrucian Brotherhood, a Masonic order influenced by the lore of the Egyptian mystery schools), the Bible, and the Quran.[24]

The end of the prophet's reign began on March 25, 1929, when one of his opponents for leadership, Sheik Claude Greene, was shot and stabbed to death at the Unity Club in Chicago. Noble Drew Ali was arrested and jailed for the murder. He died several weeks later while released on bond. His death has been variously attributed to Greene's support-ers and the Chicago Police Department. However, according to Ernest Allen Jr., he died on July 20, 1929 of tuberculosis.[25]

After Noble Drew Ali's death, his attorney, Aaron Payne, tried unsuccessfully to unify the Moorish movement. Meanwhile, several of the late prophet's disciples who became known as "Brother Prophets"—Steven Gibbons El (his chauffeur), Ira Johnson Bey (a leader from Pittsburgh, Pennsylvania), Mealy El, R. German Ali, and Kirkman Bey—fought one another for leadership positions. Steven Gibbons and Ira Johnson claimed that the dead prophet's spirit had entered their bodies. Eventually, a gun battle occurred at the Moorish Science Temple branch headquarters in which one Moorish American and two policemen died. The police arrested sixty-three Moorish Americans, and Ira Johnson was sent to the State Hospital for the Criminally Insane, where he eventually died. Steven Gibbons was also committed to the State Hospital but gained his release several years later. By 1941, he had founded a new Moorish Temple in Chicago on East 40th Street. Gibbons, along with six other Moorish leaders, still insisted that he was the Grand Sheik of the Moorish Science Temple of America. R. German Ali became the leader of a branch of the movement that recognized only Noble Drew Ali as prophet. Thus, the quest for identity resumed, and the Moorish Science Temple movement continued to grow after Noble Drew Ali's death. Major factions of the movement exist today, with their national headquarters in Baltimore, Chicago, and Los Angeles.[26]

The Ahmadiyya Mission to America

> Harlem's Moslems run into several thousands . . . Since they have no mosque, the faithful worship in private homes and hired halls, where on Saturday mornings their children study the Koran. They live quietly in Harlem, but during their festivals they don rich robes, shawls, turbans and fezzes of their native land, and the women wear gorgeous brocades and heavy decorative jewelry. Ordinarily, Moslems wear American dress, for most of them have lived in the United States more than twenty years . . . They possess a religious fervor that is expressed in much missionary work among American Negroes . . . whether they are African, Arabs, Tartars, or American Negroes, Moors, Persians or whites, Moslems intermarry. The racial flow back and forth defies classification.[27]

This is how Roi Ottley, an eminent African-American journalist, author, and reporter for the *New York Amsterdam Star News*, described the cultural richness that he observed in Harlem's Muslim community in 1943. Ottley's observations are important not only for what they tell us about the ethos of American Islam in the twentieth century, but also for what they say about the relationship between African Americans and immigrant Muslim culture. During the 1920s, positive social and religious interaction between Muslims of different racial and ethnic groups was encouraged by the Indian missionaries of the Ahmadiyya Movement in Islam. The Ahmadiyya was unquestionably one of the most sig-nificant movements in the history of Islam in the United States in the twentieth century, providing as it did the *first multiracial model* for American Islam. The Ahmadis dissemi-nated Islamic literature and converted Black and white Americans. They attacked the dis-tortions of Islam in the media, established mosques and reading rooms, and translated the Quran into English. They also constituted the link between the immigrant Muslims (whose numbers included Arabs, Persians, Africans, Tartars, Turks, Albanians, and Yugosla-vians) and Black Muslim groups such as the Nations of Islam and the Moorish Science

Temple. Thus, their goal was to permanently alter the historic patterns of racial and ethnic separation that existed among Muslims in America.

On January 24, 1920, as daybreak settled over London's streets, an elderly, light-brown-complexioned man with spectacles boarded the *S.S. Haverford* bound for America. His dark green and gold turban and his amiable but mysterious manner attracted the attention of several Chinese passengers, to whom he introduced himself as "Mufti Muhammad Sadiq, missionary for the Ahmadiyya Movement in Islam." Each day at sea, several passengers were eager to learn about this exotic stranger's religion and his plans for a Muslim mission in America.[28]

The *S.S. Haverford* arrived in Philadelphia on February 15, 1920. The United States immigration authorities seized Mufti Muhammad Sadiq and took him into custody before he could leave this ship, although he assured them that "he had not come here to teach plurality of wives. A Muslim will be committing a sin against his religion." After they had interrogated him for several hours and had established that he was a citizen of India and a representative of a religious group that practiced polygamy, the authorities asked him to leave the United States on the ship in which he had just arrived. Sadiq refused to do so and requested an appeal to the Secretariat in Washington, D.C. He was confined to the Philadelphia Detention House in Gloucester, New Jersey, until a favorable decision of the appeal was handed down several weeks later.[29]

Many men in the Detention House were impressed with Sadiq's passion and devotion to his multiracial religion, which offered dramatic changes in name and identity, and they converted. "Under curious circumstances, we got acquainted in the closed walls of the Detention House," Sadiq said of his first convert in America, R. J. H. Rochford. "Watching me praying and reciting the Holy Book, Mr. Rochford inquired of my religion, which I explained to him and I gave him some books to study. Very soon he was convinced of the truth of our religion and being converted was named Hamid.[30] Although Rochford was eventually sent back to England by the immigration authorities, during those weeks of confinement Sadiq made nineteen other coverts to Islam. These men were from Jamaica, British Guyana, Azores, Poland, Russia, Germany, Belgium, Portugal, Italy, and France. Thus, Sadiq's mission was at first generalized and only later focused almost exclusively on African Americans.[31] Sadiq's tone during his confinement was conciliatory, as he attempted to convinced the federal authorities that he could preach Islam in the United States without preaching polygamy.[32] To do so, Sadiq made a distinction between commandments and permissions in Islam. Muslims must follow the commandments of their religion, he explained, but might avoid the permissions. For instance, no government could persuade a Muslim to worship more than one God, since the worship of one God was a commandment of Islamic religion. However, polygamy was permitted only in countries whose laws sanctioned its practice. In countries that prohibited polygamy, permission for its practice was disallowed under the commandment that all Muslims must obey the laws of the country in which they lived.[33]

But if Sadiq was conciliatory, others were not so sanguine. The Ahmadiyya Movement in Islam expressed its outrage over Sadiq's detention, an outrage that Sadiq would share by the end of 1921. It cited in *The Review of Religions* the gap between America's ideas of freedom, justice, and equality and the nation's actual practices. Sher Ali proposed that if Sadiq could not preach Islam in the United States, the "American missionaries should be expelled from India." Finally, Ali warned the United States that Islam would soon spread throughout the world, with or without its cooperation.[34] After two months of confinement, Sadiq was finally allowed to enter the United States in April of 1920 on the condition that he would not preach polygamy.[35]

From 1921 to 1925 Sadiq made 1,025 American converts. Many of the Ahmadiyya converts were Black residents of Chicago and Detroit. These two cities and, to a lesser extent, Gary, Indiana, and St. Louis, Missouri, were hotbeds of Ahmadiyya activity in the 1920s. In 1922, Sadiq moved the American headquarters of the movement from Highland Park, Michigan, to Wabash Avenue on the south side of Chicago.[36]

Although the Ahmadiyya Movement in Islam secured some white American converts, there were few white American proselytizers in the early 1920s.[37] Because of the leadership roles that it gave to its Black participants, however, the movement began to attract members of Marcus Garvey's Universal Negro Improvement Association (UNIA). Brother Abdullah, a prominent convert in Chicago, was a Garveyite. There were at least six other Garveyites in the Chicago mission, and they wore their Garvey uniforms to the Ahmadi religious services and meetings. In 1923, Sadiq gave five lectures at the UNIA meetings in Detroit. Eventually he converted forty Garveyites to Islam. "Out of the converts there, an intelligent and enthusiastic young man, Rev. Sutton, has been appointed as the leader of the congregation with his Moslem name as Sheik Abdus Salaam," he wrote. "Another zealous member of ours is Mrs. Wright (Sister Nazeefa), who together with her little children is studiously learning the Arabic language."[38]

Thus there was a direct relationship between the Universal Negro Improvement Association and the Ahmadiyya Movement in Islam. But the connection between the two groups occurred on a more subtle level as well, a fact that is significant to African-American religious history and that suggests a main concern here. The Ahmadis were Indians—one of the "darker races of the world"—who were seeking their independence from the British. The Garvey movement stressed the internationalist perspective that led African Americans to think of themselves in concert with Africans and the "darker races of the world" against white Europeans and Americans. In the 1920s, this internationalist identity, which had been growing among Blacks since the late nineteenth century, began to extend to their religious consciousness as well. Christianity was increasingly criticized as a "clan religion" for whites that needed to be revised by Blacks or abandoned for another religion, such as Islam. The attraction of both the Garvey movement and the Ahmadiyya Movement in Islam was that they offered a new religious identity to African Americans who had been awakened to this perspective. Just as the UNIA was the *Universal* Negro Improvement Association with universality in the political sphere, the Ahmadis connected the faithful to a worldwide, multiracial, but "non-white" religion.

Moreover, Garveyism and the Islamic movements in the 1920s were forms of political religion. David Apter has argued that especially in Third World nations, the sacred is used to legitimate political ends and to mobilize the community for political goals. In this context, political doctrine becomes "in effect, a political religion" that gives "continuity, meaning and purpose" to a people's life. With this perspective in mind, one could say there were three historical strands in the development of Islam in the United States in the 1920s. The first, the conservative Sunni Islam of the Muslim immigrants from the Middle East and the Islamic Mission of America, orthodox, universalist, and also politically conservative. The second, the Moorish Science Temple movement, was heterodox, a racial-separatist interpretation of Islam, and Pan-Africanist with a "Moroccan" cultural base. Third, and important here, the Ahmadiyya Movement in Islam was heterodox, multiracial, and politically mixed: the Ahmadis were advocates of both Pan-Islam and Indian nationalism. Ahmadis knew that the Garvey movement was sympathetic to both of these issues; they saw the parallels between the two movements and Pan-Africanism; and to a certain extent they identified with Black people as fellow victims of European colonization and imperialism.

Pan-Islam was not a new issue for Marcus Garvey or for the UNIA. Previously, Garvey had a close relationship with Duse Mohammed Ali, the Egyptian journalist who was also an advocate of this principle, as well as of Egyptian nationalism and Pan-African business ventures. He may have influenced Garvey to allow Sadiq to give the aforementioned lectures at the UNIA meeting in Detroit in 1923.[39]

In the 1920s, the Ahmadiyya Movement in Islam had offered African Americans a multiracial Muslim identity that involved the signification of Indian cultural and political elements with aspects of Pan-Africanist identity. In this context, African-American converts were trained by Indian teachers from the East who had a global agenda that was separate and different from the Moroccan emphasis of the Moorish Science Temple of America. Thus African-American Muslims were not united but had different visions of Islamic identity and signification that involved different syntheses of religion, politics, and culture. These different visions of signification and identity multiplied in the 1930s and contributed to several decades of transition of the multiracial mission of the Ahmadiyya Movement in Islam.

The three decades between 1920 and 1950 were years of transition for the Ahmadiyya mission to America. First, during these years the Ahmadiyya movement came to terms with its failure to achieve its initial objective in the United States in the 1920s, which was to bring about a permanent departure from the historic patterns of racism and ethnic separation that existed among Muslims in America and to create a widespread multiracial movement in the United States. Second, the movement of the Indian missionaries was challenged slightly by the Black nationalist mission of the Nation of Islam, which will be discussed next. Although the latter group displaced the Ahmadiyya movement as the most prominent and popular Islamic movement among Black Americans in the 1950s, in the 1930s and 1940s it was still a private and obscure religious movement with a small following.

The Ahmadiyya Movement in Islam continues to have considerable influence among a certain segment of the African-American Muslim community today. The internationalist identities of its African-American members are extraordinary; they "are probably the most widely traveled" among Black American Muslims. Although the Ahmadiyya movement is not attracting as many African-American converts as it did in the past, partly because of the ascendancy of Sunni Islam in the United States in the 1990s, its impact on the history of African-American Islam is significant. It was the first and continues to be the most effective model of a multiracial community experience for Black people in the religion.

But now it is time to turn to the saga of the Nation of Islam, which became a model for racial-separatist identity for African-American Muslims. This religious movement began in the Black community of Detroit, Michigan, in the 1930s with the work of a mysterious street peddler, W. D. Fard.

The Early History of the Nation of Islam

In 1930, W. D. Fard, a mysterious Muslim missionary to America, began his work among poor Black people in Detroit. Assuming the guise of an Arab street peddler, Fard established the Nation of Islam. In a global context, his occupation connected him to the original Arab trading and missionary networks that had brought Islam to Black people in West Africa several hundred years earlier. It also conveyed the sense of strangeness and mystery that attracted some Americans to Eastern religious and cultures. *Street peddler, dope peddler, missionary, prophet, convict, charlatan, fraud, social reformer, Allah* and *leader of the "Voodoo Cult"* were some of the epithets used to describe Fard, who was to become one of the most important—and most mysterious—figures in the history of American Islam in the early twentieth century. Under the leadership of Elijah Muhammad, Fard's most trusted disciple, the Nation of Islam evolved from a local movement to the most powerful Islamic organization in America, establishing connections with Garveyism and espousing a unique model of racial separatism in the process. Although I shed critical light on all of these issues, the question of W. D. Fard's identity is still not answered. The many mysteries surrounding this enigmatic figure are still at the heart of the enduring question: Who was the founder of the Nation of Islam?

One evening in August 1931, W. D. Fard spoke to a gathering of several hundred followers at the former Universal Negro Improvement Association hall in Detroit. Black people were crowded in the hall and outside to hear the prophet's message. He preached that the word "negro" was a misnomer for the people of the Black African diaspora; this name was created by the white race to separate African Americans from their original Asiatic roots. Fard declared that the Blacks of North America "were not Americans but Asiatics" whose ancestors had been taken from the African-Asiatic world by European slave traders in the name of Christianity four hundred years earlier. His personality captured the imagination of his audience as he continued to tell them about their "real" name, history, and destiny. According to his captivating story, Black Americans were the "lost-found members of the tribe of Shabazz."

> The Black men in North America are not Negroes, but members of the lost tribe of Shabazz, stolen by traders from the Holy City of Mecca 378 years ago. The Prophet came to America to find and bring back to life his long lost brethren, from whom the Caucasians had taken away their language, their nation, and their religion. Here in America they were living other than themselves. They must learn that they are the original people, noblest of the nations of the earth. The Caucasians are the colored people, since they lost their original color. The original people must regain their religion, which is Islam, their language, which is Arabic, and their culture, which is astronomy and higher mathematics, especially calculus. They must live according to the law of Allah, avoiding all meat of "poison animals," hogs, ducks, geese, possums, and catfish. They must give up completely the use of stimulants, especially liquor. They must clean themselves up—both their bodies and their houses. If in this way they obeyed Allah, he would take them back to the Paradise from which they had been stolen—the Holy City of Mecca.[40]

Elijah Poole was one of the people in the audience that night. When he was introduced to Fard after the meeting he declared, "I know who you are, you're God himself." Fard replied, "That's right, but don't tell it now. It is not yet time for me to be known."[41] Poole soon became the prophet's most enthusiastic student of Islam. Fard gave him the name Elijah Karriem, and later he took the name Elijah Muhammad. Eventually, he became W. D. Fard's chief minister of Islam and his successor.[42]

Elijah Muhammad, the son of a Baptist preacher, was born in Georgia on October 7, 1897. Grown to adulthood and married, he and his wife, Clara, had eight children. The Muhammads were destined to become the most remarkable family in the history of Islam in modern America. They became a ruling dynasty in the Nation of Islam. They understood their mission as the reestablishment of Islam as a permanent religious alternative in the United States in the twentieth century, and in this mission they succeeded.[43] Their achievements will be discussed later in this paper. However, the basic social fact predisposing Blacks to conversion to the Nation of Islam during this formative period was the Great Migration (1915–1930), during which great numbers of Blacks left the South to find work in the cities of the North. The Great Migration set the stage for the cultural exchanges between different groups of people and for Black economic exploitation in the North, both of which help explain the dramatic changes in name and identity that occurred among the Black Muslims.

Migration, economic depression, and the demise of Garvey transformed the Pan-Africanist aspiration of a small but significant group of Black people in Detroit so radically that political organization alone was not enough. The dynamics of the forces that led to conversion in the Nation of Islam are still not completely understood, but certain aspects are clear. First, signification was at the center of the conversion experience for members of this movement. No other Black religious or political group up to this time had talked so explicitly and convincingly about the psychological damage that slavery had done to Black Americans. Converts were taught that they were the descendants of the "original Black nation of Asia, the Tribe of Shabazz" and that they had lost their original religion, Islam, and nationality, African Asiatic, in slavery. According to these ideas, the Asiatics were the "original" human beings, whose ancient civilization included the Nile Valley and the holy city of Mecca.

Eventually, Elijah Muhammad required all converts to change their surnames to X in order to eradicate their slave names. The X signified the original identity that was lost when Black people were taken from Africa by their enslavers. When the converts received their X, a new world of opportunities was thought to open up for them. Black Muslim leaders told them that "freedom, justice, equality, happiness, peace of mind, contentment, money, good jobs, decent homes—all these can be yours if you accept your God, Allah, now and return to His (and your original) religion, Islam."[44]

C. Eric Lincoln correctly notes that Fard and Elijah "cut the cloak to fit the cloth." Their methods of teaching Islam to the "Black victims of a new technocratic urban order" were imaginative, "controversial and sometimes ad hoc. . . . " Religious orthodoxy was not the goal of this movement. Instead, Elijah Muhammad and W. D. Fard wanted to reconstruct African-American cultural, political, and religious identity and "make Americans aware of Islam, its power and potential." In this they succeeded.[45]

In 1932, W. D. Fard was arrested and sent to jail. He was forced to leave Detroit, Michigan, on May 26, 1933. The prophet then went to Chicago, where he was again arrested and imprisoned. Sometime during 1933, Elijah Muhammad offered Fard refuge in Chicago, and the former was designated the Minister of Islam. In 1934, W. D. Fard vanished completely; to this day there are no substantive clues regarding his whereabouts, although there are several undocumented reports.[46]

After Fard's disappearance, Elijah Muhammad became the leader of the Allah Temple of Islam. He left the Detroit group and set up headquarters in Chicago, where he founded Temple No. 2 for W. D. Fard. Muhammad then deified W. D. Fard and called himself the Prophet of Allah. Muhammad's brother, Kallat Muhammad, challenged his authority and formed his own Muslim organization in Chicago in 1935.[47]

Angered by Elijah Muhammad's new claims to prophecy and leadership, some of his rivals vowed that they would "eat a grain of rice a day until Elijah was dead." Forced to leave his family behind in Chicago in order to save his life, Muhammad traveled mysteriously along the East Coast for the next seven years as an itinerant preacher for his movement. Like his teacher W. D. Fard, he assumed many names and identities to cover his tracks. During these shadowy years, Elijah Muhammad was known as Elijah Karriem, Elijah Evans, Gulam Bogans, Mr. Muckmuck, and Muhammad Rassoul. Washington, D.C., was a frequent resting place for Muhammad in this period.[48]

The Asiatic identity and global ties of the Black Muslim movement were accentuated in the 1930s and early 1940s by two outside political groups that tried to incorporate the Nation of Islam. In 1932, the Communists made an unsuccessful attempt to infiltrate the movement. Then Satokata Takahashi, a Japanese national, was successful in recruiting a small number of Muslims for his organization, Development of Our Own. Under Takahashi's leadership, Development of Our Own became the major organization in Black America for the dissemination of pro-Japanese propaganda, which sought to connect the African-American economic and political struggle against Western imperialism with that of the darker races in Asia. Ernest Allen Jr. has noted that both Abdul Muhammad and Elijah Muhammad were friends with Takahashi and admired his work. Although Elijah Muhammad never became a member of Takahashi's organization, the Allah Temple of Islam became a significant source of "pro-Japanese sentiment" among Black Americans during the World War II era. Moreover, it is noteworthy that Takahashi's wife, Pearl Sherrod, was a former member of the Nation of Islam. Other pro-Japanese African-American organizations that influenced the Asiatic identity of Elijah Muhammad's followers were the Pacific Movement of the Eastern World, the Onward Movement of America, the Peace Movement of Ethiopia, the Ethiopian Pacific Movement, and the Original Independent Benevolent Afro-Pacific Movement of the World.[49]

In the context of these pro-Japanese connections, Elijah Muhammad's various names were also intended to help him elude the federal authorities who were monitoring the Black Muslim movement for sedition and Selective Service violations. Beginning in 1942, the FBI carried out a series of raids on Black Muslim homes and mosques in Detroit, Chicago, Milwaukee, and New Jersey. Even Elijah Muhammad's thirteen-year-old son, Wallace, was under surveillance by the FBI. Finally, on May 8, 1942, in Washington, D.C., and in September 1942 in Chicago, Muhammad was arrested for refusing to register for the draft and for influencing his followers not to register. His son Emmanuel was also arrested around this time. The two men were convicted in Chicago and incarcerated in the federal penitentiary in Milan, Michigan, from 1942 to 1946, where they conducted weekly services and converted many prisoners to Islam. According to Ernest Allen Jr., the Muhammads' arrests were part of a federal sweep of African-American Muslim organizations that resulted in the arrest of more than eighty Black people in 1942 and early 1943.[50]

Elijah's wife, Clara Muhammad, became the supreme secretary of the Nation of Islam while her husband was in prison. During this time, she was the movement's cohesive force and passed down Elijah Muhammad's orders from the prison to the ministers and captains.[51]

In 1946, Elijah Muhammad was released from prison. His incarceration made him look like a martyr to the Black Muslims, and it helped to establish him as the absolute leader of his movement when he went back to Chicago. When he resumed active leadership of the

Black Muslims in the late 1940s, there were four temples in the United States—in Chicago, Detroit, Milwaukee, and Washington, D.C.[52]

During the 1950s, the Nation of Islam expanded its operations throughout the United States—dramatically increasing its membership and becoming the major voice for Islam in America. These changes occurred in the aftermath of World War II, as African Americans made the first "decisive cracks in the citadel of white supremacy" and laid the groundwork for the Black revolution of the 1950s and 1960s. Black people around the world began to redefine their identities as European colonial regimes began to fall in Asia and Africa. Also in the 1940s, a second great wave of millions of southern Blacks began to enter the so-called Promised Land of the northern cities in the United States. This demographic factor is important because it brought to the northern cities people who would become major actors in American Islam and the Black protest movement in the 1960s. In the context of these dramatic changes, American Islam became an important aspect of "the growing diversity and complexity of African-American cultural production" that occurred in America.[53]

Malcolm X and His Successors

World War II was also a watershed event in the Islamic world, for in its aftermath Syria, Jordan, Pakistan, Indonesia, and African Muslim countries achieved independence from colonialism as European power diminished. Around that time, Muslim societies began to reassert themselves and decide how to deal with the mixed legacy of Western culture.[54]

Indeed, the emergence of Malcolm X as the major international spokesperson for Black-American Muslims in the 1960s was connected with this international resurgence of Islam in world affairs, and decolonization in Asia and Africa. Malcolm X's eloquent articulation of Black America's identity crisis and its search for "a more authentic identity," its disillusionment with the socioeconomic and political agenda of the white mainstream, and its "new found sense of pride and power" reflected the agenda of contemporary Muslims all over the world.[55]

Moreover, Malcolm X was a star of the media. He was young, strong, handsome, and vibrant, and he changed his name each time he modified his religious and political identities. His "jihad of words" in defense of Islam was both forceful and seductive and echoed similar jihads of words against the West in the Muslim world. The theme of signification and identity is adumbrated through the words and ideas of Malcolm X for this redheaded genius became the primary model for the signification of Black Islamic identity in contemporary America. Indeed, in Malcolm's shifting relationships with the Nation of Islam, and with Islam in the Middle East and West Africa, and in his ambivalence between racial separation and multiracialism in these contexts, we can discern the models for the various significations of Islamic identity in the ever-changing ideologies of Louis Farrakhan and Warith Deen Mohammed—the two foremost Black Muslim leaders in America today.

The story of Malcolm X's childhood, his conversion to Islam in prison, and his years with the Nation of Islam, have received much scholarly attention in recent years. The following discussion will focus on the last year of his life as a model for the major African-American Muslim leaders who succeeded him.

Malcolm X broke all ties with the Nation of Islam on March 8, 1964, and formally announced his separation at a press conference at the Park Sheraton Hotel in New York on

March 11. The sweeping religious and political changes that he undertook from that time until his assassination on February 21, 1965, were destined to become potent models for signification and identity in contemporary African-American Islam.[56]

During this period, Malcolm underwent two dramatic changes in his religious identity that became significant models for contemporary African-American Islam. First, Malcolm X established multiracial orthodox Islam as an option for African-American Muslims. Then, he explored the religious and cultural links between African-American Islam and its West African roots. As we shall see, each of these changes in Malcolm's religious identity was accompanied by the adoption of a new name.[57]

At the very beginning of his separation from the Nation of Islam, Malcolm founded the Muslim Mosque, Inc., which was based on orthodox Muslim principles. On March 11, 1964, he discussed the religious and political significance of this new organization.

> This will give us a religious base, and the spiritual force necessary to rid our people of the vices that destroy the moral fiber of our community.
>
> Muslim Mosque, Inc. will have its temporary headquarters in the Hotel Theresa in Harlem. It will be the working base for an action program designed to eliminate the political oppression, the economic exploitation and the social degradation suffered daily by twenty-two million African-Americans.[58]

Then in April 1964, Malcolm went to Mecca to make the obligatory pilgrimage called the hajj. This experience transformed his ideas on Islam and race relations in the Muslim world. When Malcolm X saw people of different colors and races worshipping together, apparently as brothers and sisters in Islam, he came to the conclusion that the Nation of Islam's racial separation had no place in the multiracial orthodox Islam that he accepted in Mecca. Malcolm changed his name to El Hajj Malik El-Shabazz. As his wife would say later, "He went to Mecca as a Black Muslim and there he became only a Muslim."[59]

When Malcolm X departed from Mecca and North Africa, he traveled to Nigeria, which began the West African phase of his transition period. This West African tour was the most dynamic influence in his new religious and political identity for several reasons. First, West Africa was a homecoming for Malcolm in two respects—it connected him to his ancestors' land of origin and to African-American Islam's original source—the homelands of America's first African Muslim slaves. Malcolm's formulation of the spiritual and political connections between African America and West Africa was perhaps more profound than that of Edward Wilmot Blyden, the father of Pan-Africanism in the late nineteenth century. And in his connecting of African struggles for independence with the African-American liberation struggle, Malcolm's version of Pan-Africanism changed the basic goals of that struggle, from a national agenda of civil rights to an international agenda of human rights.[60]

The high point of Malcolm's trip to Nigeria occurred on May 8, 1964, at the University of Ibadan, when the Nigerian Muslim Student's Society gave him the name Omowale, which means "the son who has come home." Ruby M. and E. U. Essien-Udom were present at the event and recalled Malcolm's political impact on Nigeria:

> From the time Malcolm came to Nigeria until he left he generated an unbelievable excitement. For those of us who had known Malcolm in the United States, it was a joy to experience once

again that rare combination of oratorical brilliance and fearlessness combined with naked honesty and a genuine humility that made Malcolm so compelling and disarming. In his speech at Trenchard Hall at the University of Ibadan, Malcolm stressed the necessity for the African nations to lend their help in bringing the Afro-American's case before the United Nations. He argued that the Afro-American community should cooperate with the world's Pan-Africanists; and that even if they remained in America physically, they should return to Africa philosophically and culturally and develop a working unit between the framework of Pan-Africanism. Following his speech at Trenchard Hall, the Nigerian Muslim Student's Society had a reception for Malcolm in the Student's Union Hall and made him an honorary member of their society. They endowed him with the new name Omowale, meaning "the son who has come home." This gesture symbolized the wholehearted acceptance of Malcolm as a person and leader which we clearly observed among the radical youths and intellectuals in Nigeria. In his television and radio appearances in Nigeria, Malcolm stressed the need for African support to bring the charge of violation of Afro-American human rights by the United States before the United Nations.[61]

From Nigeria, Malcolm traveled to Ghana, which was known then as the "political Mecca" of Pan-Africanism. In Ghana, Malcolm spoke at the events sponsored by the community of African-American expatriates, the University of Ghana, the Kwame Nkrumah Ideological Institute, and the Ghanaian Parliament. He discussed Pan-Africanism with President Kwame Nkrumah, Shirley Graham DuBois, and the Chinese, Cuban, and Algerian ambassadors. On his final day in Ghana, Malcolm received an honor from the Nigerian Muslim official Al Hajj Iba Wali that signaled the Pan-Africanist connection between West Africa and African-American Muslims. He gave Malcolm the regal African turban and robe of the Nigerian Muslims and a copy of the Quran. And Malcolm donned his new African clothing as a symbol of global Black unity.[62]

Malcolm returned to the United States on May 21, 1964, after making short trips to Liberia, Senegal, and Morocco. By the time of his return, his experiences with radical political leaders in the Middle East and West Africa had convinced him of the need for an African-American political organization that would be separate from the Muslim Mosque, Inc. Thus, on June 29, 1964, he established a secular political body, the Organization of Afro-American Unity (OAAU), which was designed to unite African Americans concerned with the global issue of human rights. Although much has been made of Malcolm's attempts to reconcile his political ideas with those of the mainstream leaders of the civil rights movement during the final period of his split with the Nation of Islam, this tendency is not supported by the aims and objectives of the OAAU. These aims and objectives focused on

> the letter and spirit of the Organization of African Unity established [in] Ethiopia, May 1963 . . . Pan-Africanism, self-determination, culture, national unity, anti-imperialism, education, economic security, self-defense, and worldwide concerns.

In fact, the Black power movement that arose after Malcolm's death adopted the major principles behind the OAAU.[63]

The interrelation of religion and politics remained problematic in the religious identity that Malcolm formulated both for the Muslim Mosque, Inc., and for himself. This organization never seriously challenged the hegemony of the Nation of Islam among African-American Muslims. And there is evidence that many members of the former organization were dissatisfied with Malcolm's overwhelming political emphasis in his last days and longed for a more exclusively religious solidarity. At the same time, many African Americans who were not Muslims, but who were politically inspired by Malcolm, felt abandoned in 1964 during the long hot summer of Black urban uprisings in America. At the time of these rebellions, Malcolm was away in Africa and the Muslim world seeking support for his campaign to bring the United States government before the United Nations for its human rights violations against Black Americans. Toward the end of his life, Malcolm's jihad of words had shifted from a focus on religion to a scathing critique of capitalism as an intrinsically evil economic system with connections to global racial oppression and imperialism. He saw socialism as a possible corrective.[64]

Malcolm's political plans were never fully realized, however, because death came too soon. Stalked by the shadows of his enemies in the Nation of Islam, the FBI, the CIA, and the New York City Police Department, Malcolm knew in his final days that he was marked for death, and he was desperate. He was assassinated during a speaking engagement at the Audubon Ballroom in Manhattan on February 21, 1965, and Talmadge Hayes, Thomas 15X Johnson, and Norman 3X Butler, all former Nation of Islam members, were sentenced to life in prison. In 1977, however, Hayes confessed that he had falsely accused Johnson and Butler and that the real assassins (besides himself) were residing in New Jersey. Defense attorney William Kunstler was unsuccessful in obtaining a new trial. He suggested that the FBI and the New York City Police Department were involved in Malcolm X's murder. Indeed, the FBI had Malcolm under close observation for years and had also infiltrated the Nation of Islam. Although the full truth about Malcolm X's assassination may never be known, there has recently been a renewed interest among scholars about his assassination.[65]

During the final weeks of Malcolm's life, he began to talk about the African-American freedom struggle as an aspect of "a world-wide revolution" against racism, corporate racism, classism, and sexism. Utilizing the political lessons that he had learned from his Muslim contacts in the Middle East and Africa, he constructed a model of Black liberation that appealed to Muslims and non-Muslims alike. And aspects of his radical Black nationalism appealed to African Americans throughout the Black political spectrum—from the NAACP to the Black Left. Because of his potential (had he lived) to unite many Black Muslims and Black Christians in America and abroad in a liberation struggle that could have significantly challenged the corporate capitalist power base of the white American establishment, there is no question that the American intelligence community had the incentive to be involved in Malcolm X's murder. Indeed, since Malcolm X's death, no Muslim leader has constructed an African-American religious and political identity that has had the potential to lead Black people to liberation in America.[66]

In many respects, Malcolm X represented the culmination of the various religious identities that could be formulated in African-American Islam. His stamp on American Islam was enduring, his influence profound, as he explored the racial-separatist model of the religion in the Nation of Islam, the Arab-centric multiracial orthodox Muslim identity in Mecca, and the West African roots of African-American Islam in Ghana. Louis Farrakhan and Warith Deen Mohammed, the two most important Black Muslim leaders in America today, are in a sense the spiritual heirs of Malcolm X, for the Muslim identities that they have formulated for their movements are based on the racial-separatist model of Malcolm X during his association with the Nation of Islam and his multiracial emphasis after his pilgrimage to Mecca.

Wallace D. Muhammad became the supreme minister of the Nation of Islam immediately after his father's death on February 23, 1975. During the first years of his leadership, he mandated sweeping changes in the racial-separatist Black Muslim movement in order to bring it into line with a multiracial orthodox Muslim identity. These changes included a reinterpretation of the theology of the organization. The new leader abolished the doctrine of Black racial supremacy and for the first time allowed whites to subscribe to the religion. He refuted W. D. Fard's divinity, preferring to emphasize Fard's contributions as the founder of the movement, as a community worker, and as a reform psychologist. Wallace Muhammad held that Fard's doctrine about "white devils" was not meant to be understood literally, interpreting it as a psychological smoke screen for his community work among the Black lower class. Wallace did not consider Elijah Muhammad the "Messenger of Allah," but rather as the man who reinterpreted Fard's doctrines. He praised his father for achieving the "First Resurrection" of Black Americans by introducing them to Islam. However, he claimed that the "Second Resurrection" was to occur not as an "apocalyptic event" as his father had suggested, but instead as a change in the mission of the Nation of Islam. Now its mission was directed not only at Black America, but also at the entire American environment. Wallace recognized Malcolm X's contributions to the movement and renamed the Harlem mosque Malcolm Shabazz Mosque.[67]

Muhammad changed the terminology of the organization in order to achieve orthodox identity. He renamed the Nation of Islam the "World community of Al-Islam in the West" in 1976, the "American Muslim Mission" in 1980, and the "Muslim American Community" in the 1990s. To avoid association with Wallace D. Fard's doctrines, Wallace Muhammad changed his own name to Warith Deen Mohammed (formerly Warith Deen Muhammad). Warith Deen means "inheritor of the faith" in Arabic. At first, he called Black people Bilalians in honor of Bilal Ibn Rabah, the Ethiopian who was a close friend of the Prophet Muhammad, redesignating the newspaper *Muhammad Speaks* as *The Bilalian News*. Warith's followers now call themselves the Muslim American Community, and their newspaper is called *The Muslim Journal* (formerly *The American Muslim Journal*). Ministers of Islam were renamed "imams," and temples were renamed "mosques" and "masjids" (an Arabic word for "mosque").[68]

In 1976, Warith Deen Mohammed estimated that there were 70,000 members in his organization. However, since that time the movement has lost thousands of members who disagree with the changes that he has made and who wish to return to the racial-separatist identity prescribed by the Nation of Islam. On March 7, 1978, Louis Farrakhan announced his departure from The World Community of Islam in the West, in an interview in the *New York Times*. In 1979, he began publishing *The Final Call*, a newspaper that was named after Elijah Muhammad's publication in Chicago in 1934. *The Final Call* urges Black people to return to the belief in Allah in the person of W. D. Fard and his messenger, Elijah Muhammad. Farrakhan believes that this is an eschatological issue—it represents the last chance for Black people to attain power and freedom in the United States.[69]

Louis Farrakhan's movement shares the objectives held by the Nation of Islam under Elijah Muhammad. His program discourages integration with white people and advocates

Black control of Black community resources. It demands equal opportunities in education and employment along with economic and social justice for all Blacks in the United States. Farrakhan's organization also demands the release of Black prisoners who make up the majority of the prison population in the United States. The most extraordinary aspect of the new Nation of Islam's program is its "demand for a separate land" for Blacks. This point was also part of Elijah Muhammad's program. And Farrakhan has also reestablished the paramilitary group, the Fruit of Islam, which Warith Deen Mohammad had dismantled because of his opposition to its violent tactics. In the wake of Farrakhan's departure from the path established by Warith, "at least a dozen competing fragments" of the former Nation of Islam appeared. The three most influential are led by John Muhammad (Elijah's brother) in Detroit, Silis Muhammad in Atlanta, and Emmanuel Abdullah Muhammad in Baltimore.[70]

Louis Farrakhan and Warith Deen Mohammad underline the fact that there is more than one kind of Muslim identity in African-American Islam today, each with a different relationship to the international community and a different stance on racial-separatist and multiracial community experience.

Over the last thirty years, there has been dramatic growth in the number of Muslims in the United States. Today, experts estimate that America's Muslim population is somewhere between four and six million, which could make Islam the second-largest religion in the United States. According to Yvonne Haddad, America's Muslims operate "more than 600 mosques/Islamic centers, two Islamic colleges, scores of parochial day schools, several hundred weekend schools, women's organizations, youth groups, and professional and civic organizations." Thus, today, Islam is not just in the international news but is an integral part of the landscape of America.[71]

The shape of this new community is important for understanding the future direction of Islam in contemporary Black America. Black Americans make up about 42 percent of the Muslims in the United States. South Asian Muslims constitute almost 25 percent, Arabs approximately 12 percent, and the remaining 21 percent are from Iran, West Africa, Southeast Asia, Eastern Europe, and white America. California (one million Muslims), New York (800,000 Muslims), and Illinois (400,000 Muslims) are the states with the largest Muslim populations. Much of this dramatic growth is due to the arrival of recent Muslim immigrants who came to the United States after the American immigration laws were reformed in the 1960s. These Muslim immigrants are generally middle-class professionals who maintain cultural and linguistic ties to their countries of origin.[72]

What do these developments have to do with Islam in Black America? Although there are no conclusive statistics yet, some observers believe that the immigrant community as well as the leadership of Warith Deen Mohammed have influenced many Black American Muslims to embrace orthodox interpretations of Islam. Dawud Assad, president of the U.S. Council of Masjid, says that "eighty-five to ninety percent of our converts are Black. . . . They become better Muslims than the Muslim immigrants. The Blacks are very God-fearing." Moreover it appears that African Americans who are converting to Islam throughout the United States are learning Arabic, the universal language of the religion, and are deconstructing the racial separatism of the traditional Black Muslim movements.[73]

African-American orthodox, or Sunni, Muslims can trace their roots in the United States to African-American Sunni Islamic communities, such as Jabul Arrabiya, Ezaldeen Village and the First Pittsburgh, First Cleveland, and State Street mosques that were founded in the 1930s. Lawrence Mamiya and Amina McCloud believe that African-American Sunni Muslims are the most influential groups today.[74]

EPILOGUE

In the wake of several decades of "surveillance by the established religious authorities" and the federal government, and of "existence at the margins of public life" as the hidden transcript of the oppressed, African-American Islam has finally arrived on the center stage of American religion and politics. At the end of the twentieth century, it has developed "to new levels as an outspoken and tumultuous competitor of doctrine and practices" in both religion and politics. But what does all of this portend for African-American identity formation?[75]

Today, most African Americans are aware that Islam has deep roots in their culture. Since the 1960s, the Nation of Islam's leaders, businesses, newspapers, radio programs, food, and distinctive clothing have become visible and routinized aspects of Black communities in America's inner cities. Although most Black Americans are Christians, they tend not to share America's open hostility toward Islam. As Akbar Muhammad has pointed out, since African Americans have "no real political stake in America, political opposition to the Muslim world is unworthy of serious consideration." On the contrary, the political ideas of Black Muslim leaders—from Elijah Muhammad to Malcolm X, and from Warith Deen Mohammed to Louis Farrakhan—are the subject of constant debate in contemporary Black America.[76]

In this context, aspects of Black Muslim identity have become commodities in Black America, taking the form of stylized, media-oriented "cultural products" with little of their original religious content or substance.[77] Bean pies, incense, the television series *Roots*, Muslim clothing, Arabic names and expressions, and the speeches of Louis Farrakhan have all become products for mass consumption in contemporary Black America.

Even Malcolm X must be considered in the context of this process. After his death, he became an icon in African-American culture; Black artists, intellectuals, and celebrities tended to commodify his image and political ideas in a way that makes it easy to forget that Islam was at the center of his spiritual-political journey, beginning as Malcolm Little and progressing through Malcolm X to al-Hajj Malik Shabazz. Sonia Sanchez and Gwendolyn Brooks have written poems about his life and death. Amiri Baraka (formerly Le Roi Jones) was spiritually and artistically influenced by Malcolm X and the Nation of Islam in the 1960s. The novelists Alex Haley in *Roots* and Ishmael Reed in *Mumbo Jumbo*, inspired by Malcolm's life, have used Islam as central themes in their work. Malcolm's influence is also evident in two provocative Black autobiographies—Nathan McCall's *Makes Me Wanna Holler* and Sanyika Shakur's *Monster*. Jazz musicians such as Yusef Lateef, Ahmad Jamal, Idris Sulayman, and Sahib Shahab and professional athletes like Muhammud Ali, Kareem Abdul Jabar, Ahmad Rashad, and Jamal Wilkes have converted to Islam and adopted Arabic names. Mike Tyson reportedly converted to Islam while in prison. Grand Puba and the Islamic rap musician Lakim Shabazz, Poor Righteous Teachers, Eric B. and Rakim, King Sun, Movement X, Prince Akeem, Ice Cube, KMD, and A Tribe Called Quest all mention Malcolm X and the Nation of Islam in their lyrics. No artist, however, has commodified Malcolm X's identity more effectively than Spike Lee in his 1989 film *Do the Right Thing*, and then in *Malcolm X* in 1992. Spike Lee's superb cinematic portrayal of Malcolm X's life in the latter movie has recently inspired renewed interest and debate about Islam and Black nationalism in Black America.[78]

The film *Malcolm X* has also spurred new African-American interest in Louis Farrakhan's message. Farrakhan is "the most revered leader among the Black masses" as Ron Daniels has noted, and "his appeal is widespread." In addition to the dispossessed and disadvantaged, Farrakhan's rallies include large numbers of Black professionals, business people, and members of the Black middle class." Of course, Farrakhan's appeal is partially explained by his "militant voice" of Black separatism, which resonates throughout Black America at a time when many African Americans believe that Black elected officials are powerless to improve their lot.[79]

Commodification of identity, however, is also a provocative way to understand "the Farrakhan phenomenon." Farrakhan's message presents multifaceted significations of African-American Islamic identity that include specialized aspects for Black men, women, and children; strategies for Black economic and political empowerment; Afrocentric interpretations of history; an African-American Islamic worldview and cultural ethos; as well as potent psychological strategies to enhance Black pride and self-respect. In the context of this rich tapestry of cultural, political, economic, and spiritual offerings, African Americans have commodified selective aspects of Farrakhan's message. Ron Daniels agrees with this evaluation of the Nation of Islam leader's appeal to Black America. He writes, "In my view, many who go to hear Farrakhan or give him a favorable approval rating do not necessarily agree with all of his pronouncements or concur with every aspect of his program."[80]

Across Black America—in Black churches and mosques, in Black enclaves in cities and suburbs, in Black colleges and universities, in Black Studies departments and in Black student associations in predominantly white colleges and universities, and in Black political organizations—people are quietly acknowledging that in the future, Islam may provide some important answers to African-American economic, political, and cultural questions that have not been resolved by Black Christian leaders. Already, in Black urban areas across the country, Black Christian leaders are organizing special seminars to educate their people about Islam and to stem the tide of what they perceive as an alarming rate of African-American conversions to Islam. Mike Wilson, the founder and director of Project Joseph, which conducts "Muslim awareness seminars" for members of Black churches throughout the United States to educate them about Islam, believes that "if the conversion rate continues unchanged, Islam could become the dominant religion in Black urban areas by the year 2020."[81]

Although there is little hard evidence available to confirm or refute this assertion, Islam has recently become an increasingly significant aspect of the African-American experience. As the commodification process popularizes elements of Islamic culture among non-Muslims, Islam could indeed prevail in Black America in the twenty-first century.

NOTES

1. João José Reis, *Slave Rebellion in Brazil*, trans. Arthur Brakel (Baltimore: The Johns Hopkins University Press, 1993) This work is based on transcripts of the trials of the rebels at Conceicão da Praia, Brazil. At the Amistad Trial in New Haven, Connecticut, Richard R. Madden identified one of the African mutineers as a Muslim by saying an Islamic prayer to him. The African Muslim responded to the prayer in Arabic: "Allah Akbar"—God is Great; Howard Jones, *The Mutiny on the Amistad* (New York: Oxford University Press, 1987), 108; Madden deposition, November 20, 1839, 133 US District Court Records for Connecticut, Federal Archives and Record Center, Waltham, Massachusetts.

2. John Washington, "Some Account of Mohammed Sisei, a Mandingo, of Nyani-Mara in the

Gambia," *Journal of the Royal Geographical Society* VIII (1838): 449–54; Richard R. Madden, *A Twelve Month's Residence in the West Indies, During the Transition from Slavery to Apprenticeship, with Incidental Notices of the State of Society, Prospects and Natural Resources of Jamaica and Other Islands*, 2 vols. (Philadelphia: Carey, Lea, and Blanchard, 1835); Folarium Shyllon, *Black People in Britain, 1555–1833* (New York: Oxford University Press, 1997), 60.

3. For a brilliant analysis of intellectual resistance to slavery, see William D. Piersen, *Black Legacy* (Amherst: University of Massachusetts Press, 1993). Janet D. Cornelius has analyzed slave literacy as resistance in *When I Can Read My Title Clear* (Columbia: University of South Carolina Press, 1991). This section of the paper is a challenge to Orlando Patterson's major thesis in *Slavery and Social Death* (Cambridge: Harvard University Press, 1982) that slave systems erase social identity. Patterson fails to distinguish between what slave systems attempt to do and what they succeed in doing; he forfeits agency to the ruling/master classes and their appurtenances, thus concealing entirely the possibilities that the enslaved have any choices in the matter.

4. Charles Ball, *A Narrative of the Life and Adventures of Charles Ball, a Black Man*, 3rd ed. (Pittsburgh: John T. Skyrock, 1854), 143.

5. Reis, *Slave Rebellion in Brazil*, 154. Sidney W. Mintz and Richard Price present a pathbreaking study of how African slaves were acculturated in America in *The Birth of African-American Culture* (Boston: Beacon Press, 1992), first published by Institute for the Study of Human Issues, 1976.

6. Vincent J. Cornell, "Jihad: Islam's Struggle for the Truth," 18; Abdul Khatib, "The Need for Jihad," *Gnosis Magazine* (fall 1991): 24.

7. Allan D. Austin, *African Muslims in Antebellum America: A Sourcebook* (New York: Garland Press, 1984), 386.

8. Georgia Bryan Conrad, *Reminiscences of a Southern Woman* (Hampton, Va.: Hampton Institute, n.d.), 13.

9. Charles Spalding Wylly, *The Seed That Was Sown in Georgia* (New York: Neale, 1910). Wylly, the grandson of Thomas Spalding, recalled that his grandfather owned slaves of "Moorish or Arabian descent, devout Mussulmans, who prayed to Allah . . . morning, noon, and evening."

10. William B. Hodgson, *Notes on Northern Africa, the Sahara and Sudan* (New York: Wiley and Putnam, 1844), 73; Joseph H. Greenberg, "The Decipherment of the 'Ben Ali Diary,' a Preliminary Statement," *Journal of Negro History* (July 1940); Ella May Thornton,

"Bilali—His Book," *Law Library Journal* XLVIII (1955): 228–29. Bilali's diary is in the library of Georgia State University in Atlanta. Recently, Ronald A. T. Judy has translated Bilali's (Ben Ali's) diary and analyzed the various accounts of his life in *(Dis) Forming: The American Canon: African-Arabic Slave Narratives and the Vernacular* (Minneapolis: University of Minnesota Press, 1993). Also, see William S. McFreely, *Sapelo's People: A Long Walk into Freedom* (New York: W.W. Norton, 1994).

11. Zephaniah Kingsley, *Treatise on the Patriarchal or Co-operative System of Society*, 2nd ed. (1829); reprinted, Freeport (New York: Books for Libraries, 1970), 13–14; Wylly, *The Seed That Was Sown in Georgia*, 52; Merton Coulter, *Thomas Spalding of Sapelo* (Baton Rouge: Louisiana State University, 1940), 190–93; Caroline Couper Lovell, *The Golden Isles of Georgia* (Boston: Little Brown, 1933), 103–4.

12. Savannah Unit of the Georgia Writers' Project on the Works Projects Administration, *Drums and Shadows* (Athens: University of Georgia, 1940; Garden City, N.Y.: Doubleday-Anchor, 1972); Charles T. Davis and Henry Louis Gates Jr., eds., *The Slave's Narrative* (New York: Oxford University Press, 1985).

13. Savannah Unit of the Georgia Writers' Project, *Drums and Shadows*, 158–70.

14. Ibid.

15. "Letter of James Hamilton Couper, Esq.," in Austin, *African Muslim Slaves in Antebellum America*, 321–21; originally published by William Brown Hodgson in *Notes on Northern Africa, the Sahara, and the Sudan* (New York, 1844), 68–75; also see Curtin, *Africa Remembered*, 145–51. See Judy, *(Dis) Forming: The American Canon*, 187–207, for detailed analysis of James Hamilton Couper's writings about Salih Bilali.

16. Ibid.

17. Savannah Unit of Georgia Writers' Project, *Drums and Shadows*; Lydia Parrish, *Slave Songs of the Georgia Sea Islands* (Athens: University of Georgia Press, 1992), first published in 1942. She also met and got stories of Salih Bilali and Bilali's descendants. No one has systematically analyzed the impact of these Muslims and their traditions on Gullah culture.

18. Ibid., 154, 168–169, 170–173.

19. Booker T. Washington, *Up from Slavery*, in John Hope Franklin, ed., *Three Black Classics* (New York: Avon 1901), 41; Charles H. Lippy and Peter W. Williams, eds., *Encyclopedia of the American Religious Experience*, vol. 3 (New York: Scribner's 1988), s.v. "Black Militant and Separatist Movements," by Lawrence H. Mamiya and C. Eric Lincoln; Louis R. Harlan, *Booker T. Washington: The Making of a Black*

Leader (1856–1901) (New York: Oxford University Press, 1972) and *Booker T. Washington: The Wizard of Tuskegee, 1901–1915* (New York: Oxford University Press, 1983).

20. Akbar Muhammad, "Interaction between 'Indigenous' and 'Immigrant' Muslims in the United States: Some Positive Trends," *Hijrah Magazine* (March–April 1985): 14. Although the Moorish Science Temple began in 1913, little is known about its activities until 1925. The Moorish Science Temple has been criticized as a non-Islamic movement by some scholars and Muslims. However, McCloud has demonstrated that "Noble Drew Ali was clear on what constitutes Islam" and on "Quranic principles concerning the nature of reality as spiritual and the nature of human existence as co-eternal with the existence of time." "See McCloud, *African American Islam*, 9–13.

21. Martin Marty, *Modern American Religion: The Noise of Conflict, 1919–1941* (Chicago: University of Chicago Press, 1989), 1–14.

22. Muhammad Adullah Ahari El, *Sharif Abdul Ali (Noble Drew Ali—His Life and Teachings)*, (Chicago: University of Chicago Press, 1989), 3–4. It should be emphasized that all of the above tales are legend. Peter Lamburn Wilson, "Shoot-Out at the Circle 7 Koran: Drew Ali and the Moorish Science Temple," *Gnosis Magazine* 12 (summer 1989): 44–45.

23. Ibid., 5–7.

24. Noble Drew Ali, *The Holy Koran of the Moorish Science Temple of America* (Chicago: Author, 1927), 56–58; Ahari El, *Sharif Abdul Ali*, 12–14.

25. *Associated Negro Press*, March 20, 1929. Author's telephone interview with Ernest Allen Jr., April 1994.

26. "Negro in Illinois," 6–7. Hill, *Marcus Garvey and U.N.I.A. Papers*, Vol. VII (Berkeley: University of California Press, 1990), 82: Federal Bureau of Investigation reports on the Moorish Science Temple of America, File 62–25889; Wilson, "Shoot-Out at the Circle 7 Koran," 48; Wendell Berge, Assistant Attorney General, "Memorandum to the Director FBI," January 23, 1943. In the 1930s, a group of Moorish Americans led by Walter Smith Bey were influenced by the teachings of Dr. Yusef Kahn, an Ahmadi Muslim from India. For details about this development, see Jameela A. Hakim, "History of the First Muslim Mosque of Pittsburgh, Pennsylvania," in J. Gordon Melton and Michael A. Koszenzi, eds., *Islam in North America: A Sourcebook* (New York: Garland Publishing, 1992), 153–63; Yvonne Y. Haddad and Jane I. Smith, *Mission to America* (Gainesville: University Press of Florida, 1993), 79–106. Also see *The Moorish Chronicles*, 1. 1 (May 1993), published by the Islamic Moorish Empire of the West, Inc., in Los Angeles.

27. Roi Ottley, *New World A-Coming* (Boston: Houghton Mifflin, 1943), 56–57. This chapter is based on the author's previous research: "Islam in the United States in the 1920s: The Quest for a New Vision in Afro-American Religion," Ph.D. dissertation, Princeton University, 1986; "The Ahmadiyya Mission to Blacks in America in the 1920s," *Journal of Religious Thought* 44, no. 2 (winter–spring 1998), 50–66; and "The Ahmadiyya Movement in America," *Religion Today* (U.K.) 5, no. 3 (1990). The background material on the Ahmadiyya Movement in Islam is voluminous. Some important selected sources include **a. The published writings of Ghulan Ahmad**: *The Philosophy of the Teachings of Islam* (London: Ahmadiyya Centenary Publications, 1979), one of his most important works. *The Essence of Islam: Extracts from the Writings of the Promised Messiah*, vol. 1, trans. Muhammad Zafrullah Khan (London: Ahmadiyya Centenary Publications, 1978). *Tadkirah*, trans. Kahn (London: Saffron Books, 1976). *Tawzih-i-Maram*, trans. Iqbul Ahmad (Lahore: Anjuman Ahmadiyya, 1966). *Message of Peace* (Lahore: Anjuman Ahmadiyya, 1986). **b. Publications of the Ahmadiyya Movement**: Malawi Sher Ali, ed. and trans. *The Holy Quran* (Rabwah, Pakistan: Oriental and Religious Publishing Co., n.d.). *The Muslim Sunrise, The American Ahmadi Journal*, published continuously, with a few breaks, since the early 1920s, is the most important source of information on Ahmadiyya history in the United States. The earliest volumes of the journal can be found in the New York Public Library and its annexes. Recently a microfilm version of a full run of the earliest volumes was produced through the efforts of Ernest Allen Jr. and can be purchased through the New York Public Library. Early volumes of *The Review of Religions*, an older Ahmadi journal, also provide primary source material for the movement's early days in Armenia. The journal can be found in the annexes of the New York Public Library. A. R. Dard, *Life of Ahmad* (Lahore: Sultan Brothers, 1949). Muhammad Ali, *The Ahmadiyya Movement* (Lahore: The Ahmadiyya Anjuman Isha'at Islam, 1975). **c. Secondary Sources**: Yohannan Friedmann's pioneering book *Prophecy Continuous: Aspects of Ahmadi Religious Thought and Its Medieval Background* (Berkeley: University of California Press, 1989), builds on two earlier important works on the Ahmadiyya Movement, Humphrey J. Fisher, *Ahmadiyya* (London: Oxford University Press, 1963) and Spencer Lavan, *The Ahmadiyya Movement* (Deli: Manohar Book Service, 1974). Important secondary literature on the Ahmadiyya Movement's history in America includes Yvonne Y. Haddad and Jane I. Smith, *Mission to America: Five Islamic Sectarian*

Communities in North America (Gainesville: University Press of Florida, 1993) and the author's work cited above.

28. Sher Ali, "America's Intolerance," The Review of Religions 19 (April–May 1920): 158.

29. "Ahmadiyya Mission News," The Review of Religions 19 (July 1920): 24.

30. Mufti Muhammad Sadiq, The Moslem Sunrise 1 (April 1922): 1.

31. Mufti Muhammad Sadiq, "One Year's Missionary Work in America," The Moslem Sunrise 1 (July 1921): 12.

32. "Ahmadiyya Mission News," The Review of Religions 19 (July 1922): 24.

33. Mufti Muhammad Sadiq, "No Polygamy," The Moslem Sunrise 1 (July 1921): 9.

34. Sher Ali, "America's Intolerance," The Review of Religions 19 (April–May 1920): 158–60.

35. "Ahmadiyya Mission News," The Review of Religions 19 (July 1922): 24.

36. The Moslem Sunrise (October 1921): 36.

37. The Moslem Sunrise 2 (January 1923): 161.

38. Ibid., 3 (January 1924): 45; ibid., 2 (January 1923): 167.

39. Robert H. Hill, ed., Marcus Garvey and the Universal Negro Improvement Association Papers, vol. 1 (Berkeley: University of California Press, 1983), 521.

40. Edmann O. Benyon, "The Voodoo Cult among Negro Migrants in Detroit," American Journal of Sociology 43 (July 1937–May 1938): 897, 901. W. D. Fard, Teaching for the Lost Found Nation of Islam in a Mathematical Way, Problem Number 30.

41. Clifton E. Marsh, From Black Muslims to Muslims (Metuchen, N.J.: Scarecrow, 1984), 53. From Muhammad Speaks, Special Issue, April 1972.

42. Benyon, "Voodoo Cult among Negro Migrants in Detroit," 907.

43. C. Eric Lincoln, "The American Muslim Mission in the Context of American Social History," in Earle H. Waugh, Baha Abu-Laban, and Regula B. Qureshi, eds., The Muslim Community in North America (Edmonton: University of Alberta Press, 1983), 221; Malu Halsa, Elijah Muhammad (New York: Chelsea House, 1990), 105.

44. Elijah Muhammad, Message to the Blackman in America (Chicago: Muhammad Mosque of Islam, No. 2, 1963), iii.

45. C. Eric Lincoln, "The American Muslim Mission in the Context of American Social History," in Earle H. Waugh, Baha Abu-Laban, and Regula B. Qureshi, eds. The Muslim Community in North America (Edmonton: University of Alberta Press, 1983), 222–23.

46. Elijah Muhammad, Message to the Blackman in America, 24; Louis Lomax, When the Word Is Given (Cleveland: World, 1963), 53.

47. Lomax, When the Word Is Given, 54; Evanzz, The Judas Factor, 30.

48. Interview with Khallid Muhammad, Santa Barbara, Calif.: December 7, 1993.

49. Ernest Allen Jr., "When Japan Was Champion of the Darker Races: Satokata Takahashi and the Development of Our Own: 1933–1942," The Black Scholar 24 (winter 1994); FBI Report: "Foreign Inspired Agitation among American Negroes; 1942–1943," File 671, 179–94.

50. Ibid.; Marsh, From Black Muslims to Muslims, 60–61; Malu Halsan, Elijah Muhammad (New York: Chelsea House, 1990), 59–65.

51. Interview with Khallid Muhammad, Santa Barbara, Calif., December 7, 1993; "Cultist Riot in Courtroom," Chicago Tribune, March 6, 1935; Mazaffar Ahmad Zafr, national vice president of the Ahmadiyya Movement in Islam, has noted that the African-American jazz musicians who were converts to Islam kept the spirit of their religion alive in Black America in the 1940s and 1950s. They include Ahmad Jamal, Muhammad Sadiq (who played with Charlie Parker and Jay McShan), Dizzy Gillespie, Mustafa Daleel, and Talif Daoud. Interview with author, Chino, Calif., October 3, 1992.

52. Marsh, From Black Muslims to Muslims, 60–61.

53. Manning Marable, Race, Rebellion and Reform (Jackson: University Press of Mississippi, 1991), 15; Nicholas Lemann, The Promised Land (New York: Alfred A. Knopf, 1990).

54. Frances Robinson, Atlas of the Islamic World since 1500 (New York: Facts on File, 1982), 158–59.

55. John Esposito, Islam Straight Path (New York: Oxford University Press, 1988), 164.

56. Clayborne Carson, Spike Lee, and David Gallen, Malcolm X: The FBI File (New York: Carroll and Graf, 1991), 72–73.

57. Alex Haley, The Autobiography of Malcolm X (New York: Ballantine Books, 1965), chaps. 17 and 18.

58. George Brectman, ed., Malcolm X Speaks (New York: Grove Press, 1965), 20–21.

59. Haley, The Autobiography of Malcolm X, 80–82.

60. Ruby M. and E. U. Essien-Udom, "Malcolm X: An International Man," in Clarke, ed., Malcolm X: Make It Plain, 255–67.

61. Ibid., 246–47.

62. Alice Windom and John Henrik Clarke oral histories in Strickland and Greene, Malcolm X: Make It Plain, 180–81.

63. Brectman, ed., By Any Means Necessary, 33–67.

64. Robert Little, John Henrik Clarke, and Percy Sutton oral histories in Strickland and Greene, *Malcolm X: Make It Plain*, 174, 176, 189.

65. Marsh, *From Black Muslims to Muslims*, 83–87.

66. Clarke, *February 1965: The Final Speeches*, 106–70: Marable, "On Malcolm X," 14–15.

67. Marsh, *From Black Muslims to Muslims*, 95. Martha Lee offers the best detailed analysis of the changes in chapter 4 of *The Nation of Islam: An American Millenarian Movement*. Mohammad's theological and ritual innovations can be traced in his books: *The Teachings of W. D. Muhammad* (Chicago: Honorable Elijah Muhammad Mosque No. 2, 1976); *Book of Muslim Names* (Chicago: Muhammad Islamic Foundation, 1982); *Imam W. Deen Muhammad Speaks from Harlem, N.Y.* (Chicago: W. D. Muhammad Publications, 1984); and *An African-American Genesis* (Chicago: Progressions, 1986). See also Mattias Gardell, "The Sun of Islam Will Rise in the West: Minister Farrakhan and the Nation of Islam in the Latter Days," in Yvonne Y. Haddad and Jane I. Smith, eds., *Muslim Communities in North America* (Albany: State University of New York Press, 1994).

68. Lincoln, "American Muslim Mission in the Context of American Social History," 228. Elaine Rivera, "The Very Positive Face of Islam: Little Known Muslim Leader Has a Huge Following in U.S.," *Houston Chronicle*, May 21, 1994.

69. Lawrence H. Mamiya, "Minister Louis Farrakhan and the Final Call: Schism in the Muslim Movement," in *The Muslim Community in North America*, 237. Lee, *The Nation of Islam: An American Millenarian Movement*, 94.

70. Ibid., pp. 242–43. See Lee, *The Nation of Islam: An American Millenarian Movement*, chap. 5 for details. C. Eric Lincoln, *The Black Muslims in America*, 3rd ed. (Trenton, N.J.: Africa World Press, 1994), 267; McCloud, *African American Islam*, 83–88.

71. Yvonne Haddad, *The Muslims of America* (New York: Oxford University Press, 1997), 3.

72. Mary H. Cooper, "Muslims in America," *CQ Researcher*, April 30, 1993, 364.

73. Ari L. Goldman, "Mainstream Islam Rapidly Embraced by Black American," *The New York Times*, February 21, 1989, A1, B34.

74. Author's telephone interview with Amina McCloud, February 27, 1998.

75. James C. Scott, *Domination and the Arts of Resistance: Hidden Transcripts* (New Haven, Conn.: Yale University Press, 1990), 261.

76. Akbar Muhammad, "Interaction between 'Indigenous' and 'Immigrant' Muslims in the United States: Some Positive Trends," *Hijrah Magazine* (March–April 1985): 74.

77. Cornel West, "Postmodernism and Black America," *Zeta Magazine* (1988): 12.

78. Joe Wood, ed., *Malcolm X: In Our Own Image* (New York: St Martin's Press, 1992). Gerald Horne, "Myth and the Making of 'Malcolm X," *American Historical Review* 98 (April 1993): 445–50. Marvin X and Faruk, "Islam and Black Art: An Interview with Le Roi Jones," *Negro Digest* (January 1969): 4–10, 77–80. Ira Berkow, "After Three Years in Prison, Tyson Gains His Freedom," *New York Times*, March 26, 1995. Alex Haley, *Roots: The Saga of an American Family* (Garden City, N.Y.: Doubleday, 1976). Ishmael Reed, *Mumbo Jumbo* (New York: Macmillan, 1972). Nathan McCall, *Makes Me Wanna Holler: A Young Black Man in America* (New York: Random House, 1994). Sanyika Shakur, A.K.A. Monster Kody Scott, *Monster: The Autobiography of an L.A. Gang Member* (New York: Atlantic Monthly Press, 1993). Howie Evans, "Mike Tyson: I'll Take My Thoughts to My Grave," *Amsterdam News* 85, no. 25, June 19, 1994. Thomas Hauser, *Muhammad Ali: His Life and Times* (New York: Simon and Schuster, 1991). According to Ernest Allen Jr., many of the Islamic rappers are members of the Five Percent Nation of Islam, a splinter group of the Nation of Islam that was founded in Harlem by Clarence 13X in 1964. The Five Percenters focus on the secret literature of W. D. Fard and believe that all Black men are gods. They see themselves in the five percent of African Americans who are the "poor righteous teachers" of their race. In their significations, Harlem is Mecca, Brooklyn is Medina, and women are " 'Moons, who [bask] in the luminous wisdom of male 'Suns.' " Allen, "Making the Strong Survive: The Contours and Contradictions of Message Rap," in William Eric Perkins, ed., *Droppin' Science; Critical Essays on Rap Music and Hiphop Culture* (Philadelphia: Temple University Press, 1996). Joseph D. Eure and James G. Spudy, eds., *Nation Conscious Rap* (New York: Penguin, 1992). Julie Dash, *Daughters of the Dust: The Making of an African American Women's Film* (New York: New Press, 1992). Spike Lee with Lisa Jones, *Do the Right Thing* (New York: Fireside, 1989). Spike Lee with Ralph Wiley, *By Any Means Necessary: The Trials and Tribulations of the Making of Malcolm X* (New York: Hyperion, 1992).

79. Daniels, "The Farrakhan Phenomenon," 17. Eugene Cose, *The Rage of a Privileged Class* (New York: HarperCollins, 1993). Faith Berry, "The 'King' of the Hour at the March on Washington," *Miami Times*, September 8, 1983. Faith Berry to Minister

Louis Farrakhan, October 31, 1983; Minister Louis Farrakhan to Faith Berry, November 3, 1983.

80. Minister Louis Farrakhan, *A Torchlight for America* (Chicago: FCN, 1993). Richard Muhammad, "Farrakhan Draws 9,000 Men to Washington, D.C. Meeting: Black Men on the Move," *The Final Call*, March 16, 1994. Minister Ava Muhammad, *Your Creative Force* (1993), *Principles of Femininity* (1991), and *A Light-Giving Sun* (1991), videocassette. Daniels, "The Farrakhan Phenomenon," 18.

81. Andrés Tapia, "Churches Wary of Inner City Islamic Inroads: More Blacks See the Muslim Message as an Appealing Alternative to Christianity," *Christianity Today*, January 10, 1994, 36.

SELECTED BIBLIOGRAPHY

Beam, Joseph, ed. In The Life: A Black Gay Anthology. New York: Alyson, 1986.

Bell, Derrick. *Faces at the Bottom of the Well.* New York: Basic Books, 1992.

———, ed. *Shades of Brown: New Perspectives on School Desegregation.* New York: Teachers College Press, Columbia University, 1980.

Bobo, Jacqueline. *Black Women as Cultural Readers.* New York: Columbia University Press, 1995.

Bobo, Jacqueline, ed. *Black Women Film and Video Artists.* New York: Routledge, 1998.

———, ed. *Black Feminist Cultural Criticism.* Malden, Mass.: Blackwell Publishers, Inc., 2001.

Boyd, Herb, and Robert L. Allen, eds. *Brotherman: The Odyssey of Black Men in America.* New York: Ballantine Books, 1996.

Carbado, Devon, ed. *Black Men on Race, Gender, and Sexuality: A Critical Reader.* New York: New York University Press, 1999.

Christian, Barbara. *Black Feminist Criticism: Perspectives on Black Women Writers.* New York: Pergamon Press, 1985.

Cone, James. *A Black Theology of Liberation.* Philadelphia: J.B. Lippincott, 1970, reprinted Maryknoll, N.Y.: Orbis Books, 1990.

———, ed. *For My People: Black Theology and the Black Church.* Maryknoll, N.Y.: Orbis Books, 1984.

Davis, Angela Y. *Angela Davis: An Autobiography.* New York: Random House, 1974.

———. *Women, Race and Class.* New York: Random House, 1981.

Dent, Gina, ed. *Black Popular Culture: A Project by Michele Wallace.* Seattle: Bay Press, 1992.

DuCille, Ann. *Skin Trade.* Cambridge: Harvard University Press, 1996.

Foster, Michele. *Black Teachers on Teaching.* New York: The New Press, 1997.

Giddings, Paula. *When and Where I Enter: The Impact of Black Women on Race and Sex in America.* New York: William Morrow, 1984.

Guy-Sheftall, Beverly, ed. *Words of Fire: An Anthology of African-American Feminist Thought.* New York: The New Press, 1995.

Gwaltney, John Langston. *Drylongso: A Self-Portrait of Black America.* New York: Vintage Books, 1981.

Hemphill, Essex, and Joseph Beam, eds. *Brother to Brother: New Writings by Black Gay Men.* Boston: Alyson Publications, Inc., 1991.

Hull, Akasha Gloria. *Soul Talk: The New Spirituality of African-American Women.* Rochester, Vt.: Inner Traditions International, 2001.

Hull, Gloria T., Barbara Smith, and Patricia Bell Scott, eds. *All the Women Are White, All the Blacks Are Men, but Some of Us Are Brave: Black Women's Studies.* New York: Feminist Press at the City University of New York, 1981.

Kelley, Robin D. G. *Hammer and Hoe: Alabama Communists During the Great Depression.* Chapel Hill: University of North Carolina Press, 1990.

Lincoln, C. Eric, and Lawrence H. Mamiya. *The Black Church in the African American Experience.* Durham, N.C.: Duke University Press, 1990.

Lorde, Audre. *Sister/Outsider.* Trumansburg, N.Y.: Crossing Press, 1984.

Marable, Manning, ed. *Dispatches from the Ebony Tower: Intellectuals Confront the African American Experience.* New York: Columbia University Press, 2000.

Morley, David, and Kuan-Hsing Chen, eds. *Stuart Hall: Critical Dialogues in Cultural Studies.* London: Routledge, 1996.

Motley, Mary Penick, ed. *The Invisible Soldier: The Experience of the Black Soldier, World War II.* Detroit: Wayne State University Press, 1975.

Napier, Winston, ed. *African American Literary Theory: A Reader.* New York: New York University Press, 2000.

Robinson, Cedric J. *Black Marxism: The Making of the Black Radical Tradition.* London: Zed, 1983: reprinted Chapel Hill: University of North Carolina Press, 2000.

———. *Black Movements in America.* New York: Routledge, 1997.

Smith, Barbara. *The Truth That Never Hurts: Writings on Race, Gender, and Freedom.* New Brunswick, N.J.: Rutgers University Press, 1998.

Stuckey, Sterling. *Slave Culture: Nationalist Theory and the Foundations of Black America.* New York: Oxford University Press, 1987.

CONTRIBUTORS

Rhoda Barnes received her Ph.D. in Education from the University of California, Santa Barbara in 1994. The title of her dissertation is *African-American Parents' Involvement in Their Children's Schooling*.

Patrick Bellegarde-Smith is Associate Professor of Africology at the University of Wisconsin, Milwaukee. He is the author of *Haiti: The Breached Citadel* (1990), *In the Shadows of Power: Dantès Bellegarde in Haitian Social Thought* (1985), and coeditor (with Claudine Michel) of *The Spirit, the Myth, the Reality: Vodou in Haitian Development* (forthcoming from University Press of Florida). He is also Associate Editor of the *Journal of Haitian Studies*.

Jacqueline Bobo is Professor in the Women's Studies Program and the Department of Black Studies at the University of California, Santa Barbara. She is the author of *Black Women as Cultural Readers* (1995), editor of *Black Women Film and Video Artists* (1998), editor of *Black Feminist Cultural Criticism* (2001).

Elsa Barkley Brown is Associate Professor of History and Women's Studies at the University of Maryland, College Park. She is the coeditor of the two-volume *Major Problems in African-American History* (2000) and the two-volume *Black Women in America: An Historical Encyclopedia* (1993).

Katie Geneva Cannon is Professor of Christian Ethics at the Union Theological Seminary and Presbyterian School of Christian Education in Richmond, Virginia. She is the author of *Black Womanist Ethics* (1988) and *Katie's Canon: Womanism and the Soul of the Black Community* (1995), among other publications.

Johnnetta B. Cole is Presidential Distinguished Professor of Anthropology, Women's Studies, and African American Studies at Emory University. She was formerly President of Spelman College and is the author of *Dream the Boldest Dreams: And Other Lessons of Life* (1997) and *Conversations: Straight Talk with America's Sister President* (1994).

Angela Y. Davis is Professor in the History of Consciousness Program at the University of California, Santa Cruz. She is the author of *Blues Legacies and Black Feminism: Gertrude "Ma" Rainey, Bessie Smith, and Billie Holiday* (1999), *Women, Culture and Politics* (1987), *Women, Race and Class* (1981), and *If They Come in the Morning: Voices of Resistance* (1971).

Ann duCille is William R. Kenan Jr. Professor of the Humanities; Chair, African American Studies Program; and, Director of the Center for African American Studies at Wesleyan University. She is the author of *Skin Trade* (1996) and *The Coupling Convention: Sex, Text and Tradition in Black Women's Fiction* (1993).

Jacquelyn Grant is Professor of Systematic Theology at the Interdenominational Theological Center and Director of the Black Women in Church and Society at ITC. Her publications include *Perspectives on Womanist Theology* (1995) and *White Women's Christ and Black Women's Jesus: Feminist Christology and Womanist Response* (1989), among other publications.

Stuart Hall is Professor of Sociology at Open University, Milton Keynes, England. His books include *Minimal Selves* (1988), *The Hard Road to Renewal: Thatcherism and the Crisis of the Left* (1988), with Martin Jacques, and *Resistance through Ritual: Youth Subcultures in Post-War Britain* (1976), with Tony Jefferson. He is the coeditor of *Culture, Media, Language: Working Papers in Cultural Studies* (1980) and a special issue of *Ten.8* entitled "The Critical Decade: Black Photography of the 1980s" (1992).

Evelynn Hammonds is Professor of the History of Science and Afro-American Studies at Harvard University. Her research focuses on the history of medicine and public health in the United States, with a special focus on the study of race and gender in science and medicine. She is the author of *Childhood's Deadly Scourge: The Campaign to Control Diphtheria in New York City, 1880–1930* (1999).

Robert L. Harris Jr. is Associate Professor of African American History in the Africana Studies and Research Center at Cornell University, where he also serves as Vice Provost for Diversity and Faculty Development.

Cynthia Hudley is Professor in the Graduate School of Education at the University of California, Santa Barbara, on the faculty in Child and Adolescent Development; Special Education, Disability and Risk Studies; and the interdisciplinary doctoral emphasis in Human Development. Her research has been funded, in part, by the Centers for Disease Control and Prevention and the California Wellness Foundation, among other organizations. She is a regular contributor to scholarly literature, publishing in journals such as *Child Development*; *Developmental Psychology*; *Journal of Educational Psychology*; *Urban Education*; and *Psychology in the Schools.*

Akasha Gloria Hull has been a Professor of Literature at the University of Delaware and Professor and Chair of Women's Studies at the University of California, Santa Cruz. She is the coeditor of the groundbreaking volume *All the Women Are White; All the Blacks Are Men; But Some of Us Are Brave: Black Women's Studies* (1981) and author of *Soul Talk: The New Spirituality of African American Women* (2001), among other publications.

James Jennings is Professor of Urban and Environmental Policy and Planning at Tufts University. His books include *Understanding the Nature of Poverty in Urban America* (1994) and *The Politics of Black Empowerment: The Transformation of Black Activism in Urban America* (1992).

Deborah J. Johnson is Professor of Family and Child Ecology at Michigan State University. Her research focuses on racial socialization, racial/ethnic identity development, and children's race-related coping. She is the coeditor of *Visible Now: Blacks in Private Schools* (1988).

Robin D. G. Kelley is Professor of Anthropology at Columbia University. He is the author of *Hammer and Hoe: Alabama Communists during the Great Depression* (1990); *Race Rebels: Culture, Politics, and the Black Working Class* (1994); *Into the Fire—African Americans since 1970*; and, *Yo' Mama's Disfunctional!: Fighting the Culture Wars in Urban America* (1997), among other publications.

Phyllis R. Klotman is Professor of Afro-American Studies and Founder/Director of the Black Film Center Archive at Indiana University. Among her publications are *Struggles for Representation: African American Documentary Film and Video* (1999) and *Screenplays of the African-American Experience* (1991).

Frederick Knight is an Assistant Professor of History at the University of Memphis. He received his Ph.D. in History from the University of California, Riverside.

Alycee J. Lane is Assistant Professor of English at the University of California, Santa Barbara. Her areas of research focus on twentieth-century American literature, African-American literature and culture, gay and lesbian literature, and queer, feminist, and critical race theory.

Dwight A. McBride is Assistant Professor of English at the University of Pittsburgh. His essays in the areas of race theory and Black Cultural Studies appear in the *Harvard Blackletter Law Journal* and *Modern Fiction Studies*. He is also the author of *Impossible Witnessess: Truth, Abolitionism, and Slave Testimony* (2001) and editor of *James Baldwin Now* (1999).

Claudine Michel is Professor of Black Studies at the University of California, Santa Barbara. She is the author of *Offerings: Continuity and Transformation in Haitian Vodou* (forthcoming from Oxford University Press), author of *Aspects Educatifs et Moraux du Vodou Häitien* (1995), and coauthor of *Théories du Développement de l'Enfant: Etudes Comparatives* (1994). She is also the editor of *The Journal of Haitian Studies*.

Randi L. Miller is a faculty member and Coordinator of the Human Services Program and Coordinator of the Master of Arts in Social Sciences at California State University at San Bernardino. Her areas of research focus on race relations, school desegregation, and the training of student teachers. She has published extensively in journals such as *Public Opinion Quarterly*, *Sociology and Social Research*, *The Journal of Adolescent Research*, and *Youth and Society*.

Carol Mueller is Assistant Professor of Sociology at Arizona State University-West. She is the coeditor of *The Women's Movements in the United States and Western Europe: Feminist Consciousness, Political Opportunity and Public Policy* (1987) and editor of *The Politics of the Gender Gap: The Social Construction of Political Influence* (1988).

Harryette Mullen is Associate Professor of English at the University of California, Los Angeles. Her books of poetry include the following: *Sleeping with the Dictionary* (2002), *Muse and Drudge* (1995), *S*PeRM***KT* (1992), and *Trimmings* (1991).

Cedric J. Robinson is Professor of Black Studies and Political Science at the University of California, Santa Barbara. He is the author of *Terms of Order: Political Science and the Myth of Leadership* (1980), *Black Marxism: The Making of the Black Radical Tradition* (1987; reprinted 2000), *Black Movements in America* (1997), and *The Anthropology of Marxism* (2001).

Marlon B. Ross is Associate Professor of English at the University of Michigan, Ann Arbor. A specialist in cultural criticism and gender theory, he is the author of *The Contours of Masculine Desire: Romanticism and the Rise of Women's Poetry* (1989).

Jacqueline Shearer (1946–1993) produced and directed the 1977 landmark film *A Minor Altercation*, one of the first to be directed by a Black woman. She produced/directed "The Promised Land" and "The Keys to the Kingdom" for the PBS series *Eyes on the Prize II*, and produced, directed, and cowrote *The Massachusetts 54th Colored Infantry*, a segment of the PBS series *The American Experience*. Shearer was past president and board chairperson of ITVS (Independent Television Service), an organization that awards grants to independent television producers.

Catherine R. Squires is Assistant Professor in the Department of Communication Studies and the Center for Afro-American and African Studies at the University of Michigan. Her research centers on race, gender and media; public sphere theory; politics and media; history of African American media; and, multiracial identity issues.

Laura L. Sullivan is a Ph.D. candidate in English at the University of Florida, where she teaches courses on writing, literature, and women's studies.

Beverly Daniel Tatum is President of Spelman College and formerly Dean of the College and Professor of Psychology and Education at Mount Holyoke College. Her research is concerned with race relations in America, racial identity in teens, and race in the classroom. She is the author of *Why Are All the Black Kids Sitting Together in the Cafeteria? And Other Conversations about Race* (1997) and *Assimilation Blues: Black Families in a White Community* (1987; reprinted 1999).

Rosalyn Terborg-Penn is Professor of History and Head of the Ph.D. Program in History at Michigan State University. Her books include *The Afro-American Woman: Struggles and Images* (1978), and *Women in Africa and the African Diaspora* (1987). She is also the Associate Editor of *Black Women in America: An Historical Encyclopedia* (1993).

Richard Brent Turner is Associate Professor of African-American World Studies/Religion at the University of Iowa. He is the author of *Islam in the African American Experience* (1997).

PERMISSION ACKNOWLEDGEMENTS

The following essays were previously published. Permission to reprint in whole or in part is gratefully acknowledged here.

Bobo, Jacqueline, "The Color Purple: Black Women as Cultural Readers" is reprinted from *Female Spectators: Looking at Film and Television*, edited by E. Deidre Pribram, (London and NewYork: Verso, 1988). Reprinted with permission of Verso, an imprint of New Left Books, Ltd.

Brown, Elsa Barkeley, "Womanist Consciousness: Maggie Lena Walker and the Independent Order of Saint Luke" originally appeared in *Signs: Journal of Women in Culture and Society* 14:3 (Spring 1989): 610–633. Reprinted with permission of the University of Chicago Press.

Cannon, Katie Geneva, "Slave Ideology and Biblical Interpretation" originally appeared in *Semeia: An Experimental Journal for Biblical Criticism*. 47 (1989): 9–22. Reprinted with permission of the Society of Biblical Literature.

Cole, Johnnetta B., "Black Studies in Liberal Arts Education" is reprinted from *Transforming the Curriculum: Ethnic Studies and Women's Studies*, edited by Johnnella E. Butler and John C. Walter, the State University of New York Press © 1991 State University of New York. All rights reserved.

Davis, Angela Y., "Black Women and the Academy" first appeared in <u>*Callaloo*</u> 17:2 (1994): 422–31. © Charles H. Rowell. Reprinted with permission of The Johns Hopkins University Press.

duCille, Ann, "Dyes and Dolls: Multicultural Barbie and the Merchandizing of Difference" first appeared in *differences: A Journal of Feminist Cultural Studies* 6:1 (Spring 1994): 48–68. Reprinted with permission of Indiana University Press.

Grant, Jacquelyn, "Black Theology and the Black Woman" first appeared in *Out of the Revolution: The Development of Africana Studies*, edited by Delores P. Aldridge and Carlene Young, (Lanham, Md.: Lexington books, 2000): 427–443. Reprinted with permissions of Lexington Books.

Hall, Stuart, "What is This 'Black' in Black Popular Culture?" first appeared in *Black Popular Culture: Discussions in Contemporary Culture* #8, edited by Gina Dent, (Seattle, Wa: Bay Press, 1992): 21–33. Reprinted by permission of The New Press.

Hammonds, Evelynn, "Black (W)holes and the Geometry of Black Female Sexuality first appeared in *differences: A Journal of Feminist Cultural Studies* 6:2–3 (summer-fall 1994): 126–46. Reprinted with permission of Indiana University Press.

Harris, Robert L., Jr., "The Intellectual and Institutional Development of Africana Studies" first appeared in *Three Essays: Black Studies in the United States,* edited by Robert L. Harris, Jr., Darlene Clark Hine, and Nellie McKay. (NY: The Ford Foundation, 1990): 7–14. Reprinted with permission of the Ford Foundation.

Hull, Akasha Gloria, "Dread Path/Lock Spirit" first appeared in *My Soul is a Witness: African-American Women's Spirituality,* edited by Gloria Wade-Gayles, (Boston: Beacon Press, 1995), 229–33. Reprinted with permission of Akasha Gloria Hull.

Jennings, James, "Theorizing Black Studies: The Continuing Role of Community Service in the Study of Race and Class" is reprinted from Dispatches from the Ebony Tower, edited by Manning Marable, © 2000 Columbia University Press. Reprinted with the permission of Columbia University Press.

Johnson, Deborah J., "Racial Socialization Strategies of Parents in Three Black Private Schools" first appeared in *Visible Now: Blacks in Private Schools,* edited by Diana T. Slaughter and Deborah J. Johnson, © 1988 Greenwood Press. Reproduced with permission of Greenwood Publishing Group, Inc. Westport, CT.

Kelley, Robin D. G., "How the West Was One: On the Uses and Limitations of Diaspora" first appeared in *The Black Scholar* 30: 3–4 (fall-winter 2000): 31–35. Reprinted with permission of the Black World Foundation.

Klotman, Phyllis R. "Military Rites and Wrongs: African Americans in the U.S. Armed Forces" first appeared in *Struggles for Representation: African American Documentary Film and Video,* edited by Phyllis R. Klotman and Janet K. Cutler. © 1999 Indiana University Press. Reprinted with permission of Indiana University Press.

Knight, Frederick, "Justifiable Homicide, Police Brutality, or Governmental Repression? The 1962 Los Angeles Police Shooting of Seven Members of the Nation of Islam" first appeared in *The Journal of Negro History* 79:2 (spring 1994):182–94. Reprinted with permission of *The Journal of African American History.*

Lane, Alycee J., "Black Bodies/Gay Bodies: The Politics of Race in the Gay/Military Battle" first appeared in *Callaloo* 17:4 (1994), 1074–88. © Charles H. Rowell. Reprinted with permission of The Johns Hopkins University Press.

McBride, Dwight A. "Can the Queen Speak? Racial Essentialism, Sexuality, and the Problem of Authority," first appeared in *Black Men on Race, Gender and Sexuality: A Reader,* edited by Devon W. Carbado (NY: New York University Press, 1999). Reprinted with permission of New York University Press.

Michel, Claudine, "Teaching Haitian Vodou" first appeared in *Spring: A Journal of Archetype and Culture* 61(1997): 83–99. Reprinted by permission of Spring Audio and Journal.

Miller, Randi L., "Desegregation Experiences of Minority Students: Adolescent Coping Strategies in Five Connecticut High Schools" first appeared in *Journal of Adolescent Research*. 4:2 pp. 173–89 © 1989 by Sage Publications. Reprinted by permission of Sage Publications.

Mueller, Carol, "Ella Baker and the Origins of 'Participtory Democracy' " is reprinted from *Women in the Civil Rights Movement: Trailblazers and Torchbearers, 1941–1965*, edited by Vicki L. Crawford, Jacqueline Anne Rouse, and Barbara Woods. (Bloomington, Indiana: Indiana University Press, 1993) Reprinted by permission of Carol Mueller.

Mullen, Harryette, "African Signs and Spirit Writing" first appeared in *Callaloo* 19:3 (1996): 670–89. © Charles H. Rowell. Reprinted with permission of The Johns Hopkins University Press.

Robinson, Cedric J., "In the Year 1915: D.W. Griffith and the Whitening of America" first appeared in *Social Identities* 3:2 (1997): 161–192. Reprinted with permission of Carfax Publishing Company, a member of the Taylor and Francis Group. http://www.tandf.co.uk

Ross, Marlon B., "Some Glances at the Black Fag: Race, Same-Sex Desire, and Cultural Belonging," is reprinted from *Canadian Review of Comparative Literature* 3 (1994): 191–219.

Shearer, Jacqueline, "How Deep, How Wide? Perspectives on the Making of the *Massachusetts 54th Colored Infantry*" first appeared in *Black Women Film and Video Artists*, edited by Jacqueline Bobo, (NY: Routledge, 1998).

Squires, Catherine R., "Black Talk Radio: Defining Community Needs and Identity" first appeared in *Harvard International Journal of Press/Politics* 5:2, pp. 73–75. © 2000 by Harvard University, the President and the Fellows of Harvard College and the Massachusetts Institute of Technology. Reprinted by permission of Sage Publications.

Sullivan, Laura L., "Chasing Fae: *The Watermelon Woman* and Black Lesbian Possibility" first appeared in *Callaloo* 23:1 (2000): 448–60. © Charles H. Rowell. Reprinted with permission of The Johns Hopkins University Press.

Tatum, Beverly Daniel. "Talking about Race, Learning about Racism: The Application of Racial Identity Development Theory in the Classroom" first appeared in the *Harvard Educational Review* 62:1 (Spring 1992), pp. 1–24 Copyright © 1992 by the President and the Fellows of Harvard College. All rights reserved.

Terborg-Penn, Rosalyn, "Discontented Black Feminists: Prelude and Postscript to the Passage of the Nineteenth Amendment" first appeared in *Decades of Discontent: The Women's Movement, 1920–1940*, edited by Lois Scharf and Joan Jensen. Copyright © 1983 Greenwood Press. Reproduced with permission of Greenwood Publishing Group, Inc. Westport, CT.

INDEX